M000310589

The Beginning
Psychotherapist's Companion

# The Beginning Psychotherapist's Companion

### SECOND EDITION ■

## JAN WILLER

OXFORD
UNIVERSITY PRESS

# OXFORD
UNIVERSITY PRESS

Oxford University Press is a department of the University of Oxford.
It furthers the University's objective of excellence in research, scholarship,
and education by publishing worldwide.

Oxford   New York
Auckland   Cape Town   Dar es Salaam   Hong Kong   Karachi
Kuala Lumpur   Madrid   Melbourne   Mexico City   Nairobi
New Delhi   Shanghai   Taipei   Toronto

With offices in
Argentina   Austria   Brazil   Chile   Czech Republic   France   Greece
Guatemala   Hungary   Italy   Japan   Poland   Portugal   Singapore
South Korea   Switzerland   Thailand   Turkey   Ukraine   Vietnam

Oxford is a registered trademark of Oxford University Press in the UK and certain other countries.

Published in the United States of America by
Oxford University Press
198 Madison Avenue, New York, NY 10016

© Janet Willer 2014

All rights reserved. No part of this publication may be reproduced, stored in a
retrieval system, or transmitted, in any form or by any means, without the prior
permission in writing of Oxford University Press, or as expressly permitted by law,
by license, or under terms agreed with the appropriate reproduction rights organization.
Inquiries concerning reproduction outside the scope of the above should be sent to the Rights
Department, Oxford University Press, at the address above.

You must not circulate this work in any other form
and you must impose this same condition on any acquirer.

Library of Congress Cataloging-in-Publication Data
Willer, Jan.
The beginning psychotherapist's companion / Jan Willer.—Second edition.
   pages cm
Includes bibliographical references and index.
ISBN 978-0-19-993165-1 (pbk. : alk. paper)   1. Psychotherapy.   2. Psychotherapy—Practice.
I. Title.
RC480.W55 2013
616.89'14—dc23
2013017562

# CONTENTS

# ACKNOWLEDGMENTS

In gratitude for her courageousness in signing me for a book contract for the second edition at a new publisher, Oxford University Press, I'd like to thank my editor, Sarah Harrington. In gratitude for his bravery in signing me to a book contract for the first edition, and his many thoughtful comments and excellent advice, I'd like to thank my former editor, Arthur Pomponio, Ph.D.

For this second edition, I had remarkable help. Thanks to Shona Vas, Ph.D., for suggestions that improved Chapter 1. Many thanks to Renanah Lehner, Ph.D., and Ann Sauer, Psy.D., ABPP for their invaluable comments on Chapter 6. Many thanks to Jeffrey Barnett, Ph.D., for his expert comments on Chapter 7. Vast appreciation goes to Beeta Homiafar, Ph.D., for her many expert comments on and resource suggestions for Chapters 18 and 19. Much gratitude to Christina Holbein, my energetic and enormously helpful research assistant for this edition.

In gratitude for sharing their suggestions, input, comments, therapeutic insights, and other assistance that was helpful to the conceptualization of the first edition, I'd like to thank the following: Steve Batten, Ph.D.; Cyndy Boyd, Ph.D.; Mary Ellen Bratu, Psy.D.; Jennifer Caldwell, Ph.D.; Grayson Holmbeck, Ph.D.; Leah Horvath, Ph.D.; Zoran Martinovich, Ph.D.; Matthew Mills, M.D.; John Mundt, Ph.D.; Amberly Panepinto, Ph.D.; Vicki Seglin, Ph.D.; Suzette Speight, Ph.D.; Shona Vas, Ph.D., Rick Volden, Ph.D.; Lou Weiss, Ph.D.; Joy Whitman, Ph.D.; and Kathy Zebracki, Ph.D. I'd like to give thanks to the following friends and colleagues who helped me get the various client and psychotherapist names right throughout the book: Akira Motomura, Ph.D.; Jod Taywaditep, Ph.D.; Shona Vas, Ph.D.; and Louis Weiss, Ph.D. Any errors made in naming the clients and psychotherapists throughout the book are mine alone.

I'd also like to thank all the psychology interns who have taught me so much over the years, in chronological order: Felicity Laboy, Eric Roth, Linda Strozdas, and Mark Woodward (1995–1996); Kathryn Doheny, Jeff Lanfear, Aaron Malina, and Zoran Martinovich (1996–1997); Tim Belavich, Kristin Flynn Peters, Theresa Kiolbasa Campbell, and Beth Summerfeld (1997–1998); Charan Ranganath, Melisa Rempfer, and Delany Thrasher (1998–1999); Beth Mauer, Sherry Pagoto, Brian Ragsdale, and Donna Zaorski (1999–2000); Rodney Benson, Kim Cooper, Caroline King, and Brian Leahy (2000–2001); Sabrina Baril Young, Patricia

Espe-Pfeifer, Dawn Lindsey, and Malia Richmond (2001–2002); Alia Ammar, Samer Effarah, Mark Schneider, and Daniel Zomchek (2002–2003); and Beeta Homaifar, Renanah Lehner, Sarah Keedy, Amberly Panepinto, and Anne Wiley (2003–2004). Thank you all for your insights, your curiosity, and your feedback. I'd also like to thank all my former colleagues at the Jesse Brown VA Medical Center who have taught me so much over the years, including the library staff, who were so supportive of my many requests.

Thanks are also due to three supervisors I had in graduate school and internship who taught so much: Marilyn Robie, Ph.D., who encourages confidence and insight so well in her students; Bill Megan, Ph.D., who taught me how to think more clearly about client problems; and Bill McFall, Ed.D., who trusted me to experiment and find my own style.

My husband, Mark Osing, as always, has provided me with unwavering support. Thanks to my family for their encouragement and support throughout the years: Judy Abel, John Albright, Ann Willer, Bill Willer, Dave Willer, Fred Willer, Patricia Willer, and Robb Willer.

And finally, I'd like to thank Deb Smith for asking a very important question back in July 2005.

What I remember most about my first psychotherapy client is sitting down with her and being preoccupied with my own fears. Despite the best efforts of the faculty, I felt that I didn't know anything when I actually met my first real live client. I knew some theory and a few active listening skills. But, I had no idea how to guide the client through the psychotherapy session. I didn't know how to assess the client's problems or prioritize them. And I would have been utterly unprepared if she had walked in the door with a crisis. I believe that you, the beginning psychotherapist, can be more confident and competent with your first clients. That belief inspired me to write this book.

That first therapy session scares me even today but for a different reason. I now know much of what I was ignorant of that fateful day in 1986. If the client had a mental illness that is difficult to diagnose, like bipolar disorder or attention-deficit/hyperactivity disorder, I undoubtedly missed it. I didn't know anything about psychotropic medications, so if she could have benefited from a referral, she didn't get one. If the client came in feeling suicidal, I would have had no idea what to do. I didn't know anything about charting, so who knows what errors I made about what to include and what not to include in the chart. I doubt that anyone, myself included, told the client anything about confidentiality or informed consent. These are the reasons why that session scares me now.

Uncertainty, fear, and lack of knowledge still exist among beginning psychotherapists today. Friends who supervise beginning therapists tell of students coming into their offices and asking, "But what do I *do*?" These students know a lot about theoretical orientations. They have been taught reflective listening skills. They know about legal and ethical issues in psychotherapy. But how to start seeing a client still eludes them because there has been no one source for all the most basic information they need to know before they start seeing clients.

Often, beginning therapists have no idea how to greet a client in the waiting room or what appropriate professional boundaries are. They don't know how to deal with clients on the phone. They may have to screen new clients but not know much about how to make a diagnosis and what disorders are commonly missed. Beginning therapists (like all therapists) have a lot of emotions about doing therapy, but beginners tend to feel bad about having these feelings (Brody & Farber, 1996), and they don't know what to do about them.

Extreme differences in theoretical approaches can leave the beginning therapist confused. However, it is my belief and my hope that we are moving toward theoretical integration and balance. My focus in choosing my references for each chapter was not theoretical orientation—instead, it was clinical utility—and my view is that different theoretical approaches have different clinical strengths. Although this book is mostly atheoretical, when needed, I have drawn on the strengths of different theoretical traditions.

This is not really a book about how to *do* psychotherapy. Instead, it is a book about how to *start* psychotherapy. My goal in this volume has been to provide a well-rounded review of important topics that any beginning therapist should know *before* seeing a new client. In addition, I have included some material about the emotional complexities of doing psychotherapy for the psychotherapist. Research (Leiter & Harvie, 1996; Pearlman & Mac Ian, 1995; VanDeusen & Way, 2006) has shown that beginning psychotherapists are often overwhelmed by their emotional reactions, and this is a topic that is not typically addressed in most books about doing psychotherapy.

In many important areas, however, there is little research or professional guidance available. For example, I could hardly find any articles about the attire of health care professionals in general, much less mental health professionals. Almost everyone is strangely silent on providing guidance about how much you can tell your partner, family, and friends about your clinical work, although my utterly unscientific survey suggests that most therapists do talk about their work, at least a little, with their partners. I know that you will wrestle with these issues, so I have done my best to address these topics nonetheless. The afterword lists some questions that, perhaps, future research may answer.

None of the therapists or clients in the vignettes contained in this book actually existed as written. Some vignettes are composites, some have been altered to mask all identifying information, and others were made up simply to illustrate a point. Thus, the names of these therapists and clients are in no way meant to describe any real person, living or dead, and any resemblance is purely coincidental.

Because my expertise is with adults, that is the focus of this book. I must emphasize that I am not specifying any legal standards of care that all mental health psychotherapists should be held to, only suggestions based on current practice at the time this book was written. The clinical recommendations in this book are made with the beginning psychotherapist in mind. Experienced psychotherapists sometimes take perfectly acceptable shortcuts that I would not recommend to a beginning psychotherapist. I have attempted to introduce you to commonly used professional terms throughout; these terms are in italics. Considerable supplemental material to this book is available on this section of my website: www.drwiller.com/tbpc.

As I was writing this book, I had to wrestle with vast amounts of professional literature. I felt like the proverbial "jack-of-all-trades, master of none." As someone who is not the master of all these subjects, I certainly must have missed some important literature. For that, I apologize in advance. If you, the reader, have some information I have missed, your kindness in contacting me at jan@drwiller.com would be appreciated. I also welcome any comments.

I hope this book will help you cope with the anxieties and uncertainties inherent in becoming a psychotherapist, so you can appreciate the best reward of being a psychotherapist: the opportunity to make a positive impact on the life of another human being.

# The Psychotherapist's Self and Relationships

# The Psychotherapist's Self

The carpenter has a hammer, the surgeon has a scalpel, the therapist has the self. *(HAYES & GELSO, 2001, p. 1041)*

You probably had (or have) anxiety, even dread and terror, of your first-ever psychotherapy session. I remember that clearly myself. I knew a decent amount of theory by then, but I had no practical knowledge whatsoever. This first chapter is to help you think about how you will present yourself professionally to psychotherapy clients. I will talk about coping with the anxiety of beginning psychotherapists. I will also discuss some changes—interpersonal, cognitive, emotional, behavioral, and even spiritual and in self-concept—that you may experience as you become a psychotherapist.

Being a psychotherapist will change you and accelerate your personal growth. I was at a symposium once, many years ago, about therapist self-care. I remember one of the presenters asking the audience whether becoming psychotherapists had changed them. Everyone in the audience agreed that it had. When he asked us, we also agreed that we had not anticipated this. This process of personal growth and change will be ongoing throughout your career.

## YOUR SELF-CONCEPT AS A MENTAL HEALTH PROFESSIONAL

*Carlos Rivera is a mental health trainee. He doesn't want to assume a stuffy role. He is working in a partial hospitalization program and is assigned to help with socialization of the patients. He plays pool with them and uses curse words when he doesn't make a shot. He chats casually with patients when he is smoking with them outside. He talks about marijuana use in such a way that all the patients think he uses it regularly.*

Everyone acts differently in different relationships. For example, you may act differently with your siblings, your parents, your friends, and your teachers. A challenging aspect of becoming a psychotherapist is developing a new side to your personality. You want to be yourself, but, as with other situations you find yourself in, it is a particular version of yourself.

Your psychotherapist self should project professionalism. As you can see from the example of Carlos, many struggle with this to one degree or another. Eventually, you will see differences in how you talk and relate to others as a professional. Hopefully, you will find that your professional self can project a certain quiet authority. This is a normal progression.

## PROFESSIONAL DEMEANOR

You come to medical school like anyone else [and then] things happen that differentiate you from everyone else you know... You ask private and socially inappropriate questions of people, and they answer you. (Montross, 2007, p. 120)

As a mental health professional, you will interact differently with your clients and colleagues than you do with your family and friends. Like the medical students discussed in the previous quote, you will learn to talk openly and matter-of-factly about subjects that many people find distressing, embarrassing, or socially inappropriate. You will learn to ask clients questions that you might never dream of asking anyone else—and you will understand why these questions are necessary.

You will need to balance authenticity and empathy with a certain professional reserve. I recommend that you attempt to integrate an especially respectful and gracious manner with clients into your professional self. You should err on the side of being respectful yet empathetic to the client rather than overly familiar. Being too familiar with a client has a risk of leading to therapeutic boundary crossings (see Chapter 4). You will learn not to share many personal details of your life in professional situations (especially with clients—see the section on self-disclosure in Chapter 4 for more information). Depending on the client population, you can consider referring to the client by last name (e.g., Mr. Brown or Ms. Williams), use your best manners, and use "sir" and "ma'am" as appropriate. This type of self-presentation can often help allay clients' fears of being disrespected. Also, this will ensure that you are not inadvertently inappropriate or overly familiar to a client from a more traditional cultural background.

Your professional self may be more assertive with professional peers than you would generally be with your friends. Even if you never choose the restaurant when you are going out with friends, your psychotherapist self will need to develop a decisiveness that you can employ for your clients' benefit as needed. For example, if you find yourself with a potentially suicidal client, you must be decisive and provide appropriate guidance.

Sometimes beginning psychotherapists complain that they feel that they can't be themselves with clients because they are editing out so much of their own personal material when they talk. I suggest that you be yourself (albeit a somewhat edited version) through your *process* with the client—for example, the questions you ask, how you react, and what you focus on. As McWilliams (2004) states, "Being in a role is not the same thing as playing a role" (p. 53). But you should leave out most of your personal *content*—for example, the details of your personal life.

## PROFESSIONAL DRESS AND APPEARANCE

*Megan Edwards, a mental health trainee, is interviewing with her potential practicum supervisor, Dr. Larry Cook. The practicum entails working with low-functioning schizophrenic clients, primarily in individual and group therapy, and more informally in a clubhouse setting. Megan dressed carefully for the interview and feels that she looks great. However, during the interview, Dr. Cook can't help noticing that Megan is wearing 4-inch heels and that her skirt has ridden high on her thighs when she sat down. He wonders if she understands that the clients are low functioning and have poor impulse control. He is concerned that she will experience uncomfortable and inappropriate remarks from the clients. He also wonders about her professional judgment, since her attire seems more sexy than professional. However, he feels uncomfortable bringing up the subject with Megan, so he doesn't say anything. Another applicant ends up being matched to the practicum site.*

*Joshua Collins is a mental health trainee who has been working in a pain-management clinic in a regional medical center in a mostly rural state. He went to college in a major metropolitan area and, like most of his friends, obtained a number of colorful tattoos during that phase of his life. He has prominent tattoos on his left forearm. The temperature is in the 90s, and it is very humid. Up to now, Joshua has been wearing long-sleeved shirts to the clinic. He wears a short-sleeved shirt today. After he interviews an elderly client, the client goes into her physician's office and says that Joshua "looks like a thug."*

Business self-help books generally recommend that you dress similarly to your immediate superiors. Generally, more conservative dress is most appropriate (Morrison, 1995). Most research has shown that patients prefer their physicians to dress more formally (Lill & Wilkinson, 2005; Menahem & Shvartzman, 1998). In fact, one study found that, at least for physicians, formal attire increased patients' perceptions of their friendliness, trustworthiness, and even attractiveness (Brase & Richmond, 2004). It is reasonable to assume that the same conclusions would apply to mental health care professionals.

Of course, the therapeutic context must be considered when choosing appropriate professional clothing. What you might wear doing case management with the homeless is not what you would wear when doing smoking cessation with businesspeople. A good general guideline is to wear business casual attire when in less formal settings but to consider wearing formal business attire if you are working in a formal setting, such as a medical center that serves middle- to upper-middle-class patients. In almost all treatment settings, neither men nor women should wear tennis shoes; invest in at least one pair of comfortable yet professional-looking shoes. Slacks and a collared shirt are generally appropriate for men. More casual slacks such as chinos or corduroy slacks are usually fine. Jeans are iffy but may be okay in casual settings. Interestingly, one study found that clients preferred their male psychiatrists in more casual dress—casual collared shirt plus chinos or corduroy slacks—and female psychiatrists in more formal dress—dress shirt plus dress slacks or skirt (Nihalani, Kunwar, Staller, & Lamberti, 2006). If you are uncertain, err on the side of conservative dress and ask your supervisor for input.

Female psychotherapists have more wardrobe flexibility. Unfortunately, this means that the possibility of problematic wardrobe choices is greater. A recent research study indicated that women who are dressed in a sexy manner (more makeup, tousled hair, low-cut blouse, tight skirt, and high heels), with high-status jobs, are seen more negatively and also as less competent and less intelligent (Glick, Larsen, Johnson, & Branstiter, 2005; Wookey, Graves, & Butler, 2009). While, as psychotherapists, we do not want to cling to negative and/or sexist stereotypes, we also understand that the focus needs to be on our clients' needs rather than our own attire. So, it is wise to avoid revealing clothes, tight or form-fitting clothes, very high-heeled shoes, and skirts at or above the knee (as they will reveal much more when you sit down).

We also need to consider our clients' potential reactions to clothing choices. Women who work with predominantly male populations, especially populations that may have poorer judgment or poor impulse control, often find that they prefer to minimize their sexual stimulus value. In any setting, certain clothing choices can result in greater therapeutic time spent on the client's sexual attractions to the psychotherapist and less attention to whatever issues may have brought the client to therapy originally.

Psychotherapists should not wear perfume or cologne on the job. Strongly scented cosmetics and lotions are best avoided as well. Also, don't put potpourri or scented candles in your office. Medical conditions that can be worsened or triggered by perfumes or colognes include asthma and allergies (wheezing or an asthma attack can be induced; American Lung Association, 2011), chronic obstructive pulmonary disease (coughing or increased shortness of breath can be induced; American Lung Association, 2007), and migraines (which can be triggered; R. W. Evans, 2006).

Tattoos and piercings are becoming more common, but they are still considered daring or unprofessional by many people, such as Joshua's client mentioned previously. If you are a younger psychotherapist, you may have difficulties getting respect from older clients, a problem that can be compounded if you have a lot of obvious tattoos, piercings, or other body art. Over 80 percent of human resource managers and recruiters surveyed view persons with tattoos negatively (Swanger, 2006), so prominent tattoos may have a negative impact on your future career. For that reason, please think very carefully about getting any tattoos would be bared by business casual clothing in the summer, and get input on any plans for obvious tattoos from a trusted mentor. In addition, Newman, Wright, Wrenn, and Bernard (2005) found that emergency department patients saw physicians with facial piercings (nose, eyebrow, or lip) as inappropriate and would decrease their assessment of competence and trustworthiness.

The patients were not affected by an earring on a male physician. Thus, it is likely that if you have fewer (one or two) conservatively placed (ear) piercings, you are more likely to be seen as professional by a wider variety of clients. A tongue piercing would be inappropriate in a therapy setting because of sexual connotations.

## THE TRAINEE ROLE

*Tommy Kendall, a mental health trainee, is visiting the local university medical center for a practicum interview. He is meeting with Dr. Keesha Johnson. He enters her office, saying, "Hi, Keesha, great to meet you!" He promptly sits down in a comfortable chair and says that he has a lot of questions on his laptop, so he pulls it out and starts to turn it on. Dr Johnson has to tell him that this is her chair and she asks him to sit on the couch. He has brought in a plastic water bottle and sets it down on her table, where it proceeds to sweat during the interview and leaves a water mark behind. During the interview, his phone buzzes, and he looks at it briefly to see what the incoming text was.*

*The next interviewee is Rafaela Miller. Rafaela shakes hands and says, "It's a pleasure to meet you, Dr. Johnson." She waits for Dr. Johnson to indicate where she should sit and lets Dr. Johnson proceed to set the agenda for the interview. Rafaela keeps her portfolio handy, which contains a paper tablet for making notes, extra copies of her vita, and a printed out list of questions that she wants to ask Dr. Johnson.*

Health care settings are highly hierarchical, which can be a new cultural experience for many young adult Americans. Depending on your cultural background, you may have been brought up in a culture where you have always referred to adults by their first names and you may have been encouraged to think of yourself and your needs as being equal to those of everyone else. If this is your cultural perspective, be aware that it probably will not apply to most health care settings.

Like Tommy, above, you will make a very poor impression if you do not understand your role in the health care setting. Let me be brutally honest here. Not only are health care settings hierarchical, but as a trainee, you have the very lowest status. (If you are a psychiatry resident, your status is more ambiguous.) As a trainee, you are expected to treat all staff with the highest level of respect. Here are some specific suggestions:

- Always refer to all physicians as Dr. [last name], no matter how well or long you have known them unless they specifically request that you use a first name (this will rarely happen).
- Always refer to all psychologists and other doctoral level practitioners as Dr. [last name] when first meeting them. They will tell you if and when it is okay for you to use their first names.

- Follow the lead of other trainees in determining how to address master's level practitioners and support staff. If in doubt, use Mr. or Ms. [last name].
- Unless a personal crisis is unfolding, never check messages on a phone during a therapy session, supervision meeting, seminar, treatment team meeting, or other professional meeting. Preferably, turn your phone off.
- Paper tablets are better than laptops or computer tablets during meetings because they are less distracting and you are more likely to be paying appropriate attention, thereby demonstrating respect toward your senior colleagues.
- Be respectful of others' time. For example, if you have a question during a treatment team meeting because you don't understand something, consider waiting until your supervision session to ask about it. When you talk in meetings, be focused and concise.
- And, as all health care staff should do, be helpful to clients/patients—hold the elevator door for them, help them if they are lost, assist any disabled individuals who may need help, and so on.

## COPING WITH ANXIETY

*Kendra Hayes, a mental health trainee, is about to have her first session with a client. The clinic coordinator has already done an intake with the client, so Kendra will be starting therapy with the client. She is very anxious and can't help thinking how little she knows. She worries that she won't be able to help the client. She worries that he will see how anxious she is. She fears that her mind will go blank.*

Kendra's fears are normal. It is natural to feel anxious when first doing psychotherapy. I hope that you already know how to cope with your own anxiety in other circumstances. Use that knowledge. For example, before a therapy session, you might be able to get in a workout, a walk, meditation, or some deep breathing. Remind yourself that you know how to use active listening skills and that you can be concerned and empathetic; these alone can be healing to the client.

When you feel anxious, try to refocus on how your client will feel during the session. The client will probably be new to therapy and may be worried and fearful about what will happen during therapy. The client may be worried about having a mental illness and how you will react when symptoms are shared with you. The client may be feeling worn down, lonely, and worthless because of extended struggles with problems. The client is probably fearful and concerned about whether you will be understanding and compassionate. The client may be feeling that coming to therapy shows weakness, failure, and lack of character. Your anxiety may, to some extent, be an empathic response to the client's anxiety.

Putting yourself in the client's shoes naturally leads to some conclusions about how to act in the first therapy session. You will want to provide guidance and structure about how the session will go (which will be discussed further in Chapter 11) so that the client feels that something can be done to help. You will want to be gracious and respectful so that the client feels respected and worthy. You might want to compliment the client's wisdom or courage in coming to therapy so that the client may begin to think of coming to therapy as showing the strength to face problems head on. You will want to be empathetic so that the client feels comfortable and nurtured.

Talk to your supervisors and more advanced peers about your concerns. If your anxiety remains distressing, it would be wise to seek therapy for yourself—but I recommend this for all mental health trainees, anyway, as does Yalom (2002), among many others.

## COPING WITH CONFUSION

*Kevin Alexander, a mental health trainee, meets with his client, Joe Martin. Joe talks about going to the hardware store and feels helpless and tearful when there. This has happened to him several times before at the same hardware store. "What does it mean, doc?" asks Joe. Kevin has no idea. He feels confused and uncertain about how to respond to Joe. Joe is clearly having distress about the issue, and Kevin wants to help right now. Kevin feels that he should be able to come up with a brilliant, insightful interpretation of Joe's distress about the hardware store on the spot, yet he is utterly at a loss. He feels stuck. After a long pause, "What do you think it means?" is what he resorts to. When Kevin later meets with his supervision group, they provide a multitude of interpretations: "He is conflicted about his masculinity." "The tools represent a sense of personal agency, and he has not been able to accomplish what he wanted to in his life." "Maybe he was sexually abused in a tool shed." Kevin is more confused than ever.*

This example (which is inspired by Kottler, 2003) illustrates some of the confusion that you, the beginning psychotherapist, are likely to feel. Your clients will have personal problems that you feel you should understand and know how to solve, but you don't. Their situations and emotions prompt intense emotions in you, but you don't know how to interpret all these feelings. Sometimes you will feel so stumped in therapy sessions that you may not even know what to say. If your mind feels "blank" during a session, one helpful strategy is to summarize what the client has just been telling you.

The good news is that as you learn more, you will feel less confused and have more of an idea about how to work with your clients, understand their problems, and manage all the emotions in the room. Here's a little secret: you don't have to know all the answers. It's okay to not know what something means and even to admit that to your client. You and the client can use the process of therapy to figure it out. Thus, Kevin could say to Joe, "Joe, I don't know what your feelings in the hardware store are about, but I'm sure that if we continue to explore it together, we will figure it out."

# COPING WITH SELF-DOUBT AND FEELINGS OF INADEQUACY

*Brittany Hall is a mental health trainee at her first training placement. She is seeing Whitney Clark, a 34-year-old single mother of four. Whitney is in transitional housing with her children and is struggling to maintain her 90-day abstinence from alcohol. She is in therapy for depression and post-traumatic stress disorder (PTSD) and is attending job retraining courses. Whitney relocated to the city she lives in now after a natural disaster destroyed her uninsured home and all her personal possessions. Brittany is impressed by Whitney's strength of character and dedication to her children in the face of so many personal difficulties. She doubts how she, a 22-year-old single woman from a relatively privileged background, can help Whitney.*

At the start of the year, in his opening speech, an associate dean warned us that we would each feel ill-equipped at times over the course of these years, that we would wonder whether we are up to the challenge, whether we belong. But when these moments of intellectual disorientation and feelings of inadequacy overtake us, we are nonetheless unprepared. We know we are fraudulent. We see that our peers are not struggling in the same ways. Other students ask us to explain things to them, which we do. But we think that those are the easy things, the concepts they would figure out in another second on their own. I think, "It is this really tough stuff, which they are breezing through, that I simply cannot comprehend." (Montross, 2007, p. 145)

What he or she [the client] does in terms of changing in therapy is not an index of whether I'm doing my job right or not...sometimes when I do things very very well, the patient doesn't change at all. Other times I might be doing a half-assed job and the patient, because of being in a very good space, picks up whenever I'm into, adds a great deal of his or her own stuff and makes excellent progress, from his or her point of view. I find that to do the best work, I have to free myself from anxiety about the results. A kind of Karma yoga position, I guess. So the change is partly more respect for the patient, less arrogance about myself and more detachment about what's going on. (Kopp, 1977, p. 6)

As a beginning psychotherapist, you are likely to struggle often with feelings of inadequacy and incompetence, and experienced psychotherapists can suffer from these feelings as well (Betan, Heim, Conklin, & Westen, 2005). You wonder whether your clients will get better, and you fear that they will not improve. You may feel that the client's improvement is your responsibility. This feeling of being responsible for the client can get out of hand and feel overwhelming.

Interestingly, feeling uncertain about your competence is probably a good sign. There is a general finding that less competent psychotherapists tend to overestimate their skill level, whereas more competent psychotherapists tend to underestimate their skills; "it may be that less-competent therapists 'don't know what they don't know'" (McManus, Rakovshik, Kennerley, Fennell & Westbrook, 2011).

As the psychotherapist, your responsibility is to do the best job you can, given where you are emotionally, physically, and cognitively that particular day. If your client is not getting better, it is your responsibility to seek greater insight into how to help her. We strive to do the best we can with each client and to solve any therapeutic roadblocks that arise. But, at the same time, it is not your responsibility to make the client "get better." No one can do that but the client herself. You can be a catalyst for her change, but she is the instrument of her change.

## COPING WITH CLIENTS' SUFFERING

*Jesse Blackhawk is a mental health trainee working at a center that treats survivors of torture. Jesse's client endured 2 years of jail and torture before being released and then sponsored to come to the United States by relatives here. Before his incarceration, Jesse's client, a journalist, was under house arrest for 5 years and feared for his life every day. The client suffers from severe nightmares every night, hypervigilance, and lack of trust. The client admits to hoarding food at home, even though he knows that his relatives would never let him go hungry. Jesse feels overwhelmed by the pain of his client's suffering. He is starting to have religious doubts. He wonders how his faith can explain why innocent, well-meaning people, such as his client, endure such terrible suffering.*

Helping others with their suffering is not easy. Even experienced psychotherapists can feel overwhelmed by their clients (Betan et al., 2005). Coping with clients' suffering is a complex emotional, cognitive, and spiritual task. Feeling overwhelmed is usually an indication that you are empathizing with the client; if you are feeling overwhelmed, the client is almost certainly feeling the same thing. Knowing that this feeling emanates from your empathetic response to the client can help you cope with it: first, by reflecting the feeling back; and, second, by knowing that even though you and the client may feel overwhelmed right now, that does not mean that the situation is actually hopeless. Reevaluating and reframing the situation this way can help both you and the client escape from the trap of feeling overwhelmed.

Your client may have experienced many horrible life events: child abuse, torture, rape, domestic violence, and more. These can result in great suffering. Witnessing this pain is not easy. You may start to wonder about this pain from a spiritual perspective. If you think that may be likely, you may wish to begin the process of seeking a deepened spiritual understanding of suffering.

### Recommended Reading

Kottler, J. A. (2003). *On Being a Therapist* (3rd ed.). San Francisco: Jossey-Bass.
  *Written for the beginning psychotherapist, Kottler gives examples of the personal and professional struggles of a psychotherapist.*
Nhat Hanh, T. (1998). *The Heart of the Buddha's Teaching.* Berkeley, CA: Parallax Press.

*Psychotherapists tend to be less religious than the U.S. population as a whole. Also, many psychotherapists do not have a family religious tradition that they embrace, or are atheist or agnostic. The writings of Thich Nhat Hanh focus on Buddhist philosophy, rather than religious ideas such as deities or reincarnation, and are thus very accessible to both religious and nonreligious people interested in a Buddhist understanding of suffering.*

Yalom, I. (2002). *The Gift of Therapy: An Open Letter to a New Generation.* New York: HarperPerennial.

*While you may or may not agree with some of Yalom's thoughts about treatment and the therapeutic relationship, he thinks carefully and deeply about these issues. His insights will help bring your own thought process to the next level.*


## DISCUSSION QUESTIONS

1. What coping strategies can you use to cope with the suffering of your clients?
2. How do various religious and humanist traditions explain and address suffering?
3. What other feelings, besides anxiety and self-doubt, do you anticipate being problematic when you first see clients?

# The Supervisor–Supervisee Relationship

Your relationships with your psychotherapy supervisors will be some of the most important professional relationships of your career. Your supervisors will guide you to become an independent mental health professional. This chapter will orient you to the process of supervision. I also discuss how supervision can go awry and make recommendations about how to cope.

## THE SUPERVISION MEETING

Your supervisor's goal is to help you improve your clinical skills. You will discuss how you are working with your client. In the course of these discussions, you may review audiotapes or videotapes of the sessions or just report what happened in summary form. Your supervisor will help you understand the client and formulate effective interventions. Depending on your supervisor's theoretical orientation, you might focus more on dynamic issues, such as transference and countertransference, or you might focus more on progressing through particular behavioral and cognitive tasks that would assist your client. Unless you are adhering to a strict treatment protocol, your supervisor will generally not tell you exactly what to do in each session. Instead, he or she will help you consider interventions and interpretations that you could use with the client.

Your supervisor may also assist you with your professional development. Supervision meetings are an appropriate forum to discuss concerns, worries, or frustrations that you may have with clinical work or agency bureaucracy. Some supervisors may take a mentoring role with you, and if so, you can discuss career and professional issues.

## THE SUPERVISOR'S RESPONSIBILITIES

The first job of your new supervisor is to help orient you to your clinical work at the site. Your supervisor will guide you to learn about the clients' *presenting problem* (the problem that prompted the client to come to psychotherapy) and diagnoses.

Your supervisor will help you learn to navigate the administrative structure of the site and introduce you to other staff you need to know. Your supervisor will educate you about the necessary documentation. Ask for help and information any time you need to know about any of these topics. In the appendix at the end of this chapter, I have summarized a number of the questions that you might want to ask your supervisor when you begin at a new site.

You and your supervisor will fulfill some requirements regarding the number of supervision hours that you meet per week. Your supervisor will give you a set time for supervision every week. The supervisor will set this time aside and not let other matters encroach. Unless a client is having an emergency, your supervisor should not answer the phone, respond to e-mail, or be otherwise distracted and unfocused during the supervision hour. Additionally, your supervisor should be available for "spot supervision" as needed between meetings and should let you know who will provide backup supervision if you have a client crisis when he or she is not available or not in the office.

An effective supervisor establishes a climate of trust and honesty (Walker & Jacobs, 2004). Good supervisors are supportive, instructional, interpretive, collegial, and respectful (L. A. Gray, Ladany, Walker, & Ancis, 2001). Your supervisor may talk about his or her own experience with clinical challenges and what the impact and lessons of these challenges were.

## THE SUPERVISEE'S RESPONSIBILITIES: GETTING THE MOST FROM SUPERVISION

Your approach to supervision will influence how much you grow as a psychotherapist (Berger & Buchholz, 1993). Your supervisor is more experienced than you are and will identify issues that you missed. This is normal. Be open to suggestions and new ways of conceptualizing your clients' problems. Few things are more difficult for a supervisor to cope with than defensiveness in a supervisee.

Show your supervisor that you are responsible and motivated. Be on time to supervision meetings. If you have to cancel or reschedule a meeting, contact your supervisor well in advance. Think about what clinical issues you would like to discuss with your supervisor and be prepared with questions. If your supervisor has asked you to review your audiotapes or videotapes before the session, do that. Be sure you have finished any reading that was assigned. Write drafts of your progress notes before the supervision meeting so that your supervisor can see them and cosign them during or before the meeting. Finish your paperwork at the site on a timely basis so that your supervisor does not have to ask you about it. Keep in mind that you might want to ask your supervisor for letters of reference for you in the future.

When you start out, your supervisor is likely to want a summary of the progress of each client during the supervisory session. You may need some guidance with each client on a weekly basis. As your skills increase, you and your supervisor can devote more time to focusing on clinical concerns that you might have with one particular client. Talk to your supervisor about how to allocate time between discussion, tapes, review of progress notes, and other tasks during the supervisory hour.

Be proactive about your learning process. If you recognize that you need to learn more about relevant clinical issues, ask your supervisor to recommend readings. Increasing your knowledge will help allay your anxieties about becoming a competent psychotherapist. Be open to learning about clinical work from different theoretical perspectives. Learn how to apply research findings to clinical practice while maintaining the flexibility to tailor the treatment to the needs of each client.

Try not to be rejecting if your supervisor gives you difficult feedback. Instead, agree to think about it, then discuss the issue with friends, classmates, mentors, your psychotherapist, and anyone else you think could give you a helpful perspective. However, later, after you have given the issue sufficient thought and gotten feedback from others, if you feel that your supervisor is wrong, discuss the issue again and ask for clarification.

## HAVE REALISTIC EXPECTATIONS OF YOURSELF

Graduate students want to do well and can be perfectionistic. However, the reality is that you will need much coaching and support before you are an effective independently practicing psychotherapist. Your supervisor knows that you will be anxious about starting a new clinical experience. Your supervisor is aware of your level of training and does not expect you to completely understand how to implement therapeutic techniques that you have not yet used.

Try to have realistic expectations for yourself. A good student will not be a flawless psychotherapist (and, in fact, no one is a flawless psychotherapist). Instead, as a good student, you are open to learning, sincere, hardworking, and accepting of your limitations. As long as your skills are commensurate with your experience, you are doing fine. It is unrealistic to expect to be an excellent psychotherapist immediately. However, with good supervision, you will be competent, which is good enough.

You will make clinical errors, and you need to accept the inevitability of this. Some of the vignettes in this book were inspired by clinical errors that either I or other professionals and trainees have made. Generally these are minor errors of empathy, insight, and so on. In almost all cases, your clients will survive these minor errors just fine. The caring and rapport between you and your clients will carry you through most rough spots. When you think you have made an error, discuss the issue with your supervisor and, if you have an audiotape, play that portion of the session. A good supervisor will respect you for identifying your clinical challenges and for wanting to work on them.

If you believe that you made a more serious error, find your supervisor and talk it over immediately. For example, perhaps your client was much more depressed today, but you did not think to ask if he was feeling suicidal. Your supervisor can help you solve the problem in a timely manner.

## EVALUATIONS

You are probably anxious about being evaluated by your supervisor. This is normal. Learning more about the evaluation process can help allay your fears. Your supervisor should show you the evaluation form as part of your orientation; ask to see the form if she doesn't think of it. Whenever you would like feedback about your progress from your supervisor, ask for it.

Often trainees suffer silently, worrying about getting a bad evaluation. However, no student should ever reach the end of a training experience and be surprised by a poor evaluation. Instead, if at any time your supervisor thinks that you are having significant difficulties, the supervisor should work out a remediation plan with you so that you can work more intensively and improve in time to get a better evaluation.

## PERSONAL ISSUES IN SUPERVISION

Amanda Nakamura, a 28-year-old mental health trainee, had just experienced the prolonged and painful death of her father. One medical issue had led to another, and her father had been on a ventilator for 3 months before dying. Their relationship had been very close. The whole process had been very traumatic for all involved, and her father died only a week before the start of her next clinical placement. Amanda calls the training director to let him know about this. After some discussion, they agree that she will not be working with high-risk clients to start and that she will not be assigned any clients with loss issues until she feels she is ready.

James Green, a 24-year-old social work intern, is devastated. He learned that he did not get the scholarship he had applied for. He discusses this issue with his supervisor and is very self-critical. The supervisor attempts to point out that these decisions are very subjective and that James is an excellent student nonetheless. James continues to verbalize harsh self-criticism. The supervisor suggests that psychotherapy could help James cope with his perfectionism. James insists that he does not need therapy and is offended at the suggestion. They do not discuss it again.

One of your supervisor's responsibilities is to help you become more self-aware by recognizing when your personal issues are having a negative impact on the therapeutic process (Vasquez, 1992) or on your professional development. The student in the first example is already demonstrating her self-knowledge, and she is using it effectively. Amanda is setting realistic expectations for herself by recognizing her own emotional distress and how it could have a negative impact on client care. She has ethically taken appropriate steps to address this by contacting the training director.

Your supervisor will not and should not be your psychotherapist. However, personal issues inevitably will affect your work and your professional development, and these personal issues may arise in supervision. To preserve appropriate boundaries, while continuing to ensure your professional growth, your supervisor may recommend that you go to psychotherapy yourself. Even if you cannot understand why your supervisor recommends psychotherapy or if you disagree, personal therapy is still beneficial for any mental health trainee, because it gives you a greater understanding of your clients.

## SUPERVISOR–SUPERVISEE BOUNDARIES

*Jenna Harris is a mental health trainee who feels very comfortable with her supervisor, Jaqui Robinson, who is actually the same age as Jenna. They are both single, heterosexual women. Jenna asks Jaqui to go out to drinks and dinner with her. They do so and enjoy each other's company but at the same time feel awkward. Next week, they both realize and agree that they should not do this again while they still have a professional relationship.*

Your relationship with your supervisor should be supportive and collegial. Your supervisor may be friendly and interested in your professional development. You might have a friendly professional relationship with your supervisor, having lunch or coffee at work sometimes, seeing her at departmental social events, or your supervisor may invite you and your fellow students out for lunch or dinner once or twice. All these are appropriate interactions.

Your supervisor may self-disclose to you (Knox et al., 2008). For example, she may tell you about clinical errors that she has made and what she learned from them, in order to help you learn from your own errors. Or she might talk about her own emotional challenges with clinical work to help you realize that your challenges are normal. When your supervisor self-discloses, she hopes this will help you in your own personal and professional growth as a psychotherapist.

On occasion, supervisees and supervisors become friends after the supervision is over; this is appropriate as well. However, it is not appropriate for supervisors and supervisees to have a close friendship while supervision is ongoing. So supervisors and supervisees should not engage in friendship activities, such as one-on-one social outings, while supervision is ongoing or if supervision is expected to resume. Also, they should not engage in any joint business ventures or have a romantic relationship.

Appropriate boundaries between supervisor and supervisee are an understudied topic. Heru, Strong, Price, and Recupero (2004) found differing opinions among both psychiatry supervisors and supervisees about appropriate boundaries. One finding was that supervisors tended to see sexual topics (such as sexual attraction toward the client) as more appropriate for discussion in supervision than supervisees did. They also noted that previous studies had documented that sexual relationships between supervisors and supervisees can occur. The American Psychological Association's Ethics Code states that sexual relationships between supervisors and supervisees are inappropriate (American Psychological Association, 2010). Sexual advances from a supervisor should always be reported to your academic program and to the training supervisor at your site.

## SUPERVISOR–SUPERVISEE MATCHING

*Lisa Anderson, a mental health trainee, is meeting with her supervisor. The supervisor has a psychodynamic orientation, while Lisa's training program trained her in cognitive-behavioral interventions exclusively. Lisa is having difficulty understanding her supervisor's reasoning when he suggests that she interpret the client's transference. Lisa feels that the client's maladaptive cognitions are the best place to start therapy.*

You might feel that there is a poor match between you and your supervisor, as Lisa does. Or you may feel poorly matched temperamentally. Research indicates that psychology interns who are matched with a theoretically compatible supervisor are often happier with how supervision goes (Putney, Worthington, & McCullough, 1992). However, differences can be an opportunity for mutual learning and growth. Try to be open to the different perspectives and new insights that the supervisor brings to your clinical work.

You may wish to talk to someone you trust to get feedback about working more effectively with your supervisor. Get advice from someone who is knowledgeable, discreet, and practical. If there is someone with your graduate program whom you feel comfortable talking to, this would be a good choice, since someone in your academic program will then know that you proactively addressed the issue. Discuss the situation with your consultant in a nonblaming, nonjudgmental manner. Try to consider all options. Perhaps your expectations were too unrealistic, and you need to refocus on learning what the supervisor has to teach. Perhaps you may have some emotional issues that need to be addressed in therapy. Perhaps a different supervisor would be more helpful to you. Ask for honest feedback and practical suggestions to work more effectively with your supervisor.

## COPING WITH THE DISENGAGED SUPERVISOR

*Rebecca Goldberg is worried about her supervision. She talks to her supervisor on a weekly basis for an hour about her cases. Sometimes during supervision, he closes his eyes and appears to be napping. At times, he has even snored. She has no idea what to do during these times, so she just continues to talk about what she has done with the clients until he appears more alert.*

*Marcus White is worried about his supervision. He likes his supervisor and finds him helpful when they meet. He has supervision scheduled on a weekly basis, but the supervisor is often late, cancels at the last minute, or just does not show up. Then on some weeks, the supervisor is out of the office on other business and makes no arrangements for backup supervision coverage.*

These vignettes describe supervisors who are not meeting their responsibilities. As in these examples, the supervisor may be inattentive or unavailable.

Or the supervisor may not be timely in assisting with paperwork or reports. The supervisor may not make arrangements for supervision coverage when absent.

If you have a supervisor who is not meeting responsibilities, consider addressing this as tactfully as possible with the supervisor first. Rebecca might ask if they could talk about the process of supervision, and then say, "I'm noticing that you seem a little sleepy during some of our supervision sessions. Would it be possible to move the supervision to another time that works better for you?" Marcus might state, "I really appreciate your insights about my work with my clients, but I'm realizing that you haven't been able to meet with me every week. I feel that I really need weekly supervision. Would it be possible for us to work out some way to meet more regularly on a weekly basis?" If your efforts are not successful, consider bringing this problem to the attention of your academic program and/or the staff member who is in charge of training at the facility.

## COPING WITH THE INAPPROPRIATE SUPERVISOR

*India Turner is worried about her supervisory relationship. She has moved from New York City to a Southern state. Her supervisor tells her that she would look much more attractive if she didn't wear as much black and if she got rid of those "ugly glasses." He tells her that he wonders whether wearing black means she's depressed. India thinks that her wardrobe is chic, and she wonders why her supervisor thinks it is appropriate to tell her how to dress more attractively.*

The example of India's supervisor illustrates inappropriately critical remarks on the part of the supervisor, coupled with poor boundaries. The supervisor should not be critiquing India's wardrobe unless she is dressing unprofessionally, nor should he be advising her on what would be most attractive.

Depending on her assessment of the situation, India could consider waiting to see whether this was a one-time slip on the part of the supervisor. Depending on the quality of their relationship, she might consider discussing the remarks with the supervisor. Alternatively, she might prefer consulting with a trusted faculty member at her academic program and/or the training supervisor at the site. Depending on what happens subsequently in the supervisory relationship, she might consider asking for a different supervisor.

## COPING WITH THE INCOMPETENT SUPERVISOR

*Jessica Hill is worried about her supervision. She is working with a depressed client, who has a history of closed head injury during a car accident a few years ago and has amnesia for the accident. The client has not been able to get her life back in order and seems unable to work. Jessica's supervisor insists on doing a structured relaxation protocol with the client. Jessica asks whether she should talk to the client about her depression. The supervisor replies, "Why would we want to open that can of worms?"*

*Brandon Adams is worried about his supervision. He is working with a gay high school teacher who has not come out to his colleagues or family. His supervisor is a strict Catholic. The supervisor's first question about the client is, "Is he sexually abusing any of the kids at his school?" Brandon is offended and sees that his supervisor holds uninformed and damaging misconceptions. The supervisor goes on to insist that Brandon ask about guilt when Brandon feels that the client's primary issues revolve around coming out to his family.*

In both vignettes, the supervisees are struggling with supervisors who have inadequate knowledge or skill to address the clients' issues. Jessica can see that the supervisor is fearful of addressing the client's depression. In addition, neither Jessica nor the supervisor has sufficient clinical knowledge to realize that many of the client's problems may be due to brain injury. Both Brandon and Jessica recognize that their supervisors' clinical competence is not sufficient to assist with the current client.

When you are worried that the supervisor is not sufficiently competent, this problem is too large for you to address on your own with the supervisor. You may wish to discuss this issue first with a trusted older colleague or friend. However, it is essential that you bring this problem to the attention of faculty in your academic program. They should assist you in bringing it to the attention of the staff member who is in charge of training at the facility. These individuals should provide you with a different supervisor immediately, and they should take appropriate action to address the supervisor's knowledge deficits.

## COPING WITH THE CULTURALLY INCOMPETENT SUPERVISOR

*Joanie Stewart is worried about her supervision. She is working with an older lesbian woman who was a nurse in Vietnam during the war. Joanie is a lesbian as well. The client's presenting problem is panic disorder. Joanie asks the client whether she suffered discrimination or sexual harassment in the military. The client changes the subject. Joanie then asks about the client's relationships while in the military, and the client changes the subject again. When processing the session afterward, Joanie's supervisor (who is aware of Joanie's sexual orientation) criticizes her for bringing up these subjects, saying, "These lesbian issues aren't the point here. Why do you need to go there?" Joanie feels criticized and attacked.*

My supervisor strongly encouraged all supervisees of color to participate in the clinic-wide diversity committee. When I declined the invitation, my supervisor expressed curiosity... as he had experienced that as one of the most effective ways of educating White people about and working through racism. I acknowledged the utility of this approach as one way to promote an understanding of race, but maintained my perspective that previous experience with institutional diversity initiatives in predominantly White settings placed me in the position of teaching White people about race and racism...[which was] too psychologically and emotionally draining for me. My supervisor laughed and responded, "I don't know what they are doing to you all over at [the supervisee's university]." I felt like he was mocking me and disparaging my training program. (Jernigan et al., 2010)

Joanie's supervisor, unfortunately, is being both critical and culturally incompetent; these issues are not "lesbian issues." A helpful supervisory intervention would have been to help Joanie explore why the client avoided discussing these issues in therapy. Joanie understands that a more detailed understanding of the client's history can help put the current anxiety symptoms in context, but she was unable to elicit this information.

Negative experiences regarding cultural competence do sometimes occur in supervision. In a small qualitative study, Burkard, Johnson, et al. (2006) found that *all* supervisees of color had experienced a culturally unresponsive event, while more than *half* of European American supervisees had as well. In another qualitative study, Constantine and Sue (2007) cataloged seven types of racial microaggressions that Black supervisees experienced from White supervisors. These included invalidating racial-cultural issues that were brought up by the supervisee, making stereotypical assumptions about Black clients, offering culturally insensitive treatment recommendations, and blaming clients of color for problems stemming from oppression. Difficulties between supervisors and supervisees included making stereotypical assumptions about the Black supervisee, focusing primarily on the supervisee's clinical weaknesses (giving the impression they thought the supervisee was incompetent), or seeming reluctant to give sufficient constructive feedback (probably for fear of being seen as racist). The second vignette, cited previously, was from an article about racial identity development in supervision relationships, and both the supervisor and supervisee were of color. Thus, supervisors—whatever their ethnic backgrounds—may have insufficient training and sensitivity to multicultural issues.

Depending on your assessment of the supervisor's openness, you might give the supervisor feedback on culturally related ruptures in supervision. However, you might prefer getting input from the academic program and/or the training supervisor at the site about how to address this.

## COPING WITH THE IMPAIRED SUPERVISOR

*Michael Bell is worried about his supervision. His supervisor at the community mental health center is likable, but the supervisor talks so much about the helpfulness of Valium that Michael wonders whether she is addicted. The supervisor also has employed a former client who comes to her home and types up her psychological reports from her handwritten notes. Michael knows this former client and is aware that he has borderline traits.*

In the case of Michael, the supervisor may be impaired through prescription drug abuse and clearly has impaired judgment as well. The supervisor clearly has violated appropriate boundaries with clients, used poor judgment, and violated client confidentiality. This is an example of a supervisor who is engaging in professional misconduct. M. V. Ellis (2001) suggests that supervisees be aware of their rights and responsibilities as well as the rights and wrongs of supervision so that they can seek help if they need it. Michael should not address the issue directly with the supervisor. Instead, he should discuss his concerns with an appropriate authority and request a different supervisor.

## THE PRODUCTIVE SUPERVISORY RELATIONSHIP

*Rob Martinez, a mental health trainee, looks forward to his supervisory meetings with his supervisor, DeAngelo Williams. Rob feels supported by DeAngelo and appreciates hearing about the struggles that DeAngelo has had with his own clients. He feels that DeAngelo is interested in his ideas about how to work with his clients, and DeAngelo gives input that helps Rob enhance his own ideas and make them more workable. When Rob is confused, he finds that DeAngelo has a way of talking about clinical work that cuts through his confusion and clarifies the situation. Rob feels comfortable in the supervisory relationship and knows that he can count on DeAngelo to be there for him and his clients.*

*Vivian Medina, a mental health trainee, feels supported by her supervisor, Marianne Bishop. Vivian has had some struggles in her personal and professional life since starting graduate school. Marianne has been a mentor to Vivian and has provided her with invaluable professional advice, in addition to helpful supervision with Vivian's clients. Vivian and Marianne have had many discussions about challenging transference and countertransference issues. When Marianne suggests that Vivian seek therapy, Vivian knows that Marianne wants the best for her. While some of these discussions have been difficult, Vivian does not feel judged; instead she feels that Marianne has supported and mentored her.*

As a beginning psychotherapist, you will be anxious, and you need to be able to talk about these feelings with your supervisor. Some of the work you do with your clients may be "sensitive and challenging, and sometimes painful and difficult" (Walker & Jacobs, 2004, p. 13). Your relationship with your supervisor must be solid and supportive for you to be able to develop confidence in difficult clinical situations.

Barnett, Cornish, Goodyear, and Lichtenberg (2007) summarize the literature regarding the helpful supervisor, who will:

- Foster a nonthreatening and open relationship,
- Show empathy, support, and respect toward the supervisee,
- Validate and normalize the supervisee's experiences,
- Provide a safe environment for the vulnerable experience of learning new skills, and
- Be committed to the supervisee's professional development.

Even within a good supervisory relationship, counterproductive events can occur (Gray, Ladany, Walker, & Ancis, 2001). When there are challenges in the supervisory relationship, Nelson, Barnes, Evans, and Triggiano (2008) suggest that the best supervisors demonstrate humility, openness about personal challenges and feelings, and a willingness to talk about the problem and to acknowledge their own contributions to the challenging situation.

Give the supervisory relationship some time to grow and develop. Try to be appreciative of the strengths of your supervisor. Not all supervisors are good mentors, but they may still have helpful knowledge to impart to you that will help you grow as a professional. It is hoped that some of the examples in this chapter will help you decide whether to address these directly at the time or try to let the mistake go—since we can all make mistakes.

## RECOMMENDED READING

Berger, S. S., & Buchholz, E. S. (1993). On becoming a supervisee: Preparation for learning in a supervisory relationship. *Psychotherapy, 30*, 86–92.
> *The authors talk about appropriate education for supervisees who are beginning the supervisory process. As the supervisee, this article will inform you about important yet more advanced supervision topics, such as stages of development and parallel process.*

## DISCUSSION QUESTIONS

1. How could you work productively with a supervisor who is competent but is a mismatch with you in terms of temperament?
2. How could you work productively if you and the supervisor are not matched in theoretical orientation?
3. What policies and procedures does your academic program have if you have supervisory difficulties? How could you address this kind of problem effectively and appropriately?

## APPENDIX: QUESTIONS FOR YOUR SUPERVISOR

Whenever you get a new supervisor or go to a new training site, there are some questions that are helpful to ask. I have suggested questions throughout the text but have summarized many of them here for your convenience when meeting with a new supervisor.

Administrative and Procedural Issues

- What is the administrative structure at this site? How do I fit into that?
- Who do I need to know? Can you introduce me?
- How are fees dealt with in this setting?
- How are new clients assigned?

- How is informed consent obtained at this facility?
- How are clients educated about limits to confidentiality?
- Where are the Notice of Privacy Practices forms kept?
- Where are the informed consent forms?
- Do I discuss audiotaping verbally with clients, or is there a form they need to sign as well?
- What are the guidelines for release of information at this facility?
- Where are the release of information forms?
- What should I do if I get sick or have a personal emergency and need to cancel my clients?
- What are arrangements for vacation coverage for my clients?
- What are the clinic policies if a client brings me a gift?

## Documentation

- How are progress notes done at this facility? Do you require that I keep process notes? Are they discoverable in this state?
- How are initial intake interviews done at this facility? Are there any forms or templates that I need to fill out?
- How are treatment plans written and documented here? Can you show me a sample that has been done well?
- How do I find and access medical records at this facility?

## Electronic Communications

- Can I send e-mails to other health care professionals about clients securely at this site?
- What do you recommend about client contact by e-mail?
- Is there a clinic policy regarding e-mail with clients?
- Is there a clinic policy about online searches of clients?

## Supervisory Issues

- What is your theoretical orientation? How do you work with students who are trained in another orientation?
- How are trainee evaluations done in this setting? Can I look at your form for that?
- If I am having problems, what is the process for remediation?

## Client Care Issues

- Do you need me to do a Mental Status Exam? Can you teach me how?
- What diagnoses are particularly common in this client population?
- Do you have any recommended reading for me to learn more?

- What referrals are commonly made from this facility? Do you have brochures, business cards, or contact information for those facilities?
- How do you recommend that I deal with no-shows and cancellations?
- How do you suggest that I deal with clients' attendance problems?
- What thoughts do you have about self-disclosure with this client population?
- What are your thoughts about clients' requests for hugs?
- What do you think about attending client events?
- What should I do if a client appears prejudiced toward me?

Crisis Issues

- What are the procedures for outpatient commitment [if your state has it]?
- How can I find you if I'm having a client emergency? Who should I talk to if I can't find you?
- How are clients hospitalized voluntarily and involuntarily at this site?
- How are involuntary clients managed here?
- How are clients taken to a hospital from this setting?
- Is there a location where a client can be kept and monitored for pick-up and transportation to a hospital?
- How is essential clinical information about the client conveyed to hospital staff?
- What should I do if an agitated client—who is potentially violent, suicidal or otherwise a danger to self or others—leaves the building?
- What if a client gets violent? Should I try to help intervene after I call the police or security?
- Are trainees given training in self-defense, trained to "take down" a client, or trained how to restrain an overly agitated or potentially dangerous client?
- What steps should I take and what resources are available to me if I have an agitated, potentially violent client in my office? Are there panic buttons? Where are they?
- What should I do if a client brings any weapons to this facility?
- Is there a duty to warn law in this state? How have you addressed these issues when they come up?
- What are the procedures for child and elder abuse reporting in this state? How are these types of abuse defined in this state?

# 3

# The Therapeutic Frame

The *therapeutic frame* is a term drawn from psychodynamic literature, which likens the therapy to a painting (A. Gray, 1994). With a painting, the frame defines where the artwork begins and ends. With therapy, the *therapeutic frame* defines how, where, and when the therapy begins and ends. So the therapeutic frame refers to the structure of the session, including the location, frequency, duration, and fee for the sessions as well as what happens if the client misses or cancels any appointments. The therapeutic frame gives the client a stable structure for therapy.

When we consider the therapeutic frame, we also can think about when we are *not* doing therapy—for example, making routine phone calls, checking e-mail, and so on. Also, we do our utmost to keep psychotherapy out of situations where it does not belong (in Chapter 6, client–psychotherapist e-mail issues are covered). We never do psychotherapy with adults in inappropriate locations, such as restaurants, bars, social events, and so on.

However, in rare instances, we might consider a home visit if the client has prolonged physical illness, or we might visit a client in the hospital if ill (Gutheil & Gabbard, 1993). In addition, behavioral treatment of phobias could appropriately involve meeting in an elevator, plane, or other phobic locations. Gutheil and Gabbard (1993) counsel that "the existence of a body of professional literature, a clinical rationale, and risk–benefit documentation will be useful in protecting the clinician in such a situation from misconstruction of the therapeutic efforts" (p. 192).

## PSYCHOTHERAPIST'S RESPONSIBILITIES TO MAINTAIN THE THERAPEUTIC FRAME

To maintain the therapeutic frame, you have certain basic responsibilities. You must be on time for the scheduled therapy appointments, and you must not forget appointment times. Of course, none of us is perfect, so if you do forget a session, apologize, discuss the impact of this on the client as needed, and move on. However, if you find yourself forgetting more than one therapy appointment per year, you should talk to your supervisor to devise a better system to keep track of your responsibilities. Similarly, if you are running late, apologize, discuss the impact on the client as needed, and move on. If you find yourself running late for over 5 percent of your appointments, you should discuss this with your supervisor and address your lateness issue proactively.

Do not answer phone calls, text messages, or any other kind of message during a psychotherapy session. The session belongs to the client, and you should not be distracted. However, in rare instances, you may be expecting an emergency call; in this case, inform the client at the beginning of the session. If the emergency call comes though, allow additional time at the end of the client's session or reschedule another session the same week at no charge (paragraph informed by Gabbard, 2010).

## THE OFFICE ENVIRONMENT

Your office can tell a lot about you; "visual cues available in the therapist's office speak abundantly of the character of the occupant through the order or disorder of the office contents, the expression of taste—or lack of it—in the décor, and the comfort or discomfort of the furnishings" (Gutheil & Gabbard, 1998, p. 412). As a beginning psychotherapist, you may have little control over the actual furnishings of the office and the office may be hard-edged and institutional. However, be aware that your clients may look at your office and draw conclusions about you from what they see. If allowed at your site, the research cited below suggests that you can help your clients feel more comfortable and confident in their work with you if you can make a few minor and inexpensive adjustments to the office environment.

In a review of the limited research on the psychotherapist's office, Pressly and Heesacker (2001) recommend that the psychotherapist personalize the office with artwork focusing in nature or animals (preferably not posters) and plants. Many therapists do not put any family pictures in their offices, especially those who do psychodynamic work (Devlin et al., 2009). Comfortable furniture, rugs, and softer lighting are recommended. Soft surfaces help to reduce office noise. In an experimental study, Nasar and Devlin (2011) found that softer offices led to greater feelings of comfort, expectations of quality care, and perceptions that the therapist is well qualified. In the same study, an orderly and neat office also led to increased perceptions that the therapist is well qualified. Devlin et al. (2009) found that the display of multiple credentials (diplomas, certificates, awards) also contributed to a higher perception of the therapist's qualifications. If the client is seated on an easily movable chair or a longer couch, she can moderate the space between the two of you; comfortable interpersonal distances typically vary between individuals and cultures.

Of course, the office should be handicapped accessible whenever possible. See Chapter 20 for recommendations concerning safety issues and your office. Finally, I recommend avoiding potpourri, scented candles, and so on because they can trigger allergies, asthma attacks, and migraines.

## ATTENDANCE POLICIES

### Cancellation and No-Show Policy

*If you need to cancel, please call at least 24 hours ahead. Cancellation fees are as follows:*

- *24 hours or more: No fee*
- *Less than 24 hours: $100 fee*
- *If you do not show up for your appointment and do not call, there is a $100 fee as well.*

*Special Circumstances or Emergencies: If you have a crisis or illness and can't attend your appointment, call me, and we will talk about it.*

*My signature below shows that I understand and agree to comply with the cancellation policy.*

As a beginning psychotherapist, you will probably be first working at an agency. The agency is likely to have a pre-existing policy regarding clients canceling or not showing up for sessions. You need to know what that policy is and to be sure that the client has been informed of it in writing or verbally prior to or during the first session.

In a private-practice setting, a policy, such as the one quoted previously, might be given to the client to sign as part of the intake materials filled out prior to the first session. As recommended by Gans and Counselman (1996), this policy sets clear guidelines that the session fee is to be paid in case of absence but that the psychotherapist is willing to have some flexibility as well.

## CLIENT NO-SHOWS

*Tom Johnson has schizophrenia and lives with his mother. Tom is low functioning, and he tends to be disorganized. He has again missed his regular appointment with his psychotherapist this month. He is pleasant and engaged when he is in the office. Tom's psychotherapist calls and talks with Tom about attending his next appointment. He asks Tom if it is okay to talk to Tom's mother and ask her to help Tom remember his appointments. Tom says yes and hands the phone to his mother. She agrees to help Tom remember to attend his next appointment.*

*Greg Campbell is a high-functioning client who has dropped out of therapy on two previous occasions per his self-report. He does not show up at his weekly psychotherapy appointment. Lately, he has been canceling more frequently. Greg's psychotherapist knows that he is not a high-risk client and realizes he may be dropping out again. The psychotherapist leaves a message about the missed appointment on Greg's cell phone and requests that Greg call. When he doesn't call within a week, the case is closed.*

Do not take no-shows personally; they happen to every psychotherapist with every population, at least occasionally. Give the client 15 minutes to be late for the session, then call. If the client does not pick up, you might leave a message like this:

> "Hi Tom, this is [psychotherapist name], and I'm calling you at 2:15 Thursday afternoon. I'm calling because I had you down for an appointment at 2:00 today. Perhaps we had a miscommunication or you are running late. Can you give me a call about this soon? Thanks so much. Goodbye."

If you reach the client, just ask,

> "Hi Tom, this is [psychotherapist name]. How are you? I'm calling because I had you down for an appointment at 2 this afternoon. Is that what you had?"

Of course, you must document the no-show in the client's chart, along with whatever phone calls or other activities you did to address it. Note, however, that some supervisors will advise you not to call high-functioning clients who have no-showed; discuss this issue with your supervisor. If you have many no-shows with several of your clients, it may be helpful to discuss rapport building with your supervisor.

If the client does not show up or call, consult with your supervisor about what the next step should be. Depending on the clinic's policies, as well as the risk level and functioning level of the client, you might close the case after waiting a week or so, you might make another outreach call, or you might send a letter—with or without another appointment time.

You should never let the client develop an expectation that you will be waiting at the next regularly scheduled appointment time after a no-show. If you have a hunch that the client might show up next week, even after this week's no-show, you might leave another phone message:

> "Hi Tom, this is [psychotherapist name]. I need to let you know that I can't hold your appointment for next Thursday unless I hear from you by Monday. Please let me know what you would like to do."

## CLIENT CANCELLATIONS

*Juan Martinez is a mental health trainee. His client, Melinda Fox, has problems with chronic pain. He has been working with her on relaxation techniques and coping skills that she can use to increase her functional ability and her activity level. The client keeps canceling her appointments. She often cancels at the last minute, stating that she has medical appointments—appointments that she has probably known about for weeks. Or she leaves a vague message that "I'm not feeling well." Juan feels that she is not respectful of the time that he has dedicated to her therapy on a weekly basis. He is aggravated and resentful about these frequent cancellations. Clearly, he thinks, other matters are more important to the client than her psychotherapy or treating her psychotherapist with respect. Juan discusses the issue with his supervisor, who suggests that he broach the issue with the client nonjudgmentally. At the next session, Juan states, "Melinda, I'm noticing that you've canceled your appointments several times over the past 2 months. It seems that you've been having a lot of health problems. I'm concerned about how this is affecting you. Can you tell me about that?"*

Do not be concerned about an occasional cancellation. Clients vary. Some attend very regularly and never cancel except for extreme emergencies. However, others cancel at the last minute all too frequently. When you've gotten a cancellation message, return the call, let the client know that you got the message, and remind the client of the next appointment time. Gans and Counselman (1996) recommend that any symbolic or emotional issues about the canceled session be addressed in the next session prior to talking about any fees due.

Try not to be concerned if your client has canceled for the first time. However, make a note of the cancellation in the chart, along with the circumstances around it—specifically, what the excuse was and how much notice was given (e.g., 1 hour or 2 days). If canceling becomes a pattern, it will be helpful to have these notes to review later.

If you have a client like Juan's, you will need to address the frequent cancellations in therapy. It is likely that this will be a fruitful avenue of inquiry, informing you of other dysfunction in the client's life as well as giving you and the client an opportunity to reduce the number of cancellations.

If the client is canceling frequently (at least one session in four), the client may be thinking of dropping out of therapy. Or it may be a sign of a chaotic and disorganized lifestyle. When you suspect this, do not hesitate to comment on it:

"I've noticed that you've been missing about a fourth of your sessions. Let's talk about this. Are you missing other appointments, too?"

If several of your clients are canceling frequently, discuss this issue in supervision. Your supervisor may have some insight into any issues that you may have with building effective therapeutic relationships with the clients.

## CLIENT SHOWS UP LATE

*Kimberly Shaheen is a high-functioning client who has attention-deficit/hyperactivity disorder (ADHD). Kimberly tends to run off to her appointments after spending extra time winding up things at work. She speeds to the session in rush-hour traffic and arrives distracted and late. Problem-solving about when to leave work has not helped. So, her psychotherapist, Michelle Park, asks her about the lateness at the beginning of the session: "Kimberly, I'm noticing that you are still having problems with being late, even though we moved our appointment time back. I'm guessing you might have this problem in other areas of your life. How is that affecting you?"*

Lateness can be a rare event with a particular client, or it can be part of a pattern. In most cases, if the client is late, you should still end the session at the usual time. Extend the time only if you believe that the lateness is a fluke, you won't be late for the next client, and you aren't pressed for time. Be aware that if you extend the session, you may set up unrealistic expectations that you will extend the session every time the client shows up late. These unrealistic expectations can then lead to disappointment and conflict between you and the client later on. However, if the client is in crisis and you are concerned about risk, take whatever time is needed.

As with cancellations, lateness can be a pattern. Each time a client is late, document at the beginning of the progress note how late she was so that you can refer to it again later. Once this has become a regular pattern, it is time to address it, as Michelle did in the previous vignette.

If the client blames a logistical reason, consider problem-solving with her:

"So you get out of work at 5:00 and take the bus, which sometimes runs late, and you get here at 5:45 instead of 5:30. How about if we move your appointment to 6:30 on Wednesday instead? Then you won't be so rushed."

However, often problem-solving will not resolve the client's lateness. After a couple more episodes of lateness, you may wish to ask about it again, as Michelle did in the previous vignette. Note that the question is not whether the lateness is occurring in other areas—it almost certainly is. Instead, Michelle asks how it is affecting the client, since this is less likely to provoke defensiveness. By discussing the lateness, you are likely to elicit useful information about the client and her other life struggles.

## IRREGULAR ATTENDANCE

*Angelina Ramirez is a new psychotherapy client for Jordan Ross, a mental health trainee. Angelina came in 15 minutes late for her appointment on the first session. Before the second session, she called stating that she had forgotten the time of the session. She came on time for her third session but came an hour late for the fourth session, insisting that Jordan had made an error in his calendar.*

*Martin Brooks is another one of Jordan's new psychotherapy clients. Martin attended his first session on time. The next week, he canceled at the last minute, stating he had to take his mother to a doctor's appointment. The third week, Martin came in 25 minutes late with a crisis to talk about. The fourth week, he had a doctor's appointment for himself that conflicted with the therapy session time, and he canceled again, leaving a message the morning of the appointment. The week after that, Martin comes in 15 minutes late, saying that all the buses were running late. At that appointment, Jordan says, "Martin, I'm worried about you. I'm noticing that you're having a really hard time getting to your sessions regularly and on time. I see that you have a lot of responsibilities. I understand that, but I'm concerned because you aren't getting the treatment that you need. Realistically, we can't make much progress if I don't see you for the full session every week. Can we talk about this? I'd really like to help you with it, if I can."*

Unless there is a life-threatening crisis, do not focus on any other therapeutic issues until the attendance issue is resolved. Irregular attendance needs to be addressed first because you can't effectively treat a client who is not coming regularly to therapy. Next time you get the client in the office, bring up the subject gently, as Jordan does in the previous vignette.

When your client is not attending many appointments, it is impossible to provide an effective treatment, so you need to determine the cause. There are many reasons why clients do not regularly attend their psychotherapy sessions. Here are some of them:

- Thought disorder
- ADHD
- Client is characterologically disorganized
- Client is used to living a chaotic, disorganized lifestyle, going from one crisis to the next
- Client does not make psychotherapy a priority; others' needs come first
- Ambivalence about psychotherapy
- Anxiety about psychotherapy
- Client doesn't understand how weekly sessions can help more than occasional crisis sessions

If your client has a history of bipolar disorder, psychotic disorder, or major depression, evaluate for thought disorder and other psychotic symptoms (see Chapter 9). If any of these appear to be present, communicate with the client's psychiatrist about it. The psychiatrist can prescribe medications that will almost certainly help.

Here is how an articulate client might talk about her continued difficulties with mild thought disorder:

"I can't seem to get organized. At home, the house is a mess. I just stand there looking at it, and I can't decide what to do first, so I don't do any of it. I'm overwhelmed with e-mail at work and find myself spacing out at times. When I'm driving, other drivers honk at me because I can't seem to focus on the traffic lights all the time. I've had two accidents in the past 3 months."

Alternatively, your client may have ADHD, so screen for that as well (see Chapter 9). Medications can help concentration. In addition, you can take a skills-based approach with ADHD clients (Solanto et al., 2008).

If the client is habitually disorganized or her life has been chaotic, try a problem-solving approach. Ask if the client has a paper calendar or smartphone with her. If so, remind her to put the appointments in it. Take time during the session to do so. If not, suggest that the client get one of those, keep it with her at all times, and use it regularly. She may have some resistance to doing this ("My dad has one of those, not me!"). You can explore it as needed in the session:

> "I'm concerned that your forgetfulness might be creating problems for you in other areas of your life. How is that affecting you?"

There is also a possibility that the client does not make his needs and health a priority. Discuss what the personal costs have been to the client of ignoring his mental health. Help the client problem-solve about how to assertively address situations that might interfere with therapy.

If you suspect that the client is ambivalent about coming to therapy, this issue should be discussed immediately. Be aware that often the ambivalent client may make different excuses every week and may see your concern about attendance as criticism. Try to bring up the issue gently:

> "I've been very concerned about you, since I've noticed that you've been canceling a lot of appointments for medical reasons. It seems that these medical issues are having a negative impact on your ability to get things done that you want to do. Can we talk about this for a while? I want to know more about how this is affecting you."

You may find that, despite your best efforts, attendance has not improved. In certain situations, you may enlist the support of the client's family, or the clinic might provide reminder calls (Lefforge, Donohue, & Strada, 2007). Discuss this with your supervisor before implementing any further interventions.

Keep in mind that it is not ethical to provide a treatment that you know is ineffective. Additionally, this puts you in a problematic situation with respect to professional liability. Discuss these issues carefully with your supervisor. Perhaps you may wish to continue to schedule the client if he is high risk and seems to derive a modicum of increased stability from having a psychotherapist. Document this decision and your reasoning thoroughly in the chart. Or you may decide to be a little more confrontational:

> "I see that you are still struggling with getting to your appointments regularly and on time. I'm wondering if this is the right time in your life for you to be in therapy. Perhaps the other things in your life are more important right now. What do you think?"

Often the client will agree, and the case can be closed.

## CLIENT WON'T LEAVE AT END OF SESSION

Certain clients want to linger at the end of the session time. Many psychotherapists, consciously or unconsciously, develop behaviors that signal to the client that the session is over. Perhaps you might close your notepad, sit forward on the edge of your chair, or move to check the next appointment time in your calendar. Stand up, if necessary, to indicate that the session is over. Developing a cue such as this will help the client know that it is time to wind up. If you tend to run late with many of your clients' sessions, discuss this issue with your supervisor.

If there is a problem with ending a particular client's sessions on time, first try to problem-solve. Try to figure out why the client is likely to linger. If he lingers to pay his bill, have him pay it at the beginning of the session. If he lingers to talk about schedules, coordinate schedules at the beginning of the session. Try to figure out how long the client is lingering. If he lingers for 5 minutes, make a gesture that you are done 5 minutes before the end of the session time. If he loses track of time, arrange the office so that he can easily see a clock.

If you find that despite your best efforts to end the session on time, the client still lingers, you will need to address that with him directly:

> "I'm noticing that our sessions always seem to run late. I'm hoping that you can help me with this by trying to help me end the session on time. Since our sessions start at 1, they are scheduled to end at about 1:45. Can you help me keep track of this?"

If this is not effective, you will need to determine why the client feels a need to keep you late. (For example, a client may feel that he is special, since you are willing to stay a little late to wind up his session.) Bring this up at the beginning of another session:

> "It seems that despite our best efforts, our sessions are still running late. I'm wondering if we could talk about this for a little bit. What are your thoughts about that? Is there any way in which you feel it is helpful when our sessions run late?"

## A CRISIS INTERFERES WITH THE NEXT APPOINTMENT

*Armani Mosley is a mental health trainee. His client, Rose Washington, has come to her appointment feeling suicidal. Armani spends Rose's whole session talking with her about this and realizes that she needs to be hospitalized. He knows that he will need to spend at least the next hour working with his supervisor and Rose's psychiatrist to make this happen. Armani has a client scheduled for the next therapy session, and the client is now outside his office waiting. Rose has agreed to hospitalization and understands why it is necessary. Armani feels that it is safe to leave Rose alone for a few minutes. So Armani asks her to wait outside his office and asks the other client to come in briefly. Armani says, "I'm really sorry, but I've had an emergency come up with another client. I estimate that I'll be available in about an hour, but I can't be sure of the exact time. Would it be possible for you to wait until then, or should I reschedule you?" The client states that he understands since he has been in crisis himself in the past. The client says that he will just come back later in the week. Armani gives him another appointment and then proceeds to help Rose with her hospitalization.*

In rare events, a client's crisis or a personal crisis will interfere with another client's appointment. As Armani did in this vignette, you must evaluate this and make a plan before you can end the session. In most cases, you will feel that it is safe to leave the crisis client briefly in your office or in another location, as Armani did, and spend a few minutes addressing the other client's appointment briefly.

You may see that the crisis will be very time consuming, or you have a very tight schedule, so you can't run late all day. In that case, this would be more appropriate: "I'm sorry, but a crisis has come up with another client, and I have no idea how long this will take. I don't want to waste your time and keep you waiting. Is there any chance that you could come back later this week for your session?"

Most clients understand, but when you see the client for the session that was postponed, it is wise to apologize again and ask about the client's feelings about the canceled session.

## CLIENT CRITICIZES OTHER HEALTH CARE PROFESSIONALS

*Tim Browne, a new client, comes in for his first session. Immediately, he starts criticizing his primary care physician: "That guy's a quack. He only made me worse after seeing him." He then moved on to criticize his psychiatrist: "She's a bitch, and rude besides. She can't get my meds right. She's torturing me with all these blood tests she thinks she needs. Those people in the lab are vampires. I don't see why they need all that blood."*

Keep in mind that the client may or may not accurately represent what happened with his other health care professionals. Perhaps the client has borderline personality disorder and is now devaluing the other professional. Perhaps the client is paranoid and thinks that a professional was out to get him. Maybe the client takes minor complications like rescheduling as a personal insult. Maybe the client is suspicious of everyone because of a history of childhood trauma and neglect. Thus, you cannot know whether the other professional is actually at fault, and it is usually inappropriate and unprofessional to join in the criticism.

Try to maintain the focus on the client's emotional issues and maintain appropriate professional boundaries by empathizing with the client without necessarily agreeing with the client's perspective:

- "I'm sorry that didn't work out for you."
- "It sounds like you were disappointed in how things went with your previous psychotherapist."
- "It sounds like you're feeling angry at your psychiatrist right now."

Be wary of these criticisms. If you take them at face value, this may result in a worst-case scenario, which is commonly called "splitting." Splitting occurs when the staff has split opinions and they are arguing and in turmoil over a client. Splitting also occurs when one staff member believes that the client has to be protected from other staff whom she thinks will victimize the client. In these cases, the client's statements have spilled out of the therapy session and are disrupting the client's care and the cooperation of staff. If you recognize that splitting is happening, point this out to other staff so that it can be discussed at the staff level.

## CLIENT CHATS AT LENGTH ON PHONE

Sometimes you might need to call a client to reschedule an appointment or address another business matter. You know that the client is stable. However, the client wants to keep you on the phone and starts talking about recent personal events. What do you do?

Unless it is a crisis, it is best to confine psychotherapy material to the psychotherapy session. You are a busy health care professional and cannot be expected to talk at length on the phone. When the client takes a breath, interrupt her and state kindly, "I'm so sorry. This sounds very important, but I only had a few minutes to call you about rescheduling. I really have to go. Can we talk about this when I see you on Monday?" Do not let the client develop an expectation that if she gets you on the phone, she gets an impromptu brief mini-session.

## CANCELLATIONS DUE TO PSYCHOTHERAPIST'S MINOR ILLNESS

You will occasionally need to cancel appointments. In most cases, this will be due to a minor illness on your part. Do not try to go to therapy sessions when you are preoccupied by how unwell you feel. Minor sniffles are okay, as are occasional aches and pains, but carefully consider any illness and determine whether it will distract you too much from your clients' needs.

When you are ill, you should cancel the appointments yourself if possible. Call your supervisor if you don't have the clients' contact information. If you feel that you may be getting sick while at work, take home the clients' phone numbers so that you can cancel your appointments over the next few days. Call the clients and leave a brief message:

> "Hi, this is [psychotherapist name], and I need to cancel your appointment today because I am not feeling well. Let's meet again at your appointment next Tuesday at 5:00."

Avoid providing too many details about your illness, and if the client asks at his next session, you can usually briefly state, "I'm feeling much better, thanks for asking," and change the subject. Certain dependent or highly attached clients can become upset when you are ill. You will need to be alert to the client's emotions when asking about your illness, and if the client seems distressed, you will need to explore this issue in the next therapy session—but not over the phone when you are ill.

## CANCELLATIONS DUE TO PSYCHOTHERAPIST'S FAMILY EMERGENCY

> "...the client complained that the therapist was not paying attention to her distress about her husband forgetting her birthday. The therapist apologized and then informed the client that her granddaughter had drowned in the family pool the previous day. The embarrassed and confused client left quickly, unprepared for such a tragic disclosure. The therapist would have served her clients' needs better had she taken more time to grieve." (Pope & Keith-Spiegel, 2008, p. 647)

Eventually, you will need to cancel appointments because of a family emergency. When calling clients about this, you might say,

> "Hi, this is [psychotherapist name]. I'm afraid that I've had a family emergency, and I will need to cancel your appointment for this week. I'll see you next week as scheduled."

Always remind clients to come in at the next appointment time because otherwise they may be uncertain about the length of time you are out. If the client expresses sympathy or concern, answer briefly as you feel comfortable, say thank you, and move on. However, again, in certain circumstances, the client will have an emotional reaction to your personal situation that will need to be explored in therapy—but not over the phone during the family emergency.

Sometimes serious situations arise: a family member could be seriously ill, or you might lose a close family member to death. In these cases, you need to accept that for at least a brief period of time, you will not be able to be emotionally available to your clients. As soon as you realize that you are in this type of situation, contact your supervisor and make arrangements for coverage and cancellations as needed. Change your professional voicemail message and indicate whom your clients should contact if a crisis should arise in your absence. The voicemail should also include when you expect to be back in the office.

You may worry that your clients will see you being upset about your family emergency. Gabbard (2007) quotes the following wise advice from a colleague upon the death of his mother: "So what if your patient sees you tear up? Why would that be a terrible thing? So what if the two of you collude in avoiding the topic for a session or two? You can always come back to it [during a later session]" (p. 927).

Two types of errors can occur following a family emergency. One error is overestimating how much you can handle and not make appropriate clinical arrangements during the time when you do not have the physical or emotional resources to cope with your clients, as in the vignette above. The other error is underestimating your ability to be present with the client even though you are not feeling 100 percent back to normal. In fact, Hayes, Yeh, and Eisenberg (2007) found that recently bereaved therapists were seen by clients as less empathetic, although equally connected, credible, and capable of deep psychotherapy work. As Walker and Jacobs (2004) suggest, sometimes "competence can be good enough" (p. 101). Remember that even if you are not able to be as attentive or engaged as you typically are, your clients may still benefit from your concerned presence. Discuss this issue with your supervisor if you are unsure whether to return to work yet.

## PSYCHOTHERAPIST VACATIONS

Clients need advance notice of your vacations. I recommend at least 3 to 4 weeks' notice. Choose a specific week in which to begin notifying all clients:

"I wanted to let you know that I will be out of the office for 2 weeks starting on

April 10, so I will have to cancel two of your weekly therapy sessions next month."

See what comments the clients have. Most clients will be fine. However, certain clients, especially those who feel very dependent or have abandonment issues (Kernberg, Selzer, Koenigsberg, Carr, & Appelbaum, 1989), may have strong reactions to your absence. Many clients may ask questions about why you are out and even where you are going on vacation. Being vague can come across as overly secretive or sometimes prompt worry in a client (Barnett, 2011). Discuss how to handle client concerns and how much to disclose with your supervisor. Two weeks before the vacation, mention it again: "I just wanted to remind you that I will be out for 2 weeks, starting 2 weeks from now." One week before the vacation, remind the client once more and also remind the client of the next appointment date:

> "Since I'm going to be out starting next week, I just wanted to be sure that you have the date of our next meeting in your calendar. That will be on April 27 at 4:00 p.m. Should I write that down for you, or do you have your calendar with you?"

I have to admit that I usually remember to remind about 90% of my clients of my upcoming vacation on any one week, so starting about four weeks in advance helps assure that everyone gets at least two reminders of my upcoming vacation.

Before you go on vacation, you must obtain clinical coverage for your client caseload. All active clients need to know who will be covering their case while you are gone and how to contact the covering psychotherapist in your absence. Perhaps the covering psychotherapist will be your clinical supervisor, the client's psychiatrist, another treatment team member, or another practitioner at the facility. If the client knows the person who will be covering, just tell the client who it is. If the covering psychotherapist is not known to the client, write out the name and phone number of this person for the client. Or you can tell the client that the covering psychotherapist's name and number will be on your outgoing phone message. You should document in the chart that the client has been informed of your absence and that the client is aware of coverage arrangements.

Change your voicemail message prior to your absence. Specify on the message the exact dates that you are out and returning. Specify that you will not receive any messages during that time. Leave the name and number of the covering psychotherapist and any additional information that might be helpful in case of emergency while you are gone. State that callers can leave nonurgent messages and that you will call them back upon your return.

Work closely with your supervisor, the treating psychiatrist, and/or the treatment team to be sure that unstable clients have the treatment they need in your absence. Certain unstable clients may need to have a session or two while you are gone. Decide in consultation with your supervisor and the client whether sessions should be scheduled during your absence or whether sessions are optional and up to the client's discretion. Begin discussing these coverage plans with your supervisor 2 to 3 weeks in advance of your vacation.

## FEE ISSUES

*Holly Gibson is a mental health trainee working in a community mental health clinic affiliated with her training program. There are undergraduate assistants who work at the front desk. Clients are supposed to stop at the front desk before their psychotherapy sessions to pay their fees. The clinic director informs Holly that a client of hers has been giving excuses each time she is supposed to pay her fee and now has not paid for the past three sessions. Clinic policy is to refer clients out if they have more than three fees*

*unpaid. The clinic director tells Holly to address this issue with the client at the next ses-*
*sion. Holly feels confused about how to address this issue with the client. Holly, herself,*
*gets no money from the fees that are paid to the clinic. She worries that she is not doing*
*a good job with the client and, deep down, worries that the client may not be getting*
*her money's worth.*

Women therapists particularly, socialized to prioritize others' needs, may be
painfully mindful that we earn a living from the suffering of others. In the
short step from empathizing with our clients to identifying with our clients,
we find ourselves considering that we take a vacation or make an extravagant
purchase that our clients could not afford, using money that represents the
sacrifices they make to pay for therapy. Because the exchange of money in
therapy takes place in an intimate context, therapists, especially those paid
directly by their clients, are faced daily with questions about economic injus-
tice in a way that those who work for a paycheck are not. (Hill, 1999, p. 1)

As Hill so eloquently states, even experienced psychotherapists can struggle
with emotional and social justice issues with regard to the psychotherapy fee.
Psychotherapists with a strong impulse to nurture may feel an obligation to take
care of their clients and may have some intrapsychic conflicts about taking a fee.
Beginning psychotherapists can be insulated from most fee issues, as in the previous vignette, so when the fee needs to be addressed, they can feel especially
uncertain.

As in the previous vignette, beginning psychotherapists may be insecure about
how much they can help and not feel justified in collecting fees. In fact, in a study
of clients at a mental health training clinic (Aubry, Hunsley, Josephson, & Vito,
2000), most clients indicated that they had gone to the clinic because they could
get a reduced fee, but nearly 90 percent of clients were satisfied with paying the
reduced fee they had been charged for their psychotherapy.

McWilliams (2004) wisely points out that when the psychotherapist does not
collect a fee, the client is being exploitative of the psychotherapist. There are
undoubtedly emotional issues that contribute to the client feeling entitled in this
way, and these should be explored in therapy. However, you still need to collect the
fee. You might wish to call the client, then state the policy clearly and confidently:

"The clinic policy is that when a client owes three session fees, we need to get
payment in full to continue therapy. So please bring payment with you at the
time of your next appointment."

Two legal issues are important for psychotherapists to know about fee payment.
First, psychotherapists are sometimes tempted to accept the payment from the
insurance company as payment in full; keep in mind that you cannot do that
since it is considered insurance fraud and may get you into legal trouble (Simon,
1995). The second issue is that if you stop psychotherapy abruptly for a client who
is not paying the fee, this could be considered abandonment (R. F. Small, 1994).

In the case of a high-functioning low-risk client, who is fully capable of seeking treatment elsewhere, this is not a significant issue, although referrals should be provided (Treloar, 2010). However, if the client is low functioning or high risk, you may need to see the client again and during that session work with the client to contact an alternative low-cost or free alternative and set up an appointment. If the client is in crisis, you may need to see the client until she is stable enough to tolerate a transfer (Treloar, 2010). You should follow up by phone to ensure that the client attended the appointment (and therefore is not abandoned). Carefully document all your efforts in this regard in the chart.

## RECOMMENDED READING

Gans, J. S., & Counselman, E. F. (1996). The missed session: A neglected aspect of psychodynamic psychotherapy. *Psychotherapy, 33*, 43–50.
   *The authors discuss many of the potential meanings behind clients' cancellations and make practical suggestions about managing policies about missed sessions.*
Treloar, H. R. (2010). Financial and ethical considerations for professionals in psychology. *Ethics and Behavior, 20*(6), 454–465.
   *Treloar provides a helpful overview of common fee issues, including ethics of abandonment for nonpayment, insurance issues, pro bono treatment, barter for fees, and the impact of the federal Mental Health Parity Act.*

## DISCUSSION QUESTIONS

1. How would you like to personalize your office? What would these items say about you? What would you say if clients asked you questions about them?
2. What is the no-show and cancellation policy at the agency where you are working? What is the rationale behind this policy? If you were setting the policy, what policy would you set? Why?
3. When you are out of the office, who covers your clients? What are all the logistical steps to make that happen effectively and inform everyone who needs to know?
4. What difficulties do you expect to encounter in collecting fees from clients? How do you think Holly should collect the fee from her client? What client issues might contribute to nonpayment of fees?

# 4

# Boundaries

Like any relationship that the client has with a health care professional, the main focus of the psychotherapy relationship is the well-being of just one person: the client. But the psychotherapy relationship is unique because the focus is on the client's emotional well-being rather than physical well-being. To keep the focus on the client, refrain from talking very much about yourself. You need to maintain a *boundary* between the client and your personal activities, needs, emotional functioning, and so on. This boundary allows the client's difficulties to be addressed productively, without your personal issues intruding. This also allows your personal life to remain separate from that of the client, which is important in fostering your own emotional well-being. Therapeutic *boundaries* are defined by Gutheil (2005) as "the edge of appropriate professional conduct" (p. 89). *Boundaries* can also refer to which topics belong in the session and which do not.

## BOUNDARY CROSSINGS

*Rajiv Kumar is a psychotherapy trainee. A couple that he was treating for marital therapy canceled their termination session, since their baby was born a little earlier than had been expected. He sent the couple a card congratulating them on the birth of the baby and indicating that he'd be happy to reschedule the appointment whenever they were ready to do so.*

*Alexandra Gutierrez, a psychotherapy trainee, goes outside after her last client and finds a blizzard. As she is exiting the parking lot, she sees her last client trudging through the snow. She knows that the client walks 10 blocks to the train stop. She stops and offers him a ride to the train.*

Gutheil (2005) defines *boundary crossings* as "transient, nonexploitative deviations from classical therapeutic or general clinical practice in which the treater steps out to a minor degree from strict verbal psychotherapy" (p. 89). Glass (2003) adds that "boundary crossings relate to the psychotherapist's attempts to enhance the treatment, while boundary violations, which more grossly breach the patient's physical or psychological subjective space, often do so in the service of the therapist's interests" (p. 432). Gutheil (2005) defines *boundary violations* as "essentially harmful deviations from normal parameters of treatment—deviations that *do* harm the patient, usually through some sort of exploitation that breaks the rule 'first, do no harm' " (p. 89).

Examples of boundary crossings include offering a crying patient a tissue, helping a fallen patient up from the floor, helping an elderly patient on with a coat, writing cards to a patient during a long absence, home visits based on the patient's medical needs, calling a client who is apprehensive prior to a surgical procedure, suggesting a decreased fee for a client who has lost a job, or allowing sessions to run over the allotted time when the client is tearful, needy, or deeply upset (Glass, 2003; Gutheil, 2005). The previous two case vignettes are additional examples of boundary crossings. If limited and empathetic, occasional boundary crossings can be therapeutically appropriate. However, they should be discussed at the next psychotherapy session, and they should be carefully documented.

The context in which the boundary-related behavior occurs is of vital importance in assessing its significance (Gutheil, 2005; Gutheil & Gabbard, 1998). Gutheil (2005) goes on to clarify that "the definition is highly context-dependent. The relevant contexts might be the treater's ideology, the stage of therapy, the patient's condition or diagnosis, the geographical setting or the cultural milieu among others...Context is a critical and determinative factor" (p. 89). For example, in certain circumstances and clinical settings, it may be appropriate for the psychotherapist to engage in case management activities in addition to traditional therapy, which could entail securing services, financial assistance, or food for the client. It may be appropriate for a behavioral psychotherapist to accompany a client in his car if they are doing a desensitization hierarchy regarding driving across bridges. Alternatively, a psychodynamic psychotherapist accompanying a client in the car would generally be considered a boundary violation. Be especially cautious of boundary issues if doing home visits (see Knapp & Slattery, 2004, for further information).

When considering a boundary crossing behavior, Pope and Keith-Spiegel (2008) suggest the following considerations. Consider both the best possible outcome and the worst possible outcome of the boundary crossing; is there a risk of serious harm? Consider any uneasy feelings, doubt, and confusion. These feelings may be informing you of a risk that you are not consciously aware of; talk this over with your supervisor.

## BOUNDARY VIOLATIONS

*Lauren Smith is a psychotherapy trainee. She is getting a divorce and needs to find a new condominium. One of her clients is a real estate agent who has some similar problems. She confides some of her concerns in him, including a brief description of her marital difficulties, and asks him for advice on real estate.*

*Jonathan Paul is a psychotherapist in private practice. He has a low-income client who recently lost her job. Jonathan decides to help her out by hiring her to do his filing, clean his office, and run personal and professional errands for him.*

*Al Chavez is a psychotherapy trainee. He is working with a client, Sally Ruiz. Sally suffers from depression and has a physically abusive boyfriend. Al is concerned about Sally, who often comes in highly distraught. He violates clinic rules by staying late to see her for 2-hour sessions during her more stressful periods (the clinic forbids trainees seeing clients after clinic hours are over). He gives Sally his cell phone number, and she calls him one or two times every week to discuss her difficulties. He doesn't tell his supervisor about this because he doesn't want to hear what his supervisor will say. He feels that he is doing the right thing for Sally and that his supervisor wouldn't understand. However, he is starting to feel overwhelmed by Sally's demands for his attention. After one particularly intense session, Sally becomes very angry at Al for refusing to schedule her again later that week. Al won't stay late that day because he has preexisting plans, and he feels that it is time to set some boundaries with Sally. Sally leaves in a rage. The next week, she files a complaint at the clinic alleging that Al exploited her sexually. Al feels that now he has to admit everything to his supervisor. However, his supervisor does not know what to believe, since Al had been secretive about the other boundary violations in the past.*

Examples of boundary violations include attending a social function with a client, eating out or going to a bar with a client, employing a client, getting a client to do errands for you, violating policies for a "special" client, and sexual contact with a client (Gutheil & Gabbard, 1993, 1998). A partial list of what does *not* belong in a session includes repeated detailed descriptions of client's sex life, any significant bodily contact, any detailed personal information about your personal life, or using the client as a resource. An example of the latter would be asking your client, a financial planner, for investment advice. The previous vignettes are also examples of boundary violations. Sexual contact between psychotherapist and client is the most egregious example of a boundary violation. Note that sexual attraction alone, if not acted on, is not a boundary violation; this subject is discussed further in Chapters 22 and 23.

Psychotherapists may be especially vulnerable to boundary violations when they feel overwhelmed by a client, when they are having a life crisis, or when they feel lonely and want to confide in someone (Gabbard, 1996). They may also have a strong need to rescue others and enact this need through boundary violations (such as Al did in the previous example). If you are uncertain whether a behavior is a boundary crossing or a boundary violation, Gutheil (2005) suggests that you consider whether you would be comfortable discussing the behavior with a colleague. If not, it is probably a boundary violation.

Trainees should be aware that *"fact finders—civil or criminal juries, judges, ethics committees of professional organizations, or state licensing boards—often believe that the presence of boundary violations (or even crossings) is presumptive evidence of, or corroborates allegations of, sexual misconduct"* (Gutheil & Gabbard, 1993, p. 189). I have provided the example of Al and Sally to illustrate this point. Respecting and maintaining appropriate boundaries with clients must be a top priority of all psychotherapists. The remainder of this chapter details some common boundary challenges.

## ZERO OR ONE DEGREE OF SEPARATION

Twice I've had to decide whether or not to see the partner of a woman that I was already seeing. In both cases, I opted to see the second woman because of the difficulty they were having in finding another therapist on their insurance panel who was acceptable to them. It was troublesome in one case, where one partner was considering leaving the relationship, unbeknownst to her partner, but not in the other. (anonymous therapist quoted in Graham & Liddle, 2009, p. 18)

I got seduced into the "you're the only one who can do this" thing—for which there was a kernel of truth, as it was the early 1980s and I was at the time one of three lesbian therapists in my area who could accept insurance, and one of the other two was the client's partner and the third was their close social friend. We did a lot of talking about the potential risks and benefits, and I know that my relationship with my colleague, the client's partner, became more distant as a result of this decision—probably the right thing, but a loss for me. It's 20 years later, and we're all fine, and I wouldn't do it again. (anonymous therapist quoted in Graham & Liddle, 2009, p. 18)

These two vignettes from an article about multiple relationships encountered by lesbian and bisexual psychotherapists illustrate potential complications of zero or one degree of separation between the psychotherapist and the new client. The first vignette illustrates some of the complications of seeing a new client who is very well known by a continuing client. In almost all cases, therapeutic complications will ensue if you see an immediate family member of a continuing (or former) client, including partners, parents, children, or siblings. The second vignette illustrates a client whom the psychotherapist already knows personally prior to the onset of psychotherapy. Again, complications are almost a certainty. Always talk to your supervisor before agreeing to either of these scenarios, and be familiar with the literature on practicing psychotherapy in small communities.

A more distant one degree of separation is less likely to be a therapeutic issue; for example, if someone you know professionally, but not intimately, and do not see frequently, refers an acquaintance to you. Also, in my experience, friends and coworkers of a continuing or former client are okay as long as the first client verifies that the relationship is not conflictual in any way.

## SMALL COMMUNITIES

...my son's third-grade teacher (a former client before I had children) also serves on the library board with my spouse and is a member of the Sunday school class that we attend. She shops at the same drug store and local discount house and eats at the same restaurants. (Curtin & Hargrove, 2010, p. 550)

In my work with the Latina/o community, it is not uncommon for me to have meals, spend time with families, work with multiple members of the same family and community, and self-disclose. (Schank, Helbok, Haldeman & Gallardo, 2010, p. 509)

If you are part of a small community, often you cannot avoid running into clients in a public place and even interacting with them regularly. For example, in a rural setting, your client might work at the only gas station for 50 miles. It is unreasonable to assume that you can keep track of his work hours and get gas only when he is not there. If you are working in a rural setting, you should read about how to manage these situations effectively (C. D. Campbell & Gordon, 2003; Spiegel, 1990).

Both you and the client may be members of a small community within a larger area, with similarities in interests, religion, ethnicity, disability, or sexual orientation (Graham & Liddle, 2009; Kessler & Waehler, 2005). You may be aware of this similarity at the outset or you may discover it later. When there is a likelihood of encountering the client outside therapy, discuss the issue very early in psychotherapy.

## PSYCHOTHERAPIST SEES CLIENT IN A PUBLIC PLACE

My private practice is in the relatively small suburb where I also live. I inevitably run into clients when I am with my spouse or with a friend, be it at the grocery store, at a street carnival, leaving a movie, etc. So, part of my orientation "spiel" to new therapy clients is to point out the likelihood/possibility of this happening eventually. I let the client know that my approach will be to not acknowledge in any way that I know them, unless they approach or acknowledge me first, and even then to keep it brief and casual. If/when I run into someone this way, I always bring it up (if feasible) in our next session. Of course, there is always that one client who not only has no qualms about being recognized or encountered but who will want to strike up a detailed conversation, ask my wife questions, etc. My wife and I have agreed that if we're out somewhere, and I spot one of these situations about to happen, I say a certain innocuous word or phrase that we've agreed will signal to her that I'm about to have an awkward clinical moment. She doesn't know if it's a current client, former client, referral source, or what, but she's prepared to handle it. She doesn't ask, "So where do you guys know each other from?" She doesn't encourage conversation. She'll "rescue" me by reminding me that we're late for something and she won't ask questions about it. Being with friends is trickier, but again my good friends know what I do, what the limitations are, and don't expect me to introduce them to everyone I meet. (Anonymous private practice psychotherapist, personal communication, January 24, 2007)

My private practice, my home, and my gym are all within a couple miles of each other. So, whenever clients mention going to a gym, I ask them where they go, and if they go to the same one, we have a brief conversation about that. I might simply say tell them that I go to the same gym and say, "Occasionally I might see you or another client in a public place. My policy is not to greet you to preserve your confidentiality. If you would like to say hi, please go ahead and do so. But to preserve your confidentiality, we cannot have any discussions outside of the office." (Anonymous private practice psychotherapist, personal communication, July 23, 2012)

If I would be uncomfortable being observed by a client, I don't do it. I can go to parties, gay bars, club meetings, or the gym (which can be a bit awkward) knowing that I would never exhibit other than professional behavior in public. (Schank, Helbok, Haldeman, & Gallardo, 2010, p. 507).

Sooner or later, you will run into one of your clients in a public place. Psychotherapists who practice in a university community or a rural area have this experience frequently; in fact, 95 percent of psychotherapists at college counseling centers had encountered clients in public (Sharkin & Birky, 1992). During these encounters, psychotherapists need to be concerned about the risk for confidentiality and boundary violations. If you are aware of any situations where you are likely to run into clients, it would be helpful to address this proactively at the beginning of therapy, as in the previous vignettes.

There are two possible approaches to seeing a client in a public place. First, you could do your best to avoid any eye contact or any other signs that you have recognized the client. Move in the other direction, away from the client, as soon as possible. However, the next time you see the client in therapy, if you think there was a chance that the client might have seen you, you might bring this issue up. You can explain to the client that you thought you saw him or her but that you did not approach or say hi to protect confidentiality. Sometimes you will need to address the issue further, but usually the client will be fine with what you have done and appreciate your concern for his or her well-being.

The other approach is to greet the client in some manner appropriate to the setting. You might catch the eye of the client and simply smile and nod. On other occasions, therapists may say hello briefly or have a brief chat. While this is not the traditionally recommended response to seeing a client in a public place, the little research about this subject suggests that most clients do prefer to be acknowledged in most situations (Cochran et al, 2009). However, I would suggest avoiding the client if the client was with anyone else. Depending on the client's issues, discuss with your supervisor how to address this encounter in the next session.

If the client sees you, approaches you, and greets you, you don't introduce any family member or friend who may be with you to the client (Woody, 1999) unless the client insists and there is no way to avoid it. It is better to keep moving, smile, and say, "It was good to see you—sorry, I've got to go."

There is always a risk that a client has observed you in a public place without you knowing about it. There is a chance that the client might observe behavior that is suitable to the venue but not particularly professional (e.g., holding hands with your partner, joking loudly with friends, or trying on clothes in a large group changing room at a discount store). This may provoke feelings in the client that will then need to be explored in therapy.

## PSYCHOTHERAPIST–CLIENT TOUCHING

*Jamie Thompson, a licensed psychotherapist, has a longstanding therapeutic relationship with a high-functioning schizophrenic client. The client has always been pleasant and appropriate during their sessions, and they are clearly fond of one another. As she passes him in the waiting room, she touches him on the shoulder and tells him that she will be back to see him in about 5 minutes.*

There is considerable debate about appropriate psychotherapist–client touching (Burkholder, Toth, Feisthamel, & Britton, 2010). Until you have a chance to review the literature on this complex issue, I would suggest that you err on the side of minimal touch with clients.

If you or the client would like to shake hands at either the beginning or the end of the session, that's fine (Gutheil & Gabbard, 1993). These touches would be considered socially appropriate in almost any social setting. To be maximally safe and appropriate, I recommend that, as a trainee, you refrain from other touch with clients. However, experienced psychotherapists do not always hold themselves to this strict standard, as you can see in the case of Jamie in the previous vignette.

Prominent mental health practitioners have written about special situations of client touching. In one example, Koocher (2006) held the hand of a dying cystic fibrosis patient in a hospital. In another, Yalom (2002) ran his hands over the thin wisps of a cancer patient's remaining hair. I encourage you to read both of these examples to learn more about the specific situations and how these experienced psychotherapists handled them.

There is no single rule that every psychotherapist adheres to about physical contact with clients. Talk to peers and supervisors about the issue, asking questions about what they do and why they feel comfortable with their choices, and consider reading some professional literature. This will help you learn what feels right for you, and to balance that with what is safest from a risk-management perspective.

## CLIENT WANTS A HUG

*Melissa Roberts, a psychotherapy trainee, has just had a very emotional session with her high-functioning female client. They both feel very close to each other during the session. Melissa's client impulsively grabs her for a hug at the end of the session. Melissa accepts the hug briefly.*

*Amy Zhang, a psychotherapy trainee, has been working for several months with a client who is low functioning and has schizoaffective disorder. The client is socially isolated and is difficult to tolerate because of his angry preoccupations with paranoid ideation. However, he is very grateful to Amy for her attention to him, and at their last session, he left saying, "I love you!" She has not addressed this in today's session since he is both emotionally fragile and not very cognitively intact. At the end of the session, he says he wants a hug and starts to reach for her. Amy sticks out her right hand and tells him, "Since we have a professional relationship, I prefer to shake hands. I'll look forward to seeing you in a couple weeks."*

*Tom Taylor, a psychotherapy trainee, has been working with a client, Glenn Vanderhook. Glenn has a relationship with a girlfriend. He has borderline traits. At the end of the emotional fourth session, Glenn indicates that he would like to hug Tom. Tom quickly realizes that since Glenn has borderline traits, maintaining appropriate boundaries may be a continuing issue, and he decides to decline the hug. Tom puts his hand out instead and says, "Since we have a professional relationship, I prefer to shake hands." At the 10th session, Glenn reveals that his girlfriend abruptly ended their relationship when she discovered that he has been having casual sexual relations with men.*

Sometimes, the client will want to hug. This generally comes spontaneously at the end of the session, with little time to discuss the impulse, as in the previously mentioned cases. Be aware that refusing the hug, as Amy and Tom did, is the most conservative and safest approach from a risk-management perspective. It can *sometimes* be okay to accept a hug, as Melissa did in the previous vignette, as long as there is a longstanding therapy relationship without any signs of erotic interest on the part of the client.

Never hug a client routinely; this could slide down the slippery slope of boundary violations (Gabbard, 2010). Never hug a client if you don't think you can discuss it later with the client *and* your supervisor (Gabbard, 2010). As Amy does, never hug a client if there have been signs that the client may have some erotic feelings toward you. If the client has issues that might lead to later misinterpretation of the hug (e.g., borderline traits), do not hug. As the third vignette illustrates, even a client's initial presentation of a sexual orientation that excludes the psychotherapist (here the client, Glenn, has a girlfriend initially, and the psychotherapist is male) is not necessarily a sign that accepting a hug is an appropriate therapeutic step.

I recommend that as a beginning psychotherapist, you practice gently refusing to hug the first several clients who may want a hug, whoever they may be. As a mental health practitioner, you must develop the confidence and self-possession to refuse hugs from clients. Sooner or later, a client who should not be hugged under any circumstances will ask for a hug. You must be ready for that.

When you refuse to give a hug, or if you accept a hug that you later regret, consider addressing this in the next session. How to address the issue will need to be considered carefully. In Amy's case, because of the fragility of the client and his limited insight, the simple behavioral intervention of requesting a handshake instead is sufficient. In most other cases, you should ask the client about it if the client does not bring it up. Tom might say, "Glenn, I wanted to ask you something about your last session. At the end of the session, you asked for a hug, and I told you that since we have a professional relationship, I prefer to shake hands. I'm wondering if you have any reactions to that."

On occasion, you may wish to hug a client after a particularly emotional session or at a time when you feel that the client needs to feel your concern and comfort. If you decide to do so, be sure you ask the client if it is okay first; clients with a history of physical or sexual assault may not take a hug well (Barnett, 2011). Keep the hug quite brief anytime you do hug.

## CLIENT GIVES YOU A GIFT

*Before leaving his training site, Brian Nelson is having his last session with a client who has schizophrenia. The client is socially isolated and she became very attached to Brian during the year they worked together. The client's hobby is to collect trash and natural items, such as branches and pinecones, and put these together to make small sculptures. Brian had encouraged this artistic outlet. The client had talked about her art projects often during therapy and had brought in some of her artworks to show Brian. Brian expressed his genuine appreciation for them. At the last session, the client brings in a sculpture to give Brian. Brian thanks her graciously and accepts the gift, admiring its artistic qualities.*

*Tiffany Allen is seeing a successful businessman in therapy. The client is married and has two teenage boys. His second wife told him that she was going to divorce him unless he went to therapy and stopped cheating on her. Tiffany had noted that the client had narcissistic traits, and she had often felt that he was looking at her breasts, although his behavior had otherwise been appropriate. One of their sessions happens to fall on February 14. The client comes to the office and hands Tiffany a diamond tennis bracelet purchased from a famous jewelry store. Tiffany refuses to accept the gift, although the client insists that it cannot be returned. She suggests that they explore the meaning of this gift and how this relates to his feelings and ideas about women.*

Sooner or later, one of your clients will bring you a gift. This will almost always happen unexpectedly. Likely times for gifts are holidays, termination of psycho-therapy, or when you are leaving a training site, but it could occur at other times as well (S. Knox et al, 2009). There is no definitive rule about accepting gifts from a clinical perspective, but the facility where you are working may have some guide-lines, and if they do, you should know them.

By accepting a gift, you give the message that giving the gift is okay; this is why you would never want to accept an inappropriate gift. If you reject the gift, the client may feel rejected, and it may be more difficult to explore the mean-ing behind the gift; however, sometimes this is unavoidable. In practice, psy-chotherapists do sometimes accept gifts they consider somewhat problematic in order not to unduly disrupt the therapeutic relationship (Knox, Hess, Williams, & Hill, 2003).

Gifts may have varied and complex meanings (Hahn, 1998; Knox, Hess, Williams, & Hill, 2003). A gift could mean appreciation, gratitude, thanks, or good-bye. It could be symbolic of some aspect of therapy, such as a plant symbolizing the nurturing of the therapeutic relationship. It could also have a more complex meaning, such as garnering special treatment, equalizing power, or being "a good client."

If you personally have always had problems accepting gifts, try to address this issue before you are faced with a client with a gift. Your difficulty will be seen as rejection by the client, who will probably be feeling vulnerable at that point anyway. Talk this over with your supervisor or your psychotherapist to avoid disrupting your clients with your own issues.

When faced with a gift you must first decide whether to accept it. Acceptable gifts have these qualities:

- Cost of about $25 or less (or $5 or less for a low-income client)
- Small gift, such as a book or picture frame
- Personally handcrafted item or food
- Either given at an appropriate gift-giving occasion, such as a holiday or termination of therapy (Knox, Hess, Williams, & Hill, 2003) or gift is culturally appropriate (Brown & Trangsrud, 2008)
- Gift is the first one ever received from the client, or the first gift this year
- Gift was given after therapy has been in progress for a while and a solid relationship has been established.

Clients typically state that giving a gift expresses appreciation and gratitude (Knox et al., 2009). Accepting these gifts is affirming (Knox, 2008). Often these simple gifts do not need much more than a simple expression of appreciation (Knox et al., 2009). You might not want to explore the meaning if this could be seen as a sign of rejection to a fragile client (Hahn, 1998). You might not explore the meaning if the client is low functioning and the gift seems to have a clear meaning, as in the case of Brian's client in the previous vignette. Finally, you may not wish to explore the meaning if you do not see the gift as problematic (Knox, Hess, Williams, & Hill, 2003).

Accept gifts that do not match your taste in a heartfelt but strategic manner: "I can see a lot of skill and care went into this needlepoint pillow. Thank you so much. I will take it home with me tonight." This ensures that the client will not be expecting to see the needlepoint pillow in your office, and, if you like, you can safely give it away to someone else who would like it more than you do.

Even simple gifts may have a secondary, more complex meaning (Hahn, 1998). If you would like to explore the meaning of an acceptable gift further, your goal is to understand "the emotional meaning of the gift within the patient's subjective perspective" as it relates to the therapy relationship (Hahn, 1998, p. 79). This exploration must be empathetic and gentle. In response to an appropriate gift of an inexpensive outdoor thermometer, Hahn suggests the following comments and questions: "Oh, what a beautiful thermometer. It's the kind I can use outside [pause for patient to comment]...This is such a nice gift. What made you pick it?" (Hahn, 1998, p. 81). Later, after exploring the meaning further, the psychotherapist remarked, "No matter how you feel when you come to therapy, I am always here for you. And by taking this gift home, I will be reminded of how important our therapy has been for you."

Gifts that definitely merit further discussion, and may or may not be acceptable, can have one or more of these qualities:

- Gift is on the borderline of being too expensive to accept; you might consider accepting a somewhat more expensive gift if the client's income level was high and you are reasonably certain that no complex therapeutic issues were involved
- Gift is an item that is very personal or meaningful from the client's perspective (e.g.. a family heirloom, favorite teddy bear from childhood)
- Gift was given very early in therapy (Knox, Hess, Williams, & Hill, 2003)
- Client has already given you one gift in this calendar year (talk about it and dissuade client from further gifts, whether you accept this gift or not)

When thinking about these borderline gifts, consider what you know about the client's issues so far. Consider the impact of accepting and refusing the gift on the client and the therapy relationship—would it be wounding to the client to refuse the gift (Brendel et al., 2007)? Do you find the gift extremely desirable? If so, be especially careful because your judgment could be compromised (Brendel et al., 2007).

Unacceptable gifts, which also merit further discussion, may have one or more of these qualities:

- Gift is romantic, sexual, or too intimate or blurs boundaries in uncomfortable ways (Brown & Trangsrud, 2008; Knox, Hess, Williams, & Hill, 2003)
- Gift feels manipulative or aggressive (Knox, Hess, Williams, & Hill, 2003) or has violent themes
- Accepting the gift feels exploitative (Brendel et al., 2007)
- Gift is just too expensive (Brendel et al., 2007)

Several of these qualities apply to the case of Tiffany's gift, above. Be aware that when you explore the meaning of a gift you have refused, your client is likely to be feeling rejected or defensive and you may need to return to the subject in a later session.

Finally, always document in the chart any gift that the client has given you or attempts to give you, along with its likely cost. Document briefly in the chart why you accepted or rejected the gift and any discussion with the client about the gift.

At times, you may consider giving a gift to a client (Brown & Trangsrud, 2008). The impulse to give a gift to a client should be carefully considered and discussed with your supervisor. Any gift given should not be expensive and should mark a special occasion (e.g., birth of client's child, end of psychotherapy).

## INVITATIONS TO CLIENT PERSONAL EVENTS

I have attended a client's wedding. I did so for many reasons—though only after having a thorough discussion with the client about her interest in me being there, how I would introduce myself to others, and my decision not to attend the reception. This was a client I had worked with for quite a long time and had a good working relationship with. My attendance was important to her, as her family had rejected her because of her sexual identity and my attendance was in lieu of "family." It was only after we talked about this quite a bit that I decided to go. I sat separately from others but not so distant as to call attention to myself. I do not have a policy against this, as I think that because of cultural scripts of clients, attending a personal event can enhance the therapeutic alliance. For me it is a case-by-case basis and always understanding the intent behind the request. If confidentiality can be preserved and if it makes therapeutic sense for me to attend, I would consider it. Since I see clients from the gay/lesbian community, running into them at various events is common, and so attending something of importance for clients is something I now consider within the client's cultural frame. (Anonymous psychotherapist, personal communication, July 2, 2007)

I have attended events for patients. Working with kids, I am often invited to bar/bat mitzvahs, plays, recitals, and funerals. I don't attend them all and generally make it policy not to accept those invitations. But there are some circumstances which compel me to attend. I work with many special needs kids, and completing the effort needed for a bar/bat mitzvah or recital is very much a part of our work together. So I attend those events. I do not attend any party or reception that follows. Another part of my work is with parents who have had children die and families who have had a parent die. When my work with these people begins before the death occurs, I usually attend those funerals. For others, if there is a memorial planned at the anniversary, I attend those also. This type of work exceeds the bounds of traditional psychotherapy. In those treatment relationships, I typically do not attend events. (L. Weiss, personal communication, July 3, 2007)

I do attend those events, usually. In general, I attend the main event but not the receptions. In part, this is because I hate receptions, but on a more therapeutic level, it can be quite awkward to be asked how you know the bride, bar mitzvah boy, birthday girl, etc. I always discuss this with the client so that we have a plan and I know what they are granting me permission to say. I have no problem being an old friend of the family or some other appropriate but vague designation, but I want the client to be comfortable with how I introduce myself. Nevertheless, despite that difficulty, I consider it an honor to be invited, and if my schedule permits, I attend. I have never been asked to any event that felt inappropriate for me to attend. I know two colleagues, however, who have been asked to attend the birth (and I mean invited to be in the delivery room) of a child. They did decline! And of course, I think these decisions must be explored therapeutically, both the invitation and the declining.

I could imagine a situation in which, knowing a client, an invitation should be explored and probably declined on therapeutic grounds. Perhaps issues of boundaries or a covert agenda. The point is if we know our clients well, then we will have a sense of other issues entwined with the invitation which might make it problematic. Whether or not these issues are discussed at that time depends on our evaluation of the client's readiness to explore them. It's possible that declining with regret may be the best path to take for the moment. (V. Seglin, personal communication, July 5, 2007)

These examples from psychotherapists provide carefully thought-out rationales for attending select client events. However, a large number of psychotherapists, perhaps the majority, make it a policy to *never* attend any client events. If you decide to *never* attend client events—an equally valid choice—be prepared to explain your policy to your clients:

"Thank you so much for inviting me to your wedding. That is very thoughtful of you. However, I must explain that I have a policy of not attending any client events. This is because of my concern about preserving your confidentiality. If I am there, people may start conversations with me and ask me about my connection to you. I certainly wouldn't want to violate your confidentiality by talking about you being in therapy, and I wouldn't feel comfortable lying either. There's also a chance that we might know someone in common and that person will figure out why I am there without my saying anything. So I'd feel most comfortable that your confidentiality was best preserved if I did not attend. I'd like to see the pictures, though, so if you'd like to bring some in, e-mail me a few, or send me a link to your photo album, that would be great. And of course, I'd like to hear all about it."

Here the psychotherapist is expressing interest in the event and gratitude for being invited, yet shares the rationale for the policy: concerns about violating confidentiality by attending. If the client continues to insist, the psychotherapist might ask, "How do you feel that it would be helpful to you if I attended the wedding?" and then explore these feelings as a therapeutic issue.

If you do not attend the client's important event, you can mark the event in other ways. You might express your interest in hearing about the event and seeing pictures. In certain special circumstances, you might even mark the event with a card or a small gift, such as a picture frame.

If you are willing to consider attending the client's event, it should carefully be considered on an individual basis. The experienced psychotherapists quoted previously provide some useful guidelines. If the event is in some way a culmination of the work you have done with the client (e.g., graduation or a recital), it may be relevant to the therapeutic process to attend. There also may be some cultural reasons to attend, as the psychotherapists quoted previously have noted. However, think carefully about what your comfort level would be attending the event. Consider the following issues:

- Is the event large enough that you can remain relatively anonymous?
- What would you say if someone decided to make conversation with you? Discuss this with your client proactively. If you are uncertain whether you could cope with that kind of inquiry effectively, it might be better not to go.
- Can you get there as it is starting, sit by yourself, and leave quickly? Discuss with your client what you intend to do at the event and what to expect of your presence ("I need to leave quickly after the service to minimize any chances of inadvertently violating your confidentiality, so I'll have to provide my congratulations to you in advance.").
- Can you figure out how to gracefully avoid staying around for any reception or social interactions afterward?

As a trainee, you should never agree to attend a client event without the approval of your supervisor. If, after considering the previously mentioned issues, you would like to attend the client's event and you think your supervisor might approve, tell the client that you will consider it and that you will inform the client of your decision next week. Then discuss the issue thoroughly with your supervisor and arrive at an agreement about the appropriate course of action.

## PSYCHOTHERAPIST SELF-DISCLOSURE

I suppose I am pro self-disclosure but then I also do have an awareness that I want to protect my own privacy...If I was in more acute kind of place-ments I might be a bit more cautious of my personal information...I was quite private when I was on inpatient units. (trainee psychotherapist quoted in Bottrill, Pistrang, Barker, & Worrell, 2010 p. 172)

I think it is a really difficult balance that we try and tread...you are trying to get people to feel comfortable enough with you to trust you with things and in normal life that would mean a kind of two-way relationship, you know, a very secure foundation, and I suppose mimicking that a little bit is important because you need to give them the message that they can trust you, and self-disclosure may be quite helpful with that sort of thing. But then you do also have to be quite careful that it's boundaried. Partly because it is not a normal relationship that you are establishing, it's not a two-way relationship and it shouldn't be. (trainee psychotherapist quoted in Bottrill, Pistrang, Barker, & Worrell, 2010, p. 175)

Psychotherapist *self-disclosure* is "verbal statements that reveal something personal about the therapist" (Knox & Hill, 2003, p. 530). Additionally, Knox and Hill talk about different types of self-disclosures. You may disclose facts. Or you may disclose your feelings, insights, challenges, or coping strategies when faced with a situation similar to the client's. Or you may reassure the client that the client's feelings about a situation are common by citing your own experience. Finally, you may talk about your emotional reactions to how the client is presenting in therapy.

An appropriate self-disclosure is brief, generally no more than one or two minutes of information. Do not be too intimate in your self-disclosures; rather, give an example of your own human behavior that normalizes the client. Experienced psychotherapists will occasionally tell about personal experiences, but these have been carefully chosen and edited for therapeutic effect.

In day-to-day interactions, we are not used to the kind of self-editing that needs to transpire as part of the therapeutic interaction. Therefore, generally, for beginning psychotherapists, it is wise to err on the side of volunteering little personal information. Experts indicate that self-disclosure is a potent intervention and recommend that psychotherapists self-disclose infrequently (Knox & Hill, 2003); otherwise, it might be indicative of poor boundaries.

Never self-disclose about current personal problems, unless unavoidable (e.g., you have cancer, have to take time off for treatment, and will be looking different afterward). If you still have intense feelings about a topic, you should not self-disclose; disclose only about resolved issues.

- Wrong: "When my husband divorced me, I hated men. It took years for me to get over the pain and bitterness."
- Even more wrong: "I'm getting divorced now too. It's a terrible experience. My husband has more money than I do and is fighting for full custody. I don't know how I'm going to get through this. Sometimes I feel that I can't bear it [more details about divorce process]."
- Right: "I can sympathize. I know from personal experience that going through a divorce is an emotionally difficult period and that it takes a while to reorient your life."

Be certain that you do not disclose in a way that meets your needs more than the client's, that overburdens the client with your personal issues, or that blurs boundaries (Gabbard & Crisp-Han, 2010). An unskillful self-disclosure may make you look impaired, or may feel intrusive or annoying to the client (Howe, 2011). Be cautious about self-disclosure if you are feeling a need for validation and approval from a client (Myers & Hayes, 2006); instead, these feelings should be carefully explored in supervision or personal therapy.

If you are tempted to share a personal experience with the client, it may be wise to refrain and discuss this issue with your supervisor after the session. If you can't see yourself discussing the personal experience with your supervisor, this is a sign that you should not discuss it with your client, either. Don't worry about the delay; if the client's issue is important, another opportunity to share the experience will arise later, if you and your supervisor agree that it would be therapeutic to do so.

If used properly, research suggests that clients find self-disclosure helpful (Knox & Hill, 2003). They see the psychotherapist as more real and human, warmer, and more likeable, and they feel reassured and that their experiences are more normal (Henretty & Levitt, 2010; Knox, Hess, Peterson, & Hill, 1997). Self-disclosure can instill hope, reduce shame, and reduce feelings of isolation (Howe, 2011). Self-disclosure can be especially helpful in cross-cultural psychotherapist–client dyads (Burkard, Knox, Groen, Perez, & Hess, 2006), especially those where the psychotherapist is White and the client is of color. In a qualitative research study, they found that psychotherapists' self-disclosure of their feelings and reactions to clients' experiences of racism and oppression facilitated therapy.

## CLIENT ASKS PERSONAL QUESTIONS

*Kyle Warunrit is a psychotherapy trainee who has a client who distrusts him. The client has borderline personality traits. She tells him that she can't tell him anything about her life until she knows more about him. She starts with asking appropriate questions about his training and qualifications. Every session, she asks slightly more intrusive questions, until Kyle finds that she is asking him about his sexual orientation, relationships, and so on.*

Clients ask us personal questions for a variety of reasons. Your client might ask you questions simply because she is curious about you. Or your client might feel that he cannot share personal information of a sensitive nature with you unless he knows more about you. Or your client may fear that you will think negatively of her because of differences between the two of you. Or he might want to gain power over you by learning more about you. And there could be many other reasons for asking.

If the client asks for some simple demographic information, for example, "Are you married?" "Do you have children?" or "How old are you?" you may wish to make an initial assumption that the client is just curious. In these cases, it is okay to answer these questions briefly and move on. However, it should be noted that even these simple questions could be fraught with personal meaning for the client (Wachtel, 1993).

Wachtel (1993) points out that your response to questions from the client should depend on your assessment of why the client is asking the question. He suggests making this remark to clarify the situation: "I'd be happy to tell you, but I don't feel clear about what it is that you are really interested in knowing" (p. 227).

If there are more than a couple questions or questioning occurs frequently, it is helpful to gently ask the client about the significance of this information:

"I've noticed that you have asked me a number of personal questions and I'm wondering—how is it helpful to you to get this information?"

Never answer any question that feels too intrusive to you, even if on the surface it seems innocuous.

Even if you think that the client is asking just out of curiosity, you might not want to answer. For example, in certain instances, you might be in a treatment setting where personal information given to one client will quickly spread throughout much of the client population. In those cases, you can consider responding:

> "I'm sorry, but I have a policy of not answering personal questions. But I'm curious: would you mind telling me how it would be helpful to you to know this?"

## CLIENT ASKS ABOUT PSYCHOTHERAPIST'S MENTAL HEALTH HISTORY

*Carrie Schmidt is a mental health trainee who has just started working in an outpatient alcohol treatment program. Carrie has a history of problem drinking in the past and a family history of alcoholism. For these reasons, Carrie has abstained from drinking alcohol for the past 4 years. Many of the other counselors are open about their substance abuse histories, but Carrie does not want to discuss her past drinking with clients. One of Carrie's clients asks her, "Are you a recovering alcoholic?" Carrie says, "I know that your group psychotherapist talks a lot about his history as an alcoholic, but my approach is different. I would like to spend our time focusing on your personal problems, and it's my policy not to discuss my personal history."*

Your client may blurt out personal questions about your mental health history such as these: "Have you ever been depressed?" "Have you ever been in therapy?" "Have you ever taken antidepressants?" or "Have you ever heard voices?" Your client might be asking because she is worried that you won't understand her. If you think that this is the case, you need not answer the question—instead, show that you understand by making an empathetic remark based on the material that preceded the question (e.g., "It seems that you've been suffering from this depression for a long time and you've had a hard time getting people to understand how difficult it is.").

You may or may not have a history of mental health treatment, but in almost all cases, you should not answer these questions. However, the fact that the client is asking the question is important, and you need to understand what her motivation is. Here are some possible responses to the question:

- "I'm wondering how it would help you to know whether I've been depressed in the past."
- "It seems that you may be concerned that if I haven't been depressed, I won't be able to relate to what you're going through."

Your client may also ask you about substances: "Are you an alcoholic?" "Have you ever been a problem drinker?" or "Have you ever used cocaine?" It is, in fact, common for many substance abuse counselors to talk openly about their own past substance abuse problems. If you would like to take this approach, discuss the implications thoroughly with your supervisor first. Alternatively, you can take the approach that Carrie does in the previous vignette.

Some clients have experienced a fairly rare event and worry that you won't understand their situation: "Have you ever been in combat?" "Have you ever heard voices?" or "Have you ever been manic?" Often in these cases, the client's underlying worry may be about your knowledge base and competence. In these cases, an alternative approach can be okay:

"No, I've never been in combat, and I'm sure that I'll never understand it exactly the way that you do. However, I'm hoping that you'll give me a chance to try to help you with your problems anyway."

Sometimes the client wants a psychotherapist who has had the same problems he has. Explain that this can't always be the case ("If you had a heart attack, would you insist on having only other doctors and nurses who had had heart attacks themselves?") but that your training and knowledge can be helpful nonetheless. If this continues to be an issue, there may be underlying issues of distrust that will need further exploration over time.

If you do have a history of mental health treatment, think long and hard about revealing it to a client. Despite her questions, the client does not need to know about your emotional issues. Talk it over thoroughly with your supervisor first before revealing anything to a client. If you don't feel you can discuss the issue with your supervisor, you should not reveal it to your client.

## SEXUAL BOUNDARY VIOLATIONS

Next to suicide, boundary problems and sexual misconduct rank highest as causes of malpractice actions against mental health providers. (Norris, Gutheil, & Strasburger, 2003, p. 517)

Having occasional sexual feelings toward clients is normal (Bernsen, Tabachnick, & Pope, 1994) and is further addressed in Chapters 22 and 23. However, having sexual relations with clients or former clients is never acceptable. In his intensive study and treatment of psychotherapists who have committed sexual boundary violations, Gabbard (1996) has unearthed some important cautions that all psychotherapists should be aware of. He reports that the transgressing psychotherapists are not "bad apples" or "psychopathic" but instead psychotherapists who have started down a "slippery slope" through unexamined, seemingly minor boundary crossings with clients. These continue, leading to increasingly inappropriate personal involvement between the psychotherapist and client.

Norris, Gutheil, and Strasburger (2003) characterize some personal situations that may put a psychotherapist at risk of greater boundary crossings. A life crisis or transition, such as aging, illness, career change, marital conflict, or other personal difficulty, puts a psychotherapist at risk. The psychotherapist may feel lonely and want someone to confide in. The psychotherapist may see a particular client as "special" and particularly appealing in some way. Gabbard (1996) emphasizes that many psychotherapists who commit sexual boundary violations were emotionally vulnerable because of an impoverished social life, divorce, or loss.

Jackson and Nuttall (2001) did an anonymous survey of various mental health practitioners. They found that while only one of 200 female psychotherapists had ever had a sexual encounter with a client, one of 12 male psychotherapists had. The psychotherapists who were especially at risk were those who were male and under emotional stress *and* who had a history of having been intrusively sexually abused (these psychotherapists had a 60 percent chance of having had a sexual encounter with a client, but note that there were a very small number of psychotherapists with these characteristics in the sample, so it is unclear whether the same risk would be seen in a larger sample). All three of these risk factors alone, and in combination, increased the risk of inappropriate sexual boundary crossing. Jackson and Nuttall (2001) recommend that psychotherapists with these risk factors avoid the isolation of private practice, seek regular supervision/consultation regarding boundary issues, and get personal therapy to address trauma-related concerns.

Gabbard (1994, 1996) reports that in most cases, sexual transgression started with a nonsexual hug between the psychotherapist and client. Or the psychotherapist might have become informal, friendly, and self-revealing, perhaps talking about personal difficulties at length. Other boundaries may weaken, such as staying later than the therapy session end-time or talking to the client at night. The psychotherapist was in denial that significant boundary crossings were taking place. The psychotherapist had difficulty setting limits and felt that he or she was being aggressive when doing so. Some psychotherapists felt that they were falling in love with the client and thus justified in the sexual boundary violation (Gabbard, 1994). To prevent starting on this slippery slope, Gabbard (1996) emphasizes that "specifically, those aspects of their [the supervisee's or consultee's] thoughts, feelings, or actions that they would most like to keep secret from the supervisor are precisely the issues that should be openly discussed in supervision" (p. 317).

## PSYCHOTHERAPIST'S SERIOUS ILLNESS

During the month following the discovery of a lump in my breast, it felt urgent to me to schedule immediate medical consultations and procedures. The regularity of my schedule with patients was disrupted by my need to consult with physicians. This appeared to me to be inescapable. I typically telephoned these patients whose appointments conflicted with my doctors' appointments with a statement such as, "I need to cancel and hopefully reschedule our appointment next Wednesday." I had to reschedule some patients' appointments two to three times over the course of a few weeks. My patients had come to depend on me for my consistency; in my mind, they were no longer able to do so...It was at this point that self-disclosure appeared inescapable to me. (Kahn, 2003, p. 54)

*Ignacio Alvarez is a psychotherapist. He has cystic fibrosis (CF) and has been medically stable for several years. He needs brief occasional hospitalizations because of infections or other intermittent lung issues. He regularly reveals his CF status to clients because they occasionally notice that he wheezes a little or coughs, and they express concern; he assures them that he is medically stable, but takes the opportunity to mention that he occasionally needs to be out for more intensive treatment and that his business partner covers his practice while he is out. Because of the unpredictability of his medical condition, he regularly discusses cases with his business partner, Serena Washington. He has developed a back-up plan for when he is out: either he or Serena calls his clients to reschedule, they change his phone message, and on the message they alert callers to contact Serena.*

Illness that is serious enough to disrupt client care or personal appearance, such as Dr. Kahn's breast cancer in the previous quote, is also an example of unavoidable psychotherapist self-disclosure. Since these types of illnesses have a profound emotional impact on the psychotherapist, continuing regular consultation is recommended to ensure that the psychotherapist is coping realistically and effectively with clients' needs during the illness (Philip, 1993). For chronic conditions that can have exacerbations, Ignacio's plan above provides a model. For any serious illness, the psychotherapist must consider when treatment can be continued effectively, and clients must be prepared for any disruptions that might occur.

## PSYCHOTHERAPIST'S PREGNANCY

During the course of my pregnancy, preoccupation with the well-being of myself and baby, anxieties related to changing body boundaries, and heightened conflicts around issues of control and achievement, affected my willingness, at times, to actively explore transference material that was related to my pregnancy as well as to facilitate the expression of patients' aggressive or envious feelings toward me. In certain instances, these dynamics contributed to a tendency to distance myself from highly charged affects in the treatment and to a collusion with patients' denial and avoidance of these affects...I was retrospectively aware of my wish to withdraw from threatening aspects of patients' feelings and associations and enacted this wish by sharpening the boundaries between us. This dynamic was most apparent with patients who were either intrusive or demanding, or whose crises resonated with some personal anxiety about my pregnancy...Trying to listen to patients' ostensible concerns about my pregnancy and to hear the layered transferential meanings presented an ongoing challenge throughout my pregnancy. (Bienen, 1990, p. 611)

One borderline patient identified her feelings about my pregnancy. First there was shock, "I don't ever think of you as having a life outside of sitting in that chair," and sadness, "because it's going to interrupt our work together," also "a little bit of excitement because I'm assuming this is something that you want," and "jealousy of you because you have a life and a family and I don't," and "jealousy of your baby, since your baby gets to have you as a mom." The next time she came back, it seemed that she had dissociated because she said that she didn't remember having talked about my pregnancy at all in the previous session. (Anonymous psychotherapist, personal communication, February 16, 2012)

I am not sure that there is a 'right' answer for when to tell patients. My personal opinion is that it is a bad idea to wait to the point that they are guessing or that it is so obvious that they can't help but know. I also think that they have a right to know as your absence impacts their treatment. Also, if it's not something that you talk about openly, that promotes the atmosphere that it is not possible to discuss feelings they might have about the pregnancy and what it means for them. I have usually told patients around 16 weeks before it is quite visible and when I am ready to tell everyone—at that stage you know that things are normal and that the baby is growing OK. I could see waiting until the 20 week ultrasound to be sure, but by that point most women are showing. Once you tell patients that you are pregnant, it does open the door for more personal questions, like what pregnancy is like, how you are feeling and how the baby is. If the patient has been pregnant before, it creates a physically visible bond. (Anonymous psychotherapist, personal communication, February 17, 2012)

Pregnancy is a very personal event in the psychotherapist's life, making itself obvious to clients and forcing some self-disclosure. The psychodynamic psychotherapist, in the first quote above, describes her insights on how her pregnancy affected her clients and her emotional responsiveness to them.

As soon as you feel comfortable doing so, tell your colleagues and supervisor about your pregnancy so that everyone can work as a team to support you and your clients during this period. Keep them informed of any limitations that your obstetrician places on your activities (Tinsley, 2000).

Prior to announcing your pregnancy to your clients, you should read up on the literature in the area so that you will be prepared for some of the emotional reactions that clients may have. Would you prefer to tell your clients about your pregnancy or wait for them to ask about it? The literature is unclear about which would be the most therapeutic course of action (Tinsley, 2000), so consider this issue carefully and discuss it with your supervisor and colleagues so that you can decide what would be best for your clients. Clients may be reluctant to ask, since etiquette experts recommend that it is impolite to ask a woman if she is pregnant. However, if the client does not bring up your pregnancy, you should do it several weeks (at least) before you start making plans for coverage in your absence. Clients who have abandonment issues may have difficult reactions to the pregnancy (Tinsley, 2000).

So that your clients feel more comfortable with your impending absence, work carefully with your supervisor and colleagues to transfer clients or to provide coverage for them in your absence (Stockman & Green-Emrich, 1994). Be sure that all your clients have a plan tailored to their needs and that they know what to do if you need to stop work unexpectedly early (Tinsley, 2000). Allow yourself some flexibility concerning when you will again see your clients since many aspects of pregnancy, delivery, and infant behavior are unpredictable. Before you return to work, think about how you will handle clients' questions about the baby, baby gifts, or requests to see photos of the baby (Tinsley, 2000).

## RECOMMENDED READING

Curtin, L., & Hargrove, D. S. (2010). Opportunities and challenges of rural practice: Managing self amid ambiguity. *Journal of Clinical Psychology: In Session, 66*(5), 549–561.

*The authors update the reader on professional literature regarding rural practice and share clinical challenges.*

Gabbard, G. O. (1996). Lessons to be learned from the study of sexual boundary violations. *American Journal of Psychotherapy, 50*, 311–322.

*Dr. Gabbard talks about the slippery slope leading to sexual boundary violations.*

Graham, S. R., & Liddle, B. J. (2009). Multiple relationships encountered by lesbian and bisexual psychotherapists: How close is too close? *Professional Psychology: Research and Practice, 40*(1), 15–21.

*The authors provide a helpful description of small community critical incidents encountered by lesbian and female bisexual therapists and discuss the therapists' coping strategies.*

Gutheil, T. G., & Gabbard, G. O. (1993). The concept of boundaries in clinical practice: Theoretical and risk-management dimensions. *American Journal of Psychiatry, 150*, 188–196.

*A classic article in understanding boundary crossings versus boundary violations with regard to sexual misconduct. The article is available on the Internet in the Boundaries section of Ken Pope's website: http://kspope.com/ethics/boundaries.php.*

Gutheil, T. G., & Gabbard, G. O. (1998). Misuses and misunderstandings of boundary theory in clinical and regulatory settings. *American Journal of Psychiatry, 155*, 409–414.

*This classic article provides a sophisticated discussion of the role of context in deciding whether a psychotherapist's behavior is a boundary crossing or a boundary violation. The article is available on the internet in the Boundaries section of Ken Pope's website: http://kspope.com/payton/gutheil-gabbard.php.*

Knox, S., Hess, S. A., Williams, E. N., & Hill, C. E. (2003). "Here's a little something for you": How therapists respond to client gifts. *Journal of Consulting Psychology, 50*, 199–210.

*Knox and colleagues carefully examine 12 psychotherapists' descriptions of gifts received.*

Knox, S., & Hill, C. E. (2003). Therapist self-disclosure: Research-based suggestions for practitioners. *Journal of Clinical Psychology, 59*, 529–539.

*Knox and Hill provide a thorough discussion of psychotherapist self-disclosure with recommendations to maximize therapeutic effectiveness.*

Tinsley, J. A. (2000). Pregnancy of the early-career psychiatrist. *Psychiatric Services, 51*, 105–110.

*Although targeted at psychiatrists, Tinsley's article provides a useful review of the literature on the pregnant psychotherapist and helpful suggestions for coping.*

## ONLINE RESOURCE

http://www.kspope.com/dual/index.php

*Dr. Kenneth Pope is a psychologist and author. This page from his extensive website provides immediate access to many useful articles by a variety of authors on the subjects of dual relationships and boundaries.*

## DISCUSSION QUESTIONS

1. What personal questions from a client would you be willing to answer?
2. What if the client asked about your sexual orientation? Would your response depend on the interaction of the client's issues (e.g., homophobic or struggling with coming out) and your orientation?
3. How would you address running into a client in a public place? Would you discuss this issue with all clients ahead of time or just the ones you think you'd be more likely to see? If you do see a client in a public place and you are not sure the client has seen you, would you try to avoid her or say hi? What would this decision depend on?
4. Are you willing to touch clients (other than shaking hands)? If so, when would you feel comfortable and uncomfortable with this?
5. Would you ever be willing to attend a client event? If so, what kind of event?
6. What if you developed a serious illness? How would you address that with your clients and when? At what point is it optional to talk to clients about your illness, and at what point is it necessary?

# Psychotherapist–Client Differences and Coping with Prejudice

Applying our knowledge about individual differences to clinical practice is a complex task. Many clinical dilemmas can arise. Therapists and clients have many emotions and thoughts about their differences. Some of these feelings and thoughts are shared with each other, yet others are just below the surface and can have a negative impact on treatment effectiveness.

## RELIGIOUS DIFFERENCES

*Aaron Miller is a Jewish mental health trainee working with a predominantly African American population. He is a Reform Jew and does not wear a yarmulke. He lives and works in New York City, which has a large Jewish population. One of his clients, a Muslim, notices that he is out of the office for Yom Kippur (in areas with large Jewish populations, many people are aware of the occurrence of Jewish holidays from grocery store displays, newspaper articles, and so on). There is currently active conflict in the Middle East, and the client has been talking to Aaron about how upset he is regarding Muslims' treatment by the international community. When Aaron returns from the holiday, the client asks him, "Why didn't you tell me that you're Jewish?"*

*Crystal Cooper is a Christian mental health trainee who grew up in the rural South. She is now working at a clinic in a major metropolitan area. She has a few items of personal significance in her office to make herself feel more at home. One of them is a picture frame that her mother gave her when she moved away. It has writing about Jesus and the importance of family on the frame and a picture of her family inside. She also wears a small gold cross necklace that her parents gave her for her college graduation, which has great sentimental value to her. She is assigned a new client who is having difficulty accepting his attractions for men. She notices that the client keeps focusing in the sessions on how his family's religion does not accept gays.*

Religious symbols and behavior vary from those that are religiously required (e.g., observing certain religious holidays or a yarmulke for an Orthodox Jewish male psychotherapist) to those that are voluntary (e.g., a cross necklace worn by a Christian psychotherapist). While mental health practitioners tend to be less religious than the general population (Hage, 2006), many do actively practice within a spiritual tradition. Knowledge of the psychotherapist's religion will inevitably elicit reactions in some clients—positive and negative—including the following:

- Being happy that the psychotherapist has the same religious background
- Assuming that client and psychotherapist religious values are the same if client and psychotherapist have the same religion—which could be in error
- Not being pleased at being treated by a religious psychotherapist or a psychotherapist of a different religion (possibly the case for Aaron's client, described previously)
- Altering behavior to seek approval of the psychotherapist (e.g., Crystal's client, described previously)
- Having concerns but being unwilling to talk about them (probably also applicable to Crystal's client)
- Being concerned about differing religious values and, hence, whether the psychotherapist will be respectful of the client's religious values (also possibly the case for Aaron's client)

Because of the likelihood of negative reactions and impediments to therapy, whenever possible many psychotherapists prefer to confine their display of religious symbols to their homes and areas of their offices that are not readily observable by clients. In fact, one highly respected psychiatrist, Gabbard (2010), states, "Revealing one's religion is rarely productive in psychotherapy" (p. 57).

However, another equally valid perspective emphasizes communication, acceptance, and mutual respect. In these cases, directly addressing any questions in a very matter-of-fact manner and assuring clients that you are respectful of their differences can sometimes be sufficient. In other cases, a more detailed exploration of the client's reaction is necessary.

If you suspect that the client may be concerned about known or suspected religious issues but hasn't brought up the topic, consider asking the following:

- "I'm wondering, do you have any concerns about our religious differences?"
- "I'm thinking you've probably noticed [religious item or clothing]—I'm wondering if you have any reactions to that."

Be proactive and discuss these issues with a supervisor as soon as you recognize the relevance in any of your current (or future) cases.

A related issue is how the nonreligious psychotherapist might address religious issues with a religious client. There is a growing literature on the importance of cultural competence regarding religious differences (Hage, 2006). Addressing these issues of cultural competency is well beyond the scope of this volume, but trainees should be aware of the importance of cultural knowledge of the client's religion and seek information as needed (a good resource is Schultz-Ross & Gutheil, 1997).

## DIFFERENCES IN AGE AND LIFE EXPERIENCES

During our first year as psychiatric residents at a veterans' hospital, any patient could reliably stump my colleagues and me by asking one simple question: "If you weren't in Vietnam, how can you possibly help me?" We hadn't been to Vietnam. We were in high school during the worst years of the war. And no, we had never been ambushed, cradled a dying buddy in our arms, or dodged land mines. It was a mocking question, really—"Were you in Vietnam?"—and it left us tongue-tied and apologetic. What were the patients really saying to us? Nancy's patient, we determined, was testing her perseverance: would she really try to know him? The veteran John was seeing, it soon became clear, was keeping him at arm's length to conceal a heroin habit. Matt's patient—the one who told him haughtily at the start of every session, "Really, now, college boy, this will be pointless"—was so ashamed of his tattered life that he had to demean his therapist.

My patient, Rich B., was a former tunnel rat, a wiry soldier who could navigate the Vietcong underground networks. His diagnosis was "anxiety." Mr. B. was in the habit of quizzing me disdainfully: "What were the dates of the Tet offensive? What happened at My Lai? Do you have any idea what it's like to go down in a tunnel?"

At first I was defensive. But then I said: "Of course I don't know these things, Mr. B. You do. Tell me everything." That seemed to break the ice. Our therapy became a bit like a tutorial, and the patient realized I valued his knowledge...

I now hear the question "Have you been there, done that?" for the proxy it often is. In his practice, the psychotherapist Saul Raw finds it a common query. "I find it can reflect more profound difficulties in forming collaborative relationships based on trust," he told me, "and, at the same time, recognizing that all empathy has imperfections."

For other patients, though, the "Have you ever..." question is less a therapeutic riddle to be solved—as it was in the case of Mr. B—than an expression of genuine skepticism that they can indeed be helped.

It is the kind of question asked by a person who believes his very soul has been warped by calamity. "Sometimes a patient expresses frustration that I can't possibly help him because I never experienced the trauma that he did," said Dr. Walter Reich, a professor of psychiatry at George Washington

University and a former director of the United States Holocaust Memorial Museum, whose patients have included Holocaust survivors...

Addiction, too, can be an intense and defining experience. "I have heard patients say that if you haven't been there you can't help me," said Keith Humphreys, a Stanford psychologist. "So I tell them, 'I can help you live a sober life because it's all I have ever lived.'" (S. Patel, M.D., writing in the *New York Times*, June 12, 2007)

*Adam Robinson is a 25-year-old mental health trainee who looks somewhat younger than his age. He is working with a 55-year-old client who repeatedly asks his age and asks Adam if he's experienced enough. Since this is Adam's first clinical training experience, he has some doubts as well. He is uncertain what to say to the client.*

At times, clients with different life experiences from ours will doubt that we can be effective with them. Clients wonder whether you can understand them because your personal experiences have been different (e.g., you are not a survivor of trauma, you are of a different ethnicity, and so on).

Age difference is one difference that arises commonly with beginning psychotherapists. Your insecurity about your experience level may make you feel tongue-tied if you are asked about this unexpectedly. Older clients' concerns will usually decrease naturally over time as you demonstrate your empathy, interest, and competence (and get older).

When the client has concerns about differing life experiences, I recommend that you try something like this:

"I realize that you have many experiences that I have not had. However, I hope that you will be willing to give me a chance to learn about what you have experienced in your life and learn how this has affected you. I can assure you that I will do the very best I can to help you. I think that the things I have learned as a psychotherapist may be helpful to you as well. I hope you will be willing to give me a chance to work with you."

If the client still seems reluctant, suggest a trial period of four to eight sessions, at which point you can reevaluate and see if the client still feels the same way.

You might be working with an adult client on his child's behavior issues. Often clients will ask you at this time whether you are a parent. Depending on your theoretical orientation, you might prefer to answer this question directly, or you might prefer to inquire about the client's feelings regarding whether you are a parent first. In any event, you can take a similar approach of confirming differences while suggesting that your knowledge might be helpful and asking that the client give you a chance to help.

Be aware that sometimes a concern about differences might reflect underlying interpersonal issues. The client may be fearful of opening up to others, may have had some negative experiences with others who are demographically similar to you, may have narcissistic issues ("I want only the best, most experienced psychotherapist"), or may have other concerns.

## RACIAL, ETHNIC, AND CULTURAL DIFFERENCES

*Justin Lee is a White mental health trainee preparing to work with a predominantly Native American population for the first time. He is concerned that he will make inadvertently tactless remarks. He is trying to learn about Native American culture but is aware that there are significant differences between Native American cultural groups that are insufficiently described in the literature. He worries that his clients will not like him because he is White and still has a lot to learn about their culture. He wonders when and how best to address these differences.*

*Michelle Kim is a Korean American mental health trainee working with a substance abuse recovery program in a predominantly African American neighborhood. She asks a new client whether experiences of racism have any relationship to her substance abuse and recovery. She is surprised that the client changes the subject.*

Carefully consider the clinical needs of the client when thinking about client–psychotherapist cultural/racial or other differences. When the client is new to therapy, these issues might be too sensitive to bring up until a level of trust has been developed. If a client is in crisis, establish your concern and credibility by working to stabilize the client first. If a client is beginning to work on substance abuse recovery after "hitting bottom," his top priority must be his abstinence and recovery; all else is secondary for now. So while Michelle's question in the previous vignette might be a fruitful course of inquiry for an advanced recovery client, her new client may be more focused on basic needs, such as maintaining a job, reestablishing trust with family, financial stability, and so on.

Consider the difference between *content* and *process* when thinking about differences between the client and yourself. When you address racial, ethnic, and cultural differences through the *process* of therapy, you show through your behavior and your verbalizations that you understand, are knowledgeable about, and are respectful of the client. Through the *process* of therapy, right from the beginning, you make certain points to the client through how you treat him or her rather than by overtly discussing the interpersonal differences. If you address differences in the *content* of therapy, this means you will be asking the client directly to talk about the psychotherapist–client differences. Once trust is established, it can be helpful to overtly discuss individual differences in psychotherapy. There is a growing literature on this subject (Maxie, Arnold, & Stephenson, 2006) that you may wish to explore.

When working with racial/cultural or sexual minority groups, the majority-group psychotherapist can take three effective steps to maximize effectiveness and the therapeutic alliance. First, the psychotherapist must be sufficiently knowledgeable about cultural, societal, familial, developmental, assimilation, and spiritual issues within the minority group (Baker & Bell, 1999) and balance this knowledge with an accurate understanding of the uniqueness of the client.

Second, the psychotherapist must have done personal work on her own attitudes toward the minority group and on her own identity formation. Burkard, Ponterotto, Reynolds, and Alfonso (1999) show that White psychotherapists' identity formations are related to their effectiveness with Black clients. Gelso, Fassinger, Gomez, and Latts (1995) found that psychotherapists' homophobia was related to ineffectiveness with a lesbian client's relationship issues.

Third, Sue and Zane (1987), in a classic article, stress the importance of being *credible* and *giving* to the ethnic minority client. Being *credible* consists of being able to collaboratively form a conceptualization of the problem, means for problem resolution, and goals for treatment that are culturally relevant to your unique client. By *giving*, Sue and Zane (1987) refer to the importance of using interventions that help the client achieve significant gains early in treatment.

Research on client–psychotherapist ethnic matching has had mixed results. Some studies have found that ethnic matching can result in improved outcomes, while others found that if the client returns after the first session, there is little effect (Zane et al., 2005). Perhaps a more important consideration is agreement between the psychotherapist and client about the perception of the problem, coping orientation, and goals for treatment, referred to as *cognitive matching* (Zane et al., 2005). In a qualitative study, Chang and Yoon (2011) found that racial minority clients with White psychotherapists often assume that the White therapists could not understand their experiences as people of color, and hence they preemptively refrain from bringing up racial and cultural issues out of concern that the therapist would not respond with empathy, validation, or cultural sensitivity. Chang and Yoon also found that therapists may prescribe culturally inappropriate interventions, leading clients to feel misunderstood. Nonetheless, they found that a large majority of clients were unconcerned about the racial mismatch as long as the therapist was seen as compassionate, unconditionally accepting, and comfortable talking about racial, ethnic, and cultural issues.

When cultural differences are particularly relevant, for example when working with less acculturated individuals, there is a growing understanding that it may be helpful to augment our standard psychotherapy techniques with *culturally responsive interventions*, which are unique interventions formulated to be appropriate and therapeutic within the individual's culture (for further information see Hays, 2007, and Sue, Zane, Hall & Berger, 2009).

## SEXUAL ORIENTATION DIFFERENCES

*David Bailey is a mental health trainee who is working with young adults in a mental health training site. David's new client is a 19-year-old male who is struggling with his attraction toward other men, especially with respect to his Christian background. While David is heterosexual, he has had some struggles with his own Christian background as well. David attended a Christian university and has recently started a graduate program at a university unaffiliated with any religion. At his undergraduate university, he was aware that the gay and lesbian students were deeply closeted. As a consequence, he has never been personally acquainted with anyone who has been open about a gay, lesbian, or bisexual orientation. David is eager to learn, but he has doubts about his level of knowledge and whether he can help the client. He feels insecure about how well he will relate to the client, and he has some religious concerns as well.*

Multiple studies have confirmed that lesbian, gay, and bisexual (LGB) clients see psychotherapists at a higher rate than heterosexuals (Burckell & Goldfried, 2006). Therefore, every psychotherapist must be prepared as a part of basic cultural competency training to see LGB clients. LGB individuals probably seek psychotherapy at a higher rate because they commonly experience significant life stressors that heterosexuals do not. It is essential to understand such basic topics as the coming-out process, family adaptation to learning about the client's sexual orientation, dealing with heterosexism, and internalized homophobia (Baron, 1996). In addition, it is important to realize that gay and lesbian versus bisexual clients have some similar and different issues. For example, bisexual individuals may be less open about their sexual orientation and may be less connected with a community (Balsam & Mohr, 2007).

Psychotherapists of all sexual orientations may need to look deeply into their own personal attitudes about LGB clients and make an effort to address any internalized homophobia through psychotherapy, supervision, and education. In an analogue study, Gelso, Fassinger, Gomez, and Latts (1995) found that psychotherapists with greater homophobia tended to avoid helping a lesbian client with her relationship issues. If you have some religious concerns about working with LGB clients, consider talking to a religious leader of an LGB-affirmative religious group. It is essential that psychotherapists recognize that there is no scientific evidence that sexual orientation can be changed through psychotherapy and that efforts to do so will almost certainly result in lasting psychological harm to the client (Burckell & Goldfried, 2006).

Beginning psychotherapists may wonder when it is helpful to disclose their sexual orientation to clients. If the LGB client asks you what your sexual orientation is, in most cases you should go ahead and openly answer that question. The client is probably asking you because she wants to know if she can feel safe and accepted with you and/or she might be thinking about looking for an LGB psychotherapist. She may also ask you whether you feel comfortable working with LGB clients. Be prepared to answer that question:

- "Yes, I have a lot of experience with people who are lesbian and gay."
  (Note that it is okay if some of this experience is in your personal life.)
- "Yes, I very much hope that I can help you with your difficulties."

Research has shown that knowledgeable heterosexual psychotherapists can be seen as effective and helpful by their LGB clients (Burckell & Goldfried, 2006). If LGB clients have a strong preference for an LGB psychotherapist, they usually will look for one to begin with.

Another common scenario is the LGB psychotherapist with the heterosexual client. In general, if it isn't relevant to the client's psychotherapeutic issues, there is no reason to disclose your sexual orientation to the client. If you are LGB and feel that it would be helpful for your LGB client to know this, discuss how you might self-disclose to the client with your supervisor. In addition, you may wish to read about some of the issues that may arise when you are a member of the same LGB community as your client (L. E. Kessler & Waehler, 2005).

A client who is confused or conflicted about his sexual identity may ask you about your sexual orientation. Depending on the client's tolerance of ambiguity and the strength of the therapeutic relationship, you might want to explore the implications of your response before you self-disclose:

"I don't mind answering that question, but before I do, would you mind telling me a little bit about how it would be helpful to you to know the answer?"

The psychotherapist might follow up with the following:

"How do you think you would feel if you learned that I was gay? How would you feel if you learned I was heterosexual?"

Balance these two considerations: first, telling the client about your own orientation (especially if you are not LGB) may inhibit the client's self-exploration process; however, not telling the client while asking questions might raise his anxiety level higher than he may tolerate well. Decide what is best for your particular client's situation.

I have not addressed the treatment issues of *intersex* and *transgendered* individuals in this section; far fewer individuals identify as intersex or transgendered than lesbian, gay, or bisexual. *Intersex* individuals' sex chromosomes, genitalia, and/or secondary sexual characteristics are not exclusively male or female (in the past, the outdated term *hermaphrodite* was often used). *Transgendered* is a difficult term to define and often relates to individuals who are in the process of transitioning between genders, but it may also describe others who do not identify as strictly male or female in other ways. Psychotherapists should not treat intersex or transgendered clients without, at a minimum, an intensive effort to learn the professional literature about these groups and, preferably, knowledgeable supervision or consultation as well. Videos that provide an orientation to these issues are suggested at the end of the chapter.

## OTHER NONOBVIOUS DIFFERENCES

*Vanessa Morgan is a mental health trainee. She has been working for a year and a half with Mark Phillips, and Mark's depression and social isolation have improved significantly. In today's session, Mark tells Vanessa that he went hunting with his brother and his two nephews. He volunteers to bring her some venison next time he comes. Ordinarily,*

*Vanessa would be willing to accept a small gift from a client, and she knows that Mark simply wants to show his appreciation. However, Vanessa is a vegetarian and really does not want a large slab of deer meat in her office. She fears that if she does not tell him that she is a vegetarian, she will be presented with a gift of meat sooner or later. On the other hand, she fears that if she tells him that she is a vegetarian, he will see this as an implicit criticism of his hunting. After weighing her options, she decides that the relationship is strong enough to handle this. She states, "Thank you so much for thinking of giving me some of the meat, but since I'm a vegetarian, I'm afraid that I have to decline."*

A psychotherapist who adheres to strict Jewish or Muslim dietary standards would not eat the deer meat, either, because the deer was not killed according to the appropriate religiously specified protocol. If the relationship is more tenuous, the psychotherapist may gently indicate that the psychotherapist doesn't care for the particular food being mentioned and steer the session in another direction. Other examples of nonobvious differences would be parenting status, family-of-origin differences, and so on. At times, ethnic and cultural differences can be nonobvious differences as well.

Letting our clients know about some of our personal differences while still being able to maintain a close therapeutic relationship helps all of us learn to respect and accept these differences. However, weigh the risks and benefits of sharing nonobvious personal differences in a particular situation individually. Too much personal information can become a boundary violation over time. After the client asks several questions about your personal life, it must usually be explored as a therapeutic issue. (See Chapter 4 for further discussion of personal questions from clients.)

## COMPLEXLY DIVERSE CLIENTS

*Angelica Lopez is a mental health trainee who is being assigned a new client. Her client is a second-generation Syrian American, Jason Al-Khani, who is just realizing that he is gay. The client's parents are university professors at a major university in Texas, and he grew up there. She cannot even begin to speculate how these varying cultural influences will interact in the client.*

Modern 21st-century nations are tremendously culturally diverse. Clearly, we must have exposure and understanding of individual differences, acculturation, biculturalism, and other diversity topics. However, no textbook or article can cover all the possible interactions between different cultural, societal, and family influences in a particular client. Like Angelica, we might see clients whose multiple influences confound us. Or we might see immigrants from nations whose cultures we know little about and cannot learn much about from the psychological literature (e.g., Syrians, Greeks or Egyptians). In these situations, we must be open to learning from our clients about their cultural influences to arrive at a complete conceptualization.

## COPING WITH CLINICAL ERRORS RELATING TO CULTURAL DIFFERENCES

*Ebony Jackson is a mental health trainee working with a middle-aged female client of Puerto Rican background living in a major urban area. They have had several sessions and have developed a good rapport. Ebony has demonstrated her understanding of the client's bicultural struggles as they affect her role in the family (traditional mother vs. cobreadwinner). Her client is having problems with her adult stepdaughter, whom the family refers to as "Baby." The client feels that her husband is overly protective of "Baby." Ebony blurts out, "Well, if everyone calls her Baby, no wonder she behaves that way! What is her real name?" The client tells her the name, then gently informs her that many Puerto Rican families call the youngest child in the family "Baby," even as an adult. Ebony apologized to the client, who was amused by the error.*

*Heather Parker is a White mental health trainee with an African American young adult client. The client is very close with her sister, and they raid each other's closets all the time. The sister stays over at the client's apartment even though they live in the same city. They are often loaning each other small amounts of money back and forth. Heather conceptualizes this behavior as "enmeshed" and encourages her client to have more separation from her sister. Later Heather's supervisor reminds her that resource sharing and family closeness is common in the client's cultural group, and that the client's behavior is normal. At the next session, Heather apologized to the client for her misunderstanding.*

None of us has any desire to make the types of clinical errors that Ebony and Heather have made, but it is almost inevitable that all of us will, sooner or later. As the case of Ebony demonstrates, we might understand many cultural differences but still be surprised by unexpected traditions that mean something very different from our initial interpretation. As the case of Heather demonstrates, we might have an intellectual understanding of cultural differences, but applying this knowledge takes time and experience.

If you do make this kind of clinical error, as you can see from the previous examples, it is unlikely to cause a permanent rift in the therapeutic relationship. However, it is helpful to acknowledge that you have made an error. Then, as necessary, explore how your error has affected the client.

## COPING WITH PREJUDICED CLIENTS

*Pablo Sanchez is a mental health trainee working with a lower-functioning population. The group members do not know that Pablo is gay. He is coleading group therapy when a group member starts to use offensive language when talking about a supposedly gay person. Pablo and his cotherapists (who know that Pablo is gay) are shocked and don't know what to say so the moment passes.*

On occasion, clients will make discriminatory remarks. Commonly, this is done toward a group that the client does not belong to and thinks that the psychotherapist does not belong to. Often, when first encountering this behavior, psychotherapists may be shocked and uncertain about what to do.

In this situation we have at least two concerns about these remarks. First, these remarks are not socially appropriate. Persons making prejudicial remarks are unlikely to have positive relationships with individuals of other groups. This is dysfunctional, given the increasing diversity of 21st-century nations. Second, the psychotherapist does not want to give the client the impression that he or she agrees with the discriminatory remarks by not commenting on them. This leaves the psychotherapist with the challenge of how to address the remarks appropriately in therapy.

Laszloffy and Hardy (2000) suggest that the psychotherapist should first validate some aspect of the feelings that the client has in the situation: "It sounds as though you were very frustrated with how that other passenger treated you on the train." Note that in this reflection, the psychotherapist does not use the discriminatory language that the client used. This provides the client with an implicit message that the psychotherapist will not engage in using this language.

At this point, consider the client's functioning level. If the client is low functioning, you might simply request that discriminatory language not be used during the individual or group therapy session: "I'd appreciate it if you did not use those words during our meeting."

If you believe that the client has the capacity to tolerate it, you might ask some of these questions:

- "How do other people respond when you use that kind of language?"
- "What kinds of feelings do you have about [group]? How did you develop those? Do you know anyone who is [group]? Do you use that term around her? Why not?"

If questions about the client's experiences and language are asked gently, this will minimize defensiveness, and the client is more likely to see this behavior as inappropriate as well. In addition, consider that Hamer (2006) suggests that racist remarks of a client can often be indicative of underlying issues, often regarding transference and anger, which can be productively explored in therapy.

## COPING WITH CLIENTS WHO ARE PREJUDICED AGAINST YOU OR YOUR DEMOGRAPHIC GROUP

*Ryan Yamamoto is a Japanese American mental health trainee doing a rotation at the Veterans Affairs Medical Center. He is interested in working with the elderly, and has been assigned to work with a staff psychologist leading a psychotherapy group for Vietnam veterans. The psychologist will be Ryan's supervisor for this training experience. Before going to the group, the psychologist warns Ryan that the group may react negatively to his ethnicity. During the first group session that Ryan attends, one group member refers to him by an ethnic slur and insists that he cannot work with Ryan.*

*Dominique King is an African American mental health trainee working with a rural Southern population. She has a new White female client who has been treating her in a strange way that she can't exactly describe. She asks the client if she has any concerns about working with an African American psychotherapist. The client says, "No, of course not. I'm used to having Blacks take care of me."*

A psychotherapist's appearance, including gender, age, ethnicity, and any other obvious attributes, is a stimulus that will cause emotional reactions in some clients. Ethnic minority psychotherapists may be especially plagued with insensitive remarks and prejudicial attitudes, as noted in the previous vignettes. It is beyond the scope of this volume to thoroughly address each possible example of demographic difference, since each situation will have unique elements that need to be thoroughly explored in supervision, as well as with demographically similar peers and mentors (M. Harris, 2005).

If a client's negative reactions are trauma-based and the client is willing to continue to work with the psychotherapist (as with the example of Ryan), the relationship may be difficult at first but has the potential to be especially therapeutic for the client. The client will have an opportunity to face and resolve fears about a particular demographic group, which can foster much improved functioning.

Clients' prejudices can present themselves overly or covertly. Unfortunately, the literature on psychotherapist–client racial differences focuses almost entirely on the White psychotherapist–Black client dyad (Laszloffy & Hardy, 2000) and ignores the concerns of the racial minority psychotherapist, such as Dominique, above.

After one very overt remark or several subtly prejudicial remarks, the psychotherapist may wish to ask the client,

"I'm wondering if you may have any discomfort or concerns about working with a [fill in the blank] psychotherapist?"

In the case of an overtly prejudicial client, it can sometimes be best for the case to be transferred to a psychotherapist more demographically similar to the client, who can address dysfunctional aspects of the client's prejudicial attitudes more comfortably over time. On the other hand, if the psychotherapist is able to tolerate the client and continues to gently question the client when these issues come up, the client may be able to develop a greater maturity as well as tolerance and understanding for others. However, if the client insists on a transfer at any time, it is wise to accommodate that request.

As a supervisor and/or fellow group coleader, I would offer different feedback and assistance to the previously mentioned trainees, depending on the situation. Specifically, for Ryan and Pablo (from the previous section's vignettes), who are dealing with prejudiced group members, we would work together to establish a group rule that no prejudicial comments are allowed. Given that Pablo's clients are low functioning, the simple goal of encouraging socially appropriate behavior, such as avoiding prejudicial remarks, might be sufficient. However, Ryan's client probably has hypervigilance and post-traumatic stress disorder. These symptoms should be addressed directly, even while asking that the client talk to Ryan and the group appropriately. When the client gets used to Ryan and sees him as a helping professional, this will be a huge step in his recovery.

Dominique, on the other hand, is in a more difficult situation. The client is overtly cooperative with treatment but has an underlying prejudicial attitude toward the psychotherapist. Dominique should discuss this situation carefully with her supervisor. On the one hand, a White psychotherapist might be more accepted by the client. On the other hand, if Dominique can stick it out and gets help coping with the inevitable countertransference (since working with a client who is prejudiced against the psychotherapist is an especially emotionally taxing situation), perhaps Dominique's assistance will help this client gain respect for African Americans as professionals and individuals over time. Later, when they develop a stronger bond, it may be possible to address this comment directly.

## UNDERSTANDING UNCONSCIOUS CULTURAL PREJUDICES

I mean, you got the first mainstream African-American [Senator Barack Obama] who is articulate and bright and clean and a nice-looking guy. (Senator Joseph Biden, as quoted in the *New York Observer*, by J. Horowitz, February 4, 2007)

When whites use the word [articulate] in reference to blacks, it often carries a subtext of amazement, even bewilderment. It is similar to praising a female executive or politician by calling her "tough" or "a rational decision-maker." "When people say it, what they are really saying is that someone is articulate...for a black person," Ms. Perez said. Such a subtext is inherently offensive because it suggests that the recipient of the "compliment" is notably different from other black people. "Historically, it was meant to signal the exceptional Negro," Mr. Dyson said. "The implication is that most black people do not have the capacity to engage in articulate speech, when white people are automatically assumed to be articulate." (L. Clementson, *New York Times*, February 4, 2007)

Boding poorly for the start of his 2008 presidential campaign, Biden meant to compliment Barack Obama in the previous quote. Instead, he revealed unconscious racial prejudices by oddly describing him as "clean." And as the second quote informs us, even the seemingly positive adjective "articulate" can carry a loaded subtext.

It is easy for us to be surprised at Biden's statement. However, cognitive psychologists have learned much about prejudices in the past 20 years, and what they've learned is that everyone within the culture is well aware of negative cultural stereotypes and that, unfortunately, these stereotypes are automatically elicited (see the classic article by Devine, 1989). However, just because one is aware of stereotypes does not mean that one has any desire to implement them.

Research has shown that low-prejudice individuals establish a personal belief structure that allows them to consciously counteract the known, automatically elicited cultural stereotype. In addition, research has shown that education (Rudman, Ashmore, & Gary, 2001) is effective in reducing prejudice and stereotypes.

As psychotherapists, we acknowledge that, like everyone else in the culture, we have ingested unhealthy racial and cultural stereotypes and prejudices. Modern psychotherapy training programs emphasize multicultural education and training as an essential step in helping us to cope effectively with these negative cultural influences.

## RECOMMENDED READING

Bieschke, K. J., Perez, R. M., & DeBord, K. A. (Eds.). (2006). *Handbook of counseling and psychotherapy with lesbian, gay, bisexual, and transgender clients* (2nd ed.). Washington, DC: American Psychological Association.
  *Many contributors to this edited volume provide enhanced expertise and assist the psychotherapist in learning about cultural contexts and affirmative counseling with lesbian, gay, bisexual, and transgender clients.*
Devine, P. G. (1989). Stereotypes and prejudice: Their automatic and controlled components. *Journal of Personality and Social Psychology, 56*, 5–18.
  *In Devine's now-classic article, she describes the process of automatic racial stereotype activation.*
Hamer, F. M. (2006). Racism as a transference state: Episodes of racial hostility in the psychoanalytic context. *Psychoanalytic Quarterly, 75*, 197–214.
  *Hamer's discussion of how he, an African American psychotherapist, addressed clients' racist remarks in therapy is well worth reading for psychotherapists of all racial backgrounds and provides invaluable insights into the psychodynamics of racism.*
Larson, D. B., & Larson, S. S. (2003). Spirituality's potential relevance to physical and emotional health: A brief review of quantitative research. *Journal of Psychology and Theology, 31*, 37–51.
  *Larson and Larson provide an informative and evenhanded review of the literature on spirituality and health; this is a good introduction to the topic.*
Nesbit, R. E. (2003). *The geography of thought: How Asians and Westerners think differently... and why.* New York: Free Press.
  *This fascinating work summarizes research describing cultural and cognitive differences, showing how people from different cultures actually see the world differently.*

## TRANSGENDER INFORMATION

Documentaries are a helpful introduction to the experiences and concerns of transgendered individuals. Try: *Southern Comfort* (2001) and *TransGeneration* (2005).

## Intersex Information

The Australian documentary *The Gender Puzzle* (2006) discusses intersex biological and emotional issues, as well as transsexuality; at the time of writing, it was available on YouTube.

## DISCUSSION QUESTIONS

1. Given your age, ethnicity, sexual orientation, and other factors, what challenges do you anticipate having with clients who are different from you? Which of these challenges are more likely to be related to prejudice and which to a lack of understanding? How will you or the client know the difference?
2. What thoughts do you have about addressing a client's prejudicial remarks toward you? Would it matter if the client did or did not know that you belong to the group he is prejudiced against?
3. How would you address a client's prejudicial remarks toward others?

# 6

# Professional Electronic Communications and Data Security

> To do our job well requires that we demonstrate to our clients that we inhabit the 21st century. *(ZUR, 2012, p. 56)*

Electronic communications are fraught with potential for therapeutic problems, including misunderstandings, inappropriate remarks, legal liability, and breaches of confidentiality. While electronic communications are an essential part of modern life, the mental health literature is still wrestling with providing helpful clinical guidelines in this area.

Advances in communications technologies show promise for developing new effective treatments and for improving services to underserved populations. Online treatment is a rapidly developing area, with evolving norms and protocols. Be aware that these treatments are beyond the scope of this book and would require considerable research and consultation to practice ethically and legally. Recupero and Rainey (2005a, 2005b) discuss some of the risk issues with e-therapy.

## CHOOSING YOUR E-MAIL ADDRESS

*A training site supervisor is reviewing vitas of mental health trainees that might be matched to the site. He sees that one student's personal e-mail address is foxyshrink12345@aprovider.com. He thinks that the student has poor taste, poor judgment, or both. The student is not offered an interview for that site.*

If you can choose an e-mail ID at work, choose something simple and recognizable. For example, you might choose kellyreed@thisclinic.org or k-reed@that-clinic.com. If you enter a tagline on your work e-mail, enter your job title. This will help people learn who you are. Never choose anything religious, irrelevant, distracting, personal, or (supposedly) humorous.

Your personal e-mail address should be one that you can keep indefinitely (e.g., Hotmail, Gmail or Yahoo!). For example, you don't want your university to terminate your e-mail address when you are applying for your first job. That would impede your professional networking at a crucial point. However, some universities do let alumni keep their e-mail addresses indefinitely. Check with your university first if you plan on using an affiliated e-mail address. Be sure that your e-mail account has a strong unique password—one that you don't use for anything else and one that would be difficult to guess and hack (Fallows, 2011).

## PROFESSIONAL E-MAIL

*Two mental health trainees at a training site are good friends. They send each other e-mail about how things are going. They are using the training site's e-mail system for these messages when they are at work. One sends the other an e-mail criticizing his supervisor. When the other trainee is reading it, she is thinking about how she needs to forward a different e-mail to that supervisor and she absentmindedly forwards the negative e-mail to the very supervisor the first student is criticizing. Professional embarrassment and interpersonal difficulties ensue.*

Professional e-mail has a very different tone than personal e-mail. Many clinics and medical centers have a secure internal e-mail system where you can safely discuss patient care issues with other professionals. Keep all communications on such systems professional. Remember, all e-mail within or to a hospital or agency e-mail address can be retrieved by a superior at any time. Here are some don'ts:

- Don't ever send any e-mail that you would not want everyone in the clinic to read, even to someone you know and trust. E-mails can get mistakenly forwarded or, worse, maliciously forwarded.
- Don't talk negatively about anyone, clients or staff, on e-mail.
- Don't ever write an e-mail when you are angry. Cool off and later handle the situation tactfully, in person.
- Don't ever write anything in an e-mail that would humiliate or endanger you or anyone else if you had to talk about it in a court of law. E-mail is discoverable.
- Avoid most e-mail abbreviations (e.g., BTW [by the way] or LOL [laugh out loud]). Some of your colleagues will be old enough that they don't understand what you're saying, and others may consider it unprofessional.
- Use complete sentences and good grammar. Avoid or use very few "emoticons." These can come across as juvenile or silly, especially to your older colleagues.

- Don't use professional e-mail systems for personal chitchat. Use your personal e-mail address and the recipient's personal e-mail address for this instead. Again, if it is ever discovered or forwarded, you will regret it.
- Avoid venting in writing. It is always better to vent in person or on the phone so there is no permanent record of your momentary heated or indiscreet remarks. A written record could embarrass you later.

Your professional e-mail account should have a different password from your personal account, and it should be a strong password that is difficult to hack (Fallows, 2011).

## SENDING E-MAIL ABOUT CLIENTS TO OTHER PRACTITIONERS

E-mail can help tremendously in coordinating care between different professionals, but use it carefully. If sensitive information must be conveyed, a voicemail is preferable, as voicemail is generally more secure.

If you do send e-mail, first consider the type of e-mail system that you are sending the e-mail on. If you are sending it from one e-mail address to another within the same clinic or hospital, it is possible that the e-mail system has been protected with sufficient firewalls that you can send identifying information safely by e-mail. Never send identifying information unless you have first asked your supervisor and/or the computer network administrator about the internal security of the system.

Even on a secure e-mail system, confine your discussion of client issues to the bare facts as much as possible. Especially if they are electronic and readily accessible, let your progress notes speak for themselves and just send an e-mail pointing out that there is important information in them.

- Wrong: "Hi, Dr. Garcia. Bob was at his session today and talked about killing himself again. I'm sick and tired of all his manipulation. Anyway, can you fit him in sooner for meds?"
- Right: "Hi, Dr. Garcia. Please see my note for today on Bob. I'm concerned about recurring safety issues. Can you fit him in sooner for meds?"

The first note makes unkind negative statements about Bob, which should never be done in an e-mail (if you feel that way about Bob, you need to discuss your countertransference about him in supervision instead). The second e-mail refers to the note instead.

Never, ever, send any unsecured e-mail that mentions a client by name or that gives any identifying information about the client. Unsecured e-mail would be any e-mail account that you have personally or through your school, but other e-mail accounts can be unsecured as well. Here are two examples of unsecured e-mails that you might consider sending:

- Wrong: "Hi, Dr Garcia. I'm referring you a 27-year-old Filipino American male client, Roberto P. He's a graduate student at Xavier University and has been struggling with depression for years. I'm worried about suicide risk and want to talk to you about it before his first appointment. Call me."
- Right: "Hi, Dr. Garcia. I'm referring you a new client, R.P. I'm faxing you a release today. There are some urgent issues, so please call me about this client before the first appointment. Wednesday morning is a good time to reach me."

Even though the first example does not include the last name, too much identifying information has been included in the e-mail. The second example includes only initials—and not even the gender—which is enough information that Dr. Garcia can identify the client when he calls, especially when Dr. Garcia finds out that you referred him. Often one or two initials are sufficient for the recipient to figure out what client you are referring to, so using any names at all should be avoided.

## COMMUNICATING BY E-MAIL WITH CLIENTS

Many psychotherapists communicate with clients by e-mail. I do as well. However, before I even see new clients, they must fill out a form indicating their understanding of my e-mail policy. Be sure that clients understand that e-mail should not be used in case of emergency (Kassaw & Gabbard, 2002). Tell the client how soon he can generally expect an e-mail response from you and when e-mail will be part of the medical record (Kassaw & Gabbard, 2002). Also, clients need to be aware that e-mail is not a confidential medium, so sensitive information should be discussed during the session instead.

You should never give an e-mail address that you share with a family member to a client. If you give an e-mail address to a client, it must be one that is used by you alone (Woody, 1999).

Ask clients to confine e-mail communications to routine administrative matters, such as appointment time changes or minor billing glitches. Here is a sample of this kind of e-mail:

"Hi, Juan. I'm realizing that I have schedule problems next week. Can we move our appointment to 5:00 instead of 3:00? Thanks, [your name]"

Never give out your e-mail address without discussing it with a supervisor. Clients can have many reasons for making such requests, conscious or unconscious. Why can't the client just call? Case reports in the literature suggest that e-mail may be more subject to misinterpretation and boundary crossing than other types of communication (Gutheil & Simon, 2005).

Keep in mind that clients might be able to get your e-mail address through your university's website—so a client may decide to send you e-mail without discussing it with you first. If you think this is likely, discuss e-mail issues with the client proactively. At times, despite your requests, a client may send clinically relevant information to you by e-mail. In these cases, here is an appropriate response:

"Hi, Juan. Thanks for sending me this information. I can see that this is very important, and I look forward to hearing more about it when I see you on Wednesday. Sincerely, [your name]"

Note that the response is respectful of the importance of the e-mail without commenting on its contents. Don't comment on the information by e-mail since you will be more effective dealing with it during the therapy session. In e-mail, you lose too much detail and emotion to address therapeutic issues effectively (Gutheil & Simon, 2005). When you see the client next, you might suggest that the client write in his journal about the issue instead, then bring his writings to the therapy sessions to read to you there. Emphasize your concerns about his privacy and confidentiality as you make this suggestion.

You should save a copy of any e-mail that you have sent or received from a client that has clinically relevant information in it. E-mail can be printed out and placed physically into the chart, or you can copy it into an electronic medical record instead. Some might advise that you save every e-mail from a client, whereas other psychotherapists would not bother saving e-mails that solely deal with routine scheduling or billing issues, so opinions differ. Discuss this issue with your supervisor.

People have been found to overestimate their ability to convey emotion and tone over e-mail. This overconfidence is related to our innate egocentrism (Kruger, Epley, Parker, & Ng, 2005). The obvious implication is that we must all assume that our e-mails will be occasionally misinterpreted by others in ways that we are unable to predict. Disinhibition can occur in e-mail and other online communications that would not occur in person, leading to dangers of boundary crossings and violations (Bhuvaneswar & Gutheil, 2008).

Another reason to avoid most e-mail communications with clients is that research indicates that e-mail communication is especially vulnerable to expectancies and stereotypes (Epley & Kruger, 2005). From this, it is not a large leap to conclude that transference could become overly intense and problematic through e-mail.

A final concern about e-mail is that server problems, or unexpected absences from Internet access, can cause therapeutic disruptions if the client is dependent on e-mail as a key part of psychotherapy (Welfel & Heinlen, 2010). In the worst-case scenario, the client might send a crisis e-mail that is not received in a timely manner (Bhuvaneswar & Gutheil, 2008).

## WHAT TO DO IF AN UNKNOWN INDIVIDUAL IN CRISIS E-MAILS YOU

An individual, unknown to you, may e-mail you asking for clinical advice, distressed about suicidal thoughts, or urgently begging to become your psychotherapy client. How to respond? Ethically, you do not feel good about ignoring this call for help. Yet this is not an effective way to seek help. As a trainee, you must immediately discuss this situation with a supervisor. Having any type of online relationship with a prospective client may legally create a doctor–patient relationship (Simon, 2004), which would mean that you would have a responsibility to do appropriate assessments in case of a crisis, suicide risk, and so on, which is nearly impossible to do online, especially with someone you've never met.

Giving specific advice increases the risk of establishing a legal practitioner–patient relationship, making you potentially responsible for the outcome of the situation (Recupero, 2005). Recupero (2005), therefore, recommends that you provide only general advice and that you explicitly state that you are not engaged in a professional relationship with the individual. The following is a sample e-mail incorporating these recommendations:

"Dear John,

I cannot undertake your care or provide advice for you personally. I am not your doctor. People who are suicidal should seek help immediately. For example, they can call 911, go to an emergency room, or call their own physician.

Sincerely, Dr. Z." (Recupero, 2005, p. 473)

Do not follow up, despite your concern. Following up gives the impression that you may have a legal practitioner–patient relationship—which, I must emphasize, you should not allow in these circumstances.

## TEXT MESSAGING AND INSTANT MESSAGING

Try to avoid text messaging or instant messaging with a client. Because of their brevity, text messages are highly prone to misinterpretation, projection, and so on. If a client sends a text message containing clinically relevant information, either call the client in response or reply with a brief polite request that the client call you about the matter. As with e-mail, clinically relevant text messages should be copied into the chart. If a client communicates best by text message, as some do (Zur, 2012), consult with your supervisor about how to manage these communications. As with e-mail, try to confine text messages to scheduling and other less sensitive matters.

Under certain circumstances, and with the approval of your supervisor, it is possible that a client might have your cell phone number. In that case, the client might send a text message that he is running late. This type of text message is relatively innocuous, and you do not necessarily need to respond to it. Under no circumstances should you be checking your text messages during a psychotherapy session.

Instant messages can be too spontaneous and intimate, running the risk of veering into social chitchat. They are intrusive on the time outside the session and should also be avoided. If your clients have your e-mail address, it is wise to turn off any instant messaging feature. If you feel that you need the IM feature, your client should not have your personal e-mail address; you should give out a separate professional e-mail address instead.

Also, avoid texting other health care professionals about client issues. Many devices do not encrypt texts, opening you up to HIPAA violations (Dolan, 2011).

## YOUR INTERNET PRESENCE

*Ted Chang, a mental health trainee, and his husband, Marcos, were on vacation in Oaxaca, Mexico. Ted is an adventurous eater and enjoys trying exotic foods. He and Marcos enjoy taking goofy pictures on vacation. Marcos takes a picture of Ted with his tongue hanging out with dead crickets on it (a local delicacy). Marcos posts this picture and others from their vacation on his social networking page to share with family and friends. Ted doesn't think much about it until a professor suggests that he check what comes up on an Internet search of his name. He is shocked to see this picture on the first search result page, right under his CV. He wonders how many of his psychotherapy clients have seen this picture.*

Take the case of a man who, after developing romantic and erotic feelings toward his therapist, typed her name into a search engine and found a Web site featuring personal photographs of the therapist, including a bathing-suit shot. The man quit treatment and reported the discovery to Behnke's [American Psychological Association Ethics] office. "He knew the image of his therapist in her bathing suit was going to be so present to him that he wouldn't be able to concentrate on his psychotherapy," Behnke explained in a telephone interview. "There was material on the Internet that had an impact on this psychologist's clinical work." (Scarton, 2010)

You may have a page on a social networking site or a personal Web page. You may post vacation pictures online, or have a blog, or you may use Twitter. Maybe you do online dating. These are normal everyday activities, but as psychotherapists we need to think carefully about what we have online about ourselves.

Some experts suggest that you divide your online presence into personal and professional realms (McGee, 2011). Your professional presence might include a professional website, your online vita, or postings on LinkedIn (or other professional networking site). You may be interested in tweeting or blogging about psychology topics. This can be perfectly appropriate as long as you avoid personal topics and avoid posting any case content about psychotherapy clients. Be aware that any one of your psychotherapy clients may subscribe/follow your online content, so think carefully about posting on topics that could be hot-button issues for current psychotherapy clients.

Professional listservs can be a helpful source of professional information; however, be aware that many listservs do not check professional qualifications, so clients may get access simply through providing false credentials (Zur, 2008). Also, the information on listservs is transmitted through e-mail, not a secure medium. Listservs should be used as an informational resource only, not for discussion of psychotherapy cases. It is also fine to ask for resources for a particular client on listservs, as long as you are sufficiently vague about the client that he can never be identified (e.g. "Does anyone have information on support groups for college-age clients with social anxiety?").

Your personal online content is more challenging. I advise starting now to preserve your privacy carefully. The further you advance in your career, the more clients will be searching for information about you online—usually for perfectly appropriate reasons, such as due diligence in choosing a psychotherapist (Zur, Williams, Lehavot, & Knapp, 2009). As you may be aware, Internet giants such as Google and Facebook have unilaterally changed their privacy policies in recent years, not always offering the privacy setting options we would prefer.

Experts advise that you set your personal social networking settings to the maximum privacy level (Gabbard, Kassaw, & Perez-Garcia, 2011; Martin, 2010). If you don't, sooner or later a client will find your personal material. At best, it will be awkward or disruptive to the therapeutic process ("Hey, I see on your Facebook page that you're not single anymore—what's up with that?"). At worst, it may aid in stalking and harassing you (Zur, Williams, Lehavot, & Knapp, 2009). For these reasons, social networking entries should never be publicly available because they include too much personal information (e.g., relationship status, sexual orientation, religion, birth date) that you would not normally reveal to psychotherapy clients. Consider asking your partner and other immediate family members to set their profiles to the highest privacy level as well. Never post your home address anywhere online, but be aware that persistent clients may be able to get it online anyway.

Consider carefully what you post; you must assume that everything you post online could potentially be found by clients (Zur, 2008). On the one hand, you should have the same ability to speak out and share thoughts and information with friends as anyone else. On the other hand, it is wiser to save very personal information for phone or personal discussions rather than post it on social networking sites. Avoid posting disparaging comments about colleagues or groups of clients (Gabbard, Kassaw, & Perez-Garcia, 2011). Never, ever, mention anything specific or identifying about a client in any posting, including social networking sites (Gabbard, Kassaw, & Perez-Garcia, 2011), blogs, twitter, listservs, or anywhere else. Do not post anything related to a client's treatment or what a client has said or complain about your work (Dr. K. Kolmes, quoted in American

Psychological Association Practice Organization, 2012). Do not post on any lawsuits or administrative actions you may be involved in because this may harm your defense (Gabbard, Kassaw, & Perez-Garcia, 2011). In fact, it is wise to completely avoid discussing anything other than the most general clinical issues online.

Psychotherapists should never have blogs about their personal lives freely available; also, be aware that a private blog today could become a public blog tomorrow by unilateral privacy setting changes by the hosting site. Technologically savvy clients may be able to identify you behind your screen name (Zur, 2008) and discover personal information you have posted (supposedly) anonymously. Blogs make particularly permanent and searchable footprints on the Internet compared to some other activities such as Facebook status postings (Gabbard, Kassaw, & Perez-Garcia, 2011), although at the time of this writing, Facebook is making changes that make old status postings much more searchable. Blogs about general topics such as religion, politics, movies, or society issues will be read by some of your clients and will have some impact on the therapeutic relationship (Martin, 2010); if you have this kind of blog or post comments on others' online material, discuss it with your supervisors proactively and consider how clients may react upon reading this material.

I recommend removing all publicly accessible online videos or photos now, except for any that might be purely professional—a professional headshot or you being interviewed about a mental health topic, for example. Medical students have run into trouble for posting gallows humor videos online (Crawford, 2009). Facial recognition software, search software, and privacy policies change every day, so any online activity, posting, photo, or video that you think is anonymous today could be linked with your name tomorrow through improved technology or changed privacy settings. Given that privacy policies can change, either avoid posting snapshots online or ensure that the photos are innocuous: scenery, for example. Never post photos online showing yourself intoxicated (Gabbard, Kassaw, & Perez-Garcia, 2011), in scanty clothing or swimwear, or engaged in any activities that you don't want to share with your psychotherapy clients, and try to prevent others from posting these photos as well. Ask your friends to remove any potentially embarrassing photos now.

If you decide to do online dating, try to minimize the potential for awkward situations with single psychotherapy clients. Case examples have been reported of psychotherapists being matched to current clients (Taylor, McMinn, Bufford, & Chang, 2010). Consider not posting a picture and, instead, send it by e-mail to a select few matches whom you are interested in meeting. Consider describing yourself more generally, as a health care professional, rather than being specific so your psychotherapy clients, who may also be on the site, would not necessarily link you to your posting.

Carefully review everything you have put online. Run different variations of your name through the most common search engines to see what you find (Zur, 2008). If you don't like something, delete your online information *now* since search engine caches will keep it available to searches for a while after it is deleted. If you can't delete the item yourself, try to get it deleted by the webmaster of the site it is on (Zur, 2008). If you can't do that, at least being aware of what is out there about you will help you be prepared when clients mention it (Taylor, McMinn, Bufford, & Chang, 2010). Potential employers or supervisors may search for you online and judge you negatively. This has now become common (Finder, 2006).

## TO FRIEND OR NOT TO FRIEND

A large majority of mental health graduate students and early career psychologists maintain social networking site profiles, and it is a common experience to occasionally get "friend" requests from current and previous psychotherapy clients (Taylor, McMinn, Bufford, & Chang, 2010).

Although advice in the professional literature is not completely consistent about whether it is okay to "friend" current or past clients (Birky & Collins, 2011; Lehavot, Barnett, & Powers, 2010; O'Reilly, 2010), I agree with the experts who advise strongly never to "friend" clients on social networking sites (Gabbard, Kassaw, & Perez-Garcia, 2011; Kolmes, 2010). Kolmes (2010) states, "My belief has always been that adding clients as contacts is a big enough threat to both confidentiality and the boundaries of the therapeutic relationship to justify a blanket policy of not accepting such requests" (p. 140). Also, Kolmes (2010) lists two highly convincing reasons why it is wise to avoid "friending" current or past psychotherapy clients: first that there would be too much potential for nonsecure, nonconfidential communication, and second that messages that include health information are part of the legal record and can be difficult to document or delete on social networking sites. A third reason is that everyone who is your "friend" can see your other "friends," and if you are known to occasionally accept clients as "friends," people may wonder who on your "friend" list is a client (Kaslow, Patterson, & Gottlieb, 2011). There is nothing confidential about having a client as a "friend;" all your family and friends can see that this person has a connection to you, which violates the client's therapeutic confidentiality. In addition, it establishes a dual relationship with the client, which is unethical (Gabbard, Kassaw, & Perez-Garcia, 2011). These arguments not to ever "friend" are compelling and consistent with professional ethics.

When you receive your first request to "friend" a current or former client, here is a suggested response:

> "Dear [client]: It's kind of you to send me an invitation to connect on [site]. However, in order to maximally maintain your confidentiality, I have a policy not to connect to any current or former clients on any social media. Let me know if you have any questions about this, and we can discuss at your next session. Take care, [your name]"

At the next session, you can explore the client's responses to this e-mail. Alternatively, you can not respond by e-mail at all, but discuss the issue in person at a future session. If it is a former client, generally the e-mail will have to do; talk to your supervisor about whether to also provide a phone number in your e-mail if the former client wants to discuss the situation.

Should you "friend" a supervisor or instructor? Experts recommend not to, and to reconsider only when the supervisory relationship is over (Kaslow, Patterson, & Gottlieb, 2011). A connection on a professional networking site might be appropriate, however. Similarly, it would be wisest to connect with coworkers, staff, and fellow students only on professional networking sites. Try to "friend" only actual friends—whose discretion you trust—through personal social networking.

## WHETHER AND WHEN TO SEARCH FOR CLIENT INFORMATION ONLINE

There are many reasons why a psychotherapist might consider looking online for information relevant to a particular client:

- *To gather information relevant to the client's background and treatment:* (1) A psychotherapist has a new client who attended a historically black college. She has little experience with these colleges or their graduates, so looks online to educate herself about the experience. (2) A psychotherapist has a client with a rare autoimmune disease. He reads online to educate himself about the disease, its treatment, and common emotional reactions to the disease. (3) A psychotherapist has little experience with treating narcissistic personality traits but recognizes them in a new client. She reads several articles about treating narcissistic personality disorder that she found online.
- *Because of interest in some aspect of the client's life mentioned in a session:* A client e-mailed regarding session times. The psychotherapist saw the client's link to his fine art website at the bottom of his e-mail. The client had talked in session about revising the website and difficulties with producing the work that was showcased on the site. The psychotherapist clicked through to look at the website and the artwork. During the next session, she mentioned that she had looked at the work. The client was pleased that she took an interest.
- *As collateral information:* A psychotherapist often reviews information online about new clients to assist in orienting her to the client's life story. She finds that LinkedIn profiles give her a helpful outline of the client's professional and academic life. Since this information is public and was willingly posted by the client, she sees no problem with this practice.
- *To aid in psychotherapy:* A psychotherapist works at a college counseling center. One of his clients has admitted that she posted pictures of herself intoxicated on Facebook. She also said that she posts status updates discussing her frequent alcohol consumption. The psychotherapist expresses concern to the client that she will have personal and job placement difficulties because of these impulsive and overly revealing

posts. The client says she knows this and wants to stop. They agree that the psychotherapist will occasionally view the client's Facebook page to monitor her progress in this area.

- *To verify information because the client could be an unreliable informant:* "After the first call from a potential new client, the psychotherapist wonders whether the client, who did not present very impressively, was bragging or delusional about being the President of a Fortune 500 Company" (Zur, 2010, p. 144).

- *To verify information because the client might be deceptive:* "A 7-year-old boy began treatment for post-traumatic stress disorder after moving to a new state to live with his grandfather. The grandfather told the psychotherapist that the child's parents had been killed in a plane crash but was consistently unwilling to elaborate on the details of the event. When the child's symptoms continued to intensify, despite weeks of treatment, the clinician sought to learn more about the traumatic event via an Internet search, using the patient's name and prior residence as keywords. The search results included a newspaper article describing the murder of the child's parents by a relative. When the clinician revealed to the grandfather that she had obtained this information, he terminated the child's treatment and stated that he had hoped to give the boy a "fresh start" by not revealing the details of the parents' death, and he felt that his family's privacy had been seriously violated" (White, 2009).

- *To aid in emergency case management and client safety:* "A psychiatric nurse in an emergency room at a local hospital is attending to an unconscious young patient who, according to her family, had attempted suicide. The nurse was also told by the family that this client keeps an elaborate web site and Facebook profile. The nurse is considering going online to see if she can determine what the client may have taken as part of her suicide attempt and whether the client had posted a suicide note online" (Zur, 2010, pp. 144–145).

- *To aid if there are emergent safety concerns:* An acutely depressed client did not show up for her session and is not answering her cell phone. The psychotherapist looked to see if she had been posting on a social networking site, and what the tone of the posts was.

- *To maintain the psychotherapist's personal safety:* "Psychotherapists who utilize home offices may find that Googling new clients can help with their screening and safety-assessment protocols that are extremely important in home office settings" (Zur, 2010, p. 145).

- *Because of concerns about the safety of others:* "Dr. Jacinto Gomez, who had recently finished his training, was treating a new patient, Clara. The history she gave had many gaps, and because he suspected that she was withholding relevant information, he decided to do an Internet search rather than ask her additional questions. Clara told him that she was excited about getting a job as a staff member in a child care center after many years of having been unable to obtain such a position. What

Dr. Gomez discovered in his search was that Clara had been convicted of child abuse on two occasions twenty years earlier and had been placed on probation for five years" (Kaslow, Patterson, & Gottlieb, 2011, p. 109).

- *To be voyeuristically curious:* A psychotherapist looked up her client on a social networking site. She was interested in seeing pictures of him partying with friends and going on his recent vacation to Bermuda. The client did not have any privacy settings on his profile. The psychotherapist started to look at his postings frequently, but did not discuss this with the client.

I've given many examples to illustrate the complexity of the issue of online searches. In the very first example, when the psychotherapists are searching for information to provide a better-informed treatment, I suspect that almost every psychotherapist would agree that it is not only appropriate, but also ethically necessary, to inform oneself on therapeutic issues. In the very last case, when the psychotherapist was voyeuristically curious, again there would probably be universal agreement that the psychotherapist's behavior was a boundary violation. However, all the other examples are more or less in a gray area.

As of the time of this writing, there is no consensus in the professional literature about the appropriateness of searching for client information online. Contrast these two viewpoints:

> Although looking up information about a patient on the Internet is not unethical because it is public, psychiatrists who choose to do so must be prepared for clinical complications that require careful and thoughtful management. Some patients may experience the psychiatrist's interest in this information as a boundary-violation or a compromise of trust...It is customary when evaluating patients to often get collateral sources of data from other individuals who know the patient, usually with the permission of the patient. The treating psychiatrist may want to ask permission of the patient but can certainly access public information without a release if it is thought to be essential or helpful for the treatment. (Gabbard, Kassaw, & Perez-Garcia, 2011, pp. 172–173)

> The Internet provides psychologists with myriad opportunities to obtain information without a client's knowledge. Will information obtained in this way increase treatment effectiveness? If one believes that it will, how does the value provided by such an activity weigh against violations of evidence-based practice and treatment protocols, the client's reasonable expectation of privacy, and the integrity of the process? We do not think this is ethically, morally and/or professionally justifiable behavior. *The ends do not justify the means.*" (Kaslow, Patterson, & Gottlieb, 2011)

These two quotes illustrate that no consensus has emerged, even among experts, about Internet searches. I would tend to agree more with Gabbard et al. (2011).

The large majority of information about a person on the Internet is either information that the person herself put out there because she wants it to be publicly accessible (for example, a cooking blog, business website, or business profile) or information that is easily publicly available anyway (for example, open court records or news stories about or quoting the client). I might consider accessing online information to be comparable to: purchasing a birthday card at a gift store owned by a client because it was the nearest one, attending an art fair that you knew a client was exhibiting at, buying a cookbook authored by the client, or reading a newspaper article about a client. Considering these activities, we can see that, on the one hand, these are public activities and information, so it is unreasonable to consider them unethical; yet on the other hand, uncomfortable feelings could occur and may need to be addressed in therapy.

Many experts agree that, like any other public encounter that might occur with a client, it is wise to proactively address Internet searches through the informed consent process (Kolmes, 2010; Zur, 2010); this is discussed further in Chapter 7.

A client may mention material that he has posted online, and often this material reflects his achievements—such as the business that he built or his artwork for sale. Like any other personal progress or achievements, expressing appropriate interest can help build and sustain rapport: "Sounds like you've put a lot of work into this website showcasing your paintings. Would you like me to take a look at it?" With this statement, the therapist addresses the issue proactively, rather than after the fact as in the case example previously; this is the wisest policy but may not be essential in all cases. For many clients, who may be anxious, depressed, ruminative, or self-critical, your appropriate interest in and appreciation of their achievements and activities can be therapeutic.

Even those who advise against almost all Internet searches of clients suggest that there may be some exceptions, such as evaluations for fitness for duty or child custody (Kaslow, Patterson, & Gottlieb, 2011) or the safety of a client or a third party (Chamberlin, 2010). I would also suggest that it is appropriate to conduct an Internet search if you are concerned about your own personal safety.

Some very gray areas remain. What if you think that the client may be deceptive or withholding highly relevant personal information? Consider the previous vignette from Kaslow, Patterson, and Gottlieb (2011) in which the therapist discovers online that a new client, who recently got a job in child care, has been convicted of child abuse in the past. The point of their argument is that it would be better for the psychotherapist not to search online and to address his concerns about the gaps in the client's history directly with her. I agree that the therapist should be more direct with the client about his concerns. Yet we could argue that children's safety and welfare trumps the therapist's discomfort in addressing the abuse conviction with the client and in making a report to the state. Thus, I suspect that arguments can be made on both sides for any clinical example of possible deception or withholding, and that these issues must be considered carefully on an individual basis with consultation and supervision.

Another gray area is the client who may be an unreliable informant, possibly because of cognitive deficits, delusional ideas, or other reasons. Prior to the Internet, the psychotherapist might have worked on gaining collateral information in these cases from the client's family and significant others (and still might). Clearly, we can't adequately conceptualize and treat the client without knowing if he actually has been a president of a Fortune 500 company, he has cognitive deficits, or he is delusional. Yet, an approach that feels underhanded to the client is unlikely to result in good rapport or treatment results. Again, each of these cases may need to be considered carefully on an individual basis with consultation and supervision.

A final concern is if the psychotherapist becomes overly involved in a client's online life. This is the previous case example of voyeuristic curiosity. Appropriate interest in a client's life would not usually involve looking for updates about him online. Instead, you might look once or twice, as discussed directly with the client, and/or as covered in your informed consent process. You might check more often if the client requests it and you deem it therapeutically appropriate, as in one of the preceding examples. At the absolute most, only at the request of your client and after careful discussion with your supervisor, you might subscribe to the client's blog and look at it occasionally or at her request (but never comment publicly). Any more online interaction than this would warrant careful discussion both with your supervisor and your own psychotherapist, as it may become a significant boundary violation over time.

A related consideration is that the process of searching itself has some minor potential to endanger the client's confidentiality. Kolmes (2010) points out that entering the client's name into a search engine discloses a connection between yourself and the client to the Internet search provider. Be aware that there was a notorious episode in 2006 when AOL released supposedly anonymous search data from 500,000 users. They removed it quickly, but by then the data had been copied. Latanya Sweeney, a Harvard professor, has shown that "de-identified" data of this type can usually be re-identified (Sweeney, 2009). There is no law against this (Singer, 2011).

Consider these suggested guidelines for whether to search from Kolmes (2010):

> When psychotherapists who use search engines to look up client information describe this practice in their treatment agreement, it gives patients the opportunity to make informed consent decisions. Some patients may not feel comfortable working with clinicians who obtain information about them from search engines...Just as we document and formalize all other forms of 'consultation,' I also believe that Internet searches should be clinically justified, documented and formalized. I advise clinicians to consider whether they would be comfortable justifying such a search in the chart and disclosing to their client that they conducted the search. This is one way of distinguishing whether a search is done out of curiosity or in service to clinical care. (Kolmes, 2010, p. 141)

Be aware that these are only suggested guidelines from Kolmes, and at this point, there is no defined *standard of care* in this area (for a discussion of the concept of standard of care, see Chapter 12). As a wise psychologist once suggested,

"Think about whether you can write about the search in the chart without sounding creepy. If so, it's probably ok." Here are some suggested guidelines, incorporating the above discussions:

- Decide on a policy on Internet searches, or learn what the policy is at the site where you are working. Zur (2010) provides a range of sample policies.
- Try to be sure that clients are informed about the policy through the informed consent process (see Chapter 7 for further information about this).
- Some sites that have many clients who may be at risk of suicide, violence, or other risky behaviors may do online searches for safety reasons. Try to be sure that this is explicit in the informed consent process.
- Searches that concern emergent safety issues are least controversial, but consult with a supervisor first and document the search in the client's chart, including why the search was initiated and what was discovered. In most cases, you will also want to discuss this with the client.
- Searches that are prompted by concerns that a client may be an unreliable informant or may not be telling the truth should have the pros and cons considered carefully, and it may be wise to consult with colleagues as well as your supervisor. If you decide to search, document why you did so.
- Keep in mind that human curiosity *is* normal and that, at times, you will have normal human curiosity about clients and the things that they mention they've posted online. As previously mentioned, this is public information, and it's not unethical to look at it. However, to minimize unnecessary emotional challenges in therapy, consider mentioning your interest in looking at the material to the client, get the client's agreement (typically readily given, since the client will usually appreciate you taking an interest), and briefly document your review of the online material in the chart.
- Be cautious about becoming overly involved in a client's online life; this is likely to lead to boundary violations.

In conclusion, Zur provides the following wise advice: "we are still in an era where the standard of care regarding online searches of clients by their psychotherapists is not established yet. Therefore, proceed with caution. Be aware of your reasons for conducting online searches of your clients, construct a clinical rationale, be sensitive to your clients' culture, personality, attitudes towards privacy and technology and consult if necessary" (Zur, 2010, p. 148).

## THE HIPAA SECURITY RULE AND ENSURING DATA SECURITY

When health care practitioners are talking about HIPAA, they are usually talking about two separate rules that apply to all health care practitioners. These rules are the HIPAA Security Rule (this chapter) and the HIPAA Privacy Rule (see

Chapter 7). The Privacy Rule focuses on intentional releases of protected health information, while the Security Rule focuses on safeguarding against unintentional disclosures (American Psychological Association Practice Organization, 2007). Exploring all the implications of HIPAA rules is far beyond the scope of this volume. However, I will briefly discuss the focus of each rule and some implications for mental health trainees. Every institution or organization where you work should have a designated HIPAA Security Officer and a designated HIPAA Privacy Officer, who may be the same individual. These individuals are responsible for ensuring HIPAA compliance throughout the organization. Ask your supervisor who these officers are and ask them questions about HIPAA as needed.

*Protected health information* (PHI) is "information, including demographic data, that relates to: the individual's past, present or future physical or mental health or condition, the provision of health care to the individual, or the past, present, or future payment for the provision of health care to the individual, and that identifies the individual or for which there is a reasonable basis to believe can be used to identify the individual. Individually identifiable health information includes many common identifiers (e.g., name, address, birth date, Social Security Number)" (U.S. Department of Health and Human Services, 2003, p. 4). Thus, PHI is any information that can identify the client or that describes the client's health care.

The HIPAA Security Rule is about protecting electronic health information from unintended disclosure through breaches of security and from unintended loss, such as through fire or flood (American Psychological Association Practice Organization, 2007). This rule is implemented primarily through appropriate electronic security measures and backup procedures. Any computer, smartphone, flash drive, CD, or other device or storage media must be properly secured if it contains protected health information. Thus, if you keep your clients' phone numbers on your phone, in case you become ill and may need to cancel their appointments, the phone—and all computers it syncs with—must be password protected. Experts suggest that you not load any file-sharing apps that may access client information (such as Dropbox, Box.net, or Google Drive) on your smartphone because of the difficulty of keeping smartphones secure (HealthIT.gov, 2013). Think carefully about whether you can keep files secure if you load these applications on a laptop, and consider the alternative of accessing these files through the Internet instead.

If you share a computer that has PHI on it with anyone else, even your partner, ideally, you would be the administrator of the computer. No guest users of that computer should ever have administrator-level access. If there is a good reason for a family member to be an administrator (for example, that person has better computer skills and will do a better job keeping the computer secure against viruses and hackers), counsel that person carefully about client privacy. Be sure to set up a separate log-on for anyone besides yourself who regularly uses the computer so that they do not have ready access to the PHI.

Before disposal or donation, any device that has ever had PHI on it should have the memory completely wiped by a program designed to do so or the hard drive should be destroyed. If you don't know how to do this, hire a reputable professional to do it for you. Just deleting the files is not sufficient and is a security violation. And you should have appropriate firewalls, perform regular backups, and run updated antivirus and antispyware programs on your personal computer that contains PHI (Kibbe, 2005).

You may need to move from office to office if space is tight at your practicum site. If you use a flash drive to move clinical documents that you are working on (e.g., psychological reports), you must password protect the flash drive as well. You can purchase a secure flash drive that can be accessed only with a password.

Researchers have studied attempts to hack into computers and have seen what hackers try (M. Cukier, cited in personal communication from K. S. Pope, February 16, 2007). They have found that any computer connected to the Internet has about two attempts to hack it per *minute*. Given their research, here are some user names *not* to set up on any computer: root, admin, test, guest, info, adm, mysql, user, administrator, and oracle. For the password, do not use your user name, serial digits such as "1234," "password," "passwd," or "test." Also, note that "if a password can be found in a dictionary, that password is not safe" (Fallows, 2011). Strong passwords have all of the following characteristics:

- 10 or more characters long
- Both uppercase and lowercase letters
- One or more numbers
- One or more special characters

Don't store your passwords in a word-processing document or on a Post-it note. Invest in an encrypted program that you can use to secure them, one that will sync across at least two devices so your passwords are never lost (eWallet is one such program).

All word-processing documents that contain information about a client should be password protected with a strong password. Go ahead and use the same password over and over, as long as it is a good one.

As a general rule, any document that contains information about a client must not be viewable in a public place, even on top of your desk when other clients are in the room. Do not work on confidential documents in a public place. Secure this information in a locked drawer or filing cabinet. Do not let clients see the names of other clients on your computer screen.

Any client materials or contact information you have in your home (perhaps a case conceptualization you are preparing for class) should be under a password or kept in a locked drawer or cabinet.

## CLOUD COMPUTING AND DATA SECURITY

You are probably storing documents in the "cloud" already. For items such as research papers, articles that you are saving, and other items that do not have any

PHI in them, any cloud storage provider is fine. However, many of your documents may have client PHI in them: letters you have prepared for clients, psychological assessment reports, case studies, and so on. As of the time of this writing, the HIPAA Security Rule provides some general guidance principles—remember the importance of backups, passwords, and computer security. Saving documents in the cloud could enhance the safety of your documents by reducing the risk of document loss (especially if the cloud service saves a local copy on your computer as well as the cloud copy). However, saving documents in the cloud could also compromise your computer security if the cloud service provider does not have adequate security policies and procedures. Review the online security policies before using any cloud service provider for the following characteristics (Harauz, Kaufman, & Potter, 2009):

- Your documents are encrypted during transmission to the remote storage location.
- Your documents are encrypted when they are stored at the remote storage location.
- The cloud storage provider has strict policies about access to your documents.
- The cloud storage provider has regular backup procedures.

Consider the following: Is the main objective of the service provider's business to sell you more storage space for your documents? This would suggest that they are motivated to provide a reliable and secure storage service, which aligns with your storage aims. Or is their business model geared to advertising based on the content of your e-mail and so on? This would suggest that they may be motivated at some time to change their policies and use the content of your documents in an insecure manner.

Even when you have reviewed all the safety information for the cloud provider thoroughly, be sure to have all documents that have any client information on them are secured with a strong password as well.

### RECOMMENDED READING

Devereaux, R. L., & Gottlieb, M. C. (2012, April 30). Record keeping in the cloud: Ethical considerations. *Professional Psychology: Research and Practice.* Advance online publication. doi: 10.1037/a0028268
*This article provides a careful review of the risks of cloud computing for psychotherapists. However, they may be overly cautious about the risks, which is common whenever a new technology arises.*

Fallows, J. (2011, November). Hacked! *Atlantic Magazine.* Retrieved March 15, 2012, from http://www.theatlantic.com/magazine/archive/2011/11/hacked/8673/?single_page=true
*Fallows gives helpful and basic computer security advice in an easy-to-read article based on his wife's experience of having her e-mail account hacked.*

Gabbard, G. O. (2012). Clinical challenges in the Internet era. *American Journal of Psychiatry, 169*, 460–463.

*This article tells a cautionary tale about a client's mother posting disparaging comments regarding her son's mental health treatment online, and how the treatment team coped with that challenge.*

Gutheil, T. G., & Simon, R. I. (2005). E-mails, extra-therapeutic contact, and early boundary problems: The Internet as a "slippery slope." *Psychiatric Annals, 35*, 952–960.

*Some of the true but disguised case examples in this article will make you think very carefully about exchanging e-mail with clients.*

Recupero, P. (2005). E-mail and the psychiatrist–patient relationship. *Journal of the American Academy of Psychiatry and the Law, 33*, 465–475.

*Although explicitly written for psychiatrists, this article provides much helpful advice and cautions about legal issues involved in e-mailing psychotherapy clients.*

Zur, O. (2010). To Google or not to Google…our clients? When psychotherapists and other mental health care providers search their clients on the Web. *Independent Practitioner, 30*(3), 144–148.

*This is the best single article I've found regarding the complexities of searching for client information online. This article will help you sort out your own attitudes about the issue and provides helpful advice about informed consent. Zur provides a range of sample informed consent policies regarding online searches of clients by psychotherapists.*

## DISCUSSION QUESTIONS AND ACTIVITY

1. Some people feel that some of my advice to minimize your online presence is too risk averse. What do you think? Are you going to make the recommended changes?

2. Go through the chapter and make the recommended changes to your online presence. Did you feel resistant to any of these changes? Did you skip making any of these changes? Why?

3. Do you feel that it is too limiting of your personal life to avoid blogging about personal events? Is it too limiting to avoid posting personal photos or videos?

4. Would you ever "friend" or link to a client on a social networking site? Why or why not?

5. Would you do an online search if you felt that a client was being deceptive or leaving things out of his history? Would you do an online search if you felt that a client was being grandiose about her past? Why or why not? In which of the above examples of searching for online information about clients does the psychotherapist go too far? Which ones are okay? Why?

# Getting Started With Psychotherapy

# 7

# Confidentiality and Informed Consent

When beginning psychotherapy, your client needs to understand what psycho-therapy can and cannot do. The client needs to understand the nature of the psy-chotherapist–client relationship and how that is different from other relationships. The client also needs to learn about when information is confidential, and when it is not; laws on this vary somewhat from state to state. Given his understanding of these matters, he then agrees to pursue psychotherapy. As the psychotherapist, you need to assess whether he is capable of understanding all of this. This process is called *obtaining informed consent* from the client.

## CONFIDENTIALITY

*Confidentiality* is defined as "the duty to protect client privacy that comes from the fiduciary [legally and ethically trusting] nature of the professional relation-ship" (Younggren & Harris, 2008, p. 590). They go on to point out that "Effective psychotherapy...depends upon an atmosphere of confidence and trust in which the patient is willing to make a frank and complete disclosure of facts, emotions, memories, and fears" (Younggren & Harris, 2008, p. 590).

Professional ethics codes (e.g., American Psychological Association, 2010) require that we discuss confidentiality at the outset of psychotherapy (or any other professional services). It is essential to know what the legal limits to confidential-ity are in the state where you are practicing, and you must alert your clients to these limits as part of the informed consent process.

Research has found that many people erroneously believe that everything said in therapy is confidential (Barnett, Wise, Johnson-Greene, & Bucky, 2007); also, psychotherapists often do not educate their clients about limits to confidentiality (Braaten et al., 1993). Legal limits to confidentiality would include state-mandated reporting of child and elder abuse and (perhaps, depending on the state) intimate partner violence. Certain identifying information must be released when the psy-chotherapist makes a report of abuse. Another legal limitation to confidentiality is reporting intent of violence toward another person.

Here are some other limits to confidentiality. If the client is using insurance, the contract between the insurance company and the site typically allows some clinical information to be released to the insurance company upon the company's request. The client's diagnosis is always reported to the insurance company as a routine part of billing. If the client gets embroiled in serious legal or criminal problems, the therapy record can be subpoenaed or requested under a court order, and you cannot predict exactly what would happen to the confidentiality of the treatment notes (Younggren & Harris, 2008). The client should know that health care professionals within the facility may discuss her to coordinate care. She should also know that you are a student and you will be discussing the client's treatment with your supervisor. Although unlikely, you can legally release information that is needed to secure emergency medical care for the client, and you can release information to a coroner examining a client's death (Moline, Williams, & Austin, 1998).

All limits to confidentiality should be covered at the beginning of therapy. Many psychotherapists prefer to do this in writing because it would take a long time to go through this lengthy list with each client (for some examples of forms, see Zuckerman, 2008). The client is asked to sign the form to indicate his understanding and agreement. When using written forms, you should still provide opportunities to discuss confidentiality in the first and subsequent sessions. If you have concerns about the readability of the forms, you may wish to review most of the important points orally with the client as well.

It can also be wise to cover limits to confidentiality verbally, especially those limits that are most pertinent to a particular client. For example, you may be seeing a troubled young single parent, and you may be concerned that you might uncover some abuse or neglect during a session (see Chapter 21 for further information about child abuse and neglect). A suggested script for addressing confidentiality verbally is provided for you below. When you do this, carefully document what you discussed in the client's chart. You will need to adapt this script to your specific state laws and the situation at your training site:

"Some people think that everything we discuss in therapy is strictly confidential. Generally this is true, but I wanted to let you know that there are a few legal limitations to your confidentiality. I bring this up because I want you to be fully informed. For example, if I hear anything from you that leads me to believe that a child, dependent person, or elderly person is being harmed, I would need to report that to the state for investigation. In addition, if you are involved in any legal or criminal proceedings or if you intend to hurt someone, I might need to disclose information to the police or to a court. Do you have any questions? [Depending on the complexity of the question, you might need to advise the client to seek legal counsel.]

"I wanted to let you know that at this site, you have one electronic record that all the staff have access to. Anyone who is treating you will be able to see the progress notes that I write about our sessions. However, I want to assure you that I keep these notes brief and to the point. If at any point you would like to see them, please let me know. Do you have any questions? [Modify this paragraph to suit the specific situation at your site.]

"I will discuss your difficulties with your psychiatrist and the rest of the treatment team occasionally. This is so we can work together as a team to help you. Since I am a trainee, I will also discuss our work together with my supervisor, and we will sometimes review the audiotapes that I make of our sessions. Do you have any questions?"

Be mindful of maintaining the client's confidentiality when consulting with other professionals. Treatment planning should not occur in restaurants, elevators, or other public places. Discussions about mutual clients should not occur in agency hallways. Find a private place to talk. However, you can discuss general (not specific) clinical issues (carefully) in public locations that are not connected to the work setting, such as having lunch with a colleague at a restaurant:

- Right: "Tell me how you manage clients who aren't coming to their sessions regularly and always seem to have a good excuse."
- Wrong: "I have this 50-year-old client who lives with his mother and always cancels at the last minute because he says he has to take his mother to the hospital again for treatment. What should I do?"

In short, you can discuss principles of treatment in public, but avoid discussing the specifics of any particular client.

Special issues regarding confidentiality include working with children and adolescents, confidentiality after client death, and confidentiality when the client is at risk of spreading HIV. When these issues (or any others I have not covered) arise with your clients, be sure to discuss them with your supervisor and consider reviewing the relevant literature.

## THE HIPAA PRIVACY RULE AND THE NOTICE OF PRIVACY PRACTICES

The HIPAA Privacy Rule is a federal rule that regulates the release of confidential client data. Specifically, it controls when, under what circumstances, and to whom a health care practitioner intentionally releases *protected health information* (PHI, as defined in Chapter 6). The HIPAA Privacy Rule focuses on intentional releases of protected health information (whereas, as you remember from Chapter 6, the HIPAA Security Rule focuses on safeguarding against unintentional disclosures; American Psychological Association Practice Organization, 2007). To comply with the HIPAA Privacy Rule, health care organizations develop a Notice of Privacy Practices form, among other activities. The HIPAA Privacy Rule has implications for mental health progress notes (which will be discussed in Chapter 12). Your supervisor can guide you regarding when and how information about your clients is released from the site. (Note that there is a loophole in the HIPAA Privacy Rule indicating that sites without any electronic transmissions do not have to be HIPAA compliant—but the definition of electronic transmissions is so broad, it is unlikely you will ever work anywhere that is eligible to use the loophole.)

You may be responsible for having new clients sign a Notice of Privacy Practices form before or during the first session, and answering any questions that the clients may have about HIPAA and privacy. Also, ensure that appropriate releases are obtained from the client at any time that information about the client is sent out of your site.

## INFORMED CONSENT FOR PSYCHOTHERAPY

Informed consent requires a mentally competent person who has a good knowledge of what will occur in treatment, freely chooses to be treated, and is documented in the record as such. If any of these is lacking, its absence must be documented, explained, and responded to. (Zuckerman, 2003, p. 172)

The basic elements of informed consent are competence, information and voluntariness. (Simon, 1992, p. 123)

We engage our clients in the informed consent process because psychotherapy is a health care profession, and like other health care professions, we want our clients to understand the nature of their treatment and to make a well-informed choice to get treatment that is respectful of their autonomy. In summary, the *informed consent* process involves:

- A mentally competent client
- Education about the treatment process and treatment options, including risks and benefits
- Voluntary consent to treatment
- Documentation of the above

Our professional ethics codes require that we, as mental health professionals, obtain informed consent (American Counseling Association, 2005; American Psychiatric Association, 2010; American Psychological Association, 2010; National Association of Social Workers, 2008). Across mental health professions, differing standards are written into ethics codes about whether informed consent should be oral, written, or both. One code explicitly requires that informed consent be documented as well (American Psychological Association, 2002), although we can safely assume that other professions would also endorse documentation. Additionally, informed consent requirements encoded in law vary by state (Braaten, Otto, & Handelsman, 1993).

A client is mentally competent to provide fully informed consent if he can understand relevant information about treatment, weigh the risks and benefits against alternatives, and make a choice to participate (Eyler & Jeste, 2006). A client who is cognitively limited or has severe mental illness may not be able to provide fully informed consent. Read more about this issue if you are working in a setting where this is a concern. When you do have concerns about the client's understanding of treatment, be sure to note these carefully in your progress notes and discuss them with your supervisor.

Fully informed consent is often not obtained by psychotherapists (Somberg, Stone, & Claiborn, 1993). This can be a professional danger, since large sums have been awarded in certain legal cases where informed consent was not obtained (Beahrs & Gutheil, 2001), although in the cited cases, questionable and now-dated psychotherapy techniques were apparently used. Overall, Barnett, Wise, Johnson-Greene, and Bucky (2007) find that the informed consent process is not particularly legally risky for psychotherapists. Research suggests that professionals who engage in informed consent procedures may be seen by their clients as having more trustworthiness and expertise (Sullivan, Martin, & Handelsman, 1993). All these considerations make it necessary to obtain and document informed consent.

The process of obtaining informed consent depends on clients' characteristics and circumstances. For example, the informed consent process differs significantly with children and adolescents (Beeman & Scott, 1991); if you are working with minors, discuss this with your supervisor and consider reviewing the relevant literature. Sometimes informed consent cannot be obtained in the first session because of an emergency or other practical reasons (Fisher & Oransky, 2008). Informed consent when the client is treated with psychotropic medications involves additional considerations (Schachter & Kleinman, 2004). The growing use of technology, including the use of videoconferencing equipment for therapy or doing therapy over the Internet, may require special informed consent considerations (Recupero & Rainey, 2005a, 2005b). Finally, there are special considerations for the informed consent process when doing research (Davies, 2001; Wendler & Rackoff, 2001).

## THE CONTENT AND PROCESS OF INFORMED CONSENT

As a beginning psychotherapist, you will usually work at sites where informed consent policies are facility-wide. Your supervisor can orient you to these policies.

A large amount of information has been proposed for psychotherapists to cover as part of the informed consent process (Braaten et al., 1993; Fallon, 2006; Haslam & Harris, 2004; National Association of Social Workers, 2008; Pomerantz, 2005):

- The therapist: supervision status, training, education, licensure, specialty areas, and theoretical orientation
- The proposed psychotherapy: what it consists of, its risk and benefits, orientation to how the psychotherapist proceeds with psychotherapy, the probability of success, *length of each session, frequency of sessions*. Note that all the possible risks of treatment cannot be predicted, since you do

not know how the client's social and professional circles will react to the changes in the client (Beahrs & Gutheil, 2001).

- *The client: what the client needs to do for the therapy to be successful (this will vary depending on the type of psychotherapy offered)*
- Length of treatment recommended/expected *and external limitations that may be placed by agency or insurance*
- Alternative treatments: what they are, their risks and benefits
- *The risks of getting no treatment*
- *When confidentiality must be breached: suicide or homicide threat, child and elder abuse, and anything else specific to your state*
- *When confidentiality may be breached: what insurance companies want to know, court requests for information, consultation with other professionals about cases*
- *Fees: cost of sessions, cancellations and no-shows, methods of payment, costs for various services, payment expectations*
- *Office information and policies, including handling grievances and office hours*
- *Contact and emergency procedures: how and when to reach the psychotherapist, how to reach an on-call individual in off-hours, what to do in case of a mental health emergency*
- *Electronic communications: e-mail, social networking, online searches for client information*

Clearly, this is a very extensive list of topics to discuss. A detailed verbal examination of all these points with every client would be overly time consuming and an unnecessary burden. If you discussed all these issues verbally, you would spend the whole first session on informed consent alone, and rapport with your client could be damaged. So, the current best practice in obtaining informed consent balances these two propositions:

- Informed consent should cover basic, standardized information that all psychotherapy clients in the setting should know. In the content list above, I've italicized this type of information. A written informed consent form is useful in this regard.
- Informed consent should flexibly address what the process of psychotherapy is likely to be over time (Pomerantz, 2005), how long it is likely to last given the client's current goals, and what the client needs to do for the treatment to be successful. Verbal informed consent is most suited to this task.

## ADMINISTERING A STANDARDIZED INFORMED CONSENT FORM

Your site should have a written informed consent form already prepared. (For examples, see Zuckerman, 2008.) This form provides thorough and standardized information about clinic policies, confidentiality, forms of treatment, and so on as listed in the previous section. A signed copy of the form is kept in the client's permanent chart. You may be responsible for giving this form to the client and obtaining the client's signature after she has read the form. Be sure that the client is literate and is capable of understanding the form. Ask the client if she has any questions and document this interaction in the chart.

## VERBAL INFORMED CONSENT

Pomerantz (2005) wisely points out that informed consent is, in actuality, a process that takes place over time rather than an event that occurs at one point in time. In the first session, there is a lot about the client that you don't know yet, so you may not fully know what course of treatment you will recommend. The verbal informed consent process is better tailored to individualized needs (Beahrs & Gutheil, 2001).

As a part of psychotherapy, you will naturally engage in verbal informed consent, sometimes without fully realizing that is what you are doing. Whenever you do any of these, part of what you are doing is engaging in the informed consent process (Beahrs & Gutheil, 2001; Braaten, Otto, & Handelsman, 1993; Eyler & Jeste, 2006; Zuckerman, 2003):

- You ask the client why she came to treatment—a common question in the first session—which helps you determine whether the client made a voluntary choice to participate. Or you address any topic related to the client's voluntary choice to participate in psychotherapy.
  - "So, it sounds like you just got tired of feeling depressed off and on, and decided that you wanted to get psychotherapy to help you feel better."
  - "Of course, if you want to stop therapy, you can do so at any time; however, if you decide to stop, I'd appreciate it if we could discuss it first."
- You tell the client how you would conceptualize and treat her difficulties, and you check whether she understands what you're telling her, and whether she agrees that this treatment sounds like a good fit. Here are some of the things you might say:
  - "My recommendation is that you attend weekly individual psychotherapy sessions that last for 45 minutes. Weekly psychotherapy is best for people who are just starting out because it gives you a chance to work on your issues more intensively."
  - "In psychotherapy, we will address your current life difficulties and attempt to help you with them. I don't know yet how long treatment is likely to take, but I can give you some feedback on that when I get to know you better. I can't say for sure how much you are likely to improve, but I can tell you that most clients with similar problems improve significantly if they attend their appointments regularly and make their best effort."
  - "I'd like to give you some feedback about what we've been talking about today. You have a condition that we call generalized anxiety disorder.

There are many psychotherapy interventions that can be helpful in treating this, including examining your thought patterns and relaxation training. Also, a lot of people find that increasing their regular exercise helps decrease their overall level of anxiety. What do you think about these ideas?"

- You discuss alternatives (or adjunctive treatments) to psychotherapy—for example, psychotropic medications or self-help groups. You talk about risks to psychotherapy. Or you talk about the pros and cons of different types of treatment (e.g., you discuss her feelings and thoughts about psychotropic medications). Here are some of the things you might say:
  o "There is some risk that you may decide to make changes that important people in your life may not like, and they may have some reactions to that."
  o "Some people with similar problems to yours prefer to take medications than to come to therapy, and some people prefer to do both. Sometimes they go to self-help groups. What are your thoughts about these options?"

## ELECTRONIC COMMUNICATIONS
## AND INFORMED CONSENT

Electronic communications with the client are especially likely to be missing from your site's standardized informed consent form and will need to be discussed verbally. If no clinic policy exists about e-mailing clients or online searches of clients, discuss this with your supervisor and arrive at an agreement regarding what personal policies you will have (see Chapter 6). Here is a sample script for addressing these issues verbally with the client:

"You can e-mail me if you like, but please keep it to practical matters, such as rescheduling appointments. If something important comes up that you need to discuss before your next appointment, call me instead, okay? I also have a policy of not connecting to any clients—current or past—on social media to maximally protect your privacy. Do you have any questions? I don't usually look at clients' online information, but if there's something you want me to look at, let me know. In case of emergency, or concerns about your safety or the safety of others, I might look online for information about you, if I think it might help."

## DISCUSSING SUPERVISION WITH CLIENTS

As part of the informed consent process, you will need to alert your clients that you will be supervised. There may be a written form for this at your site, or you may need to discuss all the issues verbally. I recommend something like the following script, which is modified from Walker and Jacobs (2004):

> "Since I am a [insert type of psychotherapy student], I am regularly supervised on my clinical work. Part of getting supervision includes listening to audio recordings. I'd like you to sign a form indicating that you consent to being recorded, and then we will routinely record our sessions. Only my supervisor and I will listen to and have access to these recordings. I delete them on a weekly basis, so they are not part of any permanent record. [pause for client comment] Do you have any questions or concerns?"

You should record every session, whether you expect your supervisor to listen to it or not, so that the client becomes less self-conscious about being recorded (Walker & Jacobs, 2004). In some settings, verbal rather than written agreement is sufficient. In that case, be sure to document the client's agreement in your progress note.

Often clients will have a few brief factual questions. They may want to know who your supervisor is (tell them), why you need supervision ("It's part of my professional training and development"), and other questions. It is a good sign that the client is this curious and engaged, so answer the questions completely yet succinctly—and without defensiveness. Clients may also have some unique worries or fears about the supervisor or the supervision process. For example, some are fearful about their confidentiality, while others may fear being judged by the supervisor. These fears will often be useful clues about the client's interpersonal challenges. These fears may be allayed somewhat by describing the supervision process in slightly more detail: "Yes, we will talk about your issues to some extent, but the main focus of supervision is to help me learn how to understand you and help you better."

## DOCUMENTING INFORMED CONSENT

The professional literature provides limited guidance about the documentation of informed consent, so I would suggest the following: (1) Obtain the client's signature on the standardized written informed consent form, ask the client whether he has any questions about it, and document the content of any relevant discussions in the chart, and then be sure the form is carefully filed in the chart; (2) Discuss any particular informed consent issues that are especially pertinent to this client verbally, and document this discussion in the chart; (3) If you have any concerns about the client's mental competence, document them in the chart; (4) When you talk about what type and methods of psychotherapy you recommend, and how long it is likely to take, document this discussion; and (5) As any other issues that relate to informed consent come up during the course of psychotherapy, document that these topics were discussed. I don't think it is necessary to obsessively emphasize in the chart that a particular topic was part of the informed consent process—just one or two sentences about the content discussed should be sufficient. For example, this statement in a progress note could be seen as a part of the informed consent process: "Mr. B asked about whether I would recommend that he attend AA meetings in addition to coming to therapy. I gave him some information about AA, we talked about the pros and cons of that, and he decided that he would try one meeting and let me know how it went."

## USING CASE MATERIAL IN COURSE WORK, LECTURES, WRITINGS, AND OTHER MEDIA

Ethical considerations (American Psychological Association, 2010) require that when case material is used in communications, "(1) they [psychologists] take reasonable steps to disguise the person or organization, (2) the person or organization has consented in writing, or (3) there is legal authorization for doing so." The American Psychiatric Association (2010) has similar standards for teaching and writing: "Clinical and other materials used in teaching and writing must be adequately disguised in order to preserve the anonymity of the individuals involved" (p. 6). But the American Psychiatric Association has looser standards for presentations than the American Psychological Association: "[i]t is ethical to present a patient to a scientific gathering if the confidentiality of the presentation is understood and accepted by the audience...It is ethical to present a patient or former patient to a public gathering or the news media only if the patient is fully informed of enduring loss of confidentiality, is competent, and consents in writing without coercion" (p. 7).

Your first consideration in using case material is how far the material is distributed. Case material that is discussed within a clinical treatment team or with a supervisor should not have any masking of the client's identity. Often students may need to write up or present case material as part of their coursework. These training presentations are generally with one or two supervisors and a small group of peers. As long as you believe that there is almost no likelihood that your colleagues will know the client, a *mild disguise* will do. Mild disguise would include leaving off or changing the client's name, making the age vague (mid-20s vs. 24 years old), and omitting any extraneous identifying details that are not important to the case presentation. Note that this type of case material should never be posted anywhere on the Internet, should never be used in a larger professional format, and should never be published since it is not well disguised.

As you advance in your work, you may have the opportunity to make presentations to a larger professional group or prepare professional articles or books. Case material can be helpful in illustrating your points to the audience. Take great care to preserve the privacy of your clients in those instances. Any case material that is written in a book or journal article *must* be considered to be readily accessible by clients and the general public. Thus, in all these cases, more intensive disguising techniques must be used.

Gabbard (2000a, 2001b) suggests a number of effective strategies for *thick disguise*. In all cases, you should falsify (rather than obscure) certain external features that are not pertinent to the clinical issues at hand. For example, changing the client's profession, ethnicity, or other identifying features will make the client more difficult to identify than if you are just vague about these. He also emphasizes that brief vignettes can be as illustrative of the clinical issues as longer case descriptions are and will be more protective of the client's privacy. You can make further efforts to maintain confidentiality by using composite cases, by writing joint papers (so that it is unclear who the treating psychotherapist was), and by using case materials from other psychotherapists in your presentations or writings. As you may have noticed, all the case material in this book is presented in the form of vignettes. All the vignettes that are based on real events are heavily disguised and/or composite; however, many others are complete fiction, invented to illustrate a point. Almost all of the vignettes in this book are brief.

I advise against presenting or writing about an individual case without using thick disguise or adding/changing details with another similar case so that you present a composite case; in my personal experience, this is almost always doable. However, here are some guidelines in case you decide to proceed with one individual's detailed case nonetheless. When presenting longer case material in a professional presentation or publication, the psychotherapist should consider obtaining informed consent from the client (Gabbard, 2000a), especially when the case material is difficult to disguise. Optimally, this consent is both written and verbal and is thoroughly documented in the progress notes. In this case, the client may be given a copy of the presentation or article for review before it is presented to the profession. Be aware that this request might inspire numerous and varied emotional reactions, including feeling honored, insulted, exploited, and many more (for an insightful discussion of possible clinical ramifications, see Gabbard, 2000a). Review Sieck (2012) carefully to learn more about getting informed consent from an individual for professional case presentation. If you use an audio recording of a client in a professional presentation, because it is more identifiable, you *must* obtain verbal and written informed consent from the client (see Fischer, 2012, for helpful suggestions on doing this).

As a practical matter, you may decide not to use case material in a book or presentation until many years after you have seen the client. You may not have a way of contacting the client because of the passage of time and other barriers (e.g., you have different employment, you forgot names, and so on). In those cases, if you use the case material, you *must* use thick disguise. Although some think that the case may not be valid when using thick disguise, my view is that we present case material to each other because we believe that the case has universal interest and applicability. Generally, the interesting clinical point relates to the process of psychotherapy rather than the specific details of the client's life—which can be changed to make the case unidentifiable.

## CONFIDENTIALITY AND
## THE PSYCHOTHERAPIST'S PARTNER

Sometimes I find myself talking briefly about challenging clinical issues that have come up [with my partner], without giving any names or identifying material. I'm very careful not to give identifying info [to my partner]. I also often find myself being asked to talk about, or wanting to talk about, mental health issues that are of interest to the broader population (like PTSD in the returning soldiers, the recovered memory debate, etc.), and it's often useful to use anecdotes from cases with which I've been involved. Again, I keep it pretty non-specific, and I've even changed pertinent personal details (age, sex). I guess, in the end, the people with whom I would ever have these conversations to begin with are also going to be people who will be respectful of my boundaries, however I feel I need to draw them. (Anonymous psychotherapist, personal communication, January 21, 2007)

I tend to share experiences [with my partner] that are "out of the ordinary" or that somehow impact me personally (for example, things that hit close to home, a strong emotional reaction). I am cautious never to share any identifying information and usually focus on my reaction. (Anonymous psychotherapist, personal communication, February 3, 2007)

I think carefully about revealing the all-too-human side of the work to a spouse who has been or is currently in therapy. It's a feeling of wanting to protect without impingement the sacredness of the partner's connection w/ their own therapist without the burden of, "Hey, if my wife says that a client is frustrating, does my therapist ever find me frustrating? (boring? difficult?)." It's this need to uphold the illusion that their therapist would never have these mere-mortal reactions (and the protection that illusion affords the work). I'm especially careful to avoid at all costs being overtly critical of a client, with the possible exception of those few who have left while still owing me money. For some reason in these instances I'll have no trouble talking to my husband about the client's history of character pathology and their decision to not pay me (of course again, never jeopardizing confidentiality). I don't tend to talk to him about the nuts and bolts of the work. He's not interested on that level and I don't have the need to do it. Like the rest of us, I rely on consultation for that, have a few colleagues that I check in with whenever needed. (Anonymous psychotherapist, personal communication, January 24, 2007)

My partner is a psychotherapist as well, so we sometimes discuss clinical issues and consult with each other. When doing this in the past, we often included what we thought were benign bits of personal identifying information (profession, involvement in a community organization, etc.). On a couple of occasions, however, it seemed easy to "connect the dots" and make a pretty good guess as to who he was discussing or who I was discussing. When we

realized this, we were both quite troubled to realize our lapses—we had simply said too much that wasn't essential to the peer consultation we were seeking from one another. We have since been extremely careful about this. There
are definite advantages to being partnered with another therapist, but it is
also easy to slip into less-than-rigorous standards of privacy when discussing
our work. We have to be pretty vigilant about this, and it is not always easy.
(Anonymous psychotherapist, personal communication, February 23, 2007)

As a practical matter, it is not possible to fully withhold all information about
one's clients from one's significant other. At times, you may need to isolate yourself in a room at home and close the door to call a client in crisis; your partner is
undoubtedly savvy enough to understand what is going on. You may need to stay
late at work because of a client's crisis; you will probably need to tell your partner
why you were delayed. While you should do your best to keep client data secure
at home, you will sometimes need to work at home, and it is unrealistic to completely secure every scrap of client data at every single moment when at home. For
example, it is unreasonable to suggest that you lock away all data and close down
your computer completely when stepping away from your desk briefly to get a cup
of tea. For this reason, you will need to educate anyone living in your home carefully about confidentiality issues. It is wise to have your own desk and not share
it with anyone. On the other hand, when taking significant breaks or stopping
working for the day, be sure that all client paperwork and data is secure.

Woody (1999) advises against discussing case material with significant others, family members, or other persons who are not mental health practitioners.
However, given the emotional intimacy of one's relationship with one's partner,
it is difficult to withhold all information about one's day-to-day emotional reactions to doing psychotherapy, as the previously quoted psychotherapists describe.
When you talk to your partner about your work, focus on your emotional reaction rather than the clinical situation as much as possible. Never share any client's
identifying information with a partner, relative, or friend. Ask your partner (or
roommates or other relatives) to step out of the room when you need to talk to a
client on the phone from home. Educate them about why you need to be circum-
spect. Further research and inquiry is clearly needed in this area.

## Recommended Reading

Gabbard, G. O. (2000). Disguise or consent: Problems and recommendations concern-
ing the publication and presentation of clinical material. *International Journal of
Psychoanalysis, 81*, 1071–1086.
    *This article provides a detailed discussion of the issues involved in presenting clinical
    material to colleagues while maintaining client confidentiality.*
Woody, R. H. (1999). Domestic violations of confidentiality. *Professional Psychology:
Research and Practice, 30*, 607–610.
    *Woody describes a number of unfortunately common scenarios where confidentiality is
    violated by mental health practitioners.*

Zuckerman, E. (2008). *The paper office* (4th ed.). New York: Guilford Press.
   *This helpful and essential resource provides forms and helpful practice guidelines for
   many important clinical situations, including those discussed in this chapter.*

## ONLINE RESOURCES

http://www.hhs.gov/ocr/hipaa
   *The Department of Health and Human Services has extensive information available on
   its website about HIPAA.*
http://kspope.com/consent/index.php
   *Dr. Kenneth Pope is a prominent psychologist and author. This page from his exten-
   sive website provides immediate access to a variety of informed consent forms as well
   as standards for informed consent from many prominent mental health professional
   organizations.*

## DISCUSSION QUESTIONS

1. What are the procedures for informed consent, HIPAA, and informing
   clients about confidentiality at your site? Do you feel that these
   procedures are adequate? If not, how would you address this?
2. What information about clients is okay to talk about to your partner,
   a close friend, or a family member? What should you avoid? Does it
   matter if the partner, friend, or relative is a mental health professional or
   trainee as well?

# 8

# Making Clinical Observations

Licensed psychotherapists look at people with a trained eye. Careful observations help them zero in on the clients' problems more quickly and accurately. They learn to make a holistic evaluation of the client using how the client looks, talks, and behaves in addition to what the client says. This chapter will guide you in understanding the types of observations that trained psychotherapists make so that you can start doing this too.

## APPEARANCE, CLOTHING, AND HYGIENE

*Toni comes to the intake appointment today and meets with a mental health trainee. As Toni enters the office, the trainee notes that she is a white female of average height and weight with blonde hair. Toni's casual clothes are a bit rumpled, stained, and mismatched but apparently clean. Her hair is somewhat messy and maybe a little dirty. When asked about her ethnic background, she states that she is Polish and that both of her parents immigrated to the United States from Poland, although she was born here.*

*Alberto comes to the intake appointment today and meets with a mental health trainee. As Alberto enters the office, the trainee notes that he is neatly dressed in an immaculate dress shirt and tie. Alberto has a very dark complexion and is tall with an athletic build. His hair is carefully groomed and styled. When asked about his ethnic background, he indicates that he is a Latino of mixed black and mestizo heritage.*

*Ophelia comes to the intake appointment today at the college counseling center and meets with a mental health trainee. As Ophelia enters the office, the trainee notices that she is wearing a bright red dress with shiny black patent leather high-heeled pumps. Her dress is very low cut. She has an olive complexion and thick black, wavy hair. All the other students in the waiting room were wearing sneakers and jeans. When asked, she indicates that her mother is Mexican American and that her father is Greek American.*

You can see that even though we know nothing of these clients' backgrounds, we already can generate some hypotheses and/or questions we need to ask them from their personal appearances. Sometimes it can be helpful to describe the client's appearance in the chart. Note anything unusual about client's appearance—for example, sporting a dozen earrings on the left ear or having a prominent tattoo on the neck. Also note any obvious physical identifying characteristics, such as a missing limb or finger or a prominent burn scar on the face.

It is often unwise to guess at a client's ethnic background, as you can often be wrong. For example, the psychotherapist might have guessed that Alberto identified as African American from his appearance. Asking a client, "What is the ethnic background of your family?" can be very informative, even for apparently White clients, such as Toni.

The way clients dress can give us clues about their mental state and their ethnic and socioeconomic background. What hypotheses might you generate about the previously mentioned clients with just the information you have now?

## BEHAVIOR, MOTOR ACTIVITY, AND EYE CONTACT

*During the interview, Toni sits calmly in the chair and appears to be attending to the trainee's questions. Occasionally, she looks around the room into the corners of the ceiling, but the trainee knows that there is nothing interesting there. She has poor eye contact.*

*As Alberto walks toward his chair, he places his takeaway coffee cup precisely in the corner of the student's desk and carefully folds his jacket and drapes it over the back of the chair. During the interview, Alberto sits quietly. He tends to look down instead of at the trainee when talking.*

*As Ophelia enters the room, she is visibly bubbly. She sits down in the chair but often gestures dramatically to illustrate her points during the interview. She has good eye contact, and she appears full of energy.*

Observe any unusual behavior. What does it mean that Toni is looking around the room? What does it mean about Alberto that he is so precise with his coffee cup and his jacket? What do Ophelia's dramatic gestures mean? Given her ethnic background, you might wonder whether these gestures are normative or clinically significant.

Be alert to any unusual physical symptoms, such as tics, tremors, or an unusual *gait* (gait means how the client walks). Ask your client about any physical differences to see if the underlying condition has been diagnosed and treated.

Observe the client's eye contact. Poor eye contact can suggest many problems, from Asperger's syndrome to schizophrenia to depression to shyness. It is a sign that, for whatever reason, the client cannot adhere to all appropriate social nonverbal behavior, at least right now. However, note that appropriate eye contact does vary considerably from one cultural group to another (McCarthy, Lee, Itakura, &

Muir, 2006); for example, less acculturated Asian Americans may gaze downward when with authority figures (Ling, 1997).

Observe the *motor* (or physical) activity of the client. A low level of motor activity can be suggestive of depression. A high level of motor activity can be suggestive of mania or agitation. Agitation can be a sign of anxiety, anger, or even certain kinds of depression. Some clients with psychotic disorders can have a low level of activity, while others can be agitated.

Be aware of unusual motor activity with clients who are taking antipsychotic medications. First, clients may have a side effect to antipsychotic medication called *akathisia*, which causes them to jiggle their legs and have a profound feeling of restlessness. If you observe akathisia, discuss the issue promptly with the client and the psychiatrist because it can be so intolerable that many clients will stop taking their medications to get rid of it. Second, clients may also exhibit *tardive dyskinesia*, a mostly irreversible movement disorder that can occur in people who take antipsychotic medications for many years. Symptoms of tardive dyskinesia include involuntary wriggling of the fingers, tongue thrusting, and/or facial grimacing. When you observe any signs of tardive dyskinesia, check with the psychiatrist to confirm the diagnosis and to find out how it is being managed. Third, if the client seems particularly stiff around the head or neck area or complains of muscle pain, cramping, or stiffness, this could be a side effect of antipsychotic medications. Have the client talk to a psychiatrist immediately, because this can become medically serious.

## SPEECH AND THOUGHT PROCESSES

*During the interview, Toni attends to the trainee's questions. Occasionally, she seems to "zone out," and questions need to be repeated. Her answers tend to be brief and uninformative, necessitating many follow-up questions. She uses a simple basic vocabulary and nonstandard English words such as "ain't." Her voice is not very expressive, and the trainee cannot tell how she is feeling.*

*Alberto listens carefully to the trainee's questions and responds completely and precisely. When he describes his job in the financial sector, he uses financial jargon that the student does not fully understand. His speech flows smoothly, and he uses complex vocabulary. However, he tends to speak quietly and mumbles a bit.*

*Ophelia often interrupts before the trainee is done phrasing a question. She then talks at length and with great excitement about topics that are only peripherally related to the question. Her voice is expressive of her emotions, and she talks overly loudly and at a fast pace. When the trainee asks her to slow down, she tries, but then speeds up again.*

Observe how the client speaks. Is the client's speech fluent or impoverished? *Impoverished speech* is speech that is especially uninformative and brief.

Impoverished speech might be suggestive of mental retardation, other developmental disabilities, profound depression, or, in some cases, schizophrenia.

Observe whether the client understands what you are asking and telling her. Does she seem to understand your questions, or is she confused? Confusion can be a sign of thought disorder, dementia, or various other cognitive difficulties. Can the client remember the question that was asked? If not, she may be having some difficulties with attention and concentration. What does the client's vocabulary say about the client's likely *verbal intelligence*? (Note that it is impossible to estimate *general intelligence* from a verbal interview since *nonverbal* abilities—spatial, numerical, and others—are not observed.)

Observe whether the client can stay on the subject at hand. Repeated difficulties staying on the subject might be suggestive of mania, schizophrenia, or attention-deficit/hyperactivity disorder. Some clients have what is called *tangential* or *circumstantial* speech: they talk about multiple topics sequentially, but idiosyncratically, so that others find it difficult or impossible to follow their thought processes.

The qualities of the client's voice can be informative as well. Is the voice fast or slow? Is it quiet or loud? Is it expressive or monotone? Does the client speak clearly or mumble? What is the emotional tone of the voice? Different vocal qualities are suggestive of different problems. What do the different vocal qualities of the previously mentioned clients suggest about their problems?

Whenever you have any concerns about the client's ability to think clearly, it can help to determine whether the client is *oriented* to person, place, and date—that is, whether the client can answer these three questions:

- "What is your name?"
- "Where are we right now?"
- "What is today's date?"

If the client can answer all these questions accurately, we say that the client is *oriented in all spheres* or *oriented times three* (usually denoted "OX3" in charts). Be flexible if the client is a day or two wrong about the date. However, if the client is not oriented (e.g., he says that he is in a different location than where he is or says that the date is 2001), there is a strong likelihood of medical illness affecting cognition. Get the client medically evaluated immediately.

## AFFECT AND MOOD

*The trainee watches Toni's face carefully but cannot detect any significant mood changes. Even when Toni talks about her mother's recent death and states how sad she was about the loss, her face is unemotional.*

*Alberto's face looks drawn and sad. When talking about his daughter's recent cancer scare, his eyes become red and appear tearful, although he does not actually cry. When asked how he has been feeling, he readily states that he has been sad.*

*Ophelia is excited and even somewhat agitated. Her mood is very positive, except she appears a bit irritable when talking about her roommate, who insisted that she come to the college counseling center. She talks about her many plans for successful Web businesses that she will run out of her home and that will make a fortune for her.*

It is important to ask clients about their mood and compare that to your observations. *Mood* refers to what the client says about how she is feeling, whereas *affect* refers to your observations of the client's emotions from her facial expressions, voice, eye contact, and other aspects of her appearance (Morrison, 1995). *Flat affect*, like Toni's, means that few facial indications of emotion are present.

Comparison of mood and affect can be very informative. Toni's verbally expressed sadness coupled with her flat affect (sometimes also called *blunted affect*) suggests that she has a psychotic disorder (although flat affect can also be found in depression, Parkinson's disease, and other neurological conditions; Morrison, 1995). Alberto, on the other hand, expresses sadness in both his mood and his affect. Ophelia claims that her mood is fine, but the psychotherapist observes excessively positive mood and grandiosity. *Grandiosity* means that she has an inflated view of herself, her abilities, and her importance. This suggests that she has no insight into the likelihood that she may be getting manic.

An overly positive affect with excitement and happiness—such as Toni's—is described as *euphoric* affect, whereas a sadness—like Alberto's—can be called *dysphoric* or *dysthymic* affect. Normal affect—not notably flat, depressed, anxious, or otherwise distressed or unusual—is often described as *euthymic*.

*Labile affect* describes a client whose mood varies widely and quickly during a session from one extreme to another. For example, she could be angry one moment, then making a joke and laughing the next. When you see it, make a note of emotional lability, since it is of diagnostic importance. Most often, it is seen in clients with borderline personality disorder but also could be indicative of mania or histrionic personality disorder.

*Inappropriate affect* is also of concern. Odd emotional expressions (e.g., giggling at something profoundly sad) can be seen sometimes in individuals with schizophrenia (and sometimes neurological disorders; Morrison, 1995).

Sometimes people with post-traumatic stress disorder may talk in a strangely calm and collected manner about extremely traumatic material; unless this material has been thoroughly processed with a psychotherapist, this is probably indicative of emotional numbing. *Emotional numbing* is a psychological defense mechanism in which the client is able to talk seemingly normally, yet emotionlessly, about experiences that would normally be considered to be extremely distressing.

In more extreme cases, a client may dissociate in a session. *Dissociation* is a psychological defense mechanism in which the client's thought processes are detached from emotions or bodily sensations when faced with highly distressing material. Dissociation can sometimes involve memory repression. The dissociating client may look vague, break eye contact, or become nonverbal. Clients will often describe this as "shutting down." If a client responds this way, gently call the client's name, ask the client how she is feeling, and move on with the interview, changing the subject and avoiding the topic that triggered this response. Do not try to further discuss the topic that triggered the dissociation—it is much too distressing for the client to cope with right now. Describe this behavior and the topic that triggered it carefully in the chart. Discuss this thoroughly with your supervisor for guidance.

Be aware of how connected you feel toward the client during the interview and how the client feels about your efforts to be of assistance. If you feel unconnected to the client, this generally indicates that the client has some kind of temporary (e.g., certain individuals with acute depression) or permanent (e.g., schizophrenia or Asperger's syndrome) difficulty with social interactions. It could also be a sign that the client is ambivalent or fearful about psychotherapy.

Be aware that some affects are expressed only fleetingly. These brief facial expressions of emotion are called *microexpressions* and last for only a split second (Ekman, 2009; Ekman & O'Sullivan, 1991). These microexpressions have typically been studied in the context of detecting deception. A recent study has found that the microexpressions may occur in only the upper or lower half of the face, rather than the entire face (Porter & ten Brinke, 2008). Clients can exhibit microexpressions during psychotherapy. If you start watching carefully for them, you will probably start to notice them. Asking your client about the feeling that you observed momentarily ("For a moment there, you looked a bit disgusted when talking about your brother") can yield further insights about the complexity of his emotions.

One final caution is to be aware of cultural differences between yourself and the client. It has been commonly believed that the facial expression of six basic emotions (happiness, disgust, surprise, anger, sadness, fear) were the same across all cultures. However, a recent research study suggests that there may be heretofore unexamined cultural differences in facial emotional expression between Eastern and Western cultures (Jack, Garrod, Caldara, & Schyns, 2012).

## JUDGMENT AND INSIGHT

*When asked why she came in for treatment today, Toni states that her father told her that she needed to come. She lives with him. She says that they have been arguing about the neighbors. Toni states that she feels that her father should confront the neighbors since they have been spying on her with tiny video cameras.*

*Alberto states that he had decided to come for treatment since he knows that he is getting more depressed. He says that he decided that he needed to get help before his work performance suffered.*

*Ophelia states that her roommate insisted that she come to the counseling center. She states that she feels so good that she knows she doesn't really need to be there.*

Toni and Ophelia have very little *insight* into the fact that they are mentally ill. Toni is not exhibiting good *judgment* since she wants to feud with the neighbors over her belief that they are spying on her—which is a symptom of her mental illness. Ophelia's judgment appears impaired as well. Alberto, on the other hand, has good insight and is using good judgment to seek help before his functioning level at work deteriorates.

## DOCUMENTING YOUR OBSERVATIONS

You need not write down every single behavior that you observe. Some of these behaviors will only suggest to you that you should ask further questions. For instance, is Alberto's exactness in setting down his coffee cup and coat indicative of obsessive-compulsive symptoms? Ask him. Others are clinically significant (e.g., flat affect or euphoria). Share your observations with your supervisor and together figure out which ones are of clinical significance and how to document these in the progress notes.

## OBSERVATIONS SUGGESTIVE OF LYING

Clients may lie about certain aspects of their current life or history. This is not uncommon, as research has indicated that lying is a frequent interpersonal behavior. Here are some indicators of possible lying (adapted from DePaulo et al., 2003):

- Liars provide fewer details in a more uncertain manner.
- Liars have more silent pauses and longer response latency to questions.
- Liars seem more tense and inhibited.
- Truth tellers are more likely to spontaneously correct themselves and admit that they can't remember everything.

Note that contrary to popular thought, fidgeting and gaze aversion are not predictive of lying (Porter & ten Brinke, 2010). However, DePaulo et al. (2003) conclude, "Behavioral cues that are discernible by human perceivers are associated with deceit only probabilistically. To establish definitively that someone is lying, further evidence is needed" (p. 108).

Avoid any direct accusations of lying in the chart. However, there are certain established phrases that indicate possible lying without outright stating it: "Since Mr. R's report of his past hospitalizations differed significantly from one session to the next, I consider him to be an unreliable informant." An *unreliable informant* is a client who cannot be relied on to provide an accurate history. You can also imply that the client may be lying by contrasting the client's statement with other information:

"Ms. A stated that she had not used substances over the weekend; however, her urine toxicology screen was positive for cocaine."

Discuss with your supervisor whether you should just keep in mind that the client may be untruthful or whether you should attempt to verify the suspect information. You might consider interviewing family members to gather more reliable historical information. If you are thinking of searching online for information about the client, read the relevant portions of Chapter 6 first.

## OBSERVATIONS SUGGESTIVE OF MALINGERING

Most of your clients will have genuine problems. However, certain clients are motivated to present themselves as more ill than they actually are. *Malingerers* may fake mental illness, cognitive impairment, amnesia, pain, and/or physical disability (Chesterman, Terbeck & Vaughan, 2008). Although it is notoriously difficult to study malingerers, my clinical experience is that while malingers do not have all the issues that they present, they can have serious problems—often emotional but maybe also coping deficits—that lead them to believe that malingering is a reasonable way to address their life problems. Often, the client's motivation to malinger is connected to financial benefits, such as collecting a settlement or disability payments due to illness. Malingering is more common in certain settings such as prisons or disability evaluations.

Sometimes the reason for malingering is emotional, and it may not be wholly conscious. The client may feel a desperate need to be taken care of. One way for the client to get this need met is to be mentally ill and have mental health practitioners concerned about her well-being. The client's supposed illness may entitle the client to extra caring and caretaking from family and friends.

There is a large and complex literature about assessing malingering. It is far beyond the scope of this volume to fully address this topic. Rogers (1997) provides helpful guidance in discovering whether a client might be malingering. Here are just a few indicators of possible malingering:

- The client describes obvious symptoms (e.g., crying, sadness, or hallucinations) but does not describe, demonstrate, or endorse commonly co-occurring subtle symptoms (e.g., appetite changes or thought disorder).
- Contradictions in the account of the illness become clear over time (but remember that memory does deteriorate normally).
- The client answers, "I don't know" when normally a client would know (e.g., when asked about a hallucination: "Was that the voice of a male or female?").
- The client exhibits overly bizarre self-presentation, perhaps combining obvious symptoms of several different disorders.
- The client accuses the interviewer of thinking that he is faking.
- Symptoms that don't typically arise suddenly have a sudden onset ("I felt great on Wednesday, but on Thursday I couldn't concentrate on anything and felt incredibly anxious").

- The client describes pain or physical dysfunction that is not possible neurologically (consult a physician to be sure).
- The client exhibits disparities between reported and observed symptoms, such as an inability to sustain the symptom presentation over time when on an inpatient unit.

You must be very cautious about malingering because, unless you are a specially trained forensic psychologist or neuropsychologist, you probably do not have either sufficient evidence or the necessary clinical training to be sure.

Document your observations carefully and be factual in a way that informs a knowledgeable reader about your concerns without making explicit accusations: "Ms. T reported that she had suddenly recovered from her depression last Thursday. No signs of mania were present." Carefully document factual information that would be of assistance later: "Client stated that he was hearing voices, but when asked if they were male or female, he stated he did not know."

When you think a client may be malingering, discuss your concerns about the client's honesty with the treatment team or a trusted colleague. Refer the client for a psychological assessment with a psychologist who is knowledgeable about detecting deception (Rogers, Sewell, Martin, & Vitacco, 2003). Consult your supervisor about how to proceed in psychotherapy given your concerns.

### Recommended Reading

DePaulo, B. M., Lindsay, J. J., Malone, B. E., Muhlenbruck, L., Charlton, K., & Cooper, H. (2003). Cues to deception. *Psychological Bulletin, 129,* 74–118.
    *DePaulo and colleagues provide an interesting review of psychological research on interpersonal detection of lying.*
Rogers, R. (Ed.). (1997). *Clinical assessment of malingering and deception* (2nd ed.). New York: Guilford Press.
    *Although this volume is no longer fully current, it provides a helpful guide to the assessment of malingering.*

## DISCUSSION QUESTIONS

1. What are your diagnostic hypotheses about each of the three clients discussed in this chapter? Why?
2. List the symptoms that you have observed for each of the three clients. Have your observations confirmed enough symptoms to make a diagnosis in any of these cases?
3. How would you use your diagnostic hypotheses and what you know about the clients' symptoms so far to focus the rest of the intake interview?

# 9

# Making a Diagnosis

Knowing your client's diagnosis allows you to access the large body of clinical and research knowledge. This will help you tailor the treatment to the client's needs more effectively. Most settings require that a diagnosis be made. I have not provided any flowcharts or hierarchies; my feeling is that these would be more confusing than helpful. Your best resource in making a diagnosis quickly is your detailed knowledge of the behaviors and symptoms of mental illnesses. To make a diagnosis, there are several steps:

- Understand the format for the diagnostic interview that your site requires or choose a format if you have that latitude.
- Gather information.
- Consider alternative causes of the apparent psychological symptoms, especially medical illness or substance abuse.
- Diagnose if you have enough information to be confident.

This chapter will only begin to educate you about the complex process of making a diagnosis. I hope that you will look up the recommended readings as well, especially Morrison (2007). Your supervisor can also help guide you to consider appropriate diagnoses for your clients.

## DIAGNOSTIC SYSTEMS: DSM AND ICD

Two different systems are commonly used to diagnose mental disorders. Each one has gone through numerous revisions and has both a name and an edition number attached to it—signifying the current edition of the classification system. The International Classification of Diseases (ICD) is a compendium of descriptions of all disorders, physical and mental, compiled by the World Health Organization (current edition at the time of writing is ICD-10); it is in the public domain and is freely and readily available online. The Diagnostic and Statistical Manual is a listing of only mental and behavioral disorders that is compiled by the American Psychiatric Association, and it is proprietary—not in the public domain. At the time of this writing the DSM-V is being finalized, but it is highly controversial.

Be aware that there are a multitude of criticisms of diagnosing mental disorders in general, and of the DSM in particular. These include how to conceptualize what a mental disorder even is (Stein et al., 2010), whether a system involving more dimensional concepts would be better (Krueger & Bezdjian, 2009), whether normal human variations—such as shyness or mild social anxiety—are over-pathologized (Wakefield, Horwitz, & Schmitz, 2005), cultural insensitivity of the diagnostic systems (Wakefield, 2007), and the disproportionate influence of pharmaceutical companies (Cosgrove, Krimsky, Vijayaraghavan & Schneider, 2006). Although these critiques have merit, at present these are the diagnostic systems that we have, and they are the ones that we need to use because of institutional requirements.

## INTERVIEW FORMATS: SITE-SPECIFIC FORMATS AND STRUCTURED INTERVIEWS

The format for your initial diagnostic interview with a new client may vary by site. When starting in a new practice setting, discuss any site requirements for the initial session with your supervisor. In many settings, the psychotherapist is given a paper form (or a template in the electronic medical record) that must be filled out; the form provides an outline for the initial session. In other settings, no formal structure is provided. Beginning psychotherapists often benefit from using a list of questions or topics to address during the first session. In the appendix of Chapter 11, I provide an outline of some topics to address in the initial session. If you use this outline, ask your supervisor if there are additional subjects that you should explore with your particular client population.

When interviewing in a nonstructured manner, be aware that errors will creep in (this paragraph informed by Miller, 2010). What one psychotherapist thinks is a full-fledged panic attack might look like generalized anxiety symptoms to someone else. To minimize this type of error, you need to remember to ask about enough of the possible symptoms or, more likely, you will need to have the exact diagnostic criteria handy to use as a checklist to be sure you don't miss anything. Another type of error is that different psychotherapists ask different questions and miss different things. A final common error is stopping with your diagnostic interview when one diagnosis is made; many individuals fulfill criteria for more than one mental disorder.

The most accurate way to make a diagnosis is to administer a well-validated structured diagnostic interview, such as the current version of the Structured Clinical Interview for the DSM (SCID; First, Spitzer, Gibbon, & Williams, 2002), which requires specialized training and about 2 hours to complete. After completing the SCID, the psychotherapist is as confident as possible that an accurate and complete psychiatric diagnosis has been made.

## MENTAL STATUS EXAM

Sometimes a *Mental Status Exam* (MSE) is required. The use of the term *Mental Status Exam* is confusing, because sometimes people are referring to a comprehensive description of behavior, emotional and cognitive functioning (Daniel & Gurczynski, 2010), and at other times they are referring to a brief structured examination to assess basic cognitive functioning. Many of the observations that are part of doing an MSE (in the broader sense) are covered in Chapter 8.

For decades, most psychotherapists have used the Mini Mental State Exam when doing the brief structured examination of cognitive functioning (see http://www.minimental.com); however, copyrights on this instrument have been strictly enforced in recent years (Newman & Feldman, 2011). A public domain alternative is the Saint Louis University Mental Status (SLUMS) cognitive assessment tool; copies of this can be easily found online. In addition, some psychotherapists use a nonstandardized approach to the MSE (for instructions, see Morrison, 2007). If your site requires the MSE, your supervisor can train you to do it.

## ESSENTIAL KNOWLEDGE: COMMON DIAGNOSES AND HIGH-RISK SYMPTOMS

Certain mental illnesses are very common in the general population. One way to measure this is to determine the *lifetime prevalence*, which means the proportion of the population that has met the criteria for the illness anytime during the individual's lifetime. The following mental illnesses have at least a 4 percent lifetime prevalence in U.S. adults; the ones in italics have at least an 8 percent lifetime prevalence (R. C. Kessler, Berglund, Demler, Jim, & Walters, 2005; O'Leary & Norcross, 1998):

- *Adjustment disorder*
- Adult attention-deficit/hyperactivity disorder (ADHD)
- Agoraphobia without panic (panic disorder has a 2 to 3 percent lifetime prevalence)
- *Alcohol abuse/dependence*
- Bipolar II (also known as cyclothymic disorder)
- *Drug abuse/dependence*
- Dysthymia
- Generalized anxiety disorder
- *Major depression*
- Post-traumatic stress disorder (PTSD)

You should be familiar with the symptoms of each of these diagnoses. Learn as much as you can about how clients with specific mental illnesses look: how they talk, characteristic nonverbal behavior, what their eye contact is like, and so on (how psychotherapists systematically observe behavior was addressed in Chapter 8).

These studies have found a high prevalence of simple/specific phobias, but despite the high lifetime prevalence, many individuals with simple phobias are not bothered or impaired on a daily basis. For example, persons with phobias of heights or spiders simply avoid these things and live a normal and relatively untroubled life. A high prevalence of social phobia has been found as well; however, I agree with experts who suggest that the criteria for social phobia are overly inclusive, and the diagnosis overpathologizes people who are temperamentally shy, anxious, introverted, or from different cultures (Wakefield, 2007; Wakefield, Horwitz, & Schmitz, 2005).

Different client populations have higher rates of specific mental illnesses. For example, if you work in a prison, you may see more individuals with PTSD or antisocial personality disorder. If you work at a college counseling center, prevalences of eating disorders may be high. Ask your supervisor about the population you are working with and be familiar with diagnoses that are common within that group.

All mental health practitioners should be familiar with symptoms of psychosis and mania. These symptoms are very disabling and indicative of a need for psychotropic medication. In addition, clients with these symptoms are at higher risk for suicide (see Chapters 18 and 19 for more information).

## CHALLENGES AND CLUES IN MAKING A DIAGNOSIS

Making a full and accurate diagnosis is a time-consuming process. In an ideal world, the psychotherapist might do a structured interview and an extensive diagnostic interview, and then refer the client to psychological testing as needed to clarify any remaining questions, all this culminating in *making a disposition*, which means to arrange for appropriate treatment for the client. As you might imagine, this ideal assessment could take up to 3 hours, possibly considerably more.

In real life, agencies are often pressed for money, often resulting in psychotherapists being pressed for time. Thus, clients are usually given an intake appointment, often lasting only 45 to 50 minutes, ensuring that you will need to take shortcuts and you will miss important information. We have no choice but to accept this reality. The client's presenting problem, your clinical observations of the client, and any sleep problems the client is having will give you helpful clues about possible diagnoses. Let these clues guide your interview. Given the clues you have gathered, ask about the most likely diagnoses first.

Be alert to the potential for multiple mental health diagnoses in all your clients. *Diagnostic comorbidities* (having more than one diagnosis) are common but are often missed. Of the 26 percent of the population who have had a mental illness in the past 12 months, about half have had two or more diagnoses (R. C. Kessler, Chiu, Demler, & Walters, 2005). Since clients with comorbidity are more likely to have greater distress, they may be more likely to come for treatment.

## BE PREPARED WITH SCREENING QUESTIONS

Screening questions are a shortcut to help us make a diagnosis efficiently. We may use one or several screening questions to help us determine whether we should ask further questions about a certain diagnosis or move on to other subjects. Realize that there is potential error with all screening questions. We might have a *false positive*; in other words, our client may answer the screening question in a way that leads us to believe that the client has the diagnosis, but on further questioning, it will turn out that the client does not. Or we might have a *false negative*; in other words, we erroneously skip asking more about a particular problem because the answer to the screening question suggests that the client does not have the problem.

Why are screening questions important? Many emotional problems and psychiatric diagnoses may not be immediately obvious even to a trained professional. Here are some examples from the literature:

- *Half the cases of PTSD were missed by psychotherapists* in a study comparing diagnoses made by unstructured interview versus structured interview (Zimmerman & Mattia, 1999). *Three fourths of PTSD cases were missed* in a sample of substance-abusing veterans (Kimerling, Trafton, & Nguyen, 2006). Multiple studies have found that most clients with a history of trauma will *not* volunteer this information to a psychotherapist without being asked (Agar, Read, & Bush, 2002). These clients with undetected PTSD are not getting the correct treatment.
- *One third to one half of clients presenting with a major depressive episode will have undetected bipolar I or II disorder*, as indicated in multiple studies cited by Bowden (2005). Since bipolar individuals are more likely to seek treatment when depressed, their histories of mania can be easily missed. This is a terrifying figure because many of these clients will get inappropriate and even harmful treatment. Antidepressants alone will often send bipolar clients into mania, worsening their mental illness (Angst & Cassano, 2005). Unfortunately, mania usually feels good, so the clients may not understand that they are *not* doing better.
- *About 10 percent of cases of major depression are seasonal*, otherwise known as seasonal affective disorder (SAD, Levitt & Boyle, 2002). *Seasonal affective disorder* is a specific type of major depression that occurs in conjunction with a specific season, usually winter. It is crucial to distinguish seasonal from nonseasonal depression because the recommended *first-line treatments* are different. A treatment that you should try first, that has the highest likelihood of being effective, is called a *first-line treatment*. Bright-light treatment is the first-line treatment for SAD (Lam & Levitan, 2000) and can be supplemented by psychotherapy and medications. For nonseasonal depression, bright-light treatment is not typically used as a first-line treatment. Thus, whenever you have a client presenting with depression in the winter, screen for SAD.
- *Adults with ADHD present twice as often for treatment for emotional problems than for the ADHD itself*, so adult ADHD is easily missed by psychotherapists. This is probably because attention-deficit disorder is so often comorbid with other psychiatric disorders (R. C. Kessler,

Adler, Ames, et al., 2005; R. C. Kessler, Adler, Barkley, et al., 2005). In addition, the diagnostic criteria were developed for children and offer little guidance to the psychotherapist in assessing ADHD in adults (R. C. Kessler, Adler, Barkley, et al., 2005).

Screening questions for the disorders discussed in this chapter are available on my website at www.drwiller.com/tbpc. You can download pdfs to any device so that you have them when needed. I recommend that you review all the screening questions carefully. You may wish to construct your own list of screening questions to keep handy, drawing on the ones that are most relevant to your client population or the ones that are most difficult to remember.

## ASK ABOUT SLEEP

Sleep patterns vary depending on the client's emotional problems. Thus, asking about sleep can provide a quick clue about the client's diagnosis. When asking about sleep, you can simply say, "How has your sleep been lately?" Let the client tell you about any current sleep problems. Most of this information will be useful. If the client is having sleep problems but is having difficulty articulating what they are, you might ask some of the following questions:

- Are you able to get to sleep at night when you want to? Are you able to get to sleep within 10 to 20 minutes? [If not:] Is this because you are lying awake worrying about your problems?
- How do you feel when you wake up in the morning? Is your sleep restful?
- Can you sleep through the night? How often do you wake up? How long does it take you to get back to sleep once you're awake?
- Do you wake up earlier than you had planned?
- How many hours of sleep are you getting? [If less than 8:] Is that enough for you? (If sleep is limited but client looks energetic, ask about manic symptoms right away.) [If more than 8:] Have you always needed that much sleep? How do you feel when you sleep that much?
- Do you have any nightmares or bad dreams? How often? About how many times do you have nightmares in a week (or month)? Do they ever wake you up? What are they about?
- Does your partner say that you snore?
- Does your partner say that you kick or move around a lot at night?

One nighttime awakening is normal and not of any concern as long as the client can go back to sleep relatively easily. It is also normal in individuals who are middle-aged and older to have two or more nighttime awakenings related to medical issues (e.g., enlarged prostate necessitating urination at night, hot flashes causing nighttime awakening during perimenopause).

Each sleep problem is commonly associated with a different diagnosis. The clues that you get from the client's sleep pattern can help you zero in on the client's problems and diagnosis more quickly.

- Consider PTSD if
  - Nightmares or disturbing dreams
  - Fearful of going to sleep
- Consider depressive or anxiety disorders if
  - Difficulty getting to sleep because of rumination
  - Poor quality of sleep and/or doesn't sleep soundly
  - Wakes up at night, can't get back to sleep promptly
- Consider melancholic depression if early morning awakening
- Consider depression if sleeping 9 hours or more per night.
- Consider mania or hypomania if
  - Not feeling a need for more than 2 to 3 hours of sleep, still full of energy
  - In very rare cases, this little sleep can be normal for an individual who has no mania.
- Consider drug or alcohol intoxication or withdrawal if
  - Inability to sleep
  - Excessive drowsiness
- Consider sleep apnea (a sleep disorder) if
  - Sleep not restful
  - Partner says client snores loudly
  - Partner might notice breathing pauses
- Consider periodic limb movement of sleep (a sleep disorder) if
  - Sleep not restful
  - Partner says client is a very active sleeper
  - Partner may complain of frequent kicking of client during sleep
- Consider narcolepsy (a sleep disorder) if
  - Falls asleep suddenly in the middle of daily activities
  - Has severe difficulties with drowsiness
- Consider referral for sleep disorders and evaluation by physician for medical problems if
  - Emotional problems are mild, no reported sleep problems, good sleep habits, yet client reports daytime tiredness.

## ASK ABOUT FAMILY HISTORY OF MENTAL ILLNESS

Mental illness can run in families. However, usually it is the category of diagnoses (e.g., anxiety or psychotic disorders) that runs in the family, and the relative might have a different specific diagnosis than the client. The mental illnesses of *first-degree relatives*, who share half the client's genes (parents, siblings, and children), are most predictive, followed by *second-degree relatives*, who share one quarter of the client's genes (grandparents, aunts, uncles, nephews, nieces, and half-siblings). If the client is unsure what the mental illness of the family member was, you can ask some of these questions: "What unusual behavior did you or your family notice?" or "Do you know what kind of medication your relative is taking?" Of course, you can't diagnose this relative, whom you've never seen, but this information may provide some useful clues about genetic influences in the client's family. Be aware, however, that many people with mental illness don't have any relatives with a similar disorder.

Mental illnesses vary by how much the predisposition is inherited. The following numbers provide a rough comparison of the relative heritability of different mental illnesses. These numbers are odds ratios (the proportion of first-degree relatives of the person with mental illness who have the mental illness themselves vs. the proportion of first-degree relatives of a control—without mental illness—who have the mental illness themselves). All the odds ratios that follow are aggregates from literature reviews. A higher odds ratio indicates that the mental illness is more highly inherited:

- 3: Major depression (P. F. Sullivan, Neale, & Kendler, 2000)
- 4–6: Panic disorder, obsessive-compulsive disorder, generalized anxiety disorder, and simple phobia (Hettema, Neale, & Kendler, 2001)
- 9: Bipolar disorder (Merikangas & Yu, 2002)
- 10: Schizophrenia (P. F. Sullivan, 2005)

Since these numbers are from different studies, with undoubtedly different methodologies, please realize that any direct comparisons of heritability will necessarily be inexact. However, this gives you an idea of the relative influences of genetics on these mental illnesses.

## GATHER INFORMATION FROM ALL SOURCES, WHEN POSSIBLE

When you see a client to make a diagnosis, you are seeing the client in *cross section*; that is, you are seeing the client at just one point in time. However, to make many diagnoses, information and observations about the client's functioning over time, or *longitudinally*, is especially helpful.

Clients may or may not be *reliable informants*—that is, useful and reliable sources of honest and accurate information about themselves. They may have cognitive difficulties that impair their abilities to report their histories. They may be too mentally ill to be able to provide a coherent narrative about the past. They may be confused about what happened. They may have limited insight into their illnesses. Clients may want to minimize their mental health histories and current symptoms to convince you or themselves that they are not mentally ill. Alternatively, clients may exaggerate their mental health histories and current symptoms because they are motivated to appear mentally ill. For all these reasons, other sources of information can be invaluable in making a more accurate diagnosis. These sources include the following:

- Old chart material at your site
- Old charts from other sites
- A description of the client's current and past functioning from partner, family, roommate, or close friend
- If you want to gather information from the Internet, be sure you review the relevant portions of Chapter 6 first.

You may not have time to gather sufficient historical information from these collateral sources during the first session; you may not even have time to gather all the pertinent social history from the client during the first session. Therefore, sometimes the client will have to remain undiagnosed for now.

## ASSESS FREQUENCY, DURATION, AND SEVERITY OF SYMPTOMS

When the client talks to you about symptoms, you should then assess and document the extent of these symptoms (Morrison, 1995). The follow-up questions that you will ask will depend on the nature of the symptoms. A symptom can be *discrete*, which means that the symptom has distinct occurrences, such as nightmares, hallucinations, or panic attacks. Or a symptom can be *continuous*, which means that it seems to be occurring much of the time, such as depression or anxiety.

For discrete symptoms, ask about *frequency*: "Out of 7 nights in a week, on how many of these do you have nightmares?" "During a day, how often do you typically hear the voices?" Phrase the questions in such a way that the client can tell what kind of answer would be helpful (e.g., knowing that nightmares occur three or four nights per week is more helpful than "a lot"). For example, if your client has obsessive-compulsive disorder, you might want to know how often the client checks the stove daily or how much time is spent checking every day. If the client has panic attacks, you would want to know when the last one was and about how frequently the client has been having them. If the client has difficulty providing this information, ask more specific questions:

- "Did you have a nightmare last night?"
- "Have you heard the voices so far today? How many times?"

Panic attacks are also discrete events but are often less frequent and thus would require different questions:

- "How often do you typically have panic attacks?"
- "How many panic attacks do you have in a typical month?"
- "When was the last time you had a panic attack?"

Note that you would not want to ask these questions about panic attacks until you had determined that the client's anxiety episodes did indeed fulfill the criteria for panic attacks and you were sure that the client understood what you meant by the term "panic attack."

For symptoms that are continuous, you will want to ask about *duration* and *severity*:

- "How long have you been feeling depressed?"
- "Has it gotten worse over time?"
- "Tell me what you've noticed that lets you know you're feeling worse."

How much the mental disorder affects *adaptive functioning* (e.g., whether the client is going to work or school, taking care of routine tasks, or seeing friends and family) is another indicator of severity.

Symptoms tend to gradually decrease or increase over time. Thus, documenting the frequency, duration and severity of symptoms in the first session sets a benchmark that will help you and the client compare current to past functioning after some progress in therapy has been made.


## MEDICAL ILLNESS CAN CAUSE PSYCHOLOGICAL SYMPTOMS

Possible medical reasons for the symptoms must be thoroughly evaluated before you can make a definitive diagnosis (Morrison, 1995). Many medical issues mimic mental illness. Here are just a few examples:

- Undiagnosed brain dysfunction from a closed head injury can look like depression with motivation problems.
- Hypothyroidism can look like depression because of the client's low energy level.
- Temporal lobe epilepsy can have many unusual symptoms that resemble psychosis or other mental illnesses.
- Sleep apnea can look like depression because of poor sleep quality, which results in daytime tiredness and low motivation.

Here are some situations in which you should refer the client for a medical evaluation to clarify the diagnostic picture (informed by Morrison, 2007):

- Client is having a first episode of mental illness, especially if client is 40 or older.
- Client has recently given birth.
- Client has a current major medical illness (such as diabetes or seizure disorder), past major medical illness, or family history of major inheritable medical illness.

- Client has a current or past endocrine (hormone) disorder.
- Client has experienced a head injury, including sharp blows to the head without the skull being pierced.
- Client has neurological symptoms (such as weakness, tingling, numbing, trouble walking, tremor, involuntary movements, dizziness, or blurred or double vision).
- Client does not seem fully alert, has trouble with speech or memory, or cannot follow simple commands.
- Client is not oriented to person, place, and date (see Chapter 8).
- Client has any behaviors that could cause vitamin deficiency (limited diet, large weight loss, or self-neglect).

I would also add that if your client has not seen a physician for more than a year, it would be wise to send the client for a routine visit, especially if the client is 40 or older.

## SUBSTANCE USE CAN CAUSE PSYCHOLOGICAL SYMPTOMS

Alcohol and drug use, along with intoxication and withdrawal, can cause a plethora of symptoms mimicking mental illnesses. These include the following (American Psychiatric Association, 2000):

- Anger
- Anxiety
- Dysphoria
- Euphoria
- Hallucinations
- Impairment in attention
- Insomnia
- Paranoia
- Psychomotor agitation
- Psychomotor retardation

In addition, there is evidence (Liappas, Paparrigopoulos, Tzavellas, & Christodoulou, 2002) that alcohol abusers who are detoxing feel quite anxious and depressed at first, but feel much less so after 4 to 5 weeks of detoxification. Therefore, other diagnoses may need to be deferred in the presence of substance abuse until the client is abstinent and can be evaluated again.

## DON'T DIAGNOSE PREMATURELY

*Tomas Figuerro, a licensed psychologist, has been working with a new client, Laurie Norris, for several weeks. He knows that she has had some problems with depression, but some things continue to confuse him. He finds her charming, but at times she is disconcertingly blunt. She has an avid interest in literature. She talks about reading frequently and comes to each session carrying at least three different books. She often talks about going to websites to read book reviews. Yet despite her high verbal intelligence, she is satisfied with a job that is less than challenging. She is friendly and smiles often, yet her affect still seems somewhat blunted at times, even though she used to act in the theater semiprofessionally. She often feels confused in social situations. After a while, even though she did not seem to fit the picture he knew, he started to wonder whether she had Asperger's. He found a questionnaire in a professional research article and gave it to the client. Her answers were consistent with that diagnosis and revealed some symptoms (such as a preoccupation with numbers) that he had not been aware of. Laurie started to look up information on the Internet, and they both discussed how this syndrome had affected her life. Both of them learned about the differences between men and women with Asperger's. Laurie soon felt much better about herself, and they terminated therapy.*

Sometimes, as in the previous vignette, you will need to patiently observe the client longitudinally to gather enough data to make a diagnosis. At other times, you will need another session or two to finish gathering pertinent data. As long as the client is not in a crisis, it is okay for the client to remain undiagnosed for a while. If the client is in a crisis, gather whatever information you need to cope with the immediate crisis, then go back and finish gathering information when the crisis is over.

As you become more experienced, you will learn to recognize common mental illnesses more easily. You will also become better at realizing when you need to persist to get more information. As you can see from the previous vignette, even advanced psychotherapists can occasionally struggle to diagnose a client.

## SELECTED DIAGNOSTIC CONSIDERATIONS REGARDING ETHNICITY AND CULTURE

Diagnostic errors are common, and some are specifically tied to ethnicity. One error that has been commonly researched and cited is misdiagnosing African Americans with schizophrenia when a diagnosis of major depression with psychotic features would be more accurate (Garb, 1997, reviews the literature). Studies have indicated that this error could be due in part to the greater prevalence of psychotic symptomatology (e.g., more psychotic depression vs. nonpsychotic depression) in African Americans relative to Whites (Strakowski, 2003).

You can reduce the likelihood of misdiagnosis of schizophrenia by ensuring that you ask psychotic clients about mood as well (Strakowski, 2003) and determine the timelines of both affective and psychotic symptoms. In clients who have major depression with psychotic features, depression will occur first, followed by psychotic symptoms during the most acute period of depression. While clients with schizophrenia often become depressed, the schizophrenia occurs first, and the depression typically occurs in response to the ensuing negative life events.

Most psychotherapists are savvy to this issue now, and there is some evidence that this type of misdiagnosis may be disappearing (e.g., Neighbors, Trierweiler, Ford, & Muroff, 2003). However, these researchers do cite another diagnostic difference of possible concern: higher diagnosis of schizophrenia in African Americans versus higher diagnosis of bipolar disorder in Whites.

Another ethnic difference of concern is that Asians may express their level of distress primarily through volunteering information about somatic symptoms (K. Lin & Cheung, 1999). Possible reasons for these cultural differences in symptom expression include regarding body and mind as one (as opposed to Western dualism) and reticence about discussing one's private life. Direct questioning about psychological symptoms can elicit the needed information (K. Lin & Cheung, 1999).

A final diagnostic concern relates to culture rather than ethnicity per se. The *Canadian Journal of Psychiatry* (Lalonde, Hudson, Gigante, & Pope, 2001; Piper & Merskey, 2004) has published skeptical articles regarding the diagnosis of *dissociative identity disorder* (previously known as multiple personality disorder). The authors indicate that many Canadian mental health practitioners feel that dissociative identity disorder is culture bound (primarily to the United States) and can be *iatrogenic*, which means that it is (unwittingly) caused by the practitioner. Many American psychiatrists are skeptical about dissociative identity disorder as well (Gharaibeh, 2009). Clearly, further research is much needed in this area.

RECOMMENDED READING

Bowden, C. (2001). Strategies to reduce misdiagnosis of bipolar depression. *Psychiatric Services, 52*, 51–55.
   *Bowden's helpful and succinct article will aid you in more accurately diagnosing bipolar disorder when clients present with a depressive episode.*
Lin, K., & Cheung, F. (1999). Mental health issues for Asian Americans. *Psychiatric Services, 50*, 774–780.
   *This article provides helpful insights into culture and mental health of Asian Americans.*
Morrison, J. (2007). *Diagnosis made easier: Principles and techniques for mental health clinicians.* New York: Guilford Press.
   *This helpful and well-written volume clearly describes almost everything you will ever need to know about the process of making diagnoses. Highly recommended for all mental health trainees and professionals.*
Ramsay, J. R., & Rostain, A. L. (2005). Adapting psychotherapy to meet the needs of adults with attention-deficit/hyperactivity disorder. *Psychotherapy: Theory, Research, Practice, Training, 42*, 72–84.
   *The authors provide helpful guidance for treating adults with ADHD.*

Rosenthal, N. E. (1998). *Winter blues: Seasonal affective disorder, what it is and how to overcome it*. New York: Guilford Press.
*A definitive book about seasonal affective disorder—helpful for psychotherapists and clients alike.*

## ONLINE RESOURCES

www.drwiller.com/tbpc
*My website provides a multitude of pdfs that you can look at and download to any device that will help you with screening questions for most major types of adult mental disorders.*

http://www.med.nyu.edu/psych/assets/adhdscreen18.pdf
*The National Comorbidity Survey at Harvard University has posted self-report screening questionnaires for adult ADHD that were developed in conjunction with a World Health Organization work group. This symptom checklist is in the public domain. There is a 6-item and an 18-item version, and it is in many different languages. This checklist operationalizes ADHD symptoms in terms of adult behaviors, assisting the psychotherapist in making a diagnosis.*

http://www.dbsalliance.org/pdfs/MDQ.pdf
*The Mood Disorder Questionnaire is in the public domain and can be helpful in screening for mania. Be aware that no checklist can be used alone to make a diagnosis. Instead, use the results of the questionnaire to guide further questions on your part before you finalize any diagnoses.*

## DISCUSSION QUESTIONS

1. Annesha Banks is a new client of yours. You observe that she has difficulty maintaining eye contact with you during the interview and that her affect is flat. When asked what brought her to therapy, she indicates that she has been crying every day. When asked about her sleep, she says that she has been having vivid and disturbing dreams that disrupt her sleep. What else would you want to ask Annesha? What diagnoses would you consider for Annesha?

2. Theodore Packer is a new client. When asked what brought him to therapy, he says that he's been very anxious lately and that he can't concentrate at work and worries about losing his job. He says that his wife always complains that he doesn't listen to her, and their marriage is in trouble. His eye contact is good, and his affect is *euthymic* (normal, not depressed or manic). When asked about sleep, he says that it takes him a long time to get to sleep. What else would you want to ask Theodore? What diagnoses would you consider for Theodore?

3. Rodrigo Gutierrez is a new client. He is an Iraq War veteran. When asked why he decided to come for therapy, he said that his mother insisted that he come for help. He has been living with her. He also said that he has been arguing with everyone else in his family. He denies

feeling anxious or depressed but does say that his sleep is not restful. You notice that his eyes are bloodshot and that he keeps jiggling his leg during the session. His affect and eye contact are normal. What else would you want to ask Rodrigo? What diagnoses would you consider for Rodrigo?

# 10

# Professional Phone Contacts and the Initial Phone Call

As a beginning psychotherapist, you will probably be assigned clients by a supervisor at your training site. Once the client is assigned, you will need to contact the client to schedule an appointment time. This chapter will take you step by step through contacting the client by phone.

## PROFESSIONAL PHONE GREETINGS

Before calling the client, be sure that your voicemail is set up at your training site. That way, if you need to leave a message for the client, she will get your personal voicemail when she calls back. A short, pleasant, professional message is best. State your full name and your position. If you are not in the office every day, include any relevant information about when you will return calls. Ask your supervisor whether to include information about emergency contacts. Avoid any overly personal or religious remarks:

- Wrong: "Hi! This is Amber. Leave a message. God bless!"
- Right: "Hello, this is Amber Scott, psychology practicum student. I am in the office on Mondays and Wednesdays and will return your call next time I am in. If you need help before that, please call [alternate phone number at training site]. [Optional sentence: "If you are having an emergency, please call 911 or go to your nearest emergency room."] I'll look forward to talking with you soon. Goodbye."

When answering the phone, again, professionalism is paramount.

- Wrong: "Hello?"
- Wrong: "Hi, this is Amber."
- Wrong: "Yes?"
- Right: "This is Amber Scott, psychology practicum student."
- Right: "Hello, this is Amber Scott [or Dr. Scott if you have a doctoral degree]."

## MAKING THE INITIAL CALL

If more than one phone number is available for the client, choose the one that seems the most private to call first, generally the cell phone number. You may wish to avoid leaving a message until you have tried to contact the client directly at all the numbers that you have. If the client is not available at any of them, choose the number that seems the most private and leave a message. Sometimes you can be fairly sure that no one else has access to the voicemail that the client has given you. In these cases, the phone number the client has given you goes directly into voicemail or onto an answering machine. The client states that it is his phone number and does not name anyone else—for example, "Hi, this is Stephen. I can't come to the phone right now, so please leave a message," or, "Hello, this is Stephen Desai with ABC Manufacturing. I'm sorry I can't come to the phone right now, but please leave a message." In these cases, leave a brief message:

> "Hello, this is [your name]. I'm returning your call from [name of facility]. You can reach me at [phone number]. If you don't reach me directly, please leave me some times and numbers when I can reach you. I'll try to call you again on Thursday if I don't hear from you. I look forward to your call. Good-bye."

Issues of confidentiality are very important when making these initial contacts. Rarely will you know whether anyone else who might answer the phone knows if the client is seeking therapy. If it is unclear whether the voicemail is just for the client or whether other might be able to pick up the messages, you might want to wait and try again later. If after trying two or three times you haven't reached the client directly, you might leave a brief and uninformative message:

> "Hi, this is [your name] returning a call from [client name]. He can reach me at
>
> [phone number]. Thank you."

Generally, I will try to call a prospective client two or three times. At the last call, if he has not picked up or tried to return my call, I'll leave a message like this:

> "Hi, this is [your name] and my phone number is [phone number]. Please call me if you are still interested in scheduling an appointment. Take care."

## IF SOMEONE ELSE PICKS UP AT WORK AND CLIENT IS NOT AVAILABLE

When you call, always ask to speak to the client by name: "Could I speak to Stephen [or Stephen Desai, if clearly a work number], please?" Because of confidentiality concerns, if you reach someone else, you must be as uninformative as possible. If you are calling a work number, it is usually okay to leave a very nondescript message:

Receptionist: "Hello, this is ABC Manufacturing, Nicole speaking."
Psychotherapist: "Hi Nicole, could I speak to Stephen Desai please?"
R: "I'm sorry, he's in a meeting right now. Could I leave him a message?"
P: "Yes. Could you ask him to call [psychotherapist name] at [phone number]?"
R: "Okay. Can I tell him what this is regarding?"
P: "I'm not sure. I'm just returning his call."
R: "Okay."
P: "Thanks for your help. Good-bye."
R: "Good-bye."

The client likely receives all kinds of phone messages at work, so yours won't stand out from the others. Avoid leaving any job names or titles (e.g., doctor).

## IF SOMEONE ELSE PICKS UP AT HOME AND CLIENT IS NOT AVAILABLE

If you are calling a home number and someone else picks up, don't be hesitant. Speak briskly in a professional tone, and try to keep the initiative on your side in the conversation:

Relative: "Hello."
Psychotherapist: "Hi, can I speak to Stephen?"
R: "He's not here right now."
P [speaking quickly so relative doesn't have a chance to ask questions]: "Can you tell me when he might be back?"
R: "He'll probably be home at about 3 p.m."
P: "Thanks, I'll call back then. Goodbye!" [Then psychotherapist hangs up and doesn't wait for relative to ask questions.]

On occasion, the relative may succeed in asking some questions. Here are some possible questions and suggested responses:

Relative: "What is this call regarding?"
Psychotherapist: "I don't know, I'm just returning his call. Thanks so much for your help! Good-bye!" [Then the psychotherapist hangs up the phone, whether or not the relative has responded.]
or
R: "Would you like to leave a message?"
P: "No thanks, I'll call back later when he is at home. Thanks so much for your help! Good-bye!" [Then the psychotherapist hangs up the phone, whether or not the relative has responded.]

or

R: "How do you know Stephen?"

P: "I don't know him, I'm just returning his call. Thanks so much for your help! Good-bye!" [Then the psychotherapist hangs up the phone, whether or not the relative has responded.]

When you get a curious relative, roommate, or other person on the line, you will have to choose whether to be polite or whether to maintain confidentiality as much as possible. The more you stay on the line, waiting for the individual to be willing to say good-bye, the more you give the individual a chance to quiz you and become more curious because you are unwilling to give any substantive answers. It is better to say good-bye pleasantly, in an unrushed tone, and then hang up—although clearly it is not optimally polite.

Sometimes, you may try a couple times and still can't reach the client. In those cases, you have little choice but to leave just your name and number as a message. Again, state that you don't know what the call is regarding and that you are just returning a call.

## WHEN THE CLIENT IS AVAILABLE

When you call, know what your goals are for the conversation. Most likely, you will just want to set up a mutually convenient appointment. You might also want or need to gather a little information about the client's presenting problem. In some settings, you might also be asked to screen the client briefly to ensure that the client is appropriate for the services that the setting offers. If there are any screening issues, talk to your supervisor for advice on how to handle them.

Let's assume that you want to set up an appointment, get a little information, and also learn what the presenting problem is so that you can talk that over with your supervisor before the first session. Here is a sample transcript:

Client: "Hello."

Psychotherapist: "Hi, could I speak to Pamela, please?"

C: "This is Pamela."

P: "Hi Pamela, this is [trainee name] calling from [mental health facility]. I was returning your call regarding setting up an appointment. Is this a good time to talk?"

C: "Sure."

P: "Great. Let's first set up a time to meet. How about 2:00 this Thursday?"

C: "I'm sorry, I can't come then."

P: "What about 10:30 on Friday?"

C: "That sounds fine."

P: "Okay, I'll mark you down for that time. Could you come in about 30 minutes early to fill out some paperwork?"

C: "Sure."

P: "Okay. I'd like to get a little information from you before we meet. What is your date of birth?"

C: "October 20, 1970."

P: "Could you tell me a little bit about why you decided to come to therapy at this time?"

C: "I'm having some problems with my girlfriend, and I've been feeling depressed about it."

P: "Sounds like it's a good idea to come for therapy then. Do you know where the clinic is?"

C: "Yes."

P: "Good. I also need to tell you that the clinic requires that you pay your fee at the time of appointment and that you will be charged your fee if you cancel an appointment with less than 24 hours' notice. Do you have any questions about that?"

C: "No."

P: "So I'll look forward to seeing you this Friday at 10:30, and you'll come in at 10:00 to do the paperwork first."

C: "Okay."

P: "See you then."

C: "Good-bye."

P: "Good-bye."

Note here that the psychotherapist keeps the conversation short and to the point. The psychotherapist highlights important aspects of the payment policy to minimize any possibility of misunderstandings later. The psychotherapist is friendly but also brisk. The psychotherapist doesn't want to get into an extensive conversation with the client over the phone because it is very difficult, even for an experienced psychotherapist, to properly assess or treat an unknown client over the phone.

You will want to present yourself in a balanced manner when you are on the phone with clients. You will want to be pleasant and friendly. You will want to indicate that you are interested in what your client has to say and look forward to the session. However, maintain a professional demeanor. At times you may need to be brisk and politely redirect the client to accomplish your goal for the phone contact without veering into topics that are better addressed in therapy.

Sometimes your prospective client will want to talk at length over the phone; this may not be easy to stop. However, be aware that having a lengthy phone conversation with a prospective client may create a doctor–patient (or psychotherapist–client) relationship in the eyes of the law (Simon, 2004), which is something you should avoid doing before you have had a chance to assess the client in person (although it should be noted that giving the client an appointment could be seen as creating a doctor–patient relationship as well; Simon, 2004). Creating a doctor–patient relationship with someone you haven't met in person may increase your legal liability for negative events, such as suicide, that you cannot properly assess over the phone. That said, if you do sense that the client may be suicidal over the phone, insist that the client go to an emergency room immediately.

Most people understand that health care practitioners are busy people and don't have time to talk at length over the phone. As needed, use this intervention:

> "I have to apologize. I wanted to get back to you in a timely fashion, but I don't have much time right now. I can see that all these things you are telling me are very important, but I don't have enough time right now to do justice to these issues over the phone. Can I ask you to fill me in about all of this when we meet for our first session?"

Generally, the client will readily agree to wait until the session to discuss the issues.

## IF A CLIENT'S FRIEND OR FAMILY MEMBER CALLS YOU

Sometimes clients' friends and family members are aware that the client is seeing you. The friend or family member may then call you about the client. If this individual wants information about an adult client, gently inform the caller that psychotherapy is confidential and that you cannot provide any information. If this individual wants to tell you about the client's behavior outside the session, inform the caller that you can listen but cannot comment and that you will need to tell the client about the call at the next session.

## TALKING TO YOUR CLIENT WHEN OUT OF THE OFFICE

You may be able to retrieve messages from your clients remotely. At times, you may find it helpful to contact your client by cell phone when out of the office. Remember that if you call the client by cell phone, it is likely that the client will then have your cell phone number at her disposal. This is not optimal. So, if you must use your cell phone, enter *67 first, then enter the client's phone number. This should block your phone number from appearing on the client's caller ID. If you choose to call from your cell phone, be sure no relatives or roommates are around to hear the call. Be careful when calling from locations outside your home to assess whether you can make a confidential call. If you just need to call the client to confirm an appointment time, it may be possible to do that in a location that is not totally confidential:

> "Hi, this is [psychotherapist name]. I just wanted to call to confirm that our next appointment is at 2:00 p.m. on Tuesday."

Do not say the client's name or talk about the client's problems. If the client mentions another issue during the call, you should respond this way:

> "I'm sorry, I can't talk about that right now, because I'm not in a location where I can talk confidentially. But I just wanted to get back to you in a timely

manner about your question about the appointment time. Can we discuss it when we meet on Tuesday?"

While Pinals and Gutheil (2001) argue that you should always inform your clients and/or other professionals when you are using a cell phone, I disagree. They rightly point out that cell phone communications are subject to interception. However, the large majority of phones used now are either cell phones or cordless phones. Incidents of interception are unlikely.

## YOUR HOME AND CELL PHONE GREETINGS

*A training site supervisor is reviewing vitas of mental health trainees that might be matched to the site. She is interested in interviewing one of the candidates and calls his home phone number to leave a message. The student's voicemail replies, "Hi! You've reached Dr. Nick and Dr. Sarah at THE LOONY BIN! [Giggles, laughter, and lame jokes continue about shock therapy, meds, and so on.] Leave a message for the doctors after the beep!" The supervisor does not leave a message and decides not to offer an interview.*

Be sure you have an appropriate message at your home and cell phone voicemails, as your fellow professionals may call you there at times.

## AVOID SHARING YOUR PERSONAL PHONE NUMBERS

I recommend that you not give out your home or cell phone number to clients. Some experienced licensed practitioners may make exceptions when they are working with a low-risk population. In addition, some private practitioners may use their cell phone as a practice phone number. As a trainee, you should not do that. Instead, your site should provide a professional phone number where your clients can leave messages for you. If you feel tempted to give out a personal phone number, talk it over with a supervisor first.

## YOUR PERSONAL PHONE AND HOME ADDRESS SHOULD BE UNLISTED

If you have a landline, call your phone company now and change your phone number to unlisted. Your address should not be in the phone book, either. Also, check online directories and try to remove yourself if possible. When you buy real estate, ask your real estate attorney how to keep your name from appearing online in connection with the property. Remove your phone number and address on Facebook or other social networking sites because they cannot be considered secure. As a psychotherapist, you are at significantly greater statistical risk of being threatened, stalked, assaulted, or even killed (Berg, Bell, & Tupin, 2000). Keeping your contact information private helps keep your private life safe.

## ACTIVITIES

1. Check your social network profiles and remove your phone numbers and address (city and state is okay). Search online for your name with and without your phone number and address to see if they are online anywhere. Contact the sites and remove the information if possible.
2. If you have a landline, call the phone company and get your phone number and address unlisted.

## DISCUSSION QUESTION

1. What do you think about the recommendation to keep your phone numbers and address as private as possible? Do you think this is too paranoid? Have you done it yet?

# 11

# The First Session: Preparation, Tasks, and Structure

The first session with the client is the most important one. In this session the client will decide if she feels trusting and comfortable. Being well prepared will make a positive, professional impression so that the client feels that she is getting good quality mental health care.

Sites have varying requirements and formats for initial outpatient psychotherapy client interviews. Two basic models are usually employed. First, the client has an intake interview, and at the conclusion of the interview, the client is assigned to another psychotherapist. The goal of these intake interviews is to assess the client and refer to the appropriate health care practitioner or program. You might do some of these intake interviews, you might be assigned clients who have already had an intake interview, or both.

Second, a client may be assigned to you for treatment, but very little information may be available from the client's initial (probably phone) contact with the clinic, so you will need to spend the first session getting oriented to the client's problems. I address both of these scenarios in this chapter.

Since you have undoubtedly learned it elsewhere, I do not address rapport-building skills in this chapter. Instead, only specific rapport-building issues that are pertinent to the initial session are discussed: client ambivalence, fears, and expectations. Addressing all the details of doing an accurate and complete initial interview is far beyond the scope of this book, as entire books have been written on this subject alone (see Craig, 2005; Morrison, 1995).

## BE ORGANIZED

Before the session begins, be sure that you are organized. If the client has not already had an intake interview, have the following forms available:

- The site's informed consent form
- The site's confidentiality form (or this may be part of the informed consent form)

- The site's Notice of Privacy Practices form (as required by the Health Insurance Portability and Accountability Act)
- The site's interview outline, if there is one, or you can use a copy of the outline in the appendix for this chapter or devise your own using the screening questions on www.drwiller.com/tbpc
- Several copies of the site's release of information form.

Other items that you may wish to have handy are the following:

- A pad of paper and several pens
- Sticky notes in case you want to write down any information or referrals for the client
- A copy of the recent *Diagnostic and Statistical Manual of Mental Disorders* in case the client has a diagnosis that you are less familiar with, because you may not remember enough symptoms to make a definitive diagnosis otherwise
- Brochures, business cards, or flyers for referrals that the clinic often makes; your supervisor can help you with this.

Before the session begins, take a few moments to consider what you know about the client. Review any progress notes and other documentation that already exists. Think about what you learned from phone contact you had with the client. Think about what else you would like to learn about the client. It might be helpful to write down these thoughts to ensure that you ask about them in the intake session. You should also know what the site's procedures are for voluntary and involuntary hospitalization, should the client need it.

## TIME MANAGEMENT AND TASKS OF THE FIRST SESSION

Managing time during an initial interview can be challenging even for an experienced psychotherapist. Start out the interview with open-ended questions that will help build rapport and allow the client to tell you important material in her own words; this will help you know where to go next. Later, make the transition to more close-ended questions to help you get more information in a limited time period.

Often, we are asked to see an intake client in a 45-minute session. We are then expected to be able to make a diagnosis and send the client to whatever treatment is appropriate for his problems. Sometimes this is a realistic goal, but sometimes it isn't. Many of your psychotherapy clients will have complex mental health and social histories, and you would need two or three sessions to get all the information you need. Sometimes you have a limited time to see an intake client and refer to other treatments. In all these cases, it is important to prioritize carefully during the session.

Here is an outline of all the tasks you would ideally want to accomplish in the first session (the four most important tasks are in italics):

- Start the session.
- *Obtain written informed consent, including confidentiality, and Notice of Privacy Practices form (Chapter 7).*
- *Establish rapport.*
- *Determine the presenting problem.*
- Get an overview of current life problems the client may be having.
- Diagnose any mental illnesses (Chapter 9).
- *Evaluate the client for suicide risk and other crises (Chapters 17 through 21).*
- Obtain social, medical, and mental health histories, including getting relevant information about psychological symptoms over time and past involvement in mental health care. (Because of time constraints, you will often address these historical issues in subsequent sessions; see outline in the appendix for this chapter.)
- Give feedback to the client about diagnoses and treatment.
- Make referrals (Chapters 14 through 16). To make an appropriate referral, you will need to understand the severity of the client's symptoms and his level of distress.
- End the session.

Do not worry if you can't cover all these topics in the first session. Most clients over the age of 35 have too much life history to cover in one session, and many younger clients do too. Also, some people's history and symptoms are very complex and take a lot of time to fully observe and understand.

Even if you run over with time, you should accomplish the four italicized tasks. Note that evaluating for crisis risk can take a long time, perhaps the entire session, if the client's symptomatology and history are complex.

With experience, you will be surprised about how much important information you can get in one session. Consider how much time you have left for the interview as you complete each goal. When you see that you have only 5 to 10 minutes left in the session, start to wind it up, make referrals, and schedule the next session.

## TAKE AMPLE NOTES

During a first session, most people benefit from taking copious notes. Otherwise, you will not remember all the details of the client's symptoms and history when you write the progress note. It always helps to write down some of the client's more unusual or diagnostic statements verbatim. These give anyone reading your progress note a more nuanced view of the client. Here are some examples of statements you might write down:

- "I thought that I couldn't feel any pain, so I put cigarettes out on my arm."
- "I've always been very shy; I didn't talk at all in preschool."
- "There's high pressure from my family to do well."
- "I like to be in control."
- "My life situation sucks, and I'm sick of it."

## START THE SESSION

*Salma El Sayad is a mental health trainee working at a college counseling center. She goes to the waiting room to meet her new client, Tara Morris. She sees just one client in the waiting room and approaches her. "Hello, are you Tara?" Tara nods yes. Salma says, "I'm Salma El Sayad, it's good to meet you. Let's go to my office." Salma guides Tara through the hallways to her office. They make small talk about the women's basketball team, which has been very successful this year, in the hallway. When they reach her office, Salma gestures to indicate which seat Tara should take: "If you wouldn't mind sitting here." Salma then orients Tara to the tasks of the first session. "Today, I would like to focus on getting an overview of what is going on with you. So, I will be asking you some questions about how things have been for you lately and any symptoms you might be experiencing. This will be helpful so that we can plan what treatment will be most effective for you. How does that sound?" Tara indicates her agreement.*

*Joel Mitchell is a mental health trainee working at a community mental health center. He is doing intakes today with walk-in clients. When he finishes each intake interview, the client will be assigned to another psychotherapist for ongoing treatment. The receptionist informs him that a new client, Sharon Yang, has walked in. He checks the electronic medical record, but Sharon is new to the clinic, and there is no old chart to review before seeing her. He goes to the waiting room, which has a dozen clients in it. He says, "Ms. Yang?" Sharon gets up and comes toward him. He reaches out to shake her hand. "Hi, I'm Joel Mitchell, I'll be meeting with you today. Could you follow me to my office?" Sharon indicates her agreement and follows him. Joel indicates which chair is hers and then tells her, "Today, I'd like to talk to you and try to understand what is going on with you so that I can refer you to the treatment that is right for you. When we are done today, I will be referring you to another psychotherapist or treatment program where you can get help on an ongoing basis. I'll be taking some notes as we go along so that I don't lose track of anything important."*

At the time of the session, go to get your client from the waiting room. Depending on the setting, you might prefer to ask for the client by first name (e.g., college counseling center) or by title and last name (e.g., older or more traditional populations). Follow the lead of other psychotherapists in your setting.

Keep in mind that the client, if anything, is more anxious than you are. You might want to begin with just a minute or two of chitchat to make both of you more comfortable. If you talk with the client in the waiting room or the hall, it should be superficial, such as, "Did you have any difficulty getting here?" or

"How was traffic getting here?" Brief remarks about general impersonal topics, such as the weather, parking, or traffic encountered today, can break the ice. You might also riff off of something about the appearance or possessions of the client. For example, it might be morning—you are drinking coffee, and the client has brought coffee—so you might commiserate about needing it in the morning. Or if the client is wearing a sports logo, you could share some brief remarks about sports. Others prefer to avoid any chitchat and move directly to the interview (Morrison, 1995); both approaches are appropriate. Be sure not to chat too long, as this deemphasizes the professional nature of the relationship.

You can then segue into starting the session. Many clients know little about the therapeutic process or how psychotherapy sessions typically proceed, so it can help to spend the next few minutes of the session orienting the client to the session's tasks, as Joel and Salma do in the vignettes. Note that Joel carefully informed the client from the start that he would not be the ongoing psychotherapist. Most clients do not mind if you take notes as long as you can maintain good eye contact at appropriate times.

## INFORMED CONSENT, CONFIDENTIALITY AND HIPAA, AND CLIENT QUESTIONS

Salma asks Tara if she brought in her intake forms. Tara printed them out from the counseling center's website and has them. Salma then looks over them briefly. She sees that Tara's signature indicates that she understands the confidentiality, informed consent, and HIPAA forms, but she still asks, "Do you have any questions about therapy?" Tara asks, "What type of treatment do you recommend for depression?" Salma suspects that Tara is asking about herself. She does not know enough about Tara yet to know whether she does actually have depression, how severe it is, or what type of treatment might be appropriate. So she says, "It depends on the particular individual and how serious the depression is. How about if I try to understand what is going on with you, and then at the end, I can give you my input about what treatment I would recommend for any depression you might be experiencing?" Tara indicates her agreement. Salma then tells Tara, "I also want you to know that, since I am a student, I need to discuss all my work with a more experienced psychotherapist. I will need to audiotape our sessions after today. My supervisor will sometimes listen to those tapes. Do you have any questions about that?" Salma then answers a couple questions about the role of the supervisor in Tara's psychotherapy.

Joel asks, "Do you have any questions?" Sharon indicates that she doesn't have any questions yet. Joel then asks her if she has any questions about the clinic's standard informed consent and Notice of Privacy Practices forms. Joel tells Sharon, "After we talk, I will be discussing your situation with a more experienced psychotherapist. Do you have any questions?" Sharon does not have any questions about that.

Both clients have already read information about informed consent and confidentiality in written form. After orienting the client to the tasks of the session, the psychotherapist gives the client an opportunity to ask questions about informed consent, confidentiality, or any other therapy topics she is curious about.

Some clients will have many questions, but many will have few or none. Do the best you can to answer whatever questions arise. If you don't know the answer, it's okay to say so. As discussed in Chapter 7, also review verbally whatever information about informed consent or confidentiality you think might be especially relevant to this client; do this at the beginning of the session since it is difficult to return to it later. If you have some ideas about the client's treatment at the end of the first session, feel free to share this and get the client's reactions and agreement; this is part of the informed consent process.

## PRESENTING PROBLEM

Salma asks, "What has made you decide to come to therapy at this time?" Tara says that she has recently been "dumped" by her boyfriend and that she has been crying for hours every day. She goes on to describe sleep disturbance, overeating, and social isolation. She also says that she hasn't been doing well in school this year (she is a freshman) and that even before the breakup she was having problems concentrating and getting all her schoolwork done.

Joel says, "Please tell me what problems made you decide to come for treatment." Sharon says that she has been arguing with her elderly parents and that she doesn't like living with them anymore. Joel asks how this living arrangement came to be. Sharon says that she is on disability and has a low income. Joel asks her if she could tell him why she gets disability, but she is unable to tell him. She does tell him that it was difficult for her to get to the clinic because all the people on the bus were criticizing her on the way there.

Often the presenting problem can include clues as to the life problems and symptoms that the client is having, so it is wise to further explore whatever symptoms are suggested by the presenting problem first. Your questions about the presenting problem should be open ended (like Salma's or Joel's in the previous vignettes) and allow the client to talk for several minutes. Encourage the client to keep talking with open-ended questions as needed and use your active listening skills to get whatever information you feel is relevant.

## ESTABLISH RAPPORT—ADDRESSING AMBIVALENCE, FEARS, AND EXPECTATIONS

Tara indicates that she is uncertain whether it was right to come to therapy. Salma tells her, "It was very wise of you to come to therapy right now. I can see that this breakup is really getting you down, and you have been having a lot of trouble coping lately. I'm very hopeful that together we can figure out how to help you feel better." Tara says that she has been trying not to let her friends know how bad she feels. Salma says, "You've been very brave to talk about this; I can see that it must be difficult for you."

*Joel asks Sharon whether she has had any mental health treatment before. She indicates that she has seen five or six different psychotherapists, "but none of them did me any good." He asks her how long she attended treatment and finds that she went for no more than a few sessions. She also says that she has been given medication before but that "I didn't need it." Joel says, "I see that you've tried therapy a number of times, and you feel that it has not worked for you. But I think that I'm noticing a problem. I don't think that you've been giving it enough time. You've been coping with your problems for a long time, and none of them are going to go away overnight. So I would like to ask you to make a commitment to come weekly for at least three months. You will probably need to attend very regularly for one to three months before you start to see much improvement. It will take a lot of time and commitment on your part. Do you think you could do that?" Sharon indicates that she is willing to try. Joel also suggests that she talk to her psychotherapist if she is thinking of stopping therapy again instead of not showing up anymore. She agrees to do so.*

During the initial session, the client is likely to be quite anxious and might also be somewhat ambivalent about therapy. The client might be fearful to talk about things that she has kept secret for a long time. She may not have told even her closest friends or family how upset she has been. You can help the client engage in the therapeutic process by being alert to these concerns and addressing them as they come up. Your client might indicate that she has not been telling anyone how bad she feels. Clients who are secretive about their difficulties often feel ashamed. You can imagine how difficult it would be for a client who has been secretive to talk about her problems. It takes desperation, but also courage, to do so. Emphasize the positive with her. Compliment her on the courage that she has displayed in talking about these very personal and painful difficulties, as Salma does in the previous vignette.

Sometimes you get a client who has been in and out of therapy, like Sharon. She may begin therapy hopefully but may expect too much too soon or lose interest and, as a result, will drop out. In these cases, identify the pattern and educate the client about treatment, as Joel has done in the previous vignette.

## OVERVIEW OF CURRENT LIFE PROBLEMS

*Salma asks Tara, "Has anything else been stressing you out lately?" Tara talks about her grandmother, with whom she is very close. Her grandmother has terminal lung cancer. Tara also says she has been wondering whether she has attention-deficit disorder because of her school problems, and she is worrying that she will never finish college.*

*Joel asks Sharon, "Have any other things been bothering you lately?" Sharon says that she had been going to a community support program but that it was closed because of a lack of funds. She has a boyfriend whom she met there, but her parents do not approve since he has a history of cocaine use and psychiatric hospitalizations.*

Asking about current life problems can help you further assess the client's level of distress. This is helpful to put the client's symptoms in context; in addition, it is helpful to have this information when evaluating crisis risk.

## UNDERSTAND CULTURAL AND IDENTITY INFLUENCES

*During the interview, Salma notes the following: Tara is apparently heterosexual (although bisexuality cannot be ruled out yet); she refers to her family as "typical Italian Catholic," although her last name is not suggestive of Italian heritage; she is 20 years old and has no apparent disabilities; and her description of her family is suggestive of middle-class socioeconomic status.*

*During the interview, Joel notes the following: Sharon is apparently heterosexual; she mentions that both of her parents are elderly American-born Chinese; she is 42; and she gets disability income, although she cannot articulate the nature of her disability.*

During the initial interview, you will attend to and gather information about the client's cultural and identity influences. However, only in later sessions will you have the opportunity to work productively with this information. Hays (2009) suggests the following framework for assessing cultural and identity influences (note that these topics form the acronym ADDRESSING):

A—age, generational
D—developmental disabilities
D—disabilities acquired later in life
R—religious and spiritual orientation
E—ethnic and racial identity
S—socioeconomic status
S—sexual orientation
I—indigenous heritage
N—national origin, including refugee or immigrant status
G—gender, including transgender status

## DIAGNOSE ANY MENTAL ILLNESSES
## AND EVALUATE CRISIS RISK

*Salma observes Tara as they talk. She sees that Tara has poor eye contact and that her eyes are red from crying. Her speech is slow, and she looks sad. These symptoms are clearly suggestive of depression. At this point, Salma continues the interview by systematically asking Tara about depressive symptoms. She screens Tara for a history of manic episodes to rule out bipolar disorder and asks her about any history of depressive seasonality because it is November. Salma notices that she has just 15 to 20 minutes left in the therapy session. She says, "I need to take a few minutes to ask you some standard questions. It is okay if we do that now?" Tara indicates her agreement. Then Salma screens Tara for suicide risk, violence risk, substance abuse, psychotic symptoms, and post-traumatic stress disorder (PTSD). She knows that she has not asked about every possible disorder, but she has followed up on the presenting problem and her observations, she has asked about crises, and she has screened for diagnoses that are often comorbid with depression. Tara denies all these symptoms but has been having some thoughts of wishing for death lately. Tara denies any suicidal intent or history of suicidal behavior. They briefly review a standard suicide prevention plan and Tara agrees to it (see Chapter 19).*

*Joel observes Sharon as they talk. He sees that she sometimes looks around the room distractedly. Her affect is flat despite the fact that she clearly verbalizes that she is upset about her living situation with her parents. These symptoms are suggestive of psychosis. At this point, Joel systematically asks Sharon about psychotic symptoms as well as depressive and manic symptoms. He asks about the duration of all these symptoms so that he can make a differential diagnosis between schizophrenia, schizoaffective disorder (depressed or bipolar types), and other disorders with psychotic features. Joel needs to finish the intake interview. He tells Sharon, "Now, I need to ask you some standard questions. Can we do that now?" Sharon agrees. Sharon denies past or current suicidal or homicidal ideation. Joel had already asked her about psychotic and mood symptoms, but he screens her for trauma history and PTSD since he knows that psychotic symptoms have a high comorbidity with PTSD. Sharon indicates that she experienced date rape from a boyfriend in high school and was also raped by an acquaintance 20 years after that. He assesses PTSD symptoms and determines that she has mild symptoms of PTSD, sufficient for a diagnosis.*

The process of making a diagnosis was reviewed in Chapter 9. The above vignettes are provided to assist you in following these cases throughout the first interview. Asking about certain symptoms—such as psychosis or suicidal and homicidal ideation—can be problematic. Some clients can have these symptoms while appearing, speaking, and behaving appropriately, so the psychotherapist should routinely ask screening questions. However, certain clients can get upset if they draw the mistaken conclusion that they have said something that has led you to think that they are have serious difficulties of this sort. Prefacing your questions with a statement that they are "standard questions," as Salma and Joel do, can be helpful (Moline, Williams, & Austin, 1998). Assessing suicide and violence risk is addressed in Chapters 18 through 20.

## GIVE FEEDBACK ABOUT DIAGNOSES AND TREATMENT

*Salma says, "I'm going to try to summarize some of the things that you've told me. It sounds as though you are having some significant problems with depression. You told me about sleep problems, eating problems, crying, and feeling down; these are all symptoms of depression. Depression is very treatable, so I am hopeful that you will be feeling better soon. Right now, the best thing for you would be to resume your usual activities, even if you don't feel like it. Staying alone in bed and crying is just making your depression worse. Try to get out with your friends over the next week and go to class, okay?" Tara agrees to try. Salma says, "I'm not sure why you've been having these problems with school. It may be related to your depression, or it may be a separate problem. For now, I'd like you to fill out this questionnaire and bring it back to me next week. I'll ask you some more about how school has been going then." Tara agrees to fill out the questionnaire on attention-deficit/hyperactivity disorder for next week.*

*Joel says, "Sharon, it seems as though you have been hearing voices for some time. You also talked about your difficulties with feeling that the neighbors are spying on you. It sounds like you and your parents have been arguing about whether to confront the neighbors about this." Sharon nods. Joel continues, "I think that you have a mental illness called schizophrenia. Have you ever heard of that?" Sharon indicates that she knows she has been given that diagnosis before. She asks, "I'm not crazy, am I?" Joel replies, "I don't really like the word 'crazy,' but if you're asking whether you've lost touch with reality, I'd say you have, at times. Schizophrenia is actually a very common problem; about one out of every hundred people has it. Chances are excellent that you can feel much better if you are able to stick with treatment and work closely with your psychotherapist and your doctor."*

Giving a diagnosis can validate to the client that there is a problem that deserves to be addressed. It allows you to provide information about specific treatments that are helpful. You appear competent and knowledgeable, which is reassuring to the client. As the psychotherapist, if you know the diagnosis, you can access a large body of professional literature that will help you treat the client effectively. Providing this information so that the client can understand and agree to treatment can be conceptualized as an extended part of the verbal informed consent process (Chapter 7).

Many clients, because of their social isolation, have developed the idea that their problems and symptoms are "crazy" and totally unique and cannot be treated. They have tried to cope alone, but this has been ineffective. These clients may make remarks such as, "I'm not crazy, am I, Doc?" or "Have you ever seen anybody like me before?" Often, they fear that you will not know what their problem is or how to help them. They may fear that their problem is so unusual that you have never seen it before. They may have developed a belief that their problem cannot be treated because they have not been able to make progress with it alone. A client with these worries generally does have a diagnosable mental illness. As Joel does in the previous vignette, tell the client about her diagnosis, let her know that her difficulties are definitely not unique, and give her hope that there is an effective treatment. This is an opportunity to educate the client about her illness so that she can cope more effectively in the future. Depending on the client's comprehension and functioning level, it can also be helpful to talk to the client about her feelings about being stigmatized and to discuss cultural biases against persons with mental illness as treatment progresses.

Allay your clients' fears through assurances such as the simple ones in the previous vignettes. Talk in a calm and matter-of-fact voice. This gives an implicit message that you don't think that their problems are shameful. Reassure them that their difficulties can improve and that they can be treated. If their problems are more common than they think, let them know. Give them a chance to ask you questions about your feedback to them.

## MAINTAINING RAPPORT AND GIVING FEEDBACK WITH SUBSTANCE-ABUSING CLIENTS

Giving feedback about substance use is complex. Early in therapy, it is best to avoid putting any labels on the client's substance use (W. R. Miller & Rollnick, 2002). Instead, identify the client's concerns, reflect them back, and ask the client to elaborate on what the client has already said.

At the end of the session, you might say to the client,

> "You mentioned that you are concerned about your alcohol use. You said that you recently got a DUI and that you are embarrassed to admit that you are still driving under the influence. I am very concerned for you as well. I'm glad that you brought this issue up, and we can definitely discuss it further when we meet next. For now, what are your plans for dealing with this issue?"

At this point, because the client has already expressed his concern about the issue, he will often volunteer a plan for avoiding driving drunk. Here you can use a motivational interviewing approach (W. R. Miller & Rollnick, 2002) with the client and use the client's own statements to nudge him to be safer between now and the next session. In this type of situation, carefully document that he has agreed to take action to avoid driving drunk in the future and what that agreed-on action is (e.g., take cabs when going out with friends to bars).

## ENDING THE SESSION WITH ONGOING PSYCHOTHERAPY CLIENTS

*Salma asks, "How has it been to come in and talk about these things today?" Tara says, "I feel relieved. It wasn't as hard to talk about everything as I thought it would be." Salma indicates that she is glad to hear that. She says, "I see that it is about time to wind up today. Let's talk about schedules. I'd like you to come in twice a week until you are feeling better. What times will work for you?" They agree on a time. Salma says, "Okay, I will save 4 p.m. on Tuesdays and 1 p.m. on Thursdays for you. Those will be your scheduled times every week. When you are feeling better, we will go down to once a week. If you have to cancel, please let me know as soon as possible. Please try to give me at least 24 hours' notice. Can you do that?" Tara indicates that she understands. Salma says, "Thank you so much for coming. I enjoyed meeting you, and I'll see you next week, okay?" She leads Tara to the door, opens the door, and says good-bye.*

If the client is starting individual psychotherapy, you will want to accomplish several important goals at the end of the session. Ensure that you have gathered the most important information. Then allow about 10 minutes to finish the session. During this process, make referrals for any adjunctive treatments that you would recommend (Chapters 14 through 16), check in with the client about her perceptions of the session, and schedule your next appointment. Be sure that the agreed-on appointment is convenient for both of you. Never schedule an ongoing psychotherapy client at a time that is inconvenient for you. If the client proposes a time that is inconvenient, just state, "I'm sorry, I'm not available then." Reiterate the clinic's cancellation policy as needed. If the clinic does not have an explicit cancellation policy, feel free to clarify your expectations about cancellation to the client. Even if the clients at your site tend to be lower functioning, some will still be able to comply with a request to call to cancel. As the client leaves, shake hands if you like or if the client extends a hand. Provide directions out of the building if you think it would be helpful.

You will need between 30 and 60 minutes to write up your note for the first session (see Chapter 12). This first note should be very detailed. The process of writing it up will help you conceptualize the client better and will clarify what you need to ask more about in subsequent sessions.

## ENDING THE SESSION WITH INTAKE CLIENTS

*Joel says to Sharon, "I think it is about time to end our session. I'd like you to go back to the waiting room and wait to see the psychiatrist who is on call before you leave today. I suspect that he would like to give you some medication that will help you with the voices. Are you willing to do that?" Sharon agrees. Joel says, "Please wait in the waiting room until Dr. Moore comes to get you, okay? Also, I am giving you an appointment with Mr. Cho for next Monday at 2 p.m. Can I count on you to come in then?" Sharon says that she will be there. Joel continues, "I'm glad you came in today. I'm really hoping that Mr. Cho will be able to help you with your problems. Good luck with everything." Joel leads Sharon to the door, opens the door, shakes hands, and says good-bye. He then walks over to the psychiatrist's office to brief her on his interview with Sharon.*

Allow at least 10 minutes to finish the session. You might not want to ask for feedback about how the intake session went since you will not be working with the client on an ongoing basis, or you might ask for more general feedback: "How are you feeling about coming in for treatment now?" Set a follow-up appointment for the client or tell her how that will be done.

Part of your job as an intake worker may be deciding on appropriate treatments and referrals, which is called *making a disposition*. Before seeing any intake clients, you and your supervisor will want to have a detailed discussion about the various treatments available and who is appropriate for each one. The first few times you see an intake client, you may need to excuse yourself from the room and discuss the case with a supervisor. The supervisor will help you decide on the appropriate referrals. You can then go in and discuss these recommendations with the client. Be open to the client's input and willing to make some adjustments as needed. Allow plenty of time to discuss the options. A client who needs a treatment that she might not have been expecting or a more intensive treatment, such as inpatient or intensive outpatient, will need more time to ask questions and decide what to do.

Sometimes a client will request a treatment that you feel is inadequate to meet his needs. You should state this explicitly. Reference the client's past: "I see that you have been in individual therapy for a year, but you are still very depressed. I would like to see you get better as soon as possible. I am not sure whether individual therapy is enough for you right now since it hasn't been helping enough so far. I would like you to consider a partial hospitalization program instead. We have a good one affiliated with our clinic. How about if I set up an appointment for you to meet some of the staff there so that you can learn more about it and make a more informed decision?" Few clients will refuse a request stated in this way. You are just encouraging them to gather more information so that they can make a better decision; you are not demanding that they make any particular choice. Once they learn more, it is likely that they will accept the recommended treatment.

## CLIENT MANAGEMENT

Some clients are very talkative and want to tell you many details about their life stories. If you see that you may run out of time, think about whether it would be better to refocus or to just let the client finish, and get more information next time. If the client is unstable, or for any other reason it is essential to get the information today, you can refocus the client: "What you've just told me is very helpful in understanding your situation. Could we spend a little time focusing on some other information that I need to get from you today?" After this point, use close-ended questions as much as possible. If you need to ask an open-ended question as a follow-up, try something like this: "Could you tell me briefly what types of sleep problems you've been having?"

Certain clients are too severely mentally ill to be able to provide full historical, social, and diagnostic information in a timely manner. In these cases, try a couple of times to refocus the client, but if this is not possible, refocus yourself. Don't expect that you can get all the information you'd like to today. If the client was brought in by a friend or family member, perhaps that person can provide some useful information. Make a careful note in the chart of the symptoms that you observe and why the client is unable to participate fully. The client can be further assessed later when able to communicate more clearly. This client may need hospitalization. However, a client could be manic, agitated, depressed, or psychotic but is still coherent and able to participate meaningfully; if so, he may be able to be treated effectively as an outpatient.

Agitation is important to note and is diagnostically relevant. However, agitated people are difficult to talk to. Go ahead and ask the client to slow down when talking to you: "I'm sorry, but you're going so fast that I'm having difficulty following you, and you've said a lot of important things that I'd like to know more about. Can I ask you to slow down?" Redirect the client to the previous topic if it is not finished. Consider asking the client to take a few deep breaths together with you. See if the client can say why he feels agitated. If the client is unable to calm down and refocus, hospitalization may be needed.

Assessing manic clients is difficult. They will have pressure of speech and can talk at length about subjects that are utterly unrelated to the tasks of the first session. They are often so excited about what they are talking about or, alternatively, so irritable that it is difficult to interrupt them. Try to refocus the client a couple of times as you would with the agitated client. If this is not effective, make a note of all the manic symptoms you observe and focus on determining whether the client needs to be hospitalized (probably so if the client is that manic). Your note in the chart might include a statement like this: "Further historical information could not be gathered today since client displayed pressure of speech and was tangential, talking about unrelated topics in response to questions."

In cases of severe major depression, some clients will be too depressed to be able to participate fully in the first session. If this is the case, hospitalization will probably be needed. Get as much information about symptoms as you can and note the depressive symptoms that you observe. Again, perhaps an accompanying friend or family member could be a source of information.

A client may have prominent psychotic symptoms. Perhaps the client is preoccupied by delusional material and is unable to refocus on other topics. Perhaps the client is so cognitively disorganized that he is unable to answer questions in a coherent fashion; his responses may be nonsensical or tangential. Or the client could be distracted by auditory or visual hallucinations; in this case, you might observe the client looking around the room. In all these cases, it is likely that the client will need hospitalization if he is so mentally ill that he cannot communicate effectively. You will just need to document enough information about the severity of symptoms to clarify why admission is needed.

Do not try to gather all the background data for a client who is too mentally ill to communicate effectively. This is a waste of time and will contribute to the client's distress. This information can be gathered later when the client can participate effectively.

## THE PSYCHOTHERAPIST'S REACTION TO THE FIRST SESSION

The first session is often draining, even for experienced psychotherapists. Of course, these initial sessions are far more stressful for a beginning psychotherapist. Often, it is difficult for beginning psychotherapists to realize that they have been helpful. Let me assure you that you have, indeed, been helpful. Talking about problems to someone who cares is a very healing and validating experience. Think about how much better you feel after talking to your friends about your problems. With training, you will grow in your ability to heal the emotional pain of others. With experience, you will gain faith and trust in the therapeutic process. With time, you will become confident that psychotherapy really can help.

### RECOMMENDED READING

Morrison, J. (2007). *The first interview* (3rd ed.). New York: Guilford Press.
*This should be the next book you read about interviewing. Morrison provides an excellent introduction to making diagnoses during the first session, which is a very challenging task for beginning psychotherapists. He adeptly addresses many of the clinical challenges that can arise during a diagnostic interview.*

## DISCUSSION QUESTIONS

1. What policies and procedures does your training site have regarding intake sessions?
2. Does the site prefer that you continue the intake session as long as needed to gather all information or to gather the most important information within a 45- to 50-minute intake session? What is the most important information?
3. What do you anticipate (or what have you found) to be the most challenging aspects of meeting a client for the first time?

## APPENDIX: INTAKE INTERVIEW TOPICS

Presenting complaint

- Why coming for help now
- Current problems, including intensity, frequency, and duration of symptoms
- Ask questions as needed if client is vague

Interpersonal and coping problems; level of distress

- Legal problems
- Relationship problems
- Parenting problems
- Interpersonal problems
- Job/school problems
- How is the client coping effectively and ineffectively?
- How are symptoms affecting functioning?

Crisis evaluation (see Chapters 17 through 21)

- Suicidal ideation or behavior
- Have you ever felt that life was not worth living?
- Have you had thoughts about suicide recently? Can you tell me exactly what you've been thinking?
  - (If yes) Do you have an idea about how you would kill yourself?
  - (If yes to this question, ask whether the means to enact the plan are available)
  - (If yes) Do you think you could actually follow through with this idea?
- Have you ever attempted suicide in the past?
- Homicidal and/or violent ideation or behavior
  - Are you having any thoughts of hurting anyone? Ask follow-up questions as needed to ascertain exactly what violent or threatening behavior, if any, has already transpired recently.
  - Have you ever been violent in the past? When? Can you tell me more about what happened?
  - Have you ever had any legal problems? If so, ask the following questions: Have you ever been arrested? Have you ever been in jail or prison? What were the charges?

Diagnose mental illnesses and screen for symptoms, especially the following (see Chapter 9):

- Anxiety symptoms
  - Generalized anxiety disorder
  - Obsessive-compulsive disorder
  - Panic disorder
  - Post-traumatic stress disorder
- Substance use or abuse
- Mood symptoms: bipolar I or II, dysthymia, or major depression
- Psychotic symptoms
- Other diagnoses and symptoms
  - Adjustment disorder
  - Attention-deficit/hyperactivity disorder

    ° Eating disorders, if common in the client population
    ° Self-harm behavior
    ° Diagnoses common to the specific population at your site
    ° Other diagnoses suggested by the client's presentation

Note that this list includes the most common diagnoses in the U.S. population (see Chapter 9) as well as those that are most associated with suicide risk (see Chapter 18).

Medical problems (see Chapter 15)

- Do you have any medical problems?
- Are you taking any medications? What is that for?
- Do you have any pain? Where is it? What is causing that? How much does it bother you? How much does the pain interfere with your activities?
- Medical history

Mental health history

- Previous psychotherapy, when last seen, for how long, and how many previous psychotherapists
- Current or past use of psychotropic medication (see Chapter 14)
- Psychiatric hospitalizations, number of hospitalizations, date of first, date of most recent, why hospitalized
- Is client under the care of a psychiatrist? If so, get client to sign a release of information so that you can coordinate care.
- Other past treatment, such as substance abuse or intensive outpatient
- Family history of mental illness and substance abuse

Cultural and identity influences

    A—age, generational
    D—developmental disabilities
    D—disabilities acquired later in life
    R—religious and spiritual orientation
    E—ethnic and racial identity, including bicultural status
    S—socioeconomic status
    S—sexual orientation
    I—indigenous heritage
    N—national origin, including refugee or immigrant status
    G—gender, including transgender status

Social history

- Family of origin, including number of siblings, and family relationships
- Any history of childhood abuse, mistreatment, or neglect

- Other adult or childhood traumas
- Education, including problems suggestive of a learning disability
- Military service, including whether client observed or participated in combat
- Criminal history and legal problems
- Leisure activities, hobbies, and active participation in organizations
- Current living situation, including everyone in the home
- Children, including where they are living
- Social network and support system
- Relationship status, including sexual orientation and marital history
- Work history, including current occupation

Observe (see Chapter 8)

- Behavior
- Verbalizations and thought processes, including coherence, memory, attention, and concentration
- Apparent verbal intelligence
- Physical characteristics
- Alertness
- Orientation
- Clothing and hygiene
- Motor activity
- Voice
- Attitude toward you
- Affect
- Mood
- Judgment
- Insight

Wrap-up

- When appropriate, give feedback about diagnoses and treatment (this Chapter and Chapter 13).
- Make referrals for health care and adjunctive treatments (Chapters 15 and 16).
- Give date and time for next appointment.

References: Choca and Van Denburg (1996); Hayes (2009); Moline, Williams, & Austin (1998); Morrison (1995, 2007); Simon (2004).

# 12

# Progress Notes and the Chart

Writing a good progress note is an essential professional skill. If you ever are accused of malpractice or need to make a deposition or your notes are subpoenaed for any reason, good progress notes will save you from professional embarrassment and worse. Be sure you have read Chapters 6 and 7 and understand issues of data security and client information; those issues will not be repeated in this chapter.

## PROGRESS NOTES AND THE STANDARD OF CARE

*Julie Chen is a mental health trainee who is working for a group practice that treats high-functioning clients. She sees a marital case that ends in divorce. After the case is closed, the husband leaves a number of threatening messages demanding that she return the fees he has paid the practice. In consultation with her supervisor and the practice's lawyer, who specializes in mental health issues, she does not return the calls or the fees. The husband files suit against the group practice for malpractice, and the case goes to trial. It turns out that Julie has not maintained any progress notes after the initial session, nor did she document the threatening phone calls. She is not certain of the dates of the sessions, either, as the practice collected some payments in cash and the records are muddled. Julie's supervisor did not review Julie's (lack of) written documentation for the case contemporaneously. In court, Julie's verbal report of her treatment of the couple is found to be up to professional standards, but her supervisor and the practice are found negligent because of Julie's lack of appropriate professional recordkeeping, and the husband was given a substantial monetary award.*

*Zachary James is a mental health trainee working in a pain clinic. He coleads many treatment groups with his supervisor and does evaluations of pain patients. He is very busy and procrastinates writing the progress notes that his supervisor has assigned to him. An internal review of documentation found that Zachary was behind on group therapy notes by 6 weeks. Both Zachary and his supervisor were written up by the review committee for providing an inadequate standard of care. When his supervisor insists that he complete the documentation, Zachary is able to deduce what psychoeducational information he presented from his files but is embarrassed to admit that he no longer remembers any personal issues that the group members brought up in the sessions 3 to 6 weeks ago.*

*Standard of care* is a legal term. According to Rodgers (2009), "It does not require best practice...rather what a typical psychiatrist [or other mental health professional] would do to render adequate care to the patient" (p. 31). If you do not adhere to an appropriate standard of care, you will be vulnerable to accusations of malpractice. Of the many implications of the concept of standard of care, one is that all psychotherapy sessions (and certain other interactions relating to the client) must be documented professionally and contemporaneously.

Progress notes should always be written on the day of interaction or on the following day. Your memory will fade if you postpone the note more than one day after the session. Even better, organize your schedule to write your progress notes immediately after each session so that you don't forget important details (Cameron & turtle-song, 2002). Remember, from a legal perspective, "if it isn't written, it didn't happen" (Gutheil, 1980).

Follow the recordkeeping standards and guidelines advocated by your professional association. As indicated in the previous vignettes, no matter what you did in the session, if you don't chart the session, you are providing an inadequate standard of care.

In group, family, or couples therapy, there is a temptation to maintain just one set of progress notes. This is wrong; each individual being treated must have her own chart and her own separate set of progress notes (Knauss, 2006). Do not name other group therapy members in the notes; instead, refer to general themes discussed.


## THE USES OF PROGRESS NOTES

Keep in mind that there are many potential audiences for your progress notes: (a) yourself because you may need to look back on what you've done; (b) other members of the treatment team; (c) emergency coverage psychotherapists; (d) reviewers, such as insurers and utilization and quality assurance reviewers; (e) the legal system; and (f) the client (Gutheil & Hilliard, 2001). If the care of your client is ever transferred to another psychotherapist, the notes will be an invaluable source of information about the client's progress.


## ELECTRONIC MEDICAL RECORDS

In many facilities, there is now an *electronic medical record* (EMR) available. If your site uses an EMR, your supervisor can educate you in how to use the EMR software and to sign the note electronically. An EMR allows for improved documentation since notes are always legible. However, with an EMR system, psychotherapy notes usually become part of the general medical record, so you should ask your supervisor whether other health care providers throughout the facility will have ready access to them.

With an EMR, you can contribute to improved continuity of care. It is wise to skim all the recent progress notes, including your own, before seeing the client.

If there are any emergent psychological or medical issues, even if brought up by someone else, the EMR can inform you and you can address them as needed with the client. With an EMR, be aware that other psychotherapists will be reading your notes and be especially mindful of the level of detail. Since other psychotherapists can easily see your notes in your setting, you might add more detail that could be helpful to them. Instead of this:

"Ms. R stated that she was having problems with her medication; I suggested that she call her psychiatrist."

You might write this:

"Ms. R stated that she was having dizziness, nausea, and headaches. She believes that this is due to her medication. I suggested that she call her psychiatrist."

The second note would be much more helpful to your psychiatrist colleague.

Occasionally, everyone will make errors when charting. If you have an EMR at your facility, it is unlikely that you will be able to change notes after they are signed. If you mistakenly put a note in the wrong chart, talk to the computer experts to see if the note can somehow be made unreadable. If you have made an error in a note, you can probably put an addendum onto your previous note with the new date and the corrected information.

## PAPER CHARTS

Make an effort to write legibly in a paper chart. On each new blank page, write or stamp the client's full name, date of birth, and any numerical identifier. When you are signing a paper note, sign with your first initial or first name, your last name, and your degrees (if any). Add your title underneath your name. If your signature is not legible, I recommend that you print your name underneath the signature. As a trainee, your supervisor should be reviewing and cosigning all your notes, so leave space for the supervisor's signature below yours. Do not include any blank lines inside the body of the note or between the end of the note and your signature.

Write with black pen only in a paper chart. Black pen makes better photocopies than other colors. Do not use felt pen, as it can smear if something is spilled on the chart, or pencil, which is legally problematic because of its ease of erasure (Cameron & turtle-song, 2002).

If you make an error in a paper chart, ensure that your corrections are not done in a way that would arouse suspicion of inappropriate alteration of the chart should the chart ever be reviewed in a court of law. Cameron and turtle-song (2002) suggest the following: "Never erase, obliterate, use correction fluid or in any way attempt to obscure the mistake. Instead, the error should be noted by enclosing it in brackets, drawing a single line through the incorrect word(s), and writing the word 'error' above or to the side of the mistake. The counselor should follow this correction with his or her initials, the full date, and time of the correction. The mistake should still be readable, indicating the counselor is only attempting to clarify the mistake not cover it up" (p. 291).


## CONTENTS OF THE CHART

There is no definitive list of information that should be included in a client's chart (Moline, Williams, & Austin, 1998). However, here is a helpful list of chart items compiled from various sources (Moline, Williams, & Austin., 1998; Rivas-Vazquez, Blais, Rey, & Rivas-Vazquez, 2001). This first list comprises documents that the psychotherapist would generate or gather from the client:

- Intake forms filled out by client (if required)
- Informed consent form, including legal limits to confidentiality (if there is no written form, the first progress note should document discussion of these issues)
- Notice of Privacy Practices form
- Mental health insurance company, policy number, and phone number
- Initial note (cosigned by supervisor) that includes the following:
  ○ Referral source and reason for referral
  ○ Identifying data, including name, phone number (work and home), date of birth and age, gender, ethnicity, physical description, marital status, occupation, school or education, children living with client (ages and names), and other persons living with client (ages, relationship to client, and names)
  ○ Background/historical data
  ○ Functioning level, adequacy of coping, social support, and strengths
  ○ Diagnosis and prognosis
- Release of information forms that you and the client generate (make a copy to send out and keep the original in the chart)
- Treatment plans
- Progress notes, cosigned by a supervisor if you are being supervised
- Termination summary.

If these items come to you from the client or other sources, they should also be included in the chart:

- Release of information forms sent from other health care professionals
- Any legal documents pertaining to the client, such as subpoenas
- Any correspondence, writings, or drawings given or sent to you by the client
- Printouts or electronic copies of any e-mails sent between you and the client containing any clinically pertinent information

- Communications sent to you by other professionals regarding the client
- Chart information that other sites sent you in response to a release of information
- Any questionnaires administered to the client
- Any other documents pertaining to the client.

A separate chart should be opened for each client being treated, even if the clients are being treated jointly in marital or family therapy. This preserves the confidentiality of each family member. Many psychotherapists use abbreviations in the chart, and many common mental health abbreviations are listed in the appendix for this chapter. However, note that some experts recommend that no abbreviations be used because of the possibility of confusion or misinterpretation (Simon, 2004).


## FORMAT

*Arun Singh is a mental health trainee practicing at an outpatient clinic. He treated a client, Kenneth Lewis, for 2 years for adjustment disorder and relationship problems. About a year after therapy is terminated, Kenneth is arrested for murdering his girlfriend, which he had done during the period of treatment with Arun. Arun's progress notes are subpoenaed, and he is required to testify at the murder trial. The defense is claiming that Kenneth is not guilty by reason of insanity. Arun was not aware of the murder at the time. He is anxious about testifying but knows that he had thoroughly documented the client's stability at each session. The fact that Kenneth was emotionally stable throughout the treatment turns out to be a crucial piece of evidence.*

This vignette illustrates the importance of documenting an assessment of the client at every psychotherapy session. For that reason, I always write progress notes in the SOAP (Cameron & turtle-song, 2002) or DAP format. The sections for this type of note are as follows:

- S/O is an abbreviation for *subjective and objective,* which are generally combined into one section, or you can use D for "data" instead:
  - Subjective is what the client says.
  - Objective is what you observe about the client; include any significant behavior.
  - These two are generally combined into one section by most psychotherapists but can be written separately.
  - This section should include any interventions that you have made and how the client responded.
  - You should also include any advice that you gave to the client and the client's response ("I advised the client not to drive after he had consumed more than two drinks, and the client stated that he understood the risks and agreed that he would call a cab on those occasions.").

- A is an abbreviation for *assessment*, which includes the following:
  - Whether the client is stable today
  - If the client has been struggling with emotional stability, a statement about whether the client is worse or better than the previous session and in what way
  - Any important emotional tone to the session
  - Any risk management evaluations you had to make in this session
- P is an abbreviation for *plan*, which includes the following:
  - Any homework you have given the client (e.g., "Mr. F agreed to keep a sleep diary over the next week.")
  - Any important steps the client states he or she will accomplish by next week (e.g., "Ms. G agreed to go to an Alcoholics Anonymous meeting tomorrow.")
  - Any referrals that you have made and how they will be accomplished (e.g., "Mr. R agrees to contact his internist to be evaluated for his chronic headaches.")
  - Anything you will be doing to manage the case between now and then (e.g., "I will fax release of information to Dr. Qadir")
  - Issues or interventions to consider for the next session (e.g., "Ms. K brought up her frustration with her best friend at the end of the session. We agreed to discuss this next week.")
  - When the client will next be seen.

This progress note format forces the psychotherapist to remember to include both the assessment and the plan when documenting each session. This crucial information is often forgotten by psychotherapists who do not use this format. As you can see from the vignette, this information can be crucial if the notes are ever involved in litigation or in any internal review.

Progress notes should be well organized and easy for other psychotherapists to skim. Put each topic (e.g., depressive symptoms, anxiety symptoms, and family history) in a separate paragraph. Use simple, clear topic sentences, even if it seems a bit repetitive: "Ms. K displayed numerous symptoms of depression."

## TONE

Progress notes should be neutral and professional in tone. Avoid any implied criticism of the client or of any other health care professional. It is most respectful to refer to adult clients in the notes by their title and last name, such as "Ms. Rodriguez," or you can abbreviate this as "Ms. R."

Never make negative comments about the client or observations about the client in the chart that could be seen as value laden or overly opinionated (Cameron & turtle-song, 2002; Gutheil, 1980). Here is an example:

- Wrong: "Ms. S. was very manipulative again today. She was making her typical suicide threats in order to get more attention from the staff on the inpatient unit."
- Right: "Ms. S. made suicidal statements on the unit today. However, on questioning, she denied any suicide plan or intent. We discussed how she might verbalize her requests for help in a more prosocial manner."

I appreciate Gutheil's (1980) suggestion that, while writing progress notes, you always imagine that there is a hostile lawyer looking over your right shoulder and imagine how the lawyer might belittle you in court. I would add to this advice that you should also imagine that the client is looking over your left shoulder, and may take offense at any tactless or careless remark you make that could lead to therapeutic disruption.

## CONTENT

*Chaniya Wilson is a psychotherapy trainee working in an outpatient clinic. The clinic is part of a large academic medical center that requires all health care professionals to post progress notes in the EMR (electronic medical record). She is seeing a client, Teresa Baker, who has borderline personality traits. Today Teresa comes to her session in a rage, brandishing a printout of her progress notes. She has marked what she deems to be inaccuracies in red ink throughout the notes.*

Progress notes document whether the psychotherapy is appropriate and effective, and they are a tool to help keep psychotherapy on track. Document the client's emotional status and symptoms. Document the issues that were addressed. Use the progress notes to remind yourself of the homework assigned to the client the past week. If you make treatment recommendations, note whether the client agreed to comply. Note any plans that you have for the next session. It is wise to establish the habit of reviewing the recent chart notes before each session, as this will help you keep track of your client's progress, any homework you gave, and the goals for the client's treatment.

Progress notes should include an appropriate amount of detail. Major topics that were discussed during the session should be noted, but the details of the discussion are generally unnecessary, unless there is a crisis. Keep in mind that malpractice attorneys say, "If it isn't written, it didn't happen" (Gutheil, 1980), so anything of clinical importance must be documented. Here are some examples:

- Too much detail: "Ms. B came in upset and said that she had another fight with her brother. He said something that she thought was insulting, then she yelled at him, then they had a shoving match again, and he called her a 'bitch on wheels.' She said that she hates him. After some discussion, she calmed down and was able to hear some input about how to talk to her brother more effectively."

- Right level of detail: "Ms. B discussed a recent interpersonal conflict with her brother. We worked on effective communication skills."

Many psychotherapists have extensive training in how to interpret the meanings of the interactions between the psychotherapist and the client. We call this *process*. The actual topics discussed are referred to as *content*. Progress notes should stick to documenting content and behavior and should avoid process (Gutheil, 1980). Do not document hypotheses, dynamic issues, suppositions, or interpretations. The vignette at the beginning of this section indicates one of the benefits of keeping your notes focused on content. Another example might clarify. Instead of writing:

"Ms. N took her shoes off and put her feet up on the couch during the session. This unusual behavior symbolizes a crucial attachment change regarding her relationship with the psychotherapist."

You might write this:

"Ms. N took her shoes off and put her feet up on the couch during the session. She had not engaged in this behavior during a session before."

As is implied by this example, it can be helpful to note any unusual behavior in the chart, even if its meaning is not totally clear. However, even if you think you know the meaning of the behavior, the meaning is usually not appropriate to write in the chart.


## SAMPLE PROGRESS NOTE FOR INTAKE SESSION

7-5-20xx
  90791
  *S/O*. Ms. Ava Reid is a 26-year-old single White female who works as a waitress at Diner Z and attends community college classes. She lives by herself in an apartment; she has no children. She is tall and thin with straight medium brown hair and has a ring through her right eyebrow.
  Ms. R reports a history of chronic depression with poor self-esteem, feelings of guilt, and chronic sadness. She reported that this has worsened within the past month. Now she has difficulty falling asleep because she is ruminating about a failed relationship. She feels tired "all of the time" and has had little appetite. She has lost about 10 pounds without trying and is now markedly thin.

Although she states that she "can't take it anymore," Ms. R has been continuing to go to work and class and has apparently been coping adequately with these responsibilities. She denied any suicidal ideation and also denied ever having suicidal ideation in the past or ever engaging in any suicidal behavior. She denied feelings of hopelessness and has no relatives who died by suicide.

Ms. R has a history of childhood sexual abuse by an older cousin and has had nightmares off and on over the years, but in the past year she has had only about one per month. She reported that she rarely thinks about the traumatic incidents and has discussed them in therapy before as needed.

Ms. R denies any symptoms of psychosis or mania now or in the past. She denies significant symptoms of anxiety. She denies any past or present violent ideation or behavior.

Ms. R said that she attends Unitarian church on a weekly basis. She has a number of friends from her church group, as well as two good friends whom she has relied on for support since she was in high school. She stated that in the past week, she has been talking about her difficulties with her friends and that this has been very helpful to her.

Ms. R stated that she drinks about two times per week when with friends. She consumes between one and three drinks each time.

Ms. R comes from an intact family. Her parents live in a nearby suburb, and she has one younger brother. She characterizes her family relationships as supportive but distant. She denied any history of violent or criminal behavior.

Ms. R has been in treatment once in the past and stopped after about 6 months. She stated that she had addressed her history of childhood sexual abuse in those sessions and had stopped because she had been feeling much better.

*A.* Ms. R is suffering from symptoms of increased depression. She is not at risk for suicide, as she has no suicidal ideation or intent, and she denies any previous history of suicidal behavior or ideation. She has social supports that she is using well and she states that her involvement with her friends and her church sustains her.

*P.* I talked with Ms. R about the importance of ongoing treatment for chronic depression. She stated that she understood. She accepted appointments next week with a psychiatrist for medication evaluation and a social worker for supportive counseling. Staff will further assess PTSD symptoms as tolerated.

/signed/     Fatimah Abdul, B.S.W.

/cosigned/   Nathaniel Wood, L.C.S.W.

In the heading, the progress note is dated and given a CPT code of 90791, indicative of an initial mental health evaluation session. *CPT* stands for *current procedural terminology* and indicates what type of health care appointment the client had. CPT codes are proprietary intellectual property of the American Medical Association and are subject to occasional revision.

In the first paragraph of the "S/O" section, the psychotherapist gives basic information about the client's demographics, appearance, and life situation so that readers are oriented to Ms. R. The psychotherapist uses indentations for each paragraph and uses topic sentences that introduce the reader to the content that will be detailed in each paragraph. You can see that the psychotherapist screened for PTSD, depression, mania, substance abuse, and psychosis. The client may need further evaluation to determine whether PTSD is also a current diagnosis, since sometimes it is difficult to determine whether a client has sufficient PTSD symptoms for a diagnosis during an intake session. The psychotherapist also briefly described the client's functioning level, which is adequate despite the severity of her depression, and assessed the client's social supports. She briefly described the client's family of origin and will probably need to gather more data on that later.

In the "A" section, the psychotherapist makes whatever conclusions she can about the client's diagnosis. She clearly documents that the client is not at risk for suicidal behavior at this time.

In the "P" section, the psychotherapist documents the follow-up plan of ongoing psychotherapy and medication management and the client's agreement with that plan. The psychotherapist clarifies that staff will need to further assess PTSD symptoms in the future as tolerated by the client. Because this is an electronic progress note, it is signed electronically.

## SAMPLE PROGRESS NOTE FOR PSYCHOTHERAPY

7-1-20xx

90834

*S/O.* Ms. Njembe came in today feeling very upset. A close friend was concerned that he might have cancer.

Discussion of this issue led to the conclusion that Ms. Njembe can be more concerned about others and not have concern about her own health problems, which include poorly controlled asthma and arthritis pain. She stated that she avoids talking about her problems with others, thinking that they cannot tolerate them and will think negatively of her.

*A.* Stable but somewhat tearful today. Indicating that she often feels very depressed and anxious under stress, tends to ignore these feelings otherwise.

*P.* Return for appointment as scheduled next week. Will continue to address self-esteem and mood issues. Ms. Njembe agreed to homework of talking to a different friend about some of her concerns. She agreed to contact the physician referrals I gave her.

/signed/     Fatimah Abdul, B.S.W.

/cosigned/   Nathaniel Wood, L.C.S.W.

This note is similarly formatted to the intake note, although the CPT code of 90834 is for a 45-minute individual psychotherapy session. Note that the session summary includes significant topics discussed but is brief. The "A" section consists of an assessment of current emotional functioning today. The "P" section documents all plans agreed to in the session. Note that the psychotherapist did not include the names of either of Ms. Njembe's friends in the progress note.

## WHAT TO DOCUMENT: FULL STORY OF ATTENDANCE AND TREATMENT

*Ahmad Hakim is a mental health trainee. He is working with a suicidal client, Rachel Nghiem. Lately, Rachel has been missing her sessions. Ahmad diligently calls her after each missed appointment and leaves her a message indicating his concern and when she could come in next. Rachel's attendance continues to be irregular. Then, after two missed sessions, Rachel dies by suicide. The institution that Ahmad works for has a formal review of the case. Ahmad had thoroughly documented his outreach efforts with Rachel before her death. Here are the notes that Ahmad wrote:*

8-5-20xx
   90834
   **S/O.** Ms. N talked at length about her troubled relationship with her son. She stated that her antidepressant medications appeared to be helping her this time. She said that she had no suicidal thoughts over the past week.
   **A.** Less depressed. Ms. N has always denied intent, and today Ms. N reports that she hasn't had any suicidal thoughts in the past week.
   **P.** Attend scheduled session next week.

            /signed/     Ahmad Hakim, M.S.
                           Psychology Practicum Student

          /cosigned/  Lydia Strong, Ph.D.
                           Licensed Clinical Psychologist

8-12-20xx
   No-show
   Ms. N did not show up for her scheduled appointment. I called her home number and left a message asking her to call me. I reminded her to come in for her next session scheduled for 8-19-xx at 2:00 p.m.

            /signed/     Ahmad Hakim, M.S.
                           Psychology Practicum Student

          /cosigned/  Lydia Strong, Ph.D.
                           Licensed Clinical Psychologist

8-19-20xx
No-show
Ms N. again did not attend her scheduled appointment. I called her home
number and her cell phone number and left messages expressing my concern
and asking her to call me as soon as possible. I reminded her to attend her
next session scheduled for 8-25-xx at 2:00 p.m.

/signed/      Ahmad Hakim, M.S.
              Psychology Practicum Student

/cosigned/    Lydia Strong, Ph.D.
              Licensed Clinical Psychologist

The management of the case was found to be appropriate by Ahmad's supervisors
and peer reviewers. Later, this documentation in the chart deterred Rachel's relatives from filing a lawsuit for wrongful death against the institution.

Your notes should tell the full story of the client's treatment and attendance, as
Ahmad's did in the previous example (Cameron & turtle-song, 2002). You can
see from the notes that Ahmad was aware of Rachel's difficulties with suicidal
thoughts and had been monitoring them regularly. He appropriately documented
his outreach efforts to this client, whom he knew had some suicide risk because
she often had suicidal thoughts, although she always had denied intent.

Beginning psychotherapists are often uncertain what interactions and clinical
activities should be documented as progress notes. I have provided a partial list here:

- Psychotherapy sessions
- Cancellations by client (briefly note why, if known)
- Cancellations by psychotherapist
- No-shows
- Outreach phone calls following missed sessions
- Any phone call with significant clinical content
- Some treatment team meetings
- Some consultations between professionals
- Any clinically significant e-mails from the client (print out the e-mail
  and put it in a paper chart or copy and paste it into an electronic chart).

An example of a phone call or e-mail that may not need to be documented is a client asking a routine question, such as the time of the next appointment. An example of a phone call or e-mail that *should* be documented is a contact from a client
who missed two sessions, states that she has been depressed, and agrees to come in
later in the week. Check with your supervisor if you are unsure. It is possible that
your supervisor will want you to document every e-mail, whatever the content.

Clinically relevant phone calls are difficult to remember to document. However,
we cannot predict in advance which phone call might be the one that it is crucial
to document.

Occasionally, there may be other interactions of significance that should be documented that I have not included here. For example, under certain circumstances, a psychotherapist at a Veterans Affairs medical center might attend a benefits hearing for one of her clients. The psychotherapist would then document that this meeting had been attended and why. Your supervisor can help you figure out which infrequent activities or contacts need documenting.

## WHAT TO DOCUMENT: CLINICAL MANAGEMENT OF TREATMENT-INTERFERING BEHAVIORS

4-23-20xx
90834
*S/O.* Mr. U attended his appointment for the first time in a month. We reviewed our initial goals for him to attend weekly psychotherapy sessions. Mr. U stated that he was having financial and child care problems that were interfering with his ability to attend. We brainstormed about getting some help from his mother. After some discussion, he agreed to ask his mother to babysit every week during his scheduled appointment time. He also said that he knew she would contribute to his transportation costs if he asked her to do so. He verbalized his intent to attend on a weekly basis from now on.

*A.* Mr. U was open to discussing his attendance problems. Stable.

*P.* Attend scheduled appointment next week. Mr. U agreed to discuss child care and transportation with his mother before then.

/signed/     Ahmad Hakim, M.S.
               Psychology Practicum Student

/cosigned/    Lydia Strong, Ph.D.
               Licensed Clinical Psychologist

6-19-20xx
90834
*S/O.* Ms. Q and I discussed her difficulties taking her psychotropic medications regularly. I educated her again about how regularly taking her medication will help prevent future manic and depressive episodes and will help keep her out of the hospital. We reviewed several strategies for medication adherence. After a discussion, she agreed to keep them with her toothbrush and take them every morning before she brushed her teeth.

*A.* Stable.

*P.* Ms. Q's next appointment is scheduled in 2 weeks. We agreed to check in on her progress with taking her medications regularly then.

/signed/     Arun Singh, M.A.
               Psychology Intern

/cosigned/    Lydia Strong, Ph.D.
              Licensed Clinical Psychologist

Be sure to address *treatment-interfering behaviors* during the psychotherapy session and in the chart. These behaviors could include lack of attendance and lack of adherence to treatment recommendations. You can't effectively treat a client who doesn't attend appointments, isn't an active partner in treatment, or doesn't take needed medications and is therefore at significant risk of rehospitalization. In these situations, demonstrate in the progress notes that you are making an effort to address these issues so that you can provide an effective treatment. In the previous progress notes, the trainees have helped the clients with problem-solving and have documented their efforts.

## WHAT TO DOCUMENT: SAFETY AND RISK ISSUES

*Christina Jones is a mental health trainee in a community mental health center. Her new client has intense suicidal ideation and is on many psychotropic medications. Some of the medications have a risk of overdose. The treatment team discusses the case and agrees to give medications out on a weekly basis until the client is more stable. Christina documents this discussion in a separate note in the client's chart:*

6-25-20xx
    Treatment Team Meeting
    Present at today's treatment team meeting were Dr. Gilford, Dr. Victor, Ms. Thomas, and myself. We discussed the client's risk of overdose as well as her need for medications. The team agreed that medications are warranted because of the likelihood that they will help her depression and reduce the risk of suicide in the long term. To reduce short-term risk, Dr. Gilford agreed to prescribe a less toxic medication whenever possible and give medications out on a weekly basis. I will reinforce the suicide prevention plan with the client again at our next meeting.

/signed/      Christina Jones, M.D.
              Psychiatry Resident

/cosigned/    Laura Gilford, M.D.
              Psychiatrist

Most settings have ways of documenting routine treatment team meetings that mental health trainees do not need to worry about. However, if a psychotherapist's client is exhibiting risky behavior and the team discusses the case and comes to an agreement about it, then the team's assessment and treatment plan additions should be documented, as in the case of Christina's client.

Progress notes concerning a crisis situation should be written as soon as possible and definitely should be completed before you leave to go home for the day. Stay late if you have to. See Chapters 17 to 21 for further information on documenting crises.

## WHAT TO DOCUMENT: CLIENT'S HOSTILE OR THREATENING BEHAVIOR

*Fatimah Abdul, a mental health trainee, is treating a client who has schizophrenia. The client expresses anger and violent ideation toward Muslims. Fatimah is Muslim herself and wears a head scarf. While the client never makes any negative comments about her specifically, she feels threatened by his remarks. She wisely discusses her concerns with her supervisor. After this consultation, she carefully documents all the inappropriate comments that the client made in the last session. She also goes back and makes an addendum to several previous notes on occasions where she remembers his angry remarks but had not documented them. Fatimah and her supervisor do a careful risk assessment of the client. After determining that he has no known history of violent behavior and consulting with the psychiatrist about adjusting his medication to reduce paranoid ideation (which had been increasing in other settings as well), Fatimah decided to continue to see the client for now. However, she and her supervisor decide that, when he is more stable, they will give the client feedback about his inappropriate remarks.*

*Fatimah is interviewing a different client in the emergency room. The client stands up and begins to yell at her. Fatimah gently asks the client to calm down and asks him to lie back down on the gurney. The client complies with these requests. She carefully documents the behavior in his chart.*

If you feel threatened by a client or if the client's behavior or statements are hostile, you should document carefully and thoroughly, as Fatimah has done. This behavior is highly clinically relevant and may be crucial information in evaluating risk factors and stability of the client in the future.

## WHAT TO DOCUMENT: CLIENT'S SEXUAL STATEMENTS OR BEHAVIOR

*Jared Russell is a mental health trainee treating a female client with borderline personality disorder. At one point in a session, the client stands up and asks, "Should I take off my blouse?" Of course, Jared tells her not to. At the end of the session, he carefully documents in her chart exactly what she had said and his response to her. He discusses this issue very carefully with a supervisor and documents the discussion in the chart. During the next session, he carefully explores the client's inappropriate behavior from last time. He emphasizes to her the professional nature and professional boundaries of their relationship. Again, he carefully documents this discussion in the chart.*

There is one important exception to the rule to avoid documenting process: document statements or behavior that suggests that the client has sexual feelings toward you. On rare occasions, clients may make blatant or subtle inappropriate sexual remarks toward you. This behavior should be documented as well as what you say in response to the client. This documentation must be contemporaneous in case there is ever any question about whether your response was appropriate in the future. Jared also documents the steps he takes to address the client's behavior in supervision and in the next session.

## WHAT TO DOCUMENT: YOUR INTERVENTIONS AND RECOMMENDATIONS

1-6-20xx
90834
*S/O.* Ms. G admitted to cutting her arm with a razor, leaving superficial scratches on her arm, when she was home alone with her 2-month-old baby. I asked her to show me the scratches, which were indeed superficial. She was able to identify a feeling of loneliness and emptiness that triggered the behavior. I suggested that we review some alternative behaviors. However, she refused, stating that this has worked well for her for years and that she had no intentions of changing. After some discussion, she was willing to acknowledge that this behavior could be scary to her baby when the baby was older.

*A.* There is no evidence that the baby is in any danger, despite Ms. G's cutting; in fact, she verbalizes her desire to take good care of the baby frequently. Ms. G denied any suicidal ideation or intent during today's session. She continues to appear depressed, however.

*P.* We agreed to further discuss the issue next week. Will discuss the issue with the treatment team.

/signed/     Christina Jones, M.D.
             Psychiatry Resident

/cosigned/   Laura Gilford, M.D.
             Psychiatrist

1-13-20xx
90834
*S/O.* I asked Ms. G about cutting again. She admitted to cutting herself again with a razor and showed me superficial scratches on her arm. She was able to identify feelings of loneliness and emptiness that triggered the behavior. She verbalized her desire to stop engaging in cutting, stating, "It's such a bad influence on my daughter." We discussed some alternative behaviors

that she could engage in when feeling lonely and empty. These included calling a friend, praying, writing in her journal, and refocusing her attention on her baby. She agreed to attempt these changes and follow up on her progress next week.

*A.* While Ms. G's cutting is of concern, at this point, the scratches she has made on her arm are superficial, and she denies making any other scratches in other areas of her body. She verbalizes her intent to address the behavior. She denied any suicidal ideation or intent over the last week.

*P.* Attend scheduled appointment next week. Ms. G agreed to try some alternative behaviors and discuss how that went. She agreed that if she does cut, she will pay attention to her thoughts and feelings at that time so that we can discuss them further.

|  |  |
|---|---|
| /signed/ | Christina Jones, M.D. Psychiatry Resident |
| /cosigned/ | Laura Gilford, M.D. Psychiatrist |

While writing a progress note, many psychotherapists do not document any of the remarks or suggestions that they have made to the client during the session. This is a mistake. You will often make important interventions and therapeutic recommendations, and these should be documented. In the two previous notes, Christina documented the attempts that she made to help the client substitute more effective coping strategies for cutting. As Christina does, document when the client agrees with your recommendations and when the client doesn't. If the client refuses, document how you plan to deal with the refusal (e.g., in the first session, Christina gets the client to agree to discuss the issue again next week). Note that Christina also carefully assessed the safety of Ms. G and her baby as needed.

## WHAT NOT TO DOCUMENT

Some things should not be documented in the chart. You should avoid including the names of the client's friends or significant others in the chart. If a client is criticizing another psychotherapist at the facility where you work, this information should not be included in the chart (Cameron & turtle-song, 2002). Here is an example:

- Wrong: "Mr. R. said that his psychiatrist is 'a mean bitch who's out to get me.'"
- Right: "Mr. R. and I discussed how he can communicate more effectively with his psychiatrist."

If the client uses curse words, it is unprofessional to use them in the chart. If you feel it would be illustrative to quote a phrase of the client's when she uses a curse word, "bleep" it out:

- Right: When I asked Ms K. whether she had taken the medication prescribed by her psychiatrist, she stated, "F—— that s——!"

Finally, do not include information that could be seen as slander toward others in the chart; this could expose you to legal liability (Simon, 2004):

- Wrong: "Mr. J. talked about his suspicions that his coworker Joe Sinclair is stealing from the cash register at work. He thinks it may be blamed on him instead."
- Right: "Mr. J. talked about his worries regarding allegations that someone had been stealing on the job."

## WHEN THERE IS PRIOR MENTAL HEALTH DOCUMENTATION

A client who is new to you may not be new to your training site. My recommendation is that you review the entire chart of the client before seeing the client for the first time. If there is significant information in the chart, you will want to indicate in a progress note that you are aware of this. For example, a new client might have a history of inpatient hospitalization following a suicide attempt at the facility. You will want to indicate your own awareness of this important historical information in your first note. For example, "The client indicated that he had been previously hospitalized at this facility for acute depression. His report of this incident was consistent with the chart documentation." If there is extensive documentation, you might want to write a new note summarizing the important historical points so you have that information handy, and so that it is clear you are familiar with the past documentation.

Alternatively, this client may be new to both you and the site but may have a prior mental health history at other facilities or with other practitioners. In these circumstances, it is incumbent on you to be aware of the content of the previous mental health treatment notes. Get a release from the client during the first session and send a copy of this release to the previous practitioner or facility. Document in the chart that you sent the release. Ignorance of old documentation, even if at another site, is no excuse if you are sued for risk issues (Baerger, 2001).

Unfortunately, some facilities are negligent about responding to requests for information. Give the facility 2 to 3 weeks to respond. Then if you haven't gotten anything, document that in the chart, send another copy of the release, and document that you have done so. Again, if you don't get anything, document that the facility has not responded. Talk to your supervisor, and possibly also the site's legal counsel, for further advice at this point.

## WHEN YOUR CLIENT WANTS TO READ
## THE PROGRESS NOTES

Your client may want to read the progress notes you have been writing. Generally, state law and professional association guidelines indicate that the client has a right to read the progress notes (Moline et al., 1998), so agree to let the client read the notes. Before you show the notes to the client, it would be wise to explore in therapy why the client wants to look at the notes. Then suggest that the client read the notes *during* or *immediately before* the next scheduled session. Indicate that you recommend this so that you are immediately available to answer any questions as they come up.

Often, clients have unrealistic expectations about their progress notes. After agreeing to let the client look at the notes and providing a structure to do so, this is a good time to explore what the client's worries, ideas, and fantasies are regarding the progress notes. The client may expect that you have written sparkling and brilliant insights. However, if you limit yourself to content rather than process, this will not be the case. Most clients will actually find the progress notes quite boring. Consider warning them ahead of time, "I'm happy to show you the notes, but I have to tell you it will probably be a bunch of facts that you already know." Document that the client has reviewed the notes in the chart, along with any significant statements or emotional responses.

Sometimes the client requests changes in the chart after reading it. In most cases, you must gently refuse to make changes to the chart (Gutheil & Hilliard, 2001). The chart is a contemporaneous record of what happened in therapy. However, if you think that the client has a valid point about inaccuracies in the chart, you may agree to make an addendum, dated today, to a previous note.

## HOW TO DOCUMENT SENSITIVE ISSUES

*Jared Russell, a mental health trainee, is meeting with a long-term client who has PTSD. The client has not been talking to anyone on the treatment team about his traumatic experiences. During this session, the client tells Jared about being sexually abused by his uncle. Then the client asks Jared not to document anything that he has just said in the chart. Jared explains to the client that other psychotherapists need to know that the client has a history of trauma because they will want to provide a treatment that meets the client's needs. Jared also explains that it is unnecessary for him to include all the details in his note. He tells the client what he is likely to write: "Mr. R reported that his uncle would fondle him on occasions when his parents were not at home. He cannot remember the frequency of these abusive episodes but stated that they were too frequent to count between the ages of 6 and 10." The client says that this is okay.*

*Christina Jones, a mental health trainee, is meeting with a new client. The client reveals that her husband drinks to excess and hits her when he is very drunk. She also stated that she is afraid that the husband might some day hit her children, although she states*

*that he hasn't yet. The client then asks Christina not to document any of this informa-*
*tion in the chart. Christina says, "I know that you are bringing this up because you are*
*concerned about it. I am concerned as well. Since this issue concerns safety, I am ethi-*
*cally bound to document it. The other people who are working with you need to know*
*about this so that they can help you, too. However, I will be happy to make it clear in the*
*note that I know you are bringing it up because you are concerned about the issue and*
*you are seeking help to work on it. How does that sound?"*

Sometimes clients will ask that you not document certain things they tell you in
their charts. In some situations, the client may be aware that there is just one chart
at the facility that is shared by all the health care practitioners.

Before responding, think about the client's situation carefully. Ask yourself
these questions: Is this information a critical piece of historical information
that other psychotherapists should know? Is this information related to suicide risk, violence risk, or other potentially risky situations? Is there any other
strong reason for this information to be documented? In the first vignette,
Jared feels that the information must be documented, but he is sensitive to the
client's concerns and reassures the client that his note will be brief. In the other
vignette, the client told Christina information that is related to important risk
and safety issues. Do not skip charting a safety issue, even if the client requests
that you do so.

Often clients will tell us about upsetting experiences from the past, such as
childhood abuse, rape, other traumas, or atrocities committed in the military.
When they are ready to address these difficult issues, they may tell us considerable
detail about the episodes of trauma. Unless there is a pressing reason to do so, it is
not wise or necessary to include details. Nonetheless, it is often clinically relevant
to document that the client did experience this particular trauma. In addition,
certain aspects of the trauma might be of clinical relevance, such as the age at
which it occurred, how long, and so on. An example might clarify this. Instead
of writing:

"Mr. O stated that when the Vietnamese women did not cry enough while
being raped, [additional explicit details about Vietnam wartime atrocities]."

You might write:

"Mr. O talked about his experiences seeing Vietnam War atrocities on multiple occasions between ages 19 and 21."

At other times, the issue at hand is embarrassing to the client but has no major
bearing on any risk issues or other aspects of the treatment. In those cases, it is
fine to either record the issue in vague generalizations (Gutheil & Hilliard, 2001)
or, if it is more embarrassing than clinically relevant, to even skip documenting
the issue.

## HOW TO RELEASE RECORDS

In most circumstances, you must have a valid signed release of information to release chart materials. Then check with your supervisor before you release any records. Do not release more than is asked for. If you have some concerns about how the release of these records might affect the client, discuss this with the client before records are released. The client has the right to revoke the release at any time.

In general, you should not pass on any information that you have obtained from other facilities or practitioners; they should be contacted directly for their chart material on the client. In certain instances, you can refuse to provide records if you consider this detrimental to the client (Moline, Williams, & Austin, 1998); however, if you have followed the guidelines for writing progress notes provided in this chapter, you are unlikely to be faced with this possibility.

On rare occasions, information can be released without a written release from the client. These situations were discussed in Chapter 7.

## ENSURE SECURITY OF CLIENT INFORMATION

As the investigation into the stolen Department of Veterans Affairs (VA) data continues, the full extent and ramification of the theft has grown. It was learned last month that, aside from the information of approximately 26 million veterans contained on the laptop and external hard drive stolen from a VA employee's home, the personal information of 2.2 million military personnel was included, as well. And, while law enforcement agencies have stated that the theft was a simple burglary and that the computer equipment was likely erased and resold before its contents were ever made public, government overseers say that such a theft could easily happen again. (Spotswood, 2006)

The security of client information must be guarded at all times. Do not take written or electronic charts or progress notes home; they must remain on site at all times. The true incident in the previous quote regarding Veterans Affairs and Department of Defense records illustrates why. You cannot vouch for the security of records off-site. The only client-related material that is appropriate to take off-site would be client phone numbers paired with their initials or first names—if you anticipate an immediate possible need to cancel upcoming appointments—and written case conceptualizations for a class—that do not include or disguise identifying information. If you want to take anything else off-site that regards any clients, consult with your supervisor first.

## ENSURE APPROPRIATE DISPOSAL OF CLIENT INFORMATION

Drugstores are not supposed to put your personal health information into open dumpsters. But 13 Investigates [Indianapolis television station WTHR] has shown it happening at pharmacy after pharmacy as drug stores all across Indianapolis failed our recent test. Store workers admit if even one patient record gets into the trash, that's one too many. But what we discovered in just one trash bag this week surprised even us. It didn't contain just one patient record—it had 732 of them. That's right—732 patient records on labels, receipts, prescriptions, order forms and pill bottles, all in one garbage bag behind one pharmacy. (Segall, 2006)

Occasionally, we have client information that needs to be disposed of. Here are some examples:

- Fax cover sheet with name of patient, accompanying release, or other document
- Extra copies of chart notes (perhaps printed out from electronic chart to fax in response to a release of information)
- Written phone message to call client
- Brief jotted notes as a reminder of what to document, which are now unnecessary since you completed the progress note

This information must be shredded. Do not ever throw it in a trash bin unshredded. You might put the privacy and safety of your clients at risk. The investigation into pharmacy privacy that was cited previously began when the station found out that thieves had masqueraded as pharmacy employees to get an elderly woman's OxyContin (Tucker, 2006). The thieves had found her prescription information in the pharmacy trash bin.

## HIPAA AND PSYCHOTHERAPY NOTES

Throughout this chapter, I have been discussing how mental heath charting is traditionally done. However, there is another option described by the HIPAA Privacy Rule. It is possible to keep minimal notes in the clinical record and also keep more extensive notes (called *psychotherapy notes* by HIPAA) that contain more detailed and personal information in a separate location.

The HIPAA Privacy Rule allows these psychotherapy notes to have special privacy protections when they are kept separate from the rest of the clinical record. *Psychotherapy notes* are defined as follows: "notes recorded (in any medium) by a health care practitioner, who is a mental health professional documenting or analyzing the contents of conversation during a private counseling session or a group, joint, or family counseling session and that are separated from the rest of the individual's medical record." *Psychotherapy notes* exclude "medication prescription and monitoring, counseling sessions start and stop times, the modalities and frequencies of treatment furnished, results of clinical tests and any summary of the following items: diagnosis, functional status, the treatment plan, symptoms, prognosis and progress to date," so this information would be in the general medical record (American Psychological Association Practice Organization, 2007, p. 8).

As Brendel and Bryan (2004) indicate, what HIPAA refers to as psychotherapy notes are essentially what most psychotherapists would call *process notes*. As you've noticed, I have been advising you throughout this chapter *not* to document process issues in the chart anyway. When you reread the progress note before a session, the content will remind you of the process issues sufficiently so that you do not need process notes. I recommend that you try to do without them, unless your supervisor wants you to keep process notes as a teaching tool.

Apparently, the main point of this aspect of the HIPAA Privacy Rule was to bar insurance companies from having access to process notes on clients if we keep them separately from the rest of the chart. Ask your supervisor whether these kinds of notes can be kept separately from the rest of the clinical record at your facility. If there are no policies and procedures for doing this, psychotherapy or process notes cannot be used.

There are valid clinical reasons why you would not want to separate your progress notes into these two categories (as allowed by HIPAA) and instead keep just content notes in the one and only clinical record, as I have advised in this chapter. First, the psychotherapy notes can be subpoenaed (Brendel & Bryan, 2004), and most psychotherapists would not like to have their notes on the therapeutic process scrutinized in court; if these notes do not exist, they cannot be subpoenaed. Second, the specific conditions under which they can be disclosed are complex and vary by state (Maio, 2003); in addition, even though you can refuse to give the client access to the psychotherapy notes, the client can authorize access to these notes to anyone, even a friend (Vanderpool, 2008). Third, given the collaborative nature of much mental health treatment, it is often clinically useful to have important psychotherapy information available to other mental health practitioners at the same facility; critical information could be lost by keeping separate process notes. Fourth, the facility may have an EMR system that does not allow two separate sets of notes. Finally, important issues such as risk management must be thoroughly documented in the clinical record anyway.

## TREATMENT PLANS

Mental health professionals in medical centers and clinics and those working with certain managed care organizations are required to produce written treatment plans. Interestingly, physicians in other health specialty areas rarely have to produce any treatment plans (V. Nee, personal communication, February 23, 2007).

The format of treatment plans varies according to the requirements of your training site (Zuckerman, 2003). However, in general, treatment plans typically include the following:

- International Classification of Diseases (ICD) diagnosis, although sometimes the Diagnostic and Statistical Manual of Mental Disorders is used instead
- Behavioral description of symptoms and/or behaviors that are targets of treatment

- *Objectives*, meaning shorter-term goals, again described as behaviorally as possible
- *Goals*, meaning longer-term goals
- Target dates or number of sessions for accomplishment of objectives and goals
- Interventions and treatments that will be employed
- Who is responsible for implementing each intervention/treatment
- Referrals made and adjunctive treatments employed.

Your supervisor can show you some examples of treatment plans made according to the format and requirements of your site.

### Recommended Reading

Cameron, S., & turtle-song, i. (2002). Learning to write case notes using the SOAP format. *Journal of Counseling and Development, 80,* 286–292.
*A short and helpful article about how to write appropriate progress notes.*
Guthiel, T. G. (1980). Paranoia and progress notes: A guide to forensically informed psychiatric record-keeping. *Hospital and Community Psychiatry, 31,* 479–482.
*Despite its age, this classic article provides timeless, wise, and succinct advice about writing progress notes.*
Moline, M. E., Williams, G. T., & Austin, K. M. (1998). *Documenting psychotherapy: Essentials for mental health practitioners.* Thousand Oaks, CA: Sage.
*The authors provide a thorough discussion of documentation issues, including why good documentation is essential, what belongs in a clinical record, documenting crises, and other topics.*

## EXERCISES AND DISCUSSION QUESTIONS

1. Your client reveals that she has been taking money and drugs for sex, then asks you not to document this in her chart. Would you document it? Why or why not? What would you tell the client?
2. Your client states about his wife, "I could just kill her sometimes, I'm so angry." The client then asks you not to document this in the chart: "My psychiatrist will think I'm crazy if you write that in there." Your client has denied any history of violent behavior, and you think he wasn't literally that angry—he was just being dramatic. Would you document it? Why or why not? What would you tell the client?

## APPENDIX: COMMON ABBREVIATIONS IN MENTAL HEALTH PROGRESS NOTES

This list concentrates on common mental health abbreviations. Your training site may have a list of approved abbreviations; if so, be sure to get a copy and don't use any abbreviations that are not on the list. In addition, some sites do not allow any abbreviations in charts. Ask your supervisor about the policy at your training site. When you see medical abbreviations, you can conduct an Internet search to help you interpret the client's chart. Be cautious when interpreting medical abbreviations and ask your supervisor for help as needed. There is no standardized list, and, as you can see, some abbreviations may mean one thing in one context and another in another context.

## Medication Dosing Abbreviations

b.i.d.: twice daily
h.s.: at nighttime
prn: as needed
q.d.: every day
q.h.s.: at nighttime
q.i.d.: four times daily
t.i.d.: three times daily

## Other Common Mental Health Abbreviations

A: assessment—generally a section title for a progress note
AA or A/A: African American
A&O: alert and oriented
ADHD: attention-deficit/hyperactivity disorder
ADL: activities of daily living, such as dressing self, feeding self, grooming self, and so on
AMA: against medical advice, such as "patient was discharged AMA"
bf: boyfriend
BP: bipolar, or, more commonly, blood pressure
BPD: borderline personality disorder
CO or c/o: complains of, meaning verbalizes symptoms, such as "patient c/o frequent auditory hallucinations"
D: data, a substitute for S/O—generally a section title for a progress note
d/c: discharge or discontinue, depending on context
DD: developmental disorder
DOB: date of birth
dx: diagnosis
ETOH: short for ethanol or alcohol
F: commonly female, but also father, depending on context
GAD: generalized anxiety disorder
gf: girlfriend
H: husband
HA: headache
H&P: history and physical, a type of standardized medical screening exam

HI or H/I: homicidal ideation

HO or H/O: history of

hx: history

L: left

M: commonly male, but also mother, depending on context

MD: could be major depression or manic depression, depending on context (because of this, it is best not to use this one yourself)

MDD: major depressive disorder

mj: marijuana

NKA: no known allergies

NKDA: no known drug allergies

OCD: obsessive-compulsive disorder

O: objective—generally a section title for a progress note

OD or O/D: overdose

OX3: oriented times three; in other words, client knows own name, where client is, and what the date is

P: plan—generally a section title for a progress note

PA: generally panic attack, also could be physical abuse, depending on context

PMH: previous medical history

pt: patient

PTSD: post-traumatic stress disorder

R: right

R/O: rule out, such as "R/O PTSD," meaning that the psychotherapist should continue to consider whether the diagnosis of post-traumatic stress disorder applies to this individual

ROI: release of information

RTC: return to clinic (generally followed by a date), specifies the time of the next appointment

Rx: medication

S: subjective—generally a section title for a progress note

SA: substance abuse or sexual abuse, depending on context (another one you should not use because of ambiguity)

SAD: seasonal affective disorder, otherwise known as major depression with seasonal pattern

SI or S/I: suicidal ideation

S/O: subjective/objective—generally a section title for a progress note

Sx: symptoms

tx: treatment

UTS: urine toxicology screen, administered to detect illegal drugs (but not alcohol)

VI or V/I: violent ideation

W: wife or White, depending on context

x: times

yo: years-old

# 13

# Starting Psychotherapy and Stabilizing the Client

Beginning psychotherapists often work in settings, such as community mental health, where the clients are very complex. The sheer number of problems and diagnoses for just one client can be overwhelming. Much of the literature on how to do psychotherapy starts with the assumption that the client is stable—which is not the case with many, sometimes even most, clients in community settings.

This chapter provides you with a framework to help the client gain emotional stability. Instead of teaching you to *do* psychotherapy, which encompasses many hundreds of books, my goal is to help you think about *how to prioritize and structure* the early sessions. Be aware that for many of your clients in community settings, work on stabilization takes months or years, so try not to be too discouraged by this reality. With these clients, you can help them enormously, without ever doing anything that is considered traditional psychotherapy.

## HIERARCHY OF TREATMENT ISSUES

This hierarchy of psychotherapy issues (informed by Courtois, 1997, and Linehan, 1993) will help you decide where to start with complex clients. Start at the top of the hierarchy and work your way down. Within each step, use your judgment about where to start with that particular client. In general, avoid addressing lower-ranked issues until the higher-ranked issues are resolved or have already been addressed sufficiently earlier in the session. Italicized topics are addressed in this chapter:

- Step 1: Ensure client is alive, not dangerous, present at the session, and connected to the therapist.
  - Address risk of harm to self or others, such as suicidal ideation, violent ideation, and physical abuse of significant others (Chapters 17 through 21).
  - Ensure regular attendance (Chapter 3).
  - *Foster the therapeutic alliance.*

- Step 2: Strengthen, stabilize, reduce distress, reduce high-risk dysfunctional behavior, and agree on treatment.
  - *Build on client strengths.*
  - *Agree on goals for therapy.*
  - *Psychoeducation* about diagnosis and course of treatment
  - Referrals for psychotropic medication and other treatments (Chapters 14 and 16)
  - Referrals to stabilize client's situation, such as health-related referrals (Chapter 15), housing, income, legal, treatment for family members, and so on
  - Treat and/or refer for substance abuse or dependence (Chapter 16).
  - Reduce self-harm (Chapter 19).
  - *Reduce high-risk dysfunctional behavior.*
- Step 3: Skill-building, such as:
  - *Normalize activity level and socialization.*
  - *Improve sleep.*
  - *Relaxation training, meditation, or biofeedback*
  - *Encourage client-initiated activities, such as self-education, self-help, exercise.*
  - Other skills can be useful as well, such as assertiveness and other communication skills.
- Step 4: What we'd usually consider psychotherapy, first focused on other present-day difficulties, then focused on past issues as needed.

## FOSTER THE THERAPEUTIC ALLIANCE

The *therapeutic alliance* refers to the quality of the relationship between the psychotherapist and client, including agreement on the goals and tasks of psychotherapy (Crits-Christoph, Gibbons, & Hearon, 2006). Multiple studies have confirmed that better therapeutic alliances lead to more improvement in therapy (Crits-Christoph et al., 2006; Fluckiger, Del Re, Wampold, Symonds, & Horvath, 2012). How can you foster a good therapeutic alliance? Clearly, active listening skills are essential. Personal characteristics such as warmth and genuineness clearly contribute to the therapeutic alliance (Bachelor, 1995). Even though the scientific literature does not have definitive answers, some experts do provide us with useful advice.

Sue and Zane (1987) talk about *giving*, which is using interventions early in therapy that help the client achieve significant gains. They suggest that this can be especially helpful with cultural groups that may be skeptical toward Western psychotherapy, but all clients will benefit from your efforts to stabilize them and alleviate distress early in therapy. This will build your credibility as a psychotherapist, demonstrate your concern and attention to the client's distress, and help foster the therapeutic alliance. The interventions in this chapter help with early symptom relief.

J. S. Beck (2005) talks about the importance of a therapeutic attitude of hopeful-ness: "Patients generally respond positively when their psychotherapist maintains a consistently upbeat attitude about the probability that therapy will help" (p. 66). However, she points out that this must be done in the context of a relationship in which the client feels understood so that the client does not feel that you are being unrealistic. Often, you can integrate your psychoeducation of the client (later in this chapter) with verbalizing your expectation that the client has an excellent chance of improvement.

It is okay and, in fact, quite therapeutic to be soothing to your client (Gabbard & Westen, 2003). Being soothing can simply mean that you are accepting of the client. You can soothe by maintaining a calm attitude in the face of the client's emotional storms. You can also be soothing by your attitude, interventions, and problem-solving that show that the client's distress can be alleviated. Psychodynamic the-ory suggests that the client will start to internalize some of your reactions toward him (e.g., being accepting of self) in substitution for those the client already has (e.g., being hypercritical of self).

## WHEN YOU NEED TO SET THE AGENDA
## FOR PSYCHOTHERAPY

*Amelia Peterson is a 35-year-old woman in individual therapy. Amelia has a history of multiple suicide attempts and chronic suicidal ideation. Her diagnoses are borderline personality disorder, panic disorder, recurrent major depression, and post-traumatic stress disorder (PTSD). Currently, Amelia is living with a new boyfriend who is ver-bally abusive. When the boyfriend is abusive, Amelia's suicidal thoughts return, and she scratches herself with a razor blade. Amelia's psychotherapist has left the agency, and she is assigned to a new psychotherapy trainee, Daniel Cox. Daniel has reviewed the chart carefully, and he is aware of her risk factors. During the first session, Daniel assesses Amelia's current level of symptoms. Amelia has denied suicidal intent for about 6 months, but she has contemplated suicide plans on at least a weekly basis during that time. She usually scratches herself at least twice a month. Her depressive and panic symptoms are not well controlled by her medications, so Daniel consults with the psy-chiatrist, Dr. Torres, between sessions. At the beginning of the second session, after ask-ing Amelia how she has been doing, Daniel states, "Amelia, I'm very concerned about how you have been doing, and I'd like us to do everything we can to help you feel better. I'm especially concerned about your suicidal thoughts since I can't help you with your other issues if you're not alive. Can we start our therapy by focusing on these thoughts? I want to know when you are most likely to be thinking suicidal thoughts, what feelings you are having then, and so on."*

There are specific situations when you must set the agenda for the psychotherapy session. If you have a client who is unstable, low functioning, and/or high risk, these are situations in which you must set the therapy agenda. When there are immediate threats, such as suicidal ideation, intent to hurt others, or child abuse, you are ethically and legally required to take action to prevent harm to the client and others. In these cases, you must take the initiative.

Ensure that you have checked in with the client at the beginning of the session to see how she is doing this week. If there is a crisis, this may need to be addressed first. In conclusion, with less-stable clients, you will need to take the lead in stabilizing the client and referring to appropriate adjunctive treatments. In the above vignette, Daniel sets the agenda to discuss chronic suicidal thoughts, since the client has chronic risk for suicidal behavior (see Chapters 18 and 19).

## BUILD ON CLIENT STRENGTHS

*Client: I can't find a job and I'm going to be thrown out of my apartment. All I've been doing is isolating and playing video games for hours on end.*

*Psychotherapist: How does all that make you feel?*

*C: Completely miserable.*

*P: What about your friends and family? Who did you see before you got laid off?*

*C: We have regular family Sunday dinners, but I haven't gone for weeks because I'm too ashamed. My family's been calling and e-mailing me, but I just ignore them.*

*P: What are they saying in the messages and e-mails?*

*C: They are worried about me and want to know how I'm doing.*

*P: Do you feel that they are disgusted with you because you lost your job?*

*C: (thinks for a bit) Well, no.*

*P: Do you think they'll be critical of you because you were laid off?*

*C: Well, no. My dad was laid off 6 months ago and hasn't been able to find a job either.*

*P: How are your relationships with your family?*

*C: Well, Dad and I used to yell when I was a teenager, but we're good now. I adore my little nieces. Sis and I used to be close before all this.*

*P: Well, I don't know your family, so I can't really say much about them, but from what I'm hearing from you, it sounds like they are more concerned about you than anything.*

*C: I guess that's true.*

*P: I could be wrong, but I'm guessing that if you can swallow your pride, call your family members, and go to Sunday dinner this week, you'll probably feel a lot better. What do you think?*

*C: You're probably right. Isolating has just been making me feel more and more depressed.*

In the above vignette, the psychotherapist encouraged the client, who is becoming more depressed and dysfunctional, to reengage with her family and stop isolating. The client's family relationships have been a significant source of socialization and social support in the past. Note that the psychotherapist only briefly examines the client's dysfunctional attitudes that led the client to feel ashamed and to isolate. The psychotherapist knows that this will need to be addressed further, but also knows that if the client can be nudged to reengage with the family, this can help her mood significantly and relatively quickly. Note that the psychotherapist checked to see that the family is likely to be supportive and that the client feels that the relationships are good before encouraging more contact.

Hays (2007) emphasizes that "it is important that therapists be eclectic in their knowledge about coping strategies and diverse forms of therapy practiced in various cultures" (p. 176). Examples include religion and specific religious practices, traditional healers, and working more with the family rather than the individual. She emphasizes the importance of assessing and encouraging culturally related personal strengths (Hays, 2009). Examples include the importance of extended families and traditional celebrations. Be aware that reciting one's strengths in Asian cultures may be considered immodest (Hays, 2009).

Examples of statements can that help the client identify and apply his personal strengths are :

- "I know that you've been having difficulty getting a job, but I can see that you're a very personable and likeable guy and I bet you'd interview well."
- "Maybe you have ADHD, and these organizational skills don't come naturally to you, but I also see that you're smart and I think you can apply these smarts to the task of getting organized."
- "I can see that you've been very honest with yourself about what has led you to this difficult point in your life and you really understand what needs to change. So you've already accomplished the first step in getting better."

## AGREE ON GOALS FOR THERAPY

*Client: My daughter is driving me crazy. She's only 3 years old, but the tantrums she has in stores are humiliating. When she behaves that way, I feel that I'm the worst mother in the world, and I think about suicide all over again.*

*Psychotherapist: I can see that your daughter's tantrums are very upsetting to you. You're also concerned about her, and you know that, for her own good, her behavior needs to improve. It sounds like you haven't been able to figure out how to get her to stop. I'd be happy to help you with that. This is a very solvable problem, and I believe that we can figure out to improve her behavior if we work together on it. So one of our goals is to improve your daughter's behavior and get her to stop having tantrums.*

*C: Yes, absolutely.*

*P: Lots of parents have this problem, and it is wise of you to seek help before she gets any older. I think we also need to explore why you are so negative about yourself, calling yourself "a bad mother," even though here you are asking for help with this problem, which is exactly what you need to do about it.*

*C: Yes, I'm very hard on myself. I've always said that I'm my own worst critic.*

P: *We also need to work on your suicidal thoughts. You know, I'm wondering whether, in this situation, these thoughts may mean that you feel out of control and helpless in the situation. Is that right?*

C: *Yes, I have no idea what to do, and I think I'm never going to get it right. It's an awful feeling.*

P: *So I'm thinking that maybe if we can help you figure out some things you can do to calm down when you are distressed, it might help you feel more in control and less suicidal.*

A patient who says her goal is a satisfying romantic relationship leading to marriage has every right to seek that in life. However, the therapist can't realistically promise that she will find a suitable partner and end up happily married following therapy. The therapist can, however, offer the possibility of exploring the patient's conflicts about intimacy, her inhibitions about giving herself fully to another person, and any problematic relational styles that might interfere with her romantic pursuit (Gabbard, 2010, p. 97).

When therapy starts, you will want to help the client translate the presenting problem(s) into goals for therapy. Questions such as these can help focus the client (J. S. Beck, 1995, pp. 31–32):

- "Can you tell me specifically what problems you've been having?"
- "What would you like to accomplish in therapy?"
- "How would you like your life to be different?"

The client provides information on her problems, you provide knowledge and expertise, and together you and the client arrive at the treatment goals. In the vignette, the psychotherapist uses the client's statement about her daughter to help formulate four goals of treatment: eliminate her daughter's tantrums, address negative self-talk, reduce suicidal ideas, and improve the client's ability to cope with emotional distress.

Your conceptualization of the goals for therapy may differ somewhat from the client's life goals that bring her to therapy (Gabbard, 2010). Nonetheless, discussing and mutually agreeing on the goals of therapy helps build a strong treatment alliance. Michalak and Holtforth (2006) suggest that goals formulated be framed as positively as possible, or as *approach goals* ("to be able to go shopping by myself") rather than focusing on the negative, or *avoidance goals* ("no longer feel scared when alone outside," p. 356). Approach goals appear to contribute to a positive treatment outcome (Wollburg & Braukhaus, 2010).

Some intriguing research highlights the importance of cultural competence in setting treatment goals. Oishi and Diener (2001) found that European Americans had improved subjective well-being when focused on independent goals (focusing on the individual's preferences and enjoyment), whereas Asians and Asian Americans benefited more from *inter*dependent goals (focusing on pleasing family and friends). Note, however, that Oishi and Diener did not analyze the acculturation level of the Asian American subjects in relation to these different types of goals.

## PSYCHOEDUCATION

*Client: All my family says I'm crazy, and sometimes I feel like I am, too. I can't concentrate and I can't hold a job.*

*Psychotherapist: [after thoroughly evaluating client] I can see that you have been suffering from a combination of depression and attention-deficit/hyperactivity disorder and that this has had quite a negative impact on your life.*

*C: Is there anything that can be done for me?*

*P: Absolutely! Both of these conditions can be treated, and if you stick with weekly psychotherapy, I don't see any reason why you can't be feeling significantly better within two or three months. Let me fill you in some more about how people with these problems can feel better.*

Many clients do not have a framework for conceptualizing their difficulties, although they are aware that there is a problem. As you talk to the client, you will gain an understanding of the client's difficulties, and if the client has a mental illness, you will be able to identify it. Surprisingly, even clients who been in treatment for years may be unable to name what their mental illness is and describe how it is effectively treated.

Effective psychoeducation will inform the client (a) about what diagnoses the client has and why you think the client has that diagnosis, (b) different treatment options that can be effective, and (c) your recommendations for treatment—taking into account the client's feedback about options. Psychoeducation focuses on the client as an active partner, whose strengths can be employed most effectively when she is well informed (Lukens & McFarlane, 2004). After effective psychoeducation, the client will usually feel understood, reassured, and more hopeful about the future. Also, her stress level may be decreased (Van Daele, Hermans, Van Audenhove, & Van den Bergh, 2012). Providing useful information is a powerful intervention. A meta-analysis found that even brief psychoeducation such as a leaflet, referral to a website, or an informative e-mail can result in positive change (Donker, Griffiths, Cuijpers, & Christensen, 2009).

Often clients with *serious mental illness* (often defined as schizophrenia, bipolar disorder, and schizoaffective disorder, although sometimes more broadly) have a limited understanding of their situation. However, research has shown that when clients with serious mental illness have insight, they can work more collaboratively, have fewer hospitalizations, and have better symptom relief (Rouget & Aubry, 2007; Rusch & Corrigan, 2002). Assess the client's level of insight by asking some simple questions, such as, "What is your diagnosis? What have doctors said is your diagnosis when you were in the hospital? Do you know what that means? Tell me what you know about it. Do you believe that the voices are real? Do you think that people are really out to get you?" These types of responses are common:

- Client 1: "They say that I have schizophrenia, but I have only one personality." (In this case, you would want to explain what schizophrenia really is and get the client to articulate whether he has the symptoms.)

- Client 2: "They say I'm manic depressive, but I feel fine without my medications, and I don't think I need them. I've gone for months, and I've been fine." (In this case, you would want to explain that most people with bipolar disorder have only one or two mood episodes every year or two, and feel just like everyone else most of the time.)

As you can see from these examples, clients can have a very poor understanding of their mental illnesses. Psychoeducation can go a long way in improving treatment adherence, symptomatology, emotional well-being, social functioning and vocational functioning (Lukens & McFarlane, 2004).

## REDUCE HIGH-RISK DYSFUNCTIONAL BEHAVIOR

Clients may be engaging in a multitude of high-risk behaviors that interfere with emotional and physical health. These include the following (modified from Linehan, 1993):

- High-risk or unprotected sexual behavior
- Excessive spending
- Gambling
- Poor financial management (such as unpaid bills, poor budgeting, or not following through to get disability checks)
- Criminal behavior (such as shoplifting or embezzling)
- Staying with an abusive partner
- Dysfunctional employment-related behavior (such as quitting suddenly, getting fired, or not looking for a job when unemployed)
- Dysfunctional school-related behavior (such as not going to class or not studying)
- Poor management of physical illness (such as not taking medications, avoiding seeing doctors, or refusing to treat physical illness)
- Housing-related problems (such as inappropriate or unstable living environments or dysfunctional or abusive roommates)
- Inadequate concern for personal safety (such as going to crack houses or walking in dark alleys at night)

Psychotherapy about other life problems is usually futile in the presence of these destabilizing behaviors. The client will not be able to achieve emotional stability with these chaotic, dysfunctional problems. Help the client problem-solve and refer the client to appropriate community resources to address these problems. A motivational interviewing approach can be helpful in assisting the client to gain motivation for change (W. R. Miller & Rollnick, 2002).

## BEHAVIORAL ACTIVATION

*Scott Mladnik is a psychotherapy trainee at a large mental health clinic. A new client, Antoine Bryant, calls in a crisis, and Scott tells Antoine to come in later that day. Antoine has been depressed for 2 weeks and has been lying in bed all day ruminating about his problems. He has been calling in sick and telling everyone that he "threw out" his back. He hasn't been returning anyone's calls. Finally, he realized that something was wrong and called for help. Scott assesses Antoine for a history of manic symptoms as part of his routine assessment and finds that Antoine had a manic episode earlier this year. He has never been diagnosed with bipolar disorder before. Antoine is referred for medications immediately. Scott educates Antoine about bipolar disorder and recovery from depression. He urges him to go back to work and to call his family members and friends, who have been leaving him frantic messages. Antoine does these things, even though they are very difficult. Two weeks later, Antoine is much better. His medications are helping, he is back at work, and he has told everyone what happened. He is surprised at how supportive everyone has been. Therapy then focuses on understanding bipolar disorder and accepting the diagnosis.*

When people are feeling depressed, they tend to behave as Antoine does in the previous vignette. They withdraw from their family and friends. They don't tell anyone about what they are going through. They avoid their coworkers and may miss work. They stop going to their religious group, their book group, their bowling league, or any other group function. Often they think that they are not feeling well enough to engage in these activities. Or they may be thinking that they need to rest and that resting will help them feel better and be able to cope eventually— *this is not true.* In actuality, continued social isolation and withdrawal increases the risk of long-term social and vocational disability (Kawachi & Berkman, 2001). In addition, the client is avoiding the very things that will improve mood: the support of friends and family, enjoying the company of others, spiritual sustenance, feeling productive, being distracted from his problems for a while, and maybe even having a little fun.

*Behavioral activation* "emphasizes structured attempts at engendering increases in overt behaviors that are likely to bring the patient into contact with reinforcing environmental contingencies and produce corresponding improvements in thoughts, mood, and overall quality of life" (Hopko, Lejuez, Ruggiero, & Eifert, 2003, p. 700). In other words, one early goal of therapy, especially with depressed clients, should be to help the client normalize social and vocational functioning as well as personal activities as soon as possible. The focus is to help the client accomplish behavioral goals *even when feeling depressed.* This normalization will lead to feeling better emotionally, thinking more positive thoughts and fewer negative thoughts, and having an improved quality of life. Behavioral activation has been found to be a very effective treatment of depression (Cuijpers, van Straten, & Warmerdam, 2007; Mazzucchelli, Kane, & Rees, 2009).

Help the client brainstorm about how to cope with returning to work (e.g., how to leave early if necessary or whether it would be helpful for you to supply a letter for the Human Resources Department if any accommodations are needed). Help the client brainstorm about some goals for the next week that improve social-ization and support (Client: "Okay, this week, I'll call my best friend in Arizona and tell her how I've been feeling, and I'll go over to my sister's house and visit with her and my niece, then Saturday I'll go to the synagogue with Mom"). Help the client brainstorm about adding some enjoyable activities into her schedule (Client: "This week, I will spend half an hour doing watercolors, even if I don't feel very inspired, and I'll make an appointment for a massage").

After the client does these things, ask how it went. Sometimes clients will com-plain that they didn't feel any better afterward. Then your next question should be, "Did you feel any better *while* you were [doing the activity]?" Generally the client will say yes, providing you an opportunity to point out that it is helpful to have some time when she felt better because if she hadn't engaged in the activity, she probably wouldn't have felt very good during that time. Knowing what helps the client feel better provides an opportunity to change her schedule and activities to feel better more often, which will eventually help overall mood and functioning.

A rapid return to previous level of activities is most likely to be effective with clients such as Antoine, who very recently had a high-functioning level. Clients who are low functioning will need to work on these issues steadily over time. For a more complete description of additional components that have been included in behavioral activation treatment protocols, see Kanter et al. (2010).

## IMPROVE SLEEP

> *Psychotherapist: "It sounds as if you have been drinking a lot of coffee through-out the day and that your sleep has not been restful. I would suggest that you try not to drink any caffeinated beverages after 12:00 noon. Also, I'd suggest that you try to keep the amount of coffee to no more than two cups in the morn-ing. Would you be open to making that change? Let me know next week how your sleep is between now and then."*

This illustrates a simple behavioral intervention to help a client's sleep when the client has been drinking coffee in the late afternoon; note that the half-life of caf-feine is about 6 hours for a healthy adult (Statland & Demas, 1980) but can be much greater, depending on the health status and age of the individual. (The *half-life* of caffeine means how long it takes for half of the caffeine to leave the body. So if the client drinks two cups of coffee, 6 hours later the client still has the caffeine of one cup of coffee in her body.)

Sleep problems are very common. Insufficient or unrestful sleep decreases motivation, energy, concentration, and feelings of well-being and health. Insufficient sleep makes challenging personal problems seem much worse. Many people have poor habits that interfere with good sleep but don't realize it. Sleep habits and behaviors are often called *sleep hygiene*. Assessing these habits and helping your client change them can be an easy and highly effective early therapy intervention.

First, ask the client when she would like to get up in the morning. Assess how much sleep the client needs to be well rested. The usual amount of sleep is 7 to 9 hours; more sleep is inadvisable and is likely to be a symptom of depression. Given this, set a hoped-for bedtime. Be sure that the bedroom is quiet, dark, and restful—problem-solve with the client as needed on these issues. A fan or white noise machine can help in noisy environments.

Here are additional instructions to pass on to the client (informed by Gellis & Lichstein, 2009; Harvey & Tang, 2003; Silber, 2005; Taylor, Lichstein, Weinstock, Sanford, & Temple, 2007):

1. Refrain from caffeine after noon (possibly later if tolerated by client or the client gets up late).
2. Avoid exercise within 2 hours of bedtime.
3. Avoid alcohol within 3 hours of bedtime.
4. Other than the TV, avoid all close use of screens at least 60 minutes before the hoped-for bedtime. The brightness of LED screens on computers, tablets, and phones can interfere with sleep.
5. Engage in only calming, low-key activities in the hour before the hoped-for bedtime—no studying, video games, or work, for example. TV is ok, as long as it is not overly activating.
6. Go to bed only when sleepy.
7. Do not use the bed or bedroom for anything but sleep or sex; do not read or watch TV in bed.
8. If you do not fall asleep within about 15 to 20 minutes, leave the bed and do something low-key in another room. Avoid LED screens during this time. Return to bed only when you feel a strong urge for sleep. Then, if you do not fall asleep quickly on returning to bed, repeat as many times as necessary.
9. Use the alarm to awaken yourself at the same time every morning regardless of the amount of sleep obtained.
10. Do not nap during the day.

The rationale for these instructions is to train the body to associate bed with sleep rather than insomnia. Thus, when the client feels awake, the client gets out of bed. Naps often interfere with the next night's sleep. Awakening at the same time every morning helps reset the client's sleep to a normal healthy schedule. Warn the client of the need to stick carefully to these instructions until sleep has normalized and that it may take several weeks for sleep to normalize.

This is only a very basic introduction to working with clients who have behavioral sleep issues. Further psychological treatments can be employed, such as sleep-restriction therapy and relaxation therapy (Silber, 2005). For further guidance, see Edinger and Carney (2008).

## RELAXATION TRAINING AND MEDITATION

Relaxation training is another effective behavioral intervention that can be learned relatively quickly by the psychotherapist (see Bernstein, Borkovec, & Hazlett-Stevens, 2000). Relaxation training can help reduce chronic pain (Symreng & Fishman, 2004), anxiety (Manzoni, Pagnini, Castelnuovo, & Molinari, 2008), depression (Jorm, Morgan, & Hetrick, 2008), and anger (Deffenbacher, Oetting, & DiGiuseppe, 2002).

Research to date suggests that regular meditation can have emotional, physical, and cognitive benefits, similar to but somewhat different from those from relaxation training (Davidson et al., 2003; Jain et al., 2007; Ramel, Goldin, Carmona, & McQuaid, 2004). Some researchers suggest that depressed or anxious clients who ruminate may be especially good candidates for trying meditation (Jain et al., 2007; Ramel et al., 2004). A meta-analysis found robust improvements in anxiety through meditation practice (Manzoni, Pagnini, Castelnuovo, & Molinari, 2008). However, interestingly, a literature review of the Mindfulness-Based Stress Reduction program (of which meditation is one part) did not find improvement in depression or anxiety (Toneatto & Nguyen, 2007). If you meditate regularly or you have in the past, you may be able to teach it to your client. If you do not meditate, do not attempt to teach it; instead, refer the client to community resources.

## CLIENT-INITIATED ACTIVITIES: SELF-EDUCATION, SELF-HELP, AND EXERCISE

With your input or on their own, clients often like to take the initiative to start activities that contribute positively to their mental health. Research suggests that self-help groups, books, and exercise can be particularly helpful.

Extending your client's psychoeducation and treatment through books and films can be helpful for certain clients. See Norcross (2006) for helpful lists of top-rated self-help books, top-rated self-help autobiographies, and top-rated self-help films.

Your client may be interested in attending self-help groups. There are traditional substance-related self-help groups, such as Al-Anon and Alcoholics Anonymous (and others like these, such as Cocaine Anonymous and Narcotics Anonymous). Self-help groups for other personal problems exist as well. As a whole, research has found self-help groups to be an effective adjunct to individual therapy (Norcross, 2006). However, carefully ask your client about his self-help groups because, on rare occasions, some of them can be counterproductive (e.g., a group for "survivors of Satanic abuse" or an online group where individuals write at length about how much they appreciate cutting themselves).

Exercise has been shown to have antidepressant effects (DiLorenzo et al., 1999; Fox, 1999; Penedo & Dahn, 2005) and is helpful with anxiety as well

(Fox, 1999; Lancer, Motta, & Lancer, 2007; Penedo & Dahn, 2005). Generally, exercise and medications are equally effective interventions for depression and anxiety disorders—although medication works faster (Stathopoulou, Powers, Berry, Smits, & Otto, 2006). Exercise is better at preventing depressive relapse than medication (Stathopoulou, Powers, Berry, Smits, & Otto, 2006).

Exercise may help increase the client's resilience to stress (Salmon, 2003). Exercise may be particularly beneficial for clients with symptoms of fatigue or low energy (Puetz, O'Connor, & Dishman, 2006). It can even improve mood, alertness, concentration, sleep, and psychotic symptoms among individuals with severe mental illness (Alexandratos, Barnett, & Thomas, 2012). Generally, cardio-vascular and resistance exercise has been studied in this research.

The possible benefits of yoga have been studied as well; yoga involves both exercise and mindfulness components. Despite methodological inadequacies, a number of studies suggested that yoga could be helpful with anxiety disorders, especially obsessive-compulsive disorder (Kirkwood, Rampes, Tuffrey, Richardson, & Pilkington, 2005), and with depression (Mehta & Sharma, 2010). A trauma expert also suggests yoga for alleviating anxiety in PTSD clients (van der Kolk, 2002).

## A CAUTION ABOUT ALTERNATIVE TREATMENTS

Some alternative treatments are ineffective at best, and harmful at worst. A licensed mental health practitioner should not provide or recommend these treatments. If needed, you may want to educate the client about their lack of empirical support and the possibility to cause emotional harm. These potentially harmful treatments would include age-regression methods for treating adults who may have been sexually abused as children, chiropractic manipulation for mental/behavioral disorders, craniosacral therapy (manipulation of the skull bones) for treatment of anxiety and depression, rebirthing therapies, sexual reorientation/reparative therapy for homosexuality, Thought Field Therapy, and treatments for mental disorders resulting from Satanic ritual abuse or alien abduction (Norcross, Koocher, & Garofalo, 2006).

In addition, the licensed practitioner should be aware of the scientific reasons that certain "alternative" practices may seem to work but remain unproven (see Beyerstein, 1997, which is readily available online).

## LETTING THE CLIENT SET THE AGENDA

When working with stable and high-functioning clients, many psychotherapists prefer to let the client set the agenda for the psychotherapy session. When the client sets the agenda, he will generally choose an issue that is particularly salient that week, giving you an opportunity to explore continuing themes—such as anxiety, anger, or self-esteem—in light of that issue.

Some psychotherapists start each session with whatever question or comment feels right at the time; others use a standard opening line. Here are some opening lines (*Independent Practitioner*, 2007, p. 22, and various personal communications):

- "What brings you here today?"
- "What seems important today?"
- "Let's talk about what's on your mind."
- "So, how are things going?"
- "Well, where do we pick it up?"
- "What problems can I help you solve today?"

At times, you and the client may have ended the prior session by noting that you had more to discuss on a particular topic, or you might have realized that there was a related topic that you didn't have time for. In those cases, I might open with something like this:

"So, last time you said that you were bothered by how you were getting along with your coworkers, but we didn't have time to discuss that. I'm wondering if you'd like to discuss that or something else today?"

## EDUCATE YOURSELF ABOUT PSYCHOTHERAPY

Many beginning psychotherapists, paradoxically, have been thoroughly educated yet feel unready to start seeing clients in psychotherapy. You have learned a lot in graduate school. Yet for true competence, even more knowledge and reading is essential beyond what you learned in school.

Often, beginning psychotherapists complain that they know a lot about theory but have no idea how to apply it. Books are often the best resources at this stage, as they often start at a more basic level than journal articles and can provide a comprehensive treatment description. The list of recommended readings at the end of this chapter provides you with several suggestions of very readable books to get you started. Integrative approaches are becoming more important. Because of that, I have recommended books that illustrate a variety of approaches. These readings will help provide you with the cognitive framework that you need to be an effective psychotherapist.

## EDUCATE YOURSELF ON THE MOST RECENT UPDATES AND SPECIAL ISSUES

*Stephanie Long is a mental health student who has a new client with chronic migraine headaches and major depression. The client states that he would rather not take medications for the headaches since he already has a multitude of complex medical issues and a complicated dosing schedule. Stephanie tells the client that she will research the issue. Looking through recent journal articles, she finds that thermal biofeedback has some supporting evidence for treating migraines. She networks with colleagues and finds a health psychologist at a local medical center who is trained in administering thermal biofeedback. Next time she sees the client, she refers him to the health psychologist for adjunctive treatment. In their psychotherapy sessions, they continue to discuss the client's major depression as well as the emotional issues that sometimes trigger his migraine headaches.*

While books are essential for learning about basics of psychotherapy practice, journal articles can be helpful for learning about the most recent updates and research as well as specialized topics, such as the one researched by Stephanie in the previous vignette. Note that cognitive-behavioral and pharmacological interventions tend to be overrepresented, as these have had the greatest amount of scientific research. If you want to review how another theoretical orientation approaches the disorder, it often works to search using the name of the orientation (e.g., *psychodynamic*) with the disorder (e.g., *panic disorder*) or to look for a book on the topic instead. To be able to put what you learn from the research literature in an appropriate context, it is helpful to be knowledgeable about the empirically supported treatments debate (for an introduction, see the American Psychological Association Presidential Task Force on Evidence-Based Practice, 2006).

## RECOMMENDED READING

Edinger, J. D., & Carney, C. E. (2008). *Overcoming insomnia: A cognitive-behavioral therapy approach.* New York: Oxford University Press.
   *A brief but helpful volume on treating clients with insomnia. Gives especially helpful input regarding those who tend to ruminate at bedtime.*
Kawachi, I., & Berkman, L. F. (2001). Social ties and mental health. *Journal of Urban Health: Bulletin of the New York Academy of Medicine, 78,* 458–467.
   *This article provides a helpful overview of the relationship between socialization and mental health.*
Lukens, E. P., & McFarlane, W. R. (2004). Psychoeducation as evidence-based practice: Considerations for practice, research, and policy. *Brief Treatment and Crisis Intervention, 4,* 205–225.
   *This article provides a useful review of the evidence for psychoeducation as an effective treatment modality.*
Norcross, J. C. (2006). Integrating self-help into psychotherapy: 16 practice suggestions. *Professional Psychology: Research and Practice, 37,* 683–693.
   *Norcross provides a helpful review of how mental health professionals and clients can use various modalities of self-help (books, films, groups, and the Internet) to further treatment.*

## Helpful Books About Psychotherapy

Beck, J. S. (1995). *Cognitive therapy: Basics and beyond*. New York: Guilford Press.
*This book provides a helpful description of the therapeutic process in cognitive psychotherapy.*

Beck, J. S. (2005). *Cognitive therapy for challenging problems: What to do when the basics don't work*. New York: Guilford Press.
*Judith Beck extends the reach of cognitive psychotherapy in this helpful volume.*

Epstein, M. (1998). *Going to pieces without falling apart: A Buddhist perspective on wholeness*. New York: Broadway Books.
*Eastern philosophy has made a powerful impact on the practice and theory of mental health in the past two decades. This very readable volume introduces important concepts.*

Gabbard, G. O. (2010). *Long-term psychodynamic psychotherapy: A basic text* (2nd ed.). Arlington, VA: American Psychiatric Publishing.
*This book is written specifically for the beginning psychotherapist. Important modern principles of psychodynamic psychotherapy are outlined remarkably clearly in this text, along with ample references to research literature. Highly recommended.*

Herman, J. (1997). *Trauma and recovery: The aftermath of violence from domestic abuse to political terror*. New York: Basic Books.
*In this update to her classic volume, Herman educates the reader, in an eminently readable style, about trauma and its treatment.*

McWilliams, N. (2004). *Psychoanalytic psychotherapy: A practitioner's guide*. New York: Guilford Press.
*McWilliams writes about complex psychotherapeutic issues in highly accessible prose. Her advice is highly practical and down to earth.*

Miller, W. R., & Rollnick, S. (2002). *Motivational interviewing: Preparing people for change* (2nd ed.). New York: Guilford Press.
*If you read one thing about working with substance-abusing clients, read this book. It provides helpful guidance in establishing rapport and an effective treatment alliance with this difficult population, and the lessons are applicable to any client with ambivalence about change.*

## Online Resources

http://www.nami.org
*This website for the National Alliance on Mental Illness provides reliable psychoeducation on mental illness.*

www.ptsd.va.gov
*This is the website for the National Center for PTSD, part of Veterans Affairs. This excellent website provides useful information about PTSD for both clients and psychotherapists.*

http://www.nimh.nih.gov
*This website for the National Institute of Mental Health (part of the U.S. government) provides reliable information on a multitude of mental illnesses.*

http://mentalhelp.net/selfhelp
*This website provides client referrals to all sorts of self-help groups by type of problem.*

EXERCISES AND DISCUSSION QUESTIONS

1. What interventions might you use for each of the high-risk dysfunctional behaviors listed in this chapter? If you don't know what interventions to use, how would you find out?
2. Think about the problems that your clients often have. Make a list of psychoeducational materials (websites, books, and brochures—many can be found online) that would be particularly helpful with your client population.

# Referrals

# 14

# Psychotropic Medication: Referrals and Adherence

Psychotropic medications can help the symptoms of your clients. To refer effectively, you should understand what symptoms can be treated most effectively by medications. Reference websites are listed at the end of this chapter to help you learn more about classes of psychotropics and individual medications.

As of this writing, psychotropic medications can be prescribed by psychiatrists, other physicians, and master's level nurses. Psychiatrists have intensive advanced training in prescribing psychotropic medication for clients with mental illnesses. However, primary care physicians also often prescribe psychotropics as well. There is also a movement to allow psychologists with advanced training to prescribe psychotropic medications, but this remains quite controversial and divisive even within clinical psychology itself (Heiby, 2010; Robiner et al., 2002), although it is supported by the American Psychological Association. Psychologists can attain certifications and training that lead to prescription privileges in Louisiana and New Mexico at the time of this writing. Generally, psychiatrists will be prescribing medication for your clients, so for simplicity's sake, in this chapter I refer to practitioners prescribing the clients' medications as "psychiatrists."

## MYTHS ABOUT PSYCHOTROPICS

Some myths persist about psychotropic medications.

> *Myth*: Psychotropic medications are supposed to be sedating.
> *Fact*: Decades ago, when there were few medications available, some of the medications that were used were quite sedating. However, medications are developed with the goal of preserving or increasing alertness. Fewer modern medications are sedating, and these are generally prescribed at bedtime, so the sedative effect will assist with sleep and will mostly wear off by the next morning. In addition, the sedating effect of many medications can often wear off as the client takes the medication for a longer time period.
> *Myth*: Using psychotropic medications is wrong, cruel, or ineffective.

*Fact*: I can assure you that knowledgeable professionals, who know about the scientific literature on psychotropic medication, are in full agreement that they can be therapeutic and should be used as needed. One of your responsibilities as a mental health professional is to understand the potential benefits of psychotropic medications and use this knowledge to determine when it is appropriate to initiate a referral for a medication evaluation.

*Myth*: Schizophrenia is best treated without psychotropic medications.

*Fact*: This is totally inconsistent with the psychological and psychiatric research literature. Even with psychotropic medication, only a minority of clients with schizophrenia attain a full recovery of social and vocational functioning (Robinson, Woerner, Delman, & Kane, 2005). That said, after some years, a few individuals do seem to recover from schizophrenia (D. G. Robinson et al., 2004).

*Myth*: Antipsychotic medications cause people to look and behave in an odd manner.

*Fact*: This is misinformation, coupled with outdated information. Decades ago, Thorazine was the only medication that was available to treat schizophrenia. Thorazine had significant and distressing side effects, including muscle stiffness—which gave people a strange gait, sometimes called "the Thorazine shuffle"—and a high level of sedation. I don't know anyone who still prescribes Thorazine. Currently available antipsychotics are superior, with fewer and less severe side effects. Since there are many antipsychotics to choose from, a client who has a negative reaction to one can be easily switched to another. Most of clients' odd behavior (e.g., flat affect and eccentricity) is due to the underlying mental illness. In actuality, most people who take antipsychotic medication look relatively normal on casual observation; they blend into a crowd, and you would not notice them.

*Myth*: A client says, "If I really need my medication, I'll be able to tell right away after I stop taking it."

*Fact*: This is wrong in two ways. First, the client's mental illness may not recur immediately after medication discontinuation, even though continued medication is essential to prevent relapse and rehospitalization. This is the case for bipolar disorder and also for some clients with schizophrenia and other psychotic disorders. Bipolar clients are notorious for stopping their medications; however, they may not understand that the main purpose of ongoing medications is to *prevent recurrence* of infrequent but acute mood episodes. Second, the client who suddenly discontinues medication may have negative reactions that could have been avoided had the client collaborated with the psychiatrist. For example, antidepressants should never be stopped suddenly, as this can lead to *discontinuation reactions*, such as dizziness, insomnia, impaired concentration, irritability, and suicidal thoughts or behavior (Otis & King, 2006). Instead, they should be tapered under medical supervision. In addition, some antianxiety medications will lead to withdrawal symptoms if discontinued suddenly; if the client is taking a larger dose, sudden discontinuation might even be lethal (M. Mills, personal communication, January 29, 2008).

## CONTROVERSIES ABOUT PSYCHOTROPICS

There are a number of current controversies about psychotropic medications that you should be aware of. There is concern that psychotropics are overprescribed for children (Bonati & Clavenna, 2005; Sparks & Duncan, 2008), for the elderly (Mort & Aparasu, 2002), and for persons with intellectual disabilities (Matson & Neal, 2009). Other issues include the increased suicide risk associated with the use of antidepressants in children, teens (Reeves & Ladner, 2010), and adults under age 25, and probable overdiagnosis of attention-deficit/hyperactivity disorder (ADHD) in children accompanied by overmedication (Busch, 2009).

Many professionals are concerned about the influence of prescription drug companies over physicians who practice in the current health care climate (Coyle, 2002). There continues to be some concern about the effectiveness of antidepressants compared to placebos (Kirsch, Moore, Scoboria, & Nicholls, 2002).

## CAUTIONARY ISSUES ABOUT PSYCHOTROPICS

Primary care physicians are often urged to treat mental illness with medications. However, research has shown that physicians who do not specialize in psychiatry vary considerably in their ability to effectively prescribe psychotropics, with many of them prescribing a low and ineffective dose (Donoghue & Hylan, 2001). Adherence to antidepressants for the full recommended initial 6-month period can be very low in primary care settings (Hunot, Horne, Leese, & Churchill, 2007). In addition, primary care physicians often do not schedule needed follow-up appointments or ensure that the client has refills (E. H. B. Lin et al., 2000).

Women who are pregnant, who want to become pregnant, or who are breast-feeding should be sure to share that information with their health care practitioner any time they are going to take medication. Sometimes psychotropic medications are unsafe for the fetus, or the safety of the medication has not been sufficiently assessed. A psychiatrist specializing in these issues may need to be consulted.

Like any type of medication, psychotropics can have side effects and, in certain rare circumstances, can be dangerous. Some psychotropic medications can be fatal if the client ingests the entire bottle during a suicide attempt. Other medications carry a small risk of potentially dangerous complications and must be monitored carefully.

## SIDE EFFECTS

You will usually meet with the client more often than the psychiatrist does. The client may not distinguish, as we do, between the specialties of mental health professionals. The client may tell you about the side effects of medications even if you don't prescribe them. You may wish to have a reference work on hand so that you can look up common side effects (see suggestions at the end of this chapter). The best response to complaints about side effects is to urge the client to discuss the concerns with the psychiatrist. This is especially important if the client finds the side effects to be intolerable; urge the client to call the psychiatrist on the phone immediately to address the issue because the client is at risk of stopping the medication. If needed, assure the client that no one wants him or her to be uncomfortable with the medication and that the psychiatrist will want to know about these problems.

Selective serotonin reuptake inhibitor (SSRI) antidepressants, such as Prozac and Zoloft, are well known for their high rate of sexual side effects. You might want to screen your clients who are taking SSRIs for sexual problems. Urge clients to discuss any sexual side effects with the psychiatrist. Consult with the psychiatrist, as there may be ways to ameliorate the side effects while maintaining the gains from the medication.

If you are working with clients who take antipsychotics, discuss side effects with the psychiatrist so that you understand the risks of these medications. Here are some of the additional things you will want to learn about antipsychotics: neuroleptic malignant syndrome, tardive dyskinesia, akathisia, and how weight gain from certain antipsychotics can lead to type 2 diabetes.

## MENTAL ILLNESS AND BIOLOGY

Many different methodologies have been used over the years to study the biological basis of mental illness. Many earlier studies focused on heritability and analyzed data from studies with twins and first-degree relatives. In recent decades, with scientific advances, researchers have looked for genetic abnormalities that might predispose one to mental illness and have looked inside the workings of the brain with functional magnetic resonance imaging (fMRI), photon emission tomography (PET) scans, and so on.

We commonly think of psychotherapy as helping the client cope with the environmental and developmental factors that contributed to the client's mental illness, while we think of medications as affecting the biological basis of the mental illness. However, biological changes—due to psychotropic medication—can change thinking and self-image, and psychotherapy can measurably change the functioning of the brain (Gabbard, 2000b). Clearly, our traditional Western ideas of the mind–body dichotomy are insufficient to understand the complexities of mental illness.

As far as I know, research has shown that every mental illness that has been sufficiently studied so far has some evidence of biological and genetic basis. In addition, as far as I know, research has shown that every mental illness is more likely to occur with certain life situations and stressors. As a general rule, the more heritable or genetically influenced a disorder is, the more important psychotropic medication is to treat it (for more information about heritability of mental illnesses, see Chapter 9). For example, bipolar disorder and schizophrenia cannot be treated effectively without medications, while depression and anxiety disorders often can. In conclusion, "environmental and developmental factors must interact with genes to produce psychiatric illness" (Gabbard, 2000b, p. 117).

## COMORBID SUBSTANCE ABUSE

People who abuse substances are more likely to have rehospitalizations if they have bipolar disorder (Keck et al., 1998) or schizophrenia (G. E. Hunt, Bergen, & Bashir, 2002). Thus, recognizing and treating the substance abuse is an important step in stabilizing the client and preventing rehospitalization.

Here are several cautions regarding medicating the mentally ill substance-abusing client. A substance-abusing client is unlikely to take medications regularly. Using illegal drugs can reduce the effectiveness of psychotropic medications. Finally, dangerous drug interactions between the illegal drugs and the psychotropic medications could occur.

Antianxiety medications (benzodiazepines like Valium and Xanax) can be quite addictive and should be used with great care if the client has a past or present history of substance abuse. In those cases, ensure that you have a release of information and talk to the psychiatrist *before* the client gets a psychiatric evaluation. Nonetheless, appropriately treating anxiety can help the motivated individual to stop self-medicating through substance abuse. Most other psychotropics don't have much potential for abuse, but ask a psychiatrist if you are unsure.

## WHEN PSYCHOTHERAPY IS NECESSARY

Psychotherapy is often a necessary part of treatment, especially when the client has the following:

- Chronic interpersonal problems
- High level of emotional distress
- Deficits in ability to cope
- Maladaptive coping strategies
- Risk of violence or suicide
- Feelings of stigmatization by a diagnosis of chronic mental illness and thus being at risk of stopping psychotropic medications.

Many people think of schizophrenia and bipolar disorder as primarily biological and thus do not provide psychotherapy for those clients. On the contrary, psychotherapy is essential for these clients to achieve the highest possible level of functioning and to reduce the overall cost of their mental health care through reducing inpatient readmissions (Falloon, Barbieri, Boggian, & Lamonaca, 2007; Gabbard, Lazar, Hornberger, & Spiegel, 1997; Miklowitz et al., 2007).

## WHEN TO REFER A PSYCHOTHERAPY CLIENT FOR MEDICATION

Whether or not you prescribe psychotropic medications, you will often be the first health care professional the client sees. Thus, you will have the responsibility of determining whether a referral for psychotropic medications is needed. You need to understand when medications are optional and when they are necessary for effective treatment. Medication can facilitate more effective use of psycho-therapy. Gabbard (2006) points out that medication may improve concentration and reduce distress—which enhances the client's ability to use psychotherapy pro-ductively. As competent, effective, and ethical psychotherapists, it is our responsi-bility to ensure that our clients improve as quickly and as completely as possible. Therefore, treatment may need to include medications as well as psychotherapy. Here are some guidelines for making this decision.

Carefully consider the severity of the symptoms, determine how much the symptoms are affecting functioning, and then make a mutual decision about medications with the client. Discuss the pros and cons with the client, including when the issue should be revisited.

For many depressed and anxious clients, psychotherapy alone is a sufficient treat-ment. If a client has some depressive symptoms but the diagnosis is adjustment dis-order, psychotropics would probably be unnecessary. If the client is distressed by depressive symptoms but is functioning adequately, psychotherapy can be effective alone, but progress can be quicker with the addition of medications. For occasional panic attacks or mild obsessive-compulsive disorder (OCD), you can discuss the pros and cons of medication, psychotherapy, and combination treatment with the client and make a decision together, depending on the client's preferences.

An evaluation for medications is recommended if the client has:

- High level of subjective distress
- Sleep disruption from depression, anxiety, or post-traumatic stress disorder (PTSD) leading to exhaustion
- Poor concentration or motivation leading to deteriorating performance at work or school
- Strained interpersonal relationships because of distress and symptomatology
- Disabling panic attacks or severe OCD
- Impaired ability to fulfill obligations with work, schoolwork, or relationships

Antidepressants can help disturbed sleep in clients with depression (Saletu-Zyhlarz, Anderer, Arnold, & Saletu, 2003) and PTSD (Maher, Rego, & Asnis, 2006). Other mental illnesses, such as ADHD, eating disorders, and others, can be helped with medications. Discuss these issues with your supervisor and with a psychiatrist.

## WHEN MEDICATIONS ARE NECESSARY

Any client who has ever had an episode of hypomania or mania or a mixed-mood episode should be referred to a psychiatrist. Continued maintenance on mood-stabilizing medications (and possibly other medications, depending on the symptomatology) is essential in preventing future mood episodes and increasing the probability of functional recovery (Keck et al., 1998).

For clients with psychotic symptoms, medications are also essential to return them to a healthy state as quickly as possible. Continued medication is essential for individuals with schizophrenia and schizoaffective disorder.

The distressing and disabling symptoms for these disorders cannot be controlled by psychotherapy alone. Medications are generally considered necessary for severe major depression, especially if the client has psychotic features. *In conclusion, any client with current or past mania, hypomania, or psychotic symptoms must be referred for an evaluation for psychotropic medication.* Clients with severe anxiety and depressive disorders are likely to benefit from psychotropic medications as well.

## WORKING WITH PSYCHIATRISTS

If you don't prescribe medication, you will need to develop good working relationships with mental health practitioners who do. If you and the psychiatrist work in the same clinic or facility, you can discuss the client's treatment freely. If you don't, you will need to get a release of information from the client to talk to the psychiatrist to coordinate care. Once you make the referral for psychotropic medications, get a release signed and fax it over to the psychiatrist, along with a request to call you at the psychiatrist's earliest convenience.

You may wish to contact the psychiatrist prior to the first session with the client to provide your impressions. If there are significant risk issues or complex diagnostic issues, a call is especially warranted. Then contact the psychiatrist after the first appointment with the client to compare impressions and coordinate care. Ideally, the psychiatrist will be open to your input and will be responsive to the client during and between sessions.

In some settings, you will be expected to present oral information to the psychiatrist you are working with. Be brief and to the point. Describe the client succinctly and list all the diagnoses. Instead of suggesting any medications or types of medications, highlight any symptoms that you are concerned about.

- Wrong: "Elle lives with her two daughters and their kids. Would you believe it—there's 10 people living in a three-bedroom house? Anyway, she's feeling pretty depressed lately and kind of anxious too. I think that some Valium might do her a world of good. She doesn't know how she can continue to support all these people on her income from being a bus driver."

- Right: "Elle is a 64-year-old White female bus driver with recurrent major depression and panic disorder. Her depression and panic attacks are negatively affecting on her work functioning. In addition, her sleep is very poor, with frequent awakenings."

The information about Elle's stressors and social situation is important, but it is more pertinent to your work as the psychotherapist than it is to the psychiatrist's choice of psychotropic medications.

## ASSESSING MEDICATION ADHERENCE

Taking medications as prescribed is sometimes called *adherence* and sometimes called *compliance*; adherence is more commonly used in recent literature because it emphasizes the client as an active participant. Cramer and Rosenheck (1998) found that, on average, patients with physical disorders took 76 percent of their prescribed medications, while patients taking antidepressants took only 65 percent, and patients taking antipsychotics took only 58 percent. Bipolar clients' adherence rates can be as low as 35 percent (Osterberg & Blaschke, 2005). Thus, medication nonadherence is an even more serious problem with mental illnesses than physical illnesses.

Given these findings, *we must assume that a large proportion of our clients are not taking their medications as prescribed.* Some of them will not be taking their medications at all, whereas others are taking their medications sporadically or missing occasional doses. Thus, all clients taking psychotropic medications should be screened repeatedly for medication adherence. Avoid questions such as this: "Are you taking all your medication?" This question will probably elicit a reassurance from the client that all the medications are being taken rather than elicit the client's difficulties with adherence. Instead, try these questions:

- "How are things going with your medication?"
- "What kinds of difficulties are you having with your medication?"
- "How often are you forgetting your medication?"
- "Are you having any problems with taking your medication?"
- "Do you have any mixed feelings about taking your medication?"
- "Are you having any side effects from your medication?"

Assure the client that occasional forgetting is common and that your goal is simply to help problem-solve. Substance abuse also contributes to nonadherence (Novick et al., 2010).

If you can find out when the client has refilled the medication (which you can do if you are working in some agencies or a Veterans Affairs facility), this information can provide a rough measure of adherence. For certain medications, a blood test is routinely done to see whether the blood level of the medication is at the therapeutic dose; a physician can often determine whether the client has been adherent from that information.

## IMPROVING MEDICATION ADHERENCE

*Claire Carter is a mental health trainee working with Sheena Moore, a client with bipolar disorder. When asked, Sheena admits to not taking her medication regularly. She has good understanding of why she needs to take it and is willing to do so. After some discussion, Sheena agrees to put a note next to her toothbrush reminding her to take her medication before she brushes her teeth in the morning and evening. She agrees to keep a small pill bottle with some spare pills in her purse in case she forgets to take her medication and then remembers later when she is out of the house or in case she stays over at her mother's house.*

In the literature, no single intervention for improving medication adherence has been found to be superior (Peterson, Takiya, & Finley, 2003). Thus, I recommend that you try to gain an understanding of what unique factors are contributing to this client's nonadherence; these could include (Osterberg & Blaschke, 2005; Zeber et al., 2011):

- Depressed mood
- Substance abuse
- Inadequate follow-up or discharge planning
- Side effects
- Lack of belief in medication being beneficial
- Lack of insight into illness
- Poor relationship with psychiatrist
- Missed appointments, difficulty attending appointments
- Cost of medication, copayment, or both
- Difficulty contacting psychiatrist

Then take a personalized approach to the client's medication adherence difficulties and tailor the intervention appropriately. Try to problem-solve with the client and help the client tap into personal and community resources to address these barriers to adherence.

Many clients may have impaired concentration, attention, and memory because of their mental illnesses. This can result in difficulties with reading comprehension or poor receptive listening skills. These cognitive difficulties may mean that the client did not understand fully why the medication is important and why it needs to be taken on an ongoing basis. You can contribute to adherence by patiently explaining these issues to the client as slowly and as often as needed.

Forgetfulness or disorganization may be contributing to poor medication adherence. Here are some interventions to consider (Osterberg & Blaschke, 2005). You might urge the client to put the medication into a pillbox with separate compartments for days of the week (or times of the day if there is a more complex dosing schedule or multiple medications at different times). These are readily available in any drugstore. If the client uses a pillbox, it is obvious which medications were missed, and it gives you an opportunity to problem-solve around those incidents:

> "You always miss when you go over to your sister's house for the day? How about putting a few pills in a small container in your purse so that you'll have them when you realize that you missed your medications? Would you mind asking your sister to help you remember your medicine on those days?"

Suggest that the client keep a few pills of each medication in a purse, backpack, or briefcase that he carries around throughout the day in case the client later remembers a missed dose.

Another intervention for the forgetful client is to use cues to improve adherence (Osterberg & Blaschke, 2005). You could urge the client to identify an activity performed every day at the time that the medication needs to be taken ("I brush my teeth every morning," "I turn off the television every night before I go to bed," or "I have lunch") and have the client leave a little note by the toothbrush (or television or dining room table) to take the medication *before* brushing teeth (or turning off the television or having lunch), because if the client takes medications afterward, he may still forget. Emphasize that taking medication needs to become routine, like the toothbrushing or breakfast is.

In certain cases, these interventions with the forgetful or disorganized client are ineffective in improving adherence despite your and the client's best efforts. In these cases, you might want to involve any family members living with the client to assist with the medication. Certain antipsychotic medications can be administered in a shot rather than pills, thus ensuring adherence (Osterberg & Blaschke, 2005).

Psychiatrists will sometimes prescribe a medication (or two or more medications) on a complex dosing schedule. Complicated medication dosing schedules (e.g., three or more times per day) are inherently difficult to remember, and many clients will miss doses (Cramer & Rosenheck, 1998). Consult with the psychiatrist—perhaps a different medication or an easier dosing schedule can be tried.

Be aware that clients will sometimes set difficult dosing schedules for themselves unnecessarily: "I'm trying to take my blood pressure medication in the middle of the morning because I'm afraid that it won't mix with my Prozac." Assure the client that, as long as the psychiatrist knows about both medications and has not instructed otherwise, it is okay to take them together.

## INSIGHT, PSYCHOEDUCATION, AND ADHERENCE

*Bethany Gonzalez is a mental health trainee working with Luis Ortiz, a 50-year-old client with schizophrenia. She is trying to educate him about his mental illness and asks him if he thinks he has schizophrenia. He says, "Well, my doctor says I have schizophrenia, but I don't think so." Bethany says, "It sounds like people are telling you that you have schizophrenia, but you are uncertain and need to decide for yourself. I have a list of symptoms here, so how about if we go through them and see if you have any? Maybe it will help us sort this out." She pulls out the Diagnostic and Statistical Manual of Mental Disorders, reads through each symptom, and describes it in layman's terms. Then they discuss whether Luis has the symptom. They determine that he has hallucinations and delusions. Bethany says, "So those are the symptoms that made your doctors think that you have schizophrenia. What are your thoughts about that?" Now that Luis understands what schizophrenia is, he agrees that he probably does have it.*

Be aware that about half of individuals with schizophrenia will have limited *insight*—in other words, they will have a limited understanding that they have a mental disorder and what the symptoms and implications of that are (Lincoln, Lullmann & Rief, 2007); in these cases, there may be problems with adherence. Feel free to ask: "Do you think you need the medication?" A gentle, nonconfrontational inquiring approach, such as Bethany's in the previous vignette, can be effective in fostering greater agreement between the client and the psychotherapist. Further insight and adherence to recommended treatments can also be fostered by using motivational interviewing techniques (Rusch & Corrigan, 2002).

Insight may also be lacking when the client finds that she is asymptomatic when she stops her medication. In certain cases, this may be okay (e.g., depression or panic disorder) and the client just needs to be monitored carefully. In other cases (e.g., schizophrenia, schizoaffective disorder, or bipolar disorder), many clients can be asymptomatic for some time periods, but the symptoms will almost certainly recur, probably leading to hospitalization and/or great emotional distress. Taking the medications during even asymptomatic periods greatly increases emotional and functional stability in the long run. This issue is especially pertinent to bipolar clients, who may have one mood episode every year or two (American Psychiatric Association, 2000) and can have limited insight into the need to take their medication consistently even when they are asymptomatic. Provide additional education about the course of the illness to the client, including that there may be asymptomatic periods even if the underlying illness is still present. Discuss the importance of regular medication for keeping the client out of the hospital and as functional as possible over the long run.

## STIGMA AND ADHERENCE

*Blake Richardson is a mental health trainee working at a Veterans Affairs medical center. Blake is working with an Iraq War veteran, Todd Kelly, who has PTSD from combat. Todd says, "I don't want to take my medication because I think I should be able to snap out of it." Blake responds, "I wish you could snap out of PTSD, too, but I haven't ever met anyone who was able to do that. You didn't ask for the trauma to happen to you, but it did, and I think that it's having a powerful effect on how you're feeling. Is that right?" Todd agrees. Blake continues, "I think that there's a good chance that you won't need the medicine at some time in the future, but for right now, you're not feeling very well, you're having nightmares every night, and I think the medicine will help you feel better, which will help you get along with your wife and hold down your job. You can also get more rest so that you can think clearly and not feel so tired all the time. If you make progress in therapy, later on the medicine might not be needed. What do you think about that?"*

*Sheena Moore comes in to see her student psychotherapist, Claire Carter, the week after they talked about taking her medication regularly. Sheena says, "Every time I take my lithium, I realize that I'm manic-depressive, and I get upset about that." She and Claire talk at length about her feelings about bipolar disorder. Claire says, "It seems that you are discriminating against yourself for having bipolar disorder, but you can't help having it, and you didn't ask for it."*

Sometimes the client has strong feelings about taking medication, and these feelings should be explored in therapy. Spend as much time as you need to thoroughly explore and examine the client's feelings and thoughts. Once you have done that, further psychoeducation about the biological basis of mental illness can help the client reframe the issue. Note that Claire, in the previous vignette, has reframed Sheena's negative feelings about taking her medication as internalizing a societal discrimination and stigma against those who have chronic mental illness. Further discussion of this issue can continue at whatever depth is appropriate for the particular client.

## ETHNICITY AND ADHERENCE

Research into psychotropic medication adherence has found lower adherence rates among Latinos and African Americans than among Whites (Diaz, Woods, & Rosenheck, 2005; Zeber et al., 2011). Reasons for this difference are unclear from the research to date.

Cultural mistrust could be contributing to nonadherence among African American clients. African American clients who are high in cultural mistrust have been found to have more negative attitudes about mental health, to terminate psychotherapy prematurely (especially if with a White counselor), and to disclose less with White counselors than African American ones (Whaley, 2001).

Be attuned to any statements that may suggest concerns or mistrust on the part of your client. Ask questions to elicit further information about the concerns and validate your client's feelings. Be open to discussing these issues and avoid defensiveness. Provide more information as needed; also consider directing the client to reputable websites for further information.

### Recommended Reading

Osterberg, L., & Blaschke, T. (2005). Adherence to medication. *New England Journal of Medicine, 353,* 487–497.
    *Osterberg and Blaschke provide a thorough discussion of medication adherence .*

Otis, H. G., & King, J. H. (2006). Unanticipated psychotropic medication reactions. *Journal of Mental Health Counseling, 28,* 218–240.
   *Otis and King provide a thorough discussion of the psychotherapist's role in collaborating with the psychiatrist and client when psychotropic medications are involved. Emotional and physiological reactions are discussed.*

## ONLINE RESOURCES

http://www.fda.gov/cder/drug/DrugSafety/DrugIndex.htm
   *This page from the U.S. Food and Drug Administration website provides consumer information sheets for many commonly prescribed medications.*
http://www.epocrates.com
   *This website offers free information on drug dosage and side effects. There are Epocrates apps for smartphones.*
www.nami.org/helpline/medlist.htm
   *This page on the National Alliance for the Mentally Ill website has a handy list of commonly prescribed psychotropic medications by trade and generic names.*

## RECOMMENDED FILM

Zwerin, C. (Director). (1988). *Straight no chaser* [Motion picture]. (Available from Warner Home Video)
   *If you are interested in observing someone who is probably taking Thorazine, you might want to watch this documentary about Thelonious Monk. He was a brilliant jazz pianist and composer who also was mentally ill. From written accounts (e.g., De Wilde, 1996), it is not clear whether he had schizophrenia or schizoaffective disorder. Nonetheless, when he was functional, his wife helped him remember to take his Thorazine. He was famous for "dancing" during breaks in the music when he was not playing. In actuality, he may have had severe akathisia—a common side effect of Thorazine (much less common with newer antipsychotics) that causes a person to feel an irresistible impulse to move around, moving the legs in particular. Additionally, he was known for his stiff-fingered piano-playing technique, which he may have developed because of muscle stiffness from his medication.*

## DISCUSSION QUESTION

1. Have you ever had difficulty taking a medication regularly or completing a prescription? (Be honest! Just about everyone has.) What factors do you think contributed to this? Are there other reasons why people might not take their medications besides the ones discussed in this chapter?

# 15

# Health-Related Referrals

You will often be the first health care professional the client has seen in a while—perhaps years—so it is important that you evaluate the client holistically. You will need to recognize when to make a referral to other health care professionals, and you will need to be able to explain to clients why getting additional treatment is important.

Untreated medical issues add to the client's pain and suffering, which has a negative impact on emotional health. Untreated sleep disorders or insomnia will cause poor concentration, poor memory, headaches, and exhaustion. Unrecognized cognitive problems will impede the client's recovery. Of course, you can't be an expert in all these areas of practice. However, if you think any of these referrals are warranted, talk to your supervisor.

## MEDICAL REFERRALS

*Travis Sanders is 57-year-old man who presents with depression. His energy level has been very poor for months. He is coming at the insistence of his wife. He has gained about 10 pounds in the past 2 months and is wearing a turtleneck, although it is 77 degrees outside. He indicates that he has been feeling depressed and irritable for several months and doesn't know why. He reports that he has never been depressed before. The psychotherapist asks him when he last saw a physician. He said that he hasn't seen a doctor in over 10 years. The psychotherapist recommends a complete physical exam. The physician finds that Travis is suffering from hypothyroidism and puts him on oral hormones, which improve his mood and return him to his prior level of functioning.*

Be alert to whether your client has been in appropriate and regular contact with a physician. In the case of Travis, a medical exam was definitely needed and resolved the problem. A client can present for a mental health issue but may have unidentified medical issues contributing to or causing the mental health symptoms. All medical issues should be treated even if they do not obviously affect the client's mental health. Be alert to any behaviors that may indicate medical problems:

- Unsteady or halting gait
- Tremor
- Swelling of the extremities
- Shortness of breath

- Chronic cough, wheezing, or any difficulty breathing
- Skin abnormalities
- Clothing that is inappropriate to the climate (Morrison, 1997).

When you notice anything that suggests a possible medical problem, ask your client about it:

"I've noticed that you have a small hand tremor. Have you discussed this with your physician? Do you know what is causing this?"

Your client is used to being asked about medical symptoms by health care practitioners and is unlikely to take offense. If the client cannot identify a known medical problem that causes the symptom, inform the client that it is essential to obtain an evaluation from a physician.

A physician should evaluate any unexplained symptom, including but not limited to:

- Nausea and vomiting
- Pain
- Weakness
- Fatigue or lethargy
- Feeling too hot or too cold
- Feeling too thirsty
- Vision problems
- Rashes (Morrison, 1997).

Individuals with eating disorders need to be evaluated by a physician for potential medical complications. Do not hesitate to send the client to the emergency room if you feel it might be needed (e.g., uncontrolled gasping, shortness of breath, or chest pain); it is better to err on the side of caution.

## CHRONIC PAIN

*Melanie Diaz is a mental health trainee who is doing a practicum in a medical center outpatient therapy clinic. She has been doing intake interviews. Today Melanie is interviewing Jorge Rodriguez; her diagnostic impression is generalized anxiety disorder. She asks him whether he has any medical problems; he states that he does not. She asks him whether he has had any pain recently. He states that he often has headaches. Melanie determines that he has severe tension-type headaches almost every day. Jorge states that over-the-counter pain medications have not helped him. She refers him to a health psychologist who will evaluate him for biofeedback treatment.*

As in the previous vignette, many clients deny any medical problems but then will say that they do have pain if asked about this directly. People may deny any medical problems yet have chronic headaches, chronic back pain, arthritis, or other pain issues. You may ask clients to rate the severity of the pain on a scale from 0 (no pain) to 10 (the most severe pain they have ever had). Keep in mind that one client's rating of 10 may differ from another's. For example, a young man with a history of few medical issues may have a relatively low 10, having experienced very little severe pain in his life, while an older woman who has given birth to three children and has had a knee replacement will have experienced more severe pain and will have a much higher 10. You might also want to ask the client how bothersome the pain has been. If it appears that pain has been contributing to your client's distress or interfering with daily functioning, you should address it.

Although many definitions of chronic pain exist, researchers agree that chronic pain is "one of the most disabling and costly afflictions in North America, Europe, and Australia" (Harstall & Ospina, 2003, p. 1). A review of multinational studies found that chronic pain affects about 12 percent of the population (Harstall & Ospina, 2003). Chronic headaches and chronic back pain are common pain conditions in the United States. Since pain conditions are so frequent and because pain has a profound impact on emotional and adaptive functioning, pain should be briefly assessed in all initial psychotherapy sessions, verbally, in writing, or both.

The current prevailing model of pain is the *biopsychosocial model* (Gatchel, Peng, Peters, Fuchs, & Turk, 2007). This model hypothesizes that pain is multiply determined by biological, psychological, and social factors. The level of pain experienced is a result of filtering sensory inputs through the brain. Two other important concepts are *suffering*, referring to the emotional responses that are triggered by the pain, and *pain behavior*, which would include client's statements about the pain and avoiding activities or exercise because of pain (Gatchel, Peng, Peters, Fuchs, & Turk, 2007).

Pain can exist with no known physical cause. The biopsychosocial model recognizes the reality of this pain and does not just assume that it is "all in the patient's head." Recent research indicates that short-term chronic pain can cause the nerve pathways to be altered so that long-term chronic pain becomes more and more likely (Woolf & Salter, 2000). In other words, the client may be completely healed but still have chronic pain due to maladaptive changes in the nervous system. This pain is very real and is caused by the nervous system becoming hyperalert to pain signals. Often it is helpful to educate your client about this model and offer assurances that you understand that the pain is real and distressing even if the doctors cannot find a physical cause.

Treatment of pain can be simple or complex. In the simplest situations, the patient's primary care physician can help the patient manage the pain through use of medications. Together with psychotherapy encompassing stress management and relaxation training, this may be sufficient to alleviate the pain significantly. A health psychologist, as outlined in the next section, can help you with more complex or treatment-resistant cases. The most effective state-of-the-art treatment for chronic pain is multidisciplinary and involves psychological, medical, and physical therapy interventions (Scascighini, Toma, Dober-Spielmann, &

Sprott, 2008). Most major medical centers have specialty pain clinics that provide multidisciplinary treatment.

Chronic headaches that interfere with functioning should always be evaluated and treated. There are several types of headaches that respond to different treatments. A full discussion of this issue is beyond the scope of this book; for further information, see the resources listed at the end of this chapter. However, migraines are headaches that have a distinct pattern of symptoms: pain around the eyes, sensitivity to light, and more. When they are distressing or impair functioning, refer the client to a physician because there are many helpful medications that can prevent migraines or that can treat them quickly when they occur (Schoenen, 2001).

## HEALTH PSYCHOLOGY

*Tyler Butler is a mental health trainee evaluating Nancy Miller. Nancy is very concerned about her history of smoking because her mother has just died from emphysema. Nancy has tried to quit many times and has not succeeded. Tyler refers her to the health psychologist on staff who evaluates her and treats her in conjunction with a physician. A combination of medications, group therapy, and individual behavioral therapy finally helps Nancy quit smoking.*

*Health psychologists* are licensed psychologists (Ph.D. or Psy.D.) who have extensive additional training in the psychological management of health issues. A qualified health psychologist has received specialized pre- and postdoctoral training. Health psychologists often work in large academic medical centers and provide "psychological therapies to enhance health behaviors, manage symptoms and sequelae of disease, treat psychological symptoms and disorders, prolong survival in the face of a life-threatening illness, and improve quality of life" (Compas, Haaga, Keefe, Leitenberg, & Williams, 1998, p. 89). Compas et al. (1998) divide the field of health psychology into four broad intervention groups: (a) decreasing health-risk behaviors, such as alcohol use and smoking, along with increasing health-promoting behavior, such as exercise and a healthy diet; (b) managing specific symptoms, such as chronic pain and insomnia; (c) interventions that facilitate effective coping with chronic or life-threatening conditions, including cancer, HIV, diabetes, asthma, arthritis, and so on; and (d) addressing health-related psychological conditions, such as eating disorders and body dysmorphic disorder. Health psychologists employ a wide variety of psychological treatment techniques, including stress management training, psychoeducation, cognitive-behavioral therapy, biofeedback, and hypnosis. Health psychologists also provide psychological insight and expertise on multidisciplinary medical treatment teams (Thielke, Thompson, & Stuart, 2011).

Refer your client to a health psychologist when you identify that the client has a health-related problem that is having a negative impact on adaptive coping or emotional functioning. The health psychologist can treat the client concurrently with you and will focus on the health-related issue. Have the client sign a release so that you and the health psychologist can consult and coordinate care.

A referral should be made for any pain that interferes with functioning or causes significant distress. A health psychologist has the expertise to help the client with specialized techniques, such as cognitive therapy of pain beliefs, graded exposure, and relaxation training (Gatchel, Peng, Peters, Fuchs, & Turk, 2007). Health psychologists are often found in multidisciplinary pain clinics, which are usually based at major medical centers. At that clinic, interventions at all levels of the biopsychosocial model will be employed by a multidisciplinary team working collaboratively to get the best results in pain control and functional improvement.

One modality that some health psychologists use is *biofeedback*, which is the practice of giving the client auditory and/or visual feedback about a physiological process so that the client can learn how to consciously make physiological changes. The feedback can be about blood pressure, heart rate, the electrical conductivity of the skin, muscle tension, and others. Biofeedback is used for headaches, stress management, and other conditions where physiological relaxation improves the client's pain or functioning. Biofeedback is well validated, but other methods of relaxation training may be as effective for many clients (L. Miller, 1994).

## INSOMNIA

*Amit Patel is a graduate student in biology. He has come to the clinic because he has insomnia and acute anxiety. He tends to ruminate at night before sleeping, and then he naps during the day. His sleep schedule is not fixed, and he is exhausted all the time. After working with a psychotherapist, he has learned the importance of maintaining a regular sleep schedule, he has decreased his rumination at bedtime, he is less anxious, and his sleep has improved.*

*Insomnia* is defined as "difficulty with the initiation, maintenance, duration, or quality of sleep that results in the impairment of daytime functioning, despite adequate opportunity and circumstances for sleep" (Silber, 2005, p. 803). Chronic insomnia occurs in about 10 percent of the adult population (Roth & Roehrs, 2003). Like Amit, above, they may ruminate when getting into bed at night, which keeps them alert and awake (Gellis & Lichstein, 2009). They may have poor sleep habits (such as sleeping with the television on or taking long naps during the daytime). They may awaken at night and have difficulty getting back to sleep. Insomnia is often a symptom of a medical or emotional disorder, such as depression or anxiety.

Since insomniacs usually have poorer sleep hygiene (Jefferson, et al, 2005), insomnia can often be treated through simple sleep hygiene and stimulus control instructions by the psychotherapist, with the addition of relaxation training as necessary (see Chapter 13). Clients may also be helped by discussing the issues they are ruminating about and by learning techniques to reduce rumination.

If these interventions have not been effective in improving the client's sleep, consider these options. If you wonder whether the client has a sleep disorder, refer for evaluation by a physician who is a diplomate in sleep medicine. Alternatively, you could consider a referral for medication to help with sleep or a referral to a health psychologist.

## SLEEP DISORDERS

*Jennifer Wright, a psychiatry resident, has been treating Linda Kress in individual psychotherapy for 4 months. Initially Linda's sleep had been very disrupted by depressive symptoms, and she had difficulty getting to sleep because she was ruminating about her problems. She was sleeping only about 6 hours a night when she began therapy. After 4 months, Linda had significantly reduced depression. In addition, Linda was going to sleep promptly and getting about 7 to 8 hours of sleep every night. However, she still stated that her sleep was poor. Jennifer asked whether Linda felt rested in the morning. She stated that she did not, and in fact she never does. She also volunteered that her husband complains that she tosses and turns all night and that she kicks him when she sleeps. Jennifer referred Linda for a sleep evaluation, which confirmed that she has periodic limb movement disorder, a common sleep disorder.*

*Mike Murphy talked to his psychotherapist, John Henderson, about his difficulties with concentration and distractibility. While this was consistent with his history of depression, John also noted that Mike looked sleepy during the session, which was in the late afternoon. When asked, Mike indicated that he was sleepy much of the time and took frequent naps. John also noted that Mike was a middle-aged male who was somewhat obese and had a thick neck. John asked if Mike's wife complained about his snoring—which, in fact, she did. John sent Mike for a sleep evaluation, which confirmed that he has sleep apnea.*

Sleep disorders are much more prevalent than most people imagine. Two common sleep disorders are sleep apnea (affecting between 3 and 7 percent of the U.S. population; Punjabi, 2008) and periodic limb movement disorder (about 4 percent prevalence in Europe; Ohayon & Roth, 2002). Both of these sleep disorders are underdiagnosed and undertreated in the general population (Ohayon & Roth, 2002; Young, Peppard, & Gottlieb, 2002). Both groups of clients often report daytime sleepiness and lack of restful sleep.

In *sleep apnea*, the airway is periodically blocked during sleep, which keeps partially rousing the client (who may or may not be aware of this), so the client never gets enough deep sleep. Sleep apnea clients will usually say that their bed partners have complained about their loud snoring. They may (or may not) know that they snore, snort, or gasp during sleep. Sometimes they know that they stop breathing during sleep (Maislin et al., 1995), or they may not be aware of their sleep breathing problems. While Mike, above, is a typical sleep apnea patient (middle-aged male, heavyset, thick neck), others who don't fit this profile can have sleep apnea because of subtle facial anatomy issues (Punjabi, 2008). Untreated sleep apnea can cause sudden death, cardiac problems, or stroke (Punjabi, 2008). Sleep apnea is most commonly treated through the use of a *CPAP* (continuous positive air pressure) device. The device increases the air pressure through the nose to prevent the breathing interruptions that characterize sleep apnea. There are also some alternative and emerging treatments for sleep apnea that a sleep medicine physician can also explore with the client.

In *periodic limb movement disorder* (PLMD), individuals move frequently during sleep; the cause is suspected to be related to problems in the dopaminergic neurotransmitter system, and evidence indicates that the individual is overly physiologically aroused during sleep (Scofield, Roth, & Drake, 2008). Bed partners complain about clients tossing and turning all night or kicking when asleep. Clients may note that their bedcovers are a mess in the morning. PLMD is treated with medications, often antiseizure medications, opiates, or dopamine agonists. PLMD is often, but not always, associated with restless legs syndrome. Both PLMD and restless legs syndrome can be exacerbated by certain antidepressant medications, such as selective serotonin reuptake inhibitors.

Other sleep disorders include *narcolepsy* (falling asleep unpredictably during normal daytime activities), *bruxism* (grinding teeth while asleep), *REM behavior disorder* (leading to sleepwalking or talking in one's sleep or other seemingly alert behavior, possibly violent if acting out distressing dreams, while asleep), and *sleep-related eating disorder* (the individual gets out of bed and eats, then goes back to sleep, later having a poor memory of the incident) (MedlinePlus, 2007; National Sleep Foundation, 2007).

If you have any suspicion of a sleep disorder, ask the client to talk the issue over with a primary care physician or make a referral to a sleep clinic yourself (ask your supervisor which is most appropriate). Sleep clinics can be freestanding or associated with a major medical center. At the sleep clinic, the client will be given paper-and-pencil screening instruments. The client will probably be interviewed by a physician who specializes in sleep medicine and then will have a *sleep study*, in which the client stays overnight in a sleep lab while being monitored for symptoms of sleep disorders.

## NEUROPSYCHOLOGICAL TESTING AND NEUROLOGY REFERRALS

*Joe Preap, a clinical psychology graduate student, is treating Dorothy Peters for chronic depression. Joe notes that Dorothy never seems to complete her homework assignments. When asked, she rarely even remembers what they were. Joe also knows that Dorothy lives with a friend, is not working, and has no source of income. He is puzzled because she seems to have so little motivation. The more Joe gets to know her, the more she does not seem like a typical client with depression. Joe discusses the case with his supervisor, Dr. Gomez, who reminds him of Dorothy's history of a car accident. Dorothy had told Joe that she did not remember the actual accident itself. She regained consciousness when she was in a hospital. It was likely that she had hit her head against the windshield. Dr. Gomez told Joe that Dorothy's lack of motivation was characteristic of clients*

*with brain damage from a closed head injury. They referred Dorothy to a neuropsy-*
*chologist and a neurologist for further evaluation.*

Brain injuries can be underdiagnosed and undertreated. Symptoms of brain damage or other neurological disorders can initially be mistaken for symptoms of common emotional problems. Many people have little understanding of how a brain injury can profoundly affect the behavior, emotions, personality, and functioning of an individual. As can be seen in the previous vignette, symptoms of brain injury can be subtle and difficult to diagnose, sometimes looking like depression. Often the client and the client's family have no idea that the brain injury is still having a profound impact on functioning.

The professionals who would evaluate these issues are *neurologists,* who are physicians with specialized training in the brain and nervous system, and *neuropsychologists,* who are doctoral-level psychologists with specialized postdoctoral training in evaluating cognitive functioning.

The client may also have an undiagnosed neurological disorder that is not caused by brain damage. Some symptoms that would warrant an evaluation by a neurologist would be weakness, tingling, numbing, trouble walking, tremor, involuntary movements, dizziness, and blurred or double vision (Morrison, 2007).

Strangely, a brain injury in which the skull is not penetrated can sometimes cause quite severe impairment. This type of brain injury is called a *closed head injury* since the skull is not breached; recently it has also been referred to as *mild traumatic brain injury* or TBI (Maguen et al., 2010). During the injury, the brain rams against the skull, and then it may bounce back and ram against the skull on the other side. This can result first in a concussion and later in personality changes and profound but diffuse cognitive deficits.

TBI affects over 10 percent of Afghanistan and Iraq war veterans (Maguen et al., 2010) and often co-occurs with post-traumatic stress disorder (Taylor et al., 2012). Combat veterans should be asked whether they have ever been rendered unconscious or had a concussion or head injury of any kind. If so, they should be further evaluated by a neurologist and/or neuropsychologist. Any client who has a history of concussion, being knocked on the head, or any significant injury to the head should be evaluated.

Brain injuries in which the skull is breached usually result in a different, more focal pattern of cognitive deficits that vary depending on the location of the injury.

## REMEMBER THE MIND–BODY CONNECTION

Most medical problems, including irritable bowel syndrome, migraine headaches, asthma, and others, are more symptomatic, painful or distressing when the client is under stress because of the mind–body connection. Therefore, psychotherapy that alleviates distress may also alleviate the severity of many medical conditions. Given these considerations, concurrent treatment of mental illnesses and medical issues is highly recommended.

Pain and mental disorders influence each other. For example, pain appears to increase the likelihood of depression, anxiety, and stress; in addition, depression, anxiety, and stress appear to increase the likelihood of pain (for a more complete explanation of the relationship, see Keefe, Dunsmore, & Burnett, 1992; Symreng & Fishman, 2004; Worz, 2003). Thus, psychotherapy addressing the client's emotional problems should help your client cope with the pain and perhaps even decrease the pain's intensity. Conversely, if you help your client get appropriate medical treatment for the pain, the client's emotional problems have a greater chance of improving.

## Recommended Reading

Gatchel, R. J., Peng, Y. B., Peters, M. L., Fuchs, P. N., & Turk, D. C. (2007). The biopsychosocial approach to chronic pain: Scientific advances and future directions. *Psychological Bulletin, 133*, 581–624.
*If you are interested in learning more about current thinking regarding chronic pain, this is the article for you. Some parts are overly technical for most of us, but read the beginning, skip over the technical parts, and be sure to read these later sections: Pain and Emotion, Pain and Cognitive Factors.*

Turk, D. C., & Burwinkle, T. M. (2005). Clinical outcomes, cost effectiveness, and the role of psychology in treatments for chronic pain sufferers. *Professional Psychology: Research and Practice, 36*, 602–610.
*The authors discuss the effectiveness of various state-of-the-art treatments for chronic pain, providing a helpful overview of pain treatments for the beginning psychotherapist.*

## Online Resources

http://www.iasp-pain.org
*This website of the International Association for the Study of Pain includes a series of helpful articles under the title "Pain: Clinical Updates."*

http://health.nih.gov
*This website provides helpful information for the medical patient on a wide variety of medical diseases. It can be helpful for you as well if you have a client with a medical problem that you are unfamiliar with.*

http://www.merckmanuals.com/professional/index.html
*This is the website for the "Merck Manual of Diagnosis and Therapy." Although it is a bit technical for nonmedical practitioners, it can still be very informative about many medical conditions.*

## DISCUSSION QUESTION

1. As a health care professional, even if you are not medically trained, you will often be the point of entry into the health care system for your clients. Do you feel comfortable referring clients to other health care professionals as needed? Do you need further training? Are there any rules of thumb you can use to know when to make a referral?

# 16

# Mental Health Referrals

Clients will sometimes need more intensive mental health treatment than you can provide in weekly individual psychotherapy. In these cases, you need to understand the range of treatment options available and make an appropriate referral given the client's level of distress and level of risk to self and others.

## INPATIENT PSYCHIATRIC HOSPITALIZATION

*Sean Foster, a mental health trainee, is working in an outpatient mental health clinic. He is leading a support group for clients with chronic schizophrenia. One of the clients, Miguel Flores, looks more depressed than usual. Sean asks him how he is doing. Miguel states that he is thinking of killing himself. Sean asks him if he has a way to do that. Miguel states that he has a gun at home. Sean knows that Miguel is an Iraq War veteran and knows how to use a weapon. Sean escorts Miguel to the psychiatrist's office. Together, the psychiatrist and Sean further evaluate Miguel and decide that he should be hospitalized. Sean escorts Miguel to the emergency room while the psychiatrist fills out the necessary paperwork for admission.*

Any client who is an acute danger to himself or others should be referred to an inpatient psychiatric unit (see Chapters 18 through 20). Also, clients who have severe symptoms, such as acute psychosis or acute mania and are unable to care for themselves should be hospitalized. In some instances, highly agitated clients or clients with extreme psychomotor slowing will also be admitted because of an inability to care for themselves.

If you believe that your client needs hospitalization, you should immediately get the advice of a supervisor. Agencies and medical centers have differing policies on coping with psychiatric emergencies. Most often, clients who need hospitalization will agree to it. However, sometimes a client needs hospitalization but refuses. In those instances, you must be familiar with state law regarding involuntary hospitalization, and you must be aware of the procedures for involuntary hospitalization at your facility.

## PARTIAL HOSPITALIZATION

*Rebecca Bennett is a grocery clerk who comes to the clinic feeling acutely anxious and depressed. Both her mother and her grandmother, who were her primary sources of emotional support, have died within the past 3 months. Rebecca denies suicidal ideation, but she has been crying and spending every day in bed. She has been calling in sick to work. The intake worker suggests that Rebecca attend the partial hospitalization program.*

A *partial hospitalization program* provides intensive mental health treatment for most days of the week while allowing the client to stay at home rather than in the hospital. When clients are having an acute exacerbation of mental illness and emotional distress but are not a significant risk to themselves or others, partial hospitalization is an appropriate referral. Outcomes for these clients are not different from inpatient treatment, and satisfaction is higher (Horvitz-Lennon, Normand, Gaccione, & Frank, 2001). Many partial hospitalization programs are short term, from one week to a few weeks, and their goal is stabilization. Others are longer term, lasting for months, and are aimed at helping people with severe mental illness return to a higher-functioning level (Yanos et al., 2009). There is some evidence that certain types of partial hospitalization programs may reduce costs and hospitalizations over the long term with individuals who have borderline personality disorder (Bateman & Fonagy, 2001, 2003).

## OUTPATIENT COMMITMENT AND INVOLUNTARY MEDICATIONS

In some states, clients can be committed by the court to attend outpatient treatment and take medications even if they do not want to (Hiday, 2003). Typically, these are clients who have a history of chronic mental illness or dangerousness; they are frequent users of intensive services, with long histories of nonadherence with follow-up care. Talk to your supervisor to see what your state laws are regarding outpatient commitment.

## ELECTROCONVULSIVE THERAPY

*Lakisha Washington, a mental health trainee, has been working with Erin Fitzgerald for about 6 months. Erin is married and has three young children at home. She is married to her high school sweetheart, who is a dentist. The plan was for Erin's husband to earn the family income while she cared for the children. However, Erin has been too mentally ill with schizoaffective disorder in the past year to care for the children effectively. Erin has chronic suicidal ideation and sometimes scares the children by talking about her wish to be dead. Erin's psychiatrist, Dr. Pryor, has tried many different medications over the past 9 months and meets with Erin frequently to monitor her response. Lakisha meets with Erin and her husband frequently to monitor the suicidal ideation and do psychotherapy. Dr. Pryor and Lakisha have had to hospitalize Erin four times in the past 9 months. Finally, Dr. Pryor recommends electroconvulsive therapy (ECT). Erin is fearful, as she has heard negative things about ECT. However, the family is suffering greatly and so Erin is willing to try it. Lakisha goes to visit Erin on the inpatient psychiatric unit between treatments. Erin's mood is dramatically better, and Lakisha sees her smile and joke for the first time ever. She sees her repeatedly over the next couple weeks. Later Lakisha alludes to their first conversation immediately after the ECT. Erin does not remember any of it. However, she says that her memory is back to normal now and that she feels much better.*

You might find yourself working with a client who is not responding to medications, as in this vignette. In these cases, the psychiatrist working with the client may recommend the use of *electroconvulsive therapy* (ECT). ECT is considered an effective treatment for severe major depression, especially depression with psychotic features or prominent risk of suicide (Lisanby, 2007), but it is rarely the first treatment that is tried (Royal Australian and New Zealand College of Psychiatrists Clinical Practice Guidelines Team for Depression, 2004). Instead, ECT is often considered when the client has not responded well to multiple antidepressants (Lisanby, 2007).

Unfortunately, most of us have been exposed to ECT through overly sensational movies. The actual process of ECT is nothing like that. If you ever have a chance to observe ECT, whatever your feelings or beliefs about the treatment, I encourage you to do so. The actual process of ECT is as follows (Lisanby, 2007):

- The client is brought into the surgical suite with the medical staff.
- The client given general anesthesia and also given a short-acting medication that relaxes the muscles. A simple pumping machine is used to keep air going in and out of the lungs.
- Electrical current is generally administered only to the right hemisphere to induce a seizure. The client moves very little or not at all during the procedure.
- Effectiveness of the procedure in inducing a seizure is monitored by EEG and by observing movement in a foot, on which a tourniquet had been previously placed, so that the muscle relaxant would not enter the foot.
- The client awakens in the recovery room, remembering nothing of the procedure.
- Soon after ECT, the client may have significant cognitive issues and memory gaps, which rapidly improve over the first 3 days after treatment and are mostly gone after 2 weeks (Semkovska & McLoughlin, 2010).

ECT must be administered repeatedly to be effective. The client can be an inpatient or an outpatient. Treatment is typically administered two or three times weekly for 6 to 12 sessions (Goodman, 2011).

Be aware that considerable controversy remains about how often and how much ECT affects memory in clients over the long term (Challiner & Griffiths, 2000; Rose, Fleischmann, & Wykes, 2004). Specifically, there remains some concern that ECT may interfere with the ability to recall some personal experiences before the ECT (Goodman, 2011; Verwijk et al., 2012). On the other hand, research findings suggest that cognition is likely to improve after ECT due to alleviation of depressive symptoms (Semkovska & McLoughlin, 2010).

## VAGUS NERVE STIMULATION AND TRANSCRANIAL MAGNETIC STIMULATION

There are other medical approaches that show promise for clients with severe, intractable depression, often called *treatment-resistant depression*. These treatments are vagus nerve stimulation and transcranial magnetic stimulation. The field is changing rapidly, so talk to trusted psychiatrists to get information on the latest techniques and research the latest efficacy data.

*Vagus nerve stimulation* (VNS) is an invasive treatment in which an implanted device gives regular electrical stimulation to the vagus nerve in the neck, which sends messages to the brain. (*Invasive treatments* are those that need the body to be opened.) This procedure was initially developed for treatment of epilepsy. There is evidence that it can be helpful in treatment-resistant depression, but better-quality studies are needed (Daban, Martinez-Aran, Cruz, & Vieta, 2008). This device has been approved by the FDA for treatment of depression.

*Transcranial magnetic stimulation* (TMS) is a noninvasive treatment (it can be done from outside the individual's body) during which magnetic pulses penetrate the skull to the brain from the outside and cause changes in the electrical currents of the brain (Schutter, 2010). The treatment is administered daily for 4 to 6 weeks (Grohol, n.d.). Patients may have some pain and muscle contractions associated with the treatment (Schutter, 2010). However, it is considered safe and effective (Lopez-Ibor, Lopez-Ibor, & Pastrana, 2008) and has been approved by the FDA for use with depression.

## SUBSTANCE ABUSE PROGRAMS AND COMMUNITY RECOVERY RESOURCES

Substance abuse is comorbid with so many mental health issues and you will make many referrals for adjunctive substance abuse treatment. A large sample of British community mental health clients with mental illness found that 44 percent had a problem with alcohol or drugs within the past year (Weaver et al., 2003). In addition, substance use can cause unusual symptoms, such as cocaine psychosis, that mimic those of other mental illnesses, so substance abusers need to be evaluated with great care.

The client will first need to be motivated to seek treatment. A confrontational approach is rarely productive (Stanton, 2004). Do not tell the client that he or she is an addict or alcoholic and must seek treatment. Instead, carefully assess the client's readiness for change and tailor your intervention appropriately (Prochaska & Norcross, 2001). If the client is not yet ready, take a motivational interviewing approach (W. R. Miller & Rollnick, 2002) in which you gently assist the client in discussing concerns about the substance use.

When the client is ready for help, you will need to consider the options together. Perhaps the client is more interested in community resources such as Alcoholics Anonymous (AA). If you are unfamiliar with the principles of AA, see their website at http://www.alcoholics-anonymous.org. AA can be an effective resource for clients, and frequent attenders are more likely to abstain (Gossop et al., 2003; Straussner & Byrne, 2009). AA may help alcoholics in many ways, including reducing impulsivity (Blonigen, Timko, Finney, Moos, & Moos, 2011), increasing self-efficacy, increasing social support, and adding spirituality and meaning (Straussner & Byrne, 2009).

When the substance abuse problem is more severe and there is a physical addiction, the client may need to be medically detoxified as an inpatient. Inpatient substance abuse or dual-diagnosis (e.g., both substance abuse and mental illness) programs can be helpful for many clients who have more severe addictions and need help getting sober. Some clients also benefit from living in a recovery house or other residential program for weeks or months.

Your supervisor and colleagues can help you learn about the other recovery resources available in your community and how to refer to them. Clients who have both mental illness and substance abuse problems should have both of those difficulties treated concurrently and with an integrative approach (RachBeisel, Scott, & Dixon, 1999).

## COMMUNITY RESOURCES

Until a client's basic needs for safety, food, housing, and so on are met, the client will not be able to concentrate on addressing emotional problems. Your client then needs referrals to community resources. Depending on how your training site is organized, you might make the referrals, or a staff social worker might assist you with this. Ask your supervisor for an overview of some of the resources that are most helpful for the client population you are working with.

### RECOMMENDED READING

Straussner, S. L. A., & Byrne, H. (2009). Alcoholics Anonymous: Key research findings from 2002–2007. *Alcoholism Treatment Quarterly, 27,* 349–367.
*A good introduction to what is known about the effectiveness of AA and why it works from a psychological perspective.*

## EXERCISES AND DISCUSSION QUESTIONS

1. Have you ever seen a client who might have benefited from ECT, VNS, or TMS? Would you be willing to refer a client for any of these treatments? Why or why not?
2. Does your state allow for outpatient commitment? If so, what is the procedure to do that?
3. What is the procedure for involuntary hospitalization in your state? Get copies of the forms that are needed and see what is necessary to fill them out.

# Crisis Readiness

# 17

# Managing Crises Step by Step

*Luisa Garcia, a 28-year-old Latina, is attending her regular psychotherapy session with Katherine Mahoney, a mental health trainee. Luisa tells Katherine that she has been thinking about suicide.*

*Robert Moore, a 30-year-old White male, comes to the intake clinic. He tells the intake worker, Shane Abel, a mental health trainee, that he needs treatment since he is thinking about killing his brother over a financial disagreement. Robert is a combat veteran.*

*Ryan Fernandes, a 55-year-old male, is brought to the clinic by his elderly parents. They are Catholic first-generation immigrants from India. The intake worker, Brandi Williams, a mental health trainee, reviews the chart and sees that Ryan has a long history of schizophrenia. His parents tell Brandi that Ryan has been pacing all night for the past several nights while talking to himself.*

These three vignettes continue throughout this chapter to illustrate how to work effectively with crisis clients. The chapter also focuses on issues common to all crisis clients, such as jointly formulating a crisis management plan, deciding whether to hospitalize, and documenting appropriately. You should consult with other professionals as needed throughout this entire process. Issues pertinent to particular crises are discussed in Chapters 18 to 21. Here are the steps for crisis management:

- Establish rapport
- Assess
  - The current situation
  - Historical and demographic risk factors
- Plan and implement
  - Give and elicit feedback
  - Consult supervisor
  - Consider whether hospitalization is appropriate
  - Make a crisis management plan and secure client's verbal agreement
  - Implement plan
- Document.

## ESTABLISHING RAPPORT: COPING WITH CRISES AND THE PSYCHOTHERAPIST'S EMOTIONS

*Katherine feels very anxious about talking with Luisa about her suicidal thoughts. She has never actually assessed a client for suicide risk before, although she has done role plays in class. Katherine takes a deep breath and reminds herself that she does know how to do this. She also reminds herself that more experienced staff are available to help her. She makes reassuring statements: "Luisa, it was very wise of you to come in and ask for help. I can see that you understand that these suicidal ideas mean that you need help right away." She talks to Luisa about the assessment process in a reassuring manner while communicating to Luisa that the situation is under control: "What I'd like to do is get a better understanding of how you are doing right now so that we can make a plan that will help you as soon as possible. How does that sound to you?"*

Even experienced psychotherapists can become anxious when they are working with crisis clients. It is normal to feel anxious in a crisis situation. Take a few deep breaths if you need to. Remind yourself that the client is here to get help and will likely feel better soon.

Remember that the client feels that his or her problems are unmanageable and that help is desperately needed. Your calm reassurances will help the client feel more in control. Being with someone else who knows how to manage the situation will reassure the client. Your empathetic statements to the client will help build rapport and the therapeutic alliance (Kleespies & Richmond, 2009). Once you understand the situation and help the client get assistance, the client's emotional distress will likely be eased. Also, at any time, you can contact your supervisor or another more experienced colleague and ask for help.

Once the crisis has been resolved, discuss what happened thoroughly with your supervisor. Increasing your understanding and confidence about how to address crisis situations is the best way to reduce the stress and anxiety of coping with them.

## ASSESS THE CURRENT SITUATION

*Katherine asks Luisa how long she has been thinking about suicide. Luisa says that she has been thinking about it constantly for the past 5 days. Katherine asks more about Luisa's suicidal ideas. Luisa reveals that she is thinking about jumping off a bridge near her house and that she has walked by the spot several times while thinking about jumping. Katherine asks whether Luisa thinks she can control herself and not jump. Luisa is unsure.*

*Shane asks Robert more about his violent thoughts. Robert says that whenever he sees his brother, he thinks about "jumping him." They have been living in a small apartment together with their mother, and tensions have been running high. When Robert is out of the house, he doesn't think about his brother or their disagreement. He said that he has been trying not to act on the violent impulses since he knows he would regret it later.*

*Brandi asks Ryan about his thoughts. Ryan says that God has been talking to him and tells him that he needs to spread the Word to the heathens in the neighborhood. (They live in a mostly Hindu Indian neighborhood.)*

Whenever you have a concern that the client may be having thoughts of suicide or violence, you must ask about this (Packman, Pennuto, Bongar, & Orthwein, 2004). Not asking can put your client or someone else in danger, and not asking will put you at greater professional risk (Packman et al., 2004). You'll want to thoroughly understand your client's thought processes, level of intent, and plans regarding the risky situation (Simon, 2004).

Generally, you will want to interview the client individually, then talk to any family or friends who brought the client in, as long as the client consents—preferably using your site's standard release of information form. When the client is less functional, family members provide valuable information.

However, if culturally appropriate, you might want to interview the client together with the family. Consider that certain cultural groups (such as Ryan's) may have more intergenerational involvement and may conceptualize problems more in the context of the family than the individual (Gonzalez, 1995; Hays, 2007).

## ASSESS HISTORICAL AND DEMOGRAPHIC FACTORS

*Katherine knows from Luisa's chart that Luisa has been diagnosed for years with borderline personality disorder and chronic major depression. She also knows that last year, Luisa took an overdose of pills, had her stomach pumped, and was hospitalized for 2 weeks. She knows that Luisa has a history of three other previous attempts of varying lethality. After each attempt, Luisa was hospitalized. Luisa also reports about five other hospitalizations for severe depression and suicidal ideation.*

*Shane asks Robert if he has been violent before. Robert reveals that he is a recovering alcoholic. He has been abstinent for 15 months. When he used to drink, he was often violent, but he has not been violent since he has been sober. He denied getting into any legal trouble because of his violent behavior in the past, and, as far as he knows, no one has ever been in the hospital after a fight with him. With Robert's approval, Shane calls Robert's drug and alcohol counselor, Ms. Patterson, to get her input. She says that Robert has been very engaged with his recovery program and, to her knowledge, he has not been hostile toward anyone since becoming sober. She feels that he is very motivated and can be trusted to follow through on a crisis intervention plan. She said that she would be happy to see Robert if he could come in for an appointment tomorrow.*

*Brandi reviewed the chart and sees that Ryan has never done anything to harm himself or others. She asks his parents about this, and they confirm it. He had several past episodes when he stopped taking his medications, became psychotic, and was briefly hospitalized. When Brandi asks the family about his medications, she finds that they have been coping with a medical crisis in a grandchild and have not been monitoring Ryan's medications as closely as they often do. Ryan insists that he has been taking his medication, but he clearly has a thought disorder and may be too confused to remember his medications; Brandi knows that his insistence is more likely a statement of intention to take his medications rather than an indication that he has actually done so. Ryan wandered off by himself in the middle of the night about 2 years ago, and his family found him in his pajamas wandering the neighborhood the next morning. They are concerned that this might happen again.*

Has this same crisis situation occurred in the past with this client? If so, that is an indication that the likelihood of its happening again is greater. For example, a history of multiple suicide attempts is the best predictor that a client is at heightened risk of future attempts (Jobes, Rudd, Overholser, & Joiner, 2008).

In what circumstances has the crisis situation occurred? Are these circumstances the same today or different? For example, if the client has been violent toward family when drunk in the past and has just relapsed on alcohol, the risk is greater. If the client has never been violent when sober and has been reliably sober for several years, the risk could be less.

Consider what you know about the client. Help the client draw on his own resources by asking what has or has not worked in past crisis situations. Consider what other professionals have to say verbally and in the chart.

## PLAN: GIVE AND ELICIT FEEDBACK

*Katherine tells Luisa, "I'm concerned about what you're telling me. It was wise of you to come in and talk to me about this. I hear that you can't be sure you'd ask for help if the suicidal feelings get strong again, and you are unsure whether you can control yourself. I suspect you're talking to me about this because you know you'd be safer in the hospital." Luisa agrees.*

*Shane tells Robert, "I see that you are worried about these violent thoughts, and I am as well. Let's explore together which plan makes the most sense. It sounds to me as if you have been able to control your impulses much better since you have been sober. Is that true? Do you think you and your brother would be safer if you weren't around him right now?" Robert replies to Shane that he feels uncertain about being able to control his violent impulses right now, but he thinks that as long as he avoids his brother, he will be fine. Shane says, "I can think of a few plans that might work for you, and I'd like us to discuss them. One might be to stay with a friend and avoid all contact with your brother for now. We could also consider admitting you to the hospital or to a partial hospitalization program. What do you think?" Robert says that if he can avoid his brother, he knows he won't be violent. Shane sees that Robert is sincere and motivated not to harm his brother, so a less restrictive alternative is appropriate.*

*Brandi tells Ryan and his parents, "I'm concerned that you will end up in the hospital again. It sounds like, even though you sincerely want to take your medication, you may have been missing some doses lately. [Turning to his parents] It's likely that he will improve soon, if he can regularly get his medication over the next several days. I'm wondering if you feel you can manage him at home or if you are too worried that he might do something unsafe like wander off at night." Ryan's parents worry that he may roam the neighborhood at night again. They think that they can get him to take his medications, but they are worried about what he will do before he stabilizes. Ryan says he thinks he would be okay outside the hospital, then talks again about his intent to convert the heathens. He is observed during this discussion to be looking around the room.*

You should give the client feedback—your professional opinion about the situation. Be honest yet tactful. For example, if you determine that the client feels great because she is getting manic, say so. If you are concerned about the client's suicidal impulses and think hospitalization would be safer, say so.

Sometimes you have specific recommendations, such as Katherine has with Luisa. Here, also, the crisis management plan is equally clear to both the psychotherapist and the client. Luisa has been in this situation before and she knows what help she needs.

Eliciting feedback is important as well. The client's feedback about plans is invaluable. Several possible plans might be appropriate, depending on the client's (and family's, if present) interests and motivations. As with Robert and Ryan, in the previous vignettes, you collaborate with the client (and possibly the family) and finalize a plan jointly whenever possible.

Sometimes the input of the family is necessary. In the case of Ryan, the psychotherapist sees that the family has valid worries that he will be unsafe. Since he has a history of wandering about disoriented at night, he has the potential to be a danger to himself. His poor judgment could lead him into dangerous situations, or he could be distracted by hallucinations, wander into the street, and be killed by a vehicle. For his own safety, Brandi and the parents agree that he should be hospitalized.

## PLAN: CONSULT SUPERVISOR

*Katherine is uncertain whether she can rely on Luisa to stay in the waiting room while she consults her supervisor. They have been working together for only 2 months, and Katherine knows that Luisa is very impulsive. Katherine asks Luisa, "Can you give me a minute to call my supervisor? I need to consult with him briefly." Luisa asks if she should step out, but Katherine assures her that it is fine for her to stay in the office. Katherine calls her supervisor to ask him to come to the office. Her supervisor does not pick up the phone. Katherine then calls a fellow trainee who agrees to go to the supervisor's office and asks him to come to Katherine's office. The supervisor, Dr. Ezra Stone, knocks on the door about 5 minutes later. Luisa has met Dr. Stone before. Dr. Stone comes into the office and sits with them while Katherine summarizes Luisa's situation. Dr. Stone agrees with the plan.*

*Considering Robert's behavior and Ms. Patterson's input, Shane determines that Robert can be relied on to wait in the waiting room. He asks Robert to do so, then goes to consult with his supervisor and returns after a few minutes.*

*Given what Brandi has observed about the family relationships, she feels that Ryan's family can keep him in the waiting room for a few minutes. Brandi asks them if she can step out for a few minutes to consult with her supervisor. She asks, "Could you wait here until I get back in about 5 minutes?" They assure her that this is fine.*

If you are inexperienced at assessing crises, you will want to consult with a supervisor before giving feedback. Alternatively, if you are more experienced, it may be clear what you need to do, and you will just give your supervisor a quick call to update her on the situation at an appropriate point.

If the client agrees not to leave the facility, you and your supervisor may be able to discuss the case while the client waits in the waiting area or in your office, as with Robert and Ryan in the previous vignettes. However, if you have any concerns about the client's ability to wait for 10 to 15 minutes while you consult, as Katherine has concerns about Luisa, your supervisor can join you in the office with the client as you summarize your observations.

If you are afraid that your client will hurt himself, run off, or engage in any risky behavior and you need to step out of the office to find a supervisor, you can ask another staff person to look after the client, or you can take the client to the emergency room, if your site has one. If your site has police or security personnel, you may need to call them to escort the client.

## PLAN: CONSIDER WHETHER HOSPITALIZATION IS APPROPRIATE

*After discussing her situation with Katherine, Luisa agrees to the plan to go to the inpatient unit.*

*Brandi recommends hospitalization. Ryan agrees to be hospitalized because he sees that this is what his parents want him to do.*

Clients with acute symptoms of psychosis or mania may or may not need to be hospitalized. Each case should be considered on an individual basis. Here are some questions you will want to ask yourself to determine whether to hospitalize or treat as an outpatient:

- Is there a risk of harm to self or others? What is the risk level, and can it be readily reduced?
- Does the client have insight into his own mental illness?
- Does the client understand the need for mental health care?
- Can the client be calm and comprehend instructions?

- Does the client verbalize an intention to get and take medications?
- Do you think that the client can be relied on to follow instructions and take medication?
- If psychotic, does the client have sufficient understanding of what is real and what isn't, and can she act appropriately on this knowledge?
- Will the client agree to attend an appointment soon?
- Will the client agree to seek help if worse?
- Can the client or the client's family reliably identify if the client is worse and seek help appropriately?
- Is the family supportive and reliable, or are there supportive and reliable friends?

Outpatient treatment is appropriate when the client is engaged well, has good insight about symptoms, and can reliably follow through on appointments and any changes in medication. If there are some deficits in the client's comprehension or follow-though but the client is cooperative and the family is involved, supportive, and reliable, the client may also be able to be treated as an outpatient. If the client can be involved in an intensive partial hospitalization program rather than the more restrictive environment of the inpatient unit, the client and family are more likely to be satisfied with the care (Horvitz-Lennon, Normand, Gaccione, & Frank, 2001).

Sometimes the plan will be to hospitalize the client. Although particular details vary from state to state (Simon, 2004), clients are generally hospitalized when they are a danger to self or others or if they are so symptomatic that they cannot adequately care for their own needs and keep themselves safe. In the previous vignette, Ryan cannot ensure his physical safety because of acute psychotic symptoms, so he is considered appropriate for hospitalization.

## PLAN: MAKE A CRISIS MANAGEMENT PLAN AND SECURE CLIENT'S VERBAL AGREEMENT

*Shane asks Robert if he has a friend he can stay with for a few days. He thinks his friend Tony will let him sleep on his couch. Shane and Robert agree that this would be the best choice for now. Shane asks Robert if he has a gun. Robert says that he gave away all his guns months ago at the request of his substance abuse counselor. He agrees not to get another gun until he feels more in control of his violent ideas. Shane asks Robert who he can rely on for emotional support. Robert lists his mother, Tony, and some fellow group members. They agree that Robert could benefit from getting support from these individuals over the next week.*

As in the vignette above, collaborate with the client to formulate on an effective crisis management plan, which synthesizes your assessment, the input of the client, and, if appropriate, the client's family's input. Encourage the client get in touch with his own ability to actively problem-solve and to reach out to his social supports (Callahan, 2009). Obtain and document the client's verbal agreement to implement his portion of the plan. Observe the client carefully for signs of insincerity (e.g., hesitancy or sarcastic tone) about the plan and reconsider the plan if necessary.

## WHEN YOU AND CLIENT DO NOT AGREE ON PLAN

Because of safety issues, you might have definite ideas about what the plan should be, but the client may not like your plan. In this case, carefully explain your concerns and your reasoning to the client and ask for feedback. Then find out what the client's concerns are and do the best you can to address them:

Psychotherapist: I'm very concerned. You've told me that you can't be sure that you'd call 911 or go to the emergency room if your suicidal impulses get stronger. You've come in for help with this, and it's very important to me to take some action to help keep you safe. The only thing I know of that will keep you safe under these circumstances is for you to be in the hospital. Yet you're telling me you don't want to go. What do you suggest that we do under these circumstances?

Client: Just let me go. I'll be okay.

P: Do you have any concerns about being in the hospital?

C: I've seen the movies. I know that psych hospitals are full of dangerous psychos.

P: Actually, what's in the movies is overly sensationalized. I've visited the unit before, and I can assure you it's a very safe place. The people who are there are seeking help for their problems, just like you are.

C: Will you come see me there?

P: I can't do that because I need to be here in the intake clinic seeing other people who need help.

C: How long will I be there? Can they keep me for weeks?

P: They will probably discharge you within a week. And as soon as you don't have any intent to hurt yourself, you can ask to leave at any time, and they can't keep you.

C: Okay, I'll go.

Often, the media has promoted inaccurate and sensationalistic views of inpatient psychiatric care. When you understand and address the client's concerns, most of the time the client will agree to go to the hospital. In rare instances when there are clear safety issues for the client or others, you may have to involuntarily hospitalize a client. Be sure to ask your supervisor what the criteria are for involuntary hospitalization and how this is done in your setting so that you are prepared.

## IMPLEMENT PLAN

*Luisa expresses some concern about her cats, as she hasn't made any arrangements for them, so Katherine lets her call her sister from the office and ask her to feed the cats while Luisa is in the hospital. Then Katherine escorts Luisa to the emergency room for admission. When in the emergency room, Katherine calls Luisa's psychiatrist to give her an update on the situation. The psychiatrist will need to come to the emergency room to write an admission order.*

*Robert calls his friend Tony from Shane's office, and Tony tells him that he can stay as long as he needs to. Robert doesn't have any of his clothes or toiletries with him and agrees to ask his mother to bring them over to Tony's. He agrees to stay at Tony's at least until his next appointment with his alcohol counselor, when he can discuss this issue in more detail. Shane suggests that if he does see his brother accidentally before then, he should turn around and leave immediately. Robert readily agrees to do so but thinks this is unlikely. Robert again verbalizes his intent not to hurt his brother despite these impulses. Shane suggests that Robert call his mother as well and update her on these plans. Robert calls his mother from the office, and when he gets off the phone, he says that his mother was relieved to hear that he had taken some steps to get help and resolve this situation. His mother will bring his clothes to his friend's house tonight. Shane confirms that Robert remembers he can see his substance abuse counselor tomorrow. He also makes an appointment for Robert to see a psychiatrist in 2 days for evaluation of PTSD and other mental illnesses.*

*Since the clinic does not have an inpatient unit on site, Brandi talks to Ryan's parents about where he has been hospitalized before. They have been satisfied with the care he received at St. Joseph's. She recommends that they take him to the emergency room there. She gets a signed release from Ryan to communicate with St. Joseph's. She makes a copy of the release and prints out her progress note about her evaluation of Ryan. She puts her supervisor's pager number in the progress note in case the hospital staff members have any questions. Ryan and his family believe that he will be cooperative during the ride to the hospital, and they agree to take him directly there. Brandi calls the ER at St. Joseph's and alerts them that Ryan will be coming and that she is faxing information over. She then faxes over the release and the progress notes for today. She then documents in the chart that she has done so.*

Do whatever you can to facilitate implementing the plan. If you are in a medical center, walk the client from your office to the emergency room for admission. If the client is staying with a friend, ask him to call the friend from your office and make a plan to get to the friend's house. If the client remains an outpatient, be sure the client has an outpatient follow-up appointment scheduled and an appointment card in hand before leaving, and that he agrees to attend that appointment.

## DOCUMENT

When documenting a crisis and how it was addressed, it is important to be as thorough as possible. When documenting crises, err on the side of being overly

inclusive in your progress note. It is important to include the following items
(adapted from Rivas-Vasquez, Blais, Rey, & Rivas-Vasquez, 2001). I have sorted
them out by the section of the progress note that they go in:

- Subjective/Objective
    - Describe the client and chief complaint.
    - List all known current symptoms.
    - Summarize relevant historical information, including medical and
      substance abuse histories as well as prior mental health care.
    - If time allows, assess and document psychosocial history and family
      history of mental illness.
    - Document any consultations you made about the case.
    - Describe all known risk and protective factors and warning signs
- Assessment
    - List and describe all observed and reported symptoms of mental illness.
    - Make diagnoses, but keep in mind that making an accurate diagnosis
      may not be possible during an acute crisis. If uncertain, use a vague
      diagnosis like psychosis NOS rather than a potentially stigmatizing
      diagnosis like schizophrenia.
    - Determine a risk level and use the information you gathered to justify
      your conclusions about risk.
    - Describe, in detail, what your thought process and rationale were in
      assessing the situation and determining the plan.
- Plan
    - Document client's agreement with plan (if the client disagrees with an
      outpatient management plan, you aren't ready to document yet—you
      have to further discuss with client and you may have to hospitalize).
    - Document how the plan was or will be implemented by you and by
      the client

*When you and the client have agreed on a less restrictive plan than hospitalization,
be especially detailed about your thought process and rationale.* You want the note
to be complete and self-contained so that any mental health professional reading
it will understand exactly why you and the client made the choices that you did
and will agree that these choices were consistent with professional standards. If
sufficient risk factors or warning signs were present that you considered hospitalization but you did not hospitalize, be explicit about how you weighed the pros
and cons of outpatient versus inpatient treatment.

## PROGRESS NOTE FOR LUISA

*S/O.* Luisa Garcia is a 28-year-old Latina who has been in individual therapy
with me for 2 months. Her diagnoses are borderline personality disorder and
chronic major depression.

Ms. Garcia presents today with an exacerbation of depressive symptoms: poor eating and sleeping, feeling fatigued, and ruminating constantly about her problems. In addition, she has been thinking seriously about dying by suicide and has a plan to jump off a bridge near her home. She states that she has been thinking about this constantly for the past 5 days and has been walking past the site while thinking of jumping every day. She feels uncertain that she can control herself much longer.

Ms. Garcia has a history of multiple suicide attempts. Last year she took an overdose of her pills and had to have her stomach pumped. Additionally, she had three previous suicide attempts of varying lethalities. She has a history of eight previous psychiatric hospitalizations for depression, suicide attempts, and suicidal ideation.Ms. Garcia does not abuse substances, nor has this ever been an issue for her. Her mother, with whom she was very close, recently died from cancer, and Luisa has been despondent ever since.

**A.** Ms. Garcia is at high acute risk of suicide given her current inability to make a commitment to stay alive and her history of multiple suicide attempts.

**P.** Ms. Garcia agreed to inpatient hospitalization at this medical center. She was walked to the emergency room and was medically cleared there, then was admitted to Unit 2B.

[Signed]      Katherine Mahoney, B.A.<br>
                Psychology Trainee

[Cosigned]   Ezra Stone, Ph.D.<br>
                Licensed Clinical Psychologist

This progress note about Luisa is very brief for a crisis note. That is because it is a cut-and-dried situation of acute high suicide risk in a client with a history of multiple suicide attempts and because the client was placed in the restrictive environment of the inpatient unit, where staff will follow standard procedure and put her on suicide watch.

## PROGRESS NOTE FOR ROBERT

*S/O.* Robert Moore is a 25-year-old White male who presents at the intake clinic stating that he is having thoughts of killing his brother. He is a combat veteran.

Mr. Moore has a longstanding history of substance abuse and has been treated by the addiction clinic at this facility. With his approval, his substance abuse counselor, Ms. Patterson, was contacted. She said that he has a 15-month history of abstinence, with negative toxicology screens done at random. His adherence to treatment is good, and he has not exhibited any violent or aggressive behavior while in treatment. She stated that she felt he could be counted on to cooperate with any agreed-on crisis management plan.

Mr. Moore admits to having a long history of violent altercations, all of which occurred while he was drunk. However, he volunteered that no one was ever injured seriously, to his knowledge. Mr. Moore denied ever having been charged or convicted of any crimes, which is consistent with all chart documentation.

Mr. Moore stated that he and his brother have been living with their mother in a small one-bedroom apartment. He and his brother have been arguing about financial issues and can't get away from each other. He stated that, despite these violent thoughts, he does not want to hurt his brother, which is why he came to the clinic today. Mr. Moore said that as long as his brother is not around, he does not think about hurting him. He denied having any physical altercations with the brother.

Mr. Moore denied any thoughts about suicide or death. He has no history of suicide attempts.

**A.** Diagnostic impression: Alcohol abuse, in remission, further diagnoses deferred. Needs full mental health evaluation, including evaluation for PTSD.

Violence Risk Assessment: Mr. Moore has many violence protective factors. While Mr. Moore is having violent thoughts toward his brother, he showed good judgment coming to the clinic to get assistance in coping with this crisis. He denies any intent to hurt his brother and states that he knows that if he did, he would regret it. He also stated that he wouldn't make his mother suffer like that. He has demonstrated excellent motivation for and adherence to treatment over the past 15 months, he has a good treatment alliance, and his substance abuse counselor has indicated that she trusts him to follow any crisis management plan. Nonetheless, Mr. Moore has some significant violence risk factors. He has a history of violent behavior when intoxicated and he is a combat veteran. Given the above, my assessment is that as long as Mr. Moore stays away from his brother and continues to discuss these issues in treatment, his acute violence risk will be low.

**P.** To minimize any risk of an altercation, Mr. Moore called a friend from my office. The friend agreed to let Mr. Moore stay with him as long as he needs to. Mr. Moore agreed to go directly to the friend's house. He called his mother at work, and she agreed to bring some of his clothes and toiletries to his friend's house tonight. This arrangement will prevent him from having any interactions with his brother. He agreed to follow up tomorrow with his substance abuse counselor, who will help him further explore these issues and discuss alternative housing options. Will alert Ms. Patterson regarding above. I also referred him to Dr. Olson for further evaluation and treatment of any other emotional difficulties that may be destabilizing him. Mr. Moore stated that he has been wondering himself whether he may be suffering from PTSD because he often awakens from upsetting nightmares of combat. He agreed to attend the appointment with Dr. Olson in 2 days, on 6-15-20xx. The risk of violence should continue to be monitored.

[Signed]    Shane Abel, M.D.
             Psychiatry Resident

As you can see, this note is longer than the previous one. Since Robert will be treated as an outpatient, Shane has carefully justified the decision-making process. He carefully documents Robert's intent not to harm his brother and Robert's reasons for not doing so. He also indicates his awareness of Robert's violence risk factors. He has ensured that the plan is in place, as much as possible, before Robert leaves his office and documented that he has done so. He carefully documents Robert's collaboration and agreement on all aspects of the plan.

In this case, Shane did not evaluate Robert for symptoms of mental illness. Since Robert's substance abuse counselor could vouch for his cooperation and adherence to treatment, and Robert showed good insight and was clearly motivated, Shane felt confident that Robert would return for the evaluation in 2 days and that would be soon enough.

Note that there is no mention of Robert's brother being notified of Robert's violent thoughts against him—and, in fact, he was not. Why? First, Shane has carefully assessed Robert for violent intent and has determined that Robert has not hurt his brother and that he has no intention to do so. Second, Robert has shown good judgment in seeking help. Robert's reliability in treatment and his agreement to the plan indicate that he can be trusted to follow through appropriately. Finally, Shane's professional opinion is that the plan that he and Robert have devised has defused the situation.

## PROGRESS NOTE FOR RYAN

*S/O.* Ryan Fernandes is a 55-year-old male brought to the clinic by his parents. They are all first-generation immigrants from India, and they are Catholic.

Mr. Fernandes has a longstanding history of schizophrenia. He has been treated for it at this outpatient clinic for 12 years and apparently has had symptoms and treatment since he was 21 years old. His parents report numerous previous hospitalizations, mostly when he stopped taking his medications.

Mr. Fernandes's parents report that he has been pacing all night and talking to himself. His functioning around the house has deteriorated markedly. They admit that they have been distracted lately with the illness of a grandchild and thus haven't been monitoring his medications as closely as they usually do. They also stated that when he has gotten more symptomatic in the past, he has wandered around the neighborhood in his pajamas, talking about "converting the heathens." Today, Mr. Fernandes says that God is telling him that he has been "anointed to convert the heathens." I also observed him looking around the room as if responding to internal stimuli. Mr. Fernandes states that he has been taking his medications, but his report may be unreliable because of current symptoms of thought disorder.

Mr. Fernandes was not able to respond very coherently to questions about suicidal or violent ideation.

*A.* Mr. Fernandes is having an exacerbation of longstanding schizophrenia. There is significant risk that he could be a danger to himself by wandering the neighborhood at night when his parents are asleep. He is having auditory hallucinations, probable visual hallucinations, agitation, and delusions that he was anointed by God to convert the heathens. He has probably been missing some of his medication doses. His parents do not feel that they can manage him at home at this time. Suicide and violence risk could not be assessed at this time.

*P.* Because of the risk of unintended self-harm while he is psychotic and disorganized, Mr. Fernandes will be taken for hospitalization to St. Joseph's Medical Center. Mr. Fernandes agreed to this plan, and his parents will drive him there. He signed a release of information. I called the ER at St. Joseph's and alerted them that Mr. Fernandes is coming and that I would be faxing them a copy of this note. I consulted with Dr. Xavier about this plan, and he agreed to the disposition. His pager number is 312-555-0129 if further information is needed.

> [Signed]      Brandi Williams, M.A.
>                     Psychology Practicum Student
>
> [Cosigned]   Thomas Xavier, Ph.D.
>                     Staff Psychologist

Just because a client with schizophrenia is having an exacerbation of symptoms does not mean that the client needs hospitalization. However, in this case, because of the risk of harm through poor judgment, hospitalization is recommended. Brandi makes this reasoning clear in the progress note. Brandi documents that the client was too cognitively disorganized to assess suicidal or violent ideation; inpatient staff will follow up when Ryan is capable of answering coherently.

#### RECOMMENDED READING

See Chapters 18 to 21 for recommended readings on specific crisis assessment topics.

## EXERCISES AND DISCUSSION QUESTIONS

1. What are the procedures for initiating voluntary hospitalization at your training site? How does the client and the associated documentation get to the hospital?
2. What are the legal requirements to initiate involuntary hospitalization in your state? What are the procedures for involuntary hospitalization? Ask your supervisor to describe the details of how staff implements involuntary hospitalization at this site.
3. Ask your supervisor, your fellow trainees, and colleagues at your training site about crisis situations they have been involved in. What were all the steps they went through to assess and manage the crisis situation collaboratively with the client? Are mobile outreach services available in your area? How are they deployed in crisis situations? Different states and training sites have varying mental health resources and protocols for crisis situations. How is interagency communication facilitated with emergency rooms at local hospitals?

# 18

# Assessing Suicide Risk
# and Warning Signs

Often, beginning psychotherapists work with high suicide risk populations, such as those in community mental health centers, but this risk will occur in every client population. Thus, you must be prepared to assess and cope with suicide risk from your very first day of clinical work. Assessing suicide risk is one of the most important yet anxiety-provoking tasks that a beginning psychotherapist can do. It is also professionally risky in terms of practitioner emotional distress and risk for malpractice suits (Packman, Pennuto, Bongar, & Orthwein, 2004). Suicide is the most frequent crisis seen by mental health professionals (McAdams & Foster, 2000), and almost half the persons who die by suicide are under the care of a mental health professional (Goldsmith, Pellmar, Kleinman, & Bunney, 2002). Suicide is the 10th most common cause of death in the United States, and 0.5 percent of adults made a suicide attempt in the last year (Centers for Disease Control and Prevention, 2012).

In this chapter, I focus on the initial assessment phase for suicide risk with adult outpatients. First, some important theory and concepts about suicide risk assessment are introduced. There are seven sections of this chapter with titles that begin with the word "Understanding." These sections help you establish the conceptual framework for understanding suicide risk. Then you learn how to assess current suicidal ideation and past suicidal behavior. Finally, suicide risk factors, warning signs, and protective factors are addressed—as well as the importance of rapport and motivation for treatment.

As I discussed in the last chapter, the steps in crisis intervention are establishing rapport, assessment, plan/implementation, and documentation. Due to the sheer volume of information on suicide, only the assessment and rapport steps are addressed in this chapter. In Chapter 19, I will talk about determining suicide risk level, reducing suicide risk, and documenting your assessment.

Be aware that most of the research on suicide risk and prevention has been done on predominately White populations. Commonly accepted suicide risk factors may be less predictive among of suicide among African Americans (Abe, Mertz, Powell, & Hanzlick, 2006).

I do not address working with suicide risk in pediatric, inpatient, or emergency settings in this chapter, and if you are working in those settings, relevant literature should be reviewed (e.g., Simon, 2004).

## UNDERSTANDING THE INTERPERSONAL
## MODEL OF SUICIDE

An influential model of why people die by suicide is called the *interpersonal model of suicide* (Van Orden, K. A., et al, 2010). Joiner, Van Orden, Witte, and colleagues believe that there are two major factors involved in suicide attempts. The first major factor is a *desire for death*, which itself is due to two reasons: *thwarted belongingness* (feeling alienated from others emotionally) and *perceived burdensomeness* (feeling that one is incompetent and therefore a burden on others) (Ribeiro & Joiner, 2009). Interpersonal problems, social isolation, and social disruption (what they call *thwarted belongingness*) have been well documented as suicide risk factors in countless studies. These researchers are studying whether their burdensomeness factor is as influential as the belongingness factor.

The second major factor in this model is *acquired capability* (sometimes called *acquired capacity*) to carry out the suicide attempt. People naturally fear death and painful experiences. To make a suicide attempt, the person has to be capable of overriding fears, pain, and the idea of death (Ribeiro & Joiner, 2009). Developing this capability can be done many ways, including previous suicide attempts, rehearsing suicide through behavior or imagery, and getting used to painful or dangerous experiences in other ways (addressed in greater detail later in this chapter). The model's emphasis on this *acquired capability* factor is, I believe, its most important contribution to conceptualizing the suicide risk process.

Joiner, Van Orden, Witte, and colleagues readily acknowledge that this model does not explicitly include all of the significant risk factors and warning signs for suicide, which also include mental illness, hopelessness, substance abuse, and others (Van Orden et al., 2010). However, they do include these other factors when giving a rubric for deciding risk level (discussed further in Chapter 19).

## UNDERSTANDING SUICIDE RISK FACTORS
## AND WARNING SIGNS

Prominent researchers carefully distinguish between *suicide risk factors* and *suicide warning signs* (this discussion informed by Rudd, 2008). A *suicide warning sign* is a behavior or statement by the client that indicates that the client is at increased suicide risk within the next few days. Here are some examples of warning signs:

- Client says, "I feel hopeless."
- Client says, "I feel trapped."

- Client's spouse says that client has been hoarding medications.
- Client has been searching the Internet for information on how to die by suicide.

Suicide warning signs come and go over time. Due to their fleeting nature, suicide warning signs have been difficult for researchers to study, but warning signs show much promise to help us understand and manage suicide risk in the short term (Rudd, 2008). Experts at the American Association of Suicidology (AAS, n.d.; Rudd et al., 2006) consider these to be the most important suicide warning signs (note the acronym IS PATH WARM?):

- I—suicidal Ideation—thinking, talking, or writing about suicide, planning for suicide
- S—escalating Substance abuse
- P—Purposelessness, no reason for living
- A—Anxiety, agitation, unable to sleep or sleeping all the time
- T—feeling Trapped
- H—feeling Hopelessness
- W—social Withdrawal from friends, family, or society
- A—Anger, rage, seeking revenge
- R—Recklessness, impulsiveness
- M—dramatic Mood changes.

A *suicide risk factor* is an enduring or historical characteristic of the client that can be objectively described and indicates increased risk of suicide over the long term. Some examples of risk factors are:

- Client is widowed.
- Client has schizophrenia.
- Client has made four suicide attempts in the past, along with many episodes of cutting self.
- Client has a history of childhood sexual abuse.

Risk factors tell us that a client is at a statistically increased risk of suicide compared to others, so this *is* valuable information. However, risk factors do not tell us as much about the client's immediate level of risk *today* as warning signs do.

## UNDERSTANDING WHY PEOPLE DIE BY SUICIDE

### Hunter S. Thompson's Suicide Note

"Football Season Is Over. No More Games. No More Bombs. No More Walking. No More Fun. No More Swimming. 67. That is 17 years past 50. 17 more than I needed or wanted. Boring. I am always bitchy. No Fun—for anybody. 67. You are getting Greedy. Act your old age. Relax—This won't hurt." (Allen, 2005)

### Virginia Woolf's Suicide Note

"Dearest, I feel certain that I am going mad again. I feel we can't go through another of those terrible times. And I shan't recover this time. I begin to hear voices, and I can't concentrate. So I am doing what seems the best thing to do. You have given me the greatest possible happiness. You have been in every way all that anyone could be. I don't think two people could have been happier 'til this terrible disease came. I can't fight any longer. I know that I am spoiling your life, that without me you could work. And you will I know. You see I can't even write this properly. I can't read. What I want to say is I owe all the happiness of my life to you. You have been entirely patient with me and incredibly good. I want to say that—everybody knows it. If anybody could have saved me it would have been you. Everything has gone from me but the certainty of your goodness. I can't go on spoiling your life any longer. I don't think two people could have been happier than we have been. V."
(Brooks, 2012)

The two suicide notes, above, are from two very different authors; both died by suicide. Think about the themes in these notes in connection with people's reasons for suicide, as discussed below and later in the chapter.

There are many reasons that contribute to people dying by suicide. I have grouped these into four categories to help you conceptualize some of the most important. (This discussion is informed by Kraft, Jobes, Lineberry, Conrad, & Kung, 2010, and O'Connor, Jobes, Lineberry, & Bostwick, 2010.)

The first category of risk factors and warning signs is emotional and physical pain. Clearly, a person has to be in great pain to consider suicide to be a valid option. Often multiple painful factors combine to reach a level that the individual considers intolerable. Sometimes the person feels desperate to escape the pain (O'Connor, Jobes, Lineberry, & Bostwick, 2010). This emotional pain can be caused by disrupted relationships, painful and/or traumatic experiences, mental illness, unemployment, severe financial distress, substance abuse, chronic physical pain, medical illnesses, self-hate, or a high level of stress that overwhelms a person's ability to cope (American Association of Suicidology, n.d.). You can see the acute emotional pain caused by mental illness in Virginia Woolf's suicide note. The emotional pain of *social isolation*, whether caused by bereavement, divorce, emotional distance, rejection of others, or any other cause, is one of the most important risk factors for suicide (Van Orden et al., 2010). Hunter S. Thompson alludes to emotional distance in his suicide note. Chronic and acute stressors contribute to painful emotions. The impact of stress will be discussed in further detail later in the chapter.

The second category of risk factors and warning signs is the individual's cognitive status and cognitive evaluation of the situation. An important warning sign is the perception that one's situation is hopeless (Beck, Brown, & Steer, 1989). You can see this perception in both of the suicide notes. Certain views about one's situation contribute to suicidal thoughts: that the individual is unable to cope, that the individual is a burden to others, and that the individual is trapped and has no other options (American Association of Suicidology, n.d.). Other cognitive factors include rumination, racing thoughts, and poor problem-solving (American Association of Suicidology, n.d.; O'Connor, Jobes, Lineberry, & Bostwick, 2010). The individual may have tunnel vision about the situation, may be under the impression that the pain will last indefinitely, and may have lost track of reasons to live. Individuals who are suicidal can view the permanence of suicide as a good thing (Kraft, Jobes, Lineberry, Conrad, & Kung, 2010). Suicide can also be seen as the easy way out of a difficult situation (Kraft, Jobes, Lineberry, Conrad, & Kung, 2010). Suicidal individuals vary considerably in terms of how ambivalent they are about life, with some having much stronger reasons to live and others having stronger reasons to die (O'Connor et al., 2012).

The third category is warning signs of activation. Sometimes people feel miserable and hopeless but don't do anything about it. What might activate the individual toward making a suicide attempt? Some possibilities are impulsiveness, agitation, anxiety, aggression, a manic or mixed-mood episode, substance abuse, poor judgment, and poor self-control.

The fourth category is risk factors and warning signs that increase the individual's capability to complete suicide. This capability is increased through repeated suicide attempts, other types of suicidal behavior, various other painful or risky experiences, and mental imagery of various types.

## UNDERSTANDING THE CAPABILITY TO DIE BY SUICIDE

People who have the greatest capability to die by suicide are those who have been practicing through *multiple suicide attempts* (multiple is defined as two or more). In a person who has made multiple suicide attempts, it may take less distress to trigger a suicidal crisis. Because of that, these individuals must be considered to have chronically elevated suicide risk they must be monitored more carefully, and this monitoring requires careful documentation (Jobes, Rudd, Overholser, & Joiner, 2008).

Statistically, people with one suicide attempt are at similar risk to those with no previous attempts, but clearly some of these individuals will become multiple attempters over time. There is some evidence that individuals with borderline personality disorder and bipolar disorder are at increased risk of becoming multiple attempters after one suicide attempt (Bryan, Johnson, Rudd, & Joiner, 2008). Despite this, be aware that up to 50 percent of those who make their first suicide attempt may die (Joiner, 2005), so do not minimize suicide risk if there are no previous attempts.

Sometimes individuals haven't attempted suicide per se but have engaged in *suicidal behavior*. Although the term *suicidal behavior* includes past attempts, it also includes other behaviors that help the individual prepare or practice for a suicide attempt, without actually making a full attempt. Some experts, including those from the Centers for Disease Control and Prevention, prefer the term *self-directed violence* over *suicidal behavior* (Crosby, Ortega, & Melanson, 2011), although that term has been less commonly used to date. These case examples illustrate some types of suicidal behavior:

- *Suicide rehearsal in imagery*: A 19-year-old single male often isolates himself in his dorm room. He has post-traumatic stress disorder (PTSD) from a history of severe childhood sexual abuse, and recurrent major depression. When he has negative interactions with his family, he fantasizes about shooting himself with a gun and gaining "the peace and release of death."
- *Behavioral suicide rehearsal*: A 27-year-old combat veteran with PTSD, recurrent major depression, alcohol abuse, and panic attacks is easily overwhelmed by his 1-year-old daughter and his course work at vocational school. He keeps a loaded gun under his bed. When upset, he takes the gun out and puts it in his mouth, while contemplating pulling the trigger.
- *Behavioral preparation for suicide*: A 25-year-old with bipolar I disorder has researched on the Internet what the lethal dose of her medication would be. She is contemplating taking all her medication next time she gets a 1-month refill.
- *Passive suicide attempt*: A 37-year-old with borderline personality disorder and a history of cutting as an adolescent is overwhelmed by the demands of work and family. She feels suicidal but doesn't feel that she can kill herself, so she hooks up with unknown men from the Internet for sex, hoping that one of them will kill her.
- *Aborted suicide attempt*: A 21-year-old with borderline personality disorder, PTSD, and polysubstance abuse is upset about a recent breakup, and his family is not supportive. He has researched on the Internet how to hang himself. He ties a noose, hangs it up, and puts it around his neck, but he can't make himself jump down from the chair to die.

All of these behaviors contribute to a growing capability to die by suicide in the future.

Self-harm can contribute to the capability to die by suicide, and individuals who harm themselves are at dramatically increased risk for suicide (Simon, 2009). Self-harm behavior is discussed further in a separate section later in this chapter.

Any experience that involves *habituation* to (or getting used to) pain or fear—whether the person voluntarily chose to engage in the experience or not—might increase a person's capability to die by suicide (Joiner, 2005; Van Orden, Witte, Gordon, Bender, & Joiner, 2008). These experiences include knowledge of how to use a gun, learning about how to kill oneself in other ways, frequent tattooing or piercing, compulsive multiple surgeries, chronic physical pain, getting involved in physical fights, contact sports, tying a noose, intentionally hurting animals, jumping from high places, self-injecting drug use, being a survivor of abuse, or any history of experiencing pain or violence or inflicting pain or violence on others (Joiner, 2005; Van Orden, Witte, Gordon, Bender, & Joiner, 2008). These experiences and activities have been found to be correlated with the number of previous suicide attempts (Van Orden, Witte, Gordon, Bender, & Joiner, 2008).

Even frequent, vivid, and intense suicidal ideation can increase capacity to die by suicide. Be aware that this ideation is especially risky when suicide is envisioned positively—as something that is easy, relaxing, or peaceful. Also, be aware that some suicidal individuals daydream about suicide to help themselves feel better (Selby, Anestis, & Joiner, 2007); this daydreaming or mental suicide rehearsal can increase capability to complete suicide.

## UNDERSTANDING INSTRUMENTAL BEHAVIOR

Sometimes an individual has engaged in what appears to be a suicide attempt, but the individual, others around him, or the professional staff feel that it is a *suicide gesture*, specifically an ineffective, insincere act, aimed at demonstrating to others the appearance of a suicide attempt, with little chance of death and with low or no intent to die (Crosby, Ortega, & Melanson, 2011; Heilbron, Compton, Daniel, & Goldston, 2010).

Please do not use the term *suicide gesture*: it has negative connotations and therefore can contribute to underestimating suicide risk. Instead, describe the client's exact suicidal behavior and whether the client acknowledged any intent to die.

When the client acknowledges that there was no intent to die, although there was the appearance of a suicide attempt, Rudd (2006) calls this *instrumental behavior*, which is "potentially self-injurious behavior for which there is evidence . . . that the person did not intend to kill himself/herself (i.e. zero intent to die) and that the person wished to use the appearance of intending to kill himself/herself in order to attain some other end (e.g. to seek help, to punish others, or to receive attention)" (p. 14). Here is a case example of instrumental behavior:

> An intoxicated young female takes an overdose in her dorm room while her two college roommates are in the next room. Within a few minutes, she walks into the living area, obviously drunk, and tells her roommates that she took something because she wants her boyfriend to know how much she loves him. Her friends call 9-1-1 and she is taken to the local emergency room for evaluation but is released within a few hours. (Rudd, 2006, p. 13)

If you are unsure whether a behavior was instrumental or a suicide attempt, ask the client if she thought that it would kill her (Rudd, 2006). Like any self-harm behavior, instrumental behavior can contribute to the individual's capability for suicide. Instrumental behavior can also have more risk of lethality than the client realizes.

## UNDERSTANDING THE TWO KINDS OF SUICIDAL THOUGHTS

When we talk about *suicidal intent,* we are trying to assess the degree to which a client actually intends to die by suicide. Most clients with suicidal thoughts have mixed feelings about suicide. Usually, the client is coming for treatment on his own. Sometimes the client has displayed behavior that caused a family member or friend to become concerned, and that person prompted a referral for treatment and evaluation. Sometimes the client has engaged in suicidal behavior, which might have been interrupted by someone else or by the client, and somehow this led up to you evaluating him. In whatever way the client came to treatment, assessing whether there is current suicidal intent, and if so, its severity, is a crucial portion of the suicide risk assessment process.

There are the two kinds of suicidal thoughts, those with and without suicidal intent. The first is a vague wish for death without any actual intent to kill oneself; this is called *suicidal desire* (Joiner, 2005; Wingate et al., 2004). In most clinical settings, clients who have suicidal desire but do not have any suicidal intent are often said to have *passive suicidal ideation.* They will talk about their suicidal ideation in this way:

- "I wish I were dead."
- "Everyone would be better off if I were gone."
- "I wish I had never been born."
- "I don't care about my life anymore."

Unless they have other significant suicide risk factors, these clients are usually at low risk of suicide. However, even when the client denies suicidal intent, you should still continue to perform and document a full suicide risk assessment (Simon, 2004). Here is a case example of *suicidal desire*:

A Mexican American male, 25 years old, experienced the recent death of his mother and father in a fatal car accident. He had close and supportive relationships with both parents. He had no siblings because his mother needed a hysterectomy after he was born. He is an American citizen and is a native speaker of both English and Spanish. The rest of his extended family lives in Mexico, and they are not U.S. citizens. He is highly distressed, misses his parents desperately, and states, "I wish I was killed in the car accident, too. Now I have nobody." He denies any suicidal intent.

To clarify, these statements mean the same thing:

- The client has *passive suicidal ideation.* (This statement is most commonly used in clinical settings, but is inexact.)
- The client has *thoughts of death without suicidal plan or intent.* (I recommend use of this statement in your documentation.)
- The client has *suicidal desire.* (The term *suicidal desire* is typically used in research, but not in clinical settings.)

The other kind of suicidal thoughts, when the client has some signs of suicidal intent, is *resolved plans and preparations* (Joiner, 2005; Wingate et al., 2004). In most clinical settings, we usually say that these clients, who have some suicidal intent, have *active suicidal ideation*. If clients have suicidal intent, they talk about suicidal ideation like this:

- "Whenever I go over that bridge, I think that if I was really brave, I would drive the car off into the water."
- "I've got a gun, and I often think I should kill myself with it."
- "Sometimes I think of hanging myself off the rafters in the garage. No one would find me until I was dead."
- "I think about taking an overdose of my pills, but I know that my children would be devastated."
- "If I killed myself, then my boyfriend would understand how he hurt me."

Clients with suicidal intent can be at any risk level. If they have a lot of protective factors, their risk level can possibly be low. However, any significant risk factors or warning signs increase their risk level. To clarify, these statements mean the same thing:

- The client has *active suicidal ideation*. (This statement is most commonly used in clinical settings, but is inexact.)
- The client has *suicidal intent*. (I recommend use of this statement in your documentation.)
- The client has *resolved plans and preparations*. (The term *resolved plans and preparations* is used in research, but not in clinical settings.)

## UNDERSTANDING SUICIDAL INTENT

"You've told me that you really don't want to die, but all of your behavior over the last few weeks suggests otherwise. You've been drinking heavily, you've written a letter to your husband saying you wanted to die, and several weeks ago you took an overdose when you knew no one would be home and waited three days to tell me about it. I need for you to help me make some sense of this contradiction. It almost seems like you're telling me one thing and doing another? Frankly, I'm more inclined to consider your behavior as the more important variable here, particularly since I'm very concerned about your safety and well being." (Rudd, 2006, pp. 17–18)

Once you know that a client has some suicidal intent, you will want to understand the degree of this intent. Both what the client *says* about intent and what the client's *behavior has shown* about intent are important (Rudd, 2006). Sometimes these don't match up. When they don't, an intervention like the one above is helpful in clarifying the situation. Be aware that what the client *does* is more important than what he or she *says* regarding suicidal intent (Rudd, 2006).

Here are some signs of higher suicidal intent (American Psychiatric Association, 2003; Rudd, 2006):

- Preparing for death—for example preparing letters for loved ones, organizing financial records, obtaining or modifying insurance policies, preparing or modifying a will, writing a suicide note
- Making efforts to avoid discovery during a suicide attempt or when planning a suicide attempt
- Choosing a suicide method that the client thinks is particularly lethal
- Suicide rehearsal or aborted attempt
- Vividly imagining going through with the suicide plan
- Obtaining means to commit suicide or making a plan to obtain means (e.g., pills, gun).

## SUICIDE RISK SCREENING QUESTIONS

*Tony Sanchez, a mental health trainee, is working in a walk-in intake clinic. He is assigned a new client, Phil Thomas, to interview. Phil has never been to the clinic before, and there is no chart for Tony to review. Phil is a 66-year-old White male who is accompanied by his 64-year-old sister, Susie. Tony speaks with both of them. Susie says she has been worried about Phil's mental health since he lost his wife to lung cancer 3 months ago. Lately, she says, Phil has not been taking care of himself, and when she comes by, he is sitting alone in the dark with the television on but doesn't appear to be actually watching it. Phil says, "I'm no good to anyone and I'm just a burden on Susie." Tony asks Susie to step outside and wait, then assesses Phil for depressive symptoms. He then screens Phil for suicide risk: "Are you having any thoughts about hurting yourself?" Phil tells him that he sometimes thinks of blowing his head off with his gun. Tony asks Phil how long he has had these thoughts. Phil says that he has been thinking of hurting himself ever since his wife's funeral. Tony asks whether Phil has ever had thoughts of hurting himself before his wife died. Phil denies it. Tony asks whether Phil thinks he could follow through on this suicide plan. Phil says he's not sure. Tony asks whether any family members of Phil's have died by suicide. Phil says that his paternal grandfather died by suicide many decades ago. Tony asks Phil whether he has been feeling hopeless. Phil answers, "Yes."*

*Fred Takahashi is a mental health trainee who has been assigned a new client, Crystal Hughes, a 27-year-old White female. At their first session, Fred notices that Crystal has five parallel superficial scratches on her left forearm and asks her about them. Crystal says that she loves her girlfriend and does not want to leave her, but she is certain that the girlfriend has not been sexually faithful because she snooped last week and found suspicious messages on her e-mail and cell phone. The girlfriend denied being unfaithful when she accused her last night, and they argued. After their fight, Crystal felt intense distress and anxiety. Fred asks Crystal whether she has been thinking of killing herself. She says that last night she was thinking of slashing her wrists but ended up cutting*

*herself instead. She locked herself in the bathroom, took out a razor blade, and scratched*
*her arm until it bled. Fred asks Crystal whether she thinks that she might follow through*
*on these suicidal ideas. Crystal says that she's afraid that she would, and that's why she*
*came to the clinic today. When Fred asks Crystal whether she has been feeling hopeless,*
*she says that she is feeling hopeless and wants to die. Fred asks her if she has any relatives*
*who have died by suicide, and she denies this.*

Often, beginning psychotherapists are afraid to ask clients about suicidal thoughts. They fear that asking about suicide might implant ideas in the client's mind. However, there is no scientific evidence that this is the case (Moline, Williams, & Austin, 1998). In fact, if you do not ask about suicidal thoughts, you may miss an opportunity to intervene to prevent a suicide, and you may put your professional career at risk.

Every time you meet a new client, it is necessary to do a suicide assessment (Moline et al., 1998). Your client may have been prescreened for you by your supervisor and/or the clinic, but life circumstances can change quickly, so you also should assess for suicide risk. Asking the following seven screening questions should be an adequate initial screening for suicide risk (Jobes, Rudd, Overholser, & Joiner, 2008; Rudd, 2006):

- Have you been feeling hopeless?
- Have you ever felt that life was not worth living?
- Have you had thoughts about suicide recently? Can you tell me exactly what you've been thinking?
  - (If yes) Do you have an idea about how you would kill yourself?
  - (If yes to this question, ask whether the means to enact the plan are available)
  - (If yes) Do you think you could actually follow through with this idea?
- Have you ever attempted suicide in the past?

*Remember these questions; they are the most important information in this chapter.* You do not need to memorize the exact wording of each question, but you should understand and remember everything that these questions are asking about. To reiterate, these questions assess whether there is hopelessness, whether there is a wish for death, whether there is *suicidal ideation* (and if so, whether there is a *plan* and whether there is *intent* to follow through), and whether there have been *past suicide attempts*. If there is a plan, you should also ask about *means*. For example, if a client's suicide plan is shooting himself with a gun, ask whether the client has access to a gun; in this case, the gun would be the means. Again, it is essential to screen for (1) hopelessness—an emotional state that typically precedes emergence of suicidal thoughts, (2) desire for death and (3) suicidal ideation, and if it is present (4) whether there is a suicide plan, (5) whether the individual has the means to carry it out, and (6) whether there is intent to follow through with the plan; also assess (7) past suicide attempts or behavior (Jobes, Rudd, Overholser, & Joiner, 2008). The next section provides follow-up questions that you can use to get further detail about each of these issues. Simon (2004) suggests adding the following question to your screening procedure as well: "Have you had any family members who have died by suicide?"

The way that you ask these questions is important. Use exact terms such as "suicide" or "kill yourself" (Rudd, 2006). Being matter-of-fact about suicidal thoughts communicates to the client that you can handle the situation (Granello, 2010a). Acknowledge to the client that you understand that it can be difficult to discuss these thoughts and feelings (Granello, 2010a). Emphasize that you and the client are collaborators in addressing the suicidal crisis (Jobes, 2006).

Most clients will answer "no" to all the screening questions, and you are done in just a couple minutes. If the answer to any of these questions is positive, though, a thorough suicide risk assessment should be done. The first part of the risk assessment involves assessing for mental illness and other suicide risk and protective factors, as well as warning signs (this chapter). The second part of the risk assessment involves determining the risk level, making a suicide prevention plan, deciding on the level of treatment, working with the client to reduce suicide risk, and then documenting everything you've done (Chapter 19).

Do not rely on a written intake form to screen for suicidal ideation. A classic study (Morrison & Downey, 2000) found that many individuals who have suicidal ideation will not reveal this information on an intake form but will be more revealing in the context of the intake interview. Of note, ethnic minority individuals may be at increased risk of not disclosing suicidal ideation on written forms.

If the client hesitates when you've asked about suicide but then answers "no," remark on that: "Are you sure? I noticed that you were hesitant." In addition, if the client has hopelessness or significant depressive symptomatology, further probing about suicidal thoughts may be indicated, even if denied (Jacobs & Brewer, 2006). Note that studies have found that many clients who have suicidal ideation will deny it when asked, so if the client has other significant risk factors, you may want to talk to family members or significant others and/or ask again when there is a stronger therapeutic alliance. Be aware that "[n]egative cultural attitudes about suicide can lead to the suppression of information about suicide thoughts and behaviors" (Granello, 2010b, p. 368). For example, African American women can be reluctant to disclose suicidal thoughts upon intake (Granello, 2010b). Closeness to the family, coupled with shame about suicidal thoughts, can make Asian Americans less likely to disclose suicidal thoughts and suicide attempts (Choi, Rogers, & Werth, Jr., 2009).

Both of the clients in the above vignettes have suicidal ideation, a plan for how they would hurt themselves, and access to the means to do so. Phil does not have previous suicide attempts, while Crystal does. Both are feeling hopeless. So both clients need a detailed suicide assessment. Note that a disrupted relationship is a key factor in the development of suicidal ideation for both clients. Also, note that Phil volunteered that he thinks he is a burden on his sister.

Note that assessing for suicide risk is an ongoing process. Suicide risk varies from minute to minute, hour to hour, and day to day because suicidal behaviors are impulsive and transient (Simon, 2006). Clients with a recent suicidal crisis should have their suicidal ideation reevaluated every time they are seen until they are stable and the suicidal ideation has been absent for several sessions, at a minimum. Use your judgment, and consult carefully with your supervisor, about how often to assess for suicidal ideation if a client has had multiple suicide attempts or has developed a significant capability for self-harm, even when the client denies current suicidal ideation. Some clients with chronic suicidal ideation may need to be assessed at every session indefinitely. Be sure to discuss the specific details of the client's risk with your supervisor so that you have a plan for how often to reassess.

## ASSESS CURRENT SUICIDAL IDEATION IN DETAIL

*Tony asks Phil more questions about his current suicidal ideation: "Phil, tell me some more about your thoughts about hurting yourself." Phil says, "I think about taking out my gun, putting it in my mouth, and pulling the trigger." Tony ascertains that there is a gun in the house, along with ammunition, and that it is kept in a locked cabinet in the basement. Tony asks Phil, "Do you think you would ever actually pull the trigger?" Phil says that he doesn't know. Tony asks Phil how often he thinks about hurting himself. Phil says that he thinks about it off and on every day.*

*Fred asks Crystal more about her suicidal ideation. Crystal says that she has been thinking about taking all her Prozac, but at other times she thinks about slitting her wrists. She says that it would "serve my girlfriend right" to come in and find her bleeding to death in the tub. Fred asks her whether she thinks she would act on these thoughts. Crystal says that she thinks she might. Fred asks how often she is thinking about killing herself. Crystal says that she has had these thoughts off and on for years but that she has been thinking about this much more frequently since she found the messages last week.*

The presence of current suicidal ideation is the most important predictor of suicide risk. When asking about suicidal thoughts, you will want to understand how distressing the thoughts are to the client by assessing frequency, intensity, and duration. (This section is informed by Bryan & Rudd, 2006; Jacobs & Brewer, 2006; and Rudd, 2006.) Here are some sample questions:

- Frequency—How often?
  - How often do you think about suicide?
  - Are the thoughts every day? How often throughout the day? When was the last suicidal thought—today? Yesterday? Last week?
- Intensity—How distressing?
  - Could you rate the intensity of your suicidal thoughts on a scale of 1 to 10, with 1 being not at all intense and 10 being extremely intense?
  - How much are these suicidal thoughts bothering you?

- Duration—How long?
  - When did the suicidal ideas start?
  - How long have these thoughts lasted?

You will also want to assess suicidal intent, a plan to die by suicide, and the means to make it happen. Here are some sample questions (informed by American Psychiatric Association, 2003; Rudd, 2006):

- Plans
  - Have you made a specific plan to kill yourself?
  - Have you thought about *when* you would kill yourself?
  - Have you thought about *where* you would kill yourself?
  - Do you have any other ideas about how you would kill yourself? (Keep asking this question until the client denies that there are any other methods under consideration.)
  - Have you made any preparations to hurt yourself (e.g., stockpile medications)?
  - Have you taken any steps to prepare for suicide, such as write a note, get your financial affairs in order, or do anything else?
  - Have you thought about how you would prevent anyone from finding or stopping you?
- Means
  - Do you have access to a gun or other weapons?
  - Do you have any pills that you might take? What are they?
  - Have you made arrangements or planned to get access to [method]?
  - What is the likelihood that would actually kill you? (Client could over- or under-estimate lethality.)
- Intent
  - Do you think you would ever act on those thoughts? Why or why not?
  - Are these passing thoughts or are you serious about them?
  - Do you feel that you have the determination to follow through with killing yourself? Do you think you are capable of doing it?
  - If you begin to have thoughts about hurting yourself again, what would you do?
  - Have you started to hurt yourself but stopped before doing anything?
  - Have you rehearsed suicide in any way? Have you gotten [method] out and gone through the steps to kill yourself?
  - What is the closest you've come to hurting yourself?
  - What stops you from killing yourself? What has kept you alive until now?
  - What makes your life worth living?
  - If you have those thoughts again, what would you do?

You do not need to ask every one of these questions to every client—these are just to give you an idea what you may need to ask to get the full picture. Once you have this information, you need to consider what the likelihood is that the client will act on the ideation (see next chapter). Cultural or religious beliefs about suicide may influence an individual's willingness to discuss suicidal thoughts, so it may be helpful to explore these beliefs as part of the assessment process (American Psychiatric Association, 2003).

## ASSESS PAST SUICIDE ATTEMPTS AND SUICIDAL BEHAVIOR

*When asked by Tony, Phil denies any history of suicidal ideation, behavior, or self-harm prior to his wife's death.*

*When asked, Crystal says that she has been hospitalized twice in the past after making suicide attempts. She points out very faint scars on her wrists that Fred had not noticed before and said that she cut her wrists when she was 16 years old after being rejected by a boyfriend. She then admits to numerous other episodes of cutting. She said that the second hospitalization was last year and that she had taken a half-bottle of Xanax but then got scared and called 911.*

Past suicide attempts are the second most important predictor of current suicide risk, after the presence of current suicidal ideation. Persons who have made past suicide attempts are at a much higher risk than any other group to die by suicide. Past attempters have a risk of completed suicide that is 38 times (in an aggregate of many studies; E. C. Harris & Barraclough, 1997) to over 100 times (in a review of international studies; Owens, Horrocks, & House, 2002) greater than the general population. Persons who have attempted suicide at least twice, known as *multiple attempters*, are the group at greatest risk of future suicide and suicide attempts (Joiner et al., 1999). Thus, past suicide attempts must be thoroughly evaluated, and clients with past attempts, especially those with more than one attempt, must be very carefully monitored and treated. *Note that past suicidal ideation, without any history of suicidal behavior, is so common that it is a poor predictor of risk,* although it can still be informative to assess.

To assess past suicide attempts, ask the following:

- "Have you had any thoughts of killing yourself in the past?"
- "Have you ever attempted suicide in the past?"
- "How close did you get to suicide in the past?"
- "When was your most serious attempt to harm or kill yourself?"

If the client appears to be confused or you suspect forgetfulness or minimizing, ask further specific questions, such as, "Have you ever been hospitalized for an emotional problem?" or "What was going on when you went to the hospital?"

When the client reveals a past episode(s) of suicide attempts or suicidal behavior, gather as much information about that episode as possible (American Psychiatric Association, 2003; Rudd, 2006):

- What were the circumstances of the attempt?
  - "How old were you?" (or "When was that?")
  - "Were you using drugs or alcohol then?"
- Precipitant—what triggered the crisis?
  - "What triggered your thinking about suicide?"
  - "Why did you think about killing yourself? Why did you think suicide was the best option?"
- Nature of the attempt
  - "Please tell me exactly what you did."
  - "What happened then?"
  - "Did you want to die?"
- Outcome
  - "Did you get any help? Did you go to the hospital? How did you get there? Did you call someone?"
  - "Were you injured? Was medical care required? Did you get that care? Why or why not?"
  - "Did you take steps to try and prevent your discovery or rescue when you made the suicide attempt?"
- Reaction to surviving the attempt
  - "How did you feel about surviving your suicide attempt?"
  - "Did you think that would kill you?"

Then ask the client: "Other than that, were there any other times in the past when you made a suicide attempt, injured yourself, or made a plan to die by suicide?" Keep asking this question and then asking about the specific episodes until the client denies that there are any other previous episodes of suicidal behavior. Try to identify any patterns in the attempts—are there specific types of crises that precipitate suicide attempts in this individual? Have the attempts become more lethal over time? Are the life circumstances similar now or different?

To understand any continued risk, ask how the person feels about surviving the attempt. If the person is relieved, there is less risk. If the person regrets surviving, there is more risk and greater likelihood of future attempts (Jobes, Rudd, Overholser, & Joiner, 2008).

You should always review any mental health records that are immediately available regarding past suicidal behavior. If ongoing treatment is anticipated, send releases to get records from past treatment facilities for any client with any suicide risk (Packman, Pennuto, et al., 2004). If the family is available, consider getting a written or oral (crisis situation) agreement from the client to talk to them (and document that agreement in the chart), then ask them for their perspectives on the client's past suicidal behavior (Simon, 1988).

## ASSESS MENTAL ILLNESS

*Tony assesses Phil for symptoms of depression. Phil has poor appetite and has lost 15 pounds in the past 2 months. He is not sleeping well. He is feeling either numb or depressed most of the time and cries uncontrollably when thinking about how much he misses his wife. He feels guilty and says that he did not appreciate her enough when she was alive. Tony screens Phil for bipolar disorder, PTSD, and psychotic symptoms, but these are denied.*

*Fred assesses Crystal for mental illness. She had a history of bulimia in high school but denied any problems with that in recent years. She has many symptoms of major depression. When asked about manic symptoms, she describes an episode in the past that might have been hypomanic, but Fred is not sure. Clearly, Crystal is in great distress.*

Almost all mental illnesses have been associated with increased mortality from suicide (E. C. Harris & Barraclough, 1997; Goldsmith, Pellmar, Kleinman, & Bunney, 2002). Emotional distress is likely to be the connection between mental illness and suicide. Therefore, in addition to noting the client's diagnosis, carefully attend to the client's level of distress about current symptoms. More than one diagnosis and more severe symptoms can increase suicide risk (Simon, 2004). Adjusting to the reality of having a mental illness is often very distressing for high-functioning clients; being in the midst of this adjustment process may put them at greater suicide risk (Simon, 2004).

In a classic article that is still frequently cited, E. C. Harris and Barraclough (1997) reviewed the research and derived combined risks of suicide for a number of mental illnesses (based on criteria from the *Diagnostic and Statistical Manual of Mental Disorders*, 3rd ed., revised) by aggregating numbers across studies. These numbers indicate the degree of increased risk compared to the general population. Here are the findings of this study:

- Eating disorders, 23 times (23 times the rate of suicide in the general population)
- Major depression, 20 times
- Bipolar I disorder, 15 times (since the diagnostic criteria of the studies that were aggregated were based on *DSM-III-R*, bipolar II was not included)
- Brief reactive psychosis, 15 times
- Adjustment disorder, 14 times
- Dysthymia, 12 times
- Obsessive-compulsive disorder, 10 times (the authors suspect that number should be higher)
- Panic disorder, 10 times
- Schizophrenia, 8.5 times
- Personality disorders, 7 times

Anorexia nervosa may have the highest risk of suicide for all mental illness, estimated to be about 58 times that of the general population (American Association of Suicidology, n.d.); individuals with anorexia are more likely to die from suicide than from complications of their disorder. Less data and research are available regarding individuals with bulimia, but it is clear that they have an increased risk of suicide over the general population, while having much less risk than anorexic individuals (American Association of Suicidology, n.d.).

A review of suicide risk in depression (Goldsmith, Pellmar, Kleinman, & Bunney, 2002) indicated that some depressive symptoms are more predictive of suicide: suicidal ideation, hopelessness, guilt, loss of interest in usual activities, low self-esteem, cognitive distortions, and few perceived reasons for living. Hopelessness is a significant warning sign for suicide in the general U.S. population (Packman, Marlitt, Bongar, & Pennuto, 2004) and has been validated in an African American sample as well (Davidson, Wingate, Slish, & Rasmussen, 2010). The combination of severe depression along with anxiety and/or panic attacks can be especially distressing and predictive of suicide risk (Simon, 2004).

Individuals with either bipolar I or bipolar II are at significant risk for suicide, and up to 10 percent may eventually die from suicide. A current depressive mood episode significantly increases suicide risk (Rihmer, 2007; Valtonen et al., 2008). However, note that clients with mixed-mood episodes have an even greater risk of suicide (Rihmer, 2007; Valtonen et al., 2008). During a mixed episode, the individual has all of the misery of a depressive episode, accompanied by the activation of a manic episode—no wonder they are at such high risk.

People with schizophrenia are at significant risk of suicide, with estimates ranging from 5 to 10 percent dying from suicide (Bolton, Gooding, Kapur, Barrowclough, & Tarrier, 2007). The highest rate of suicide is in the first 5 to 10 years after diagnosis, when the individual has not yet adapted. Most at risk are males, Whites, those with postpsychotic depression, those who are now incapable of working after a high level of premorbid functioning, those with multiple relapses and/or hospitalizations, and those with poor treatment adherence (Bolton, Gooding, Kapur, Barrowclough, & Tarrier, 2007; Pompili et al., 2007).

Experts suggest that suicide as a result of *command hallucinations* (auditory hallucinations commanding the individual to do something, in this case to commit suicide) is actually rare (Pompili et al, 2007); still, these hallucinations should not be ignored. Find out if the client feels that the commands can be resisted, if the client wants to resist the command, how often the voices are occurring, and if there is a known voice (client may be more likely to act if the voice seems to be that of someone he or she knows).

The personality disorders that are most at risk are borderline personality disorder and antisocial personality disorder (Joiner, 2005; Wingate, Joiner, Walker, Rudd, & Jobes, 2004). Psychotherapists can get used to repeated suicidal statements from individuals with borderline personality disorder and can then underestimate the risk—or may even believe that the repeated statements mean that the individual will not follow through with suicide (Jobes, Rudd, Overholser, & Joiner, 2008). These ideas are incorrect; be aware that around 10 percent of those with borderline personality disorder will end up dying from suicide. The individuals with antisocial personality disorder who are most at risk of suicide are those who are impulsive, aggressive, and irresponsible, but not emotionally detached (Wingate, Joiner, Walker, Rudd, & Jobes, 2004).

Note that Harris and Barraclough (1997) did not include PTSD in their study. However, multiple lines of evidence show that trauma and PTSD increase risk of completed suicide and suicide attempts (Krysinska & Lester, 2010). A history of sexual abuse significantly increased suicide risk in a large British sample (Bebbington et al., 2009).

Body dysmorphic disorder was not included in the study by Harris and Barraclough (1997) either; however, subsequent studies have found an extremely high suicide risk in this group, potentially 45 times the rate of the general population (Phillips & Menard, 2006).

Clients are usually discharged quickly from inpatient units and are often not completely stable. The week after discharge is an especially high-risk period for suicide, and the 3 months after discharge continues to be a high-risk period (Appleby et al., 1999; Links, 2005). Be aware that suicidal inpatients may feign improvement in the hopes that they will be discharged so that they can act on their suicide plans (Simon & Gutheil, 2009). Finally, in a Danish population study, a history of psychiatric hospitalization was found to be a significant risk factor for suicide (Qin, Agerbo, & Mortensen, 2003).

## ASSESS STRESSORS, EMOTIONAL AND PHYSICAL PAIN

*Tony asks Phil about his stress. Phil talks about how he has had to learn how to do his own laundry and cooking since his wife died. His wife managed all the finances as well, and he has been ignoring the bills. Phil has arthritis in both hips, which has been very painful lately. He has been putting off getting the hip replacements that his doctors recommended. He is uncertain if he can afford to keep his home, given the loss of his wife's pension and Social Security.*

*Crystal tells Fred that she has been under a lot of stress. Her younger sister has been staying with her and would otherwise be homeless, but they argue all the time. Crystal is distressed about the recent argument with her girlfriend and fears that they will break up. She hasn't gone to her job for the last 3 days and fears that she will be fired.*

Ask the client about recent stressors: "Has anything stressful been going on in your life lately?" Both Phil and Crystal have experienced significant stressors lately that have contributed to distress, emotional instability, and suicidal ideation.

Many stressors have been linked to suicide attempts. These include losing a job, poverty, sickness-related absence from work, and chronic illness or disability (American Association of Suicidology, n.d.; K. L. Knox, Conwell, & Caine, 2004). Serious medical problems can increase suicide risk two to seven times, especially those that may cause functional impairment or chronic pain such as AIDS, seizure disorder, spinal cord injury, Huntington's chorea, and multiple sclerosis

(American Association of Suicidology, n.d.; E. C. Harris & Barraclough, 1997, Krakowski & Czobor, 2004). Traumatic brain injury increases the risk of suicide (American Association of Suicidology, n.d); athletes and combat veterans, among others, should be screened for signs of brain injury. So carefully evaluate the emotional impact of serious medical problems.

Interpersonal trauma, whether recent (e.g., domestic violence) or remote (e.g., childhood physical or sexual abuse), increases risk of suicide (Packman, Marlitt, et al., 2004). Social isolation increases risk of suicide in general (Packman, Marlitt, et al., 2004)—those who are single or live alone are at greater risk of suicide (Goldsmith, Pellmar, Kleinman, & Bunney, 2002)—and the loss of a spouse is a particularly salient stressor that can precipitate suicide (Louma & Pearson, 2002), especially among men under 35 years old. Family problems, such as family discord, domestic violence, family stress, and feeling that one is a burden on one's family, increase risk of suicide (Van Orden et al., 2010). Even the stress of frequent moves from one locale to another can increase suicide risk (American Association of Suicidology, n.d.).

People who are unemployed have two to four times the risk of suicide as those who have a job (American Association of Suicidology, n.d.), and the longer an individual is unemployed, the greater the suicide risk (Classen & Dunn, 2012). More anecdotally, loss or contraction of one's small business (Povoledo & Carvajal, 2012); severe indebtedness, often caused by gambling (Yip, Yang, Ip, Law, & Watson, 2007); shame (Van Orden et al., 2010); and reputation damage (Pridmore & McArthur, 2008) have been linked to suicide.

## ASSESS WARNING SIGNS OF ACTIVATION

*Tony assesses Phil for substance abuse. Phil admits that he has often been drinking a six-pack of beer every day, sometimes followed by hard liquor. Phil says that the alcohol dulls the pain of his loss. However, he states that lately his sister Susie has been bringing him to her Alcoholics Anonymous (AA) meetings with her, as Susie is a recovering alcoholic herself. He stated that he has been trying to cut down on the alcohol, and that he had 2 days last week when he did not drink.*

*Crystal admits that she occasionally uses cocaine and marijuana. She said that she was drunk when she made the two previous suicide attempts. She stated that she drinks alcohol on the weekend when out with friends. When screened for psychotic symptoms, Crystal says that she sometimes hears a voice telling her to kill herself. Crystal says that she hasn't slept much since becoming worried about her girlfriend's faithfulness last week. She alternates between being very angry and being tearful about the situation.*

Signs of being activated include impulsivity, anxiety, anger, aggression, agitation, and substance abuse. Client characteristics that are indicative of greater impulsivity or less self-control are generally linked to greater risk of suicide (Joiner et al., 1999). In an Austrian study of inpatients who had made a suicide attempt, nearly half reported that 10 minutes or less passed between thinking of making a suicide attempt and actually making the attempt (Deisenhammer et al., 2009). If the degree of impulsivity is not clear from the client's history, feel free to ask (Rudd, 2006, p. 59): "Do you consider yourself an impulsive person? When have you felt out of control in the past?" However, note that one study of elderly suicide attempters found that less impulsive individuals made more lethal suicide attempts (Dombrovski et al., 2011), so suicide risk among less impulsive individuals should not be ignored.

Certain symptoms may also contribute to lack of self-control; the client may not be getting much sleep or may have reduced concentration. Intense feelings of anger and aggressive behavior can be a warning sign of suicide (American Association of Suicidology, n.d.). Those who are incarcerated and those with anti-social personality disorder are at increased risk (Verona, Sachs-Ericsson, & Joiner, 2004).

Alcohol and drug abuse significantly increase the risk of suicide (and other impulsive behaviors as well; all risks from E. C. Harris & Barraclough, 1997):

- Sedative dependence and abuse, 20 times (20 times the rate of suicide in the general population)
- Multiple substance dependence and abuse, 20 times
- Opioid dependence and abuse, 14 times
- Alcohol dependence and abuse, 6 times
- Cannabis heavy use, 4 times

## ASSESS SELF-HARM AND OTHER CAPABILITY FACTORS

*Phil admits that when he is very drunk, he will sometimes take out the gun and cradle it on his lap, thinking of killing himself.*

*Crystal reports that after she cut herself yesterday, she felt relief and could "float above my problems." She said that she didn't feel any pain at all from the scratches. Crystal says that when she is upset, she will daydream about dying by suicide and "relaxing into death," which calms her down.*

"Have you ever done anything to hurt yourself?" will usually elicit self-harm behavior as well as suicidal behavior. However, initially the client may deny this but volunteer it later, or you may see suspicious injuries and ask about them, as Fred did earlier in the chapter.

Self-inflicted injuries are often burns or scratches on the skin; they are often on the arms but may also be on the legs, abdomen, or other areas of the body. Clients may wear clothing that covers the area when in public. If the client admits to self-injury, ask where the injuries are. If there are cuts or other injuries in an area that you can observe without the client inappropriately disrobing, you might ask if you can see them. Even if you are not a physician, it is likely that you will be able to see whether the cuts are superficial or whether it would be wise to have a medical evaluation. If you have any doubt whether the client caused significant tissue damage, a physician or nurse should be consulted. If the self-inflicted injury is in a more private location, such as the inner thigh, you should get a nurse, psychiatrist, or another physician to examine the injuries. If none of these health professionals is on site, you may need to obtain a release of information to talk to the client's physician.

Crystal's positive view of suicide, saying that it would be "relaxing," and her tendency to daydream about suicide to cope with negative feelings are both risky and increase her capability to die by suicide (Selby, Anestis, & Joiner, 2007). Phil's suicide rehearsal behavior of cradling the gun and thinking of killing himself increases his capability to die by suicide.

## ASSESS CULTURAL, DEMOGRAPHIC, AND HISTORICAL RISK FACTORS

*Tony considers Phil's demographic and historical risk factors. Phil is a White male, over the age of 65, and thus is in a very high-risk group. He has recently become a widower, increasing his risk. He also has a family member who died by suicide, which again increases his risk. Phil is a Vietnam combat veteran; Tony is aware that he needs to understand the impact of this experience on Phil, but Tony also knows that this combat history is significantly less likely to be a suicide risk factor for Phil than for a recent combat veteran.*

When looking at ethnicity and suicide rates, consider age group and gender as well. The U.S. suicide rate for 2005 to 2009 was 12.4 suicide deaths per 100,000 persons in the population (most data for this paragraph from Centers for Disease Control and Prevention, 2012). The *group at the very highest risk is White men over the age of 65* (CDC, 2012); White men over 85 are at even greater risk (Simon, 2004). The group at the next highest risk is White and Native American male teenagers and adults. African American and Latino men of all ages have about an average suicide risk compared to the general population. White females have a relatively low risk that *decreases* as they become elderly, whereas Asian females and males have a low risk that *increases* as they become elderly, especially among Chinese Americans (Duldulao, Takeuchi, & Hong, 2009). The groups at the very lowest risk are African American and Latina females of all ages. Asian men under the age of 65 have a relatively low suicide rate as well.

Be aware of the so-called paradox of lower suicide rates in the African American population. Even though they have increased suicide risk factors (Davidson & Wingate, 2011), they may have offsetting protective factors of increased hope (Davidson & Wingate, 2011), religiosity/spirituality (Griffin-Fennell & Williams, 2006), and social support (Utsey, Hook, & Stanard, 2007) relative to Whites. However, suicide risk has increased for African Americans over recent decades (Compton, Thompson, & Kaslow, 2005), especially for young males (Joe &

Niedermeier, 2008), and there is significant evidence that suicide rates are underestimated among African Americans (Osiezagha, Kaur, Barker, & Bailey, 2009). African Americans' family members may be inattentive to suicide risk, seeing it as not applicable to their community (Day-Vines, 2007).

Asian American and Latino groups have considerable within-group variation in suicide attempts and completed suicides. For Asian Americans, higher acculturation indicates greater risk; those born in the United States have the highest rate of suicide attempts, followed by those who migrated to the United States when they were younger than 13; those who migrated at age 13 or older have the fewest suicide attempts (Borges, Orozco, Rafful, Miller, & Breslau, 2012). However, among Latinos, immigrants are more likely to complete suicide than native-born individuals (Wadsworth & Kubrin, 2007). Interestingly, while foreign-born Asian Americans are at the lowest risk of suicidal ideation in the Asian American population (Duldulao, Takeuchi, & Hong, 2009), among immigrants, less acculturation and poorer English language skills have been linked to increased suicidal ideation (Leong, Leach, Yeh, & Chou, 2007).

Asian cultural groups may be at more risk for enacting suicide out of shame (Simon, 2011b). Shame suicides are also possible in Western cultures as a result of public scandals, criminal charges, significant loss of money, or loss of reputation (Saxby & Anil, 2012; Simon, 2011b). Previously high-functioning and high-achieving individuals who become unable to work and become hospitalized for the first time may be at increased risk of suicide (Simon & Gutheil, 2002), which may be shame-based as well.

Men are three to four times more likely to die by suicide then women, although women make three to four times as many attempts (Callanan & Davis, 2012). Interestingly, gender tends to modify the impact of other suicide risk and protective factors. Women's suicide risk can be less affected by unemployment than men's (Classen & Dunn, 2012). Having a young child is more of a protective factor for women than men (Qin, Agerbo, & Mortensen, 2003). Being single was more associated with suicide risk in men than women (Qin, Agerbo, & Mortensen, 2003).

People who live in more rural areas are at increased risk (Singh & Siahpush, 2002). People who are divorced, single, or widowed are at greater risk than those who are married (Goldsmith, Pellmar, Kleinman, & Bunney, 2002).

Lesbian, gay, and bisexual (LGB) individuals have been found to have an increased rate of suicide attempts compared to heterosexuals in the United States (Bolton & Sareen, 2011, Haas et al, 2011), perhaps twice the rate (King et al., 2008). A large Danish study found increased rates of completed suicide among LGB individuals (Mathy, Cochran, Olsen, & Mays, 2011), but studies have been inconclusive whether LGB individuals die by suicide more often than heterosexuals in the United States (Haas et al., 2011). Two studies found that in stark contrast to the heterosexual U.S. population, African American and Latino LGB individuals had made *more* suicide attempts than White LGB individuals (Meyer, Dietrich, & Schwartz, 2008; O'Donnell, Meyer, & Schwartz, 2011)—usually these ethnic groups are at lower risk.

Studies have also found that one sixth to one third of transgendered individuals have attempted suicide (Clements-Nolle, Marx, & Katz, 2006; Mathy, Lehmann, & Kerr, 2003; Xavier, Bobbin, Singer, & Budd, 2005).

Rates of mental illness and substance abuse are higher in LGBT populations as well (Bolton & Sareen, 2011; Clements-Nolle, Marx, & Katz, 2006). LGBT individuals aged 25 or younger have the highest risk for suicide attempts (Clements-Nolle, Marx, & Katz, 2006; Haas et al., 2011; Paul et al., 2002). Increased mental illness and suicidal behavior in LGBT individuals is generally agreed to be caused by distress due to stigma, prejudice, and interpersonal rejection (Bolton & Sareen, 2011; Clements-Nolle, Marx, & Katz, 2006).

Some historical factors associated with suicide risk include suicide in a parent, which is estimated to increase risk in the client by six times (Brent et al., 2002). Suicide in other family members increases the risk of suicide in the client as well (Simon, 2004). Strangely, women who have breast implants have about two to three times the rate of suicide as comparable women in the general population (McLaughlin, Wise, & Lipworth, 2004).

While some disagreement remains, most studies conclude that both military veterans and active-duty military personnel during wartime are at increased risk for suicide (Gibbons, Brown, & Hur, 2012; Kaplan, McFarland, Huguet, & Newsom, 2012). Suicide among soldiers reached record levels during deployments in Iraq and Afghanistan (Kauffman & Chedekel, 2008). Even among high-functioning Iraq/Afghanistan veterans attending college, almost half think about suicide often, and about one fifth think about a suicide plan (Rudd, Goulding, & Bryan, 2011). In one study, more combat experiences were associated with more depressive and PTSD symptoms, a greater history of suicidal thoughts, feeling like a burden to others, being distanced from others, and having a higher score on a measure of capability to die by suicide (Bryan, Cukrowicz, West, & Morrow, 2010). However, research suggests that as more years pass since the combat experience, the veteran's suicide risk level approximates that of similar individuals in the general population (Gibbons, Brown, & Hur, 2012).

## ASSESS PROTECTIVE FACTORS

*Tony asks Phil what has kept him alive until now. Phil talks about how much he loves his two grandsons, who live nearby. They used to get together every week to play catch and board games. Phil learned to play their favorite video games, "although I always lose," he says with a smile. He says, "I know what it is like to lose a grandfather to suicide and don't know if I can do that to them. But maybe they'd be better off without me." He says that he has been avoiding his grandsons "because they shouldn't see me like this." Tony tells Phil that he is sure that his grandsons would not be better off without him and that, in fact, if he died by suicide, that would put them at greater risk of suicide later in life. Phil says that he would not want that to happen. Tony suggests that Phil and his grandsons can be a comfort to each other, and Phil agrees that this might be true. Tony asks Phil about his relationship with his sister. They have always been close and raised*

*their children and grandchildren together. Susie has been looking in on Phil and making*
*him eat and go out to AA meetings every day. Phil says that he feels that she has helped*
*keep him alive. Tony asks Phil, "Would you be willing to come for treatment regularly,*
*for your family, if not for yourself?" Phil says that he would.*

*Fred asks Crystal what has been keeping her alive. She says that she has a close relation-*
*ship with her younger sister and has been trying to help out since the sister lost her job*
*last month. Both of their parents have died, and she feels responsible for her sister. She*
*says, "I think about killing myself, but then I think about how my little sister would be*
*all alone."*

Each client has unique protective factors. In general, as protective factors decrease,
suicidal intent and emotional symptoms tend to increase (Rudd, 2006). Ask about
the client's reasons to live (Rudd, 2006):

- "What has kept you alive so far?"
- "What are your reasons for living?"
- "What keeps you going in difficult times like this?"
- "What made you decide to come in and talk to me today?"
- "Why do you say that you couldn't die by suicide?"
- "Are you hopeful about the future?"
- "What would need to happen to help you be more hopeful about the future?"
- "Do you have family or friends you can talk to, who are supportive?"
- "Who can you turn to in a crisis?"
- "Has treatment been effective for you in the past?"

Protective factors often involve social and family support. Having young dependent children, being pregnant, or having a caring partner can be protective
(Goldsmith, Pellmar, Kleinman, & Bunney, 2002; Rudd, 2006). A close circle of
friends or any other supportive group can be protective. Being actively involved in
organized religion can be protective (Goldsmith, Pellmar, Kleinman, & Bunney,
2002), especially for African Americans (Anglin, Gabriel, & Kaslow, 2005). An
emotionally supportive family can be protective. Being in a low-risk suicide group
(e.g., young African American women) can be considered a protective factor, but
do not underestimate risk because of the client's demographic group.

Clients who have greater self-control, greater self-efficacy, intact reality-testing,
and more adaptive coping skills are at less risk (Goldsmith, Pellmar, Kleinman, &
Bunney, 2002; Rudd, 2006). Feeling hopeful, having future plans or events to look
forward to, and having satisfaction in life are protective (Rudd, 2006).

Negative reactions to suicide can be protective. Thinking about the pain that
suicide would cause to one's close family members can be protective. Being fearful
of death or suicide is a good sign.

Some religions have explicit prohibitions against suicide that clients may take
very seriously (American Psychiatric Association, 2003), but research has been

mixed about whether religion is a protective factor in general (Griffin-Fennell & Williams, 2006), and little is known about suicide risk among minority religious groups such as Buddhists or Hindus (Leong, Leach, Yeh, & Chou, 2007). Cultural or moral prohibitions against suicide may not be protective, as had previously been assumed (Richardson-Vejlgaard, Sher, Oquendo, Lizardi, & Stanley, 2009).

Engagement in treatment is a powerful protective factor. Psychotherapy—especially cognitive behavioral therapy and Dialectical Behavior Therapy, focused on improving problem-solving, coping skills, self-control, and emotion management—can reduce the intensity of suicidal ideation, suicidal intent, and suicide attempts (Rudd, Joiner, Trotter, Williams, & Cordero, 2009). Therefore, the following treatment characteristics, if present, can be considered protective factors: good treatment alliance, good motivation for treatment, hopefulness about treatment, willingness to seek emergency treatment as needed, and willingness to ask for additional sessions as needed. A history of treatment adherence is also protective, such as a history of regular attendance at sessions, adherence to treatment recommendations, adherence to medications, and demonstrated past adherence to the crisis management plan.

## ASSESS OTHER SOURCES OF INFORMATION

> *Tony feels that Phil is not at immediate risk to hurt himself or leave the facility, because Phil has verbalized his willingness to get help. He asks Phil to wait in the waiting room and asks if it is okay for him to talk to Susie for a few minutes. Phil gives his verbal agreement. Tony then asks Susie some questions. He briefly verifies Phil's report that he has not been suicidal in the past and has never gotten any mental health treatment. Susie says that Phil was not bathing regularly after the funeral until she started stopping by each day. She said that he recognizes now that he needs to get professional help and stop drinking. However, she worries about him a great deal. He has been refusing to go anywhere with her but to the grocery store and AA meetings until today.*

Talking to the client's family and significant others, as Tony does in the previous vignette, will sometimes reveal significant information that the client did not volunteer. Often, clients are more forthcoming about their suicidal thoughts with family members than with psychotherapists (Simon, 2011b). Collateral information from the family can be especially useful when no other historical documentation is available, as in the case of Phil.

Whenever you are working with a client, you should be aware of information that is already in the client's chart. This is even more important with any potentially suicidal client. You must thoroughly review the chart, document that you did so, and be aware of any relevant information from the chart that is pertinent to the suicide risk assessment. You should also be in regular communication with other mental health professionals at your facility who have regular contact with the client and be aware of what they have learned regarding the client's suicide risk. Keep up-to-date with current chart notes from other health care professionals as treatment progresses.

If the client was treated in private practice, chart records can sometimes be unavailable or insufficient. In those cases, obtain a signed release, call the previous psychotherapist and discuss any suicidal behavior or ideation during the previous episode of treatment, and then document the call thoroughly in the client's current chart. If the client was treated at other facilities, you should obtain copies of those records and review that information as well; failure to do so may result in legal liability (Roberts, Monferrari, & Yeager, 2008). Again, document this in the chart.

## RAPPORT AND MOTIVATION FOR TREATMENT

*Tony is concerned, but he also sees positive signs regarding Phil's engagement and motivation for treatment. It is a good sign that Phil has been willing to follow his sister's recommendations and go to AA as well as come to the clinic today. As the interview progresses, Phil appears relieved and more willing to get help. Phil even smiled when talking earlier about his grandsons.*

As you progress with evaluating the suicidal client, you will discuss a suicide prevention plan and you will attempt to work with the client to reduce risk factors and enhance protective factors, as discussed in the next chapter. Your goal is to establish rapport with the client, so the client can see that you care. You also want to let the client know that, with professional assistance, his problems are manageable. This instills hope and helps to counteract the client's idea that suicide might be the only way out. As you do this, you will notice the emotions and responses of the client. Ask yourself these questions:

- Is the affect of the client becoming brighter as the session progresses?
- Does the client readily collaborate on and agree to implement treatment recommendations?
- Does the client readily agree to the suicide prevention plan?
- Is the client open to your reframing of the situation (e.g., that coming in for evaluation and treatment was wise and courageous)?

All these would indicate that the client is becoming more hopeful as the evaluation session progresses and thus will now be at lower risk. This means that outpatient treatment could be considered for this client, if careful consideration of other risk factors does not contraindicate it.

Be concerned if you notice signs that the client is unlikely to engage in continued treatment, including these:

- The client seems unconnected to you.
- The client seems uninterested in treatment recommendations and uninvolved in the treatment process.

- The client repeatedly talks about barriers to mental health treatment (e.g., "I can't come in because I have to take care of my elderly mother").
- The client indicates that only weak people need treatment.
- The client has a history of stopping treatment immediately after past crises had resolved.
- The client has a history of involuntary inpatient commitments.

Clients with a history of poor follow-through in treatment are at greater risk of completed suicide (Joiner et al., 1999). As Simon (1988) states, "The presence of a therapeutic alliance is a bedrock indicator of the patient's willingness to seek help and sustenance through personal relationships during emotional crisis, and is one of the most important nonverbal statements of a desire to live" (pp. 92–93). So be aware of any signs that your client is not engaging in treatment, because this may be indicative of a greater risk of completed suicide (Joiner et al., 1999).

Even if the client is interpersonally challenging, try to reinforce his efforts to communicate with you: "I know it's difficult to talk about such personal issues, particularly with someone you've just met. It takes a lot of personal courage to do so" (Rudd, 2006, pp. 34–35). Simply reaching out for help from a mental health professional is a sign of some hope for the future (Rudd, 2006).

## RECOMMENDED READING

Crosby, A. E., Ortega, L. & Melanson, C. (2011). *Self-directed violence surveillance: Uniform definitions and recommended data elements.* Centers for Disease Control and Prevention: Atlanta, GA.

*Despite its dry title, this publication helpfully describes many forms of suicidal behavior and provides state-of-the art recommendations for the most accurate terminology to use when describing this behavior. This document is readily available for free online at http://www.cdc.gov/violenceprevention/pdf/Self-Directed-Violence-a.pdf*

Van Orden, K. A., et al (2010). The interpersonal theory of suicide. *Psychological Review, 117,* 575–600.

*This article presents the most current version of the interpersonal theory of suicide, previously called the interpersonal-psychological theory of suicide. Also, it provides an informative update regarding research on various suicide risk factors.*

## EXERCISES AND DISCUSSION QUESTIONS

1. List all of the warning signs, risk factors, and protective factors for both Phil and Crystal.
2. Would you feel comfortable treating Crystal as an outpatient? Why or why not? What about Phil?
3. Take the quiz on page 75 (pdf page 77) of Crosby, Ortega, and Melanson (2011). Were you able to correctly classify different types of suicidal behavior, otherwise known as self-directed violence?

# 19

# Suicide Prevention, Risk Reduction, and Documentation

Once you've assessed the risk factors, protective factors, and warning signs (Chapter 18), the next step is to determine the client's acute suicide risk level. You then tailor your interventions to the risk level. Finally, you carefully and thoroughly document your assessment and what you and the client have agreed to.

As previously mentioned in Chapter 7, an element of informed consent is that you can break confidentiality if you believe the client is at significant risk of death by suicide (Berman, 2006). When the client is at high acute suicide risk, you can legally break confidentiality and obtain the assistance of the client's significant others to prevent suicide (Simon, 2011b). This information should be part of the standardized written informed consent process and should be reiterated verbally as needed to ensure the client's understanding.

Talk to your supervisor about managing suicidal clients in your clinical setting. Where could a client wait safely for transportation to a hospital? How are clients taken to a hospital from the setting? What should you do if an agitated, suicidal client leaves the building (Granello, 2010a)? Throughout the suicide risk assessment process, consult with your supervisor or another trusted colleague whenever you feel uncertain. Remember this wise advice: "The clinician should not worry [about suicide risk] alone" (Simon, 2011b, p. 117).

Working with suicidal clients can bring up intense feelings in the psychotherapist, including insecurities, anxiety, fear, anger, and helplessness (Granello, 2010a). Be sure you care for yourself through seeking supervision, consultation, and emotional support from colleagues and using your own psychotherapy to process these challenging emotions (Granello, 2010a).

## UNDERSTANDING CHRONIC SUICIDE RISK

People who have made two or more suicide attempts are *multiple attempters*. Research indicates that multiple attempters remain at much higher risk for completed suicide throughout their lifetimes. For that reason, we consider them to be at some risk of suicide indefinitely, otherwise known as *chronic risk* of suicide (Joiner, Van Orden, Witte, & Rudd, 2009; Rudd, 2006).

Individuals with signs of high capability (Chapter 18) are also considered to be at chronic risk (Joiner, Van Orden, Witte, & Rudd, 2009), especially those with three or more of the following:

- Single suicide attempt
- Aborted suicide attempt
- Self-injecting drug use
- Self-harm (nonsuicidal self-injury)
- Frequent exposure to, or participation in, physical violence (Joiner, Van Orden, Witte, & Rudd, 2009, p. 70)

I would also add *instrumental behavior* (appearance of a suicide attempt with no intent to die) and *behavioral suicide rehearsal* to the above list of signs suggestive of chronic suicide risk (see Chapter 18 for examples of these)

Most clients have no chronic suicide risk. In that case, just document in the chart that you asked about previous suicide attempts, self-harm, and other topics related to chronic risk but that the client denied these had occurred. There is no need for further explicit discussion of chronic risk in the chart when it is not an issue.

## UNDERSTANDING ACUTE SUICIDE RISK LEVELS

Each client is a unique individual and has unique risks and protective factors. No one risk factor can be used alone to determine risk level, and a thorough evaluation is needed in every case. Keep in mind that no particular suicide can be predicted with accuracy. Suicide is a low-base-rate event (Goldsmith, Pellmar, Kleinman, & Bunney, 2002), meaning that it happens so infrequently that accurate prediction is impossible. Literally thousands of research studies have evaluated various aspects of suicide and suicidal thoughts, yet still, with any single client, it remains impossible to accurately predict suicide. We can only ascertain whether the client is at risk and what the level of risk is.

I recommend that you use the following risk levels. I describe the typical signs of each risk level below (American Psychiatric Association, 2003; Joiner, Van Orden, Witte, & Rudd, 2009; Rudd, 2006). Note that suicidal intent escalates as the risk level increases.

- *No signs of acute suicide risk*
  - This individual has no current suicidal ideation and no significant risk factors that need to be monitored. No one with chronic risk should be given this acute risk level. Most psychotherapy clients are in this group.
  - Case example: *Karen Price, a 30-year-old White female, presents at the clinic with depression. She has no history of previous depression but is undergoing a stressful divorce and is now a single mother of a 3-year-old boy. She denies any current suicidal ideation. She had thoughts of suicide*

*when 15 years old but never engaged in any suicidal behavior or self-harm. She is doing well at work and has a network of friends who have been a great comfort to her.*

- *Low acute suicide risk*
  - If no chronic suicide risk: This individual has thoughts wishing for death, or thoughts about suicide, and may have a vague plan. However, she denies any intent to act on the suicidal ideas, and there are no behavioral signs of intent (such as rehearsal or preparation). Risk factors and warning signs are low and there are multiple protective factors, including social support. She readily agrees to treatment recommendations and is well engaged in treatment and hopeful that treatment will help her. This type of client is often described as having *passive suicidal ideation*, specifically suicidal ideation without intent, in many mental health settings. Most people who have suicidal ideation are in this group.
  - Case example: *Emily Chu, an 18-year-old Asian female, comes to the student counseling center with depression. She is separated from her family for the first time and is having some difficulty meeting others. She states that she has never been depressed before, nor has she ever had suicidal ideation, but she is now occasionally wishing that she were dead. She denies any intent to hurt herself and does not have a plan.*
  - If chronic suicide risk: This individual is stable and well engaged in treatment without thoughts of death or suicide.
  - Case example: *Toni Howard is a 35-year-old African American female with a longstanding diagnosis of borderline personality disorder. She has a history of five psychiatric hospitalizations, two suicide attempts, cutting, and chronic suicidal ideation, so she has chronic suicide risk. However, she has been in treatment for 6 months and is well engaged with her psychotherapist. She has denied any suicidal ideation and self-harm consistently for 2 months. She talks frequently about her desire to be a good mother to her 10-year-old daughter.*
- *Moderate acute suicide risk*
  - If no chronic suicide risk: This individual may have a clear suicide plan. He has significant risk factors and warning signs of suicide. The suicidal thoughts are escalating in intensity and frequency. On the other hand, there are significant signs that the individual is or will be well engaged in treatment and is motivated for treatment. When you suggest treatment, he expresses signs of hope, and he agrees to a suicide prevention plan. He denies intent, at least for today. Some protective factors are present.
  - Case example: *Phil, who was presented in Chapter 18 and later in this chapter*
  - If chronic suicide risk: This individual has thoughts about the desirability of death or suicide. However, she denies suicidal intent and has significant protective factors, including signs of good treatment engagement.

- ○ Case example: *Roger is an elderly White male who is a Vietnam combat veteran. Twenty years ago, he tried to commit suicide with a mix of cocaine and alcohol, but survived. He has a history of suicide rehearsal with his handgun many times before his wife of 34 years left him. Also, 2 years ago, he drunkenly ran his car into a tree after his wife left him. He admits that this was a suicide attempt, but he survived unscathed. The two suicide attempts put him in the chronic suicide risk category. He says that he's thinking about death again since being given a diagnosis of hepatitis C, but that he needs to survive because his unemployed adult daughter and 10-year-old granddaughter are living with him and are financially dependent on him. Since the car accident, he has been attending AA and has gotten a sponsor. He readily agrees to go to an intensive outpatient program and to the suicide prevention plan. He is an active and engaged participant in his treatment.*

- *High acute suicide risk*
  - ○ This individual has significant signs of suicidal intent, probably including both verbal and behavioral signs. Multiple risk factors and warning signs are present and there are few—if any—protective factors. Social support is usually low. You and/or your client may be unsure whether the client would be willing to follow through with a suicide prevention plan instead of acting on the suicidal thoughts. You may see signs of impulsivity, high activation, mania, unpredictability, psychosis, or otherwise being unwilling or unable to follow through with outpatient treatment. The individual may have a history of nonadherence to treatment. The individual has tunnel vision about his situation and feels hopeless.
  - ○ Case example: *Carlos, a 40-year-old Latino, has been laid off from his job at a meatpacking plant. His family members here and in Mexico were dependent on his income. He feels that he has failed all of them and that his life is therefore not worth living. He has told all of his family that he has failed them and deserves to die. He took his first unemployment check and bought a gun, then went to a bar and drank to excess to try to work himself up to kill himself, but he passed out at home before doing so. The next morning, his wife insists that he accompany her to the emergency room.*
  - ○ If chronic suicide risk: This individual has any signs of suicidal intent or an unmanageable level of distress.
  - ○ Case example: *Crystal, who was presented in Chapter 18 and later in this chapter.*

Suicidal desire or vague thoughts of death should be taken very seriously in individuals who are at chronic suicide risk. These clients can very rapidly escalate from having no suicidal ideation to having intense and frequent suicidal ideation with significant intent—in other words, they can rapidly escalate from low acute risk to high acute risk. So, any suicidal thoughts in these individuals will raise them to either moderate or high acute suicide risk (Joiner, Van Orden, Witte, & Rudd, 2009).

## ASSESS THE LEVEL OF RISK AND DETERMINE
## THE APPROPRIATE INTERVENTION LEVEL

*Tony's initial assessment is that Phil is at moderate acute suicide risk. Phil has significant risk factors: he is a recently bereaved older White man. Phil also has a suicide plan; specifically, he been thinking about using a gun, a very lethal method of suicide. Phil has been drinking, which puts him at greater risk.*

*However, Tony sees that Phil has expressed and demonstrated willingness for treatment. Phil has significant protective factors, including feeling supported by his family members. Phil expressed his growing attachment to the AA program and his intent to "work the steps" and get a sponsor. Phil also has no previous history of suicidal ideation or behavior. Tony suspects that if he can engage Phil in treatment, his acute suicide risk will decrease quickly. Tony is willing to revise his risk assessment to high acute risk if Phil does not readily agree with all his recommendations and the suicide prevention plan.*

*Tony asks both Phil and Susie (Phil's sister) back into his office since he sees that they are close, and he realizes that involving Susie in the treatment will enhance the likelihood of success. He says to Phil, "I see that you have been suffering a lot lately. Unfortunately, your grief has been so severe that it has turned into ongoing depression. Depression is very treatable. I can see that we need to take what is going on with you very seriously. I suggest that you attend an intensive daily program that we have here at this facility. You would come every weekday for intensive treatment, but you'd get to stay in the comfort of your own home at night. Would you be interested in doing that?" Phil readily agrees to this plan and seems relieved that there is a treatment option other than hospitalization.*

*Fred's initial assessment is that Crystal is at high acute risk. Crystal is a multiple attempter—she has two previous suicide attempts—so she has chronic suicide risk. In addition, she recently abused substances, engaged in self-harm, and is in acute distress. Crystal has two suicide plans that she has been thinking about frequently every day. Fred sees that Crystal needs hospitalization.*

These two case examples are continued from the previous chapter. Crystal's risk level, above, is easy to figure out: it is clear that she is high risk and needs to be in the hospital. Phil's risk category, on the other hand, is more difficult to determine. For the most part, he fits the description of moderate risk early in this chapter. However, his suicide plan is more vivid than we would like for someone classified as moderate risk and he's been engaging in suicide rehearsal. Tony wisely decides to use Phil's reaction to treatment recommendations to help him finalize his determination of risk level. So far, signs are good that Phil is open to and will adhere to treatment recommendations.

Together with your supervisor, you will consider three levels of intervention for your clients who have suicidal ideation:

1. Individual weekly psychotherapy as usual: suitable only for clients with no signs of suicide risk or those with low acute risk
2. More intensive outpatient treatment: suitable for clients with moderate acute risk who readily and believably agree to the suicide prevention plan and show positive signs of treatment engagement. Together, you and the client can consider the following options:
   - Two or three individual therapy sessions per week
   - Phone contact between sessions
   - Partial hospitalization program
   - Substance abuse treatment
   - Dialectical behavior therapy (DBT) or other psychotherapy group
   - Community support groups (such as AA)
   - Psychotropic medication
   - Family psychoeducation
   - Suicide prevention hotline number provided (National Suicide Prevention Lifeline at 1-800-273-TALK)
3. Hospitalization: suitable for a client with high acute suicide risk.

For clients at low acute risk, weekly psychotherapy is generally sufficient. Try reframing the suicidal ideation as a sign that the client is in distress and needs help, rather than a genuine wish to be dead.

For clients at moderate risk, a higher intensity of treatment is needed. Consult with your supervisor to determine the appropriate course of action. You might be providing all of the treatment, or more likely you will refer the client for intensive treatments and will continue to see her weekly (or more frequently). Get signed releases so you can coordinate care with the other professionals and programs (American Psychiatric Association, 2003). You may need to monitor the client occasionally by phone or have family sessions. Joiner, Van Orden, Witte, and Rudd (2009) emphasize the helpfulness of between-session phone calls for clients at moderate risk. One recommendation is to consider scheduling midweek phone check-ins to assess risk and reinforce coping skills. These calls should be brief (no more than 15 minutes) but empathetic. Interestingly, research has shown that therapists who are more willing to receive phone calls from clients are actually less likely to get these calls (Reitzel, Burns, Repper, Wingate, & Joiner, 2004).

If you are on the fence between high acute risk and moderate acute risk, be concerned if you notice any signs of continued suicidal intent or low adherence to treatment:

- The client has tunnel vision and is unable to accept your input or reframing about his situation.
- The client seems reluctant, sarcastic, or hopeless about treatment recommendations.
- The client's affect or verbalizations suggest reluctance to comply with the suicide prevention plan.

If you notice any of these, the client may be high risk after all and need hospitalization; consult carefully with your supervisor.

If you do need to hospitalize the client, be sure that all the relevant risk information gets communicated to the hospital staff verbally or in writing. If you do not provide this information, you may be held legally liable (Granello, 2010a).

## MAKE A SUICIDE PREVENTION PLAN AND SECURE CLIENT'S VERBAL AGREEMENT

*Tony says to Phil, "I'm still concerned about your suicidal thoughts. We can't help you if you aren't alive to be helped. I know that it has been painful to lose your wife, but I also know that you have a lot of family members who love you and want you to be around for them." Phil nods his agreement. Tony continues, "I'd like to ask you to make a suicide prevention plan with me. I'd like you to agree to give up the gun and let Susie keep it in a safe place at her home for you to have later when you are feeling better. Would you be okay with that?" Phil agrees. Tony continues, "I'd also like you to agree to call 911 or go to the nearest emergency room if you are having suicidal thoughts and you think that you might be at risk of killing yourself. Can I count on you to do that?" Phil readily agrees.*

Should you suggest that the client call you when he is feeling more suicidal? I do not recommend it. You cannot be available 24/7, so if the client is depending on you and you are not available by your phone, then what should the client do? This uncertainty may confuse someone who is feeling acute distress. Do not take responsibility for saving your client's life; this is a clinical mistake (Simon & Gutheil, 2004), and it is not realistic. If you can't trust the client with that responsibility, the client should be hospitalized.

I agree with McWilliams (2004), who says that an appropriate suicide prevention plan is one that is available to the client 24/7 and is not dependent on your constant availability. If the client will be treated as an outpatient, the client must agree to a suicide prevention plan. Give the client two alternatives if the suicidal ideation worsens: either call 911 or go to the nearest emergency room. The 911 operators can dispatch appropriate personnel to the client's home to take the client for evaluation. Any emergency room will be able to evaluate the client and hospitalize as needed. Obtain and document the client's verbal agreement to adhere to this plan. If the client has any hesitation, ask what the concerns are and address them thoroughly until the client accepts the plan. If the client cannot accept the plan, there may be more ambivalence about continuing to live than the client initially revealed. This should be further evaluated and addressed as you decide whether to treat the client as an outpatient or whether to initiate hospitalization.

An alternative suicide prevention plan is asking the client to call you first, but if you are not available, then to seek help from the suicide hotline (National Suicide Prevention Lifeline at 1-800-273-TALK), 911 or the nearest emergency room (Simon, 2004). However, that plan can be problematic with certain borderline clients who might decide to call you, tell you that they are going to die by suicide, and then expect that you will exert all efforts to rescue them by phone while they are actively resisting your efforts. The client needs to work out any ambivalence about the suicide plan in the psychotherapy session, not act it out when in a crisis. If you sense that the client may act out ambivalence about suicide in this way, do not tell the client to call you when suicidal; instead, use the 911/emergency room suicide prevention plan and address ambivalence about living at every psychotherapy session until it is resolved.


## UNDERSTANDING THE LETHALITY OF SUICIDE MEANS

Different means of making a suicide attempt have different lethalities. Research has found that people who have greater suicidal intent usually choose more lethal means (Haw, Hawton, Houston, & Townsend, 2003; Horesh, Levi, & Apter, 2012). The most lethal suicide means are guns (Stanley & Brown, 2012), hanging (death can occur in under one minute; Gilbert, Jensen, & Byard, 2008), drowning (Elnour & Harrison, 2008), jumping in front of a train or car (although relatively rare; Krysinska & De Leo, 2008), inhaling lethal gases (Elnour & Harrison, 2008), and jumping from bridges and other heights (Reisch, Schuster, & Michel, 2008). Less common suicide methods in the United States of varying lethalities include suffocation, electrocution, hypothermia (dying from being too cold), car crashes, driving a vehicle off a drop-off, and self-immolation (burning oneself to death).

Some individuals seek death by putting themselves in harm's way, perhaps through angering an armed gang member or acting in a threatening manner so that the police are called; these are called *victim-perpetrated suicides*. However, these suicides are classified as homicides and are not included in suicide statistics, so the frequency of these suicides is unknown (Osiezagha, Kaur, Barker, & Bailey, 2009).

Cutting oneself with a knife is generally of lower lethality, unless at least one of these is present: (1) through practice, the person has acquired the capability of making sufficiently deep cuts, (2) the person has acquired enough knowledge of physiology to know where to cut for maximum lethality, or (3) the person has arranged not to be found, so there is sufficient time for blood loss and death to occur.

Prescription and over-the-counter medications and toxins vary considerably in lethality; some—including some psychotropic medications—are highly lethal in sufficient doses (Berman, Shepherd, & Silverman, 2003). A suicide attempt with pills can be highly lethal when the person has (1) researched the amount of pills to ingest to cause death and (2) made efforts to avoid being found until the pills have caused death. Impulsive suicide attempts involving pills, perhaps in combination with alcohol or street drugs, vary considerably in lethality depending on what was ingested and whether the person then called for help or was found by another individual.

In the United States, 60 percent of suicides are by firearms, which is the most frequently used method of suicide for men (56 percent), whereas poisoning by pills or other toxic substances is the most common means of completed suicide for women (37 percent), followed by firearms (Centers for Disease Control and Prevention, 2012). Just having guns in the home increases suicide risk fivefold (Simon, 2007). Note that the client may have been engaging in suicide rehearsal with the gun, as Phil has in the vignette.

Suicide methods vary significantly by country. For example, in India, ingesting pesticides is the most common means of suicide attempt in many regions (Banerjee et al., 2009; Bhattacharya et al., 2011), while self-immolation was the most common means at another Indian hospital (Kumar, Mohan, Ranjith, & Chandrasekaran, 2006). In Europe, hanging is the most common method of suicide (Varnik, 2008).

The client's *perception* of the lethality of the means used in a suicide attempt might differ from the *actual* lethality of the means. In other words, the client might think that a low-lethality method, such as cutting wrists, would kill her when she does not have the knowledge and capability to implement that method. Alternatively, the client might think that drinking heavily and taking a handful of sedatives is unlikely to kill her, when it actually could cause death. The best way to ascertain the client's perception of lethality is to ask her: "Did you think that [method] could actually kill you?" (Rudd, 2006).

## RESTRICT ACCESS TO LETHAL MEANS, ESPECIALLY GUNS

*Tony turns to Susie, "Susie, can I count on you to go to Phil's house right after we meet today and take the gun and the ammunition away with you?" Susie indicates her agreement. Tony cautions, "Could you be sure that the gun is secured in a locked area and that Phil has no access to it?" Susie agrees to do so. Tony asks if there are any other guns available to Phil, but both of them indicate that there aren't.*

The time between a suicidal impulse and a suicide attempt can be very short, often only a few minutes (Deisenhammer et al., 2009). To treat a client with suicidal ideation safely as an outpatient, you will want to make a plan to remove his access to lethal means as much as possible (Simon, 2004). *Means restriction* is a suicide prevention strategy that makes the means to die by suicide more difficult to obtain. Suicidal intent fluctuates rapidly (Bryan, Stone, & Rudd, 2011), and not having any means available can provide an opportunity for the client's suicidal impulse to pass.

Be aware that gun owners usually have more than one gun; on average they have four (Bryan, Stone, & Rudd, 2011). Simon (2011b, p. 138) recommends asking the following questions routinely:

- "Do you have guns at home or at any other place?"
- "Can you get a gun easily?"
- "Do you intend to obtain or purchase a gun?"

Ideally, guns should be removed from the home and disposed of, or removed from the home and locked up elsewhere by a responsible adult (Bryan, Stone, & Rudd,

2011). Hiding the guns or locking them up in the client's home is not sufficient because a determined client will get to them (Simon, 2007, 2011b). If the client is resistant, consider removing ammunition completely from the home or dismantling the gun and giving a critical piece to a supportive other (Bryan, Stone, & Rudd, 2011). Neither the client nor the psychotherapist should remove the guns; instead, it should be a trusted responsible adult, such as a family member or friend (Bryan, Stone, & Rudd, 2011). Schedule a phone call with this responsible adult to be sure that the guns have been removed and secured, and then document this information (Simon, 2011b). If you are working with inpatients, read Simon (2007) to learn more about managing gun risk upon discharge with that population.

Too many medications in the home can be a suicide risk, so others in the home should dispose of unneeded medications and consider securing any personal medications. The psychiatrist may wish to limit the client's medications to a week's supply, depending on potential toxicity. Clients who have been having thoughts of suicide by car would be wise to take public transportation or have others do the driving for now. To achieve these goals, you may need to meet with a responsible friend, relative, or significant other of the client and obtain that person's assistance (Joiner, Van Orden, Witte, & Rudd, 2009). Determine whether the client is motivated to adhere to these interventions.

No environment can be made 100 percent safe for someone who is intent on dying by suicide; all that can be done is to remove means that could be used impulsively so that the client can have more time to think clearly and obtain professional help. If you find yourself obsessing over how to make the client's home safer, that might be a sign that you don't trust the client to seek help if needed; in that case, the client should be hospitalized instead.

## CREATE A COPING CARD TOGETHER

*Tony says to Phil, "I'd like us to work together to come up with some steps you can take when you're upset and thinking about suicide. It can be hard to think clearly when you're feeling so upset, so I'd like us to devise a coping card you can use if you get upset or start thinking about suicide"(adapted from Joiner, Van Orden, Witte, & Rudd, 2009, p. 96). Tony asks Phil what has helped him feel better when he was upset in the past. Tony ensures that some of the options involve connecting with other people. Then Tony writes out the following coping card for Phil:*

*When I'm upset and thinking of suicide, I'll take the following steps:*

- *Call Susie and talk.*
- *Go to an AA meeting.*
- *Call one of the people who have given me their phone numbers at AA meetings.*
- *Take a walk.*
- *Go to church to pray.*
- *Take a nap.*
- *Do a Sudoku puzzle.*

*If I still feel distressed and have suicidal ideas, I can call the National Suicide Prevention Lifeline at 1-800-273-TALK. If I feel that I cannot control my suicidal behavior, I'll go to the emergency room or call 911.*
*(Adapted from Jobes, 2006, pp. 81–82, and Joiner, Van Orden, Witte, & Rudd, 2009, p. 98)*

A *coping card* (sometimes called a crisis card) provides written directions for the client who is coping with severe emotional distress and suicidal ideation. The card should be small enough that the client can easily keep it in a purse or wallet (Joiner, Van Orden, Witte, & Rudd, 2009). (Of course, you can also use a standard piece of paper and fold it up.) You can see how the sample coping card above is personalized to Phil and his needs. Some other possible interventions for the coping card could include (some from Jobes, 2006):

- Writing in my journal
- Taking a nice, hot bath
- Listen to uplifting or cheerful music
- Talking to a friend
- Petting my cat
- Taking my dog to the dog park and chatting with other dog owners
- Chat with a neighbor
- Take the kids to the playground

The coping card can be helpful to reinforce positive coping strategies and reinforce the suicide prevention plan. The hotline number, above, is a national number in the United States that you can provide to your clients.

Note that *the use of a coping card is not required*—although it is highly recommended by suicide prevention experts. You can address these issues verbally during the session without using the actual written card, although having the card to refer to can be helpful, since the client's thoughts are usually confused during crisis periods.

## EMPHASIZE RAPPORT AND HOPEFULNESS

*Tony says, "As I mentioned before, depression is very treatable, and I think that there is an excellent chance that you can feel much better within the next few weeks. In order for this to happen, I'd suggest several things. First, it's very important that you attend regular weekly psychotherapy sessions. Can I count on you to do that? Let's schedule a regular session time for you [takes a few minutes to schedule session]."*

Throughout your assessment of the client, use your active listening skills and reflect what you hear: "I hear that you feel overwhelmed by the situation, and I understand that from where you sit, you cannot see a way out of this other than suicide. It is clear to me that you are in such tremendous psychological pain that you feel you simply cannot face another day" (Granello, 2010a, p. 224). Empathy can calm the client down so that other interventions are possible and the suicidal crisis is defused (Granello, 2010a). Often people feel weak for seeking help; reframe help-seeking as wise and courageous.

Once the client feels understood, you can follow up with interventions that increase hope. As Tony does, above, help the client realize that the problems are treatable. Tony has mobilized resources within the mental health system to improve Phil's emotional functioning as soon as possible. He is clarifying that treatment is possible, available, and likely to help. Emphasize that positive life change can occur, even in the presence of negative emotions. Note that Tony emphasizes the likelihood of improvement without making promises, since each client is different and improvement cannot be predicted with certainty.

Look for other opportunities to reestablish hope. Encourage the client to develop plans, hopes, and goals for the future, which can serve as a protective factor (Jobes, 2006). Improving symptoms and daily functioning will reduce hopelessness, which is strongly linked to suicide risk (Beck, Brown, & Steer, 1989; Joiner et al., 2005).

Basic problem-solving about current life problems may help. The client's emotional problems may interfere with cognition, or she may have had problem-solving deficits all along. Consider this: "I am hopeful that there is a way out other than suicide. I believe that if we work through this together, we'll figure it out" or "I'm willing to stay with you as we work through the problem together" (Granello, 2010a, pp. 229–230). These statements emphasize your dedication to teaming up together and emphasize that problem-solving is possible.

Hope can be especially difficult for people with schizophrenia (Mamo, 2007). It can be difficult to assess negative mood because schizophrenic individuals have blunted affect. The symptoms of schizophrenia may make the client feel out of control. You must have sufficient knowledge about the treatment of schizophrenia to be able to tell the client what is necessary for her to do, in order to be as healthy as possible and give her hope. Talk to your supervisor about these issues if you are working with this population.

## INCREASE SOCIAL SUPPORT

*Tony says to Phil, "I think it is great that you have been going to AA with Susie. Can I count on you to continue to do that every day for the next few weeks?" Phil says that he will. Tony then says, "One last thing that I think is crucially important is for you to start seeing your grandsons again. I suspect that they miss you a lot and would like to see you. How soon can you go over and see them?" Susie says that she can drive him over to see the grandsons this evening. Phil agrees to go even though he seems somewhat reluctant. Tony asks why Phil is reluctant. Phil again says, "I don't want them to see me like this." Both Tony and Susie emphasize how much the grandsons have been missing him and need him. They suggest that just seeing the grandsons might help cheer him up. After hearing this, he agrees to go.*

Assess the current level of social support and make a plan to increase the client's social support over the next few days or weeks. If there are any supportive family members, ask the client how to enlist their emotional support (Packman, Pennuto, et al., 2004). In the vignette, Tony asks Susie to help Phil attend AA and see his grandchildren. Even small increases in social support can decrease suicidal desire (Joiner, Van Orden, Witte, & Rudd, 2009).

Sometimes it can be helpful to educate a partner or other family members about the importance of social support and to encourage them to check in on the client and to make plans to engage in pleasant activities together (Joiner, Van Orden, Witte, & Rudd, 2009). Be sure that the family member has a healthy relationship with the client (Rudd, 2006). A written release to talk to these individuals is recommended. Cultural considerations can be important in determining social support. If the client belongs to an ethnic group where there is strong family interdependence and/or extended family support, this can help support the client (unless there is significant conflict). Of concern, White clients may be the most socially isolated since they are less likely to be embedded in an actively involved extended family and may not be highly engaged with a religious community.

If the client has a history of being interested in religion and has a religious group that he has found uplifting in the past, reengaging with that group can be helpful. However, note that certain religious involvements might add to the client's distress (e.g., the client is gay and the church preaches against it) and should not be encouraged.

## ALLEVIATE DISTRESSING SYMPTOMS

*Tony says, "I would like to help you see a psychiatrist today and get some medication so you can sleep better. Usually, getting better sleep makes a significant impact on how a person is feeling. How does that sound?" Phil indicates that he is willing to see the psychiatrist. Tony says, "At your next appointment, we will talk about other strategies that you can use to help improve your sleep."*

Psychotropic medications can quickly reduce symptoms and acute distress (Simon, 2004). Symptoms that can be treated quickly with medications include insomnia, agitation, anxiety, panic attacks, and psychotic symptoms. Educate the client about how these medications should help within days and address any concerns that the client may have about medications. However, note that antidepressants can increase suicidal ideation and behavior in young adults under age 25 (Geddes, Barbui & Cipriani, 2009).

Depressed individuals tend to lie around the house ruminating and feeling miserable. They stop engaging in their regular activities and in the activities that they enjoy the most. Educate the client about the importance of behavioral activation (see Chapter 13), and work together to increase socialization and reengage in work and activities. Improve mood by reengaging with daily activities: work, hobbies, exercise, clubs, religious groups, and meetings.

Identify any other current issues that contribute to risk and target interventions to them. Tony plans on addressing sleep hygiene to improve sleep at Phil's next session (Chapter 13). If the client has been abusing alcohol, explore whether she is ready for treatment or detoxification. If the client is agitated, encourage exercise—and so on.

## DEVELOP AND SUMMARIZE THE ACTION PLAN

*Tony summarizes, "So you'll see the psychiatrist today, you're going over to see your grandsons this evening, and we've got an intake interview scheduled with the intensive outpatient program for tomorrow. Does all this sound doable? Is there anything else that you might be able to do in the next few days that would feel like a sign of progress to you?" Phil seems unsure. Tony continues, "What regular activities did you used to do?" Phil says he used to have breakfast with "the guys" on Wednesday mornings. Tony asks, "Do you think that breakfast with the guys is something you can actually do, given how you've been feeling?" Phil says yes, because the guys know he's been going through a hard time after losing his wife.*

The *action plan* summarizes what the client will do over the next few days to move toward problem resolution and away from suicide (Granello, 2010a). The two questions about what activity the client would see as a sign of progress and whether the client sees the activity as doable are key (Granello, 2010a). If the client does not do the activity, she may see it as "another failure." You can inoculate against that view: "Next time I see you, let me know how things go with the plan. If would be great if you were able to do these things, but if not, no worries. If you don't do something, make a mental note of how you were feeling and thinking when it didn't happen. If we better understand those feelings and thoughts, it will really help us understand what you're wrestling with. So either way it goes is okay."

Other things that could be part of the action plan include increases in physical activity, relaxation exercises, self-care behaviors, or any coping skills that worked for the client in the past (Granello, 2010a).

## TIME MANAGEMENT WITH SUICIDE RISK CLIENTS

When a client tells you about her suicidal ideation, you *must* accomplish some essential tasks before the client leaves your office—primarily for the safety of the client, but also to reduce your own legal risk. All other activities must wait or be cancelled—meetings, other clients, even picking up your kids from day care (if you have kids). For this reason, if you are on a tight deadline to leave the office, be very cautious about how you schedule the end of your workday. Do not schedule intakes or higher-risk clients then. You cannot leave the building for the day until you have thoroughly assessed the suicidal ideation, made whatever treatment plans are necessary, and documented the interaction. The only way you can leave is if you can find a trustworthy psychotherapist, with whom the client has sufficient rapport and who is willing to take on this responsibility.

Someone, preferably your usual supervisor, must be available to supervise your handling of the case. In many electronic systems (for example, the one used by Veterans Affairs), a trainee's progress note cannot be seen until a supervisor has signed it. All crisis-related progress notes, including those assessing acute suicide risk, must be cosigned and available to other staff before you leave the site for the day.

Here is a list of the essential tasks you must accomplish when any client has suicidal ideation:

- Ask all suicide risk screening questions (Chapter 18).
- Determine whether client has two or more previous suicide attempts.
- If the client has one or no previous suicide attempts, are there signs of high capability for an attempt?
- Ask in detail about the most severe attempt.
- Determine how severe the warning signs are, especially substance abuse, hopelessness, and activation.
- Assess the client's level of suicidal intent.
- Determine the intensity of the client's mental illness symptoms, stress, and emotional and physical pain.
- Determine what the protective factors are. What has kept the client alive up to now? What is the client's level of treatment engagement?
- Determine a risk level.

If the client is an ongoing client, much of this you will already know or can assess relatively easily, given your knowledge of the client's current and past functioning. If the client is new or is an intake case, this may take you an hour or more.

If the client is at low acute risk, use your judgment (in consultation with your supervisor) about what interventions from this chapter to use today and which to do at the next session. Be sure to have an agreement with the client about a suicide prevention plan. Also, it is best for the client to have at least a couple items on an action plan. You might want to schedule an extra session before the client's next weekly session so that you can implement more of the interventions in this chapter.

If the client is at high acute risk, you will need to hospitalize. Your supervisor can assist you with that.

If the client is at moderate acute risk, this is the most difficult situation. On the one hand, you don't think the client needs hospitalization, but she does need intensive intervention to stabilize her. In this case, you *must* stay at the site until you are satisfied that the client has a workable plan, you (and your supervisor) feel confident about this initial plan, the client seems more hopeful and engaged, and all of this is fully documented and cosigned in the chart.

## ONGOING PSYCHOTHERAPY FOR SUICIDE RISK

The informed consent process continues over the course of the treatment (see Chapter 7). Therefore, when you become aware of suicide risk, discuss how suicide risk is treated and find out whether the client agrees to this treatment. One of the primary targets of treatment will be reducing suicidal behavior and impulses. To do this, some difficult feelings may need to be addressed and the client will have to be willing to learn new skills and participate in crisis management (Rudd et al., 2009). In rare cases, when the client refuses to adhere to necessary portions of the treatment (for example, coordinating care with the psychiatrist), it *can* be ethical to terminate treatment (Jobes, 2006); however, *never* do this without consulting with your supervisor and carefully considering legal abandonment issues.

As you work with a client who has had a suicidal crisis, you want to reduce the likelihood of future attempts. Dialectical behavior therapy (DBT) has been shown to be helpful in reducing suicide attempts and reducing hospitalizations for suicidal ideation (Linehan et al., 2006). Cognitive therapy can help improve problem-solving and coping abilities (Stellrecht et al., 2006).

You will also want to help the client reduce self-harm behaviors, since these increase the client's capability to die by suicide in the future (Joiner, Van Orden, Witte, & Rudd, 2009). Self-harm is a dysfunctional way of coping with distressing feelings. In a classic study, clients were asked why they harmed themselves (Briere & Gil, 1998). After engaging in self-harm, the subjects felt less anger at themselves, less anger at others, and less fear, emptiness, hurt, loneliness, and sadness. After self-harm, they had more feelings of relief and shame (Briere & Gil, 1998). The findings of this study clearly indicate that individuals who harm themselves need alternative coping methods. In fact, research has found that individuals who engage in self-harm have deficits in their problem-solving abilities (J. Evans, 2000). Until the client learns alternatives and is motivated to use them, the self-harm will likely continue.

Given these findings about coping deficits, here are some early interventions you can consider using to deescalate self-harm behavior:

- Maintain your empathy to the client throughout, and gently emphasize the importance of addressing self-injurious behavior consistently in therapy.
- Ask the client how the self-injurious behavior helps: "How were you feeling before you burned yourself with the cigarette?" "What was happening that led you to have that feeling?" "How did you feel after you burned yourself?"
- Agree that the client needs effective ways to ease distress and acknowledge the client's feeling that self-injurious behavior has helped: "I certainly agree that you need something effective to do when you feel fearful or when you are having flashbacks. I can see that you feel that biting yourself has really helped you when you felt like that."

- Educate the client about the dangers of the self-injurious behavior: "I'm concerned because you could end up getting a serious infection or permanent scarring, or you could cut too deep and injure a blood vessel or a nerve."
- If appropriate, reframe the relationship between the client's trauma history and the self-injurious behavior: "You've already suffered more than enough hurt in your life. I don't think you deserve to suffer any more injuries."
- Suggest that alternative ways of coping can be used when the client is feeling in distress: "I'm hoping that we can work together and help you figure out healthier ways to cope when you are upset. I understand how important it is to have something you can do to feel better."
- Recognize that the self-injurious behavior may not stop immediately. Discuss how to reduce its dangerousness—perhaps by substituting holding an ice cube in the hand or snapping a rubber band on the wrist (Linehan, 1993).
- Tell the client in a nonjudgmental way that you'd like to discuss the self-injurious behavior after every time it occurs and help the client think about other ways to cope.
- Enroll client in a DBT group or teach DBT skills on an individualized basis. DBT has the most research supporting its effectiveness in treating self-harm (Burns, Dudley, Hazell, & Patton, 2005), probably because it is a structured approach that directly addresses coping effectively with distress.

## HOSPITALIZE CLIENTS WITH HIGH ACUTE SUICIDE RISK

*Fred suggests to Crystal that hospitalization is best given how distressed she has been. Crystal agrees but says she feels discouraged that she needs hospitalization again. Fred takes steps to initiate hospitalization.*

When starting at a new mental health training site, learn the procedures for how clients are hospitalized before starting to see any clients. Paperwork and procedures for hospitalization vary from site to site and from state to state. In some states, out-patient commitment is also possible. Be aware of the laws regarding involuntary inpatient and outpatient treatment in your state. Talk to your supervisor about how involuntary hospitalization is initiated at your facility. Your supervisor should orient you to both the voluntary and the involuntary hospitalization procedures.

*Voluntary hospitalization* is when your client agrees to be hospitalized. When hospitalizing, do not leave the client alone and unattended unless you have a very good reason to assume that the client will not leave and will not engage in self-harm in your absence. If you work at a site that has an emergency room and an inpatient unit, you or another staff member should walk the voluntary client down to the emergency room and ensure that the client is under observation before leaving. If the site does not have these services, a reliable individual, such as a family member or friend, should escort the client directly to the agreed-on hospital (Simon, 2011b). Personal items can be brought to the client later; the top priority is for the client to be taken to the hospital immediately and directly.

An *involuntary hospitalization* is the hospitalization of a client who refuses to be hospitalized but whom psychotherapists believe is a danger to self or others. Involuntary hospitalization generally requires considerable paperwork, often including the agreement of two mental health professionals. The client will then wait in a secure location that is monitored by staff and will be transported to a facility that accepts involuntary psychiatric patients. In extreme cases, staff may need to restrain the client during the wait.

## DOCUMENT YOUR INITIAL SUICIDE RISK ASSESSMENT

Thorough documentation is an essential portion of the suicide risk assessment (Moline et al., 1998). In the future, you or others may need this information when assessing another suicidal crisis in the same client. In addition, you will want to document all the risk factors, warning signs and protective factors so the treatment team can work together to reduce the client's risk.

You must document completely so that—in case of legal action—your documentation proves that your evaluation and actions were up to your profession's *standard of care* (Packman, Pennuto, Bongar, & Orthwein, 2004), defined as "the professional practice that one would expect of a reasonable and prudent clinical practitioner, in similar circumstances, with a similar patient" (Jobes, 2006, p. 117). Remember that, in a legal context, "if it wasn't written down, it didn't happen" (Gutheil, 1980, p. 479). As Moline et al. (1998) assert, "Clear, specific and objective written documentation of treatment and preventative actions taken by you are a good safeguard against liability" (p. 74). Remember, your progress note documenting suicide assessment and prevention is your *only* proof that you adhered to the appropriate standard of care.

Your thought processes in clinical decision-making must be thoroughly documented. If you did not hospitalize, make your reasons for this perfectly clear in the chart (Packman, Pennuto, Bongar, & Orthwein, 2004), and make a good case for why you think that outpatient treatment is the best treatment choice. If you do not hospitalize, you must be feeling that the client shows sufficient potential to engage well with intensive outpatient treatment and shows sufficient personal strengths and protective factors to stay in the community. There is a tendency to forget to document protective factors that relate to the client's treatment, such as good treatment alliance, history of regular attendance, or client's hopefulness about treatment. These protective factors can reduce the client's acute risk level from high to moderate.

I recommend that *if you do not hospitalize, the client's acute risk level should be no more than moderate.* Be sure to carefully differentiate between high *acute* risk and *chronic* risk; it is usually appropriate for individuals with chronic risk to be outpatients, but it is not appropriate for someone with high acute risk to be an outpatient. If you really think the client is at high acute risk, then hospitalize. Think about the worst-case scenario: Would you like to sit in the witness box and be asked by a prosecutor why you did not hospitalize a client whom you documented was at high acute risk?

The main issues that should be documented are:

- An assessment of suicide risk, with all details about risk factors, warning signs, and protective factors thoroughly described, including positive treatment signs
- If the client is at chronic risk, note why this is.
- The client's acute suicide risk level, and why you think that acute risk level is appropriate
- The treatment that has been planned, and why you think that treatment will reduce risk
- Any immediate safety or other interventions that you made today
- The suicide prevention plan (call 911 or go to the nearest emergency room if suicidal impulses are at risk of not being controlled)
- The client's agreement to and collaboration in all of the above
- Plans—when the next appointment is and what the client agrees to do before then.

Document all suicide risk assessments contemporaneously to protect against lawsuits because a suicide may occur despite your best efforts. *Documentation of a suicide risk assessment must be completed (and cosigned if necessary) before you leave the facility for the day.* If your client dies by suicide and you haven't written a note documenting your earlier suicide assessment, you are in a highly problematic legal position. If you work in a medical center, your client may come to the emergency room when you are not available. Your notes will help another mental health professional decide what to do.

Be sure to specify whether the client agreed to follow through on your recommendations. For continuing clients with suicidal ideation, be sure to document whether the client followed your recommendations between psychotherapy sessions.

Your goal for suicide risk documentation is that any other professional reading your note can see and understand exactly what you found out as well as why you did what you did—*and* that the professional will agree that what you did adhered to appropriate professional standards. The following outlines what to address in the progress note that documents a suicide risk assessment (informed by Jobes, 2006; Rudd, 2006). These items are *in addition* to the usual items that would be covered in each section. This outline is for a client who will be treated as an outpatient:

Subjective/Objective Section of note

- [Describe in complete detail all current and historical information that is relevant to Ms. A's suicide risk.]

- [Include everything the client says about why suicide is and is not an option for her.]
- Ms. A's current suicidal ideation is...[describe intent, plans, means]
- Either:
  - Ms. A denied any suicidal intent. Or,
  - Ms. A has the following signs of suicidal intent [describe both behavioral and verbal signs of intent].
- Ms. A reported the following past suicide attempts...[include whether there were injuries sustained, how lethal the attempt was, how lethal the client thought the attempt was, whether medical care or hospitalization was needed, if needed medical care or hospitalization was obtained, and if not, why not (Rudd, 2006). It may take several sessions to get all this information, so you may need to get the outline of just the most severe attempt in the first session.]
- Ms. A reported the following past suicidal ideation...[past suicidal ideation is not very informative of suicide risk because it is so common, but it can still be informative in understanding the client]
- Ms. A's past adherence to treatment is...[be sure to note any episodes of nonadherence, for example refusing medical care or hospitalization after a past suicide attempt]
- Ms. A's current engagement in treatment is...
- I consulted with Ms. A's family member...[specify the family member(s) consulted and what they said about Ms. A's functioning, as well as any actions they will take to assist Ms. A over the next few days]
- I consulted with [other professionals] regarding Ms. A and [their agreement/input regarding plan]

Assessment Section of note

- The suicide risk factors for Ms. A are...
- The suicide warning signs for Ms. A are...
- The suicide protective factors for Ms. A are...
- Ms. A verbalizes that she does not intend to act on her suicidal ideation because...
- Given the above, Ms. A is at [specify level] risk for suicide at the present time because...
- I did not hospitalize Ms. A because...[if client has chronic risk or moderate acute risk, this reasoning should be especially detailed]

Plan Section of note

- Ms. A verbalized her agreement to enact the following suicide prevention plan: if she feels tempted to act on suicidal ideas, she will come to the emergency room or call 911 for assistance.

- Ms. A has agreed to participate in the following treatments to reduce her risk of suicide...[include what interventions you chose—including psychotropic medication referral, why you chose them, timeframes for interventions, and why you didn't choose alternative interventions (Simon, 2004)]
- Ms A agreed to take the following actions...[describe any recommendations you've made and the client agreed to regarding increased activity level, reengagement with social network, attending support groups, and so on]
- During the session...[detail means restriction and any other actions or plans undertaken during session; e.g., sister agreed to remove gun from home]
- Ms. A will be next seen by [insert person] at [insert date].

If you feel that you cannot make a persuasive argument for managing the client as an outpatient, then the client should be hospitalized.

Here are a few Do's and Don'ts when documenting suicide risk:

- Don't: "Client did not express any suicidal ideation."
- Don't: "Client reported no suicidal ideation."
- Don't: "There is no evidence that client is suicidal."

The statements above are Don'ts because it is not clear that you asked directly about suicide.

- Don't: "No SI, HI, CFS." (in other words, "no suicidal ideation, no homicidal ideation, contracts for safety;" Simon, 2011b)

The above statement with all these abbreviations is commonly found in charts (Simon, 2011b), but it only documents that the client was insufficiently assessed and that an ineffective treatment (no-suicide contract) was administered.

- Do: "Client *denied* any current or past suicidal thoughts or behaviors."
- Do: "Client *denied* any current or past suicidal thoughts or behaviors, but the veracity of this statement is unclear. His wife stated that he has been acutely depressed and has made hopeless remarks in the last week, and that he purchased a handgun for the first time yesterday."

Why are only these two statements a Do? Because they are the only ones that make it clear that you have directly asked about current and past suicidal thoughts and behaviors. Be sure to use the key word *denied*. The last statement shows that you are carefully considering the client's recent behavior and symptoms, in addition to what he has told you.

- Don't: "Client promised not to shoot himself or others with his gun."
- Do: "Client *agreed* to the following risk management plan: he called his brother during the meeting, who agreed to meet him and remove the

gun from his home and take it to [specify secure location] for at least the next month."

Why is the second statement a Do? Because the psychotherapist has engaged in means restriction, which may help prevent an impulsive suicide attempt. *Agrees* is another key word; when the client *agrees* to your recommendations, be sure that you have documented this.

## DOCUMENT FOLLOW-UP SUICIDE RISK ASSESSMENTS

When treating the client as an outpatient, identify triggers for suicidal ideation and discuss coping skills for these situations. Explore the client's ambivalence about suicide carefully in therapy—why the client wants to die, and why the client wants to stay alive (Jobes, 2006).

Continue to assess suicide risk during every session until three sessions have passed without any suicidal ideation (Jobes, 2006). After that, decide together with your supervisor how often to reassess. Reassess suicidal ideation whenever the client presents with increased symptoms. Document each week what the nature of the suicidal ideation was and why it continues to be appropriate to treat the client as an outpatient. If the client is not improving, or is deteriorating, discuss this with your supervisor, perhaps before the client leaves the facility that day. The two of you can think carefully about whether he should be hospitalized (Rudd, 2006).

Also, as you progress with treatment, be sure to document whether the client followed through on the referrals that you gave her and whether she is following treatment recommendations (Jobes, 2006). If not, explore the client's reluctance or difficulties with following though, document that you've done so, and encourage the client to try again.

Be sure you've got a release of information to talk to the client's psychiatrist, and document your initial and every subsequent consultation with the psychiatrist in the chart. Document every phone call that has clinically relevant information, especially if you are making an effort to check in with the client between sessions by phone.

If a client with significant suicide risk drops out of treatment, make a good-faith effort to reengage the client in treatment. In consultation with your supervisor, consider sending appointments by mail, contacting the client on the phone, and/or contacting family members for assistance in getting the client to attend. Document all these efforts carefully before you close the case.

## SHOULD YOU USE NO-SUICIDE CONTRACTS?

A *no-suicide contract* (NSC) is a form that a psychotherapist asks a client to sign attesting that the client agrees not to die by suicide. I agree with Simon (1988, 2004), who feels that the primary purpose of a suicide contract is to alleviate the anxiety of the psychotherapist. He goes on to caution that making a suicide contract "may falsely relieve the therapist's concern and lower vigilance without having any appreciable effect on the patient's suicidal intent" (Simon, 1988, p. 93).

In a review of the literature, McMyler and Pryjmachuk (2008) found that most clinicians in hospitals and high-risk settings use NSCs and *think* that a NSC is a valid alternative when time and resources are tight, that the NSC protects them legally, and that the NSC lowers the risk of suicide. All of the ideas are *false*. Legally, a contract cannot be enforced that would limit an individual's liability from negligence, so a NSC cannot protect you from negligence in inadequately assessing suicide risk, which then leads to suicide (Simon, 2006). There is absolutely no evidence that written contracts reduce suicidal behavior, and repeated studies show that many clients will die by suicide even with a written contract (Simon, 2004). In fact, up to half of clients with NSC inflict self-harm; indeed, NSCs may actually *increase* the rate of self-harm, especially in clients with borderline personality disorder (McMyler & Pryjmachuk, 2008). Therefore, your best risk management strategy for dealing with suicidal clients is to follow the recommendations in this chapter.

In conclusion, if anything, the NSC actually increases your legal risk. It documents that you have concern about a particular client who has suicidal ideation. Yet, it does not show that you've done an adequate suicide risk assessment (Simon, 2011b), as outlined in these two chapters. In other words, you've documented both that the client is at risk of suicide and that you did not do an adequate assessment. This is why experts consider NSCs to be an "utterly inadequate intervention" (Jobes, 2008, p. 406) at best, and a legal liability at worst.

If you are working in a setting where NSCs are commonly used, consider sharing this chapter and the previous one or McMyler and Pryjmachuk (2008) with the staff for discussion. If you can figure out how to do this tactfully, you could make a significant impact on quality of care.

## COPING IF A CLIENT ATTEMPTS SUICIDE OR DIES BY SUICIDE

> I felt helpless, not knowing what to do. My thoughts and feelings ran into each other. What did I think of her? What did I think of myself: my failure, my incompetence, my grandiosity, my stupidity? Had I killed her? I always thought I was careful, responsible, able to see inside my clients. I could understand their pain and help them. No client of mine would ever kill herself. I'm too careful…I was shocked at the rage that washed over me…. I knew I would never be the same. There was no way to explain my shame. I felt haunted by every detail of the story. (Alexander, 2007)

The vignette above is from a psychotherapist's response to her client's suicide attempt (Alexander, 2007). Research suggests that the suicide of a client is one of the most stressful professional events (Horn, 1994). Trainees and early-career professionals may be especially vulnerable to intense emotional reactions and stress after a client's suicide (Horn, 1994) or suicide attempt.

Experiencing a client's suicide is common. Psychotherapists who work with inpatients or clients with severe mental illness are more likely to have a client who dies by suicide (Kleespies, 1993). All mental health professionals have at least a 25 percent chance of having at least one client dying by suicide in their careers, and psychiatrists have at least a 50 percent chance (Chemtob, Bauer, Hamada, Pelowski, & Muraoka, 1989; Gulfi, Dransart, Heeb, & Gutjahr, 2010; McAdams & Foster, 2000). Three studies found that during psychology training alone, the risk for client suicide was 10 to 17 percent (Kleespies, 1993; Kleespies, Penk, & Forsyth, 1993; Kleespies, Smith, & Becker, 1990), and one sample of psychology trainees found that about 30 percent had a client attempt suicide during their training years (Kleespies, 1993).

If your client has died by suicide, there are several practical matters you must address (for a thorough treatment of these issues, see Simon, 2004). Tell your clinical supervisor and your administrative supervisor. The malpractice insurer who covers your training site should be contacted by the appropriate person within 30 days. You need to understand that confidentiality does not expire with the client's death, and you need to consider how you will relate to the family through this difficult time. Risk management, unfortunately, needs to be considered carefully. Read more about these complex issues immediately if a client dies by suicide.

The suicide of a client will affect your emotional functioning (this entire paragraph is informed by Gulfi, Dransart, Heeb, & Gutjahr, 2010; Horn, 1994). You have the feelings that go along with losing a significant person to suicide, and you experience the suicide as a critical event in your professional development. Ordinary emotional reactions to suicide may begin with shock, disbelief, and denial and then progress to guilt, shame, sadness, and blame. On a professional level, you may worry about your professional competence and you may experience self-doubt and anxiety. You may fear that fellow professionals are being silently critical. You may be preoccupied with intrusive thoughts about the client and worry about legal issues as well. When working with other suicidal clients, you may feel anxious or helpless. You may also have some avoidance symptoms or repeated thoughts about the suicide (Gulfi, Dransart, Heeb, & Gutjahr, 2010; McAdams & Foster, 2000). These are typically short-term reactions that fade over time.

Do not share all your feelings with the grieving family; they have enough emotional distress already. Talking about your worries with the client's family will sow inaccurate concerns that poor treatment contributed to the suicide, so don't do it. Talk to your supervisor and colleagues about these issues instead. Saying the words "I'm sorry" to the family could be problematic as well (Simon, 2004). On the other hand, having some contact with the family could be an opportunity for you to refer them to needed treatment, since they will now be at risk of maladaptive coping and even suicide themselves (Ellis & Patel, 2012). In addition, if you keep your distance, the family could feel abandoned or treated coldly or believe that your have something to hide (Ellis & Patel, 2012). If your supervisor approves, you can consider attending the client's funeral if the family feels it is appropriate, or you might write a note of condolence to the family. Talk to your supervisor about these issues, then tailor a plan to the particular needs of your client's family.

Address the emotional and professional impact with trusted colleagues, including supervisors and consultants, especially those who have also lost a client to suicide (Kleespies, 1993). Feelings of fear and helplessness when treating suicidal clients and becoming overly protective of higher-risk clients are common reactions (Horn, 1994); personal therapy and consultation can help. The emotional support of your family, friends, and peers can be helpful as well (S. Knox, Burkard, Jackson, Schaack, & Hess, 2006) as long as you are careful not to violate the deceased client's confidentiality.

Later, you will regain emotional equilibrium and reach acceptance and understanding of the event. When you are ready, consider reviewing the case in detail with a supervisor or with a consultation group to gain more understanding of what transpired. As a result of the suicide, you may be more attuned to clients' emotional pain and more aware of suicide risk and are likely to be motivated to learn more about effectively managing suicidal clients (Gulfi, Dransart, Heeb, & Gutjahr, 2010; S. Knox et al., 2006). You may be more careful with clinical recordkeeping and more aware of legal liabilities, and you may be more willing to seek consultation regarding high-risk cases (Gulfi, Dransart, Heeb, & Gutjahr, 2010; McAdams & Foster, 2000). These responses can lead to improved sensitivity and quality of care.

## CONCLUSION

These two chapters on suicide risk are just an introduction to the complex subject of assessing and managing suicide risk in clients. Unfortunately, the effectiveness of suicide risk interventions is an underresearched subject overall (Rudd, Joiner, Trotter, Williams, & Cordero, 2009), especially among ethnic minority groups (Joe & Niedermeier, 2008). It is essential that you continue to learn more about this subject through reading, consultation, and lectures. The following list of recommended readings will help you get started on this process.

### RECOMMENDED READING

Granello, D. H. (2010a). A suicide crisis intervention model with 25 practical strategies for implementation. *Journal of Mental Health Counseling, 32,* 218–235.
*Granello details many strategic interventions that assist the psychotherapist with addressing the suicide crisis effectively. Highly recommended.*
Packman, W. L., Pennuto, T. O., Bongar, B., & Orthwein, J. (2004). Legal issues of professional negligence in suicide cases. *Behavioral Sciences and the Law, 22,* 697–713.
*Packman and colleagues provide a thorough discussion of legal malpractice issues relevant to client suicide and how the psychotherapist can practice to minimize risk.*
Rudd, M. D. (2006). *The assessment and management of suicidality.* Sarasota, FL: Professional Resource Press.

*This 99-page volume summarizes the main points in suicide assessment and manage-
ment in more detail than was possible in these two chapters. Well written in an accessible
format, this is an essential resource.*

Simon, R. I. (2011). *Preventing patient suicide: Clinical assessment and management.*
Washington, DC: American Psychiatric Publishing.

*Although targeted to fellow psychiatrists, Simon's volume is essential reading for any psy-
chotherapist who wants to be well informed and confident in the clinical management
of suicide risk. Simon provides helpful details on inpatient management of suicide risk.*

### ONLINE RESOURCE

www.drwiller.com/tbpc

*This section of my website has sample progress notes for crisis situations for your
review.*

## EXERCISES AND DISCUSSION QUESTIONS

1. Does your facility use no-suicide contracts with clients? Do you think
   this is a good idea with these particular clients? Why or why not?
2. Do you know any psychotherapists who have lost a client to suicide?
   Has your supervisor or any of your coworkers lost a client to suicide?
   Ask these colleagues how they dealt with it.
3. If a client were to die by suicide, what would you need to do from a
   procedural standpoint at the facility? What do you think would help you
   cope personally and professionally with this tragedy?
4. Write a progress note documenting Tony's assessment of Phil.
5. Write a progress note documenting Fred's assessment of Crystal.

# 20

# Violence Risk Management

In this chapter, I focus on management of violence risk in the adult outpatient mental health setting. The violence could be either psychological—such as threats or insults—or a physical assault—such as intimate partner violence, physical fights, or homicide.

If you plan to work in another setting (e.g., corrections, schools, or with children or adolescents), review the literature regarding violence risk management in that setting. Because of the level of risk on inpatient units, all mental health practitioners working on the unit should have specialized training in self-defense. Inpatient professionals should also be trained in how to "take down" a violent patient and know how to use physical restraints appropriately (Yeager et al., 2005).

## FIRST, MAXIMIZE YOUR OWN SAFETY

[After considering extended hospitalization] the patient told me that she had seen the hospital and decided that she would like to live on a houseboat while in treatment. The request was not one that I had expected, so I was a bit taken aback. Topeka, after all, is a landlocked city. I explained to her that it wouldn't be possible to accommodate her request. She then looked at me in a menacing way and asked, "Are you proposing marriage to me?" Although the situation was filled with uncertainties, I was clearheaded about one thing: I was not proposing marriage to her. I told her so, and she came at me with several swift karate kicks, one of which hit me in the right thumb [and broke it]. (Gabbard, 2004, p. 427)

In the hour before he was killed, on Sunday, Sept. 3, Dr. Wayne S. Fenton, a prominent schizophrenia specialist, was helping his wife clear the gutters of their suburban Washington house. He was steadying the ladder, asking her to please stop showering debris on his clean shirt; he had just made an appointment to see a patient and wanted to look presentable.... At 4:52 p.m. that Sunday, the Montgomery County police found the 53-year-old psychiatrist dead in his small office, a few minutes' drive from his house. They soon tracked down the patient he had agreed to meet that afternoon, Vitali A. Davydov, 19, of North Potomac, who admitted he had beaten the doctor with his fists, according to charging documents. (Carey, 2006)

BLS [Bureau of Labor Statistics] rates measure the number of events per 10,000 full-time workers—in this case, assaults resulting in injury. In 2000, health service workers overall had an incidence rate of 9.3 for injuries resulting from assaults and violent acts. The rate for social service workers was 15, and for nursing and personal care facility workers, 25. This compares to an overall private sector injury rate of 2.... The average annual rate for non-fatal violent crime for all occupations is 12.6 per 1,000 workers. The average annual rate for physicians is 16.2; for nurses, 21.9; for mental health professionals, 68.2. (Occupational Safety and Health Administration, 2004, p. 5)

Mental health care professionals are at significant risk for workplace violence. Fatal attacks are very rare (Reid, 2008), but minor physical assaults and threats are common (Pieters, Speybrouck, De Gucht, & Joos, 2005). Clients are most violent toward family and significant others (Anderson et al., 2004) or psycho-therapists (Barlow, Grenyer, & Ilkiw-Lavalle, 2000). Psychotherapists who work in inpatient settings, emergency rooms, community mental health clinics, non-profit settings, corrections, or drug/alcohol treatment programs are at greater risk, while attacks in private practice are rare (Jayaratne, Croxton, & Mattison, 2004; Petit, 2005). Psychotherapists who are younger than 45 years old, male, or less experienced are more likely to be threatened or assaulted; one study found that one third of psychiatric residents had been physically assaulted by a patient (Jayaratne et al., 2004; Schwartz & Park, 1999). There is no evidence that the race or ethnicity of the psychotherapist influences the likelihood of being assaulted (Jayaratne et al., 2004).

While violence risk cannot be eliminated, steps can be taken to increase safety (Berg, Bell, & Tupin, 2000). Chairs should be arranged so that either you or the client could easily exit the office without being blocked (Dubin & Jagarlamudi, 2010). Neither sharp objects (scissors, letter openers) nor heavy decorative objects (sculptures, paperweights) should be easily available. When working with high-risk populations, panic buttons should be installed (Berg et al., 2000).

Severely mentally ill individuals who appear highly agitated or who are not responsive to verbal direction should be sent directly to the emergency room and not seen in the office (Simon, 2011a). Do not work in a secluded area alone with any clients at moderate, high, or unknown acute risk for violence (Reid, 2008). At least one other psychotherapist should always be nearby, within earshot. No trainee should be working alone in a clinic, or when a supervisor is not present, because you never know when you may need to consult regarding a crisis.

If you ever experience an assault by a client, discuss this thoroughly with your supervisor afterwards and please consider getting psychotherapy for yourself to help you process the many complicated feelings you are likely to have about the attack (Reid, 2008). It may be appropriate to make a police report or press charges; again, discuss this with your supervisor.

## VIOLENCE RISK AND INFORMED CONSENT

At the outset of treatment and as part of the informed consent process (as discussed in Chapter 7), address limits to confidentiality regarding violence. In a population that is at low acute risk for violence, a brief mention of these limitations in written informed consent documents that the client signs at the outset of treatment would be sufficient. However, in a higher-risk population (e.g., community mental health clinic, corrections settings, or substance abuse treatment), a written document, followed by a brief oral review, may be helpful to ensure that the client understands. When your client has been informed, it will not be a surprise if you need to take steps to ensure anyone's safety. Prior informed consent will help maintain the therapeutic alliance if you need to take any precautions. If you forgot to address limits of confidentiality earlier, you can address it at the time that the client reveals violent ideation, although this is not ideal.

## CLIENTS AT ACUTE RISK OF BECOMING VIOLENT

Several client groups have an increased risk of violent behavior, and there can be overlap between these groups. Some individuals are at risk of *affective violence*—violence that is impulsive, defensive, angry or fearful, physiologically arousing, and in response to a perceived immediate threat (McEllistrem, 2004; Meloy, 2006). The goal of affective violence is to neutralize the threat. Persons who engage in affective violence may have decreased verbal skills and/or executive functioning (Meloy, 2006). They may have a history of combat or interpersonal trauma, which can make them hypervigilant to threats.

Persons experiencing an acute exacerbation of serious mental illness with manic or psychotic symptoms can be at increased violence risk. Bipolar clients in a manic phase are at greater risk of violence, especially when agitated and irritable.

There has been a longstanding debate about whether psychosis is related to greater violence risk. McNiel (2009) suggests that findings may be inconsistent because only individuals with acute symptom exacerbations may be at a statistically greater violence risk. Psychotic individuals who are at the greatest risk of violent behavior are those who abuse substances and have a diagnosis of schizophrenia (Douglas, Guy, & Hart, 2009). Of particular concern are command hallucinations to be violent (McNiel, Eisner, & Binder, 2000) and certain delusions—that others intend harm, that others could control one's thoughts, that others could insert thoughts in one's head (Norko & Baranoski, 2005); sometimes these delusions can focus on specific individuals perceived to present a serious threat (Mullen & Ogloff, 2009). However, keep in mind that "most violent individuals are not psychotic, and most psychotic individuals are not violent" (Douglas, Guy, & Hart,

2009, p. 697). Individuals are assessed to be a potential danger to others because of an acute exacerbation of mental illness should be hospitalized for everyone's safety. Once they are stabilized on medication, the violence risk is usually dramatically reduced.

Persons who abuse substances can be at increased risk of violent behavior, especially those who have a major mental illness and substance use issues (McNiel, 2009). They are at higher risk when intoxicated or during withdrawal. Signs of intoxication include "incoordination, unsteady gait, slurred speech, flushed face, change in pupil size, fluctuating level of consciousness and disorientation. Common features of withdrawal include sweating, tremors, hypervigilance, anxiety, hallucinations and elevated vital signs including pulse, blood pressure and heart rate" (McNiel, 2009, p. 129). Medical intervention for acute symptoms can reduce violence risk, and ongoing substance abuse treatment can keep violence risk low.

Cognitively compromised individuals are at greater risk of violence, including those with a history of head injuries, delirium from a medical condition, or dementia in the elderly (McNiel, 2009). Medical intervention to improve cognitive status or reduce impulsiveness can be a good initial intervention for these individuals. Be aware that many Iraq and Afghanistan combat vets sustained head injuries in combat (Maguen et al., 2010) and may have subsequent cognitive dysfunction.

Psychopathic individuals—a subset of those who have antisocial personality disorder—are at increased risk of violent behavior. These individuals lack empathy with the victim, are emotionally detached, and perpetuate violence to achieve a goal (McEllistrem, 2004; Meloy, 2006). They may have superficial charm and a grandiose sense of self-worth, pathologically lie, and may con or manipulate others (McNiel, 2009). The literature often refers to these individuals as engaging in *predatory violence* because of the affectless, premeditated nature of their violent behavior (Meloy, 2006). Unless you are working in corrections, you will not often see these individuals in mental health settings, so I do not focus on them in this chapter.

Certain rare situations can also be a violence risk (Mullen & Ogloff, 2009):

- An individual who is suicidal but still cares enough to take a final revenge, resulting in a murder-suicide risk
- Morbid jealousy of a former partner
- Some stalking situations
- Depressed suicidal mothers of young children
- Also, postpartum psychosis has been known in rare cases to cause child abuse, child neglect, and murder of children (Doucet, Jones, Letourneau, Dennis, & Blackmore, 2011).

## VIOLENCE RISK LEGAL ISSUES: THE *TARASOFF* CASE

Prosenjit Poddar, raised in rural India, arrived in Berkeley, California, in September 1967 to study graduate electronics and naval architecture.

Beginning in the fall of 1968, Poddar began romantically pursuing Tatiana Tarasoff, a community college student who lived with her parents nearby. Tarasoff was never really interested, but cultural differences produced much misunderstanding. In March 1969, Poddar blurted out a marriage proposal, which was promptly rejected. Angry and humiliated, he returned home and voiced to his roommate thoughts of killing Tarasoff. Over the next few months, Poddar's behavior was plainly paranoid: taping telephone conversations with Tarasoff, then staying in his room for days on end listening to them, and telling coworkers that he would like to blow up Tarasoff's house.

Finally, in June 1969, Poddar's roommate persuaded him to see a university health service psychiatrist. At the initial interview, Poddar told the psychiatrist of his thoughts of killing an unnamed young woman with whom he was obsessed. Antipsychotic and sleep medication were prescribed and weekly therapy appointments with a psychologist were scheduled. Poddar kept these appointments for eight weeks, repeatedly confessing his homicidal ideas toward the unidentified woman. In August 1969, the therapist told Poddar that he would take steps to restrain him if he continued such talk. Poddar immediately stopped coming to therapy. The therapist conferred with the treating psychiatrist (and with another university psychiatrist) and then wrote a letter to university police stating that Poddar [should be committed for observation in a mental hospital].

The campus police tracked Poddar down at his new apartment (very near Tarasoff's house) and interviewed him in front of his new roommate, Tarasoff's brother, about the death threats. Poddar acknowledged a troubled relationship with an unidentified young woman but denied any death threats. The brother knew that the alleged threats were against his sister but did not take them seriously. The officers, "satisfied that Poddar was rational, released him on his promise to stay away from Tatiana."

The university health service's chief of psychiatry, astonishingly, "then asked the police to return [the psychotherapist's] letter, directed that all copies of the letter and notes that [he] had taken as therapist be destroyed, and 'ordered no action to place…Poddar in [a] 72-hour treatment and evaluation facility.'"

Poddar purchased a gun and began to stalk Tarasoff. One evening just before Halloween 1969, he found her at home alone and killed her, called the police, and waited to be arrested.

Tarasoff's parents sued the university health service's chief of psychiatry; the psychiatrist who initially interviewed Poddar; the psychologist who saw him for the eight sessions, along with one other campus psychiatrist who had the misfortune to have taken part in one discussion about what to do at the time Poddar broke off treatment; and the campus police. Their complaint alleged that "defendant therapists did in fact predict that Poddar would kill and were negligent in failing to warn." (Herbert, 2002, pp. 417–418; reference notes removed for clarity)

In the 1970s, this legal case in California established the following case law prec-edent in that state: If the psychotherapist's client makes violent threats against a specific individual, the psychotherapist must warn that intended victim. This case is generally referred to by one name, *Tarasoff*, the last name of the woman who was killed and her parents, who sued. The events leading up to the case are described in detail in the previous quote.

Note that Poddar's psychologist and psychiatrist clinically managed Poddar's violent threats appropriately. They were concerned about his potential for violence. The psychiatrist prescribed antipsychotic medications to attempt to reduce delusional thoughts. They conferred appropriately about the case and even consulted with an additional psychiatrist. When Poddar dropped out and still appeared to be a violence risk, they directed the police to detain him and hospitalize him involuntarily (although the police did neither). Also note that Poddar didn't kill Tarasoff until weeks after this and after terminating therapy. The only clinical error was that the chief of psychiatry ordered clinical docu-ments to be destroyed; destroying documentation is always a very serious clinical error.

At least one of Tarasoff's family members knew about the threats, since Tarasoff's brother was Poddar's roommate and heard the interview with the police. It also should be noted that Tatiana Tarasoff was not even in the United States at the time of the psychologist's request for Poddar's hospital-ization (Gutheil, 2001). What was being alleged in the case was that the treat-ing mental health professionals should have, nonetheless, contacted Tatiana Tarasoff directly and warned her personally of the threat against her. The court upheld that Ms Tarasoff should have been warned even though it was an unprecedented demand that was not consistent with confidentiality laws of the time.

## VIOLENCE RISK LEGAL ISSUES: DUTY TO WARN

State laws regarding *Tarasoff*-type situations vary dramatically (Herbert & Young, 2002). In most states there is statute law, while in other states there is case law, and in still other states there may be no law at all (Fox, 2010). In some states, existing laws contradict the *Tarasoff* ruling (Herbert & Young, 2002; Walcott, Cerundolo, & Beck, 2001). Which mental health professionals are covered by *Tarasoff* statutes varies as well (Herbert & Young, 2002).

*Statute law* is law that is passed by legislators, such as state senators and representatives, and is codified by the state or federal legal system. *Case law* is a body of law based on judicial decisions of legal cases; new law can be made or existing law interpreted and clarified. Thus, the original *Tarasoff* ruling was California case law. However, it has since been supplanted by statute law in California (Herbert, 2002). Case law in one state is not technically law in another state, but it may be cited in rulings in the other states nonetheless (Walcott et al., 2001).

A *duty to warn* is written into some state statutes (this paragraph is informed by Herbert & Young, 2002; Soulier, Maislen, & Beck, 2010). Here are some of the ways these statutes differ:

- The psychotherapist may either be required or permitted to make a warning.
- Whether the warning goes to the intended victim, the police, or both varies.
- Whether the psychotherapist can exercise professional judgment and expertise to decide whether the threat is credible varies.
- Whether the psychotherapist can take alternative action to contain the threat without making a warning varies.
- Some require a specific identifiable victim, whereas others do not.

*Thus, no general guidelines can be given for making a report to an intended victim or victims, the police, or both, since state statutes vary so much.* Read the statute for your state (if there is one). Unfortunately, experts conclude that in states where there is no law, "the clinician is continuously in jeopardy: warn, and face breach-of-confidentiality exposure; keep silent, and risk a *Tarasoff* suit" (Herbert & Young, 2002, p. 280). In some states, imminence of a specific threat is required, which bars the psychotherapist from warning of a serious threat that may not yet be imminent (Fox, 2010). Even when there is statute law, the legal application of the statute can be in a state of flux due to specific legal cases being decided on the state and federal levels (Cunningham & Ciccone, 2011; Klinka, 2009).

The term *duty to protect* is often used in statutes rather than *duty to warn*. However, when this term is used in a state statute, the laws of most states indicate that the psychotherapist's duty is discharged solely by warning the intended victim and/or law enforcement (Herbert & Young, 2002) and that direct actions to actually protect the victim from the client (such as civil commitment) are not mandated, although these actions are sometimes suggested. In other words, even though psychotherapists may interpret the terms *duty to warn* and *duty to protect* differently, they are used essentially interchangeably in state laws. Herbert and Young (2002) conclude, "Much has been made of this [difference in terminology]. In fact, the earlier phrase [duty to warn] was accurate, the later one [duty to protect] rhetorical and misleading" (p. 275).

Think again about the actual case where Poddar murdered Tarasoff. In this case, the psychotherapists took many steps to protect Tarasoff from Poddar. In most clinical situations, the steps they took would have contained Poddar and, through effective treatment, would have kept him from murdering anyone. Herbert and Young (2002) conclude, "If anything, *Tarasoff* thus weakens the case for a duty to protect by providing a potential defense (if a warning was given) against a suit for negligent noncommitment" (p. 275). This leaves psychotherapists in a peculiar state of affairs: in some states, a warning to the intended victim and/or law enforcement is required, but actual clinical steps to contain the potential perpetrator of murder or violence are not. Therefore, because we do not want our clients murdering anyone, we *cannot* rely on state law for guidance about appropriate case management; we must also consider ethics and our clinical expertise to manage the situation effectively. Remember, when a client has made a credible threat against someone's life, make all efforts to hospitalize the client to contain the threat. Later in the chapter, I will provide some vignettes that address these issues further.

Sometimes, there is no specific person who is at risk. Everyone in the client's life, especially the psychotherapist and the client's family, may be at risk of being a victim. This client may be a violence risk because of her history of violent behaviors and because of current warning signs of violence. In most states, no warnings are legally required when no specific person is threatened (but check your state laws to be sure). However, as a practical matter, collaboration with close family and any family members in the client's residence is advised for everyone's optimal safety.

In one study, most psychologists were found to be misinformed about their state laws. In certain states, half of the psychologists wrongly believed that they were legally mandated to make a warning when other options were equally suitable under the law (Pabian, Welfel, & Beebe, 2009). Furthermore, in these cases, "options such as negotiating voluntary hospitalization or intensifying outpatient treatment are more likely to maintain therapeutic trust and may be of more value in assisting the client to resist destructive actions over the long run" (Pabian, Welfel, & Beebe, 2009, p. 12). Surprisingly, there is no actual evidence that warning a potential victim actually decreases the risk of violence against that person (Pabian, Welfel, & Beebe, 2009). All these points highlight the importance of consultation with your supervisor and other colleagues regarding violence risk management and duty to warn.

## VIOLENCE RISK SCREENING QUESTIONS: HISTORY OF VIOLENCE

Past violent behavior is more predictive of future violence than anything else, by far (Barlow, Grenyer, & Ilkiw-Lavalle, 2000; Bonta, Law, & Hanson, 1998). All clients should have an initial screening for past violent behavior in the first session. (In low-risk populations, you can skip asking about violent behavior verbally if it has been thoroughly addressed on written intake forms and the client did not endorse any violent behavior on those forms.) You can precede these difficult questions by stating, "Now, I am going to ask you a few standard questions that I ask everyone." Here are suggested screening questions:

- "Have you ever been violent or threatened anyone?"
- "Have you ever had any legal or criminal problems?"
- If so, "Were you arrested? What were the charges? Were you in jail or prison?"

If the client answers yes to any of these questions, you should do a full assessment of violence risk. When a client has admitted to a past incidence of violence, ask follow-up questions to learn more (Flannery, 2005; Kumar & Simpson, 2005):

- "When? Can you tell me more about what you did? Did you use a weapon?"
- "Why did you decide to do that?" or "What triggered you to do that?"
- "What was your relationship to [victim]?"
- "Did you plan this, or was it a spur of the moment thing? Tell me more about that."
- "What ended up happening? How injured was [victim]?"
- "How do you feel about that now?"

You do not need to ask all these questions exactly, but they illustrate the type of information that you should gather. For past violence, you will want to know how many separate times the client has been violent and the details of each occurrence.

During this assessment, a client may disclose past incidents of crime and violence, such as physical assault, sexual assault, or murder. In some cases, you will learn that the client was never charged or prosecuted for the crime (Walfish, Barnett, Marlyere, & Zielke, 2010). What are your obligations in that case? Experts advise that you do not report these crimes; in fact, they advise that reporting them would be a breach of confidentiality and a breach of your ethical obligation to the client (Walfish, Barnett, Marlyere, & Zielke, 2010). However, be sure to discuss your client's disclosures of past crimes with your supervisor. Planned future crimes, however, can be another matter, especially if there is an identifiable victim. Immediately discuss with your supervisor any planned crimes that your client reveals.

You should also ask about childhood: "Did you ever have behavior problems as a child?" The following childhood violent behaviors and behavior problems are predictive of adult violent behavior (Buchanan, Binder, Norko, & Swartz, 2012): truancy or conduct problems, first arrest under age of 18, cruelty to animals or people, and fire-setting.

If the client denies a history of violence but you still have some suspicions or concerns, ask the following:

- "What is the most violent thing you have ever done?"
- "What is the closest you have ever come to being violent?"
- "Do you ever worry that you might physically hurt someone?" (Monahan, 1993)
- "Have you ever been hospitalized for having thoughts about hurting someone else?"
- "Have you ever been hospitalized or jailed for violent behavior?"

If significant others are available for interview, you can question them as well, such as, "Are you concerned that [client name] might hurt someone?" (Monahan, 1993, p. 244). You will also want to review past chart records at your facility and send for chart records at other facilities; remember that you are legally responsible for knowing what is in these records if you know that they exist (Baerger, 2001).

## VIOLENCE RISK SCREENING QUESTIONS: VIOLENT IDEATION AND INTENT

Next, you will want to ask about violent ideation, violent intent, and who is at risk of victimization:

- "Are you having any thoughts of hurting anyone?" If so: "Would you act on these thoughts? Why or why not?"
- "Who are you having thoughts about being violent towards?"
- "Have you been able to refrain from acting on these violent thoughts? How?"

A client who feels unable to control herself from being violent needs to be in the hospital.

Just because a client has violent ideation, this does not mean that she has any violent intent. Gellerman and Suddath (2005) carefully reviewed the relevant research and case law regarding violent ideation versus threats of violence and conclude, "The research suggests that violent fantasies [violent ideation] are present in a large number of 'normal' individuals who presumably have not acted criminally based on these fantasies. There is insufficient scientific evidence that violent fantasies [ideation] should be considered absolutely predictive of future dangerousness" (p. 293). Therefore, violent ideation, without any violent intent, should not be considered a threat. Instead, violent ideation is one piece of evidence that must be considered in making a well-balanced assessment of violence risk. Gellerman and Suddath (2005) suggest that when a client reveals violent ideation, the psychotherapist should evaluate further, including assessing the nature and quality of the ideas, the degree to which a person is preoccupied with them, whether foreseeable victims can be identified, and what the client's potential is of acting on the violent ideas.

## ASSESS VIOLENCE WARNING SIGNS—SIGNS THAT VIOLENCE RISK MAY BE ESCALATING

These violence warning signs were mostly derived from studies of individuals who had a previous history of violence. Use them to differentiate between low, moderate, and high acute risk. Violence warning signs (Buchanan et al., 2012; Bonta, Law, & Hanson, 1998; Douglas & Skeem, 2005; Hanson, 2009, Harvard Medical School, 2011; Silver, Mulvey, & Monahan, 1999) include:

- Substance abuse
- Impulsiveness
- Acute stressors (e.g., unemployment, homelessness, divorce, or health problems)

- Anger—perhaps also irritability and agitation
- Ready access to weapons, especially guns—particularly when client knows how to use them (Kumar & Simpson, 2005)
- Poor relationships in the home, family dysfunction, lack of family support
- Exacerbation of psychotic symptoms, especially paranoid ideas that others intend harm or command hallucinations to be violent.
- Poor work adjustment
- Nonadherence to treatment or poor therapeutic alliance
- Exposure to and social support for crime and violent behavior (e.g., lives in high-poverty neighborhood, associates with gang members)
- Cognitive appraisal
  - Sees self as victim
  - Hostile, suspicious, believes others intend harm
  - Antisocial attitudes, such as lack of concern over consequences of violent acts and lack of compassion.

## ASSESS OTHER VIOLENCE RISK FACTORS

The following is a summary list of other violence risk factors (Anderson, Bell, Powell, Williamson, & Blount, 2004; Barlow, Grenyer, & Ilkiw-Lavalle, 2000; Bonta, Law, & Hanson, 1998; Buchanan et al., 2012; Flannery, 2005; Flannery, Schuler, Farley, & Walker, 2002; Harvard Medical School, 2011; Krakowski & Czobor, 2004; Swanson et al., 2002):

- Demographic factors
  - Male under age 40
  - Older age: Geriatric patients with dementia can also be at risk of violent behavior.
  - Low socioeconomic status
  - Race: When socioeconomics status is controlled for, race is not a risk factor.
  - Gender: Males and female clients are at equal risk for violence in mental health settings (Anderson et al., 2004), although males are at more risk in the general population.
- Childhood history factors
  - Physical abuse
  - Intimate partner violence in the home
  - Parent with severe mental illness
  - Parent with criminal record
  - Placed in foster care
  - School problems: truancy, poor school adjustment, dropping out of school

- Mental illness factors
  - ◦ Post-traumatic stress disorder (PTSD)
  - ◦ Antisocial/psychopathic personality
  - ◦ Borderline personality is associated with criminal activity and intimate partner violence (Logan & Johnstone, 2010).
  - ◦ Acute exacerbation of bipolar disorder or schizophrenia
- Neurological status: Clients with neurological abnormalities or a history of head trauma can be at greater risk.
- Admission status: Patients admitted involuntarily are at greater violence risk on the inpatient unit.
- Combat veteran status: Among veterans, those who had killed or seen killing during combat were at higher risk for violent behavior (Elbogen et al., 2010).

Psychotherapists tend to underpredict violence for Whites, overpredict violence risk for non-Whites (Hicks, 2004), and underpredict violence in women (Skeem et al., 2005).

## ASSESS VIOLENCE PROTECTIVE FACTORS

If the client has good treatment engagement and good treatment adherence, the likelihood for violence is lessened (Douglas & Skeem, 2005). Thus, certain characteristics of the treatment can be protective factors: good treatment alliance, good motivation for treatment, history of adherence to treatment recommendations, history of adherence to medications, willingness to seek emergency treatment as needed, willingness to ask for additional sessions as needed, and so on.

Other protective factors include:

- Prosocial attitudes: the individual believes that violent behavior would be wrong, understands the negative consequences of behaving violently, and wants to avoid these consequences by controlling his behavior
- Family, cultural, or religious values supporting nonviolence
- Having empathy for the potential victim (Kumar & Simpson, 2005)
- Social support (Douglas & Skeem, 2005).
- A supportive marriage (de Ruiter & Nicholls, 2011)
- Avoiding stressful relationships and those that promote criminal behavior (de Ruiter & Nicholls, 2011)
- Being employed (de Ruiter & Nicholls, 2011).

## ASSESS VIOLENCE WARNING SIGNS—RISK TOWARD A SPECIFIC INDIVIDUAL

If a client makes violent threats toward another person or otherwise appears dangerous toward a specific person, we must further assess the client to determine whether that person is at significant risk (Borum & Reddy, 2001). Consider these six factors, which form the mnemonic ACTION (Borum & Reddy, 2001):

- A—Attitudes that support or facilitate violence: Does the client believe that the use of violence is justified under the circumstances? Does the client believe that there have been intentional provocations by others? Does the client think that being violent will be successful in accomplishing her stated goals? Does the client have personal attitudes (such as antisocial, patriarchal, misogynistic, or prejudicial) consistent with violent behavior? Does the client feel that there are no other options or that there is nothing to lose?
- C—Capacity: Does the client have the physical and intellectual capacity to carry out the threat? Does the client have access to means, access to the target individual, and the opportunity to commit the act? How well does the client know the target's routines and whereabouts?
- T—Thresholds crossed: Has the client already engaged in behaviors to further the plan of attack? Have any of these behaviors broken any laws already (showing a willingness to engage in antisocial behavior)?
- I—Intent: After weighing this information and other statements made by the client, does there appear to be actual intent to engage in the violent act?
- O—Others' reactions: Does the client report that significant others are encouraging or discouraging of the violent plan? Are significant others immediately available to provide input about the client's behavior and likelihood to act? Are they fearful that the client will act on violent statements?
- N—Nonadherence versus adherence to risk-reduction interventions: Is the client willing to participate in interventions to reduce or mitigate risk? Is the client motivated to prevent this violent act? Does the client feel that treatment will be effective? Does the client have a good treatment alliance? Has the client adhered to treatment recommendations in the past? Does the client have insight into the need for treatment and potential for violence?

## ASSESS BEHAVIORAL WARNING SIGNS OF VIOLENCE, DE-ESCALATE OR CONTAIN THE THREAT

[Physical signs of imminent violence include]...a clenched jaw, flared nostrils, flushed face and clenched or gripping hands.... Demanding immediate attention, pacing, restlessness, pushing or slamming things, yelling, profanity, physical aggressiveness and verbal threats can all be early indicators of pending violence. Bell (2000) further elaborates warning signs of imminent violence including eye movement and appearance (such as dilation of the pupil or darting eye movements), proximity (such as a patient invading the clinician's personal space), inability to comply with reasonable limit setting and patient's perception of fear in the clinician. (Anderson et al., 2004, p. 387)

The previous description is a helpful summary of verbal and nonverbal warning signs of anger and aggression that indicate a risk of imminent violence. Also, the client might make physical or sexual threats against you; unfortunately, over 80 percent of mental health workers in one study had experienced a threat against them, mostly from male clients (Hatch-Maillette, Scalora, Bader, & Bornstein, 2007).

If you feel that a client is becoming threatening toward you in a session, use your judgment about whether you can talk the client down or whether you need help. Stay at least two steps or an arm's distance away from clients who may be aggressive (Dubin & Jagarlamudi, 2010). You could try to de-escalate the client, which is most effective when you already have a good treatment alliance. Don't respond to yelling or angry statements with sharp, angry statements of your own. If you get angry, you will probably escalate the situation; avoid arguing back or ordering the client to stop yelling or talking to you in that manner (Fauteux, 2010). Instead, use a quiet, soothing tone of voice. Reflect the client's feelings: "I can see that you are feeling very upset and angry right now." Reassure the client that she has done the right thing and that you plan to help: "You did the right thing coming in to the clinic to ask for help. I'd really like to get a better understanding of what is going on with you and see if we can make a plan together that will help you." Remember to remain at a safe physical distance and stay within reach of a panic button, if your facility has them (Petit, 2005).

Once the client has started to de-escalate, you can then ask the client to calm down and behave appropriately: "Calm down. Sit down, please. It's difficult for me to get an understanding of what's wrong when you are yelling and pounding on the desk. Can I ask you to take a few deep breaths and then try to tell me what's wrong in a quieter voice? I can help you better if I can understand what's going on more."

Consider offering medication empathetically (Anderson et al., 2004): "I can see that you are very distressed. Perhaps our psychiatrist can help you with some medication that will help you calm down. Would you like me to help you look into that?" Antipsychotics and benzodiazepines can be used as sedatives in emergency situations (Fulde & Preisz, 2011).

A client who is too agitated and angry to calm down should probably be hospitalized. If this is an intake client, do not frustrate yourself and the client by trying to fully assess all the history and symptoms because it is clear that hospitalization is needed right now. Inpatient staff can assess the client later when she is calm. If you think the client will cooperate, say something like this:

"Ms. Thomas, I can see that you are very upset right now. It was very wise of you to come here and ask for help. Given what you've told me so far, I think that the safest place for you would be the hospital. Could you come to [location] with me so I can get that started for you?"

Ask another staff person to accompany you and escort the client to the emergency room or a quiet, secure location so that arrangements can be made for hospitalization.

At any time, if you feel in physical danger, excuse yourself by saying that you need to go to the bathroom (Munsey, 2008), giving another excuse, or just exiting the office, and then call police or security staff. If you have a panic button, you could push it. In corrections settings, you might have a mobile alarm system that you carry on your person. You will have to trust your judgment in any particular situation, but don't be a hero—be safe and call for police, security, and/or additional staff assistance.

Ask your supervisor what to do in your setting if you have a client who is agitated and at immediate risk of being violent yet refuses to agree to hospitalization. In general, you would want to move away from the client and be sure that assistance is available. If possible, the area should be cleared of other patients and staff who are not needed for the crisis. Appropriately trained staff, security personnel, or police should be the ones who restrain the client if necessary.

## IF VIOLENCE IS OCCURRING OR IMMINENT

*Monique Brown is a mental health trainee who is in her office writing some progress notes. Suddenly, she hears thumping from the next office and hears her colleague cry for help.*

When you hear a potentially violent situation, call the police or security immediately. Do not hesitate. It is far worse to hesitate in a dangerous situation than to call the police unnecessarily. If your facility has security staff, call them, because they can arrive quickly. If not, call 911 for help. You might be trained to assist appropriately in a violent situation, or you might not be. Discuss with your supervisor what you should do if this arises.

You might also hear an ambiguous situation, such as a client yelling in an angry manner in the next office. In that situation, you may wish to assess the situation first. Knock on the door (even if there is a do-not-disturb sign) and assess the situation. If the psychotherapist appears calm and in control, you may simply ask the psychotherapist if everything is okay. You may also wish to politely ask the client to be quiet: "I'm not sure that you realize it, but everyone can hear you. Could I ask you to talk more quietly, so as not to disturb other clients and staff?" If the situation looks tense, ask the psychotherapist to step out for a minute and ask if everything is okay. If not, ask what you can do to help.

## UNDERSTANDING VIOLENCE RISK LEVELS

As with suicide risk, violence risk can be either chronic or acute. People with *chronic violence risk* have a significant history of violent criminal behavior and/or a history of multiple violent episodes. The violent history could include physical fights, physical abuse of family members, gang activity, sexual aggression, homicide, or attempted homicide. The person could have a history of verbal threats of violence, behavioral intimidation, or stalking.

I recommend that you use the following acute risk levels. I have written these risk levels to be parallel to what you learned in the suicide risk chapter:

- *No signs of violence risk*
  - This individual has no signs of violent ideation, no history of violent behavior, and no significant risk factors that need to be monitored.
  - Case example: *Barry Wilhelm is a 40-year-old married father of three young boys, who manages a local grocery store. When he was a teenager, he unwittingly drove the getaway car after two friends robbed a convenience store. He was on court-ordered supervision for 1 year after that. He deeply regrets this history. He is coming to therapy now for depression and anxiety. He denies any violent ideation or behavior now or in the past.*
  - Comment: Here Barry has a distant history of criminal involvement. However, he has no history of violent behavior and no violent ideation, and he has many protective factors. He has no discernible violence risk.
- *Low acute risk of violence*
  - This individual has violent ideation but denies any intent to act on the violent thoughts. There are no signs that he is preparing to act on the violent thoughts, and there are indicators of good impulse control. There is no significant recent history of violence. If there are past episodes of violence they are in the distant past (e.g., violent fights as a teen) or caused little physical harm (e.g., minor shoving of partner during argument), or the client has made dramatic life changes since then (e.g., now sober and employed). There may be some warning signs or risk factors. There are multiple protective factors. He readily agrees to treatment recommendations and is well engaged in treatment.
  - Case example: *Gilberto Flores is a law student who has been having difficulties with one of his professors. The professor gave him a very poor grade in his Constitutional Law course. Gilberto has been having thoughts of throwing bricks through the windows of this professor's home and hitting his professor with his fists when he sees the professor in the hallway. Gilberto admits that he recently had a loud verbal altercation with his girlfriend and left the house to cool off because he was afraid he would hurt her. Gilberto denies any history of violent or criminal behavior. He denies any intent to act on his violent ideation, stating that he knows that it is wrong and would not solve his problems. He scared himself by how angry he was at his girlfriend and he very much wants professional help.*

- ∘ Comment: Gilberto is in significant distress and needs help with anger and stress management. However, he doesn't have any history of violence, nor does he have any violent intent. He is very motivated to get help. This puts him in the low acute violence risk category.
- ∘ Also see case example of Casey in next section.
- *Moderate acute risk of violence*
  - ∘ This individual is having thoughts about being violent in general, and perhaps also toward a specific individual, at least several times per week. She has chronic violence risk and some significant recent warning signs for violence. However, there are signs that she is or will be well engaged in treatment and is motivated to do so. She readily agrees to a violence prevention plan and other interventions to reduce risk of violence. Some protective factors are present. She denies intent and verbalizes that she wants to live a life free of violent behavior.
  - ∘ See case example of Richard in the next section.
- *High acute risk of violence*
  - ∘ This individual has significant signs of violent and/or homicidal intent, probably including violent threats or planning to engage in violence. The violent intent is likely toward at least one specific individual. Or you see behavioral signs of agitation and warning signs of immediate general violent risk toward anyone near the client. Multiple risk factors and warning signs are present and there are few—if any—protective factors. The individual may be either socially isolated or surrounded by others who believe in using violence to solve problems. Probably the individual has chronic violence risk as well.
  - ∘ See case examples of Georgette in the next section and Samantha later in the chapter.

As with suicidal clients, I suggest that you don't label a client as high acute risk if you are planning on treating the client as an outpatient. If you think the client can be effectively treated as an outpatient, you must believe that there are protective factors present, including a good treatment alliance and good motivation for treatment. These protective factors enable you to classify the client as moderate acute risk for violence. In the chart, carefully describe the protective factors that indicate outpatient treatment is the best treatment choice.

## ASSESS THE LEVEL OF ACUTE RISK AND DETERMINE THE APPROPRIATE INTERVENTION LEVEL

*Efram Rosenberg is a mental health trainee working with a substance-abusing Iraq War veteran, Casey Simmons. Casey has been living with his family since returning from the war. Casey is having a difficult time getting a job. He has longstanding* conflicts with his father, who had been physically abusive when he was a child. Casey tells Efram, "I just want to hit him sometimes, I get so mad," but denies ever having been violent toward his father or having any actual intent to do so. Casey says, "I know how much Dad's violence messed me up, so I'd never do that to anyone, not even him." While Efram sees that Casey has no violent intent and sees Casey at low acute risk of violence, he is concerned because Casey has some risk factors—namely, his high level of stress, his history of childhood physical abuse, continued family discord, his combat veteran status, and substance abuse. Efram gives Casey a referral to obtain alternative housing that supports his abstinence, and Casey agrees to follow through with this today. No report of a violent threat is made, although Efram is practicing in a state with a statute mandating duty to warn.

Ashley Evans is a mental health trainee working with Richard Walker, a client who has a long history of polysubstance abuse. Richard has been incarcerated for burglary and for assault. Richard continues to abuse marijuana and cocaine intermittently. These drugs can make him paranoid, and at those times, he thinks that others are out to get him, feels angry, and thinks about attacking others. However, he verbalizes his understanding that attacking is wrong and would lead to incarceration, which he wants to avoid. He states that he therefore does not want to be violent to anyone. Because Richard has a history of violence and significant risk factors, Ashley considers him to be at both chronic risk for violence and moderate acute risk of violence. She sees him for individual therapy weekly. Richard also has daily community recovery groups and a weekly psychotherapy group, and he has frequent contacts with his psychiatrist. All these interventions encourage prosocial behavior and help to minimize his substance use and monitor his paranoid thinking.

Komal Singh is a mental health trainee who has been working with Georgette Yeager, a client who has schizoaffective disorder, bipolar type. Georgette has a long history of being hospitalized with exacerbations of her mental illness. She lives with her elderly parents. On numerous occasions, she has stopped taking her medications. Soon after stopping medications, she would argue loudly with her parents, threaten them with bodily harm, and smash dishes, claiming that her parents were poisoning her. When these incidents occurred, her parents would call the police and she would be committed to inpatient care. Today, Georgette has attended her appointment with Komal. She is pacing Komal's office and highly agitated; despite Komal's best efforts, she cannot calm down. She is expressing paranoid ideas about her parents, again claiming that they want to poison her. Komal considers Georgette to have a high acute risk of violence. Komal knocks on the office door next to hers and asks for help. Both psychotherapists escort Georgette to the facility's locked "quiet room." While the other psychotherapist observes Georgette, Komal calls her supervisor, and together they call the police and an ambulance to transport Georgette for hospitalization. Komal and the supervisor decide that they need to work on arranging other housing for Georgette when she is discharged because she presents a chronic danger to her elderly parents. Komal calls the parents to alert them to the situation. They are well aware of the danger that Georgette poses and thank Komal for initiating hospitalization.

Choose between three levels of intervention for your clients who have violence risk:

1. Individual weekly psychotherapy: suitable only for clients without any signs of violence risk or those with low acute risk
2. More intensive outpatient treatment: suitable for clients with moderate acute risk who readily and believably agree to a violence prevention plan and show positive signs of treatment engagement. Together, you and the client can consider the following options:
   o Two or three individual therapy sessions per week
   o Phone contact between sessions
   o Partial hospitalization program
   o Substance abuse treatment
   o Group psychotherapy targeted to specific issues, such as anger management or substance abuse
   o Community support groups (such as AA)
   o Psychotropic medication
   o Family therapy, marital therapy, or psychoeducation to reduce conflict in the home
   o Long-term residential treatment facilities
   o Depending on state law, you may need to consider duty to warn (discussed later in this chapter)—consult with your supervisor.
3. Hospitalization: suitable for a client with high acute violence risk. You may need to consider duty to warn, depending on your state's laws— consult with your supervisor.

In the first vignette, the client is not threatening his father but instead is revealing violent ideation. Efram has done a violence risk assessment and determined that although the client has some violence risk factors, he has no history of violence outside of combat, nor does he have any intent to be violent. Given this, the acute violence risk is assessed as low. Taking appropriate clinical steps to reduce the client's overall risk is thus the most appropriate step. In conclusion, *having violent ideation (or fantasies) does not constitute making a threat* (Gellerman & Suddath, 2005). Violent ideation must be evaluated within the context of a full violence risk assessment to determine whether anyone is actually in danger.

In the second vignette, the client has chronic violence risk and moderate acute violence risk but is not immediately dangerous to anyone. Ashley and the treatment team keep him as stable as possible through more intensive interventions and monitoring: weekly individual sessions, weekly group therapy, and medication sessions with his psychiatrist. Community mental health centers, nonprofit agencies, and Veterans Affairs settings tend to have a significant number of chronic violence risk clients. Frequent consultation with your supervisor and other treatment staff is essential in these cases.

In the third vignette, Komal and her supervisor find that Georgette is having another exacerbation of mental illness, and they need to hospitalize her. Remember that most people with schizophrenia are not dangerous to anyone, even when they are having an exacerbation of mental illness, but a small number, like Georgette, can be a violence risk. Talk to your supervisor about how to manage the hospitalization of potentially violent clients at your site.

## MAKE A VIOLENCE PREVENTION PLAN AND SECURE CLIENT'S VERBAL AGREEMENT

Talk with the client about this violence prevention plan: if the client feels at risk of becoming violent, he should leave the provoking situation and call 911 or go to the nearest emergency room. If the client readily agrees to the plan and verbalizes a sincere motivation to avoid violent behavior, this is a positive sign that it may be possible to treat the client as an outpatient. Document what the violence prevention plan is and that the client agreed to it. The client's motivation to avoid violent behavior can be seen as a protective factor as well.

## RESTRICT ACCESS TO WEAPONS

If weapons are accessible, help the client obtain the assistance of a reliable family member or friend to remove the weapons from the home and secure them in another location (similar to procedures addressed with suicidal clients, see Chapter 19). In addition, ask if the client has any weapons with him right now and, if your supervisor approves, ask the client to give them to you and secure them in a locked desk or filing cabinet. Later, you can follow your site's policies for disposal of weapons obtained from clients. Obtain the client's agreement not to obtain any more weapons until both of you agree that it is safe to do so. Document all of these actions carefully.

## ONGOING PSYCHOTHERAPY FOR VIOLENCE RISK

Since your client is seeing you in a mental health facility, the client has demonstrated some degree of cooperation and insight so far. Build on that by asking the client to collaborate on a treatment plan that reduces violence risk (Flannery, 2005). Maintain good communication about current level of risk among all staff involved with the client (Kumar & Simpson, 2005). As appropriate, involve the client's family.

The client should be engaged in substance abuse treatment as needed. Substance abuse is one of the most important risk factors for violence. An anger management group may be appropriate, or anger management and assertiveness skills can be addressed in individual therapy. Treatment that targets antisocial attitudes and impulsivity can reduce the risk of violent behavior (Hanson, 2009).

Since certain symptoms may increase risk, effective treatment may reduce a client's violence risk to match that of the general population (Friedman, 2006).

Thus, if your client has been violent in the past when experiencing paranoia or command hallucinations or when manic, one way to prevent violence is to control these symptoms effectively with medications. Schedule the client frequently, and work with the client and the client's family to improve medication adherence (Chapter 14). Work closely with the psychiatrist, who can adjust the medication to control symptoms better. Consider antipsychotics that can be given as a long-acting shot every 2 to 4 weeks, which may lead to improved treatment adherence and symptom control.

If a potentially violent client is dropping out of treatment and has not attended one or more psychotherapy sessions, make a good-faith effort to reengage the client in treatment (Monahan, 1993) for the safety of the client and society, and for the sake of your own legal liability. In consultation with your supervisor, consider sending the client additional appointments by mail, contacting the client on the phone, and/or contacting family members for assistance if you have previously obtained a signed release to talk to them. Document all these efforts carefully in the days or weeks before you close the case.

## VIOLENCE RISK LEGAL CASE EXAMPLE: ILLINOIS STATUTES

As an example of law regarding duty to warn, here are some excerpts from the relevant Illinois statutes:

- There shall be no liability on the part of, and no cause of action shall arise against, any person who is a physician, clinical psychologist, or qualified examiner based upon that person's failure to warn of and protect from a recipient's threatened or actual violent behavior except where the recipient has communicated to the person a serious threat of physical violence against a reasonably identifiable victim or victims. Nothing in this Section shall relieve any employee or director of any residential mental health or developmental disabilities facility from any duty he may have to protect the residents of such a facility from any other resident.
- Any duty which any person may owe to anyone other than a resident of a mental health and developmental disabilities facility shall be discharged by that person making a reasonable effort to communicate the threat to the victim and to a law enforcement agency, or by a reasonable effort to obtain the hospitalization of the recipient. (all excerpts from Whitted, Cleary & Takiff, n.d.)

Let me mention a couple key points and clinical implications from the above for psychotherapists practicing in Illinois:

- The psychotherapist only needs to consider reporting "a serious threat of physical violence." *Note that if the client believably denies intent, this*

*is not a serious threat and does not need to be reported; if you do, you will
unnecessarily violate her confidentiality.* Instead, help the client without
violent intent work on reducing violence risk while you reassess and
document the violent ideation regularly, as directed by your supervisor.

- The psychotherapist could *either* make a reasonable effort to
communicate the threat *or* could make a reasonable effort to hospitalize
the client. *So if you hospitalize the client and contain the threat that way, it
does not necessarily need to be reported.*

When the client verbalizes violent ideation, we have two ethical goals: to maintain
client confidentiality and to maintain the safety of everyone involved. In Illinois, if
the client has violent intent, you can choose to hospitalize the client, while ensuring that the inpatient staff is informed of the violent intent, and documenting that
you've informed them. In Illinois, this is sufficient to fulfill both the legal and ethical obligations, as well as being the best way to manage the situation from a psychotherapeutic perspective. Check your state's laws to see if the same principles apply.

Under Illinois state law, I would make a report to the intended victim and law
enforcement if a client made a believable threat of physical harm against a specific
individual and then refused further treatment and fled the office. Do not try to
contain a potentially violent client who is fleeing the office; that is a job for properly trained law enforcement personnel.

In other cases, under Illinois law, when a client communicates violent ideation,
I carefully assess the violent intent of the client. If the client believably denies
intent, I do not consider her to be making a threat, so my obligation under Illinois
statute law is not triggered (Gellerman & Suddath, 2005). In those cases, I do a
violence risk assessment and consider what interventions would be effective given
the level of violence risk.

## VIOLENCE RISK LEGAL ISSUES:
## WHEN TO MAKE A REPORT

*Samantha Jenkins is a 24-year-old psychotherapy client. She comes in for her regular
session with her student psychotherapist, DeShawn Taylor. Samantha is angry and loud.
She curses when talking about her live-in boyfriend, whom she suspects of being unfaithful. DeShawn knows that Samantha has been violent toward her boyfriend in the past
when they were having arguments. Samantha says, "I've decided now. I've got to shoot
him. There's nothing you can do to stop me." She then abruptly leaves the office before
DeShawn can further assess her intent, whether she actually has a gun, or anything else.
DeShawn practices in a state with no statute or case law about duty to warn. He goes
to his supervisor's office right away and appropriately interrupts his supervisor's session
with another client ("I'm very sorry, but I have to talk to you about a crisis immediately") to consult. Since both agree that Samantha has made a serious threat toward
her boyfriend and is at high acute risk for violence, DeShawn calls the home and warns
the boyfriend of Samantha's threat. Although not required by law, DeShawn provides*

*the boyfriend with specific advice: "I believe that this is a sincere threat against your life. I recommend that you leave your apartment immediately and go to a location that Samantha will not associate with you. This location could be a motel or a friend's house or, even better, go out of town for a few days until she has been found and detained. I want to be sure you are safe until a mental health professional determines that you are no longer at risk of being harmed." He then contacts the police, tells them of the threat, and asks them to pick up Samantha and take her to the state hospital for commitment.*

*A hospitalized client, Maria Barnes, is angry because her psychotherapist is on vacation. She rages to Allison Wolinski, a mental health trainee on the unit, "I'm going to kill him." Allison is concerned and tells the rest of the unit staff. Allison then calls the psychotherapist's supervisor at the outpatient clinic at the same medical center. They practice in a state with a duty to warn statute that indicates that a warning must be made to the intended victim if the psychotherapist assesses a threat is serious. Allison and the supervisor agree that they trust the judgment of the unit staff, and they know that the staff will not release Maria while she still verbalizes threats. Thus, they consider the risk to the psychotherapist to be low. Nonetheless, they agree to call the psychotherapist, thinking that he would want to know what transpired. Allison called the psychotherapist and told him about the threat. In this case, the psychotherapist was unconcerned since he knows that Maria is very labile and that this is just her way of expressing anger. When the psychotherapist returns, therapy resumes as before, including discussions of separation, abandonment, and anger management.*

In the first vignette, DeShawn and his supervisor must make an appropriate decision about how to manage this emergency. No law guides them. However, they believe that Samantha's threat could have been sincere, so they feel ethically compelled to protect her boyfriend's life, even if this means violating Samantha's confidentiality. Samantha is clearly unable to control her own behavior appropriately since she made threats in the session. They agree that she needs to be hospitalized to protect others. Our ethical concerns for the safety and well-being of others and the client dictate this action because, clearly, an involuntary hospitalization would be better for the client than a conviction of murder. As Mossman (2004) states, "The existence of a moral obligation to save others, and the absence of clear standards to define the obligation does not mean that there are never clear cases where we know another person is in danger and should do something reasonably simple to avert the danger" (p. 363). In addition, as Gutheil (2001) states, "Because the clinician works, not for the patient, but for the healthy side of the patient, the use of a *Tarasoff* warning may be seen to take place in service to that side of the patient that wishes not to harm another person" (p. 349).

In the second vignette, Allison contacts the psychotherapist whom the client made threats against, even though she felt that the acute risk was low because the client was hospitalized and carefully watched by inpatient staff. In this case, she felt that the psychotherapist would want to be informed, and she cannot be sure that the psychotherapist will check the chart notes before going to see the client on the unit. Since they all practiced at the same facility, no breach of confidentiality issues were involved, so there is no downside to reporting the threat. Allison is also aware that mental health professionals are at significant risk of violence from clients, in general, so she wisely wanted to be extra cautious. In conclusion, it is wise to maintain good communication between professionals by keeping fellow health care practitioners aware of changes in violence risk for mutual clients (Kumar & Simpson, 2005).

## DOCUMENTATION

Good documentation is essential in violence risk situations for two reasons. First, your documented assessment of violence risk is essential clinical information that must be preserved to help you and other psychotherapists who work with the client in the future. If the client is at risk of behaving violently again, studying this information will help other psychotherapists evaluate future risk more knowledgably. Second, lawsuits regarding the client's subsequent violent behavior could be brought against you in the future. A good contemporaneous violence risk assessment is the best defense (Elbogen, Tomkins, Pothuloori, & Scalora, 2003). As opposed to general progress notes, where brevity is a virtue, progress notes that discuss violence risk should include every relevant detail and may be quite lengthy. *Documentation of any violence risk must be completed and cosigned before you leave the facility for the day.* The times to do a violence risk assessment include at intake, upon discharge from inpatient or intensive outpatient programs, whenever there are significant changes in risk factors, and whenever the client verbalizes violent ideation.

The main issues that should be documented are:

- An assessment of acute and chronic violence risk, with all details about risk factors, warning signs, and protective factors thoroughly described
- The client's acute violence risk level, and why you think that risk level is appropriate
- The treatment that has been planned for the client, and why you think that treatment will help contain risk
- Any immediate safety or other interventions that you made today
- The violence prevention plan (call 911 or go to the nearest emergency room if client feels she may not be able to control violent impulses)
- The client's agreement to all of the above
- Follow-up plans—when the next appointment is, what the client agrees to do before then.

For a general violence risk assessment, the assessment for an outpatient can be outlined as follows:

Subjective/Objective Section of note

- [Describe in complete detail all current and historical information that is relevant to Mr. B's violence risk.]

- [Include everything the client says about why violence is and is not an option for him.]
- Mr. B's current violent ideation is... [describe intent, plans, whether weapons are available]
- Either:
  - Mr. B denied any violent intent.
  - Mr. B has the following signs of violent intent [describe both behavioral and verbal signs of intent].
- Mr. B's attitudes about violence are...
- Mr. B reported the following past violent behaviors and criminal activity... [include whether there were injuries and if the victim needed medical care. If the client has an extensive history of violent behavior, it may take several sessions to get all this information, so you may need to get information about the most severe violence in the first session.]
- Mr. B's past adherence to treatment is... [be sure to note any episodes of noncompliance, for example refusing medical care or hospitalization]
- Mr. B's current engagement in treatment is...
- I consulted with Mr. B's family member... [specify the family member(s) consulted and what they said about Mr. B's functioning, as well as any actions they will take to assist him over the next few days]
- I consulted with [other professionals] regarding Mr. B and [their agreement/input regarding plan]

Assessment Section of note

- The violence risk factors for Mr. B are...
- The violence warning signs for Mr. B are...
- The violence protective factors for Mr. B are...
- Mr. B verbalizes that he does not intend to act on his violent ideation because...
- Given the above, Mr. B is at [specify either low or moderate] acute risk for violence at the present time because...
- I did not hospitalize Mr. B because... [if client has moderate acute risk, this reasoning should be especially detailed]

Plan Section of note

- Mr. B verbalized his agreement to enact the following violence prevention plan: if he feels that he cannot control his violent thoughts, he will come to the emergency room or call 911 for assistance.
- Mr. B has agreed to participate in the following treatments to reduce his risk of violence... [include what interventions you chose— including psychotropic medication referral, why you chose them, timeframes for interventions, and why you didn't choose alternative interventions]

- Mr. B agreed to take the following actions...[describe any recommendations you've made and the client agreed to—attending support groups and so on]
- Mr. B will be next seen by [insert person] at [insert date].

If you feel that you cannot make a persuasive argument, using this outline, for managing the client as an outpatient, then the client should be hospitalized.

If there is specific risk against an individual, all the factors assessed (remember the ACTION acronym) should be carefully documented, as should the reasoning for any clinical decision-making and ensuing treatment plans. If you make a *Tarasoff* warning to anyone, document whom you warned (the intended target, the police, or both), when you made the warning and why, and your clinical efforts to reduce risk to that individual.

If you have been involved in a violent or potentially violent situation with a client, document what the circumstances were, what you did, and what happened as soon as possible after the incident. If a colleague was attacked by a client, the colleague might be injured and not be able to document in a timely manner; someone else may need to document the attack instead. This timely documentation is essential for the safety of other psychotherapists.

Be certain that all documentation is completed contemporaneously; do not go back and add details weeks or months later. Complete this documentation before you go home for the day; if you were concerned enough to assess violence risk, you should be concerned enough to document it the same day. Other psychotherapists may need this information after hours and will not have it unless you've written it up. In the worst-case scenario, if you do not document immediately and the client is subsequently violent, you are in an untenable legal situation.

## COPING IF YOUR CLIENT KILLS

In my capacity as expert witness for the defense, I reviewed the discharge summary. It was a superb document, including a carefully justified risk-management plan and detailed recommendations to the patient and family members regarding adherence to the plan.... Then I noticed the secretarial inscription at the bottom of the last page.... The summary had obviously been written on the day after the killing and back-dated to appear as if it had been written before the patient had been discharged.... When I informed the defense counsel of the ruse, she immediately decided to settle the case— which she had previously thought was eminently winnable—for the amount the plaintiff was asking, rather than risk a trial at which the tainted discharge summary would be placed before the jury. (Monahan, 1993, p. 248)

I was retained on a case in which the patient discharged from a community mental health center later killed a stranger. On the day after the killing made the front page of the local newspaper, the director of the facility wrote numerous comments, in black ink, across the only copy of the discharge summary. These are some of them: "How could we have missed this!" "Somebody should have gotten his records," "Really shoddy work on our part." One can imagine the dollar signs glistening in the plaintiff's attorney's eyes when she saw this subpoenaed document. The case, needless to say, was settled on very generous terms. While unburdening one's conscience and self-flagellation may do wonders for the psyche, they are very hard on the net worth. Indeed after this case, the mental health center in question was no longer able to buy liability insurance. No one would sell it to them. (Monahan, 1993, p. 249)

The worst-case scenario may happen: Your client may murder someone, and then there is a lawsuit. If your client kills, there are some things you should never do. Monahan (1993) advises that you not make any written or verbal statements of guilt or responsibility for what happened. Never go back and alter or add chart documents to include more information, even if they were incomplete. "It is, in short, much better to admit that you didn't keep good records and hope that the jury believes you when you tell them what happened than to manufacture good records after the fact at the cost of your own integrity and credibility" (Monahan, 1993, p. 248).

Discuss the case thoroughly with your supervisor. You are likely to have many feelings about your inability to foresee and prevent the crime. You may even be preoccupied by thoughts and even dreams of the crime. These reactions are normal. To regain your personal and professional functioning, seek professional support through supervision and personal therapy.

## CONCLUSION

I want to provide you with a few caveats about violence risk in the professional literature. In this chapter, I have chosen to be consistent with the terminology you've learned in the previous two chapters on suicide risk, rather than use the differing terminology for the same concepts that exists in the violence risk literature.

The literature on violence risk focuses mostly on correctional settings (Kumar & Simpson, 2005). Much effort has been devoted to various structured risk assessment devices that are focused on helping correctional workers predict who will be violent over time if released from a correctional setting (Coid et al., 2011). While this is certainly a worthwhile endeavor, it is not particularly helpful to those of us who need to assess acute violence risk in outpatients (Douglas & Skeem, 2005). In clinical settings, we are primarily concerned with preventing immediate physically violent behavior, and secondarily concerned with other violent crime (such as robbing a store at gunpoint); the violence risk literature consolidates both of these types of behaviors when assessing violence risk. I hope that future research might differentiate these two, which would be more useful for clinical settings.

Also, most research efforts have been devoted to risk factors that do not change (age, history of violence). Warning signs of acute violence risk (called *dynamic risk factors* in the violence risk literature) and violence risk levels (called *risk state* in the violence risk literature) are only starting to be examined more (e.g., Douglas & Skeem, 2005).

## RECOMMENDED READING

Borum, R., & Reddy, M. (2001). Assessing violence risk in *Tarasoff* situations: A fact-based model of inquiry. *Behavioral Sciences and the Law, 18,* 375–385.
   *Borum and Reddy discuss the process of evaluating an individual for immediate violence risk toward a specific individual. Careful review and consideration of the assessment process discussed in this article is recommended for all psychotherapists.*
Petit, J. (2005). Management of the acutely violent patient. *Psychiatric Clinics of North America, 28,* 701–711.
   *Petit thoroughly discusses the management of a client with acute risk of being immediately violent in the clinical setting.*
Simon, R. I. (2011). Patient violence against health care professionals: Safety assessment and management. *Psychiatric Times, 28,* retrieved August 14, 2012, from http://www.psychiatrictimes.com/schizophrenia/content/article/10168/1813471#
   *Simon shares cases of violence against mental health professionals and what we can learn from these cases.*

## ONLINE RESOURCE

www.drwiller.com/tbpc
   This section of my website has sample progress notes for crisis situations for your review.

## EXERCISES AND DISCUSSION QUESTIONS

1. Find and review your state laws for *Tarasoff*-type situations. You may need to contact your state professional association if only case law exists or to verify if there is no law.
2. Given the laws in your state, how would you proceed with the situations in this chapter's vignettes? Would you do anything differently? Why? How would you document these situations?
3. Ask your supervisor to discuss several cases with you in which he or she assessed a potentially violent client. If hospitalization was needed, how was this implemented at your training site? Was anyone warned of violence risk? Why or why not, under your state's laws? When was outpatient treatment appropriate?

# 21

# Child and Elder Maltreatment, Intimate Partner Violence, and Rape Crises

All psychotherapists need to know how to address child and elder maltreatment, intimate partner violence, and rape. These crises involve legal, ethical, and clinical considerations. Because the legal considerations vary from one state to another, I have attempted to highlight the greatest variations. Note that there are two types of law that might apply: statutes, which are laws that are passed by the state legislature, and case law, which is law that is established through judicial rulings on particular cases. Some sources for legal information by state are highlighted at the end of this chapter; your supervisor and your state professional organization can also assist you.

## BEING A MANDATED REPORTER AND LEGALLY REQUIRED BREACHES OF CONFIDENTIALITY

When the client has been informed of limits to confidentiality at the start of treatment and then reveals a problematic situation, your obligation to report abuse will not be a surprise. In fact, Steinberg, Levine, and Doueck (1997) found that when the informed consent process had been clear and explicit about limits to confidentiality, clients reacted significantly more positively to the psychotherapist making a report of child abuse, and there was a trend toward these clients being more likely to remain in treatment.

A *mandated reporter* has the individual responsibility to ensure that a report of child maltreatment is made to the state authorities. Interestingly, in some states all citizens are mandated reporters (Mathews & Kenny, 2008). State laws are sometimes not explicit regarding whether trainees are mandated reporters; however, since your supervisor is almost certainly a mandated reporter, the two of you must address these legal requirements. Sometimes institutional policies dictate that one individual in the institution makes all the reports to the appropriate state authority. But be aware that, depending on your state's laws, you could be the sole person who is legally responsible for ensuring that the report was made and that it was made in a timely fashion (Alvarez, Donohue, Kenny, Cavanaugh, & Romero, 2004).

## CHILD MALTREATMENT: OVERVIEW

Determining whether to make a report of child maltreatment can be a very difficult decision. As a beginning psychotherapist, you may feel particularly confused. In this section, I review some reporting recommendations based on current literature. This is a basic overview, and further professional education is essential. Psychotherapists who work extensively with children or families need to be especially well informed and need to gain more extensive professional training than is provided in this chapter.

Child maltreatment comes in many different forms. The types of child maltreatment are sexual abuse, physical abuse, emotional abuse, neglect, and endangerment (this paragraph is informed by Alvarez, Kenny, Donohue, & Carpin, 2004; Lambie, 2005). Note that if one sibling is being maltreated, in over half the cases, others are as well (Hamilton-Giachritsis & Browne, 2005).

- *Sexual abuse* includes contact (fondling, intercourse, or inappropriate touching of genitalia) and noncontact (exposure to pornography or sexual acts).
- *Physical abuse* that results in injury is reportable, and other acts that have the potential for injury, such as shaking, striking, or kicking, are reportable in most cases.
- *Emotional abuse* is a "pattern of behavior that impairs a child's emotional development or sense of self-worth, including constant criticism, threats, or rejection, as well as withholding love, support, or guidance" (Lambie, 2005, p. 254); note that some states do not require that emotional abuse be reported (Marshall, 2012).
- *Neglect* is when the child's basic needs for food, clothing, health care, supervision, education, emotional care, and so on are not being met.
- *Endangerment* is when a child's safety is at unnecessary risk.

Be aware that while we as psychotherapists would consider all these acts to be child maltreatment, not all of them may be legally defined as child abuse in your state. Also, some states consider child abandonment and parental substance abuse to be forms of child abuse, whereas others do not (Child Welfare Information Gateway, 2011).

Find and refer to the exact wording of your state law regarding reporting of child maltreatment, since state laws vary considerably (Kalichman, 1999). Because research has shown that many students do not recognize certain signs of child abuse and neglect (Smith, 2006), Appendix 1 of this chapter provides specific examples and signs of maltreatment. Please review the appendix and your state's statute on child abuse carefully and discuss any uncertainties you have with your supervisor.

Be sure that all clients have given written informed consent at the beginning of therapy and that the informed consent process directly addresses mandated reporting of child abuse and neglect (Kalichman, 1999). Have the hotline number for your state's child protective services readily available. It is likely that your state will require a follow-up written report (Alvarez, Donohue, et al., 2004). If so, keep blank copies of the form on hand. Families that are the most at risk for child maltreatment include those with at least one child with developmental issues, low maternal education, maternal drug use, maternal depressive symptoms, and more children in the family (Dubowitz et al., 2011). I would also be alert for child maltreatment when any parent or caretaker uses alcohol or drugs to excess or has significant dysfunction from mental illness.

## CHILD MALTREATMENT: GRAY AREAS

*Statutory rape* is sexual activity in which one partner is below the state's legal age of consent for sexual activity; generally statutory rape is between an adult and a minor. Some state laws can be unclear as to whether statutory rape is considered child sexual abuse (Bean, Softas-Nall, & Mahoney, 2011). Talk to your supervisor and call your state child abuse hotline for advice if you have questions about this issue.

There is a gray but important area between spankings and beatings that are administered with fists or an object (e.g., a hairbrush or a belt). Generally, spankings are not considered child abuse (Renninger et al., 2002). If your client talks about administering or receiving "whoopings," you may need to ask what this consists of.

The line between poor parenting skills and child emotional abuse can be difficult to draw. See Hamarman and Bernet (2000) and Marshall (2012) for further advice on this issue. They suggest that, if state laws allow, cases of poor parenting, which result in mild psychological maltreatment without malicious intent, should be treated with family therapy and parent skills training, rather than reported to the state.

Cultural differences, especially in immigrant populations, need to be carefully considered. Here are some examples of cultural practices that could be considered child maltreatment in the United States:

- Leaving children alone at home, or outside playing alone, might be common in the country of origin when one's neighbors could be expected to watch them (Hughes, 2006).
- Vigorous skin rubbing with a spoon or coin is a folk remedy in Vietnam (Davis, 2000) and other Asian countries. This rubbing may significantly bruise the child.
- Moxibustion, an Asian folk remedy, involves using a burning cone or stick that may cause the child's skin to burn (Karageorge & Kendall, 2008).

- Facial cutting to create scars, followed by rubbing charcoal into the lacerations, is an induction rite into adulthood within certain East African tribes (Feldman, 2003).
- Cupping, a folk remedy involving suction against the skin, leaves a round mark on the skin.

If you observe these practices or other unfamiliar cultural practices that may affect children's well-being, consult with your supervisor about whether to make a report.

## CHILD MALTREATMENT: MAKING A DECISION TO REPORT

> Excerpt from Illinois Abused and Neglected Child Reporting Act: "Any physician, resident, intern...substance abuse treatment personnel,...social worker,...licensed professional counselor, licensed clinical professional counselor, registered psychologist and assistants working under the direct supervision of a psychologist, psychiatrist...having *reasonable cause to believe* a child known to them in their professional or official capacity may be an abused child or a neglected child shall *immediately* report or cause a report to be made to the Department." (emphases added; Illinois General Assembly, n.d.)

From the above excerpt, you can see that in Illinois, you need not be certain that abuse took place; you need to have only a *reasonable cause to believe* that the child may be being abused or neglected. Note that under the law, it is not your job to further assess the situation and make a determination as to whether abuse actually took place; that is the job of child protective services (Renninger, Veach, & Bagdade, 2002). The statute states that once you develop a reasonable cause to believe abuse or neglect transpired, you must immediately make a report to the state.

Do not go beyond your professional competence and question extensively to gain certainty that a child has been maltreated (Kalichman, 1999); certainty is not necessary to make a mandated report. If you are not a medical professional, do not undertake any physical examinations. If you do not have extensive forensic training in validating abuse through interviews, do not attempt to do so; your untrained efforts will contaminate the investigation process. If you work primarily with adults, do not have the child come in and attempt to interview him. *When you feel compelled to gather more information, it is a probably a sign that you have a reasonable suspicion of abuse, and you should make a report* (Kalichman, 1999).

If you are uncertain about whether to make a report, consult with your supervisor or another trusted licensed professional. Be sure that you consult on the very same day that you obtained the information from the client. You can also call child protective services in your state and discuss the concerns with a worker, who will help you decide whether a report is warranted. These discussions will help clarify whether to make a report. If you decide in consultation with a colleague or with a worker at child protective services not to make a report, carefully document whom you consulted with, what the content of the consultation meeting was, and what the reasoning was behind the decision not to report, with specific reference to state laws.

Be careful not to underreport. If you have been informed that maltreatment has occurred but you know that another professional already reported it, you still have a legal liability to initiate a report yourself (M. A. Small, Lyons, & Guy, 2002). When you call, insist that the worker document your call; some workers may not fully understand that you are legally required to report, even if a report has been made already. In addition, receiving more than one report provides child welfare workers an indication of the seriousness of the situation. In some states, there is no requirement to report unless you have actually seen the maltreated child yourself; however, some experts suggest that professional ethics dictate that you make a report nonetheless if you have a reasonable suspicion (Kalichman, 1999). Sometimes psychotherapists underreport because they aren't aware of different types of child maltreatment. Child physical or sexual abuse can come from siblings or peers as well as adults. Children can sometimes be maltreated while in foster care (Gelles, 2006) or in an institution (Kalichman, 1999). Psychotherapists must also be aware that in rare events, caregivers can intentionally produce illness in a child or other dependent person; this is called *Munchausen syndrome by proxy* (Pasqualone & Fitzgerald, 1999).

On the other hand, be careful not to overreport. Overreporting contributes to overtaxing your state's already overburdened child protective system. Overreporting leads to unnecessary emotional distress on the part of the child and the child's family. An example where a report is not warranted is a child who has emotional symptoms that could possibly be suggestive of abuse (e.g., is withdrawn or fearful) but there are no other signs of abuse (Besharov & Laumann, 1996). These emotional symptoms could be due to childhood mental illness or to a chaotic but not abusive family situation, and your report would likely be unsubstantiated and would cause unneeded distress to the family; however, continue to be alert to indicators of abuse in these cases.

Research shows that many suspected cases of abuse are never reported (Alvarez, Kenny, et al., 2004). Cultural factors may result in White psychotherapists and those born in the United States being more likely to make reports than non-White psychotherapists and immigrant psychotherapists (Ashton, 2004).

Psychotherapists may worry that they will be sued for making a report, but all states provide legal immunity for reports made in good faith (Alvarez, Kenny, et al., 2004). On the other hand, depending on state law, psychotherapists can risk facing charges, jail time, or loss of license for failure to report, or a psychotherapist might also be sued by a victim or the victim's family for failure to report (Alvarez, Kenny, et al., 2004). Finally, and by far most important, failure to report will result in the child experiencing continued maltreatment and emotional distress.

Remember that it is not your job, legally, to determine the full facts in the case; that is the job of child protective services.

## CHILD MALTREATMENT: MAKING A REPORT

When a mandated report is made, there are two goals. First, we are motivated compassionately, ethically, and legally to be sure that children are safe. Second, we want to maintain the therapeutic relationship so we can help alleviate the family situation that led to the maltreatment. Some psychotherapists fear that that reporting will hurt the therapeutic relationship. However, Steinberg, Levine, and Doueck (1997) found that only one-quarter of clients drop out following a report, whereas in three-quarters of cases, the therapy relationship is unchanged or improved.

Prepare to call by gathering together all the relevant contact information that you have regarding the child and the child's family (this paragraph is informed by Kalichman, 1999). This information could include the name of the child, the child's age, sex, address, and current whereabouts. Other helpful information would include ages and names of other children in the home, names and addresses of the child's parents, information of the circumstances and nature of the maltreatment, and the identity of the suspected perpetrator. Of course, you may not have all this information. If not, that is okay; simply supply as much information as you have. Do not provide confidential information about the client that is not directly relevant to the episode of maltreatment (e.g., adult client's own history of abuse).

Your client may be the child, the perpetrator, or another family member. When deciding how to proceed, first ask yourself whether the child will be at more risk if the family is aware that a report is being made (Kalichman, 1999). If so, do not tell the family that you will be making a report before you do so. However, if the risk to the child will not increase if the family is aware of the report, involving them in the reporting process can help maintain trust in the therapeutic relationship.

When you involve your adult client in the reporting process, first explain the necessity of making a report. Positive therapeutic outcomes were associated with this reporting strategy: Inform the client yourself that you need to make a report and explain why in terms of your own clinical assessment rather than as a requirement imposed by state law (Weinstein, Levine, Kogan, Harkavy-Friedman, & Miller, 2001). If you have appropriately informed the client of limits to confidentiality at the beginning of treatment, the need to make this report will probably not be a surprise. You should also explain what is likely to happen when a report is made.

Second, alternatives can be offered to the client to participate in or observe the process of reporting. The client could make the call to report the abuse in the office with you observing (do not rely on the client to report the abuse later). Or the client could observe you making the call so that the client knows exactly what you said during the call. If the client does not want to participate in either of these options, you should make the report immediately when the session ends.

When you or the client make the call, be sure to obtain the name, position, and contact information for the worker who takes the call. If the client calls, follow this up with a call of your own or talk to the worker yourself with the client there so that it is documented by child protective services that you have made the mandated call.

## CHILD MALTREATMENT: DOCUMENTATION AND FOLLOW-UP

Make a note in the chart of any other professional you consulted with prior to making the call. Document the circumstances of the call: Had you informed the client that you were making the call? Did the client participate in making the call? Note the time of the call and the name or employee number of the person you talked to (Kalichman, 1999). Document exactly what information you provided to the worker. *Document that you made the call on the day that you made it.*

If your state requires a written form, keep a copy of that. Document any follow-up calls you made to child protective services or that they made to you. Document any activities related to the case as they happen.

## ELDER MALTREATMENT

Margaret, an 82-year-old retired musician, lives with her 65-year-old son, Maurice. Maurice is a pathological gambler who spends all of his time at the racetrack. Margaret suffers from congestive heart failure and mild dementia. She is unable to dress, wash, or feed herself without assistance. Margaret's physicians have advised Maurice that she should not be left alone at home. Maurice ignores their advice, frequently fails to feed or bathe his mother, and uses the money she gives him to refill her prescriptions to bet on the horses. Consequently, Margaret is not able to obtain needed medication and her heart condition has worsened significantly. Her nutrition is poor, and she is mildly dehydrated. Margaret has also burned herself several times while trying to prepare her own meals. (Welfel, Danzinger, & Santoro, 2000, p. 285)

In a caregiver support group for elderly people, group members were discussing stressful caregiving situations. Mr. Smith began talking about how he sometimes became frustrated with his wife, a victim of Alzheimer's disease. "When you say you're frustrated, what do you mean exactly," the facilitator asked him. "Well," he answered, "I guess I mean I have to do things I would rather not have to do." "Such as what?" the facilitator probed. "Well sometimes she won't get dressed, just real stubborn she is. I'll try showing her what I mean by taking off my clothes, but it doesn't register. So then

I'll try to take off her blouse, gently, but she'll back away from me. I'll try talking to her, but nothing. So I'll slap her a few times, I'll say 'You have to listen to me' then she cooperates. It's real frustrating." (Bergeron & Gray, 2003, p. 96)

Evidence suggests that elder abuse is significantly underreported and underidentified. *Neglect*, the most common form of elder abuse, is defined as "withholding of necessary food, clothing, and medical care to meet the physical and mental needs of an elderly person" (Jayawardena & Liao, 2006, p. 128). Caretakers may neglect elders intentionally or unintentionally. Caretakers may be unable to provide adequate care. Physical, emotional, and financial abuse are also common, and different forms of abuse often co-occur:

- *Physical abuse* includes "pushing, striking, or causing bodily injury, force-feeding, or improper use of physical restraints" (Jayawardena & Liao, 2006, p. 128).
- *Emotional abuse* involves threats, humiliation, or insults.
- *Financial abuse* entails misappropriating the elder's funds or property for the caretaker's own financial gain. Perpetrators of elder financial abuse can also be individuals "outside the family, such as contractors, salesmen, attorneys, caregivers, insurance agents, clergy, accountants, bookkeepers, and friends" (Kemp & Mosqueda, 2005, p. 1123).
- *Sexual abuse* of the elderly is rare, although it may be more underreported than other types of elder maltreatment (Loue, 2001); it is any unwanted sexual contact, perhaps with an elder who is too cognitively impaired to consent.

Elders can also be neglected or abandoned by caregivers. See Appendix 2 for detailed signs and examples of elder maltreatment. Be aware that while psychotherapists would consider all of the above to be elder maltreatment, not all of them may be legally defined as elder abuse in your state.

Abusers of the elderly in the home can be spouses, adult children, spouses of adult children, and other relatives (Jayawardena & Liao, 2006; Rudolph & Hughes, 2001). Abuse by the spouse is sometimes a continuation of longstanding domestic violence (Loue, 2001). Abuse can also take place in an institutional setting (Loue, 2001). The elderly who most at risk have dementia, short-term memory problems, mental illness, or alcohol abuse (Selwood & Cooper, 2009; Shugarman, Fries, Wolf, & Morris, 2003) or are dependent or aggressive (Loue, 2001). Maltreatment risk factors associated with the caregivers are "advanced age, alcoholism, intellectual deficits, inadequate communication skills, substance abuse, depression, poor physical health, stress, social isolation, financial difficulties, and dependence on the elderly individual" (Loue, 2001, p. 167).

Even more than with child maltreatment, laws regarding elder abuse vary considerably from state to state (Jogerst et al., 2003), although in the large majority of cases, licensed mental health professionals are mandated reporters (Stiegel & Klem, 2007). Review your state statute on elder abuse and keep the number for reporting elder abuse handy. Consider and document the same issues as you would in the case of child maltreatment: obtaining proper informed consent, effectively using consultation, and involving the client in making the report. Intervene to ensure safety if the elderly person is in imminent danger; interventions could include an emergency housing referral or involvement of other family members—with the client's consent (Donovan & Regehr, 2010).

## ELDER SELF-NEGLECT

[Self-neglecting elders in the United Kingdom lived in homes with] conditions of extreme disrepair with buildings in a state of collapse, holes in the roof, ceilings, walls and broken windows. Interiors were often sparsely furnished with bare floorboards and makeshift stoves/cooking facilities including open fires on the floor. In many cases there was no electricity, running water, or proper sanitation.... [Elders lived with] blocked toilets, offensive household odours, and infestations of fleas, flies, rats, and maggots. There were reports of large numbers of pets, particularly cats, within dwellings. A commonly reported feature involved houses being crammed full of belongings, which spilled over into the garden area. Such clients hoarded rubbish, clothes, newspapers, family belongings and miscellaneous items. (Lauder, Anderson, & Barclay, 2005, p. 320)

Elder self-neglect appears to occur at a much greater frequency than elder maltreatment from others (Lauder et al., 2005). *Self-neglect* is defined as "not engaging in those self-care actions that are required to produce socially acceptable levels of personal and household cleanliness and personal health and well-being" (Lauder et al., 2005, p. 317). Possible contributing factors to self-neglect include a strong value of personal independence and control, diminished physical abilities, and dementia. Inattention to safety, as well as lack of healthy and sufficient food and water, can also constitute self-neglect (Mosqueda & Dong, 2011). The elderly person's home is likely to be "dirty, full of rubbish and in a general state of disrepair" (Lauder et al., 2005, p. 320). Self-neglecting clients may be socially isolated, and they may be difficult to treat because they may not attend appointments or open their mail. Self-neglect is more common in women and the very old (Thompson & Priest, 2005).

About half the states require that self-neglect be reported to adult protective services as well (Loue, 2001). But often the issue of the elderly person's competency to make his own decisions, in the context of self-neglect, is not adequately addressed in state reporting laws (Loue, 2001).

## MALTREATMENT OF VULNERABLE ADULTS

Some adults who are not elderly are nonetheless considered *vulnerable adults* because of their disability status (Teaster, 2000). In most states, adult protective services programs serve both elderly and other vulnerable adults (National Committee for the Prevention of Elder Abuse & National Adult Protective Services Association, 2007). The vulnerable adults' disabilities can be physical, mental, or emotional. Self-neglect, physical abuse, and caregiver abandonment or neglect were the most common categories of investigated reports, each encompassing about 20 percent of the total (National Committee for the Prevention of Elder Abuse & National Adult Protective Services Association, 2007).

If you feel that it may be appropriate to make a report regarding a vulnerable adult, talk to your supervisor. Further information can be obtained from the link to your state on www.ncea.aoa.gov/ or by calling your state elder abuse hotline (since this hotline is likely to handle cases with vulnerable adults as well).

## INTIMATE PARTNER VIOLENCE

*Pannee Raksuwan is a mental health trainee working in an emergency intake clinic. Her intake client, Sandra Johnson, states that her husband tried to strangle her. She has prominent bruises and is feeling dizzy, perhaps from a mild concussion. Sandra tells Pannee about her history of chronic depression with multiple suicide attempts. Sandra states that she plans to leave; she is upset and crying. She admits to a history of returning to her husband a week or two after the abuse.*

*Shoshanna Rosenberg is a mental health trainee working with a client, Frank. The client repeatedly describes arguments with his male partner. Shoshanna asks whether these arguments have been physical at times. With some reluctance, Frank admits that he and his partner hit each other when they are angry. Frank had to go to the emergency room for a dislocated finger once after his partner pushed him against a wall.*

Intimate partner violence (IPV) is a common phenomenon worldwide and within every American cultural group, although there is some international variation in rates (Loue, 2000). One multiracial study of heterosexual couples found that men were most commonly the primary perpetrator of violence (54 percent), but mutual violent perpetration (35 percent) is common as well, and female primary perpetration (11 percent) is not unusual (Weston, Temple, & Marshall, 2005). Another study found that mutual violence in heterosexual couples is the most common pattern (Williams & Frieze, 2005). However, the negative emotional and physical impact of IPV may be stronger on women (K. L. Anderson, 2002; Weston et al., 2005). IPV can also occur in gay and lesbian couples (McKenry, Serovich, Mason, & Mosack, 2006).

Perpetrators are likely to have childhood trauma, adult mental illness, and/or substance abuse (Stuart, Moore, Gordon, Ramsey, & Kahler, 2006). The victims suffer disproportionately from post-traumatic stress disorder (PTSD), substance abuse, depression, and other anxiety disorders (Robertiello, 2006) as well as brain injuries (Valera & Berenbaum, 2003) and physical health problems (Dutton et al., 2006). Women with disabilities are twice as likely to experience IPV (D. L. Smith, 2008).

Evidence suggests that IPV is underdetected by health care professionals. A chart review of women's emergency visits found that fewer than 30 percent of charts documented that the woman was screened for IPV (Richter, Surprenant, Schmelzle, & Mayo, 2003). A survey of licensed psychologists found that less than 20 percent of psychologists screened routinely for IPV (Samuelson & Campbell, 2005). So, if you do not ask about IPV, you will probably miss it.

IPV and child abuse often co-occur (Knickerbocker, Heyman, Slep, Jouriles, & McDonald, 2007), so the presence of one type of abuse should trigger awareness that there may be violence, abuse, and neglect within the family. Observing IPV as a child leads to a higher rate of childhood problems (Kitzmann, Gaylord, Holt, & Kenny, 2003), adult psychopathology (Diamond & Muller, 2004), and adult perpetration of IPV (Ehrensaft et al., 2003).

Often victims come to psychotherapists with depression or anxiety symptoms. One simple screening procedure for domestic violence is the Partner Violence Screen, which consists of the following three questions:

1. "Have you been hit, kicked, punched, or otherwise hurt by someone within the past year? If so, by whom?"
2. "Do you feel safe in your current relationship?"
3. "Is there a partner from a previous relationship who is making you feel unsafe now?" (Feldhaus et al., 1997, p. 1358)

If the client has experienced IPV, Samuelson and Campbell (2005) recommend that safety be assessed through these types of questions:

- "What threats have been made?"
- "Do you and [name of abuser] live together? How often do you see each other? Does he/she have a key to your apartment?" (and other questions to assess accessibility of client to abuser)
- "Do you want immediate protection by law enforcement or the safety of a shelter?" "Do you have a plan to protect yourself [and your children] if the danger escalates?"
- "Do you know how to access community resources if you feel unsafe?"

It is common knowledge that resources are available for victims of domestic violence. Often, those who are ready to leave the perpetrator have already taken steps to contact law enforcement, leave the partner, or go to a domestic violence shelter. Therefore, clients who are experiencing ongoing domestic violence may be ambivalent about leaving the partner or do not intend to leave. In those cases, sometimes all the psychotherapist can do is provide support, concern, education, and information to the client.

The client may not realize that physical attacks are a crime and might not understand the negative impact of IPV on the client's own mental health and that of the children. Samuelson and Campbell (2005) recommend having the following information ready to provide to victims of interpersonal violence: hotline numbers, local shelters, domestic violence therapy groups, law enforcement, legal aid, advocacy groups, educational and financial services, and food and housing assistance. Couples therapy can be considered, but the couples psychotherapist should be highly knowledgeable about the research on conjoint treatment of IPV (such as McCollum & Stith, 2008). If you do couples therapy, be sure to assess the couple for IPV; research has found that almost 50 percent of psychotherapists don't (Schacht, Dimidjian, George, & Berns, 2009).

In some states, IPV is mandated to be reported to the state. In other jurisdictions, there may be requirements that certain types of injuries (e.g., gunshot wounds) be reported (Loue, 2000). However, in still other states, there is no mandate for reporting IPV at all. Talk to your supervisor about what the laws are in your state.

## RAPE

*Dante Rogers, a mental health trainee, is getting to his office at the college counseling center early in the morning. He checks his voice mail to find a distraught and not entirely coherent message from his client, Michelle Barnes. He listens to the message several times, and it becomes clear that Michelle was calling in the early morning hours stating that she had experienced date rape. He calls Michelle's cell phone right away. She is still distressed, but her roommate is with her. He tells Michelle to come in to the office right away, and she agrees to do so. He then calls his first two scheduled clients to reschedule them.*

*Angelica Willis, a mental health trainee, is working in a state prison for men. An inmate whom she does not know requests to speak with her. She meets with him, and he starts crying, stating that he has been raped. He asks her not to tell anyone since he is fearful of being killed by the rapist and his gang.*

The mental health practitioner can encounter a rape crisis in any clinical setting. The client may seek mental health treatment first rather than medical treatment. Most communities have rape crisis centers that can send a volunteer or paraprofessional to assist the rape victim throughout the emergency medical assessment and treatment process.

Rape is underrecognized and undertreated in men; one survey found that 5 percent of rape victims were male (Azikiwe, Wright, Cheng, & D'Angelo, 2005). Men appear to be most at risk of rape in prison (Wiwanitkit, 2005), although it is becoming clear that rape of men by men is a problem in the U.S. military (Ellison, 2011). Adult male survivors of rape were raped by men in over

85 percent of cases, and in almost all cases there was forced anal penetration (Wiwanitkit, 2005).

As a health care practitioner, you need to be informed about all the issues that a sexually assaulted client will need to address: emotional, medical, and legal. Cybulska and Forster (2005) delineate the tasks that should ideally be accomplished in the immediate aftermath of rape:

- Treat severe injuries (e.g., the client may need antibiotics or a tetanus shot for bite wounds)
- Assess safety
- Forensic medical examination
- Emergency contraception with testing to rule out preexisting pregnancy as needed
- Prophylaxis against sexually transmitted diseases, including HIV
- Screen for sexually transmitted diseases, including HIV
- Counseling and psychological support
- Support for the victim's partner and family if appropriate

To this list, I would add making a report of the crime, if the client is willing to do so. Clearly not all rape victims will be willing to participate immediately—or sometimes ever—in all aspects of this process.

As you probably know, emergency departments have trained professionals available to gather forensic medical evidence in rape cases. After the rape occurs, the client has a limited time in which there is any chance that valid evidence can be gathered. The passage of time, defecating, showering, and changing clothes all reduce the chances of obtaining evidence (A. Anderson, 1999; Cybulska & Forster, 2005). Sperm survives in the vagina for 7 days and in the rectum for 3 days (Cybulska & Forster, 2005). After 7 days, no forensic evidence can be gathered; however, any injuries that are healing can still be documented medically (Cybulska & Forster, 2005). A rape victim advocate from the local rape crisis center may be able to knowledgably help support the client throughout this process.

Whether or not forensic evidence has been gathered, the client needs to be evaluated for pregnancy (if a fertile female), for sexually transmitted diseases, and for injury. The emergency room staff should offer emergency contraception. Emergency contraception can be administered in the emergency room, reducing the chances that the distressed rape victim misses filling her prescription (Azikiwe et al., 2005). Medications can be administered to reduce the chance that HIV and other sexually transmitted diseases could infect the client (Linden, 2011). It is important that you know about these treatments because you may need to educate the client to ask for them; in many cases, medical care for rape victims is incomplete, especially with regard to emergency contraception (R. Campbell, Wasco, Ahrens, Sefl, & Barnes, 2001).

If the client wishes to make a police report and press charges, it is helpful to obtain the assistance of a rape victim advocate. Unfortunately, many negative outcomes can occur for the rape victim in the legal arena. First, the case may be dismissed against the client's wishes, and if the client succeeds in prosecuting, the legal process of doing so can sometimes be retraumatizing (R. Campbell et al., 2001). Second, when a government's finances are tight, rape kits can go years without being processed; some rape kits in Los Angeles passed the 10-year statute of limitations for prosecuting the crime (PBS, 2009).

In counseling the client, the first goal is to reduce the client's immediate level of distress. Let the client talk to you at her own pace. Listen nonjudgmentally and provide validation and support; this will help calm her. Assist the client in calling the rape crisis center from your office if she hasn't already. Educate the client about her medical and legal options. Help the client activate her social support network if she hasn't done so already (e.g., the client may want to call her sibling, parent, best friend, or other individual to support her through the legal and medical aftermath). Help the client figure out how to reestablish a feeling of safety; perhaps she would like to stay with a close friend or her family for a few days. She may need prescriptions for medications to manage anxiety, agitation, or sleeplessness. Before she leaves, make a plan for follow-up treatment no later than 1 week from now. You may wish to have the client check in by phone between sessions in the first week or two.

Whatever the client decides to do from a medical or legal perspective, clear and careful records should be made of the client's statements about the assault since the client might need these records to press charges later (Cybulska & Forster, 2005). The information to document includes:

- Date and time of the assault
- Circumstances of the assault
- Location
- Type of assault (physical and/or sexual)
- Orifices involved, condom use, and whether ejaculation occurred
- Client's actions after the assault (Cybulska & Forster, 2005).

Completely document whatever the client tells you about the assault. Remind her of relevant confidentiality issues as needed. At some point, she might need this documentation if she presses charges or if she has sustained ongoing physical or emotional injuries from the assault.

Use great care in asking about details of the trauma because it may be overly distressing for the client to repeatedly discuss it or to discuss it in detail. Any medical professionals who treat her must ask her most of these questions in order to provide effective medical care based on her specific situation. If your supervisor thinks it is appropriate, it might be helpful for you to be present during that interview to provide support. Consult carefully with your supervisor about how to manage the immediate aftermath of your client's rape so as not to exacerbate current or future symptoms.

Rape causes a higher rate of PTSD than most other traumas and can also lead to depression, substance abuse, suicidal behavior, and chronic physical health problems (Campbell, 2008). Normal reactions to rape can include passivity during the assault itself, forgetting part or all of the experience, delaying or avoiding disclosing the rape, and social isolation after the rape (Freyd, 2008). After the initial crisis and stabilization phase, specialized forms of cognitive therapy can be helpful (see Resick et al., 2008; Vickerman & Margolin, 2009), but close supervision by a supervisor well trained in trauma treatment is essential.

Much more commonly, you will see a psychotherapy client who has a more distant history of rape. Be aware that knowledge of the trauma treatment literature and knowledgeable supervision is essential to effectively treat trauma survivors.

## COPING WITH MALTREATMENT, VIOLENCE, AND NEGLECT

Addressing traumatic experiences with clients is distressing. Thoroughly discuss what has transpired with your supervisor and seek support from trusted colleagues and in personal therapy. In addition, read about psychotherapist self-care in Chapter 23.

### RECOMMENDED READING: CHILD MALTREATMENT

Alvarez, K. M., Donohue, B., Kenny, M. C., Cavanaugh, N., & Romero, V. (2004). The process and consequences of reporting child maltreatment: A brief overview for professionals in the mental health field. *Aggression and Violent Behavior, 10,* 311–331.

*Alvarez and colleagues provide a detailed portrayal of the nuts and bolts of the child protective services reporting and investigation process. This article should be essential reading for all mental health professionals.*

Kalichman, S. C. (1999). *Mandated reporting of suspected child abuse: Ethics, law, and policy.* Washington, DC: American Psychological Association.

*Kalichman provides an in-depth discussion of mandated reporting of child maltreatment, including helpful case discussions and reports of legal cases. Read this book if you anticipate working with families or children or if you will be working with a high-risk population.*

### RECOMMENDED READING: ELDER MALTREATMENT

Loue, S. (2001). Elder abuse and neglect in medicine and law: The need for reform. *Journal of Legal Medicine, 22,* 159–209.

*Loue provides a detailed review of the area of elder abuse, including current legal complexities.*

Thompson, H., & Priest, R. (2005). Elder abuse and neglect: Considerations for mental health practitioners. *Adultspan Journal, 4,* 116–128.

*Thompson and Priest provide helpful information, including how to assess the home situation, cultural considerations, and suggestions for intervention.*

Welfel, E. R., Danzinger, P. R., & Santoro, S. (2000). Mandated reporting of abuse/maltreatment of older adults: A primer for counselors. *Journal of Counseling and Development, 78,* 284–292.

*Provides a detailed overview of the process of mandated reporting for elder abuse and neglect.*

## Recommended Reading: Intimate Partner Violence

Samuelson, S. L., & Campbell, C. D. (2005). Screening for domestic violence: Recommendations based on a practice survey. *Professional Psychology: Research and Practice, 36,* 276–282.
*Samuelson and Campbell assess current practices and give helpful recommendations for screening and intervention.*

McCloskey, K. & Grigsby, N. (2005). The ubiquitous clinical problem of adult intimate partner violence: The need for routine assessment. *Professional Psychology: Research and Practice, 36,* 264–275.
*The authors provide useful questions to assess the history and dangerousness of the IPV situation. The final appendix provides a useful handout that you can copy to give to clients for safety planning.*

## Recommended Reading: Rape

Campbell, R., Wasco, S. M., Ahrens, C. E., Sefl, T., & Barnes, H. E. (2001). Preventing the "second rape": Rape survivors' experiences with community service providers. *Journal of Interpersonal Violence, 16,* 1239–1259.
*Campbell and colleagues research and discuss the actual experiences of rape survivors in the mental health, medical, and legal arenas.*

Cybulska, B., & Forster, G. (2005). Sexual assault: Examination of the victim. *Medicine, 33,* 23–28.
*Cybulska and Forster describe in detail the process of medical examination of the female sexual assault victim.*

## Online Resources

http://www.childwelfare.gov
*This website provides a comprehensive review of all state-mandated reporting laws for child abuse and neglect as well as other information about child welfare. The website is a project of the U.S. Department of Health and Human Services.*

www.ncea.aoa.gov/
*Website for the National Center on Elder Abuse. Provides guidance in finding state statutes regarding elder abuse reporting and more information about elder abuse.*

## EXERCISES AND DISCUSSION QUESTIONS

1. Find your state laws for child and elder maltreatment. Save a copy in a safe place. Find the phone numbers for reporting child and elder maltreatment and put them in a handy place as well.
2. Are there situations in your state where you might become aware of child abuse yet not be required to report it? What would you do then?

Are written reports required? What is the statute of limitations? How soon do you need to call after you learn about abuse? Does the statute specify any differences between information learned as part of your professional duties and personally obtained information?

3. Answer the above questions for elder abuse.

4. How is statutory rape defined in your state? Do you need to report this as child abuse? What number would you call to report it?

5. Does your state mandate reporting of elder self-neglect? How is that defined? What number would you call to report it?

6. Does your state mandate reporting of domestic violence? Under what circumstances? What number would you call to report it?

## APPENDIX 1

## EXAMPLES AND SIGNS OF CHILD MALTREATMENT

*Caution: Be aware that, while we as psychotherapists would consider all these acts to be child maltreatment or signs of probable child maltreatment, not all of them may be legally defined as child abuse in your state.*

Physical Abuse

- Eyewitness observations of a caregiver's abusive or neglectful behavior (e.g., staff secretary reports that she observed father hitting boy in waiting room)
- The child's description of being abused or neglected
- The caregiver's own description of abusive or neglectful behavior (e.g., "Then I hit him upside the head.")
- Accounts of child maltreatment from partner or other family members (e.g., partner reports physically abusive behavior toward child)
- Peer or anyone else reports to you that child told him about physical abuse
- "Suspicious" injuries suggesting physical abuse (e.g., extensive and unexplained bruises, burns, lacerations, welts, human bite marks, bald spots, or abrasions)
- Injuries inconsistent with information provided by caregiver
- Newborns with medical evidence of fetal exposure to drugs or alcohol
- Munchausen syndrome by proxy (see Pasqualone & Fitzgerald, 1999)

Sexual Abuse

- Evidence or reports of commercial exploitation through prostitution or the production of pornographic materials
- Female genital mutilation
- Sexual trafficking

- Child reports indecent exposure, fondling, penetration, oral sex, masturbation, or other sexual activity with an adult
- Peer or anyone else reports to you that child told him about sexual abuse
- Any sexual activity with a peer that was precipitated by force, threats, or coercion (depending on ages and specific state laws, an adult having sex with an adolescent may be statutory rape)
- If you are a medical professional: medical findings suggesting sexual abuse (e.g., pain, itching, bruising, or bleeding in the genitalia; venereal disease; frequent urinary tract or yeast infections; or pregnancy)

Neglect and Endangerment

- Newborns denied nutrition, life-sustaining care, or other medically indicated treatment
- Demonstrated caregiver inability to care for a newborn baby
- Young children left alone (e.g., 7-year-old left in charge of younger siblings all day)
- Abandoned children (e.g., 8-year-old left with neighbor for 2 days, caregiver's whereabouts unknown)
- Demonstrated caregiver disabilities (e.g., mental illness or retardation or alcohol or drug abuse) severe enough to make child abuse or child neglect likely (e.g., parent is out abusing drugs with friends most evenings, leaving 12-year-old alone at home)
- Signs of physical deprivation suggesting child neglect (e.g., child is notably too thin)
- Consistent hunger, sometimes resulting in stealing or begging for food
- Inappropriate dress, poor hygiene, or lice
- Children in physically dangerous situations (e.g., caregiver is unconcerned that child is often found exploring a construction site in the evening)
- Apparently untreated physical injuries, illnesses, or impairments suggesting medical neglect (e.g., child is not taken to the emergency room promptly after breaking bone in foot)
- Apparent caregiver indifference to a child's severe psychological or developmental problems (e.g., caregiver doesn't bother to enroll previously suicidal child in psychotherapy)
- Chronic and unexplained absences from school suggesting parental responsibility for the nonattendance
- Caregiver is unconcerned about child's difficulties, which could include school, medical, or mental health problems, among others
- Caregiver keeps child out of school to work or care for siblings
- Parent or caretaker expels child or adolescent from home (e.g., parent is angered with 15-year-old girl returning home 20 minutes after curfew,

refuses to let teen into home, and teen walks to friend's house alone and
in the dark and stays there overnight)
- Home environment which puts health of the child at risk
- "Accidental" injuries suggesting gross inattention to the child's need
  for safety
- Caregiver drives while intoxicated with child in car

Emotional Abuse (Not required to be reported in all states)

- Caregiver encourages self-destructive, criminal or deviant behaviors (e.g.,
  parent seems pleased that child has stolen small items from the local
  grocery store or parent encourages child to use substances)
- Habitual belittling, humiliating, insulting, hostile, shaming or rejecting
  statements (e.g., "You're stupid" or "You'll never amount to anything")
- Child is locked in closets or rooms alone
- Child or child's loved one is threatened with harm, killing, abandonment
  or dangerous situations
- Violation of parental visitation rights
- Exposure to domestic violence

*No list can be complete or appropriate to every state's specific laws; use your judg-*
*ment and consult appropriately to make a determination whether to report child*
*maltreatment, given the details of each specific case.*
References: Besharov and Laumann (1996); Kalichman (1999); Lambie (2005);
Marshall (2012); Renninger, Veach, and Bagdade (2002); Rodriguez-Strednicki
and Twaite (2004a, 2004b).


## APPENDIX 2

## EXAMPLES AND SIGNS OF ELDER MALTREATMENT

Physical Abuse

- Caretaker slaps, hits, bites, pinches, pulls hair, burns, or scalds elder
- Caretaker force-feeds elder, sometimes resulting in choking
- Caretaker overmedicates elder as a chemical restraint, giving more of
  psychotropic medication than was prescribed
- Caretaker withholds pain medications
- Caretaker improperly uses physical restraint: inappropriate restraint type
  or forceful application, prolonged positioning, or the use of restraints to
  ensure isolation or unnecessary immobility
- Caretaker's report of injury not consistent with physical findings
- Multiple injuries in various states of healing

- Injuries to the eye, nose, or mouth are suspect
- Bruising to the head or neck is suspect

## Sexual Abuse

- Unexplained vaginal or anal bleeding
- Bruises around the breasts or genital area
- Unexplained venereal disease/genital infections

## Neglect

- Caretaker deprives elder of needed assistance in activities of daily living, such as getting meals and drinks, washing, and toileting
- Evidence of malnutrition, starvation, or dehydration
- Poor hygiene, dirty clothes or bedding, or inadequate clothing

## Medical Neglect or Abuse

- Caretaker does not bring elder for needed medical treatment, delays in seeking treatment, or does not provide needed care for the elder's diseases in the home
- Presence of bedsores
- Needed eyeglasses, hearing aids, or dentures are withheld
- Caretaker undermedicates elder, misuses medication or administers medication improperly
- Medical professional may note multiple unused medications
- Munchausen syndrome by proxy

## Emotional Abuse

- Yelling, swearing, verbal, or nonverbal insults or humiliation
- Threats to institutionalize or abandon the elder
- Threats of violence
- Caretaker socially isolates elder

## Financial Abuse

- Theft or misappropriation of money, property, or valuables
- Abrupt changes in or sudden establishment of wills or changing of deeds
- Elder lacks amenities, (e.g., television) that elder should be able to afford
- Shortage of money or unpaid bills despite adequate income or funds
- Reluctance of caretaker to pay for needed clothes and other necessities

- Signed checks when the older person is unable to write and no one is designated with financial power of attorney
- Suspicious use of funds by individual with elder's financial power of attorney
- Forged signatures on legal documents
- The signing of legal documents (wills, deeds, or trusts) by a cognitively impaired individual
- Caretaker neglects elder in the home yet refuses placement because of financial dependence on elder
- Financial abusers can be individuals outside the family, such as contractors, salespeople, attorneys, caregivers, insurance agents, religious organizations, charitable organizations, political interest groups, accountants, bookkeepers, and friends

References: Buka & Sookhoo (2006); K. A. Collins (2006); Cooney, Howard, and Lawlor (2006); D. Harris (2006); Jayawardena and Liao (2006); Kemp and Mosqueda (2005); Loue (2001); Neno and Neno (2005); Thompson and Priest (2005).

# Caring for Yourself and Your Clients

# 22

# Challenging Relationships and Emotions

Strong feelings on your part or the client's part can arise even during the very first session. These emotions are the first clue that key relationship patterns may be occurring within the session. Relationship patterns are expressed through thinking, emotions, behavior, and physiological reactions (J. S. Beck, 2005). The client may express emotions about significant others, or even toward you, which may cause you to have strong feelings in return.

Often your feelings in psychotherapy will be positive—for example, you like the client, you empathize with the client, or you are pleased with the client's effort in therapy. At other times, your feelings may be perplexing or troubling—for example, the client is boring you, or the client makes you feel anxious. Sometimes psychotherapists are even ashamed about some of the feelings that they have in therapy—for example, feeling disgust toward the client or feeling attracted to the client.

Different theories of psychotherapy conceptualize these emotions and relationships differently. In this chapter, as in the rest of this book, I attempt to frame clinical issues in a theoretically integrative manner. In this chapter, my terminology—although I hope not my conceptualization—departs from this ideal. Psychodynamic psychotherapists have a long history, dating back to Freud, of naming these emotions. The clients' emotional reactions and relationships patterns in therapy are called *transference* and psychotherapists' emotional reactions and relationships patterns in therapy are called *countertransference*. I am not aware of any similarly useful terms in other traditions.

## COGNITIVE-BEHAVIORAL CONCEPTUALIZATION OF RELATIONSHIPS IN PSYCHOTHERAPY

A great deal of evidence exists that some of Freud's (1965) theories of transference and countertransference, though somewhat exaggerated and distorted, often exist in practically all forms of psychotherapy. For example, we can in all likelihood endorse these clinical findings: (a) Clients and psychotherapists bring influences of their personal history to the therapeutic encounter; (b) they consciously, and especially unconsciously, project their feelings and wishes onto each other; (c) consequently, clients and psychotherapists often have a biased or prejudiced view of each other's personality and effectiveness; and (d) they both can use their transference and countertransference thoughts, feelings, and behaviors to help and/or hinder the therapeutic process.... Psychotherapists often are obsessively and compulsively convinced that their particular theory and practice of therapy is the only one capable of helping their clients. Therefore, they rigidly and inefficiently stick to its narrow ways and refuse to use other methods that would be more helpful. (Albert Ellis, 2001, pp. 1000–1001)

They [patients] usually have very negative ideas about themselves, others, and their worlds—views that they developed and have maintained since childhood or adolescence. When these beliefs dominate their perceptions, patients then tend to perceive, feel and behave in highly dysfunctional ways, across time and across situations—including in the therapy session itself. (Judith S. Beck, 2005, p. 4)

When noticing their own discomfort or maladaptive behavior (for example, avoiding important topics, overcontrolling or undercontrolling patients, speaking sharply or without empathy), therapists should identify their dysfunctional thoughts and beliefs and conceptualize their area of vulnerability.... Because therapists are human, it is inevitable, and sometimes even helpful, that they occasionally have a dysfunctional reaction toward their patients. As professionals, therapists need to conceptualize why the problem arose so they can take stock of their contribution to the problem and solve it. (Judith S. Beck, 2005, pp. 114, 127)

As Albert Ellis stated in the first quote, transference and countertransference are well-recognized phenomena in psychotherapy. As far as I know, however, he never integrated his recognition of them into his theoretical perspective. The second quote, from Judith Beck, emphasizes the importance of examining the client's ideas about relationships with others during therapy. This quote could even be interpreted as a description of transference from a cognitive-behavioral perspective. The third quote, also from Judith Beck, describes a phenomenon very much like countertransference from a cognitive-behavioral perspective.

## RESEARCH EVIDENCE OF TRANSFERENCE

Classically, transference has been considered an unconscious process in which the patient displaces or "transfers" onto the therapist feelings and thoughts originally directed toward the important people of childhood. (Goldstein, 2000, p. 167)

[Transference occurs when] a perceiver's mental representation of a significant other is activated in an encounter with a new person, leading the perceiver to interpret the person in ways derived from the representation and also to respond emotionally, motivationally, and behaviorally to the person in ways that reflect the self–other relationship. (Andersen & Chen, 2002, p. 620)

Transference was first recognized by Sigmund Freud back in the late 19th century. Research and clinical practice have supported the concept of transference since then. The previous two quotes indicate that *transference* entails transferring feelings, thoughts, and behaviors from a past significant relationship to a current relationship. And, as Andersen and colleagues have shown (e.g., Andersen & Chen, 2002), transference can happen in an individual's personal life as well as within the therapy relationship.

A growing body of research scientifically demonstrates the presence of transference in the therapeutic relationship. Andersen and Berk (1998) have found that "mental representations of significant others serve as storehouses of information about given individuals from one's life, and can be activated (made ready for use) and applied to (used to interpret) other individuals, and that this is especially likely when the new individual in some way resembles a significant other" (p. 81).

Research by Beach and Power (1996) demonstrated that transference occurs in all types of psychotherapy. They transcribed psychotherapy sessions from psychotherapists of varying theoretical orientations and discovered comments indicative of transference in each. Interestingly, fewer transference statements were voiced by clients in the cognitive and cognitive-behavioral groups. They also found that psychoanalytic psychotherapists responded to client transference statements with more detailed comments.

A different research approach toward transference was taken by Bradley, Heim, and Westen (2005). They used standardized instruments to survey psychologists and psychiatrists regarding the thoughts, feelings, motives, conflicts, and behaviors expressed by clients toward psychotherapists. They then subjected the resulting data to factor analysis, which is a statistical method of identifying categories in data. Five groups of transference feelings emerged:

- Angry/entitled: The client makes excessive demands on the psychotherapist while also being angry and dismissive; generally found with borderline and narcissistic clients.
- Anxious/preoccupied: The client fears the psychotherapist's disapproval and rejection and may be overly compliant or dependent.
- Avoidant: The client seems to want to avoid connecting with the psychotherapist emotionally.
- Sexualized: The client appears to have sexual feelings toward the psychotherapist and may behave in a seductive manner.
- Secure/engaged: The client feels comfortable with the psychotherapist, and they have a positive and secure working alliance.

Interestingly, the researchers were concerned that these findings might be an artifact of the significant number of psychodynamically oriented psychotherapists in the sample, so they reanalyzed the data excluding those psychotherapists and found basically the same results. Note that there are many possible emotional reactions that are not categorized by this research; probably only the most common transference patterns showed up in the factor analysis.

These different research projects have one commonality: that transference exists and that it is a normal event that occurs during psychotherapy and in the client's personal life. Thus, as psychotherapists, we must be prepared to recognize it and use it therapeutically to help clients understand their relationships more deeply. Then clients can choose to change longstanding relationship patterns that they feel are unhealthy.

## USING TRANSFERENCE IN THERAPY

> It is the establishment and working through of the transference that is thought to be crucial to the attainment of insight in psychoanalysis and psychoanalytic psychotherapy. Traditionally, the therapist strove to serve as a "blank screen," in an atmosphere of neutrality, abstinence, and anonymity, thus providing a setting most conducive to the displacement of feelings.... [Now therapy is considered] a process that is more interactional, interpersonal, and subjective in nature, characterized by a mingling of transference and countertransference between patient and therapist. The therapist, like the patient, is viewed as a unique individual with his own theory of how therapy works, his own idiosyncrasies, his own conflicts and his own past, all of which contribute to the unfolding of the transference. (Goldstein, 2000, p. 168)

Initially, you might take your clients' emotional reactions toward you very personally. You are concerned about your clients and you just want to help. To have your clients feel fearful, angry, or distant in response can be confusing and frustrating. Learn to cope with your client's emotions by using them to gain greater insight into the client's life problems.

Although transference can occur toward anyone and is not simply a phenomenon of therapy, it is more likely to occur when there is some resemblance to an individual who was very influential to the client (Andersen & Berk, 1998). By virtue of your professional authority and your caretaking for the client, your role already has some resemblance to that of the client's parent (or other significant childhood caretaker). This role will contribute to transference arising during the psychotherapy session. In addition, the client may have rigid, inflexible ways of dealing with interpersonal situations and may demonstrate this toward you in the session (J. S. Beck, 2005).

In psychodynamic approaches, as indicated in the previous quote, the psychotherapist uses insights about the client's transference to make *transference interpretations.* When you make a transference interpretation, you are trying to verbally describe some aspect of the relationship between you and the client that is occurring implicitly (Hobson & Kapur, 2005). Another definition of transference interpretations is "an explicit reference to the patient's ongoing relationship with the therapist" (Høglend, 2004, p. 280). Here are some examples of transference interpretations of the relationship between the client and the psychotherapist:

- "I'm noticing that you are hesitant to talk to me about your difficulties with your classes. I'm wondering how you are expecting me to react if we discuss that."
- "[H]ow did you feel when I suggested that you might have some influence [on your husband]? (pause) Did you feel a little anxious?...What did it mean to you when I said it?" (J. S. Beck, 2005, p. 71)
- "You seem a little different this week. I wonder, are you feeling less connected to therapy and to me?...Are you also thinking that I feel less connected to you?" (J. S. Beck, 2005, p. 82)

Note that these transference interpretations are more often questions than statements. You may not even know what the answers would be; you need only identify that a reaction arose in the client that signifies transference and begin the process of inquiring about it. While there are many ways to make transference interpretations, these interpretations are phrased as "inviting a mutual exploration of possibilities rather than...talking 'at' the patient or prescribing the truth" (Hobson & Kapur, 2005, p. 277).

Høglend (2004) notes that transference can be explored in therapy without direct transference interpretations. Instead, you might "interpret conflicts and/or interpersonal patterns in the patient's contemporary relationships or search for memories of past relationships, without including a reference to the patient-therapist interaction" (p. 281). Høglend terms these therapeutic interventions *extratransference interpretations.* Some examples of extratranference interpretations of the relationship between the client and significant others:

- "I've noticed that you often do not talk about your difficulties with your friends. Are you worried that they would react negatively if you did so? [After client reacts to that point] How do you think you developed these expectations of other people?"
- "What were you thinking when you talked to your mother on the phone?" (J. S. Beck, 2005, p. 211)
- "So you were trying to e-mail your sister and you began to feel bad. What was going through your mind?" (J. S. Beck, 2005, p. 213)

Note that the psychotherapist is actually helping to guide the client in constructing her own extratransference interpretations. The client's views about others can then be examined using cognitive therapy techniques if you choose (J. S. Beck, 2005).

You don't need to present a transference interpretation that dazzles your client with your insight and therapeutic brilliance ("You treat me as if I were your mother, expecting me to be harsh and controlling"). I suspect that it was this type of comment that Høglend (2004) examined when he found that there is a significant risk that clients will not take transference interpretations well. Clients may be defensive or anxious in response to transference interpretations or find them intrusive and unpleasant. They can see the psychotherapist as critical, hostile, or dominant. And they can feel that the psychotherapist is focusing too much on the therapy relationship and ignoring the client's very real current interpersonal problems, symptoms, and difficulties in coping. All these reactions pose some threat to the continuation of therapy, the strength of the therapeutic alliance, and hence the therapy outcome.

In his review of the research on transference, Høglend (2004) concluded that research suggested that a high level of transference interpretations (five or more per session) is poorly tolerated by clients, often resulting in dropout and/or lack of improvement. Extratransference interpretations were much more readily tolerated by the clients. Interestingly, two research studies found (contrary to theoretical expectations) that clients with more severe interpersonal problems responded better to therapy that included transference interpretations and that clients who were higher functioning responded better to therapy without any transference interpretations (Høglend, Johansson, Marble, Bogwald, & Amlo, 2007; Høglend et al., 2011). Some promising research has recently been done on using transference-focused psychotherapy with clients with personality disorders, especially borderline personality disorder (Clarkin, Levy, & Schiavi, 2005; Doering et al., 2010).

Clearly, transference interpretations are powerful interventions that are not fully understood in the current research paradigm. So how can the beginning psychotherapist use transference interpretations when starting to see a new client? In summary, here are some suggestions:

- Be gentle when making either transference or extratransference interpretations. Ask questions or wonder what is happening, rather than making statements.
- Since transference interpretations can be challenging to the client (Høglend, 2004), you may wish to avoid them until you feel that rapport is sufficient that the client can tolerate them. Then provide no more than one transference interpretation per session until you feel confident that the client can handle more (a low level of interpretation as defined by Høglend, 2004).
- Take your time before you make any interpretations. Let several instances accrue before suggesting a specific interpretation and "postpone the interpretation of transference until it is close to the

patient's awareness. If it is prematurely interpreted, the patient may be totally unable to relate to what the psychotherapist is saying and might feel misunderstood. One useful adage suggests that one should formulate the interpretation and think about it four times before verbalizing it" (Gabbard, 2010, p. 76).

- If the client does not tolerate transference interpretations, it is okay to avoid them; still, you can use your conceptualization to inform therapy because the client will report the same challenges with significant others that you observe in the therapy relationship.
- Use extratransference interpretations as frequently as needed and tolerated.
- Clients with borderline personality disorder may find transference interpretations especially beneficial (Levy et al., 2006). Other clients with significantly disturbed interpersonal relations can benefit as well.
- Subsequent work on the issues that emerge from these interpretations can be done from different theoretical perspectives. For references, see the list of recommended readings at the end of this chapter.
- Even if no transference or extratransference interpretations are ever made in therapy, the client's habitual ways of reacting to others can be transformed over time. The therapeutic relationship itself can be a powerful vehicle for learning about interpersonal relationships (Gabbard, 2010). If the psychotherapist is nurturing, understanding, kind, and helpful, clients can internalize new ideas about significant relationships, helping them to have more healthy relationships in other spheres of life.

## COUNTERTRANSFERENCE

Therapists working with borderline clients are likely to discover that, from time to time, interactions with clients elicit in themselves strong emotional reactions ranging from empathetic feelings of depression to strong anger, hopelessness, or attraction. It is important for the therapist to be aware of these reactions and to look at them critically so that they do not unduly bias his or her responses. However, far from being an impediment, these feelings can be quite useful if the therapist is able to understand his or her emotional responses to the client. Emotional responses do not occur randomly. If a therapist experiences an unusually strong response to a client, this is likely to be a response to some aspect of the client's behavior, and it may provide valuable information if it can be understood. It is not unusual for a therapist to respond emotionally to a pattern in the client's behavior long before that pattern has been recognized intellectually. (Freeman, Pretzer, Fleming, & Simon, 1990, p. 194)

The therapist whose reactions are countertransference-based is faced with the task of deciphering which of his or her personal issues is being stimulated and how.... I propose that countertransference be conceptualized as therapist reactions that stem from areas of personal conflict within the therapist.... [This definition] does not require that therapist conflicts be unresolved. Rather, it allows for the possibility that countertransference might also arise from therapist issues or conflicts that are partially resolved (I do not believe that one's issues are ever completely resolved). (Hayes, 2004, pp. 23, 31)

Psychotherapists of all theoretical stripes recognize that it is normal to have emotional reactions to clients. One of the most challenging tasks before you is learning to understand your feelings about the client. Sometimes these feelings will be helpful in therapy, and at other times they will confuse you; this is normal. There are many ways to conceptualize types of countertransference (Dalenberg, 2000), so I have selected just one for simplicity's sake.

The first major type of countertransference involves your emotional reactions to the client that are based on the client's presentation: the client's behavior, what the client says, how it is said, and so on. This is the type of countertransference being described by the cognitive therapists in the first of the previous quotes. These are emotional reactions that anyone is likely to have with the client. These emotions give you important clues about the client's interpersonal world outside the session. As Judith Beck (2005) states, "It is useful for therapists to use their own negative reactions to patients as a cue to assess the degree to which patients' behavior and attitudes in the session are representative of their behavior and attitudes outside of the session" (p. 84). This type of countertransference is sometimes called *objective countertransference* (Kiesler, 2001).

The second major type of countertransference is based on your personal issues. In other words, something is stimulating your personal emotional reaction. Fauth (2006) defines this type of countertransference: "therapists' idiosyncratic reactions (broadly defined as sensory, affective, cognitive, and behavioral) to clients that are based primarily in therapists' own personal conflicts, biases, or difficulties (for example, cognitive biases, personal narratives, or maladaptive interpersonal patterns)" (p. 17). This type of countertransference is sometimes called *subjective countertransference* (Kiesler, 2001). (Note: If you read more about countertransference in the literature, you will see that some researchers and theorists [e.g., Fauth, 2006; Hayes, 2004] define the term *countertransference* as *only* this second type of emotional reaction to the client—explicitly excluding the psychotherapist's emotional reactions that are based on the client's presentation.)

Unfortunately, countertransference is underresearched as a clinical phenomenon (Hayes, 2004). Perhaps this is because "countertransference emanated from psychoanalysis, a field traditionally disinclined toward empirical inquiry" (Hayes, 2004, p. 21). Betan, Heim, Conklin, and Westen (2005) surveyed the emotional responses of a sample of psychiatrists and psychologists toward one selected client each and mathematically categorized the results into eight distinct patterns of psychotherapist emotional reactions:

- Disengaged: The psychotherapist feels distracted, withdrawn, annoyed, or bored in sessions.
- Helpless/inadequate: The psychotherapist feels inadequate, incompetent, hopeless, and anxious.
- Overwhelmed/disorganized: The psychotherapist desires to avoid or flee the patient and has strong negative feelings, including dread, repulsion, and resentment. Clients are likely to have borderline personality disorder or narcissistic personality disorder.
- Parental/protective: The psychotherapist has a wish to protect and nurture the patient in a parental way above and beyond normal positive feelings toward the client.
- Criticized/mistreated: The psychotherapist feels unappreciated, dismissed, or devalued by the client.
- Special/overinvolved: The psychotherapist sees the client as special, relative to other clients, and has "soft signs" of problems in maintaining boundaries, including self-disclosure, ending sessions on time, and feeling guilty, responsible, or overly concerned.
- Sexualized: The psychotherapist has sexual feelings toward the patient or experiences sexual tension.
- Positive: The psychotherapist and client have a positive working alliance and a close connection.

This research demonstrates that it is normal to have strong feelings toward clients, even negative or sexual feelings. Your challenge is to understand why you are having these feelings and to use them therapeutically if appropriate. Even positive countertransference can create therapeutic challenges (see case examples at www.drwiller.com/tbpc for more on this topic).

Since countertransference can be in response to the client's presentation or can be based on your own personal idiosyncratic reactions, having the insight to tell the difference is an essential psychotherapy skill. Keep in mind that it is something of an arbitrary distinction to divide countertransference into these two major categories because, as Gabbard (2001a), states, "countertransference is a jointly created phenomenon that involves contributions from both patient and psychotherapist. The patient draws the therapist into playing a role that reflects the patient's internal world, but the specific dimensions of that role are colored by the therapist's own personality" (p. 984).

## COUNTERTRANSFERENCE BASED ON THE CLIENT'S ISSUES

*Anita Cook is a mental health trainee who is working with Laura Ward, a woman who is living with her husband. Laura is battered by her husband about once a month.*

*Laura has shared all her abusive experiences with Anita. She also says that she is afraid to leave him because he might kill her. Anita feels sympathy for Laura's fear and pain. Anita then starts to suggest how Laura can effectively leave her husband. Laura says, "But I love him, and the children need their father." They repeatedly take these two opposing stands for several sessions. Anita tells her supervisor that Laura is "stubborn and resistant."*

*Aaron Webb is a mental health trainee who is working with Eugene Turner, a recovering alcoholic and addict. Eugene has been convicted for selling crack, and he is on parole. Aaron likes Eugene and sympathizes with his struggles. Eugene grew up in poverty, and he has post-traumatic stress disorder from being physically abused by a stepfather in his youth. Eugene lives in a halfway house under very strict rules. He is supposed to be in every night at a certain time. Eugene has an ambivalent and conflictual relationship with his mother, who is his primary emotional and financial support. Eugene tells Aaron that he has been sticking to all the halfway house rules. Then Eugene urges Aaron to call the halfway house. Aaron gets a release of information and does so. After faxing the release over, Aaron talks to a staff member who informs him that Eugene has been coming in late for several nights and is at risk of having his parole violated. Aaron feels intense rage when he hears that Eugene has been lying to him but is also confused because this is not a typical feeling for him. Aaron is well aware that addicts can struggle with telling the truth. Since Aaron recognizes that this rage is unusual for him, he understands that it is probably a countertransference reaction. Aaron does not know exactly how he came to experience the rage; however, he uses the feeling as a guide for the next session without acting it out. Aaron says to Eugene, "I've been somewhat confused after our last session. You told me that you were sticking to all the house rules, but you also encouraged me to call the house, where you knew I would learn otherwise. I'm wondering what was going on with you when you decided to do that? How have others reacted to you when you've told them things that aren't true in the past?" Aaron discovers that Eugene is fearful of trusting others out of concern that they will be angry and then lies to avoid their rage, increasing the chances that they will be angry later. This pattern apparently first developed between Eugene and his stepfather.*

Countertransference must be attended to carefully, because unexamined feelings on your part can lead the therapy astray. For example, you may begin to react to the client like everyone else does instead of offering the client an opportunity to think about how his behavior affects others and how the behavior can be changed. Or you may fall into the trap of reenacting the client's important relationships from the past rather than exploring the client's current interpersonal challenges that stem from those relationships.

As I noted before, there are many different definitions of countertransference. For simplicity, I describe three types of countertransference that are based on the client's issues.

The first type of countertransference based on the client's issues relates to empathy; in this case, you are simply empathetically feeling the same feelings that the client is feeling. This type is sometimes called *concordant countertransference* (Kernberg, Selzer, Koenigsberg, Carr, & Appelbaum, 1989). The therapeutic response is to simply reflect the feelings of the client: "It sounds like you're feeling quite anxious about that."

The second type of countertransference based on the client's issues is also about empathy, but in a more complicated way. Here the client has mixed feelings about a situation. In the first of the previous vignettes, Laura has mixed feelings about leaving her abusive spouse. However, instead of exploring these mixed feelings, she says, "But I love him!" while the psychotherapist focuses on the danger. In this case, both of these feelings (love and fear of danger) really belong to the client, but the client's ambivalence is being acted out between the client and the psychotherapist. The feelings that the psychotherapist has enacted are the ones that are most difficult for the client to tolerate—fear of her dangerous husband. Clearly Laura is worried about the situation because she is actively seeking help from a psychotherapist and has talked about her fears. This type of countertransference is traditionally called *projective identification* in the psychoanalytic literature (Gabbard, 2001a). The client's recognition of her own ambivalence will be the key to effective change, and getting the client to explore her ambivalence in therapy is the most effective intervention. This interpersonal dynamic is also commonly experienced when working with individuals with substance abuse problems. To most effectively address this type of countertransference, learn about motivational interviewing (W. R. Miller & Rollnick, 2002).

Check to see if projective identification is occurring when you and the client are arguing, or are in a power struggle, or when you feel that the client is being stubborn or resistant. When you do find yourself enacting this, as you inevitably will at some point, you can always change tactics. Address this type of countertransference by reflecting the ambivalence that you see and try to get the client to be more aware of the struggle within her. In the previous vignette, Anita could say,

> "This seems like a terribly painful situation. I see that you love your husband and you want to stay with him, yet you are also afraid that he might hurt or even kill you, so you are uncertain about what to do."

The third type of countertransference is about reenacting the client's relationships from the past. In the second of the previous vignettes, the psychotherapist experiences an unexpected rage reaction. He recognizes that this is not typical of him, so he hypothesizes that it is countertransference. He uses this emotion to guide the next session, discovers important issues about trust and learns about an important relationship pattern between the client and his stepfather. Had the psychotherapist acted out his anger toward the client, it would have been a therapeutic mistake (although a common one, according to research by Gelso, Hill, Mohr, Rochlen, & Zack, 1999). This type of countertransference is called *role responsiveness* (Gabbard, 2001a), although often (confusingly) it is considered another form of projective identification.

## COUNTERTRANSFERENCE BASED ON THE PSYCHOTHERAPIST'S PERSONAL ISSUES

[In a qualitative research study] Therapist 4 possessed strong values related to independence and strength that she identified as potential sources of countertransference. The client with whom she worked for 12 sessions looked frequently to the therapist for guidance and advice, generating recurrent frustration in the therapist. Furthermore, the therapist seemed to experience difficulty identifying with the client, stating on one postsession interview, "I have never, ever, ever" been as dependent as the client. A second theme for this dyad involved death. The client's mother was in the process of dying and the therapist's mother had died within the previous year. The therapist felt some connection with the client around death but found from her own experience that it was not helpful "to get lost in the grieving." Because the therapist found information about death and dying to be helpful in her recovery process, she assumed the client would benefit from the same. Consequently, the therapist was predominately didactic and intellectual in addressing the client's concerns about her mother's impending death. (Hayes et al., 1998, p. 476)

Therapist 5 struggled for control throughout his work with a female client who looked to him for guidance and rescuing but who angrily rejected his advice because she saw it as controlling. This tapped into the therapist's countertransference issues of needing to gratify and help others and caused him to feel overly responsible for the client. The therapist struggled throughout their 17 sessions with how directive he should be, and he vacillated between empathizing with the client and distancing himself from her. (Hayes et al., 1998, p. 476)

Therapist 2 described three countertransference origins in her 17 postsession interviews: needs to nurture, perform well, and be a good parent. The therapist used her countertransference reactions [based on these three personal issues] to deepen her understanding of the client, remain patient, and nurture the client. In fact, approximately half of her countertransference manifestations [based on the therapist's personal issues] were classified as approach responses that increased closeness with her client. (Hayes et al., 1998, p. 476)

The second major type of countertransference is emotional reactions to the client due to your own personal issues. These personal issues could be related to your current life situation or your past life experiences. This type of countertransference should not be used in therapy; instead, these reactions point out areas of self-exploration for you.

The three previous quotes are from a qualitative research study in which eight psychologists were interviewed immediately following their sessions of brief therapy with eight clients (Hayes et al., 1998). The themes illustrated in the quotes emerged over time. The anonymous psychotherapists in this study showed great compassion and courage by sharing their most personal feelings with the researchers so that others could learn. These three cases (from the eight in the article) illustrate some universal issues about how countertransference (the kind that is based on a psychotherapist's personal issues) can affect therapy.

In the first quote, therapist 4 ends up distancing herself emotionally from the dependent client with the dying mother. In the second quote, therapist 5 alternates between moving closer to the client by gratifying her desire for advice, then distancing himself when she was rejecting of him. In the third quote, therapist 2 uses her countertransference reactions to identify with and move closer to the client. Note that countertransference based on personal issues is typically manifested through moving closer to the client or distancing oneself from the client (Hayes, 2004). Distancing is generally detrimental to the therapy, while sometimes moving closer is helpful, and sometimes it is not—if one moves too close.

Note that Hayes et al. (1998) found that the psychotherapists in the study experienced reactions toward the client that were due to their personal issues in fully 80 percent of sessions. This illustrates that this type of countertransference is normative and universal and cannot be avoided.

Since all of us must expect to experience this type of countertransference, we must learn to manage it appropriately. Do not try to ignore these feelings, as they will impede your work with clients if you do. Research suggests that acting out this type of countertransference is damaging to the therapy (Hayes, Gelso, & Hummel, 2011).

## UNDERSTANDING AND UTILIZING COUNTERTRANSFERENCE

> CT [countertransference] that is not understood or controlled by the therapist is likely to injure the therapeutic process.... [T]he therapist's internal experience may also be acted out in the treatment, and this is usually harmful. In such cases, the therapist is taking care of his or her own needs, enacting his or her own defenses, and not attending to the patient's issues and needs. (Gelso & Hayes, 2001, pp. 418, 419)

> When patients display dysfunctional behavior in session, therapists should realize that their patients' behaviors likely stem from difficult (often traumatic) life circumstances and extreme, negative core beliefs. Such a stance allows therapists to regard patients more positively, display empathy, and behave more adaptively themselves.... And the therapeutic relationship itself can be a vehicle for helping these patients develop a more positive

view of themselves and others and learn that interpersonal problems can be solved. (J. S. Beck, 2005, pp. 43, 63)

The first quote illustrates some ways in which countertransference can negatively affect the therapeutic process. The second quote encourages us to use our understanding of the client's difficulties to be empathetic, despite their dysfunctional behavior toward us.

Judith Beck (2005) encourages you to monitor yourself during the therapy session by asking:

- Negative emotionality: Do I feel annoyed, angry, anxious, sad, hopeless, overwhelmed, guilty, embarrassed, or demeaned?
- Getting too close or too distant: Am I engaging in dysfunctional behaviors, such as blaming, dominating, or controlling the patient? Or am I being too passive?
- Behavior: Is my volume/tone of voice, facial expression, and body language appropriate?
- Physiological reaction: Am I feeling tense? Is my heart beating faster? Is my face becoming hot?

Before determining whether to use countertransference in therapy, you must have a good understanding of it and whether it is related to your issue, the client's, or both. Here are some questions that you can use to help understand the countertransference:

- Am I having an atypical feeling or reaction toward this client or behaving in a way that is not typical of my therapy style? If yes, clearly some kind of countertransference is operating.
- Am I having a stronger emotional reaction to this client than to other clients? This could be due either to some intense emotional issues of the client (e.g., homicidality or borderline or narcissistic traits), or to countertransference regarding your personal issues, or both.
- Do I think that others in the client's life are probably having the same emotional reaction to him that I am having now? If yes, some measure of countertransference due to the client's issues is likely operating.
- Have I noticed myself feeling emotionally distant from this client or ignoring some issues? If yes, it is likely that some countertransference due to your personal issues is involved.
- Have I noticed myself becoming too involved with this client, perhaps by trying to solve problems, extending sessions too long, or doing special favors? If yes, it is again likely that some countertransference due to your personal issues is involved.
- Do I feel like the client is "pushing my buttons"? If yes, probably some countertransference regarding your personal issues is involved.

When your countertransference feelings are negative, even if you are certain that they are based on the client's issues, your interventions must be framed with care. It is okay to wait until you can discuss your reactions with your supervisor before sharing your insights with the client in a later session. The same dynamic will recur if it is important.

When you identify countertransference that is based on the client's personal issues, it helps to attempt to understand the client more deeply. Try to understand how this pattern of difficult interpersonal interactions developed through the client's distressing negative experiences of the past. Try to understand how the client has found this (now mostly dysfunctional) way of relating to others to be helpful in some way. You can use this understanding to become more empathetic to the client and explore the issue productively in therapy rather than falling into the trap of reenacting it.

## MANAGING COUNTERTRANSFERENCE BASED ON THE PSYCHOTHERAPIST'S ISSUES

Gelso and Hayes (2001) conclude that "the ten studies [done so far] support the idea that unmanaged CT [countertransference due to the psychotherapist's personal issues] adversely affects treatment outcomes" (p. 419). They also concluded that research evidence supports that "awareness of CT [countertransference] feelings [due to the therapist's personal issues] was associated with fewer CT behaviors" (p. 418). So, when you identify countertransference that is based on your own personal issues, work to understand your own reactions more deeply; otherwise, you will reduce your therapeutic effectiveness (Gelso & Hayes, 2001).

According to Gelso, Latts, Gomez, and Fassinger (2002), effective countertransference management—based on the psychotherapist's own issues—encompasses these five skills:

- Empathy: Being able to maintain empathy with the client despite the countertransference feelings that are also in the psychotherapist's awareness
- Self-insight: Understanding the origins of the psychotherapist's personal issues that lead to the emotional reaction to the client
- Self-integration: Maintaining healthy boundaries between the psychotherapist and client—specifically, not acting in the therapy session on countertransference that is based on the psychotherapist's personal issues
- Anxiety management: Sufficient management of the psychotherapist's anxiety
- Conceptualizing ability: The psychotherapist's ability to conceptualize his own reaction from a theoretical perspective.

Psychotherapy trainees who most effectively managed their countertransference based on personal issues were found to have the best psychotherapy outcomes with their clients (Gelso, Latts, Gomez, & Fassinger, 2002). As you can infer from these five skills, good supervision or consultation, personal psychotherapy, and a dedication to continuing to increase one's conceptual knowledge of psychotherapy can be invaluable in developing one's ability to manage countertransference. So if you are seeing a client and you see that you are having strong emotional reactions, ask yourself these questions (derived from these five skills):

- Can I maintain empathy with the client? Or am I acting out my feelings in a way that can interfere with therapy?
- Do I understand which of my own issues are related to the client's issues? Or do I feel distressed and confused?
- Am I able to see the client as a separate person from me? Or am I telling the client how to handle the situation based on my own personal experience—and not the client's experience?
- Am I able to stay focused during the session? Or do I feel too anxious or distressed to concentrate at times?
- Can I understand, from a theoretical perspective, why I am having the reactions that I am having? Or am I confused about why the client is "pushing my buttons"?

If you are struggling with these issues and the client's treatment is being negatively affected, discuss this with your supervisor. The client may need to be referred to someone else, or perhaps your supervisor can help you with your conceptualizations and interventions enough that you can be effective with the client. Your struggle also indicates that you need to address these issues in your own personal therapy.

Your personal experiences—if sufficiently resolved—can help you understand your clients' difficulties more deeply and, thus, serve as a source of healing (Hayes et al., 1998). (See discussion about self-disclosure in Chapter 4.) And, in fact, Hayes et al. (1998) hypothesized, based on their qualitative research, that "when therapists' countertransference is triggered by clients' family of origin issues, therapists will generally respond with compassionate understanding" (p. 478). As McWilliams (2004) states, "psychotherapy is one of the few professions in which one's greatest misfortunes can be retooled into professional assets" (p. 70).

## THE FUTURE OF TRANSFERENCE AND COUNTERTRANSFERENCE RESEARCH AND THEORY

[The science of cognitive neuroscience has recognized] the existence of two ways that memory can be expressed, either explicitly (via conscious recall or recognition) or implicitly (in behavior, independent of conscious control). Explicit memory refers to conscious memory for ideas, facts and episodes. Implicit memory refers to memory that is observable in behavior but is not consciously brought to mind.... The existence of unconscious or implicit networks—which tend to be resistant to change because they reflect long-standing regularities in the person's experience and allow him or her to navigate the world in ways that feel predictable (even if sometimes rigid, inaccurate or otherwise maladaptive)—provides perhaps the best empirical justification for long-term therapies.... The connectionist notion of representations as potentials for reactivation—as sets of neurons that have been activated in the past and are hence more readily activated as a unit in the future—offers a mechanism to explain the long-held psychoanalytic position that patients are likely to express important conflicts, defenses, motives, and interpersonal patterns in their relationship with the therapist. (Westen, 2005, pp. 444–446)

The discovery of mirror neurons lends a new dimension of understanding to empathy, countertransference, and projective identification that was not previously available. Both conscious and unconscious physical processes are elicited through synchronization with clients.... Social psychology studies have demonstrated time and again that it is common for people to unconsciously copy one another's facial expression, synchronize breathing rates, and mimic the other's partial or complete posture. Through doing so, emotions have also been shown to be shared. This happens regularly in the therapy room as well and can go either way: therapist to client, or client to therapist. (Rothschild, 2004, n.p.)

In the first of the previous quotes, Westen (2005) relates transference to recent research findings in cognitive neuroscience. These findings have determined that there are separate brain pathways for explicit (conscious) processes and implicit (unconscious or automatic) processes. Explicit (or conscious) processes have been traditionally targeted by cognitive psychotherapists, while implicit (or unconscious) processes (including transference) have traditionally been targeted by psychodynamic psychotherapists (Gabbard & Westen, 2003). There is a growing consensus that addressing both processes is a productive therapeutic approach.

There are interesting hints that socioeconomic status (Dougall & Schwartz, 2011) and cross-cultural issues (Nagai, 2009) may affect transference and countertransference, but these relationships remain little understood and are in need of further research. Chapter 5 addressed some practical issues that arise when there are psychotherapist–client differences.

As Rothschild (2004) indicates in the second of the previous quotes, scientists are tantalizingly close to explaining how countertransference occurs. She cites a confluence of neuroscience research and social psychology research that hints toward a near-future scientific understanding of how the psychotherapist's emotions can resonate so acutely with those of the client.

## RECOMMENDED READING

Beck, J. S. (2005). *Cognitive therapy for challenging problems: What to do when the basics don't work.* New York: Guilford Press.

*While Beck does not use the terms "transference" and "countertransference," she none-theless provides a very helpful and thorough discussion of these phenomena from a cognitive therapy perspective. Note that Beck focuses on discussing the psychotherapist's emotional reactions that are in response to the client's presentation.*

Berenson, K. R., & Andersen, S. M. (2006). Childhood physical and emotional abuse by a parent: Transference effects in adult interpersonal relations. *Personality and Social Psychology Bulletin, 32,* 1509–1522.

*While a bit technical, this report of contemporary transference research provides the reader with insight into how transference is detected experimentally.*

Chu, J. (1988). Ten traps for therapists in the treatment of trauma survivors. *Dissociation, 1,* 24–32.

*In this classic article, Chu clearly describes many countertransference challenges that confront the psychotherapist who works with trauma survivors.*

Comas-Diaz, L., & Jacobsen, F. M. (1991). Ethnocultural transference and counter-transference in the therapeutic dyad. *American Journal of Orthopsychiatry, 61,* 392–402.

*A multitude of helpful vignettes illustrate clinical examples of ethnocultural transference and countertransference emerging in psychotherapy. A classic article for the psychotherapist who wants to achieve cultural competency.*

Gabbard, G. O. (2001). A contemporary psychoanalytic model of countertransference. *Journal of Clinical Psychology/In Session: Psychotherapy in Practice, 57,* 983–991.

*Gabbard briefly provides an update on the current theoretical status of countertransference from a psychoanalytic perspective. Read this if you would like a more sophisticated understanding of how countertransference is a jointly created phenomenon between client and psychotherapist.*

Gabbard, G. O. (2010). *Long-term psychodynamic psychotherapy: A basic text* (2nd ed.). Arlington, VA: American Psychiatric Publishing.

*This book is written specifically for the beginning psychotherapist. Important modern principles of psychodynamic psychotherapy are outlined remarkably clearly in this text, along with ample references to research literature. Highly recommended.*

Gelso, C. J., & Hayes, J. A. (2001). Countertransference management. *Psychotherapy, 38,* 418–422.

*Two prominent researchers on countertransference use insights derived from their research and the research of others to describe how to effectively manage countertransference that is based on the psychotherapist's personal issues.*

Hayes, J. A., & Gelso, C. J. (2001). Clinical implications of research on countertransference: Science informing practice. *Journal of Clinical Psychology/In Session: Psychotherapy in Practice, 57,* 1041–1051.

*Hayes and Gelso describe their theory and research on countertransference with an emphasis on informing the practitioner. Note that Hayes and Gelso focus exclusively on countertransference that is due to the psychotherapist's personal emotional reactions in this paper and in their research.*

Hobday, G., Mellman, L., & Gabbard, G. O. (2008). Complex sexualized transferences when the patient is male and the therapist female. *American Journal of Psychiatry, 165*(12), 1525–1530.

*This article explores a difficult psychotherapy case with sexualized transference toward a female psychotherapist.*

Kernberg, O. F., Selzer, M. A., Koenigsberg, H. W., Carr, A. C., & Appelbaum, A. H. (1989). *Psychodynamic psychotherapy of borderline patients*. New York: Basic Books. *While explicitly about treating borderline clients, this volume presents useful, thought-provoking discussions regarding boundaries, establishing a therapeutic contract, coping with countertransference, and addressing threats to treatment, among other topics, that can be applied to many challenging clients.*

## ONLINE RESOURCE

www.drwiller.com/tbpc
   *My website has a document entitled Challenging Emotions in Psychotherapy: Case Studies. The document describes many common emotional issues between psychotherapists and clients.*

## DISCUSSION QUESTIONS

1. Can you reconcile the research on transference and countertransference discussed in this chapter with your theoretical orientation? Why or why not?
2. What characteristics of a supervisor would lead you to feel comfortable discussing your feelings toward a client? What if these feelings were embarrassing (e.g., you detest a client or feel sexually attracted to a client)?
3. How can you deal with your distressing feelings toward a client if you feel too inhibited—for whatever reason—to discuss them with your supervisor?

# 23

# Becoming a Psychotherapist: Challenges, Rewards, and Growth

As psychotherapists, our professional and personal developments are closely linked. Psychotherapy is an emotionally demanding profession. We need to learn how to be happy, healthy, and fulfilled and avoid getting burned out and exhausted. The process of doing therapy will change us in profound ways. People invite us into their innermost lives and we learn how to help them. But there are some risks to your mental health from being a psychotherapist. I hope that the knowledge in this chapter will help you avoid or minimize these emotional risks, variously called vicarious traumatization, traumatic countertransference, secondary traumatic stress, compassion fatigue, and burnout—with some overlap between these concepts (see S. Collins & Long, 2003; Jenkins & Baird, 2002). To simplify, I focus on two of these interrelated concepts: burnout and vicarious traumatization.

The profession of psychotherapy provides us with opportunities for personal growth and rewarding professional experiences. We can gain a unique perspective on the commonalities of human experiences. Our clients honor us by the depth of the emotions and experiences that they are willing to have with us. We can delve into vast resources of professional knowledge about subjects that interest us. We continually learn more about how to have rewarding personal and professional relationships.

## BURNOUT

I could see I was burning out. I looked at the other therapists who had been with the agency longer than I had. They were apathetic, depressed and avoided work, whenever possible. The patient assignment system gave everyone new patients regularly, no matter how high their current caseload. This system rewarded those who clearly didn't care about their clients—the clients would drop out, and the clinician had less work. Those who engaged well with their clients were chronically overworked and overstressed. When staff retired or left, they were rarely replaced, resulting in higher workloads for everyone.

We never had any real input into what was going on in the agency. Occasionally, they would ask for our input, but it was clearly ignored, and the higher-ups did what they had wanted to do all along. Those with the most power were physically isolated in remote offices, and had no known contact with anyone on the "front lines." The paperwork increased significantly every year, and we joked that eventually we'd treat one patient per week and spend the other 39 hours on paperwork. We were frequently told to "do more with less."

We wondered whether anyone in charge cared if we did a good job. There were never any rewards or promotions available. No opportunities for professional advancement or development were offered by the administration. A coworker posted a cartoon on her door of a door to a padded cell; the sign on the door to the padded cell said, "Do not disturb any further." We could all relate.

We wondered whether the administrators became administrators, in part, because they wouldn't have to deal with patients any more. They seemed burned out themselves. At best, the bosses were pleasant but ineffectual, at worst, they were punitive and harsh.

I got to the point that when a client talked about feeling suicidal, I felt exhausted and overburdened. I started to have difficulty caring anymore. I knew I had to leave to preserve my sanity and my professional competence. (Anonymous psychotherapist, personal communication, March 10, 2007)

This portrait of a psychotherapist who is burning out illustrates that *burnout* is "a prolonged response to chronic emotional and interpersonal stressors on the job, and is defined here by the three dimensions of exhaustion, cynicism, and a sense of inefficacy" (Maslach, 2003, p. 189). Most frequently found in human services workers, burnout generally includes extreme emotional fatigue, disillusionment, and apathy toward work. Gradually, productivity and concern for clients decrease. As the period of burnout progresses, the psychotherapist may exhibit emotional problems, substance abuse, interpersonal problems, or increased physical illness (S. Collins & Long, 2003; Felton, 1998; Maslach, 2003).

Random samples of psychologists have found that 40 to 44 percent had high emotional exhaustion (Ackerly, Burnell, Holder, & Kurdek, 1988; Rupert & Morgan, 2005), indicating that burnout is extremely common in mental health practitioners. Certain client issues increase burnout. Treating too many clients and having more client contact hours increase burnout (Leiter & Harvie, 1996). High stress contributes to burnout (D'Souza, Egan, & Rees, 2011). Clients with the potential for aggressive behavior or suicide were found to be the most emotionally exhausting (Rupert & Morgan, 2005), while clients who did not improve also contributed to burnout (Shinn, Rosario, Morch, & Chestnut, 1984).

Psychotherapists who are perfectionistic (D'Souza, Egan, & Rees, 2011) may be more susceptible to burnout. When the demands of work conflict with family life, this may lead to burnout. Conversely, when the psychotherapist gets emotional support at home, this leads to less burnout (Rupert, Stevanovic, & Hunley, 2009).

Organizational contributions to burnout have been extensively studied, and, in fact, administrative and bureaucratic factors have been found to contribute more to burnout in mental health professionals than patient care issues do. Working long hours, heavy work demands ("do more with less"), spending more time on administrative tasks and paperwork, and having less control over work activities increase burnout (Rupert & Morgan, 2005), as does low salary (Jenaro, Flores, & Arias, 2007). Certain interpersonal issues on the job contribute to burnout as well: little appreciation for a job well done, interpersonal problems with coworkers, and abuse or harassment in the workplace. Finally, negative aspects of the organization as a whole, such as reorganization, downsizing, and a lack of resources, contribute to burned-out workers (Maslach, 2001, 2003; Rupert & Morgan, 2005). Settings that are most prone to burnout are government (Emery, Wade, & McLean, 2009), hospital or agency (Raquepaw & Miller, 1989), and correctional settings (Senter, Morgan, Serna-McDonald, & Bewley, 2010), probably due to the above factors. Settings less prone to burnout are university counseling centers (Senter, Morgan, Serna-McDonald, & Bewley, 2010) and private practice (Raquepaw & Miller, 1989).

## INSTITUTIONAL POLICIES TO PREVENT BURNOUT

Burnout is more accurately seen as an organizational problem rather than an individual problem. About 30 years ago, a study found that agencies rarely made any efforts to reduce burnout among staff (Shinn et al., 1984). Unfortunately, most agencies and hospitals have not made any progress since then. Interventions aimed at increasing individual coping to reduce burnout have had little success, leading to the likelihood that reductions in burnout will be seen only if greater individual coping skills are coupled with organizational change (Maslach, Schaufeli, & Leiter, 2001).

The organization must support the psychotherapists to prevent burnout. Communication in healthy organizations is characterized by a democratic, informed decision-making style—instead of being exclusively hierarchical—and administrators are supportive and help provide structure as needed (Leiter & Harvie, 1996). Good health insurance that covers mental health and chemical dependency is necessary so that the psychotherapists can seek professional help themselves to reduce the likelihood of a burned-out staff (Felton, 1998). Psychotherapists must have some control over their workload and how their time is allocated. Psychotherapists must not be overworked, since overwork often leads directly to burnout. Overwork also prevents psychotherapists in engaging in positive coping during their personal time, which helps them manage stress.

## VICARIOUS TRAUMATIZATION

When the main focus of my work shifted to working with rape victims... Suddenly, I found myself experiencing nightmares of being raped. Or I would turn a dark corner in my home and imagine a rapist coming toward me just like he had for my client. The more clients I had, the less sleep I got. I found myself becoming tense and irritable. I began to take extra safety precautions and began to view others, especially men, more circumspectly. In short, hearing other women tell me about how they were sexually assaulted was, in small ways, traumatizing and disruptive for me....

I find myself thinking, "Why didn't you scream when you knew people were nearby?" or "How could you have chosen not to even tell him to stop?" I know the answers, but always have to go over them in my head to convince myself. The truth is people in danger sometimes freeze just like the rabbit in the car headlights. If she ran, she might survive, but fear has frozen her in place. And even if she had not been frozen, no one knows if it would have helped or made the situation worse. Intellectually, the answer is satisfying to me, but on a more visceral level, I find it unacceptable. If I accept this reality, I have to give up my notion of my own invulnerability and my competence to take care of myself. My schemas are challenged. I don't want to contemplate the possibility that I, too, might freeze or be unable to do anything to rectify the situation. It goes against my cherished notion that whatever bad comes my way, I will be able to handle it and overcome it. Each time I help a client accept her vulnerability and the fact that she "just froze," I have to accept that possibility for myself. I don't like it and resist it every time....

When I first began working with rape victims, I found it puzzling that I experienced some symptoms of vicarious traumatization, but had never experienced this while working with other victims. As I thought about it, I came to realize that with other victims I had been able to set myself apart from them and maintain my sense of invulnerability. "Perhaps that client was abused as a child, but I am an adult and it can't happen to me." "Maybe she got caught up in an abusive relationship, but I never have, so it is unlikely that I ever will." (One might debate the latter as an illusion, but on some level, whether accurate or not, it allowed me to maintain a sense of invulnerability.) With rape, I could not maintain my distance. As I helped my clients to see that bad things happen to people randomly, I could no longer keep my invulnerability intact. I was just as vulnerable as anyone else. That realization made me more susceptible to symptoms of vicarious traumatization. It also has brought me closer to the struggles of my clients. For that I am grateful. (Astin, 1997, pp. 103, 105–106, 108)

In this quote, Dr. Astin was caught by surprise by her strong emotional reaction to the rape survivors. She had treated survivors of other traumas before, she said, but had not been so personally affected. We are all indebted to her for her honest and fearless report of her experiences.

*Vicarious traumatization* (VT), otherwise known as *secondary traumatic stress*, has been characterized as "a special form of countertransference stimulated by exposure to the client's traumatic material" (Courtois, 1993). While countertransference has multiple different definitions, Courtois is referring to it in the broadest of ways, as encompassing any emotional reaction the psychotherapist has to the client. The psychotherapist begins to take on the emotional, behavioral, and cognitive changes of her traumatized clients. This phenomenon was first described by McCann and Pearlman (1990).

VT can cause changes in the psychotherapist (McCann & Pearlman, 1990). The psychotherapist could become more suspicious of others' motives and become cynical and distrustful. The psychotherapist could develop a heightened sense of vulnerability and often feel unsafe. The psychotherapist may become profoundly aware of the lack of control that we sometimes have over unexpected life events. The psychotherapist could grow to see others as malevolent, cruel, and dangerous. The psychotherapist may feel emotionally estranged from her loved ones by the need to keep her clients' horrors confidential. In response to a previously neutral stimulus, the psychotherapist could be triggered to remember the client's traumatic material. Emotional numbing could occur, and the psychotherapist could begin to engage in numbing behaviors, such as overeating, overspending, overworking, and alcohol use (Hesse, 2002). Clearly, post-traumatic stress disorder (PTSD) can result from VT; however. only a small minority of psychotherapists have the full diagnosis of PTSD (Bride, 2007), and among those, it is unclear how many may have had PTSD prior to seeing any trauma clients.

It is impossible to avoid treating clients with PTSD and thus incurring some risk of intense countertransference. Why? Because there is a very high prevalence of PTSD in the population and an even higher prevalence in psychotherapy clients; a significant number of clients in *all* treatment settings will turn out to have PTSD. Therefore, all psychotherapists must be prepared to treat PTSD effectively. As I've discussed earlier (Chapter 9), PTSD can be a hidden problem, and the psychotherapist can unknowingly (or unconsciously) conspire to keep it that way by not screening for it on a routine basis.

It is likely that each psychotherapist has a different tolerance for working with traumatized clients. To function effectively, discover your tolerance and keep the number of traumatized clients safely below that. Like any emotional resource, this tolerance may fluctuate depending on what is occurring in your personal life. Agencies should avoid having any psychotherapist's caseload consist entirely of traumatized clients, since this puts the psychotherapist at an increased risk of emotional distress.

Controversies remain about VT. Studies of VT tend to assume that all emotional disruption is due to the stresses of working with trauma survivors, but there is evidence that some—or even most—of this emotional disruption may be simply due to the stresses of clinical work in general (Elwood, Mott, Lohr, & Galovski, 2011) or burnout in particular (Devilly, Wright, & Varker, 2009). Also, it is not clear when symptoms of VT are serious and need intervention, and when they are simply transitory emotional reactions to the stresses of working with traumatized populations that will resolve on their own (Elwood, Mott, Lohr, & Galovski, 2011) or with supervision and further training. Some even fear that placing such emphasis on the emotional dangers of treating trauma survivors may cause psychotherapists to experience more and unnecessary emotional distress (Devilly, Wright, & Varker, 2009).

Seasoned psychotherapists, who have sought out specialized knowledge, training, and supervision and who have good self-care and wellness habits, can treat trauma survivors without any notable emotional distress (Dunkley & Whelan, 2006; Harrison & Westwood, 2009). It helps to appreciate that trauma survivors often show great resilience and strength. Seeing our clients improve over time is gratifying and fulfilling. The client's emotional healing will have ripple effects through the client's family, friends, and offspring for years to come.

## MONITOR YOUR EMOTIONAL NEEDS

As psychotherapists, we are not immune to mental health problems. In fact, you may have gone into mental health because your own history of emotional distress has given you compassion for others who have suffered similarly. Our work can provoke challenging emotional reactions and has been described as "grueling and demanding" (Norcross, 2000). It can take an emotional toll and contribute to depression, anxiety, emotional exhaustion, and disrupted relationships if appropriate self-care is not undertaken (Norcross, 2000). A consistent finding is that those who are younger or newer to therapy work are at increased risk of burnout or VT (Leiter & Harvie, 1996; Pearlman & Mac Ian, 1995; VanDeusen & Way, 2006). Beginning psychotherapists can be more easily overburdened by a high caseload and difficult clients until they develop more therapeutic knowledge and increased positive personal coping skills to balance their professional stresses.

Research has found that emotional problems are common in mental health practitioners and trainees. Many psychotherapists and psychotherapy trainees have experienced problems with anxiety, depression, or substance abuse (Kuyken, Peters, Power, & Lavender, 2003). A higher baseline level of anxiety puts one at greater risk for burnout (Maslach, 2003). Pope and Tabachnick (1993) found that over 60 percent of their sample of psychologists had experienced at least one episode of clinical depression, over 25 percent had suicidal ideation at some point in the past, and almost 4 percent had made at least one suicide attempt. In a study of impaired mental health professionals, Katsavdakis, Gabbard, and Athey (2004) found that the most common problems—in order of frequency—were marital problems, suicidal behavior, work problems, boundary violation, drug abuse, and alcohol abuse. In a different study, Brooks, Holttum, and Lavender (2002) found that although a sample of British psychology trainees had better adjustment scores overall than the general population, 40 percent had problems in at least one of these areas: depression, anxiety, self-esteem, and work adjustment; also, a significant proportion had some problems with substance abuse. Johnston, Smethurst, and Gowers (2005) found that one third of mental health professionals treating eating disorders in their U.K. sample had a history of an eating disorder themselves.

We psychotherapists try to pay meticulous attention to detail since our clients depend on us to provide good care and assess their emergencies carefully. It is adaptive for us to be active problem-solvers and to often think about how to improve the care that we provide. Unfortunately, in the extreme, these adaptive traits can be maladaptive, becoming perfectionism (Wittenberg & Norcross, 2001) and self-blame (Norcross, 2000).

Ethnic minority students may also experience unique stressors during their training years, including overt and covert racism, feeling alone, worries about fitting in, lack of acknowledgment of one's identity, and feeling vulnerable (Vasquez et al., 2006). Whether compounded with ethnic differences or not, other differences between students and their teachers, peers, and clients, such as those of social class, disability status, and sexual orientation, can be challenging as well.

International students can struggle with cultural adjustment, distance from family, and social alienation (Mittal & Wieling, 2006). Specific challenges that mental health graduate students discussed included stresses due to level of English proficiency, feeling like an outsider, different interpersonal norms, and being judged according to national stereotypes. Positive experiences of international students included support from fellow students and faculty, as well as encouragement for cross-cultural research.

## UNDERSTAND YOUR TRAUMA HISTORY
## (IF YOU HAVE ONE)

This afternoon, as my patient sat before me describing his difficult emotions and concerns, my brain went into lockdown. I stared at his face, saw his lips move, and heard his voice, but my ability to process information was lost. Instead, my mind was hijacked by a stream of disturbing images from my own experiences in Iraq: a young marine burning alive in his armored vehicle, the guard outside our dining facility who had her head taken off by a rocket-propelled grenade, one of my long-term clients literally blown to pieces by an IED shortly before he was to return home. Flooded by a sudden onset of these memories, I briefly lost all awareness of the marine sitting in front of me. When my patient said, "Sir, are you okay?" I stared back blankly, feeling nothing. For the first time in seven months, I had nothing to offer, not compassion, not hope, not encouragement; some invisible boundary had been crossed and I was no longer able to relate to anyone else's sadness or process any more tragedy. (Anonymous military psychologist as quoted in Johnson et al., 2011, p. 96)

Like any other group of adults, many mental health professionals have a history of childhood physical or sexual abuse. The rate of childhood sexual or physical abuse for psychotherapists appears similar to or perhaps slightly greater than the rate in the general population (Feldman-Summers & Pope, 1994; Little & Hamby, 1996; Pope & Feldman-Summers, 1992). In addition, many psychotherapists have experienced other traumas: rape, domestic violence (Pope & Feldman-Summers, 1992), and combat (Johnson et al., 2011), as described above.

If you are a psychotherapist who has a history of trauma, you will have a greater intuitive understanding of what your traumatized clients have experienced. However, you also face some risks. While it is normal to have strong emotional reactions at times when working with traumatized clients, psychotherapists who were new to working with traumatized clients and had a history of sexual trauma displayed significantly greater emotional disruption (Dunkley & Whelan, 2006; Nelson-Gardell & Harris, 2003; Pearlman & Mac Ian, 1995). Compared to other psychotherapists, psychotherapists who have a history of childhood sexual abuse reported that they made more boundary mistakes in therapy and cried more with clients (Little & Hamby, 1996). They also sometimes shared their experiences of sexual abuse with clients, and they usually felt angrier with the client's perpetrator than other psychotherapists did (Little & Hamby, 1996). If you have a history of trauma, do not share this with clients. Instead, thoroughly discuss your thoughts about taking this step with a supervisor (or a consultant) *and* your own psychotherapist. If you cannot envision discussing your trauma history with your supervisor, do not discuss it with clients either.

While sexual feelings are equally common in male and female psychotherapists, male psychotherapists are at greatest risk for sexual boundary violations; the most recent research I found estimates that about 9 percent of male psychotherapists but less than 1 percent of female psychotherapists have had sexual relations with a client (Jackson & Nuttall, 2001). Although the number of male psychotherapists with a history of childhood sexual abuse was too small to draw any definitive conclusions, the researchers found that men with a history of childhood sexual abuse, especially those with more severe sexual abuse *and* emotional distress, may be at greatest risk of sexual boundary violations (Jackson & Nuttall, 2001).

In conclusion, if you have a trauma history, understand that you may be more vulnerable to emotional distress when working with clients, especially when you are less experienced. You must also pay very close attention to boundary issues, especially when you are tempted to self-disclose or when there is sexual transference or countertransference. Seek out psychotherapy, consultation, and supervision as needed.

## GET PERSONAL PSYCHOTHERAPY

When I was a graduate student, my academic director of training recommended that I get personal psychotherapy in a rather punitive way. Later I realized that—despite its tone—this advice was some of the best I ever got. I found a nurturing and accepting therapist who helped me explore the emotional and interpersonal impact of my trauma history. The gains I made in my own psychotherapy over the years have led to fulfillment that I could never have imagined thirty years ago on that fateful day in graduate school. (Anonymous psychotherapist, personal communication, October 27, 2007)

For our own mental health and the mental health of our clients, it is essential that we monitor ourselves adequately for stress and take appropriate steps to address our emotional difficulties. For the reasons cited previously (and others), about half of psychology graduate students seek psychotherapy during their graduate studies (Dearing, Maddux, & Tangney, 2005), and 75 to 85 percent of psychotherapists have been in psychotherapy themselves, generally on more than one occasion (Bike, Norcross, & Schatz, 2009; Norcross, 2005; Pope & Tabachnick, 1993).

The potential benefits of personal psychotherapy for the psychotherapist are numerous (Norcross, 2005): improved emotional functioning, reduced countertransference potential, alleviating the stress of being a psychotherapist, demonstrating the transformative power of psychotherapy through personal experience, developing increased sensitivity to the struggles of clients, and developing clinical skills by observing one's own psychotherapist. One study found that those psychotherapists who had received personal psychotherapy reported more personal growth and less burnout (Linley & Joseph, 2007).

If you are interested in seeking psychotherapy, ask a trusted peer, supervisor, or colleague for some recommendations. Many private practitioners are happy to see mental health graduate students for a reduced fee, especially if you can arrange your schedule to come during the daytime hours, which are more difficult to fill. Many graduate programs already provide all their students with a list of recommended psychotherapists in the local community. Avoid seeking psychotherapy at any agency or setting that trains students from your graduate program.

## GAIN PROFESSIONAL COMPETENCE

Gaining knowledge will help allay your anxiety about treating difficult populations. Getting consultation or supervision can also be helpful at any stage in one's professional development. As you become more experienced and knowledgeable, your professional competence and confidence will grow. One of the advantages of being a mental health professional is that there is always something new and interesting to learn about in our field.

Professionals who work in a medical center setting are at an advantage, as there are often grand rounds and other professional presentations readily available. Professionals in medical center and university settings have ready access to professional libraries and academic search databases and search tools to help them stay current.

Important developments, both research and theoretical, occur every year, and we must figure out how to gain and use this knowledge for the benefit of our clients. Attending at least one professional conference every year or two will help keep you up on the latest developments in the field. Popular press items can be informative, including the magazines *Scientific American, Mind,* and *Discover* as well as the *New York Times,* especially the Tuesday science section. Reading several professional books per year is helpful. When you graduate, you might want to join or start a book or journal club so that you can keep current with the help of colleagues.

## DEVELOP AREAS OF EXPERTISE

Many psychotherapy graduate students are overwhelmed by the amount of information that they do not know. It is true that the professional literature is vast, and no one of us can know any more than a fraction of it. However, competent professionals develop certain areas of practice that they are interested in and become especially knowledgeable about these topics. Perhaps you might have an intrinsic interest in a particular topic, or maybe you've had a training placement that sparked an interest in a certain client population. Go ahead and nurture this professional interest. Go to specific conferences about the topic. When you have to do a research paper, do one in your interest area whenever possible.

Your enthusiasm about your areas of interest and expertise will be helpful to you in several ways. This enthusiasm will help carry you through any difficult professional periods. You will be more motivated to keep up with the field because of your interest level. You will find it easier to get a job because you know what you are interested in and you will seek it out. Employers will appreciate your level of knowledge and your enthusiasm.

Don't worry if you don't have an area of expertise right now. If you are right for the psychotherapy field, one area of interest (or probably more than one) will make itself known sooner or later. Just be patient and be alert for it to develop.

## DEVELOP SUPPORTIVE PROFESSIONAL RELATIONSHIPS

Supportive relationships with other mental health professionals are an essential portion of your professional development. It helps to have relationships with others who have various levels of experience. Many mental health professionals also end up with a life partner who is a psychotherapist as well. Greater professional support leads to better professional functioning (Kuyken et al., 2003). In addition, as a beginning psychotherapist, open and supportive relationships with your supervisors can be invaluable in your personal and professional development.

Developing good professional relationships is also a form of networking. These relationships may help you obtain recommendations and even employment in the future.

Ethnic minority students and professionals often have professional challenges that White students do not (Vasquez et al., 2006). Family members often tell the ethnic minority student, "You have to work twice as hard to be thought half as good" (Vasquez et al., 2006, p. 161), which can result in workaholism and greater work stress. Ethnic minority psychotherapists can find it particularly helpful to seek out additional mentoring and supportive relationships with other professionals of similar ethnicity, even if they are at a geographic distance (Gonzalez-Figueroa & Young, 2005; Vasquez et al., 2006), and certain White mentors can be found who will have confidence in the abilities of the ethnic minority student as well (Vasquez et al., 2006).

Your supportive colleagues will provide helpful validation and consultation for you as you progress professionally. When you have a professional ethics question, you will have someone to call. When you need support with a difficult client, you can readily get professional consultation. When you are making a professional transition, you will have others who can advise you—and you can do the same for your colleagues.

## MAKE PROFESSIONAL CONTRIBUTIONS

Making professional contributions helps you give back to the mental health community and encourages you to maintain your competence as well. You may be interested in volunteering your time and expertise at a community organization with a worthy cause. Or you may be interested in lobbying your state or federal representatives on mental health–related issues. There is a way to make a contribution for every psychotherapist's temperament: writing, lecturing, teaching, research, supervising, consulting, and involvement in professional organizations.

## DEVELOP RESILIENCY IN RESPONSE TO ADVERSE PROFESSIONAL EVENTS

As psychotherapists, we are at risk of a multitude of adverse events. We might be embroiled in the legal system through malpractice suits, subpoenas, and dispositions; I have recommended a resource at the end of the chapter for giving testimony. We could experience adverse client events, such as having clients die by suicide, being stalked by a client, or being threatened by a client. Many of these adverse events are unfortunately common. For example, nearly 20 percent of a random sample of Australian psychologists had been stalked for at least 2 weeks by a client (Purcell, Powell, & Mullen, 2005), and 21 percent of a sample of U.K. psychiatrists had been stalked (McIvor, Potter, & Davies, 2008). Having a client die by suicide is all too common, with 25 to 50 percent of licensed psychotherapists experiencing a client suicide (McAdams & Foster, 2000); psychiatrists have the highest risk because of the number of clients they see for medication management. Various U.S. and international studies have found that the majority of mental health practitioners will experience at least one physical threat or assault in their careers; psychiatrists and nurses are at greatest risk (Arthur, Brende, & Quiroz, 2003; Lawoko, Soares, & Nolan, 2004; Pieters, Speybrouck, De Gucht, & Joss, 2005).

Being knowledgeable about how to manage these crises from clinical, legal, and ethical perspectives can help us be prepared for whatever may happen. If the worst does happen, do not hesitate to seek support from colleagues, friends, and family. Discuss the event with sympathetic and informed colleagues to gain perspective.

## KEEP BALANCED AND REPLENISH YOURSELF

As we all know, graduate students often have a streak of perfectionism and/or workaholism. These traits are often coupled with what I call "graduate student guilt," the idea that there is work that you *should* be doing at every waking moment and that, if you aren't, you deserve to feel guilty. If you are tired, exhausted, and burned out, you can't be helpful to your clients because you aren't taking care of yourself.

Keeping yourself emotionally replenished is an essential personal task for the psychotherapist. Allow yourself personal time to maintain a balance between your personal and professional lives and pursue activities that refresh you. Endeavor to set aside a significant period of time every week when you do not work on classwork. If you are religious, this could perhaps be Shabbat or Sunday. If not, choose any other time period that works for you, preferably lasting at least 24 hours. You might do some housework then or spend time with your friends, children, and/or partner. During the rest of the week, try to have a little personal or family time every day. Other wellness activities that psychotherapists find helpful include physical activity, varying your work responsibilities, spending time with friends, and spending time with family (Lawson & Myers, 2011), as well as maintaining a sense of humor, personal/professional balance, and engaging in hobbies (Rupert & Kent, 2007).

There is nothing wrong with television, but use it in moderation when you choose to, not just to avoid schoolwork. If you need time away from schoolwork, try to use that time mindfully and choose activities that you will really enjoy. Perhaps you might want to develop and pursue a hobby even if it is only for an hour every week or two.

Research shows that many simple things increase happiness, or subjective well-being, as some authors prefer to call it. People who are more socially connected (Kawachi & Berkman, 2001) tend to be happier. People who consciously practice gratitude are happier (Seligman, Steen, Park, & Peterson, 2005). Flow experiences increase happiness. Flow is "a particular kind of experience that is so engrossing and enjoyable that it becomes...worth doing for its own sake even though it may have no consequence outside itself. Creative activities, music, sports, games and religious rituals are typical sources for this kind of experience" (Csikszentmihalyi,

1999, p. 824). People who experience flow are invigorated and have a greater sense of well-being (Csikszentmihalyi, 1999).

Recharge your batteries by taking a weeklong vacation at least twice each year—and don't take any work with you. Be sure your clients know that you will not be available to them by phone or e-mail when on vacation (Webb, 2011) and what your coverage arrangements are.

There is some preliminary evidence that mindfulness practices such as yoga, qigong, and meditation can be helpful self-care practices for psychotherapists (Christopher et al., 2011; Christopher, Christopher, Dunnagan, & Schure, 2006; Newsome, Christopher, Dahlen, & Christopher, 2006). Sitting meditation can be helpful in reducing depression and increasing positive mood states (Jain et al., 2007), and case reports suggest that meditation may help you gain perspective in difficult countertransference situations (Christensen & Rudnick, 1999; Cooper, 1999). Recent research also suggests that sitting meditation may be especially helpful in alleviating distress by reducing ruminative thoughts (Jain et al., 2007; Ramel, Goldin, Carmona, & McQuaid, 2004) and increasing positive affect (Davidson et al., 2003).Walking meditation can be helpful when you are feeling agitated, anxious, or frustrated. It can be helpful to get instruction in meditation, and meditating regularly with others strengthens that practice.

The research in well-being and religion shows mixed and inconsistent findings (Lewis & Cruise, 2006). This research tends to equate Christianity and/or mono-theism with spirituality, which is inappropriate in our 21st-century multicultural society. For example, Hinduism, one of the world's five major religions, is polythe-istic, as are many indigenous religions, and many Buddhists consider themselves agnostic or atheist. Of course, you are the best judge of whether religious practice would be an uplifting and replenishing experience for you; if so, make time to participate actively with your preferred religious group.

## APPRECIATE THE REWARDS OF BEING A PSYCHOTHERAPIST

There are profound rewards that come from a career as a psychotherapist. I will leave you with the words of a colleague and the words of two prominent psycho-therapists, teachers, and writers on the subject.

> On a regular basis I'm given the chance to bear witness to the most personal, moving and ultimately the most profound struggles that are part and parcel of the human condition for all of us. I'm allowed to participate in and to influence in some small—and at times not so small—way the unfolding of another person's life, all the while being profoundly influenced myself by the whole process. This work has brought a depth and breadth to my own life and personhood that I can't imagine being afforded to me in any other line of work. How lucky is that? (M. E. Bratu, personal communication, June 8, 2007)

To my mind, the ultimate satisfaction in being a therapist is the opportunity to earn a living by being honest, curious, and committed to trying to do right by others.... While many professions involve service to others, the vocation of psychotherapy allows for a particularly intimate, organic, integrated kind of helping that makes one's work meaningful and fulfilling, no matter how tiring. I am grateful that such a role exists in my era and culture, a role that allows me to earn a living by doing what I enjoy doing and find consonant with my temperament.... Watching a client grow psychologically is the closest analogue we have in professional life to the experience of watching a beloved child change into a self-assured adult. There is nothing like it. (McWilliams, 2004, pp. 282–283)

Those who are cradlers of secrets are granted a clarifying lens through which to view the world—a view with less distortion, denial and illusion, a view of the way things really are.... When I turn to others with the knowledge that we are all (therapist and patient alike) burdened with painful secrets—guilt for acts committed, shame for actions not taken, yearnings to be loved and cherished, deep vulnerabilities, insecurities and fears—I draw closer to them. Being a cradler of secrets has, as the years have passed, made me gentler and more accepting. When I encounter individuals inflated with vanity of self-importance, or distracted by any of a myriad of consuming passions, I intuit the pain of their underlying secrets and feel not judgment but compassion, and above all, connectedness.... [W]e are the midwife to the birth of something new, liberating and elevating. We watch our patients let go of old self-defeating patterns, detach from ancient grievances, develop zest for living, learn to love us, and through that act, turn lovingly to others.... What a treat it is to watch them open doors to rooms never before entered, discover new wings of their house containing parts in exile—wise, beautiful, and creative pieces of identity. (Yalom, 2002, pp. 257–258)

## CONCLUSION

I began this book by telling you about my feelings of anxiety as well as my hunch that I was somehow ill prepared when I saw my first psychotherapy client as a graduate student. Since then, as a teacher and supervisor, I have thought long and hard about what beginning students need to know when they walk into that first psychotherapy session. This book has been the culmination of those thoughts. My sincerest hope is that this book helps you, in some way, on your journey to become a well-prepared, competent, and confident psychotherapist.

### Recommended Reading

Astin, M. C. (1997). Traumatic therapy: How helping rape victims affects me as a therapist. *Women and Therapy, 20,* 101–109.

*Astin powerfully describes the personal impact of working with rape victims and how she has learned to cope.*

Brodsky, S. L. (1991). *Testifying in court: Guidelines and maxims for the expert witness.* Washington, DC: American Psychological Association.

*Brodsky's books, including this one, provide helpful and practical advice for any mental health professional (whether you are an expert witness or not) who has become embroiled in the legal system. If you are ever subpoenaed and you have to give testimony in court or give a deposition, read this first. In addition, talk to a lawyer about the difference between an expert witness and a witness of fact.*

Csikszentmihalyi, M. (1999). If we are so rich, why aren't we happy? *American Psychologist, 10,* 821–827.

*In this well-written article, Csikszentmihalyi summarizes much of the research on happiness, income, and flow and draws some profound conclusions about human existence and well-being.*

Glinkauf-Hughes, C., & Mehlman, E. (1995). Narcissistic issues in therapists: Diagnostic and treatment considerations. *Psychotherapy, 32,* 213–221.

*Despite its off-putting title, this article is simply about gaining insight into common emotional issues among psychotherapists, such as parentification, perfectionism, and the imposter phenomenon.*

Nhat Hanh, T. (1975). *The miracle of mindfulness: A manual on meditation.* Boston: Beacon Press.

*A short classic volume to introduce the reader to basic meditation practices.*

Norcross, J. C., & Guy, J. D. (2007). *Leaving it at the office: A guide to psychotherapist self-care.* New York: Guilford Press.

*The authors discuss helpful issues for psychotherapists, such as nurturing relationships, setting boundaries, fostering creativity and growth, and others.*

## ONLINE RESOURCE

http://www.authentichappiness.sas.upenn.edu

*This is the website for the University of Pennsylvania Positive Psychology Center, which has numerous interesting resources regarding the psychological study of happiness.*

## DISCUSSION QUESTIONS

1. Have you met any mental health professionals who appear to be suffering from burnout and/or vicarious traumatization? Without naming any names, what signs have they given that suggest this to you?
2. Considering what you have learned from this chapter and your own personal temperament, what do you think would be most helpful to you in managing or avoiding burnout and vicarious traumatization?
3. What are the costs to you of being a psychotherapist?
4. How has the process of becoming a psychotherapist changed you personally? Has it changed your personal relationships? How?
5. Have you found it rewarding to be a psychotherapist? If so, in what ways?

One of my struggles in writing this book was a striking lack of literature about certain practical concerns. Some authors helpfully shared their personal experiences and insights, and I referenced these when possible.

However, there is little to no research about certain clinically important topics. I have listed some of my questions about those topics here. I hope that this might inspire research and further writing by mental health professionals.

- What do clients think about what their psychotherapists wear? Do they care about earrings and tattoos? Do these opinions change with the client's age?
- What coping strategies—adaptive and maladaptive—do psychotherapists use to cope with their clients' emotional pain? Can trainees be taught these coping strategies?
- How do clients react to the psychotherapist's office decor? What about plants? Family pictures? Religious symbols? Color schemes? Presence or absence of "ethnic" art? Does it matter whether this "ethnic" art matches the client's ethnicity?
- What are typical attendance, cancellation, no-show, and fee policies in different therapy settings? What is the impact of different policies on client retention?
- What factors predict no-shows and cancellations? What methods of addressing these in therapy are most effective?
- How do clients react to psychotherapists' pregnancies? Do these reactions differ by client? How? Do men have any similar issues with taking paternity leave?
- What are common boundary crossings in therapy (e.g., gifts, hugs, and attending client events)? How often do they occur? How are these boundary crossings typically handled? Why did the psychotherapist allow the boundary crossing, and what was the effect on therapy?
- Which personal questions are psychotherapists willing to answer, and which ones do they refuse? How much does this vary by theoretical orientation?

- How many psychotherapists have a history of treatment for more serious mental illnesses (e.g., major depression, bipolar disorder, schizophrenia, or post-traumatic stress disorder)? Do these psychotherapists ever reveal this to their clients? Under what circumstances?
- How often do mental health professionals have to cope with prejudicial behavior on the part of clients? What are the best ways of coping with this?
- How much do psychotherapists typically tell their partners, friends, and relatives about their work? Does this differ depending on whether the partner is a psychotherapist as well? How much is unavoidable? How much is too much?
- What kind of personal Internet presence do psychotherapists have? What do they think is appropriate? Does this vary by age?
- What do psychotherapists say to start a psychotherapy session? Do they say the same thing every time? What are the differences in how therapy sessions start by theoretical orientation?
- How much do beginning psychotherapists suffer from vicarious traumatization and burnout? How much do they simply feel overwhelmed?

And, finally, while there is some interesting and informative research on transference and countertransference, far too few researchers are working on it, and there is clearly promise for interdisciplinary research with cognitive neuroscientists and social psychologists that remains to be done.

# ABOUT THE AUTHOR

Jan Willer is an adjunct faculty member at DePaul University in Chicago. As a former psychology internship training director, she has lectured, taught, and published on mental health training. She has a private practice in Chicago. Her website is www. drwiller.com.

Abe, K., Mertz, K. J., Powell, K. E., & Hanzlick, K. L. (2006). Characteristics of Black and White suicide decedents in Fulton County, Georgia, 1988–1992. *American Journal of Public Health, 96*, 1794–1798.

Ackerly, G. D., Burnell, J., Holder, D. C., & Kurdek, L. A. (1988). Burnout among licensed psychologists. *Professional Psychology: Research and Practice, 19*, 624–631.

Agar, K., Read, J., & Bush, J. (2002). Identification of abuse histories in community mental health centre: The need for policies and training. *Journal of Mental Health, 11*, 533–543.

Alexander, J. L. (2007). Client suicide: This is not happening to me: A clinical report and personal memoir. *Smith College Studies in Social Work, 77*(2/3), 67–78.

Alexandratos, K., Barnett, F., & Thomas, Y. (2012). The impact of exercise on the mental health and quality of life of people with severe mental illness: A critical review. *British Journal of Occupational Therapy, 75*(2), 48–60.

Allen, H. (2005, September 9). Last words: A testament to Hunter Thompson. Washington Post. Retrieved August 28, 2012, from http://www.washingtonpost.com/wp-dyn/content/article/2005/09/08/AR2005090801993.html

Alvarez, K. M., Donohue, B., Kenny, M. C., Cavanagh, N., & Romero, V. (2004). The process and consequences of reporting child maltreatment: A brief overview for professionals in the mental health field. *Aggression and Violent Behavior, 10*, 311–331.

Alvarez, K. M., Kenny, M. C., Donohue, B., & Carpin, K. M. (2004). Why are professionals failing to initiate mandated reports of child maltreatment, and are there any empirically based training programs to assist professionals in the reporting process? *Aggression and Violent Behavior, 9*, 563–578.

American Association of Suicidology. (n.d.). *Eating disorders and suicide.* Washington, DC: American Association of Suicidology. Retrieved from http://www.suicidology.org.

American Association of Suicidology. (n.d.). *The economy and suicide.* Washington, DC: American Association of Suicidology. Retrieved from http://www.suicidology.org.

American Association of Suicidology. (n.d.). *Risk factors for suicide and suicidal behaviors.* Washington, DC: American Association of Suicidology. Retrieved from http://www.suicidology.org.

American Association of Suicidology. (n.d.). *Suicide and asthma.* Washington, DC: American Association of Suicidology. Retrieved from http://www.suicidology.org.

American Counseling Association. (2005). ACA code of ethics. Retrieved January 11, 2007, from http://www.counseling.org/Resources/aca-code-of-ethics.pdf.

American Lung Association. (2007). When COPD symptoms get worse. Retrieved January 20, 2012, from http://www.lungusa.org/associations/states/minnesota/events-programs/mn-copd-coalition/patient-toolkit/when-symptoms-get-worse.pdf

American Lung Association (2011). Asthma triggers. Retrieved January 20, 2012, from http://www.lungusa.org/lung-disease/asthma/living-with-asthma/take-control-of-your-asthma/asthma-triggers.html

American Psychiatric Association. (2000). *Diagnostic and statistical manual of mental disorders* (4th ed., text revision). Washington, DC: Author.

American Psychiatric Association. (2003). *Practice guideline for the assessment and treatment of patients with suicidal behaviors.* Arlington, VA: American Psychiatric Association.

American Psychiatric Association. (2010). *The principles of medical ethics with annotations especially applicable to psychiatry.* Arlington, VA: American Psychiatric Association.

American Psychological Association. (2002). Ethical principles of psychologists and code of conduct. *American Psychologist, 57*(12), 1060–1073.

American Psychological Association. (2010). Ethical principles of psychologists and code of conduct 2010 Amendments. Retrieved January 26, 2012, from http://www.apa.org/ethics/code/index.aspx

American Psychological Association Practice Organization. (2007, Winter). Putting HIPAA into Practice. *In Good practice: Topical edition.* Washington, DC: Author.

American Psychological Association Practice Organization. (2012, Spring/Summer). Social media: What's your policy? *Good Practice*, pp. 10–11, 18.

American Psychological Association Presidential Task Force on Evidence-Based Practice. (2006). Evidence-based practice in psychology. *American Psychologist, 61,* 271–285.

Andersen, S. M., & Berk, M. S. (1998). Transference in everyday experience: Implications of experimental research for relevant clinical phenomena. *Review of General Psychology, 2,* 81–120.

Andersen, S. M., & Chen, S. (2002). The relational self: An interpersonal social-cognitive theory. *Psychological Review, 109,* 619–645.

Anderson, A. (1999). "Don't scream, Miss Annie, don't scream." *American Family Physician, 59,* 213–215.

Anderson, K. L. (2002). Perpetrator or victim? Relationships between intimate partner violence and well-being. *Journal of Marriage and Family, 64,* 851–863.

Anderson, T. R., Bell, C. C., Powell, T. E., Williamson, J. L., & Blount, M. A. (2004). Assessing psychiatric patients for violence. *Community Mental Health Journal, 40,* 379–399.

Anglin, D. M., Gabriel, K. O. S., & Kaslow, N. J. (2005). Suicide acceptability and religious well-being: A comparative analysis in African American suicide attempters and non-attempters. *Journal of Psychology and Theology, 33*(2), 140–150.

Angst, J., & Cassano, G. (2005). The mood spectrum: Improving the diagnosis of bipolar disorder. *Bipolar Disorders, 7,* 4–12.

Appleby, L., Shaw, J., Amos, T., McDonnell, R., Harris, C., McCann, K., et al. (1999). Suicide within 12 months of contact with mental health services: National clinical survey. *British Medical Journal, 318,* 1235–1239.

Arthur, G. L., Brende, J. O., & Quiroz, S. E. (2003). Violence: Incidence and frequency of physical and psychological assaults affecting mental health providers in Georgia. *Journal of General Psychology, 130*, 22–45.

Ashton, V. (2004). The effect of personal characteristics on reporting child maltreatment. *Child Abuse and Neglect, 28*, 985–997.

Astin, M. C. (1997). Traumatic therapy: How helping rape victims affects me as a therapist. *Women and Therapy, 20*, 101–109.

Aubry, T. D., Hunsley, J., Josephson, G., & Vito, D. (2000). Quid pro quo: Fee for services delivered in a psychology training clinic. *Journal of Clinical Psychology, 56*, 23–31.

Azikiwe, N., Wright, J., Cheng, T., & D'Angelo, L. J. (2005). Management of rape victims (regarding STD treatment and pregnancy prevention): Do academic emergency departments practice what they preach? *Journal of Adolescent Health, 36*, 446–448.

Bachelor, A. (1995). Clients' perception of the therapeutic alliance: A qualitative analysis. *Journal of Counseling Psychology, 42*, 323–337.

Baerger, D. R. (2001). Risk management with the suicidal patient: Lessons from case law. *Professional Psychology: Research and Practice, 32*, 359–366.

Baker, F. M., & Bell, C. C. (1999). Issues in the psychiatric treatment of African Americans. *Psychiatric Services, 50*, 362–368.

Balsam, K. F., & Mohr, J. J. (2007). Adaptation to sexual orientation stigma: A comparison of bisexual and lesbian/gay adults. *Journal of Counseling Psychology, 54*, 306–319.

Banerjee, S., Chowdhury, A. N., Schelling, E., Brahma, A., Biswas, M. K., & Weiss, M. G. (2009). Deliberate self-harm and suicide by pesticide ingestion in the Sundarban region, India. *Tropical Medicine and International Health, 14*(2), 213–219.

Barlow, K., Grenyer, B., & Ilkiw-Lavalle, O. (2000). Prevalence and precipitants of aggression in psychiatric inpatient units. *Australian and New Zealand Journal of Psychiatry, 34*, 967–974.

Barnett, J. E. (2011). Psychotherapist self-disclosure: Ethical and clinical considerations. *Psychotherapy, 48*(4), 315–321.

Barnett, J. E., Cornish, J. A. E., Goodyear, R. K., & Lichtenberg, J. W. (2007). Commentaries on the ethical and effective practice of clinical supervision. *Professional Psychology: Research and Practice, 38*(3), 268–275.

Barnett, J. E., Wise, E. H., Johnson-Greene, D., & Bucky, S. F. (2007). Informed consent: Too much of a good thing or not enough? *Professional Psychology: Research and Practice, 38*(2), 179–186.

Baron, J. (1996). Some issues in psychotherapy with gay and lesbian clients. *Psychotherapy, 33*, 611–616.

Bateman, A., & Fonagy, P. (2001). Treatment of borderline personality disorder with psychoanalytically oriented partial hospitalization: An 18-month follow-up. *American Journal of Psychiatry, 158*(1), 36–42.

Bateman, A., & Fonagy, P. (2003). Health service utilization costs for borderline personality disorder patients treated with psychoanalytically oriented partial hospitalization versus general psychiatric care. *American Journal of Psychiatry, 160*(1), 169–171.

Beach, K., & Power, M. (1996). Transference: An empirical investigation across a range of cognitive-behavioural and psychoanalytic therapies. *Clinical Psychology and Psychotherapy, 3*, 1–14.

Beahrs, J. O., & Gutheil, T. G. (2001). Informed consent in psychotherapy. *American Journal of Psychiatry, 158*, 4–10.

Bean, H., Softas-Nall, L., & Mahoney, M. (2011). Reflections on mandated reporting and challenges in the therapeutic relationship: A case study with systematic implications. *The Family Journal, 19*, 286–290.

Bebbington, P. E., Cooper, C., Minot, S., Brugha, T. S., Jenkins, R., Meltzer, H., & Dennis, M. (2009). Suicide attempts, gender, and sexual abuse: Data from the 2000 British Psychiatric Morbidity Survey. *American Journal of Psychiatry, 166*(10), 1135–1140.

Beck, A. T., Brown, G., & Steer, R. A. (1989). Prediction of eventual suicide in psychiatric inpatients by clinical ratings of hopelessness. *Journal of Consulting and Clinical Psychology, 57*, 309–310.

Beck, J. S. (1995). *Cognitive therapy: Basics and beyond.* New York: Guilford Press.

Beck, J. S. (2005). *Cognitive therapy for challenging problems: What to do when the basics don't work.* New York: Guilford Press.

Beeman, D. G., & Scott, N. A. (1991). Therapists' attitudes toward psychotherapy informed consent with adolescents. *Professional Psychology: Research and Practice, 22*, 230–234.

Berg, A. Z., Bell, C. C., & Tupin, J. (2000). Clinician safety: Assessing and managing the violent patient. *New Directions for Mental Health Services, 86*, 9–28.

Berger, S. S., & Buchholz, E. S. (1993). On becoming a supervisee: Preparation for learning in a supervisory relationship. *Psychotherapy, 30*, 86–92.

Bergeron, L. R., & Gray, B. (2003). Ethical dilemmas of reporting suspected elder abuse. *Social Work, 48*, 96–105.

Berman, A. L. (2006). Risk management with suicidal patients. *Journal of Clinical Psychology, 62*(2), 171–184.

Berman, A. L., Shepherd, G., & Silverman, M. M. (2003). The LSARS-II: Lethality of Suicide Attempt Rating Scale-Updated. *Suicide and Life-Threatening Behavior, 33*(3), 261–276.

Bernsen, A., Tabachnick, B. G., & Pope, K. S. (1994). National survey of social workers' sexual attraction to their clients: Results, implications, and comparison to psychologists. *Ethics and Behavior, 4*, 369–388.

Bernstein, D. A., Borkovek, T. D., & Hazlett-Stevens, H. (2000). *New directions in progressive relaxation training: A guidebook for helping professionals.* Westport, CT: Praeger Paperback.

Besharov, D. J., & Laumann, L. A. (1996). Child abuse reporting. *Society, 33*, 40–46.

Betan, E., Heim, A. K., Conklin, C. Z., & Westen, D. (2005). Countertransference phenomena and personality pathology in clinical practice: An empirical investigation. *American Journal of Psychiatry, 162*, 890–898.

Beyerstein, B. L. (1997). Why bogus therapies often seem to work. *Skeptical Inquirer, 21*, 29–34. Retrieved August 12, 2007, from http://www.csicop.org/si/show/why_bogus_therapies_seem_to_work/.

Bhattacharya, A. K., Bhattacharjee, S., Chattopadhyay, S., Roy, P., Kanji, D., & Singh, O. P. (2011). Deliberate self-harm: A search for distinct group of suicide. *Indian Journal of Psychological Medicine, 33*(2), 182–187.

Bhuvaneswar, C. G., & Gutheil, T. G. (2008). E-mail and psychiatry: Some psychotherapeutic and psychoanalytic perspectives. *American Journal of Psychotherapy, 62*(3), 241–261.

Bienen, M. (1990). The pregnant therapist: Countertransference dilemmas and willingness to explore transference material. *Psychotherapy, 27*, 607–612.

Bieschke, K. J., Perez, R. M., & DeBord, K. A. (Eds.). (2006). *Handbook of counseling and psychotherapy with lesbian, gay, bisexual, and transgender clients* (2nd ed.). Washington, DC: American Psychological Association.

Bike, D. H., Norcross, J. C., & Schatz, D. M. (2009). Processes and outcomes of psychotherapists' personal therapy: Replication and extension 20 years later. *Psychotherapy Theory, Research, Practice, Training, 46*(1), 19–31.

Birky, I., & Collins, W. (2011). Facebook: Maintaining ethical practice in the cyberspace age. *Journal of College Student Psychotherapy, 25*, 193–203.

Blonigen, D. M., Timko, C., Finney, J. W., Moos, B. S., & Moos, R. H. (2011). Alcoholics Anonymous attendance, decreases in impulsivity and drinking and psychosocial outcomes over 16 years: Moderated-mediation from a developmental perspective. *Addiction, 106*(12), 2167–2177.

Bolton, C., Gooding, P., Kapur, N., Barrowclough, C., & Tarrier, N. (2007). Developing psychological perspectives of suicidal behaviour and risk in people with a diagnosis of schizophrenia: We know they kill themselves but do we understand why? *Clinical Psychology Review, 27*(4), 511–536.

Bolton, S. L., & Sareen, J. (2011). Sexual orientation and its relation to mental disorders and suicide attempts: Findings from a nationally representative sample. *Canadian Journal of Psychiatry, 56*(1), 35–43.

Bonati, M., & Clavenna, A. (2005). The epidemiology of psychotropic drug use in children and adolescents. *International Review of Psychiatry, 17*, 181–188.

Bonta, J., Law, M., & Hanson, K. (1998). The prediction of criminal and violent recidivism among mentally disordered offenders: A meta-analysis. *Psychological Bulletin, 123*(2), 123–142.

Borges, G., Orozco, R., Rafful, C., Miller, E., & Breslau, J. (2012). Suicidality, ethnicity and immigration in the USA. *Psychological Medicine, 42*(6), 1175–1184.

Borum, R., & Reddy, M. (2001). Assessing violence risk in *Tarasoff* situations: A fact-based model of inquiry. *Behavioral Sciences and the Law, 18*, 375–385.

Bottrill, S., Pistrang, N., Barker, C., & Worrell, M. (2010). The use of therapist self-disclosure: Clinical psychology trainees' experiences. *Psychotherapy Research, 20*(2), 165–180.

Bowden, C. (2001). Strategies to reduce misdiagnosis of bipolar depression. *Psychiatric Services, 52*, 51–55.

Bowden, C. (2005). A different depression: Clinical distinctions between bipolar and unipolar depression. *Journal of Affective Disorders, 84*, 117–125.

Braaten, E. B., Otto, S., & Handelsman, M. M. (1993). What do people want to know about psychotherapy? *Psychotherapy, 30*, 565–570.

Bradley, R., Heim, A. K., & Westen, D. (2005). Transference patterns in the psychotherapy of personality disorders: Empirical investigation. *British Journal of Psychiatry, 186*, 342–349.

Brase, G. L., & Richmond, J. (2004). The white-coat effect: Physician attire and perceived authority, friendliness and attractiveness. *Journal of Applied Social Psychology, 34*, 2469–2481.

Brendel, D. H., Chu, J., Radden, J., Leeper, H., Pope, H. G., Samson, J.,…Bodkin, J. A. (2007). The price of a gift: An approach to receiving gifts from patients in psychiatric practice. *Harvard Review of Psychiatry, 15*(2), 43–51.

Brendel, R. W., & Bryan, E. (2004). HIPAA for psychiatrists. *Law and Psychiatry, 12,* 177–183.

Brent, D. A., Oquendo, M., Birmaher, B., Greenhill, L., Kolko, D., Stanley, B., et al. (2002). Familial pathways to early-onset suicide attempt: Risk for suicidal behavior in offspring of mood-disordered suicide attempters. *Archives of General Psychiatry, 59,* 801–807.

Bride, B. E. (2007). Prevalence of secondary traumatic stress among social workers. *Social Work, 52*(1), 63–70.

Briere, J., & Gil, E. (1998). Self-mutilation in clinical and general samples: Prevalence, correlates and functions. *American Journal of Orthopsychiatry, 68,* 609–620.

Brodsky, S. L. (1991). *Testifying in court: Guidelines and maxims for the expert witness.* Washington, DC: American Psychological Association.

Brody, E. M., & Farber, B. A. (1996). The effects of therapist experience and patient diagnosis on countertransference. *Psychotherapy, 3,* 372–380.

Brooks, J., Holttum, S., & Lavender, A. (2002). Personality style, psychological adaptation and expectations of trainee clinical psychologists. *Clinical Psychology and Psychotherapy, 9,* 253–270.

Brooks, R. (2012, February 1). Virginia Woolf's suicide. *The Virginia Woolf Blog* [online]. Available: http://virginiawoolfblog.com/when-virginia-went-missing/

Brown, C., & Trangsrud, H. B. (2008). Factors associated with acceptance and decline of client gift giving. *Professional Psychology: Research and Practice, 39*(5), 505–511.

Bryan, C. J., Cukrowicz, K. C., West, C. L., & Morrow, C. E. (2010). Combat experience and the acquired capability for suicide. *Journal of Clinical Psychology, 66*(10), 1044–1056.

Bryan, C. J., Johnson, L. G., Rudd, M. D., & Joiner, T. E. (2008). Hypomanic symptoms among first-time suicide attempters predict future multiple attempt status. *Journal of Clinical Psychology, 64*(4), 519–530.

Bryan, C. J. & Rudd, M. D. (2006). Advances in the assessment of suicide risk. *Journal of Clinical Psychology: In Session, 62*(2), 185–200.

Bryan, C. J., Stone, S. L., & Rudd, M. D. (2011). A practical, evidence-based approach for means-restriction counseling with suicidal patients. *Professional Psychology: Research and Practice, 42*(5), 339–346.

Buchanan, A., Binder, R., Norko, M., & Swartz, M. (2012). Resource document on psychiatric violence risk assessment. *American Journal of Psychiatry, 169*(3), data supplement.

Buka, P., & Sookhoo, D. (2006). Current legal responses to elder abuse. *International Journal of Older People Nursing, 1*(4), 194–200.

Burckell, L. A., & Goldfried, M. R. (2006). Therapist qualities preferred by sexual-minority individuals. *Psychotherapy: Theory, Research, Practice, Training, 43,* 32–49.

Burkard, A. W., Johnson, A. J., Madson, M. B., Pruitt, N. T., Contreras-Tadych, D. A., Kozlowski, J. M., et al. (2006). Supervisor cultural responsiveness and unresponsiveness in cross-cultural supervision. *Journal of Counseling Psychology, 53,* 288–301.

Burkard, A. W., Knox, S., Groen, M., Perez, M., & Hess, S. A. (2006). European American therapist self-disclosure in cross-cultural counseling. *Journal of Counseling Psychology, 53,* 15–25.

Burkard, A. W., Ponterotto, P. G., Reynolds, A. L., & Alfonso, V. C. (1999). White counselor trainees' racial identity and working alliance perceptions. *Journal of Counseling and Development, 77,* 324–329.

Burkholder, D., Toth, M., Feisthamel, K., & Britton, P. (2010). Faculty and student curricular experiences of nonerotic touch in counseling. *Journal of Mental Health Counseling, 32*(2), 168–185.

Burns, J., Dudley, M., Hazell, P., & Patton, G. (2005). Clinical management of deliberate self-harm in young people: The need for evidence-based approaches to reduce repetition. *Australian and New Zealand Journal of Psychiatry, 39*, 121–128.

Busch, S. H. (2009). Medication treatment for ADHD: Controversy abounds. *Health Affairs, 28*(5), 1549–1550.

Callahan, J. (2009). Emergency intervention and crisis intervention. In P. Kleespies (Ed.), *Behavioral emergencies: An evidence-based resource for evaluating and managing risk of suicide, violence, and victimization* (pp. 13–32). Washington, DC: American Psychological Association.

Callanan, V. J., & Davis, M. S. (2012). Gender differences in suicide methods. *Social Psychiatry and Psychiatric Epidemiology, 47*(6), 857–869.

Cameron, S., & turtle-song, i. (2002). Learning to write case notes using the SOAP format. *Journal of Counseling and Development, 80*, 286–292.

Campbell, C. D., & Gordon, M. C. (2003). Acknowledging the inevitable: Understanding multiple relationships in rural practice. *Professional Psychology: Research and Practice, 34*, 430–434.

Campbell, R. (2008). The psychological impact of rape victims' experiences with the legal, medical, and mental health systems. *American Psychologist, 63*(8), 702–717.

Campbell, R., Wasco, S. M., Ahrens, C. E., Sefl, T., & Barnes, H. E. (2001). Preventing the "second rape": Rape survivors' experiences with community service providers. *Journal of Interpersonal Violence, 16*, 1239–1259.

Carey, B. (2006, September 19). A psychiatrist is slain, and a sad debate deepens. *New York Times*. Retrieved June 22, 2006, from http://www.nytimes.com/2006/09/19/health/psychology/19slay.html

Centers for Disease Control and Prevention. (2012). Suicide facts at a glance. Retrieved August 2, 2012, from http://www.cdc.gov/violenceprevention/pdf/Suicide-DataSheet-a.pdf

Challiner, V., & Griffiths, L. (2000). Electroconvulsive therapy: A review of the literature. *Journal of Psychiatric and Mental Health Nursing, 7*, 191–198.

Chamberlin, J. (2010). Is it ever OK for a therapist to snoop on clients online? *GradPSYCH*, Web-only Features.

Chang, D. F., & Yoon, P. (2011). Ethnic minority clients' perceptions of the significance of race in cross-racial therapy relationships. *Psychotherapy Research, 21*(5), 567–582.

Chemtob, C. M., Bauer, G. B., Hamada, R. S., Pelowski, S. R., & Muraoka, M. Y. (1989). Patient suicide: Occupational hazard for psychologists and psychiatrists. *Professional Psychology: Research and Practice, 20*, 294–300.

Chesterman, L. P., Terbeck, S., & Vaughan, F. (2008). Malingered psychosis. *Journal of Forensic Psychiatry & Psychology, 19*(3), 275–300.

Child Welfare Information Gateway. (2011). *Definitions of child abuse and neglect.* Washington, DC: U.S. Department of Health and Human Services, Children's Bureau.

Choca, J. P., & Van Denburg, E. J. (1996). *Manual for Clinical Psychology Trainees* (3rd ed.). New York: Brunner/Mazel.

Choi, J. L., Rogers, J. R., & Werth, Jr., J. L. (2009). Suicide risk assessment with Asian American college students: A culturally informed perspective. *The Counseling Psychologist, 37*(2), 186–218.

Christensen, A., & Rudnick, S. (1999). A glimpse of Zen practice within the realm of countertransference. *American Journal of Psychoanalysis, 59,* 59–69.

Christopher, J. C., Chrisman, J. A., Trotter-Mathison, M. J., Schure, M. B., Dahlen, P., & Christopher, S. B. (2011). Perceptions of the long-term influence of mindfulness training on counselors and psychotherapists: A qualitative inquiry. *Journal of Humanistic Psychology, 51*(3), 318–349.

Christopher, J. C., Christopher, S. E., Dunnagan, T., & Schure, M. (2006). Teaching self-care through mindfulness practices: The application of yoga, meditation and qigong to counselor training. *Journal of Humanistic Psychology, 46,* 494–509.

Chu, J. (1988). Ten traps for therapists in the treatment of trauma survivors. *Dissociation, 1,* 24–32.

Clarkin, J. F., Levy, K. N., & Schiavi, J. M. (2005). Transference focused psychotherapy: Development of a psychodynamic treatment for severe personality disorders. *Clinical Neuroscience Research, 4*(5-6), 379–386.

Classen T. J., & Dunn R.A. (2012). The effect of job loss and unemployment duration on suicide risk in the United States: a new look using mass-layoffs and unemployment duration. *Health Economics, 21,* 338–350.

Clements-Nolle, K., Marx, R., & Katz, M. (2006). Attempted suicide among transgender persons. *Journal of Homosexuality, 51*(3), 53–69.

Clementson, L. (2007, February 4). The racial politics of speaking well. *New York Times.* Retrieved April 12, 2007, from http://www.nytimes.com/2007/02/04/weekinreview/04clemetson.html?ex=1328245200&en=b0c0215875608f7a&ei=5088&partner=rssnyt&emc=rss.

Cochran, B. N., Stewart, A. J., Kiklevich, A. M., Flentje, A., & Wong, C. C. (2009). The impact of extratherapeutic encounters: Individual reactions to both hypothetical and actual incidental contact with the therapist. *Professional Psychology: Research and Practice, 40*(5), 510–517.

Coid, J. W., Yang, M., Ullrich, S., Zhang, T., Sizmur, S., Farrington, D., & Rogers, R. (2011). Most items in structured risk assessments do not predict violence. *Journal of Forensic Psychiatry & Psychology, 22*(1), 3–21.

Collins, K. A. (2006). Elder maltreatment: A review. *Archives of Pathology and Laboratory Medicine, 130,* 1290–1296.

Collins, S., & Long, A. (2003). Working with the psychological effects of trauma: Consequences for mental health-care workers—A literature review. *Journal of Psychiatric and Mental Health Nursing, 10,* 417–424.

Comas-Diaz, L., & Jacobsen, F. M. (1991). Ethnocultural transference and countertransference in the therapeutic dyad. *American Journal of Orthopsychiatry, 61,* 392–402.

Compas, B. E., Haaga, D. A. F., Keefe, F. J., Leitenberg, H., & Williams, D. A. (1998). Sampling of empirically supported psychological treatments from health psychology: Smoking, chronic pain, cancer and bulimia nervosa. *Journal of Consulting and Clinical Psychology, 66,* 89–112.

Compton, M. T., Thompson, N. J., & Kaslow, N. J. (2005). Social environment factors associated with suicide attempt among low-income African Americans: The protective role of family relationships and social support. *Social Psychiatry and Psychiatric Epidemiology, 40*(3), 175–185.

Constantine, M. G., & Sue, D. W. (2007). Perceptions of racial microaggressions among black supervisees in cross-racial dyads. *Journal of Counseling Psychology, 54,* 142–153.

Cooney, C., Howard, R., & Lawlor, B. (2006). Abuse of vulnerable people with dementia by their carers: Can we identify those most at risk? *International Journal of Geriatric Psychiatry, 21*, 564–571.

Cooper, P. C. (1999). Buddhist meditation and countertransference: A case study. *American Journal of Psychoanalysis, 59*, 71–85.

Cosgrove, L., Krimsky, S., Vijayaraghavan, M., & Schneider, L. (2006). Financial ties between DSM-IV panel members and the pharmaceutical industry. *Psychotherapy & Psychosomatics, 75*(3), 154–160.

Courtois, C. (1993, Spring). Vicarious traumatization of the therapist. *NCP Clinical Newsletter*, 8–9.

Courtois, C. (1997). Healing the incest wound: A treatment update with attention to recovered-memory issues. *American Journal of Psychotherapy, 51*, 464–496.

Coyle, S. L. (2002). Physician-industry relations. Part 1: Individual physicians. *Annals of Internal Medicine, 136*, 396–402.

Craig, R. J. (Ed.). (2005). *Clinical and diagnostic interviewing*. New York: Jason Aronson.

Cramer, J. A., & Rosenheck, R. (1998). Compliance with medication regimens for mental and physical disorders. *Psychiatric Services, 49*, 196–201.

Crawford, L. S. (2009). *Doctors, patients, and social networks*. Retrieved from http://www.law.com/tech.

Crits-Christoph, P., Gibbons, M. B. C., & Hearon, B. (2006). Does the alliance cause good outcome? Recommendations for future research on the alliance. *Psychotherapy: Theory, Research, Practice, Training, 43*(3), 280–285.

Crosby, A. E., Ortega, L., & Melanson, C. (2011). *Self-directed violence surveillance: Uniform definitions and recommended data elements*. Atlanta, GA: Centers for Disease Control and Prevention.

Csikszentmihalyi, M. (1999). If we are so rich, why aren't we happy? *American Psychologist, 10*, 821–827.

Cuijpers, P., van Straten, A., & Warmerdam, L. (2007). Behavioral activation treatments of depression: A meta-analysis. *Clinical Psychology Review, 27*, 318–326.

Cunningham, E. A., & Ciccone, J. R. (2011). Illinois supreme court finds no duty to warn. *Legal Digest, 39*(2), 266–268.

Curtin, L., & Hargrove, D. S. (2010). Opportunities and challenges of rural practice: Managing self and ambiguity. *Journal of Clinical Psychology, 66*(5), 549–561.

Cybulska, B., & Forster, G. (2005). Sexual assault: Examination of the victim. *Medicine, 33*, 23–28.

Daban, C., Martinez-Aran, A., Cruz, N., & Vieta, E. (2008). Safety and efficacy of vagus nerve stimulation in treatment-resistant depression: A systematic review. *Journal of Affective Disorders, 110*(1-2), 1–15.

Dalenberg, C. (2000). *Countertransference and the treatment of trauma*. Washington, DC: American Psychological Association.

Daniel, M., & Gurczynski, J. (2010). Mental status examination. In D. L. Segal & M. Hersen (Eds.), *Diagnostic interviewing* (4th ed., pp. 61–88). New York: Springer.

Davidson, C. L., & Wingate, L. R. (2011). Racial disparities in risk and protective factors for suicide. *Journal of Black Psychology, 37*(4), 499–516.

Davidson, C. L., Wingate, L. R., Slish, M. L., & Rasmussen, K. A. (2010). The Great Black Hope: Hope and its relation to suicide risk among African Americans. *Suicide and Life-Threatening Behavior, 40*(2), 170–180.

Davidson, R. J., Kabat-Zinn, J., Schumacher, J., Rosenkranz, M., Muller, D., Santorelli, S. F., et al. (2003). Alterations in brain and immune function produced by mindfulness meditation. *Psychosomatic Medicine, 65,* 564–570.

Davies, T. (2001). Informed consent in psychiatric research. *British Journal of Psychiatry, 178,* 397–398.

Davis, R. E. (2000). Cultural health care or child abuse? The Southeast Asian practice of cao gio. *Journal of the American Academy of Nurse Practitioners, 12*(3), 89–95.

Day-Vines, N. L. (2007). The escalating incidence of suicide among African Americans: Implications for counselors. *Journal of Counseling & Development, 85*(3), 370–377.

Dearing, R. L., Maddux, J. E., & Tangney, J. P. (2005). Predictors of psychological help seeking in clinical and counseling psychology graduate students. *Professional Psychology: Research and Practice, 36,* 323–329.

Deffenbacher, J. L., Oetting, E. R., & DiGiuseppe, R. A. (2002). Principles of empirically supported interventions applied to anger management. *The Counseling Psychologist, 30,* 262–280.

Deisenhammer, E. A., Ing, C. M., Strauss, R., Kemmler, G., Hinterhuber, H., & Weiss, E. M. (2009). The duration of the suicidal process: How much time is left for intervention between consideration and accomplishment of a suicide attempt? *Journal of Clinical Psychiatry, 70*(1), 19–24.

DePaulo, B. M., Lindsay, J. J., Malone, B. E., Muhlenbruck, L., Charlton, K., & Cooper, H. (2003). Cues to deception. *Psychological Bulletin, 129,* 74–118.

De Ruiter, C., & Nicholls, T. L. (2011). Protective factors in forensic mental health: A new frontier. *International Journal of Forensic Mental Health, 10*(3), 160–170.

Devereaux, R. L., & Gottlieb, M. C. (2012). Record keeping in the cloud: Ethical considerations. *Professional Psychology: Research and Practice.* Advance online publication.

Devilly, G. J., Wright, R., & Varker, T. (2009). Vicarious trauma, secondary traumatic stress or simply burnout? Effect of trauma therapy on mental health professionals. *Australian and New Zealand Journal of Psychiatry, 43,* 373–385.

Devine, P. G. (1989). Stereotypes and prejudice: Their automatic and controlled components. *Journal of Personality and Social Psychology, 56,* 5–18.

Devlin, A. S., Donovan, S., Nicolov, A., Nold, O., Packard, A., & Zandan, G. (2009). "Impressive?" Credentials, family photographs, and the perception of therapist qualities. *Journal of Environmental Psychology, 29,* 503–512.

De Wilde, L. (1996). *Monk.* New York: Marlowe.

Diamond, T., & Muller, R. T. (2004). The relationship between witnessing parental conflict during childhood and later psychological adjustment among university students: Disentangling confounding risk factors. *Canadian Journal of Behavioural Science, 36,* 295–309.

Diaz, E., Woods, S. W., & Rosenheck, R. A. (2005). Effects of ethnicity on psychotropic medications adherence. *Community Mental Health Journal, 41,* 521–537.

DiLorenzo, T. M., Bargman, E. P., Stucky-Ropp, R., Brassington, G. S., Frensch, P. A., & LaFontaine, T. (1999). Long-term effects of aerobic exercise on psychological outcomes. *Preventive Medicine, 28,* 75–86.

Doering, S., Hörz, S., Rentrop, M., Fischer-Kern, M., Schuster, P., Benecke, C.,... Buchheim, P. (2010). Transference-focused psychotherapy v. treatment by community psychotherapists for borderline personality disorder: Randomised controlled trial. *British Journal of Psychiatry, 196,* 389–395.

Dolan, P. L. (2011, Oct. 31). Physician texting provides quick communication—and an easy way to violate HIPAA. *American Medical News.* Retrieved from http://www.ama-assn.org/amednews/2011/10/31/bica1031.htm.

Dombrovski, A. Y., Szanto, K., Siegle, G. J., Wallace, M. L., Forman, S. D., Sahakian, B.,... Clark, L. (2011). Lethal forethought: Delayed reward discounting differentiates high- and low-lethality suicide attempts in old age. *Biological Psychiatry, 70*(2), 138–144.

Donker, T., Griffiths, K. M., Cuijpers, P., & Christensen, H. (2009). Psychoeducation for depression, anxiety and psychological distress: A meta-analysis. *BMC Medicine, 7,* 70.

Donoghue, J., & Hylan, T. R. (2001). Antidepressant use in clinical practice: Efficacy v. effectiveness. *British Journal of Psychiatry, 879,* s9–s17.

Donovan, K., & Regehr, C. (2010). Elder abuse: Clinical, ethical, and legal considerations in social work practice. *Clinical Social Work Journal, 38*(2), 174–182.

Doucet, S., Jones, I., Letourneau, N., Dennis, C. L., & Blackmore, E. R. (2011). Interventions for the prevention and treatment of postpartum psychosis: A systematic review. *Archives of Women's Mental Health, 14*(2), 89–98.

Dougall, J. L., & Schwartz, R. C. (2011). The influence of client socioeconomic status on psychotherapists' attributional biases and countertransference reactions. *American Journal of Psychotherapy, 65*(3), 249–265.

Douglas, K. S., Guy, L. S., & Hart, S. D. (2009). Psychosis as a risk factor for violence to others: A meta-analysis. *Psychological Bulletin, 135*(5), 679–706.

Douglas, K. S., & Skeem, J. L. (2005). Violence risk assessment: Getting specific about being dynamic. *Psychology, Public Policy, and Law, 11*(3), 347–383.

D'Souza, F., Egan, S. J., & Rees, C. S. (2011). The relationship between perfectionism, stress and burnout in clinical psychologists *Behaviour Change, 28*(1), 17–28.

Dubin, W. R., & Jagarlamudi, K. (2010). Safety in the evaluation of potentially violent patients: Decreasing the clinician's risk. *Psychiatric Times, 27*(7).

Dubowitz, H., Kim, J., Black, M. M., Weisbart, C., Semiatin, J., & Magder, L. S. (2011). Identifying children at high risk for a child maltreatment report. *Child Abuse & Neglect, 35*(2), 96–104.

Duldulao, A. A., Takeuchi, D. T., & Hong, S. (2009). Correlates of suicidal behaviors among Asian Americans. *Archives of Suicide Research, 13*(3), 277–290.

Dunkley, J., & Whelan, T. A. (2006). Vicarious traumatisation: Current status and future directions. *British Journal of Guidance & Counselling, 34*(1), 107–116.

Dutton, M. A., Green, B. L., Kaltman, S. I., Roesch, D. M., Zeffiro, T. A., & Krause, E. D. (2006). Intimate partner violence, PTSD, and adverse health outcomes. *Journal of Interpersonal Violence, 21,* 955–968.

Edinger, J. D., & Carney, C. E. (2008). *Overcoming insomnia: A cognitive-behavioral therapy approach workbook.* New York: Oxford University Press.

Ehrensaft, M. K., Cohen, P., Brown, J., Smailes, E., Chen, H., & Johnson, J. G. (2003). Intergenerational transmission of partner violence: A 20-year prospective study. *Journal of Consulting and Clinical Psychology, 71,* 741–753.

Ekman, P. (2009). Lie catching and microexpressions. In C. Martin (Ed.), *The philosophy of deception* (pp. 118–135). New York: Oxford University Press.

Ekman, P., & O'Sullivan, M. (1991). Who can catch a liar? *American Psychologist, 46,* 913–920.

Elbogen, E. B., Fuller, S., Johnson, S. C., Brooks, S., Kinneer, P., Calhoun, P. S., & Beckham, J. C. (2010). Improving risk assessment of violence among military veterans: An evidence-based approach for clinical decision-making. *Clinical Psychology Review, 30*(6), 595–607.

Elbogen, E. B., Tomkins, A. J., Pothuloori, A. P., & Scalora, M. J. (2003). Documentation of violence risk information in psychiatric hospital patient charts: An empirical examination. *Journal of the American Academy of Psychiatry and the Law, 31,* 58–64.

Ellis, A. (2001). Rational and irrational aspects of countertransference. *Journal of Clinical Psychology, 57,* 999–1004.

Ellis, M. V. (2001). Harmful supervision, a cause for alarm: Comment on Gray et al. (2001) and Nelson and Friedlander (2001). *Journal of Counseling Psychology, 48,* 401–406.

Ellis, T. E., & Patel, A. B. (2012). Client suicide: What now? *Cognitive and Behavioral Practice, 19*(2), 277–287.

Ellison, J. (2011, April 3). The military's secret shame. *Newsweek.* Retrieved August 24, 2012, from http://www.thedailybeast.com/newsweek/2011/04/03/the-military-s-secret-shame.html

Elnour, A. A., & Harrison, J. (2008). Lethality of suicide methods. *Injury Prevention, 14*(1), 39–45.

Elwood, L. S., Mott, J., Lohr, J. M., & Galovski, T. E. (2011). Secondary trauma symptoms in clinicians: A critical review of the construct, specificity, and implications for trauma-focused treatment. *Clinical Psychology Review, 31*(1), 25–36.

Emery, S., Wade, T. D., & McLean, S. (2009). Associations among therapist beliefs, personal resources and burnout in clinical psychologists. *Behaviour Change, 26*(2), 83–96.

Epley, N., & Kruger, J. (2005). When what you type isn't what they read: The perseverance of stereotypes and expectancies over e-mail. *Journal of Experimental Social Psychology, 41,* 414–422.

Epstein, M. (1998). *Going to pieces without falling apart: A Buddhist perspective on wholeness.* New York: Broadway Books.

Evans, J. (2000). Interventions to reduce repetition of deliberate self-harm. *International Review of Psychiatry, 12,* 44–47.

Evans, R. W. (2006). Precipitating factors. Retrieved December 28, 2006, from http://www.migraines.org/treatment/pdfs/migraine-1.pdf.

Eyler, L. T., & Jeste, D. V. (2006). Enhancing the informed consent process: A conceptual overview. *Behavioral Sciences and the Law, 24,* 553–568.

Fallon, A. (2006). Informed consent in the practice of group psychotherapy. *International Journal of Group Psychotherapy, 56*(4), 431–453.

Falloon, I. R. H., Barbieri, L., Boggian, I., & Lamonaca, D. (2007). Problem solving training for schizophrenia: Rationale and review. *Journal of Mental Health, 16,* 553–568.

Fallows, J. (2011, November). Hacked! *The Atlantic.* Retrieved from http://www.theatlantic.com/magazine/archive/2011/11/hacked/8673/?single_page=true.

Fauteux, K. (2010). De-escalating angry and violent clients. *American Journal of Psychotherapy, 64*(2), 195–213.

Fauth, J. (2006). Toward more (and better) countertransference research. *Psychotherapy: Theory, Research, Practice, Training, 43,* 16–31.

Feldhaus, K. M., Koziol-McLain, J., Amsbury, H. L., Norton, I. M., Lowensteine, S. R., & Abbot, J. T. (1997). Accuracy of 3 brief screening questions for detecting partner violence in the emergency room. *Journal of the American Medical Association, 277,* 1357–1361.

Feldman, I. (2003). *Information packet: Cultural sensitivity with immigrant families and their children.* New York: City University of New York (CUNY), National Resource Center for Family-Centered Practice and Permanency Planning at the Hunter College School of Social Work.

Feldman-Summers, S., & Pope, K. S. (1994). The experience of "forgetting childhood abuse": A national survey of psychologists. *Journal of Consulting and Clinical Psychology, 62,* 636–639.

Felton, J. S. (1998). Burnout as a clinical entity—Its importance in health care workers. *Occupational Medicine, 48,* 237–250.

Finder, A. (2006, June 11). For some, online persona undermines a resume. *New York Times.* Available at http://www.nytimes.com/2006/06/11/us/11recruit.html?pagewanted=all

First, M. B., Spitzer, R. L., Gibbon, M., & Williams, J. B. W. (2002). *Structured Clinical Interview for DSM-IV-TR Axis I Disorders, Research Version, Patient Edition (SCID-I/P).* New York: Biometrics Research, New York State Psychiatric Institute.

Fischer, C. T. (2012). Comments on protecting clients about whom we write (and speak). *Psychotherapy, 49*(1), 19–21.

Fisher, C. B., & Oransky, M. (2008). Informed consent to psychotherapy: Protecting the dignity and respecting the autonomy of patients. *Journal of Clinical Psychology, 64*(5), 576–588.

Flannery, R. B. (2005). Precipitants to psychiatric patient assaults on staff: Review of empirical findings, 1990–2003, and risk management implications. *Psychiatric Quarterly, 76,* 317–326.

Flannery, R. B., Schuler, A. P., Farley, E. M., & Walker, A. P. (2002). Characteristics of assaultive psychiatric patients: Ten-year analysis of the assaulted staff action program (ASAP). *Psychiatric Quarterly, 73,* 59–69.

Fluckiger, C., Del Re, A. C., Wampold, B. E., Symonds, D., & Horvath, A. O. (2012). How central is the alliance to psychotherapy? A multilevel longitudinal meta-analysis. *Journal of Counseling Psychology, 59*(1), 10–17.

Fox, K. R. (1999). The influence of physical activity on mental well-being. *Public Health Nutrition, 2,* 411–418.

Fox, P. K. (2010). Commentary: So the pendulum swings—Making sense of the duty to protect. *Journal of the American Academy of Psychiatry and the Law, 38*(4), 474–478.

Freeman, A., Pretzer, J., Fleming, B., & Simon, K. M. (1990). *Clinical applications of cognitive therapy.* New York: Plenum Press.

Freyd, J. J. (2008, Fall). What juries don't know: Dissemination of research on victim response is essential for justice. *Trauma Psychology Newsletter,* 15–18.

Friedman, R. A. (2006). Violence and mental illness—How strong is the link? *New England Journal of Medicine, 355,* 2064–2066.

Fulde, G., & Preisz, P. (2011). Managing aggressive and violent patients. *Australian Prescriber, 34*(4), 115–118.

Gabbard, G. O. (1994). Psychotherapists who transgress sexual boundaries with patients. *Bulletin of the Menninger Clinic, 58,* 124–135.

Gabbard, G. O. (1996). Lessons to be learned from the study of sexual boundary violations. *American Journal of Psychotherapy, 50,* 311–322.

Gabbard, G. O. (2000a). Disguise or consent: Problems and recommendations concerning the publication and presentation of clinical material. *International Journal of Psychoanalysis, 81,* 1071–1086.

Gabbard, G. O. (2000b). A neurobiologically informed perspective on psychotherapy. *British Journal of Psychiatry, 177,* 117–122.

Gabbard, G. O. (2001a). A contemporary psychoanalytic model of countertransference. *Journal of Clinical Psychology/In Session, 57,* 983–991.

Gabbard, G. O. (2001b). Editorial: Preserving confidentiality in the writing of case reports. *International Journal of Psychoanalysis, 82,* 1067–1068.

Gabbard, G. O. (2004). The illusion of safety. *American Journal of Psychiatry, 161,* 427–428.

Gabbard, G. O. (2006). The rationale for combining medication and psychotherapy. *Psychiatric Annals, 36*(5), 315–319.

Gabbard, G. O. (2007). Flexibility of the frame revisited: Commentary on Tony Bass's "when the frame doesn't fit the picture." *Psychoanalytic Dialogues, 17*(6), 923–929.

Gabbard, G. O. (2010). *Long-term psychodynamic psychotherapy: A basic text* (2nd ed.). Arlington, VA: American Psychiatric Publishing.

Gabbard, G.O. (2012). Clinical challenges in the Internet era. *American Journal of Psychiatry, 169,* 460–463.

Gabbard, G. O., & Crisp-Han, H. (2010). Teaching professional boundaries to psychiatric residents. *Academic Psychiatry, 34*(5), 369–372.

Gabbard, G. O., Kassaw, K. A., & Perez-Garcia, G. (2011). Professional boundaries in the era of the internet. *Academic Psychiatry, 35*(3), 168–174.

Gabbard, G. O., Lazar, S. G., Hornberger, J., & Spiegel, D. (1997). The economic impact of psychotherapy: A review. *American Journal of Psychiatry, 154,* 147–155.

Gabbard, G. O., & Westen, D. (2003). Rethinking therapeutic action. *International Journal of Psychoanalysis, 84,* 823–841.

Gans, J. S., & Counselman, E. F. (1996). The missed session: A neglected aspect of psychodynamic psychotherapy. *Psychotherapy, 33,* 43–50.

Garb, H. N. (1997). Race bias, social class bias, and gender bias in clinical judgment. *Clinical Psychology: Science and Practice, 4,* 99–120.

Gatchel, R. J., Peng, Y. B., Peters, M. L., Fuchs, P. N., & Turk, D. C. (2007). The biopsychosocial approach to chronic pain: Scientific advances and future directions. *Psychological Bulletin, 133*(4), 581–624.

Geddes, J. R., Barbui, C., & Cipriani, A. (2009). Risk of suicidal behaviour in adults taking antidepressants. *BMJ, 339,* 411–414.

Gellerman, D. M., & Suddath, R. (2005). Violent fantasy, dangerousness, and the duty to warn and protect. *Journal of the American Academy of Psychiatry and the Law, 33,* 484–495.

Gelles, R. J. (2006). Child maltreatment and foster care. *Gender Issues, 23,* 36–47.

Gellis, L. A., & Lichstein, K. L. (2009). Sleep hygiene practices of good and poor sleepers in the United States: An Internet-based study. *Behavior Therapy, 40*(1), 1–9.

Gelso, C. J., Fassinger, R. E., Gomez, M. J., & Latts, M. G. (1995). Countertransference reactions to lesbian clients: The role of homophobia, counselor gender, and countertransference management. *Journal of Counseling Psychology, 42,* 356–364.

Gelso, C. J., & Hayes, J. A. (2001). Countertransference management. *Psychotherapy, 38,* 418–422.

Gelso, C. J., Hill, C. E., Mohr, J. J., Rochlen, A. B., & Zack, J. (1999). Describing the face of transference: Psychodynamic therapists' recollections about transference in cases of successful long-term therapy. *Journal of Counseling Psychology, 46,* 257–267.

Gelso, C. J., Latts, M. G., Gomez, M. J., & Fassinger, R. E. (2002). Countertransference management and therapy outcome: An initial evaluation. *Journal of Clinical Psychology, 58,* 861–867.

Gharaibeh, N. (2009). Dissociative identity disorder: Time to remove it from DSM-V? *Current Psychiatry, 8*(9), 30–36.

Gibbons, R. D., Brown, C. H., & Hur, K. (2012). Is the rate of suicide among veterans elevated? *American Journal of Public Health, 102*(S1), S17–S19.

Gilbert, J. D., Jensen, L., & Byard, R. W. (2008). Further observations on the speed of death in hanging. *Journal of Forensic Sciences, 53*(5), 1204–1205.

Glass, L. I. (2003). The gray areas of boundary crossings and violations. *American Journal of Psychotherapy, 57,* 429–444.

Glick, P., Larsen, S., Johnson, C., & Branstiter, H. (2005). Evaluations of sexy women in low- and high-status jobs. *Psychology of Women Quarterly, 29,* 389–395.

Glinkauf-Hughes, C., & Mehlman, E. (1995). Narcissistic issues in therapists: Diagnostic and treatment considerations. *Psychotherapy, 32,* 213–221.

Goldsmith, S. K., Pellmar, T. C., Kleinman, A. M., & Bunney, W. E. (2002). *Reducing suicide: A national imperative.* Washington, DC: National Academy Press.

Goldstein, W. N. (2000). The transference in psychotherapy: The old vs. the new, analytic vs. dynamic. *American Journal of Psychotherapy, 54,* 167–171.

Gonzalez, F. (1995). Working with Mexican-American clients. *Psychotherapy, 32,* 696–706.

Gonzalez-Figueroa, E., & Young, A. M. (2005). Ethnic identity and mentoring among Latinas in professional roles. *Cultural Diversity and Ethnic Minority Psychology, 11,* 213–226.

Goodman, W. K. (2011). Electroconvulsive therapy in the spotlight. *New England Journal of Medicine, 364*(19), 1784–1787.

Gossop, M., Harris, J., Best, D., Man, L., Manning, V., Marshall, J., et al. (2003). Is attendance at Alcoholics Anonymous meetings after inpatient treatment related to improved outcomes? A 6-month follow-up study. *Alcohol and Alcoholism, 38,* 421–426.

Graham, S. R., & Liddle, B. J. (2009). Multiple relationships encountered by lesbian and bisexual psychotherapists: How close is too close? *Professional Psychology: Research and Practice, 40*(1), 15–21.

Granello, D. H. (2010a). A suicide crisis intervention model with 25 practical strategies for implementation. *Journal of Mental Health Counseling, 32*(3), 218–235.

Granello, D. H. (2010b). The process of suicide risk assessment: Twelve core principles. *Journal of Counseling & Development, 88*(3), 363–370.

Gray, A. (1994). *An introduction to the therapeutic frame.* London: Routledge.

Gray, L. A., Ladany, N., Walker, J. A., & Ancis, J. R. (2001). Psychotherapy trainees' experience of counterproductive events in supervision. *Journal of Counseling Psychology, 48,* 371–383.

Griffin-Fennell, F., & Williams, M. (2006). Examining the complexities of suicidal behavior in the African American community. *Journal of Black Psychology, 32*(3), 303–319.

Grohol, J.M. (n.d.). TMS treatment for depression gains FDA approval. Retrieved on July 20, 2012, from http://psychcentral.com/blog/archives/2008/10/09/tms-treatment-for-depression-gains-fda-approval/

Gulfi, A., Dransart, D. A., Heeb, J. L., & Gutjahr, E. (2010). The impact of patient suicide on the professional reactions and practices of mental health caregivers and social workers. *Crisis, 31*(4), 202–210.

Gutheil, T. G. (1980). Paranoia and progress notes: A guide to forensically informed psychiatric record-keeping. *Hospital and Community Psychiatry, 31*, 479–482.

Gutheil, T. G. (2001). Moral justification for *Tarasoff*-type warnings and breach of confidentiality: A clinician's perspective. *Behavioral Sciences and the Law, 19*, 345–353.

Gutheil, T. G. (2005). Boundary issues and personality disorders. *Journal of Psychiatric Practice, 11*, 88–96.

Gutheil, T. G., & Gabbard, G. O. (1993). The concept of boundaries in clinical practice: Theoretical and risk-management dimensions. *American Journal of Psychiatry, 150*, 188–196.

Gutheil, T. G., & Gabbard, G. O. (1998). Misuses and misunderstandings of boundary theory in clinical and regulatory settings. *American Journal of Psychiatry, 155*, 409–414.

Gutheil, T. G., & Hilliard, J. T. (2001). "Don't write me down": Legal, clinical and risk-management aspects of patients' requests that therapists not keep notes or records. *American Journal of Psychotherapy, 55*, 157–165.

Gutheil, T. G., & Simon, R. I. (2005). E-mails, extra-therapeutic contact, and early boundary problems: The Internet as a "slippery slope." *Psychiatric Annals, 35*, 952–960.

Haas, A. P., Eliason, M., Mays, V. M., Mathy, R. M., Cochran, S. D., D'Augelli, A. R., ... Clayton, P. J. (2011). Suicide and suicide risk in lesbian, gay, bisexual, and transgender populations: Review and recommendations. *Journal of Homosexuality, 58*(1), 10–51.

Hage, S. M. (2006). A closer look at the role of spirituality in psychology training programs. *Professional Psychology: Research and Practice, 37*, 303–310.

Hahn, W. K. (1998). Gifts in psychotherapy: An intersubjective approach to patient gifts. *Psychotherapy, 1*, 78–86.

Hamarman, S., & Bernet, W. (2000). Evaluating and reporting emotional abuse in children: Parent-based, action-based focus aids in clinical decision-making. *Journal of the American Academy of Child & Adolescent Psychiatry, 39*, 928–930.

Hamer, F. M. (2006). Racism as a transference state: Episodes of racial hostility in the psychoanalytic context. *Psychoanalytic Quarterly, 75*, 197–214.

Hamilton-Giachritsis, C. E., & Browne, K. D. (2005). A retrospective study of risk to siblings in abusing families. *Journal of Family Psychology, 19*, 619–624.

Hanson, R. K. (2009). The psychological assessment of risk for crime and violence. *Canadian Psychology, 50*(3), 172–182.

Harauz, J., Kaufman, L. M., & Potter, B. (2009). Data security in the world of cloud computing. *IEEE Security and Privacy, 7*(4), 61–64.

Harris, D. (2006). Elder abuse. *Update, 73.*

Harris, E. C., & Barraclough, B. (1997). Suicide as an outcome for mental disorders. A meta-analysis. *British Journal of Psychiatry, 170*, 205–228.

Harris, M. (2005, August). What your supervisees want you to know about racial diversity. Paper presented at the annual meeting of the American Psychological Association, Washington, DC.

Harrison, R. L., & Westwood, M. J. (2009). Preventing vicarious traumatization of mental health therapists: Identifying protective practices. *Psychotherapy Theory, Research, Practice, Training, 46*(2), 203–219.

Harstall, C., & Ospina, M. (2003). How prevalent is chronic pain? *Pain: Clinical Updates, 11*, 1–4.

Harvard Medical School. (2011, January). Mental health and violence. *Harvard Mental Health Letter, 27*, 1–3.

Harvey, A. G., & Tang, N. K. Y. (2003). Cognitive behavior therapy for primary insomnia: Can we rest yet? *Sleep Medicine Reviews, 7,* 237–262.

Haslam, D. R., & Harris, S. M. (2004). Informed consent documents of marriage and family therapists in private practice: A qualitative analysis. *American Journal of Family Therapy, 32*(4), 359–374.

Hatch-Maillette, M. A., Scalora, M. J., Bader, S. M., & Bornstein, B. H. (2007). A gender-based incidence study of workplace violence in psychiatric and forensic settings. *Violence and Victims, 22*(4), 449–462.

Haw, C., Hawton, K., Houston, K., & Townsend, E. (2003). Correlates of relative lethality and suicidal intent among deliberate self-harm patients. *Suicide and Life-Threatening Behavior, 33*(4), 353–364.

Hayes, J. A. (2004). The inner world of the psychotherapist: A program of research on countertransference. *Psychotherapy Research, 14,* 21–36.

Hayes, J. A., & Gelso, C. J. (2001). Clinical implications of research on countertransference: Science informing practice. *Journal of Clinical Psychology/In Session: Psychotherapy in Practice, 57,* 1041–1051.

Hayes, J. A., Gelso, C. J., & Hummel, A. M. (2011). Managing countertransference. *Psychotherapy, 48*(1), 88–97.

Hayes, J. A., McCracken, J. E., McClanahan, M. K., Hill, C. E., Harp, J. S., & Carozzoni, J. S. (1998). Therapist perspectives on countertransference: Qualitative data in search of a theory. *Journal of Counseling Psychology, 45,* 468–482.

Hayes, J. A., Yeh, Y. J., & Eisenberg, A. (2007). Good grief and not-so-good grief: Countertransference in bereavement therapy. *Journal of Clinical Psychology, 63*(4), 345–355.

Hays, P. A. (2007). *Addressing cultural complexities in practice: Assessment, diagnosis, and therapy* (2nd ed.). Washington, DC: American Psychological Association.

Hays, P. A. (2009). Integrating evidence-based practice, cognitive-behavior therapy, and multicultural therapy: Ten steps for culturally competent practice. *Professional Psychology: Research and Practice, 40*(4), 354–360.

HealthIT.gov (2013). Mobile device privacy and security. Retrieved Jan. 10, 2013, from http://www.healthit.gov/providers-professionals/how-can-you-protect-and-secure-health-information-when-using-mobile-device.

Heiby, E. M. (2010). Concerns about substandard training for prescription privileges for psychologists. *Journal of Clinical Psychology, 66*(1), 104–111.

Heilbron, N., Compton, J. S., Daniel, S. S., & Goldston, D. B. (2010). The problematic label of suicide gesture: Alternatives for clinical research and practice. *Professional Psychology: Research and Practice, 41*(3), 221–227.

Henretty, J. R., & Levitt, H. M. (2010). The role of therapist self-disclosure in psychotherapy: A qualitative review. *Clinical Psychology Review, 30*(1), 63–77.

Herbert, P. B. (2002). The duty to warn: A reconsideration and critique. *Journal of the American Academy of Psychiatry and the Law, 30,* 417–424.

Herbert, P. B., & Young, K. A. (2002). *Tarasoff* at twenty-five. *Journal of the American Academy of Psychiatry and the Law, 30,* 275–281.

Herman, J. (1997). *Trauma and recovery: The aftermath of violence from domestic abuse to political terror.* New York: Basic Books.

Heru, A. M., Strong, D. R., Price, M., & Recupero, P. R. (2004). Boundaries in psychotherapy supervision. *American Journal of Psychotherapy, 58*(1), 76–89.

Hesse, A. (2002). Secondary trauma: How working with trauma survivors affects thera-pists. *Clinical Social Work Journal, 30*, 293–309.

Hettema, J. M., Neale, M. C., & Kendler, K. S. (2001). A review and meta-analysis of the genetic epidemiology of anxiety disorders. *American Journal of Psychiatry, 158*, 1568–1578.

Hicks, J. W. (2004). Ethnicity, race, and forensic psychiatry: Are we color-blind? *Journal of the American Academy of Psychiatry and the Law, 32*(1), 21–33.

Hiday, V. A. (2003). Outpatient commitment: The state of empirical research on its out-comes. *Psychology, Public Policy and Law, 9*, 8–32.

Hill, M. (1999). For love and money. *Women and Therapy, 22*, 1–3.

Hobday, G., Mellman, L. & Gabbard, G.O. (2008). Complex sexualized transferences when the patient is male and the therapist female. *American Journal of Psychiatry, 165*(12), 1525–1530.

Hobson, R. P., & Kapur, R. (2005). Working in the transference: Clinical and research perspectives. *Psychology and Psychotherapy: Theory, Research and Practice, 78*, 275–293.

Høglend, P. (2004). Analysis of transference in psychodynamic psychother-apy: A review of empirical research. *Canadian Journal of Psychoanalysis, 12*, 280–300.

Høglend, P., Hersoug, A. G., Bøgwald, K. P., Amlo, S., Marble, A., Sørbye, Ø., . . . Crits-Christoph, P. (2011). Effects of transference work in the context of therapeutic alli-ance and quality of object relations. *Journal of Consulting and Clinical Psychology, 79*(5), 697–706.

Høglend, P., Johansson, P., Marble, A., Bogwald, K., & Amlo, S. (2007). Moderators of the effects of transference interpretations in brief dynamic psychotherapy. *Psychotherapy Research, 17*, 162–174.

Hopko, D. R., Lejuez, C. W., Ruggiero, K. J., & Eifert, G. H. (2003). Contemporary behavioral activation treatments for depression: Procedures, principles, and progress. *Clinical Psychology Review, 23*, 699–717.

Horesh, N., Levi, Y., & Apter, A. (2012). Medically serious versus non-serious suicide attempts: Relationships of lethality and intent to clinical and interpersonal character-istics. *Journal of Affective Disorders, 136*(3), 286–293.

Horn, P. J. (1994). Therapists' psychological adaptation to client suicide. *Psychotherapy, 31*, 190–195.

Horowitz, J. (2007, February 4). Biden unbound: Lays into Clinton, Obama, Edwards. *New York Observer*. Retrieved May 29, 2008, from http://observer.com/2007/02/biden-unbound-lays-into-clinton-obama-edwards/.

Horvitz-Lennon, M., Normand, S. T., Gaccione, P., & Frank, R. G. (2001). Partial versus full hospitalization for adults in psychiatric distress: A systematic review of the pub-lished literature (1957–1997). *American Journal of Psychiatry, 158*, 676–685.

Howe, E. (2011). Should psychiatrists self disclose? *Innovations in Clinical Neuroscience, 8*(12), 14–17.

Hughes, T. (2006). The neglect of children and culture: Responding to child maltreat-ment with cultural competence and a review of "Child Abuse and Culture: Working with Diverse Families." *Family Court Review, 44*(3), 501–510.

Hunot, V. M., Horne, R., Leese, M. N., & Churchill, R. C. (2007). A cohort study of adherence to antidepressants in primary care: The influence of antidepressant con-cerns and treatment preferences. *Primary Care Companion to the Journal of Clinical Psychiatry, 9*(2), 91–99.

Hunt, G. E., Bergen, J., & Bashir, M. (2002). Medication compliance and comorbid substance abuse in schizophrenia: Impact on community survival 4 years after a relapse. *Schizophrenia Research, 54*, 253–264.

Illinois General Assembly (n.d.). Illinois compiled statutes. Retrieved January 16, 2013, from http://www.ilga.gov/legislation/ilcs/ilcs3.asp?ActID=1460&ChapterID=32.

Independent Practitioner. (2007, Winter). Opening lines in therapy—Div 42 members share their favorites. *Independent Practitioner, 27*, 22.

Jack, R. E., Garrod, O. G. B., Caldara, R., & Schyns, P. G. (2012). Facial expressions of emotion are not culturally universal. *Proceedings of the National Academy of Sciences of the United States of America.* Advance online publication.

Jackson, H., & Nuttall, R. L. (2001). A relationship between childhood sexual abuse and professional sexual misconduct. *Professional Psychology: Research and Practice, 32*, 200–204.

Jacobs, D. G., & Brewer, M. L. (2006). Application of the APA Practice Guidelines on Suicide to clinical practice. *CNS Spectrums, 11*, 447–454.

Jain, S., Shapiro, S. L., Swanick, S., Roesch, S. C., Mills, P. J., Bell, I., et al. (2007). A randomized controlled trial of mindfulness meditation versus relaxation training: Effects on distress, positive states of mind, rumination and distraction. *Annals of Behavioral Medicine, 33*, 11–21.

Jayaratne, S., Croxton, T. A., & Mattison, D. (2004). A national survey of violence in the practice of social work. *Families in Society: The Journal of Contemporary Social Services, 85*, 445–453.

Jayawardena, K. M., & Liao, S. (2006). Elder abuse at end of life. *Journal of Palliative Medicine, 9*, 127–136.

Jefferson, C. D., Drake, C. L., Scofield, H. M., Myers, E., McClure, T., Roehrs, T., & Roth, T. (2005). Sleep hygiene practices in a population-based sample of insomniacs. *Sleep, 28*(5), 611–615.

Jenaro, C., Flores, N., & Arias, B. (2007). Burnout and coping in human service practitioners. *Professional Psychology: Research and Practice, 38*(1), 80–87.

Jenkins, S. R., & Baird, S. (2002). Secondary traumatic stress and vicarious traumatization: A validational study. *Journal of Traumatic Stress, 15*, 423–432.

Jernigan, M. M., Green, C. E., Helms, J. E., Perez-Gualdron, L., & Henze, K. (2010). An examination of people of color supervision dyads: Racial identity matters as much as race. *Training and Education in Professional Psychology, 4*(1), 62–73.

Jobes, D. A. (2006). *Managing suicidal risk: A collaborative approach.* New York: The Guilford Press.

Jobes, D. A., Rudd, M. D., Overholser, J. C., & Joiner, T. E. (2008). Ethical and competent care of suicidal patients: Contemporary challenges, new developments, and considerations for clinical practice. *Professional Psychology: Research and Practice, 39*(4), 405–413.

Joe, S., & Niedermeier, D. M. (2008). Social work research on African Americans and suicidal behavior: A systematic 25-year review. *Health & Social Work, 33*(4), 249–257.

Jogerst, G. J., Daly, J. M., Brinig, M. F., Dawson, J. D., Schmuch, G. A., & Ingram, J. G. (2003). Domestic elder abuse and the law. *American Journal of Public Health, 93*, 2131–2136.

Johnson, W. B., Johnson, S. J., Sullivan, G. R., Bongar, B., Miller, L., & Sammons, M. T. (2011). Psychology *in extremis*: Preventing problems of professional competence in dangerous practice settings. *Professional Psychology: Research and Practice, 42*(1), 94–104.

Johnston, C., Smethurst, N., & Gowers, S. (2005). Should people with a history of an eating disorder work as eating disorder therapists? *European Eating Disorders Review, 13*(5), 301–310.

Joiner, T. E. (2005). *Why people die by suicide.* Cambridge, MA: Harvard University Press.

Joiner, T. E., Conwell, Y., Fitzpatrick, K. K., Witte, T. K., Schmidt, N. B., Berlim, M. T., et al. (2005). Four studies on how past and current suicidality relate even when "everything but the kitchen sink" is covaried. *Journal of Abnormal Psychology, 114,* 291–303.

Joiner, T. E., Van Orden, K. A., Witte, T. K., & Rudd, M. D. (2009). *The interpersonal theory of suicide.* Washington, DC: American Psychological Association.

Joiner, T. E., Van Orden, K. A., Witte, T. K., Selby, E. Z., Ribeiro, J. D., Lewis, R., & Rudd, D. M. (2009). Main predictions of the Interpersonal-Psychological Theory of suicidal behavior: Empirical tests in two samples of young adults. *Journal of Abnormal Psychology, 118*(3), 634–646.

Joiner, T. E, Walker, R. L., Rudd, M. D., & Jobes, D. A. (1999). Scientizing and routinizing the assessment of suicidality in outpatient practice. *Professional Psychology Research and Practice, 30,* 447–453.

Jorm, A. F., Morgan, A. J., & Hetrick, S. E. (2008). Relaxation for depression. *Cochrane Database of Systematic Reviews,* (4), CD007142.

Kahn, N. E. (2003). Self-disclosure of serious illness: The impact of boundary disruptions for patient and analyst. *Contemporary Psychoanalysis, 39,* 51–74.

Kalichman, S. C. (1999). *Mandated reporting of suspected child abuse: Ethics, law, and policy.* Washington, DC: American Psychological Association.

Kanter, J. W., Manos, R. C., Bowe, W. M., Baruch, D. E., Busch, A. M., & Rusch, L. C. (2010). What is behavioral activation? A review of the empirical literature. *Clinical Psychology Review, 30,* 608–620.

Kaplan, M. S., McFarland, H., Huguet, N., & Newsom, J. T. (2012). Estimating the risk of suicide among US veterans: How should we proceed from here? *American Journal of Public Health, 102*(S1), S21–S23.

Karageorge, K., & Kendall, R. (2008). *The role of professional child care providers in preventing and responding to child abuse and neglect.* Washington, DC: U.S. Department of Health and Human Services, Children's Bureau.

Kaslow, F. W., Patterson, T., & Gottlieb, M. (2011). Ethical dilemmas in psychologists accessing Internet data: Is it justified? *Professional Psychology: Research and Practice, 42*(2), 105–112.

Kassaw, K., & Gabbard, G. O. (2002). The ethics of e-mail communication in psychiatry. *Psychiatric Clinics of North America, 25,* 665–674.

Katsavdakis, K. A., Gabbard, G. O., & Athey, G. I. (2004). Profiles of impaired health professionals. *Bulletin of the Menninger Clinic, 68*(1), 60–72.

Kauffman, M., & Chedekel, L. (2008, Summer). Probing the high suicide rate among soldiers in Iraq. *Nieman Reports,* 73–76.

Kawachi, I., & Berkman, L. F. (2001). Social ties and mental health. *Journal of Urban Health: Bulletin of the New York Academy of Medicine, 78,* 458–467.

Keck, P. E., McElroy, S. L., Strakowski, S. M., West, S. A., Sax, K. W., Hawkins, J. M., et al. (1998). 12-month outcome of patients with bipolar disorder following hospitalization for a manic or mixed episode. *American Journal of Psychiatry, 5,* 646–652.

Keefe, F. J., Dunsmore, J., & Burnett, R. (1992). Behavioral and cognitive-behavioral approaches to chronic pain: Recent advances and future directions. *Journal of Consulting and Clinical Psychology, 60*, 528–536.

Kemp, B. J., & Mosqueda, L. A. (2005). Elder financial abuse: An evaluation framework and supporting evidence. *Journal of the American Geriatrics Society, 53*, 1123–1127.

Kernberg, O. F., Selzer, M. A., Koenigsberg, H. W., Carr, A. C., & Appelbaum, A. H. (1989). *Psychodynamic psychotherapy of borderline patients.* New York: Basic Books.

Kessler, L. E., & Waehler, C. A. (2005). Addressing multiple relationships between clients and therapists in lesbian, gay, bisexual, and transgender communities. *Professional Psychology: Research and Practice, 36*, 66–72.

Kessler, R. C., Adler, L. A., Ames, M., Barkley, R., Birnbaum, H., Greenberg, P., et al. (2005). The prevalence and effects of adult attention deficit/hyperactivity disorder on work performance in a nationally representative sample of workers. *Journal of Occupational and Environmental Medicine, 47*, 565–572.

Kessler, R. C., Adler, L. A., Barkley, R., Biederman, J., Conners, K. C., Faraone, S. V., et al. (2005). Patterns and predictors of attention-deficit/hyperactivity disorder persistence into adulthood: Results from the National Comorbidity Survey Replication. *Biological Psychiatry, 57*, 1442–1451.

Kessler, R. C., Berglund, P., Demler, O., Jin, R., & Walters, E. E. (2005). Lifetime prevalence and age-of-onset distributions of DSM-IV disorders in the National Comorbidity Survey Replication. *Archives of General Psychiatry, 62*, 593–602.

Kessler, R. C., Chiu, W. T., Demler, O., & Walters, E. (2005). Prevalence, severity and comorbidity of the 12-month DSM-IV disorders in the National Comorbidity Survey Replication. *Archives of General Psychiatry, 62*, 617–627.

Kibbe, D. C. (2005). 10 steps to HIPAA security compliance. Retrieved January 19, 2007, from http://www.aafp.org/fpm/20050400/43tens.html.

Kiesler, D. J. (2001). Therapist countertransference: In search of common themes and empirical referents. *Journal of Clinical Psychology/In Session, 57*, 1053–1063.

Kimerling, R., Trafton, J. A., & Nguyen, B. (2006). Validation of a brief screen for post-traumatic stress disorder with substance use disorder patients. *Addictive Behaviors, 31*, 2074–2079.

King, M., Semlyen, J., Tai, S. S., Killaspy, H., Osborn, D., Popelyuk, D., & Nazareth, I. (2008). A systematic review of mental disorder, suicide, and deliberate self harm in lesbian, gay, and bisexual people. *BMC Psychiatry, 8*, 70.

Kirkwood, G., Rampes, H., Tuffrey, V., Richardson, J., & Pilkington, K. (2005). Yoga for anxiety: A systematic review of the research evidence. *British Journal of Sports Medicine, 39*, 884–891.

Kirsch, I., Moore, T. J., Scoboria, A., & Nicholls, S. S. (2002). The emperor's new drugs: An analysis of antidepressant medication data submitted to the U.S. Food and Drug Administration. *Prevention and Treatment, 5*(1), n.p.

Kitzmann, K. M., Gaylord, N. K., Holt, A. R., & Kenny, E. D. (2003). Child witnesses to domestic violence: A meta-analytic review. *Journal of Consulting and Clinical Psychology, 71*, 339–352.

Kleespies, P. M. (1993). The stress of patient suicidal behavior: Implications for interns and training programs in psychology. *Professional Psychology: Research and Practice, 24*, 477–482.

Kleespies, P. M., Penk, W. E., & Forsyth, J. P. (1993). The stress of patient suicidal behavior during clinical training: Incidence, impact and recovery. *Professional Psychology Research and Practice, 24,* 293–303.

Kleespies, P. M., & Richmond, J. S. (2009). Evaluating behavioral emergencies: The clinical interview. In P. Kleespies (Ed.), *Behavioral emergencies: An evidence-based resource for evaluating and managing risk of suicide, violence, and victimization* (pp. 33–55). Washington, DC: American Psychological Association.

Kleespies, P. M., Smith, M. R., & Becker, B. R. (1990). Psychology interns as patient suicide survivors: Incidence, impact and recovery. *Professional Psychology: Research and Practice, 21,* 257–263.

Klinka, E. (2009). It's been a privilege: Advising patients of the *Tarasoff* duty and its legal consequences for the federal psychotherapist-patient privilege. *Fordham Law Review, 78*(2), 836–931.

Knapp, S., & Slattery, J. M. (2004). Professional boundaries in nontraditional settings. *Professional Psychology: Research and Practice, 35*(5), 553–558.

Knauss, L. K. (2006). Ethical issues in recordkeeping in group psychotherapy. *International Journal of Group Psychotherapy, 56*(4), 415–430.

Knickerbocker, L., Heyman, R. E., Slep, A. M. S., Jouriles, E. N., & McDonald, R. (2007). Co-occurrence of child and partner maltreatment: Definitions, prevalence, theory and implications for assessment. *European Psychologist, 12,* 36–44.

Knox, K. L., Conwell, Y., & Caine, E. D. (2004). If suicide is a public health problem, what are we doing to prevent it? *American Journal of Public Health, 94,* 37–46.

Knox, S. (2008). Gifts in psychotherapy: Practice review and recommendations. *Psychotherapy: Research, Theory, Practice, Training, 45*(1), 103–110.

Knox, S., Burkard, A. W., Edwards, L. M., Smith, J. J., & Schlosser, L. Z. (2008). Supervisor's reports of the effects of supervisor self-disclosure on supervisees. *Psychotherapy Research, 18*(5), 543–559.

Knox, S., Burkard, A. W., Jackson, J. A., Schaack, A. M., & Hess, S. (2006). Therapists-in-training who experience a client suicide: Implications for supervision. *Professional Psychology: Research and Practice, 37,* 547–557.

Knox, S., Dubois, R., Smith, J., Hess, S. A., & Hill, C. E. (2009). Clients' experiences giving gifts to therapists. *Psychotherapy Theory, Research, Practice, Training, 46*(3), 350–361.

Knox, S., Hess, S. A., Peterson, D. A., & Hill, C. E. (1997). A qualitative analysis of client perceptions of the effects of helpful therapist self-disclosure in long-term therapy. *Journal of Counseling Psychology, 44,* 274–283.

Knox, S., Hess, S. A., Williams, E. N., & Hill, C. E. (2003). "Here's a little something for you": How therapists respond to client gifts. *Journal of Consulting Psychology, 50,* 199–210.

Knox, S., & Hill, C. E. (2003). Therapist self-disclosure: Research-based suggestions for practitioners. *Journal of Clinical Psychology, 59,* 529–539.

Kolmes, K. (2010). Developing my private practice social media policy. *Independent Practitioner, 30*(3), 140–142.

Koocher, G. (2006). On being there. *Monitor on Psychology, 37,* 5. Retrieved October 18, 2006, from http://www.apa.org/monitor/apr06/pc.html.

Kopp, S. (1977). *Back to one: A practical guide for psychotherapists.* Palo Alto, CA: Science and Behavior Books.

Kottler, J. A. (2003). *On being a therapist* (3rd ed.). San Francisco: Jossey-Bass.

Kraft, T. L., Jobes, D. A., Lineberry, T. W., Conrad, A., & Kung, S. (2010). Why suicide? Perceptions of suicidal inpatients and reflections of clinical researchers. *Archives of Suicide Research, 14*(4), 375–382.

Krakowski, M. I., & Czobor, P. (2004). Psychosocial risk factors associated with suicide attempts and violence among psychiatric inpatients. *Psychiatric Services, 55,* 1414–1419.

Krakowski, M., & Czobor, P. (2004). Gender differences in violent behaviors: Relationship to clinical symptoms and psychosocial factors. *American Journal of Psychiatry, 161*(3), 459–465.

Krueger, R. F., & Bezdjian, S. (2009). Enhancing research and treatment of mental disorders with dimensional concepts: Toward DSM-V and ICD-11. *World Psychiatry, 8*(1), 3–6.

Kruger, J., Epley, N., Parker, J., & Ng, Z. (2005). Egocentrism over e-mail: Can we communicate as well as we think? *Journal of Personality and Social Psychology, 89,* 925–936.

Krysinska, K., & De Leo, D. (2008). Suicide on railway networks: Epidemiology, risk factors, and prevention. *Australian and New Zealand Journal of Psychiatry, 42*(9), 763–771.

Krysinska, K., & Lester, D. (2010). Post-traumatic stress disorder and suicide risk: A systematic review. *Archives of Suicide Research, 14*(1), 1–23.

Kumar, C. T., Mohan, R., Ranjith, G., & Chandrasekaran, R. (2006). Characteristics of high intent suicide attempters admitted to a general hospital. *Journal of Affective Disorders, 91*(1), 77–81.

Kumar, S., & Simpson, A. I. F. (2005). Application of risk assessment for violence methods to general adult psychiatry: A selective literature review. *Australian and New Zealand Journal of Psychiatry, 39,* 328–335.

Kuyken, W., Peters, E., Power, M. J., & Lavender, T. (2003). Trainee clinical psychologists' adaptation and professional functioning: A longitudinal study. *Clinical Psychology and Psychotherapy, 10,* 41–54.

Lalonde, J. K., Hudson, J. I., Gigante, R. A., & Pope, H. G. (2001). Canadian and American psychiatrists' attitudes toward dissociative disorders diagnoses. *Canadian Journal of Psychiatry, 46,* 407–412.

Lam, R. W., & Levitan, R. D. (2000). Pathophysiology of seasonal affective disorder: A review. *Journal of Psychiatry Neuroscience, 25,* 469–480.

Lambie, G. W. (2005). Child abuse and neglect: A practical guide for professional school counselors. *Professional School Counseling, 8,* 249–258.

Lancer, R., Motta, R., & Lancer, D. (2007). The effect of aerobic exercise on obsessive-compulsive disorder, anxiety, and depression: A preliminary investigation. *The Behavior Therapist, 30, 53,* 57–62.

Larson, D. B., & Larson, S. S. (2003). Spirituality's potential relevance to physical and emotional health: A brief review of quantitative research. *Journal of Psychology and Theology, 31,* 37–51.

Laszloffy, T. A., & Hardy, K. V. (2000). Uncommon strategies for a common problem: Addressing racism in family therapy. *Family Process, 39,* 35–51.

Lauder, W., Anderson, I., & Barclay, A. (2005). Housing and self-neglect: The responses of health, social care and environmental health agencies. *Journal of Interprofessional Care, 19,* 317–325.

Lawoko, S., Soares, J. J. F., & Nolan, P. (2004). Violence towards psychiatric staff: A comparison of gender, job and environmental characteristics in England and Sweden. *Work and Stress, 18,* 39–55.

Lawson, G., & Myers, J. E. (2011). Wellness, professional quality of life, and career-sustaining behaviors: What keeps us well? *Journal of Counseling & Development, 89*(2), 163–171.

Lefforge, N. L., Donohue, B., & Strada, M. J. (2007). Improving session attendance in mental health and substance abuse settings: A review of controlled studies. *Behavior Therapy, 38,* 1–22.

Lehavot, K., Barnett, J. E., & Powers, D. (2010). Psychotherapy, professional relationships, and ethical considerations in the MySpace generation. *Professional Psychology: Research and Practice, 41*(2), 160–166.

Leiter, M. P., & Harvie, P. L. (1996). Burnout among mental health workers: A review and a research agenda. *International Journal of Social Psychiatry, 42,* 90–101.

Leong, F. T., Leach, M. M., Yeh, C., & Chou, E. (2007). Suicide among Asian Americans: What do we know? What do we need to know? *Death Studies, 31*(5), 417–434.

Levitt, A. J., & Boyle, M. H. (2002). The impact of latitude on the prevalence of seasonal depression. *Canadian Journal of Psychiatry, 47,* 361–367.

Levy, K. N., Clarkin, J. F., Yeomans, F. E., Scott, L. N., Wasserman, R. H., & Kernberg, O. F. (2006). The mechanisms of change in the treatment of borderline personality disorder with transference focused psychotherapy. *Journal of Clinical Psychology, 62,* 481–501.

Lewis, C. A., & Cruise, S. M. (2006). Religion and happiness: Consensus, contradictions, comments and concerns. *Mental Health, Religion and Culture, 9,* 213–225.

Liappas, J., Paparrigopoulos, T., Tzavellas, E., & Christodoulou, G. (2002). Impact of alcohol detoxification on anxiety and depressive symptoms. *Drug and Alcohol Dependence, 68,* 215–220.

Lill, M. M., & Wilkinson, T. J. (2005). Judging a book by its cover: Descriptive survey of patients' preferences for doctors' appearance and mode of address. *British Medical Journal, 331,* 1524–1527.

Lin, E. H. B., Katon, W. J., Simon, G. E., Von Korff, M., Bush, T. M., Walker, E. A., et al. (2000). Low-intensity treatment of depression in primary care: Is it problematic? *General Hospital Psychiatry, 22,* 78–83.

Lin, K., & Cheung, F. (1999). Mental health issues for Asian Americans. *Psychiatric Services, 50,* 774–780.

Lincoln, T. M., Luellmann, E., & Rief, W. (2007). Correlates and long-term consequences of poor insights in patients with schizophrenia. A systematic review. *Schizophrenia Bulletin, 33*(6), 1324–1342.

Linden, J. A. (2011). Care of the adult patient after sexual assault. *New England Journal of Medicine, 365*(9), 834–841.

Linehan, M. M. (1993). *Cognitive-behavioral treatment of borderline personality disorder.* New York: Guilford Press.

Linehan, M. M., Comtois, K. A., Murray, A. M., Brown, M. Z., Gallop, R. J., Heard, H. L.,...Lindenboim, N. (2006). Two-year randomized controlled trial and follow-up of dialectical behavior therapy versus therapy by experts for suicidal behaviors and borderline personality disorder. *Archives of General Psychiatry, 63,* 757–766.

Linehan, M. M., Goodstein, J. L., Nielsen, S. L., & Chiles, J. A. (1983). Reasons for staying alive when you are thinking of killing yourself: The Reasons for Living Inventory. *Journal of Clinical and Consulting Psychology, 51,* 276–286.

Ling, C. W. (1997). Crossing cultural boundaries. *Nursing, 27,* 32d–32f.

Links, P. S. (2005). Suicide risk peaks in first week of psychiatric hospitalisation and post-discharge. *Evidence-Based Mental Health, 8*(4), 114.

Linley, P. A., & Joseph, S. (2007). Therapy work and therapists' positive and negative well-being. *Journal of Social and Clinical Psychology, 26*(3), 385–403.

Lisanby, S. H. (2007). Electroconvulsive therapy for depression. *New England Journal of Medicine, 357*(19), 1939–1945.

Little, L., & Hamby, S. L. (1996). Impact of a clinician's sexual abuse history, gender, and theoretical orientation on treatment issues related to childhood sexual abuse. *Professional Psychology: Research and Practice, 27,* 617–625.

Logan, C., & Johnstone, L. (2010). Personality disorder and violence: Making the link through risk formulation. *Journal of Personality Disorders, 24*(5), 610–633.

Lopez-Ibor, J. J., Lopez-Ibor, M. I., & Pastrana, J. I. (2008). Transcranial magnetic stimulation. *Current Opinion in Psychiatry, 21*(6), 640–644.

Loue, S. (2000). Intimate partner violence: Bridging the gap between law and science. *Journal of Legal Medicine, 21,* 1–34.

Loue, S. (2001). Elder abuse and neglect in medicine and law: The need for reform. *Journal of Legal Medicine, 22,* 159–209.

Louma, J. B., & Pearson, J. L. (2002). Suicide and marital status in the United States, 1991–1996: Is widowhood a risk factor? *American Journal of Public Health, 92,* 1518–1522.

Lukens, E. P., & McFarlane, W. R. (2004). Psychoeducation as evidence-based practice: Considerations for practice, research, and policy. *Brief Treatment and Crisis Intervention, 4,* 205–225.

Maguen, S., Cohen, G., Cohen, B. E., Lawhon, G. D., Marmar, C. R., & Seal, K. H. (2010). The role of psychologists in the care of Iraq and Afghanistan veterans in primary care settings. *Professional Psychology: Research and Practice, 41*(2), 135–142.

Maher, M. J., Rego, S. A., & Asnis, G. M. (2006). Sleep disturbances in patients with post-traumatic stress disorder: Epidemiology, impact and approaches to management. *CNS Drugs, 20,* 567–590.

Maio, J. E. (2003). HIPAA and the special status of psychotherapy notes. *Lippincott's Case Management, 8*(1), 24–29.

Maislin, G., Pack, A. I., Kribbs, N. B., Smith, P. L., Schwartz, A. R., Kline, L. R., et al. (1995). A survey screen for prediction of apnea. *Sleep, 18,* 158–166.

Mamo, D. C. (2007). Managing suicidality in schizophrenia. *Canadian Journal of Psychiatry, 52*(S1), 59S–70S.

Manzoni, G. M., Pagnini, F., Castelnuovo, G., & Molinari, E. (2008). Relaxation training for anxiety: A ten-years systematic review with meta-analysis. *BMC Psychiatry, 8*(1), 41.

Marshall, N. A. (2012). A clinician's guide to recognizing and reporting parent psychological maltreatment of children. *Professional Psychology: Research and Practice, 43*(2), 73–79.

Martin, S. (2010, July). The Internet's ethical challenges. *Monitor on Psychology, 41,* 32.

Maslach, C. (2001). What have we learned about burnout and health? *Psychology and Health, 16,* 607–611.

Maslach, C. (2003). Job burnout: New directions in research and intervention. *Current Directions in Psychological Science, 12,* 189–192.

Maslach, C., Schaufeli, W. B., & Leiter, M. P. (2001). Job burnout. *Annual Review of Psychology, 52,* 397–422.

Mathews, B. P., & Kenny, M. (2008). Mandatory reporting legislation in the USA, Canada and Australia: A cross-jurisdictional review of key features, differences and issues. *Child Maltreatment, 13*(1), 50–63.

Mathy, R. M., Cochran, S. D., Olsen, J., & Mays, V. M. (2011). The association between relationship markers of sexual orientation and suicide: Denmark, 1990–2001. *Social Psychiatry and Psychiatric Epidemiology, 46*(2), 111–117.

Mathy, R. M., Lehmann, B. A., & Kerr, D. L. (2003). Bisexual and transgender identities in a nonclinical sample of North Americans: Suicidal intent, behavioral difficulties, and mental health treatment. *Journal of Bisexuality, 3*(3-4), 93–109.

Matson, J. L., & Neal, D. (2009). Psychotropic medication use for challenging behaviors in persons with intellectual disabilities: An overview. *Research in Developmental Disabilities, 30*(3), 572–586.

Maxie, A. C., Arnold, D. H., & Stephenson, M. (2006). Do therapists address ethnic and racial differences in cross-cultural psychotherapy? *Psychotherapy: Theory, Research, Practice, Training, 43*, 85–98.

Mazzucchelli, T., Kane, R., & Rees, C. (2009). Behavioral activation treatments for depression in adults: A meta-analysis and review. *Clinical Psychology: Science and Practice, 16*(4), 383–411.

McAdams, C. R., & Foster, V. A. (2000). Client suicide: Its frequency and impact on counselors. *Journal of Mental Health Counseling, 22*, 107–121.

McCann, I. L., & Pearlman, L. A. (1990). Vicarious traumatization: A framework for understanding the psychological effects of working with victims. *Journal of Traumatic Stress, 3*, 131–149.

McCarthy, A., Lee, K., Itakura, S., & Muir, D. W. (2006). Cultural display rules drive eye gaze during thinking. *Journal of Cross-Cultural Psychology, 37*, 717–722.

McCloskey, K., & Grigsby, N. (2005). The ubiquitous clinical problem of adult intimate partner violence: The need for routine assessment. *Professional Psychology: Research and Practice, 36*(3), 264–275.

McCollum, E. E., & Stith, S. M. (2008). Couples treatment for interpersonal violence: A review of outcome research literature and current clinical practices. *Violence and Victims, 23*(2), 187–201.

McEllistrem, J. E. (2004). Affective and predatory violence: A bimodal classification system of human aggression and violence. *Aggression and Violent Behavior, 10*(1), 1–30.

McGee, S. J. (2011). To friend or not to friend: Is that the question for healthcare? *American Journal of Bioethics, 11*(8), 2–5.

McIvor, R. J., Potter, L., & Davies, L. (2008). Stalking behaviour by patients towards psychiatrists in a large mental health organization. *International Journal of Social Psychiatry, 54*(4), 350–357.

McKenry, P. C., Serovich, J. M., Mason, T. L., & Mosack, K. (2006). Perpetration of gay and lesbian partner violence: A disempowerment perspective. *Journal of Family Violence, 21*, 233–243.

McLaughlin, J. K., Wise, T. N., & Lipworth, L. (2004). Increased risk of suicide among patients with breast implants: Do the epidemiologic data support psychiatric consultation? *Psychosomatics: Journal of Consultation Liaison Psychiatry, 45*, 277–280.

McManus, F., Rakovshik, S., Kennerley, H., Fennell, M., & Westbrook, D. (2011). An investigation of the accuracy of therapists' self-assessment of cognitive-behaviour therapy skills. *British Journal of Clinical Psychology, 51*(3), 292–306.

McMyler, C., & Pryjmachuk, S. (2008). Do "no-suicide" contracts work? *Journal of Psychiatric and Mental Health Nursing, 15*(6), 512–522.

McNiel, D. E. (2009). Assessment and management of acute risk of violence in adult patients. In P. Kleespies (Ed.), *Behavioral emergencies: An evidence-based resource for evaluating and managing risk of suicide, violence, and victimization* (pp. 33–55). Washington, DC: American Psychological Association.

McNiel, D. E., Eisner, J. P., & Binder, R. L. (2000). The relationship between command hallucinations and violence. *Psychiatric Services, 51,* 1288–1292.

McWilliams, N. (2004). *Psychoanalytic psychotherapy: A practitioner's guide.* New York: Guilford Press.

MedlinePlus. (2007). Sleep disorders. Retrieved April 6, 2007, from http://www.nlm.nih.gov/medlineplus/sleepdisorders.html.

Mehta, P., & Sharma, M. (2010). Yoga as a complementary therapy for clinical depression. *Complementary Health Practice Review, 15*(3), 156–170.

Meloy, J. R. (2006). Empirical basis and forensic application of affective and predatory violence. *Australian and New Zealand Journal of Psychiatry, 40*(6-7), 539–547.

Menahem, S., & Shvartzman, P. (1998). Is our appearance important to our patients? *Family Practice, 15,* 391–397.

Merikangas, K., & Yu, K. (2002). Genetic epidemiology of bipolar disorder. *Clinical Neuroscience Research, 2,* 127–141.

Meyer, I. H., Dietrich, J., & Schwartz, S. (2008). Lifetime prevalence of mental disorders and suicide attempts in diverse lesbian, gay, and bisexual populations. *American Journal of Public Health, 98*(6), 1004–1006.

Michalak, J., & Holtforth, M. G. (2006). Where do we go from here? The goal perspective in psychotherapy. *Clinical Psychology: Science and Practice, 13*(4), 346–365.

Miklowitz, D. J., Otto, M. W., Frank, E., Reilly-Harrington, N. A., Kogan, J. N., Sachs, G. S., . . . Wisniewski, S. R. (2007). Intensive psychosocial intervention enhances functioning in patients with bipolar depression: Results from a 9-month randomized controlled trial. *American Journal of Psychiatry, 164,* 1340–1347.

Miller, C. (2010). Interviewing strategies, rapport, and empathy. In D. L. Segal & M. Hersen (Eds.), *Diagnostic interviewing* (4th ed., pp. 23–38). New York: Springer.

Miller, L. (1994). Biofeedback and behavioral medicine: Treating the symptom, the syndrome or the person? *Psychotherapy, 31,* 161–169.

Miller, W. R., & Rollnick, S. (2002). *Motivational interviewing: Preparing people for change* (2nd ed.). New York: Guilford Press.

Mittal, M., & Wieling, E. (2006). Training experiences of international doctoral students in marriage and family therapy. *Journal of Marital and Family Therapy, 32*(3), 369–383.

Moline, M. E., Williams, G. T., & Austin, K. M. (1998). *Documenting psychotherapy: Essentials for mental health practitioners.* Thousand Oaks, CA: Sage.

Monahan, J. (1993). Limiting therapist exposure to *Tarasoff* liability. *American Psychologist, 48,* 242–250.

Montross, C. (2007). *Body of work: Meditations on mortality from the human anatomy lab.* New York: Penguin.

Morrison, J. (1995). *The first interview: Revised for DSM-IV.* New York: Guilford Press.

Morrison, J. (1997). *When psychological problems mask medical disorders: A guide for psychotherapists.* New York: Guilford Press.

Morrison, J. (2007). *Diagnosis made easier: Principles and techniques for mental health clinicians.* New York: Guilford Press.

Morrison, L. L., & Downey, D. L. (2000). Racial differences in self-disclosure of suicidal ideation and reasons for living: Implications for training. *Cultural Diversity and Ethnic Minority Psychology, 6*(4), 374–386.

Mort, J. R., & Aparasu, R. R. (2002). Prescribing of psychotropics in the elderly: Why is it so often inappropriate? *CNS Drugs, 16,* 99–109.

Mosqueda, L., & Dong, X. (2011). Elder abuse and self-neglect: "I don't care anything about going to the doctor, to be honest…." *JAMA, 306*(5), 532–540.

Mossman, D. (2004). How a rabbi's sermon resolved my *Tarasoff* conflict. *Journal of the American Academy of Psychiatry and the Law, 32,* 359–363.

Mullen, P. E., & Ogloff, J. R. (2009). Assessing and managing the risks of violence towards others. In M. G. Gelder, N. C. Andreasen, J. J. Lopez-Ibor, & J. R. Geddes (Eds.), *New Oxford textbook of psychiatry* (2nd ed., vol. 2, pp. 1991–2002). New York: Oxford University Press.

Munsey, C. (2008). Stay safe in practice. *Monitor on Psychology, 39*(4), 36.

Myers, D., & Hayes, J. A. (2006). Effects of therapist general self-disclosure and countertransference disclosure on ratings of the therapist and session. *Psychotherapy: Research, Theory, Practice, Training, 43*(2), 173–185.

Nagai, C. (2009). Ethno-cultural and linguistic transference and countertransference: From Asian perspectives. *American Journal of Psychotherapy, 63*(1), 13–23.

Nasar, J. L., & Devlin, A. S. (2011). Impressions of psychotherapists' offices. *Journal of Counseling Psychology, 58*(3), 310–320.

National Association of Social Workers. (2008). Code of ethics of the National Association of Social Workers. Retrieved August 26, 2012, from http://www.socialworkers.org/pubs/code/code.asp

National Committee for the Prevention of Elder Abuse & National Adult Protective Services Association. (2007). *The 2004 survey of state adult protective services: Abuse of vulnerable adults 18 years of age and older.* Washington, DC: National Center on Elder Abuse. Retrieved December 17, 2007, from http://www.ncea.aoa.gov/Resources/Publication/docs/APS_2004NCEASurvey.pdf

National Sleep Foundation. (2007). T*opics A to Zzzzs.* Retrieved April 6, 2007, from http://www.sleepfoundation.org/site/c.huIXKjM0IxF/b.2450839/k.BA4F/Topics_A_to_Zzzzs/apps/nl/newsletter2.asp.

Neighbors, H. W., Trierweiler, S. J., Ford, B. C., & Muroff, J. R. (2003). Racial differences in DSM diagnosis using a semi-structured instrument: The importance of clinical judgment in the diagnosis of African Americans. *Journal of Health and Social Behavior, 44,* 237–256.

Nelson, M. L., Barnes, K. L., Evans, A. L., & Triggiano, P. J. (2008). Working with conflict in clinical supervision: Wise supervisors' perspectives. *Journal of Counseling Psychology, 55*(2), 172–184.

Nelson-Gardell, D., & Harris, D. (2003). Childhood abuse history, secondary traumatic stress, and child welfare workers. *Child Welfare, 82,* 5–26.

Neno, R., & Neno, M. (2005). Identifying abuse in older people. *Nursing Standard, 20,* 43–47.

Nesbit, R. E. (2003). *The geography of thought: How Asians and Westerners think differently… and why.* New York: Free Press.

Newman, A. W., Wright, S. W., Wrenn, K. D., & Bernard, A. (2005). Should physicians have facial piercings? *Journal of General Internal Medicine, 20*, 213–218.

Newman, J. C., & Feldman, R. (2011). Copyright and open access at the bedside. *New England Journal of Medicine, 365*(26), 2447–2449.

Newsome, S., Christopher, J. C., Dahlen, P., & Christopher, S. (2006). Teaching counselors self-care through mindfulness practices. *Teachers College Record, 108*, 1881–1900.

Nhat Hanh, T. (1975). *The miracle of mindfulness: A manual on meditation.* Boston: Beacon Press.

Nhat Hanh, T. (1998). *The Heart of the Buddha's Teaching.* Berkeley, CA: Parallax Press.

Nihalani, N. D., Kunwar, A., Staller, J. & Lamberti, J. S. (2006). How should psychiatrists dress? A survey. *Community Mental Health Journal, 42*, 291–302.

Norcross, J. C. (2000). Psychotherapist self-care: Practitioner-tested, research-informed strategies. *Professional Psychology: Research and Practice, 31*, 710–713.

Norcross, J. C. (2005). The psychotherapist's own psychotherapy: Educating and developing psychologists. *American Psychologist, 60*, 840–850.

Norcross, J. C. (2006). Integrating self-help into psychotherapy: 16 practice suggestions. *Professional Psychology: Research and Practice, 37*, 683–693.

Norcross, J. C., & Guy, J. D. (2007). *Leaving it at the office: A guide to psychotherapist self-care.* New York: Guilford Press.

Norcross, J. C., Koocher, G. P., & Garofalo, A. (2006). Discredited psychological treatments and tests: A Delphi poll. *Professional Psychology: Research and Practice, 37*, 515–522.

Norko, M. A., & Baranoski, M. V. (2005). The state of contemporary risk assessment research. *Canadian Journal of Psychiatry, 50*(1), 18–26.

Norris, D. M., Gutheil, T. G., & Strasburger, L. H. (2003). This couldn't happen to me: Boundary problems and sexual misconduct in the psychotherapy relationship. *Psychiatric Services, 54*, 517–522.

Novick, D., Haro, J. M., Suarez, D., Perez, V., Dittmann, R. W., & Haddad, P. M. (2010). Predictors and clinical consequences of non-adherence with antipsychotic medication in the outpatient treatment of schizophrenia. *Psychiatry Research, 176*(2-3), 109–113.

Occupational Safety and Health Administration. (2004). *Guidelines for preventing workplace violence for health care and social service workers.* Retrieved July 3, 2007, from http://www.osha.gov/Publications/osha3148.pdf.

O'Connor, S. S., Jobes, D. A., Lineberry, T. W., & Bostwick, J. M. (2010). An investigation of emotional upset in suicide ideation. *Archives of Suicide Research, 14*(1), 35–43.

O'Connor, S. S., Jobes, D. A., Yeargin, M. K., FitzGerald, M. E., Rodriguez, V. M., Conrad, A. K., & Lineberry, T. W. (2012). A cross-sectional investigation of the suicidal spectrum: Typologies of suicidality based on ambivalence about living and dying. *Comprehensive Psychiatry, 53*(5), 461–467.

O'Donnell, S., Meyer, I. H., & Schwartz, S. (2011). Increased risk of suicide attempts among Black and Latino lesbians, gay men, and bisexuals. *American Journal of Public Health, 101*(6), 1055–1059.

Ohayon, M. M., & Roth, T. (2002). Prevalence of restless legs syndrome and periodic limb movement disorder in the general population. *Journal of Psychosomatic Research, 53*, 547–554.

Oishi, S., & Diener, E. (2001). Goals, culture, and subjective well-being. *Personality and Social Psychology Bulletin, 27*(12), 1674–1682.

O'Leary, B. J., & Norcross, J. C. (1998). Lifetime prevalence of mental disorders in the general population. In G. P. Koocher, J. C. Norcross, & S. S. Hill (Eds.), *Psychologists' desk reference* (pp. 3–5). New York: Oxford University Press.

O'Reilly, K. B. (2010, Sept. 6). Social media pose ethical unknowns for doctors. *American Medical News.* Retrieved from http://www.ama-assn.org/amednews/2010/09/06/prl20906.htm.

Osiezagha, K., Kaur, A., Barker, N. C., & Bailey, R. K. (2009). Suicide and African Americans: An overview. *Challenge, 15*(1077-193-X2), 29–39.

Osterberg, L., & Blaschke, T. (2005). Adherence to medication. *New England Journal of Medicine, 353,* 487–497.

Otis, H. G., & King, J. H. (2006). Unanticipated psychotropic medication reactions. *Journal of Mental Health Counseling, 28,* 218–240.

Owens, D., Horrocks, J., & House, A. (2002). Fatal and non-fatal repetition of self-harm: Systematic review. *British Journal of Psychiatry, 181,* 193–199.

Pabian, Y. L., Welfel, E., & Beebe, R. S. (2009). Psychologists' knowledge of their states' laws pertaining to *Tarasoff*-type situations. *Professional Psychology: Research and Practice, 40*(1), 8–14.

Packman, W. L., Marlitt, R. E., Bongar, B., & Pennuto, T. O. (2004). A comprehensive and concise assessment of suicide risk. *Behavioral Sciences and the Law, 22,* 667–680.

Packman, W. L., Pennuto, T. O., Bongar, B., & Orthwein, J. (2004). Legal issues of professional negligence in suicide cases. *Behavioral Sciences and the Law, 22,* 697–713.

Pasqualone, G. A., & Fitzgerald, S. M. (1999). Munchausen by proxy syndrome: The forensic challenge of recognition, diagnosis, and reporting. *Critical Care Nursing, 22,* 52–64.

Patel, S. (2007, June 12). "Been there?" Sometimes that isn't the point. *New York Times.* Retrieved July 1, 2007, from http://www.nytimes.com/2007/06/12/health/psychology/12essa.html.

Paul, J. P., Catania, J., Pollack, L., Moskowitz, J., Canchola, J., Mills, T., ... Stall, R. (2002). Suicide attempts among gay and bisexual men: Lifetime prevalence and antecedents. *American Journal of Public Health, 92*(8), 1338–1345.

PBS (2009, August 21). Justice delayed. Retrieved August 24, 2012, from http://www.pbs.org/now/shows/517/index.html

Pearlman, L. A., & Mac Ian, P. S. (1995). Vicarious traumatization: An empirical study of the effects of trauma work on trauma therapists. *Professional Psychology: Research and Practice, 26,* 558–565.

Penedo, F. J., & Dahn, J. R. (2005). Exercise and well-being: A review of mental and physical health benefits associated with physical activity. *Current Opinion in Psychiatry, 18*(2), 189–193.

Peterson, A. M., Takiya, L., & Finley, R. (2003). Meta-analysis of trials of interventions to improve medication adherence. *American Journal of Health-System Pharmacy, 60,* 657–665.

Petit, J. (2005). Management of the acutely violent patient. *Psychiatric Clinics of North America, 28,* 701–711.

Philip, C. E. (1993). Dilemmas of disclosure to patients and colleagues when a therapist faces life-threatening illness. *Health and Social Work, 18,* 13–19.

Phillips, K. A., & Menard, W. (2006). Suicidality in body dysmorphic disorder: A prospective study. *American Journal of Psychiatry, 163*(7), 1280–1282.

Pieters, G., Speybrouck, E., De Gucht, V., & Joos, S. (2005). Assaults by patients on psychiatric trainees: Frequency and training issues. *Psychiatric Bulletin, 29,* 168–170.

Pinals, D. A., & Gutheil, T. G. (2001). Sanctity, secrecy and silence: Dilemmas in clinical confidentiality. *Psychiatric Annals, 31,* 113–118.

Piper, A., & Merskey, H. (2004). Dissociative identity disorder. Part 1. The excesses of an improbable concept. *Canadian Journal of Psychiatry, 49,* 592–600.

Pomerantz, A. M. (2005). Increasingly informed consent: Discussing distinct aspects of psychotherapy at different points in time. *Ethics & Behavior, 15*(4), 351–360.

Pompili, M., Amador, X. F., Girardi, P., Harkavy-Friedman, J., Harrow, M., Kaplan, K., . . . Tatarelli, R. (2007). Suicide risk in schizophrenia: Learning from the past to change the future. *Annals of General Psychiatry, 6,* 10.

Pope, K. S., & Feldman-Summers, S. (1992). National survey of psychologists' sexual and physical abuse history and their evaluation of training and competence in these areas. *Professional Psychology: Research and Practice, 23,* 353–361.

Pope, K. S., & Keith-Spiegel, P. (2008). A practical approach to boundaries in psychotherapy: Making decisions, bypassing blunders, and mending fences. *Journal of Clinical Psychology, 64*(5), 638–652.

Pope, K. S., & Tabachnick, B. G. (1993). Therapists' anger, hate, fear, and sexual feelings: National survey of therapist responses, client characteristics, critical events, formal complaints, and training. *Professional Psychology: Research and Practice, 24,* 142–152.

Porter, S., & ten Brinke, L. (2008). Reading between the lies: Identifying concealed and falsified emotions in universal facial expressions. *Psychological Science, 19*(5), 508–514.

Porter, S., & ten Brinke, L. (2010). The truth about lies: What works in detecting high-stakes deception? *Legal & Criminological Psychology, 15*(1), 57–75.

Povoledo, E., & Carvajal, D. (2012, April 14). Increasingly in Europe, suicides by "economic crisis." *New York Times.* Retrieved from http://www.nytimes.com/2012/04/15/world/europe/increasingly-in-europe-suicides-by-economic-crisis.html?pagewanted=all.

Pressly, P. K., & Heesacker, M. (2001). The physical environment and counseling: A review of theory and research. *Journal of Counseling and Development, 79,* 148–160.

Pridmore, S., & McArthur, M. (2008). Suicide and reputation damage. *Australasian Psychiatry, 16*(5), 312–316.

Prochaska, J. O., & Norcross, J. C. (2001). Stages of change. *Psychotherapy, 38,* 443–448.

Puetz, T. W., O'Connor, P. J., & Dishman, R. K. (2006). Effects of chronic exercise on feelings of energy and fatigue: A quantitative synthesis. *Psychological Bulletin, 132,* 866–876.

Punjabi, N. M. (2008). The epidemiology of adult obstructive sleep apnea. *Proceedings of the American Thoracic Society, 5*(2), 136–143.

Purcell, R., Powell, M. B., & Mullen, P. E. (2005). Clients who stalk psychologists: Prevalence, methods and motives. *Professional Psychology: Research and Practice, 36,* 537–543.

Putney, M. W., Worthington, E. L., & McCullough, M. E. (1992). Effects of supervisor and supervisee theoretical orientation and supervisor-supervisee matching on interns' perceptions of supervision. *Journal of Counseling Psychology, 39,* 258–265.

Qin, P., Agerbo, E., & Mortensen, P. B. (2003). Suicide risk in relation to socioeconomic, demographic, psychiatric, and familial factors: A national register-based study of all suicides in Denmark, 1981–1997. *American Journal of Psychiatry, 160*(4), 765–772.

RachBeisel, J., Scott, J., & Dixon, L. (1999). Co-occurring severe mental illness and substance use disorders: A review of recent research. *Psychiatric Services, 50*, 1427–1434.

Ramel, W., Goldin, P. R., Carmona, P. E., & McQuaid, J. R. (2004). The effects of mindfulness meditation on cognitive processes and affect in patients with past depression. *Cognitive Therapy and Research, 28*, 433–455.

Ramsay, J. R., & Rostain, A. L. (2005). Adapting psychotherapy to meet the needs of adults with attention-deficit/hyperactivity disorder. *Psychotherapy: Theory, Research, Practice, Training, 42*, 72–84.

Raquepaw, J. M., & Miller, R. S. (1989). Psychotherapist burnout: A componential analysis. *Professional Psychology: Research and Practice, 20*, 32–36.

Recupero, P. R. (2005). E-mail and the psychiatrist-patient relationship. *Journal of the American Academy of Psychiatry and Law, 33*, 465–475.

Recupero, P. R., & Rainey, S. E. (2005a). Forensic aspects of e-therapy. *Journal of Psychiatric Practice, 11*(6), 405–410.

Recupero, P. R., & Rainey, S. E. (2005b). Informed consent to e-therapy. *American Journal of Psychotherapy, 59*, 319–331.

Reeves, R. R., & Ladner, M. E. (2010). Antidepressant-induced suicidality: An update. *CNS Neuroscience & Therapeutics, 16*(4), 227–234.

Reid, W. H. (2008). Assaults against psychiatrists and other mental health professionals. *Journal of Psychiatric Practice, 14*(3), 179–181.

Reisch, T., Schuster, U., & Michel, K. (2008). Suicide by jumping from bridges and other heights: Social and diagnostic factors. *Psychiatry Research, 161*(1), 97–104.

Reitzel, L. R., Burns, A. B., Repper, K. K., Wingate, L. R., & Joiner, T. E. (2004). The effect of therapist availability on the frequency of patient-initiated between-session contact. *Professional Psychology: Research and Practice, 35*(3), 291–296.

Renninger, S. M., Veach, P. M., & Bagdade, P. (2002). Psychologists' knowledge, opinions, and decision-making processes regarding child abuse and neglect reporting laws. *Professional Psychology: Research and Practice, 33*, 19–23.

Resick, P. A., Galovski, T. E., Uhlmansiek, M. O., Scher, C. D., Clum, G. A., & Young-Xu, Y. (2008). A randomized clinical trial to dismantle components of cognitive processing therapy for posttraumatic stress disorder in female victims of interpersonal violence. *Journal of Consulting and Clinical Psychology, 76*(2), 243–258.

Ribiero, J. D., & Joiner, T. E. (2009). The Interpersonal-Psychological Theory of suicidal behavior: Current status and future directions. *Journal of Clinical Psychology, 65*(12), 1291–1299.

Richardson-Vejlgaard, R., Sher, L., Oquendo, M. A., Lizardi, D., & Stanley, B. (2009). Moral objections to suicide and suicidal ideation among mood-disordered Whites, Blacks, and Hispanics. *Journal of Psychiatric Research, 43*(4), 360–365.

Richter, K. P., Surprenant, Z. J., Schmelzle, K. H., & Mayo, M. S. (2003). Detecting and documenting intimate partner violence: An intake form question is not enough. *Violence Against Women, 9*, 458–465.

Rihmer, Z. (2007). Suicide risk in mood disorders. *Current Opinion in Psychiatry, 20*(1), 17–22.

Rivas-Vazquez, R. A., Blais, M. A., Rey, G. J., & Rivas-Vazquez, A. A. (2001). A brief reminder about documenting the psychological consultation. *Professional Psychology: Research and Practice, 32*, 194–199.

Robertiello, G. (2006). Common mental health correlates of domestic violence. *Brief Treatment and Crisis Intervention, 6*, 111–121.

Roberts, A. R., Monferrari, I., & Yeager, K. R. (2008). Avoiding malpractice lawsuits by following risk assessment and suicide prevention guidelines. *Brief Treatment and Crisis Intervention, 8*(1), 5–14.

Robiner, W. N., Bearman, D. L., Berman, M., Grove, W. M., Colon, E., Armstrong, J., et al. (2002). Prescriptive authority for psychologists: A looming health hazard? *Clinical Psychology: Science and Practice, 9,* 231–248.

Robinson, D. G., Woerner, M. G., Delman, H. M., & Kane, J. M. (2005). Pharmacological treatments for first-episode schizophrenia. *Schizophrenia Bulletin, 31,* 705–722.

Robinson, D. G., Woerner, M. G., McMeniman, A., Mendelowitz, A., & Bilder, R. M. (2004). Symptomatic and functional recovery from a first episode of schizophrenia or schizoaffective disorder. *American Journal of Psychiatry, 161,* 473–479.

Rodgers, C. (2009). Keys to avoiding malpractice. *Psychiatric Times, 26*(12), 31–32.

Rodriguez-Srednicki, O., & Twaite, J. A. (2004a). Understanding and reporting child abuse: Legal and psychological perspectives: Part one: Physical abuse, sexual abuse and neglect. *Journal of Psychiatry and the Law, 32,* 315–359.

Rodriguez-Srednicki, O., & Twaite, J. A. (2004b). Understanding and reporting child abuse: Legal and psychological perspectives: Part two: Emotional abuse and secondary abuse. *Journal of Psychiatry and the Law, 32,* 443–481.

Rogers, R. (Ed.). (1997). *Clinical assessment of malingering and deception* (2nd ed.). New York: Guilford Press.

Rogers, R., Sewell, K. W., Martin, M. A., & Vitacco, M. J. (2003). Detection of feigned mental disorders: A meta-analysis of the MMPI-2 and malingering. *Assessment, 10,* 160–177.

Rose, D., Fleischmann, P., & Wykes, T. (2004). Consumers' views of electroconvulsive therapy: A qualitative analysis. *Journal of Mental Health, 13,* 285–293.

Rosenthal, N. E. (1998). *Winter blues: Seasonal affective disorder, what it is and how to overcome it.* New York: Guilford Press.

Roth, T., & Roehrs, T. (2003). Insomnia: Epidemiology, characteristics and consequences. *Clinical Cornerstone, 5,* 5–15.

Rothschild, B. (2004). The physiology of empathy. *Counseling and Psychotherapy Journal, 15,* n.p.

Rouget, B. W., & Aubry, J. (2007). Efficacy of psychoeducational approaches on bipolar disorders: A review of the literature. *Journal of Affective Disorders, 98*(1-2), 11–27.

Royal Australian and New Zealand College of Psychiatrists Clinical Practice Guidelines Team for Depression. (2004). Australian and New Zealand clinical practice guidelines for the treatment of depression. *Australian and New Zealand Journal of Psychiatry, 38,* 389–407.

Rudd, M. D. (2006). *The assessment and management of suicidality* (1st ed.). Sarasota, FL: Professional Resource Exchange.

Rudd, M. D. (2008). Suicide warning signs in clinical practice. *Current Psychiatry Reports, 10*(1), 87–90.

Rudd, M. D., Berman, A. L., Joiner, T. E., Nock, M. K., Silverman, M. M., Mandrusiak, M., ... Witte, T. K. (2006). Warning signs for suicide: Theory, research, and clinical applications. *Suicide and Life-Threatening Behavior, 36*(3), 255–262.

Rudd, M. D., Goulding, J., & Bryan, C. J. (2011). Student veterans: A national survey exploring psychological symptoms and suicide risk. *Professional Psychology: Research and Practice, 42*(5), 354–360.

Rudd, M. D., Joiner, T. E., Brown, G. K., Cukrowicz, K. C., Jobes, D. A., Silverman, M., & Cordero, L. (2009). Informed consent with suicidal patients: Rethinking risks in (and out of) treatment. *Psychotherapy Theory, Research, Practice, Training, 46*(4), 459–468.

Rudd, M. D., Joiner, T. E., Trotter, D., Williams, B., & Cordero, L. (2009). The psychosocial treatment of suicidal behavior: A critique of what we know. In P. Kleespies (Ed.), *Behavioral emergencies: An evidence-based resource for evaluating and managing risk of suicide, violence, and victimization* (pp. 33–55). Washington, DC: American Psychological Association.

Rudman, L. A., Ashmore, R. D., & Gary, M. L. (2001). "Unlearning" automatic biases: The malleability of implicit prejudice and stereotypes. *Journal of Personality and Social Psychology, 81,* 856–868.

Rudolph, M. N., & Hughes, D. H. (2001). Emergency assessments of domestic violence, sexual dangerousness, and elder and child abuse. *Psychiatric Services, 52,* 281–306.

Rupert, P. A., & Kent, J. S. (2007). Gender and work setting differences in career sustaining behaviors and burnout among professional psychologists. *Professional Psychology: Research and Practice, 38*(1), 544–550.

Rupert, P. A., & Morgan, D. J. (2005). Work setting and burnout among professional psychologists. *Professional Psychology: Research and Practice, 36,* 544–550.

Rupert, P. A., Stevanovic, P., & Hunley, H. A. (2009). Work-family conflict and burnout among practicing psychologists. *Professional Psychology: Research and Practice, 40*(1), 54–61.

Rusch, N., & Corrigan, P. W. (2002). Motivational interviewing to improve insight and treatment adherence in schizophrenia. *Psychiatric Rehabilitation Journal, 26,* 23–32.

Saletu-Zyhlarz, G. M., Anderer, P., Arnold, O., & Saletu, B. (2003). Confirmation of the neurophysiologically predicted therapeutic effects of trazodone on its target symptoms depression, anxiety and insomnia by postmarketing clinical studies with a controlled-release formulation in depressed outpatients. *Neuropsychobiology, 48,* 194–208.

Salmon, P. (2003). Anxiety, depression and sensitivity to stress: A unifying theory. *Clinical Psychology Review, 21,* 33–61.

Samuelson, S. L., & Campbell, C. D. (2005). Screening for domestic violence: Recommendations based on a practice survey. *Professional Psychology: Research and Practice, 36,* 276–282.

Saxby, P., & Anil, R. (2012). Financial loss and suicide. *Malaysian Journal of Medical Sciences, 19*(2). Retrieved January 11, 2013, from http://www.ncbi.nlm.nih.gov/pmc/articles/PMC3431736/.

Scarton, D. (2010, March 30, 2010). Google and Facebook raise new issues for therapists and their clients. *Washington Post.* Retrieved from http://www.washingtonpost.com/wp-dyn/content/article/2010/03/29/AR2010032902942.html.

Scascighini, L., Toma, V., Dober-Spielmann, S., & Sprott, H. (2008). Multidisciplinary treatment for chronic pain: A systematic review of interventions and outcomes. *Rheumatology, 47*(5), 670–678.

Schacht, R. L., Dimidjian, S., George, W. H., & Berns, S. B. (2009). Domestic violence assessment procedures among couple therapists. *Journal of Marital and Family Therapy, 35*(1), 47–59.

Schachter, D. C., & Kleinman, I. (2004). Psychiatrists' attitudes about and informed consent practices for antipsychotics and tardive dyskinesia. *Psychiatric Services, 55,* 714–717.

Schank, J. A., Helbok, C. M., Haldeman, D. C., & Gallardo, M. E. (2010). Challenges and benefits of ethical small-community practice. *Professional Psychology: Research and Practice, 41*(6), 502–510.

Schoenen, J. (2001). Migraine. *Pain: Clinical Updates, 9*(3), 1–9.

Schultz-Ross, R. A., & Gutheil, T. G. (1997). Difficulties in integrating spirituality into psychotherapy. *Journal of Psychotherapy Practice and Research, 6,* 130–138.

Schutter, D. J. (2010). Quantitative review of the efficacy of slow-frequency magnetic brain stimulation in major depressive disorder. *Psychological Medicine, 40*(11), 1789–1795.

Schwartz, T. L., & Park, T. L. (1999). Assaults by patients on psychiatric residents: A survey and training recommendations. *Psychiatric Services, 50,* 381–383.

Scofield, H., Roth, T., & Drake, C. (2008). Periodic limb movements during sleep: Population prevalence, clinical correlates, and racial differences. *Sleep, 31*(9), 1221–1227.

Segall, B. (2006). Hundreds of patient records found in pharmacy dumpster. Channel 13, WTHR, Indianapolis. Retrieved January 1, 2007, from http://www.wthr.com/story/5207597/hundreds-of-patient-records-found-in-pharmacy-dumpster.

Selby, E. A., Anestis, M. D., & Joiner, T. E. (2007). Daydreaming about death: Violent daydreaming as a form of emotion dysregulation in suicidality. *Behavior Modification, 31*(6), 867–879.

Seligman, M. E. P., Steen, T. A., Park, N., & Peterson, C. (2005). Positive psychology progress: Empirical validation of interventions. *American Psychologist, 60,* 410–421.

Selwood, A., & Cooper, C. (2009). Abuse of people with dementia. *Reviews in Clinical Gerontology, 19*(1), 35–43.

Semkovska, M., & McLoughlin, D. M. (2010). Objective cognitive performance associated with electroconvulsive therapy for depression: A systematic review and meta-analysis. *Biological Psychiatry, 68*(6), 568–577.

Senter, A., Morgan, R. D., Serna-McDonald, C., & Bewley, M. (2010). Correctional psychologist burnout, job satisfaction, and life satisfaction. *Psychological Services, 7*(3), 190–201.

Sharkin, B. S., & Birky, I. (1992). Incidental encounters between therapists and their clients. *Professional Psychology: Research and Practice, 23,* 326–328.

Shinn, M., Rosario, M., Morch, H., & Chestnut, D. E. (1984). Coping with job stress and burnout in the human services. *Journal of Personality and Social Psychology, 46,* 864–876.

Shugarman, L. R., Fries, B. E., Wolf, R. S., & Morris, J. N. (2003). Identifying older people at risk of abuse during routine screening practices. *Journal of the American Geriatrics Society, 51,* 24–31.

Sieck, B. C. (2012). Obtaining clinical writing informed consent versus using client disguise and recommendations for practice. *Psychotherapy, 49*(1), 3–11.

Silber, M. H. (2005). Chronic insomnia. *New England Journal of Medicine, 353*(8), 803–810.

Silver, E., Mulvey, E. P., & Monahan, J. (1999). Assessing violence risk among discharged psychiatric patients: Toward an ecological approach. *Law and Human Behavior, 23*(2), 237–255.

Simon, R. I. (1988). *Concise guide to clinical psychiatry and the law.* Washington, DC: American Psychiatric Press.

Simon, R. I. (1992). *Clinical psychiatry and the law* (2nd ed.). Washington, DC: American Psychiatric Publishing.

Simon, R. I. (1995). Deviant billing is risky business. *Psychotherapy Letter, 7*, n.p.

Simon, R. I. (2004). *Assessing and managing suicide risk: Guidelines for clinically based risk management.* Washington, DC: American Psychiatric Publishing.

Simon, R. I. (2006). Imminent suicide: The illusion of short-term prediction. *Suicide and Life-Threatening Behavior, 36*, 296–301.

Simon, R. I. (2007). Gun safety management with patients at risk for suicide. *Suicide and Life-Threatening Behavior, 37*(5), 518–526.

Simon, R. I. (2009). Enhancing suicide risk assessment through evidence-based psychiatry. *Psychiatric Times, 26*(1), 42–45.

Simon, R. I. (2011a). Patient violence against health care professionals: Safety assessment and management. *Psychiatric Times, 28*(2), 16.

Simon, R. I. (2011b). *Preventing patient suicide: Clinical assessment and management.* Washington, DC: American Psychiatric Publishing, Inc.

Simon, R. I., & Gutheil, T. G. (2004). Clinician factors associated with increased risk for patient suicide. *Psychiatric Annals, 34*, 750–754.

Simon, R., & Gutheil, T. G. (2009). Sudden improvement among high-risk suicidal patients: Should it be trusted? *Psychiatric Services, 60*(3), 1–3.

Singer, N. (2011, April 30). Data privacy, put to the test. *New York Times.* Retrieved February 2, 2012, from http://www.nytimes.com/2011/05/01/business/01stream. html?_r=1&ref=health.

Singh, G. K., & Siahpush, M. (2002). Increasing rural-urban gradients in US suicide mortality, 1970–1997. *American Journal of Public Health, 92*, 1161–1167.

Skeem, J. L., Schubert, C., Stowman, S., Beeson, S., Mulvey, E., Gardner, W., & Lidz, C. (2005). Gender and risk assessment accuracy: Underestimating women's violence potential. *Law and Human Behavior, 29*(2), 173–186.

Small, M. A., Lyons, P. M., & Guy, L. S. (2002). Liability issues in child abuse and neglect reporting statutes. *Professional Psychology: Research and Practice, 33*, 13–18.

Small, R. F. (1994). How can I legally and ethically avoid abandoning my client? *Psychotherapy Letter, 6*, n.p.

Smith, D. L. (2008). Disability, gender, and intimate partner violence: Relationships from the behavioral risk factor surveillance system. *Sexuality and Disability, 26*(1), 15–28.

Smith, M. (2006). What do university students who will work professionally with children know about maltreatment and mandated reporting? *Children and Youth Services Review, 28*, 906–926.

Solanto, M. V., Marks, D. J., Mitchell, K. J., Wasserstein, J., & Kofman, M. D. (2008). Development of a new psychosocial treatment for adult ADHD. *Journal of Attention Disorders, 11*(6), 728–736.

Somberg, D. R., Stone, G. L., & Claiborn, C. D. (1993). Informed consent: Therapists' beliefs and practices. *Professional Psychology: Research and Practice, 24*, 153–159.

Soulier, M. F., Maislen, A., & Beck, J. C. (2010). Status of the psychiatric duty to protect, circa 2006. *Journal of the American Academy of Psychiatry and the Law, 38*(4), 457–472.

Sparks, J. A., & Duncan, B. L. (2008). Do no harm: A critical risk/benefit analysis of child psychotropic medication. *Journal of Family Psychotherapy, 19*(1), 1–19.

Spiegel, P. B. (1990). Confidentiality endangered under some circumstances without special management. *Psychotherapy, 27*, 636–643.

Spotswood, S. (2006, July). DoD personnel info part of VA data theft. *U.S. Medicine.* Retrieved January 1, 2007, from http://www.usmedicine.com/article.cfm?articleID= 1346&issueID=89.

Stanley, B., & Brown, G. K. (2012). Safety planning intervention: A brief intervention to mitigate suicide risk. *Cognitive and Behavioral Practice, 19*(2), 256–264.

Stanton, M. D. (2004). Getting reluctant substance abusers to engage in treatment/self-help: A review of outcomes and clinical options. *Journal of Marital and Family Therapy, 30*, 165–182.

Stathopoulou, G., Powers, M. B., Berry, A. C., Smits, J. A., & Otto, M. W. (2006). Exercise interventions for mental health: A quantitative and qualitative review. *Clinical Psychology: Science and Practice, 13*(2), 179–193.

Statland, B. E., & Demas T. J. (1980). Serum caffeine half-lives. Healthy subjects vs. patients having alcoholic hepatic disease. *American Journal of Clinical Pathology, 73*, 390–393.

Stein, D. J., Phillips, K. A., Bolton, D., Fulford, K. W. M., Sadler, J. Z., & Kendler, K. S. (2010). What is a mental/psychiatric disorder? From DSM-IV to DSM-V. *Psychological Medicine, 40*(11), 1759–1765.

Steinberg, K. L., Levine, M., & Doueck, H. J. (1997). Effects of legally mandated child-abuse reports on the therapeutic relationship: A survey of psychotherapists. *American Journal of Orthopsychiatry, 67*, 112–122.

Stellrecht, N. E., Gordon, K. H., Van Orden, K., Witte, T. K., Wingate, L. R., Cukrowicz, K. C., . . . Joiner, T. E. (2006). Clinical applications of the interpersonal-psychological theory of attempted and completed suicide. *Journal of Clinical Psychology, 62*(2), 211–222.

Stiegel, L., & Klem, E. (2007). *Reporting requirements: Provisions and citations in adult protective services laws, by state.* Washington, DC: American Bar Association Commission on Law and Aging.

Stockman, A. F., & Green-Emrich, A. (1994). Impact of therapist pregnancy on the process of counseling and psychotherapy. *Psychotherapy, 31*, 456–462.

Strakowski, S. (2003). How to avoid ethnic bias when diagnosing schizophrenia. *Current Psychiatry, 2*(6), n.p.

Straussner, S. L. A., Byrne, H., CASAC, & LMHC. (2009). Alcoholics Anonymous: Key research findings from 2002–2007. *Alcoholism Treatment Quarterly, 27*(4), 349–367.

Stuart, G. L., Moore, T. M., Gordon, K. C., Ramsey, S. E., & Kahler, C. W. (2006). Psychopathology in women arrested for domestic violence. *Journal of Interpersonal Violence, 21*, 376–389.

Sue, S., & Zane, N. (1987). The role of culture and cultural techniques in psychotherapy: A critique and reformulation. *American Psychologist, 42*, 37–45.

Sue, S., Zane, N., Hall, G. C. N., & Berger, L. K. (2009). The case for cultural competency in psychotherapeutic interventions. *Annual Review of Psychology, 60*(1), 525–548.

Sullivan, P. F. (2005). The genetics of schizophrenia. *PLoS Medicine, 2*, 614–618.

Sullivan, P. F., Neale, M. C., & Kendler, K. S. (2000). Genetic epidemiology of major depression: Review and meta-analysis. *American Journal of Psychiatry, 157*, 1552–1562.

Sullivan, T., Martin, W. L., & Handelsman, M. M. (1993). Practical benefits of an informed-consent procedure: An empirical investigation. *Professional Psychology: Research and Practice, 24*, 160–163.

Swanger, N. (2006). Visible body modification (VBM): Evidence from human resource managers and recruiters and the effects on employment. *International Journal of Hospitality Management, 25*, 154–158.

Swanson, J. W., Swartz, M. S., Essock, S. M., Osher, F. C., Wagner, R., Goodman, L. A., et al. (2002). The social-environmental context of violent behavior in persons treated for severe mental illness. *American Journal of Public Health, 92*, 1523–1531.

Sweeney, L. (2009). Policy and law: Identifiability of de-identified data. Retrieved February 2, 2012, from http://latanyasweeney.org/work/identifiability.html

Symreng, I., & Fishman, S. M. (2004). Anxiety and pain. *Pain: Clinical Updates, 12*, 1–6.

Taylor, B. C., Hagel, E. M., Carlson, K. F., Cifu, D. X., Cutting, A., Bidelspach, D. E., & Sayer, N. A. (2012). Prevalence and costs of co-occurring traumatic brain injury with and without psychiatric disturbance and pain among Afghanistan and Iraq war veteran VA users. *Medical Care, 50*(4), 342–346.

Taylor, D. J., Lichstein, K. L., Weinstock, J., Sanford, S., & Temple, J. R. (2007). A pilot study of cognitive-behavioral therapy of insomnia in people with mild depression. *Behavior Therapy, 38*, 49–57.

Taylor, L., McMinn, M. R., Bufford, R. K., & Chang, K. B. T. (2010). Psychologists' attitudes and ethical concerns regarding the use of social networking web sites. *Professional Psychology: Research and Practice, 41*(2), 153–159.

Teaster, P. (2000). A response to the abuse of vulnerable adults: The 2000 Survey of State Adult Protective Services. Washington, DC: National Center on Elder Abuse. Retrieved December 17, 2007, from http://www.ncea.aoa.gov/Resources/Publication/docs/apsreport030703.pdf.

Thielke, S., Thompson, A., & Stuart, R. (2011). Health psychology in primary care: Recent research and future directions. *Psychology Research and Behavior Management, 4*, 59–68.

Thompson, H., & Priest, R. (2005). Elder abuse and neglect: Considerations for mental health practitioners. *Adultspan Journal, 4*, 116–128.

Tinsley, J. A. (2000). Pregnancy of the early-career psychiatrist. *Psychiatric Services, 51*, 105–110.

Toneatto, T., & Nguyen, L. (2007). Does mindfulness meditation improve anxiety and mood symptoms? A review of the controlled research. *Canadian Journal of Psychiatry, 52*(4), 260–266.

Treloar, H. R. (2010). Financial and ethical considerations for professionals in psychology. *Ethics and Behavior, 20*(6), 454–465.

Tucker, E. (2006, December 1). Report sparks changes at pharmacy chains. Associated Press. Retrieved January 1, 2007, from http://www.washingtonpost.com/wp-dyn/content/article/2006/12/01/AR2006120100193.html.

Turk, D. C., & Burwinkle, T. M. (2005). Clinical outcomes, cost effectiveness, and the role of psychology in treatments for chronic pain sufferers. *Professional Psychology: Research and Practice, 36*, 602–610.

U.S. Department of Health and Human Services. (2003). Summary of the HIPAA Privacy Rule. Retrieved January 19, 2007, from http://www.hhs.gov/ocr/privacy/hipaa/understanding/summary/privacysummary.pdf.

Utsey, S. O., Hook, J. N., & Stanard, P. (2007). A re-examination of cultural factors that mitigate risk and promote resilience in relation to African American suicide: A review of the literature and recommendations for future research. *Death Studies, 31*(5), 399–416.

Valera, E. M., & Berenbaum, H. (2003). Brain injury in battered women. *Journal of Consulting and Clinical Psychology, 71*, 797–804.

Valtonen, H. M., Suominen, K., Haukka, J., Mantere, O., Leppämäki, S., Arvilommi, P., & Isometsä, E. P. (2008). Differences in incidence of suicide attempts during phases of bipolar I and II disorders. *Bipolar Disorders, 10*(5), 558–596.

Van Deale, T., Hermans, D., Van Audenhove, C., & Van den Bergh, O. (2012). Stress reduction through psychoeducation: A meta-analytic review. *Health Education & Behavior, 39*(4), 474–485.

van der Kolk, B. A. (2002). In terror's grip: Healing the ravages of trauma. *Cerebrum, 4,* 34–50.

Vanderpool, D. (2008). Do patients have access to therapy or personal notes? *Psychiatric News, 43*(8), 24.

VanDeusen, K. M., & Way, I. (2006). Vicarious trauma: An exploratory study of the impact of providing sexual abuse treatment on clinicians' trust and intimacy. *Journal of Child Sexual Abuse, 15*, 69–85.

Van Orden, K. A., Witte, T. K., Cukrowicz, K. C., Braithwaite, S. R., Selby, E. A., & Joiner, T. E. (2010). The interpersonal theory of suicide. *Psychological Review, 117*(2), 575–600.

Van Orden, K. A., Witte, T. K., Gordon, K. H., Bender, T. W., & Joiner, T. E. (2008). Suicidal desire and the capability for suicide: Tests of the interpersonal-psychological theory of suicidal behavior among adults. *Journal of Consulting and Clinical Psychology, 76*(1), 72–83.

Varnik, A. Kolves, K., van der Feltz-Cornelis, C.M., Marusic, A., Oskarsson, H. . . . Hegerl, U. (2008). Suicide methods in Europe: A gender-specific analysis of countries participating in the European Alliance Against Depression. *Journal of Epidemiological Community Health, 62,* 545–551.

Vasquez, M. J. T. (1992). Psychologist as clinical supervisor: Promoting ethical practice. *Professional Psychology: Research and Practice, 23*(3), 196–202.

Vasquez, M. J. T., Lott, B., Garcia-Vasquez, E., Grant, S. K., Iwamasa, G. Y., Molina, L. E., et al. (2006). Personal reflections: Barriers and strategies in increasing diversity in psychology. *American Psychologist, 61*, 157–172.

Verona, E., Sachs-Ericsson, N., & Joiner, T. E. (2004). Suicide attempts associated with externalizing psychopathology in an epidemiological sample. *American Journal of Psychiatry, 161*, 444–451.

Verwijk, E., Comijs, H. C., Kok, R. M., Spaans, H. P., Stek, M. L., & Scherder, E. J. A. (2012). Neurocognitive effects after brief pulse and ultrabrief pulse unilateral electroconvulsive therapy for major depression: A review. *Journal of Affective Disorders, 140*(3), 233–243.

Vickerman, K. A., & Margolin, G. (2009). Rape treatment outcome research: Empirical findings and state of the literature. *Clinical Psychology Review, 29*(5), 431–448.

Wachtel, P. L. (1993). *Therapeutic communication: Knowing what to say when.* New York: Guilford Press.

Wadsworth, T., & Kubrin, C. E. (2007). Hispanic suicide in U.S. metropolitan areas: Examining the effects of immigration, assimilation, affluence and disadvantage. *American Journal of Sociology, 112*(6), 1848–1885.

Wakefield, J. C. (2007). The concept of mental disorder: Diagnostic implications of the harmful dysfunction analysis. *World Psychiatry, 6*(3), 149–156.

Wakefield, J. C., Horwitz, A. V., & Schmitz, M. F. (2005). Are we overpathologizing the socially anxious? Social phobia from a harmful dysfunction perspective. *Canadian Journal of Psychiatry, 50*(6), 317–319.

Walcott, D. M., Cerundolo, P., & Beck, J. C. (2001). Current analysis of the *Tarasoff* duty: An evolution towards the limitation of the duty to protect. *Behavioral Sciences and the Law, 19,* 325–343.

Walfish, S., Barnett, J. E., Marlyere, K., & Zielke, R. (2010). "Doc, there's something I have to tell you": Patient disclosure to their psychotherapist of unprosecuted murder and other violence. *Ethics & Behavior, 20*(5), 311–323.

Walker, M., & Jacobs, M. (2004). *Supervision questions and answers for counsellors and therapists.* London: Whurr Publishers.

Weaver, T., Madden, P., Charles, V., Stimson, G., Renton, A., Tyrer, P., et al. (2003). Comorbidity of substance misuse and mental illness in community mental health and substance misuse services. *British Journal of Psychiatry, 183,* 304–313.

Webb, K. B. (2011). Care of others and self: A suicidal patient's impact on the psychologist. *Professional Psychology: Research and Practice, 42*(3), 215–221.

Weinstein, B., Levine, M., Kogan, N., Harkavy-Friedman, J. M., & Miller, J. M. (2001). Therapist reporting of suspected child abuse and maltreatment: Factors associated with outcome. *American Journal of Psychotherapy, 55,* 219–233.

Welfel, E. R., Danzinger, P. R., & Santoro, S. (2000). Mandated reporting of abuse/maltreatment of older adults: A primer for counselors. *Journal of Counseling and Development, 78,* 284–292.

Welfel, E. R., & Heinlen, K. T. (2010). Ethics in technology and mental health. In M. A. Cucciare & K. R. Weingardt (Eds.), *Using technology to support evidence-based behavioral health practices: A clinician's guide* (pp. 267–290). New York: Routledge.

Wendler, D., & Rackoff, J. E. (2001). Informed consent and respecting autonomy: What's a signature got to do with it? *IRB: Ethics and Human Research, 23,* 1–4.

Westen, D. (2005). Implications of research in cognitive neuroscience for psychodynamic psychotherapy. In G. O. Gabbard, J. S. Beck, & J. Holmes (Eds.), *Oxford textbook of psychotherapy* (pp. 447–454). New York: Oxford University Press.

Weston, R., Temple, J. R., & Marshall, L. L. (2005). Gender symmetry and asymmetry in violent relationships: Patterns of mutuality among racially diverse women. *Sex Roles, 53,* 553–571.

Whaley, A. L. (2001). Cultural mistrust and the clinical diagnosis of paranoid schizophrenia in African American patients. *Journal of Psychopathology and Behavioral Assessment, 23,* 93–100.

White, H. (2009). Locating clinical boundaries in the World Wide Web. *American Journal of Psychiatry, 166*(5), 620–621.

Whitted, Cleary & Takiff, LLC (n.d.). Duty to warn—When can I break confidentiality? Retrieved on August 14, 2012, from http://www.wct-law.com/for-professionals/144.html

Williams, S. L., & Frieze, I. H. (2005). Patterns of violent relationships, psychological distress, and marital satisfaction in a national sample of men and women. *Sex Roles, 52,* 771–784.

Wingate, L. R., Joiner, T. E., Walker, R. L., Rudd, M. D., & Jobes, D. A. (2004). Empirically informed approaches to topics in suicide risk assessment. *Behavioral Sciences and the Law, 22*(5), 651–665.

Wittenberg, K. J., & Norcross, J. C. (2001). Practitioner perfectionism: Relationship to ambiguity tolerance and work satisfaction. *Journal of Clinical Psychology, 57,* 1543–1550.

Wiwanitkit, V. (2005). Male rape, some notes on the laboratory investigation. *Sexuality and Disability, 23,* 41–46.

Wollburg, E., & Braukhaus, C. (2010). Goal setting in psychotherapy: The relevance of approach and avoidance goals for treatment outcome. *Psychotherapy Research, 20*(4), 488–494.

Woody, R. H. (1999). Domestic violations of confidentiality. *Professional Psychology: Research and Practice, 30*, 607–610.

Wookey, M. L., Graves, N. A., & Butler, J. C. (2009). Effects of a sexy appearance on perceived competence of women. *Journal of Social Psychology, 149*(1), 116–118.

Woolf, C. J., & Salter, M. W. (2000). Neuronal plasticity increasing the gain in pain. *Science,* 2000, 1765–1768.

World Health Organization (1990). International Classification of Diseases-10. Retrieved August 26, 2012 from http://www.who.int/classifications/icd/en/

Worz, R. (2003). Pain in depression; Depression in pain. *Pain: Clinical Updates, 11*(5), 1–4.

Xavier, J. M., Bobbin, M., Singer, B., & Budd, E. (2005). A needs assessment of transgendered people of color living in Washington, DC. *International Journal of Transgenderism, 8*(2-3), 31–47.

Yalom, I. (2002). *The gift of therapy: An open letter to a new generation.* New York: HarperPerennial.

Yanos, P. T., Vreeland, B., Minsky, S., Fuller, R. B., & Roe, D. (2009). Partial hospitalization: Compatible with evidence-based and recovery-oriented treatment? *Journal of Psychosocial Nursing, 47*(2), 41–47.

Yeager, K. R., Saveanu, R., Roberts, A. R., Reissland, G., Mertz, D., Cirpili, A., & Makovich, R. (2005). Measured response to identified suicide risk and violence: What you need to know about psychiatric patient safety. *Brief Treatment and Crisis Intervention, 5*(2), 121–141.

Yip, P. S., Yang, K. C., Ip, B. Y., Law, Y. W., & Watson, R. (2007). Financial debt and suicide in Hong Kong SAR. *Journal of Applied Social Psychology, 32*(12), 2788–2799.

Young, T., Peppard, P. E. & Gottlieb, D. J. (2002). Epidemiology of obstructive sleep apnea: A population health perspective. *American Journal of Respiratory and Critical Care Medicine, 165,* 1217-1239.

Younggren, J. N., & Harris, E. A. (2008). Can you keep a secret? Confidentiality in psychotherapy. *Journal of Clinical Psychology: In Session, 64*(5), 589–600.

Zane, N., Sue, S., Chang, J., Huang, L., Huang, J., Lowe, S., Srinivasan, S., Chun, K., Kurasaki, K., & Lee, E. (2005). Beyond ethnic match: Effects of client-therapist cognitive match in problem perception, coping orientation, and therapy goals on treatment outcomes. *Journal of Community Psychology, 33*(5), 569–585.

Zeber, J.E., Miller, A.L., Copeland, L.A., McCarthy, J.F., Zivin, K., Valenstein, M., Greenwald, D. & Kilbourne, A. (2011). Medication adherence, ethnicity, and the influence of multiple psychosocial and financial barriers. *Administration and Policy in Mental Health and Mental Health Services Research, 38,* 86-95.

Zimmerman, M., & Mattia, J. I. (1999). Is posttraumatic stress disorder underdiagnosed in routine clinical settings? *Journal of Nervous and Mental Disease, 187*(7), 420–428.

Zuckerman, E. L. (2003). *The paper office* (3rd ed.). New York: Guilford Press.

Zuckerman, E. L. (2008). *The paper office* (4th ed.). New York: Guilford Press.

Zur, O. (2008). The Google factor: Therapists' self-disclosure in the age of the internet. *Independent Practitioner, Spring,* 82–85.

Zur, O., Williams, M. H., Lehavot, K., & Knapp, S. (2009). Psychotherapist self-disclosure and transparency in the internet age. *Professional Psychology: Research and Practice, 40*(1), 22–30.

Zur, O. (2010). To Google or not to Google...our clients? When psychotherapists and other mental health care providers search their clients on the Web. *Independent Practitioner, 30*(3), 144–148.

Zur, O. (2012). Ethics in the digital age. *Psychotherapy Networker, July/August*, 26–33, 56.

CPSIA information can be obtained
at www.ICGtesting.com
Printed in the USA
BVHW031333180820
586501BV00002B/8

9 780199 931651